Lecture Notes in
Computer Science

Lecture Notes in Computer Science

Lecture Notes in Computer Science

Edited by G. Goos and J. Hartmanis

432

N. Jones (Ed.)

ESOP '90

3rd European Symposium on Programming
Copenhagen, Denmark, May 15–18, 1990
Proceedings

Springer-Verlag

Berlin Heidelberg New York London Paris Tokyo Hong Kong

Editor

Neil Jones
DIKU, University of Copenhagen
Universitetsparken 1, DK-2100 Copenhagen, Denmark

CR Subject Classification (1987): D.3.1–4, F.3.1–3, F.4.1

ISBN 3-540-52592-0 SpringerVerlag Berlin Heidelberg New York
ISBN 0-387-52592-0 Springer-Verlag New York Berlin Heidelberg

Printing and binding: Druckhaus Beltz, Hemsbach/Bergstr.
2145/3140-543210 – Printed on acid-free paper

Preface

This volume contains the Proceedings of the Third European Symposium on Programming (ESOP '90), held jointly with the Fifteenth CAAP (Conference on Trees in Algebra and Programming) May 15-18, 1990 in Copenhagen. The CAAP '90 Proceedings are published in another LNCS volume, a twin to this one.

Two previous ESOP symposia have been held, the first in Saarbrücken in 1986 and the second (also jointly with CAAP) in Nancy in 1988. They continue lines begun in France and Germany under the names *Colloque sur la Programmation* and the GI-workshops on *Programmiersprachen und Programmentwicklung*.

ESOP '90 addresses fundamental issues and important developments in the design, specification and implementation of programming languages and systems on topics including those listed below. Especially encouraged were papers that describe practical work based on theory, or computer experiments implementing theoretical concepts and formal models.

- *Program development*
    specification, methodology, tools, environments
- *Programming language concepts*
    types, data abstraction, parallelism, real-time
- *Language implementation techniques*
    compilers, interpreters, abstract machine design, optimization
- *Programs as data objects*
    abstract interpretation, program transformation, partial evaluation
- *Programming styles*
    imperative, functional, predicative, object-oriented

Seventy-five papers were submitted, of which twenty-four were selected by the program committee. The choice was made on the quality of the papers, but it turns out that they are a representative sample of the submitted ones. On the average the submitted papers were rather good and the task of the Program Committee was not always easy. In particular several papers contained new and interesting ideas, but were not worked out well enough.

The two invited lecturers are Henk Barendregt (University of Nijmegen, Holland) and Robert Paige (Courant Institute, New York). I am pleased to thank these two outstanding scholars for accepting the invitation to address the conference.

I thank the ESOP Program Committee members and referees for all the work they did in selecting the contributions; Klaus Grue for help at Copenhagen in organizing the paper selection process; André Arnold, chairman of the CAAP Program Committee; and Max Dauchet and F. Bossut for hosting the program committee meeting at Lille.

I also thank Nils Andersen, the CAAP/ESOP Local Arrangements Chairman, for efficiently and cheerfully handling the arrangements and planning needed to make such a conference a success; Torben Mogensen for designing the logo; Lars Ole Andersen for organizing the system demonstrations; and last but not least, three secretaries at Copenhagen who solved a thousand practical problems: Hjørdis Gundermann, Eileen Møller Nielsen and Lisa Wiese.

The conferences were sponsored by EATCS (the European Association for Theoretical Computer Science), who help in bringing this meeting to the attention of the worldwide community in theoretical computer science. Finally, thanks are due to the Danish Natural Science Research Council (Det Naturvidenskabelige Forskningsråd) for paying the expenses of the four invited speakers.

Neil Jones

Program Committee

Neil D. Jones (Copenhagen, Chairman)	Tom Maibaum (London)
Guy Cousineau (Paris)	Jan Maluszynski (Linköping)
Harald Ganzinger (Dortmund)	Peter Mosses (Århus)
Chris Hankin (London)	Bengt Nordström (Göteborg)
Bernard Lang (Paris)	Philip Wadler (Glasgow)
Pierre Lescanne (Nancy)	Reinhard Wilhelm (Saarbrücken)
Bernd Mahr (Berlin West)	Glynn Winskel (Århus)

The program of ESOP '90 offered two invited talks which are included in this volume. The Program Committee thanks the invited lecturers:

Henk P. Barendregt (University of Nijmegen, Holland)
Robert Paige (Courant Institute, New York University, USA)

List of Referees for ESOP '90

A. Aasa

S. Abramsky

Ascander

R. Backhouse

K.-J. Backström

S. Blott

S. Bonnier

G.L. Burn

D.R. Busch

K. Clenaghan

M. Cole

T. Coquand

R.J. Cunningham

M. Dawson

P. Dybjer

P. Fritzson

D. Galmiche

I. Gnaedig-Antoine

V.D. Gouge

T. Hallgren

M. Hanus

Hermann

P. Harrison

L. Hascoet

R. Heckmann

C.J. Hogger

K.H. Holm

S. Holmström

C.K. Holst

R.J.M. Hughes

S. Hughes

S. Hunt

J. Jaray

T. Johnsson

S.B. Jones

M. Jourdan

A. Jung

M. Kamkar

P.H.J. Kelly

C. Kirchner

H. Kirchner

J. Kramer

T. Lehmann

G. Lindström

D. Lugiez

P. Lundgren

J. Löwgren

F.G. McCabe

L. Maranget

M. Mauny

Mery

H. Miki

T. Mogensen

F. Müller

A. Nilsson

C. Paulin

K. Petersson

S. Peyton-Jones

R. de Queiroz

Quere

J.L. Remy

B. Richards

F. Rouaix

J. Rouyer

S. Sagib

J.-B. Saint

H. Sander

A. Schmitt

R. Schott

H. Seidl

N. Shahmekri

K. Sieber

A. Sua'rez

S. Todd

S. Vickers

P. Viry

Q. Win

Table of Contents

TYPES IN LAMBDA CALCULI AND PROGRAMMING LANGUAGES

Henk Barendregt

Faculty of Mathematics and Computer Science, University Nijmegen, Toernooiveld 1,

6525 ED Nijmegen, The Netherlands

Kees Hemerik

Department of Mathematics and Computer Science, Eindhoven University of Technology, Den Dolech 2,

5600 MB Eindhoven, The Netherlands

1. INTRODUCTION

The lambda calculus was originally conceived by Church as part of a general theory of functions and logic, intended as a foundation for mathematics. Although the full system turned out to be inconsistent, the subsystem dealing with functions only turned out to be a successful model of the computable functions. For an introduction to the subject and its relation to functional programming, see Barendregt [1990]. Some books on the lambda calculus are Barendregt [1984] and Hindley and Seldin [1986]. A major problem with the lambda calculus as functional programming language is the great amount of freedom in combining terms. A way to restrict this combinatorial freedom is the use of *types,* which are characterisations of classes of terms. The first type systems for lambda calculus were introduced in Curry [1934] and Church [1941]. Since then many typed lambda calculi have been proposed for different purposes.

The evolution of programming languages shows a similar pattern. The oldest varieties, like assembler and LISP, were essentially typefree and allowed too much combinatorial freedom. In languages like ALGOL 68 and Fortran simple but rather rigid type systems were introduced. For various applications these type systems were too restrictive and they have been extended in many ways. Type theory is currently an active research area. Publications, like the IEEE-LICS and ACM-POPL proceedings and papers like Cardelli and Wagner [1985] and Reynolds [1985], show that the developments in lambda cacluli and programming languages are converging. It also displays a bewildering variety of systems and confusion of notations and nomenclature. What is clearly needed is a classification or taxonomy of these systems on the basis of a common frame of reference. This paper presents a contribution towards such a classification. The exposition is based on the extensive treatment in Barendregt [199-], but because of space limitations proofs have been omitted. Although the paper concentrates on typed lambda calculi, at many places the relations with programming languages are illustrated.

The main criterion for the classification is based on the original systems of Curry and Church, which might be called *implicit* typing and *explicit* typing, respectively. This division is the subject of section 2. Section 3 systematically discusses the main ingredients of implicit type systems, and section 4 does the same for explicit type systems. Section 4 concludes with a taxonomy of explicit systems by means of generalised type systems, including the 'λ-cube' introduced in Barendregt [1989]. Since all systems discussed in this paper are ultimately based on the type-free lambda calculus, we conclude this introduction with a short review of that system for reference purposes.

1.1 TYPE-FREE LAMBDA CALCULUS

The aspects of lambda calculus important for functional programming consist of the syntax of terms and the reduction (rewrite) relation on these.

1.1.1. Definition. The sets of (term) variables V, of constants C and of lambda terms Λ are defined by the following abstract syntax.

$$V = x \mid V'$$
$$C = c \mid C'$$
$$\Lambda = V \mid C \mid \Lambda\Lambda \mid \lambda V.\Lambda$$

So $V = \{x, x', x'', ...\}$ and $C = \{c, c', c'', ...\}$.

1.1.2. Conventions.

(i)   x, y, z,...   range over V.

(ii)   a, b, c,...   range over C.

(iii)   M, N, L,... range over Λ.

(iv) $\equiv$ stands for syntactic equality.

(v) $MN_1...N_k \equiv (..((MN_1) N_2)...N_k)$, association to the left.

(vi) $\lambda x_1...x_k.M \equiv \lambda x_1. (\lambda x_2. ...(\lambda x_k. (M))..)$, association to the right.

1.1.3. Examples. The following are lambda terms.

(i) $\lambda x.x$.

(ii) $y(\lambda x.x)$.

(iii) $(\lambda x.xx)(\lambda x.xx)$

1.1.4. Definition

(i)   FV(M) is the set of free variables of M.

(ii)   M [x : = N] is the result of substituting N for the free occurrences of x in M.

1.1.5. Definition (Reduction).

(i)   A binary relation $\to_\beta$ (one step reduction) is defined on Λ as follows.

$$(\lambda x.M)N \to_\beta M [x : = N];$$

$$\frac{M \to_\beta M'}{MN \to_\beta M'N}; \qquad \frac{M \to_\beta M'}{NM \to_\beta NM'}; \qquad \frac{M \to_\beta M'}{\lambda x.M \to_\beta \lambda x.M'}.$$

(ii)   Many step reduction $\twoheadrightarrow_\beta$ is the reflexive transitive closure of $\to_\beta$.

(iii)   Conversion $=_\beta$ is the equivalence relation generated by $\lambda \twoheadrightarrow_\beta$.

Instead of $\to_\beta$, $\twoheadrightarrow_\beta$ and $=_\beta$ we often write $\to$, $\twoheadrightarrow$ and $=$, respectively.

1.1.6. Examples.

(i) $(\lambda x.xx)(\lambda y.y)z \to (\lambda y.y)(\lambda y.y)z$
$$\twoheadrightarrow z.$$

(ii) $(\lambda xy.x)\, z\, w \twoheadrightarrow z.$

(iii) $(\lambda x.xx)(\lambda y.y)z = (\lambda xy.x)zw.$

1.1.7. Definition.

(i) $M \in \Lambda$ is called a *normal form* (nf) if for no N one has $M \to N$.

(ii) M *has* a nf N if $M \twoheadrightarrow N$ and N is a nf.

(iii) M is *strongly normalising*, notation SN(M), if for no infinite sequence $M_1, M_2, \ldots$ one has $M \to M_1 \to M_2 \to \ldots$.

1.1.8. Examples.

(i) $(\lambda x.xx)y$ has yy as nf.

(ii) $\Omega \equiv (\lambda x.xx)(\lambda x.xx)$ has no nf.

(iii) $(\lambda xy.x)\, a\, \Omega$ has a as nf, but is not strongly normalising since $\Omega \to \Omega \to \ldots$.

1.1.9. Theorem (Church-Rosser property).

(i) If $M \twoheadrightarrow M_1$, and $M \twoheadrightarrow M_2$ then for some $M_3 \in \Lambda$ one has $M_1 \twoheadrightarrow M_3$ and $M_2 \twoheadrightarrow M_3$.

(ii) If $M_1 = M_2$, then for some $M_3 \in \Lambda$ one has $M_1 \twoheadrightarrow M_3$ and $M_2 \twoheadrightarrow M_3$.

1.1.10. Corollary (Unicity of normal forms). A lambda term has at most one nf.

There are certain terms in normal form $\ulcorner 0 \urcorner$, $\ulcorner 1 \urcorner$, ... (*numerals*) that represent the elements of $\mathbb{N}$, the set of natural numbers.

1.1.11. Theorem (Lambda definability of computable functions).

(i) Let $f : \mathbb{N} \to \mathbb{N}$ be a computable function. Then for some $F \in \Lambda$ one has for all $n \in \mathbb{N}$

$$F \ulcorner n \urcorner \twoheadrightarrow \ulcorner f(n) \urcorner.$$

(ii) More generally, if $f : \mathbb{N}^k \to \mathbb{N}$ is computable, then for some $F \in \Lambda$ one has for all $n_1, \ldots, n_k \in \mathbb{N}$

$$F \ulcorner n_1 \urcorner \ldots \ulcorner n_k \urcorner \twoheadrightarrow \ulcorner f(n_1, \ldots, n_k) \urcorner.$$

This is the basis of evaluation of functional programs. The input and program form together one expression and by the Church-Rosser theorem it does not matter how reductions are done, as long as one cares to find the normal form (if it exists). For this there are several possible normalising strategies, for example leftmost reduction.

One way (but not the only) of obtaining representations of recursive functions is to use the so called fixed point operator Y.

1.1.12. Theorem. Let $Y \equiv \lambda f.(\lambda x.f(xx))(\lambda x.f(xx))$. Then Y produces fixed points, i.e. for every F one has $F(YF) = YF$. Turing's fixed point operator $\Theta \equiv (\lambda ab.b(aab))(\lambda ab.b(aab))$ even has the property $\Theta F \twoheadrightarrow F(\Theta F)$.

2. IMPLICIT VERSUS EXPLICIT TYPING

There are two ways in which expressions denoting algorithms can be typed: the implicit way, originating with Curry [1934], and the explicit way, originating with Church [1941].

In the systems of implicit typing the expressions are the type-free lambda terms. To each such term a set of possible types is assigned. The number of elements in this set may be zero, one or more. If type σ is assigned to term M, then one writes $M : \sigma$ (pronounce 'M in σ'). An example (to be treated in detail later) is
$$(\lambda x.x) : (\alpha \to \alpha),$$
that is, the identity is of type $\alpha \to \alpha$. This means that if $y : \alpha$, then $((\lambda x.x)y) : \alpha$. Also one has
$(\lambda x.x) : ((\alpha \to \beta) \to (\alpha \to \beta))$. Indeed, if $f : \alpha \to \beta$, then $((\lambda x.x)f) : (\alpha \to \beta)$. Therefore one, says that the identity is *polymorphic*.

In the systems of explicit typing the expressions are annotated versions of lambda terms. Such an expression has a type that usually is uniquely determined by the annotations. An example is
$$(\lambda x{:}\alpha.x) : (\alpha \to \alpha).$$
One may write $I_\sigma \equiv (\lambda x{:}\sigma.x) : (\sigma \to \sigma)$ for the identity on σ. In particular $I_{\alpha \to \beta} : (\alpha \to \beta) \to (\alpha \to \beta)$.

The components of an algorithm as given by a term usually have a fixed intended meaning. Therefore the explicitly typed terms are rather natural. However, it is often space and time consuming to annotate programs with types. Moreover, the annotation often can be constructed from the type-free expression by automatic means. Therefore the implicit typing paradigm is rather convenient.

Now we will introduce the most basic typed system, the *simply typed lambda calculus*, both in the style of Curry and that of Church. These systems will be denoted by $\lambda \to$-Curry and $\lambda \to$-Church.

2.1 THE IMPLICIT VERSION OF $\lambda \to$

Types and terms of $\lambda \to$-Curry.

There are many systems of types. The set of types for $\lambda \to$, notation Type $(\lambda \to)$, is defined by the following abstract grammar. We write T = Type $(\lambda \to)$.

2.1.1. Definition

$V = \alpha \mid V'$	(type variables)
$C = \gamma \mid C'$	(type constants)
$T = V \mid C \mid T \to T$	(types)

Notice that $V = \{\alpha, \alpha', \alpha'', ...\}$. We will use $\alpha, \beta, \gamma, ...$ to denote arbitrary type variables. Similarly $C = \{\gamma, \gamma', \gamma'', ...\}$. We will use $\boldsymbol{\alpha}, \boldsymbol{\beta}, \boldsymbol{\gamma}, ...$ to denote arbitrary type constants. Elements of T are $\alpha, \alpha \rightarrow \alpha, \boldsymbol{\beta} \rightarrow \alpha \rightarrow \alpha$. Here and elsewhere we use association to the right for $\rightarrow$; that is, the last type is really $\boldsymbol{\beta} \rightarrow (\alpha \rightarrow \alpha)$. The letters $\sigma, \tau, \rho, ...$ denote arbitrary elements of T.

2.1.2. Definition. (i) A *statement* is of the from $M : \sigma$ with $M \in \Lambda$ and $\sigma \in T$. In this case M is called the *subject* and σ the *predicate*.

(ii) A *basis* is a set of statements with as subjects distinct (term) variables. The letters $\Gamma, \Delta, ...$ range over bases.

Some of the type constants are given special names, like **int, bool, char**. These are used for formulating extensions of $\lambda \rightarrow$ in which certain elements are highlighted. For example term constants **0, s** may be selected and $\lambda \rightarrow$ can be extended with the axioms

$$o : \textbf{int}, s : \textbf{int} \rightarrow \textbf{int}$$

Of course everything could be done with free variables. Indeed term variables x_0 and x_s and a type variable α_{int} can be selected and one can consider as a basis

$$x_0 : \alpha_{\text{int}}, x_s : \alpha_{\text{int}} \rightarrow \alpha_{\text{int}}$$

In fact a constant is nothing but a variable that is not and will not be bound.

Assignment rules of $\lambda \rightarrow$-Curry

2.1.3 Definition. A statement $M : \sigma$ is derivable in $\lambda \rightarrow$ form a basis Γ, notation $\Gamma \vdash_{\lambda \rightarrow} M : \sigma$ or simply $\Gamma \vdash M : \sigma$ if there is no danger of confusion, if $\Gamma \vdash M : \sigma$ can be produced by the following assignment rules.

(Start)　　$\Gamma \vdash x : \sigma$,　if $x{:}\sigma$ is in Γ;

$$(\rightarrow E) \quad \frac{\Gamma \vdash M : (\sigma \rightarrow \tau) \quad \Gamma \vdash N : \sigma}{\Gamma \vdash (MN) : \tau};$$

$$(\rightarrow I) \quad \frac{\Gamma, x{:}\sigma \vdash M : \tau}{\Gamma \vdash (\lambda x.M) : (\sigma \rightarrow \tau)}.$$

Here $\Gamma, x{:}\sigma$ stands for $\Gamma \cup \{x{:}\sigma\}$. If $\Gamma = \emptyset$, then $\Gamma \vdash M : \sigma$ is written as $\vdash M : \sigma$. Pronounce $\vdash$ as yields. $\Gamma \not\vdash M : \sigma$ means that $\Gamma \vdash M : \sigma$ does not hold. The rule $\rightarrow E$ stands for $\rightarrow$-elimination; $\rightarrow I$ for $\rightarrow$-introduction.

2.1.4. Examples.

(i)　　The following derivation shows that $\vdash_{\lambda \rightarrow} (\lambda xy.x) : (\sigma \rightarrow \tau \rightarrow \sigma)$. The derivation is written in a version of natural deduction, due to N.G. de Bruijn, in which the scope of assumptions is made explicit.

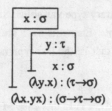

$$(\lambda y.x) : (\tau \rightarrow \sigma)$$
$$(\lambda x.yx) : (\sigma \rightarrow \tau \rightarrow \sigma)$$

(ii)   Similarly one has $\vdash_{\lambda \rightarrow} (\lambda xy.y) : (\sigma \rightarrow \tau \rightarrow \tau)$.

(iii) $\vdash_{\lambda \rightarrow} (\lambda x.x) : (\sigma \rightarrow \sigma)$.

(iv) $y{:}\sigma \vdash_{\lambda \rightarrow} ((\lambda x.x)y) : \sigma$.

Properties of $\lambda \rightarrow$-Curry.

There are several valid properties of $\lambda \rightarrow$ in which reduction and type assignment play a role. Since several (but not all) of these are valid also for other systems, we will indicate them by an acronym for quick reference. Not all versions of some property are exactly the same though and the precise formulation is given in case the statement differs from the standard meaning.

2.1.5.   Definition. The following acronyms are used for properties of type systems.

(i)   CR (Church-Rosser property).

This refers to the set of terms and reduction and conversion. The formulation is in 1.1.9.

(ii)   SR (Subject reduction property). This states the following. Let $M \rightarrow\!\!\!\!\rightarrow M'$. Then

$$\Gamma \vdash M : \sigma \Rightarrow \Gamma \vdash M' : \sigma.$$

(iii)   SN (Strong normalisation property). This is

$$\Gamma \vdash M : \sigma \Rightarrow SN (M).$$

(iv)   UT   (Unicity of types). This is

$$\Gamma \vdash M : \sigma \ \& \ \Gamma \vdash M : \sigma' \Rightarrow \sigma \equiv \sigma'.$$

(v) $\Gamma \vdash M{:}\sigma$? is decidable. This states that given, Γ, M, σ it is decidable whether $\Gamma \vdash M{:}\sigma$.

(vi) $\Gamma \vdash M{:}?$ is computable. This states that given Γ, M it can be decided whether there is a σ such that $\Gamma \vdash M : \sigma$ and moreover one such σ can be computed from Γ, M.

Property 2.1.5 (iii) implies that not every computable function is lambda definable, see Barendregt [1990], theorem 4.2.15.

2.1.6.   Theorem. For $\lambda \rightarrow$-Curry the following properties hold.

(i)   CR, for Λ and β-reduction/ -conversion.

(ii)   SR.

(iii)   SN.

(iv) $\Gamma \vdash M : \sigma$? is decidable.

(v) $\Gamma \vdash M : ?$ is computable.

2.1.7. Remarks. (i) The converse of SR does not hold for $\lambda\rightarrow$. Let $S \equiv \lambda xyz.xz(yz)$ and $K \equiv \lambda pq.p$. Then $SK \twoheadrightarrow \lambda xy.y$ and $\vdash (\lambda xy.y) : (\sigma\rightarrow\tau\rightarrow\tau)$ but $\nvdash SK : (\sigma\rightarrow\tau\rightarrow\tau)$.

(ii) M is called typable if $\Gamma\vdash M : \sigma$ for some Γ and σ. SN states that if M is typable, then M is strongly normalising. The converse is not true. E.g. $\lambda x.xx$ is not typable.

(iii) Computability of $\Gamma\vdash M : ?$ has been established independently by Hindley [1969] for a combinator version of $\lambda\rightarrow$ and by Milner [1978] for the closely related programming language ML. The ML-algorithm analyses the term M and generates a set E of equations between types in such a way that M is typable iff E has a solution. Moreover, the most general type of M corresponds to the most general solution of E. The latter solution can be found by applying a unification algorithm to E. A clear description of such an algorithm has been given by Wand [1987].

Pragmatics of $\lambda\rightarrow$ - Curry

There exist various programming languages with type systems closely resembling $\lambda\rightarrow$-Curry, such as ML (Harper [1986]), Hope (Burstall [1980]) and Miranda (Turner [1985]). The ML type system, invented by Milner [1978] independently from Hindley's work, has been discussed extensively in the literature (Damas [1982], Mycroft [1984], Kfoury [1988, 1989]). The system is based on an extension of $\lambda\rightarrow$-Curry with a declaration mechanism of the form **let** $x = M$ **in** N, which allows a form of polymorphism in the sense that different occurrences of x in N may have different types which are instances of a type scheme for x and M. In this section we consider the basic system introduced by Milner and some of its extensions. All systems are based on the following sets of terms, types and type schemes.

$$\Lambda \quad =V\,|\,C\,|\,\lambda\,V.\Lambda\,|\,\textbf{let}\,V = \Lambda\,\textbf{in}\,\Lambda\,|\,\textbf{fix}\,V\,.\,\Lambda$$

$$T \quad =V\,|\,C\,|\,T \rightarrow T$$

$$\Sigma \quad =T\,|\,\forall V.\Sigma$$

It follows that universal quantifiers may only occur at the top level of type schemes. In the remainder of this section we shall use metavariables τ and σ to range over types and type schemes, respectively. It will be necessary to consider 'generic instances' of type schemes. Let $\sigma = \forall\alpha_1...\alpha_m.\,\tau$ and $\sigma' = \forall\beta_1...\beta_n.\tau'$. Then σ' is a generic instance of σ, written $\sigma\leq\sigma'$, iff there is a substitutor S acting only on $\{\alpha_1...\alpha_m\}$ sucht that $\tau' = S(\tau)$ and no β_i is free in σ. If we consider $\sigma=\sigma'$ iff $\sigma\leq\sigma'\leq\sigma$, then $(\Sigma, \leq)$ is a partial order with least element $\forall\alpha.\alpha$. The following graph, taken from Mycroft [1984], illustrates the order $\leq$.

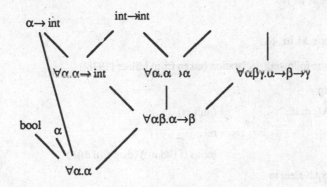

The first type assignment system we consider for this language is the one of Milner [1978] in the form of Damas [1982]. Once more we note that τ ranges over types and σ over type schemes.

(var) $\Gamma \vdash x : \sigma$,   if $(x : \sigma) \in \Gamma$;

(inst) $\dfrac{\Gamma \vdash M : \sigma}{\Gamma \vdash M : \sigma'}$ if $\sigma \leq \sigma'$;

(gen) $\dfrac{\Gamma \vdash M : \sigma}{\Gamma \vdash M : \forall \alpha . \sigma'}$ if $\alpha \notin FV(\Gamma)$;

(m-app) $\dfrac{\Gamma \vdash M : \tau_1 \rightarrow \tau_2 \quad \Gamma \vdash N : \tau_1}{\Gamma \vdash MN : \tau_2}$;

(m-abs) $\dfrac{\Gamma, x : \tau_1 \vdash M : \tau_2}{\Gamma \vdash \lambda x.M : \tau_1 \rightarrow \tau_2}$;

(m-fix) $\dfrac{\Gamma, x : \tau \vdash M : \tau}{\Gamma \vdash \mathbf{fix}\, x.M : \tau}$;

(p-let) $\dfrac{\Gamma, x : \sigma \vdash N : \tau \quad \Gamma \vdash M : \sigma}{\Gamma \vdash \mathbf{let}\, x = M \,\mathbf{in}\, N : \tau}$.

The intended meaning of **fix** x.M is in terms of the type-free lambda calculus $\Theta(\lambda x.M)$. The meaning of **let** x=M **in** N is N[x:=M]. For practical purposes this basic language can be extended with other language constructs defined in terms of the given ones. For example, the construct

letrec x = M **in** N

can be defined as

let x = **fix** x.M **in** N.

Consider as an example the following declaration (taken from Milner [1978])

letrec map =

      λf, m.if   (null m)

                              nil

                              (cons (f (hd m)) (map f (tl m)))

which is equivalent to

let map =

  fix map'.λf,m. if   (null m)

             nil

             (cons (f (hd m)) (map' f (tl m)))

Assuming the following basis

null	:	$\forall\alpha.(\text{list } \alpha \rightarrow \text{bool})$
nil	:	$\forall\alpha.(\text{list } \alpha)$
cons	:	$\forall\alpha.(\alpha \rightarrow \text{list } \alpha \rightarrow \text{list } \alpha)$
hd	:	$\forall\alpha.(\text{list } \alpha \rightarrow \alpha)$
tl	:	$\forall\alpha.(\text{list}\alpha \rightarrow \text{list } \alpha)$
if	:	$\forall\alpha.(\text{bool} \rightarrow \alpha \rightarrow \alpha \rightarrow \alpha)$

one can deduce

  map : $\forall\alpha\forall\beta.((\alpha \rightarrow \beta) \rightarrow (\text{list } \alpha \rightarrow \text{list } \beta)).$

To every occurrence of the variable map within the scope of the declaration must be assigned a type which is a generic instance of this type scheme. E.g., if we assume a type xxx and variables

x	:	list xxx
f	:	$\text{xxx} \rightarrow \text{int}$
odd	:	$\text{int } \rightarrow \text{bool}$

then in the expression

  map odd (map f x)

the inner and outer occurrence of map will have types

  $(\text{xxx}\rightarrow\text{int})$ $\rightarrow(\text{list xxx} \rightarrow \text{list int})$

  $(\text{int} \rightarrow \text{bool})$ $\rightarrow(\text{list int} \rightarrow \text{list bool})$

respectively.

The first extension to the system above has been suggested by Mycroft [1984] in order to remedy some unexpected consequences of the basic system. E.g. if the definition of map as given above is followed by a definition

  let oddlist = λl.map odd l

then the ML system will derive the types

  map : $\forall\alpha\forall\beta.\ ((\alpha\rightarrow\beta) \rightarrow (\text{list}.\alpha) \rightarrow (\text{list } \beta))$

  oddlist : $(\text{list int}) \rightarrow (\text{list bool})$

whereas, if they are defined simultaneously by

  letrec map = λf. m ...

  and oddlist = λl. map odd l

the system will derive

$$\text{map} \quad : \quad (\text{int} \to \text{bool}) \to (\text{list int}) \to (\text{list bool})$$

$$\text{oddlist} \quad : \quad (\text{list int}) \to (\text{list bool}).$$

This phenomenon is due to the fact that a simultaneous recursive definition

$$\textbf{letrec } f_1 \quad = \lambda x_1.M_1$$

$$\textbf{and } f_2 \quad = \lambda x_2.M_2$$

is equivalent to

$$\textbf{let} < f_1, f_2> = \textbf{fix} \ <f_1, f_2>.<M_1,M_2>$$

and according to the type assignment rule (m - fix) bound variables of a fix-expression should have types rather than type schemes. In Mycroft [1984] and Kfoury [1988] it has been suggested to replace rule (m - fix) by

$$(p\text{ - fix}) \quad \frac{\Gamma, x{:}\sigma \vdash M : \sigma}{\Gamma \vdash \textbf{fix } x \, . \, M : \sigma}$$

The resulting system is sometimes referred to as the Milner-Mycroft system. Mycroft could not prove the decidability of type derivation for this system. In Kfoury [1988] a proof is given, but it does not result in a practical algorithm.

A second extension to the basic system has been inspired by another problem, mentioned in Milner [1978] and Kfoury [1989]. Consider a declaration of the form

$$\textbf{let m} \quad = \lambda f.\lambda x.\lambda y. \ <f \ x, f \ y>.$$

One would expect that application of m to arguments

$$(\lambda x.x) \quad : \ \forall \alpha.\alpha \to \alpha$$

$$M_1 \quad : \ \tau_1$$

$$M_2 \quad : \ \tau_2$$

results in

$$<M_1, M_2> : \tau_1 \times \tau_2$$

but in ML the term

$$\textbf{let m} = \lambda f.\lambda x.\lambda y. \ <fx, fy> \textbf{ in } m \ (\lambda x.x) \ M_1 M_2$$

cannot be typed, because according to rule (m-abs) all occurrences of f should have the same type. In Kfoury [1989] it is proposed to replace (m-abs) and (m-app) by

$$(p\text{-abs}) \quad \frac{\Gamma, x{:}\sigma \vdash M : \tau}{\Gamma \vdash \lambda x.M : \sigma \to \tau}$$

$$(p\text{-app}) \quad \frac{\Gamma \vdash M : \sigma \to \tau \quad \Gamma \vdash N : \sigma}{\Gamma \vdash MN : \tau}$$

thus allowing functions to accept polymorphic arguments. For the resulting system the computability of type derivation is open. In fact that system comes close to the system $\lambda2$-Curry, which is the subject of section 3.1.

2.2. THE EXPLICIT VERSION OF $\lambda\to$

Unless stated otherwise, in this subsection $\lambda\to$ stands for the explicit (Church) version of the simply typed lambda calculus.

Types and terms of $\lambda\to$ - Church

The set of types for this version of $\lambda\to$, notation $T = \text{Type}\,(\lambda\to)$, is the same as for the implicit version of $\lambda\to$, viz.

$$T = V \mid C \mid T \to T.$$

2.2.1 **Definition.** The set of pseudoterms of $\lambda\to$, notation Λ_T, is defined as follows.

$$\Lambda_T = V \mid C \mid \Lambda_T\Lambda_T \mid \lambda V{:}T.\Lambda_T.$$

For example $\lambda x{:}\alpha.x$ and $y\,(\lambda x{:}\alpha\to\alpha\cdot xy)$ are in Λ_T. The first one will turn out to have a type, the second one not.

Assignment rules of $\lambda\to$ - Church.

2.2.2 **Definition.** $\Gamma\vdash_{\lambda\to} M : \sigma$ is defined by the following axiom and rules.

$$\text{(start)} \qquad \Gamma\vdash x : \sigma, \text{ if } (x{:}\sigma) \in \Gamma;$$

$$\text{($\to$E)} \qquad \frac{\Gamma\vdash M : (\sigma\to\tau) \quad \Gamma\vdash N : \sigma}{\Gamma\vdash (MN) : \tau};$$

$$\text{($\to$I)} \qquad \frac{\Gamma, x{:}\sigma \vdash M : \tau}{\Gamma\vdash (\lambda x{:}\sigma.M) : \sigma\to\tau}.$$

2.2.3 **Examples.**

(i) $\vdash_{\lambda\to} (\lambda x{:}\sigma\,\lambda y{:}\tau.x) : (\sigma\to\tau\to\sigma).$

(ii) $\vdash_{\lambda\to} (\lambda x{:}\sigma\lambda y{:}\tau.y) : (\sigma\to\tau\to\tau).$

(iii) $\vdash_{\lambda\to} (\lambda x{:}\sigma.x) : (\sigma\to\sigma).$

(iv) $y{:}\sigma \vdash_{\lambda\to} ((\lambda x{:}\sigma.x)y) : \sigma.$

2.2.4 **Definition.** A pseudoterm M is called *legal* if for some Γ and σ one has $\Gamma\vdash_{\lambda\to} M : \sigma.$

For example $(\lambda x{:}\sigma.x)$ and $(\lambda x{:}\sigma.x)y$ are legal, but $(\lambda x{:}\alpha.xx)$ is not.

The notations of β-reduction and β-conversion are extended to pseudoterms. First of all the notion of substitution is extended to Λ_T in the obvious way. Then the contraction rule on pseudoterms

$$(\lambda x{:}\sigma.M)N \to M\,[x := N] \qquad\qquad (\beta)$$

generates β-reduction, denoted again by →», and β-conversion, denoted by =. Note that in (β) the term N does not need to match the type σ.

Properties of λ→ - Church

2.2.5 Theorem. The following properties hold for λ→.

  (i)   CR,for the extended notion of reduction and conversion on Λ_T.

  (ii)   SR.

  (iii)   SN.

  (iv) $\Gamma\vdash_{\lambda\to} M{:}\sigma$? is decidable.

  (v) $\Gamma\vdash_{\lambda\to} M{:}?$ is computable.

Relation between λ→-Curry and λ→-Church

There is a relation between the implicit and explicit version of λ→. In order to express this we need a map from pseudoterms to type-free terms.

2.2.6. Definition. A map $|-|: \Lambda_T \to \Lambda$ is defined by erasing all type annotations.

  $|x| = x, |c| = c,$

  $|MN| = |M||N|,$

  $|\lambda x{:}\sigma.M| = \lambda x.|M|.$

2.2.7. Proposition.

  (i) $\Gamma\vdash_{\lambda\to\text{-Church}} M{:}\sigma \Rightarrow \Gamma\vdash_{\lambda\to\text{-Curry}} |M| : \sigma.$

  (ii) $\Gamma\vdash_{\lambda\to\text{-Currry}} M{:}\sigma \Rightarrow \exists M' [|M'| \equiv M \ \& \ \ \Gamma\vdash_{\lambda\to\text{-Church}} M'{:}\sigma].$

Pragmatics of λ→ - Church

Edinburgh LCF, a Logic of Computable Functions, see Gordon et al.[1979], is essentially λ→-Church, extended with a fixed point combinator.

3. IMPLICIT TYPING

In this section three systems of typed lambda calculus à la Curry will be introduced. These systems are all extensions of the implicit version of λ→. The three systems are the polymorphic lambda calculus λ2, the system with recursive types λμ and the system with intersection types λ∩. The system λ2 will also be encountered in section 4.1 in an explicit version. A system à la Curry that includes all of λ2, λμ and λ∩ as subsystems has been described in MacQueen, Plotkin and Sethi [1986].

3.1. POLYMORPHISM

In λ→-Curry one has that $\vdash_{\lambda\to} (\lambda x.x) : (\sigma\to\sigma)$ for every type σ. The fact that λx.x has several types is called polymorphism. This can be made explicit by allowing as type ∀α.α→α and as statement (λx.x) :

$\forall\alpha.\alpha\to\alpha$. The system $\lambda2$, introduced by Girard [1972] and Reynolds [1974] in the Church version, will be able to express this. In this subsection we will introduce $\lambda2$-Curry.

Types and terms of $\lambda2$- Curry

The terms of $\lambda2$ are those of $\lambda\to$, see definition 1.1.1.

3.1.1   Definition. The types of $\lambda2$, notation $T = $ Type $(\lambda2)$, are defined by the following abstract grammar.

$$T = V \mid C \mid T \to T \mid \forall V.T$$

Notation.   (i) $\forall\alpha_1...\alpha_n.\sigma \equiv \forall\alpha_1.(\forall\alpha_2. ...(\forall\alpha_n.(\sigma))...)$.
       (ii) $\perp = \forall\alpha.\alpha$.

Examples of types
       $\forall\alpha.\alpha\to\alpha$;
       $\forall\alpha\beta.\alpha\to\beta$;
       $\forall\alpha.\perp\to\beta$.

Assignment rules of $\lambda2$-Curry

3.1.2.   Definition.

(Start) $\Gamma\vdash x:\sigma$,   for $(x:\sigma) \in \Gamma$;

$(\to E)$ $\dfrac{\Gamma\vdash M : \sigma\to\tau, \Gamma\vdash N : \sigma}{\Gamma\vdash MN:\tau}$; $(\to I)$ $\dfrac{\Gamma, x:\sigma\vdash M : \tau}{\Gamma\vdash (\lambda x.M) : \sigma\to\tau}$;

$(\forall E)$ $\dfrac{\Gamma\vdash M : \forall\alpha.\sigma}{\Gamma\vdash M : \sigma[\alpha:=\tau]}$; $(\forall I)$ $\dfrac{\Gamma\vdash M : \sigma}{\Gamma\vdash M : \forall\alpha.\sigma}$, if $\alpha\notin FV(\Gamma)$.

3.1.3   Examples
       $\vdash_{\lambda2} (\lambda x.x)$ $: (\forall\alpha.\alpha\to\alpha)$
       $\vdash_{\lambda2} (\lambda xy.x) : (\forall\beta.\alpha\to\beta\to\alpha)$
       $\vdash_{\lambda2} (\lambda x.xx) : (\forall\beta.\perp\to\beta)$

This last fact has the following derivation

$$\begin{array}{|l}
\text{x} : \bot \\ \hline
\quad \text{x} : \bot \\
\quad \text{x} : \bot \rightarrow \beta \\
\quad \text{xx} : \beta \\ \hline
\end{array}$$

$$(\lambda\text{x.xx}) : \bot \rightarrow \beta$$

$$(\lambda\text{x.xx}) : \forall\beta. \bot \rightarrow \beta$$

Properties of λ2-Curry

3.1.4.   Theorem. The following properties hold for λ2.

   (i)   CR.

   (ii)   SR.

   (iii)   SN.

It is not known whether the properties

   $\Gamma \vdash M : \sigma$? is decidable

   $\Gamma \vdash M : ?$ is computable

are valid. (R. Milner calls them 'embarrassing open problems'.)

3.2. RECURSIVE TYPES

If we had a type σ such that $\sigma = \sigma \rightarrow \sigma$, and moreover an x:$\sigma$, then x can be applied to itself to obtain xx:σ. Therefore for such a σ one has $(\lambda\text{x.xx}) : (\sigma \rightarrow \sigma)$ and hence $(\lambda\text{x.xx}) : \sigma$. Solutions of the equation $\sigma = \sigma \rightarrow \sigma$ are obtained axiomatically by writing $\sigma \equiv \mu\alpha.\alpha \rightarrow \alpha$ which has to be interpreted like 'some solution of $\alpha = \alpha \rightarrow \alpha$'.

Types and terms of λμ-Curry

The terms of λμ are those of λ→, see definition 1.1.1.

3.2.1.   Definition. The set of types of λμ, notation T = Type (λμ), is defined as follows.

$$T = V \mid C \mid T \rightarrow T \mid \mu V. \, T$$

Notation. $\mu\alpha_1...\alpha_n.\sigma \equiv \mu\alpha_1.(\mu\alpha_2. \, ... \, (\mu\alpha_n.(\sigma))..)$.

Assignment rules of λμ-Curry

In order to state that the μ types satisfy what they are intended to do, some congruence relation $\approx$ on types is defined such that for example $\sigma \approx (\sigma \rightarrow \sigma)$ for $\sigma \equiv \mu\alpha.\alpha \rightarrow \alpha$. This relation $\approx$ is defined using trees corresponding to types. The definition of the trees is somewhat informal, but clear enough when seeing the examples.

3.2.2. Definition. Let $\sigma \in$ Type $(\lambda\mu)$. The *tree* corresponding to σ, notation $T(\sigma)$, is defined as follows.

$$T(\delta) \quad = \quad \delta, \qquad\qquad\qquad \text{if } \delta \text{ is a type variable or constant;}$$

$$T(\sigma\rightarrow\tau) \quad = \quad \begin{array}{c} \rightarrow \\ \diagup \quad \diagdown \\ T(\sigma) \quad T(\tau) \end{array} \quad ;$$

$$T(\mu\alpha.\sigma) \quad = \quad T(\sigma[\alpha:=\mu\alpha.\sigma]) \qquad \text{if defined; else..}$$

Examples.

$$T(\alpha\rightarrow\beta\rightarrow\alpha) = \begin{array}{c} \rightarrow \\ \diagup \quad \diagdown \\ \alpha \quad\; \rightarrow \\ \qquad \diagup \; \diagdown \\ \qquad \beta \quad \alpha \end{array} \quad ;$$

$$T(\mu\alpha.\alpha\rightarrow\alpha) = \begin{array}{c} \rightarrow \\ \diagup \quad\quad \diagdown \\ T(\mu\alpha.\alpha\rightarrow\alpha) \quad T(\mu\alpha.\alpha\rightarrow\alpha) \end{array} \quad = \quad \begin{array}{c} \rightarrow \\ \diagup \quad \diagdown \\ \rightarrow \quad\; \rightarrow \\ \diagup\,\diagdown \quad \diagup\,\diagdown \\ \cdots \;\; \cdots \;\; \cdots \;\; \cdots \end{array} \quad ;$$

$$T(\mu\alpha.\alpha) \quad = \quad T(\alpha[\alpha:=\mu\alpha.\alpha]) = T(\mu\alpha.\alpha) = . \; ;$$

$$T(\gamma\rightarrow\mu\alpha\beta.\beta) = \begin{array}{c} \rightarrow \\ \diagup \; \diagdown \\ \gamma \quad . \end{array}$$

3.2.3. Definition. Let $\sigma, \tau \in$ Type $(\lambda\mu)$. Then σ and τ are *equivalent*, notation $\sigma \approx \tau$, if $T(\sigma) = T(\tau)$.

Examples. If $\sigma \equiv \mu\alpha.\alpha\rightarrow\alpha$, then $\sigma \approx \sigma\rightarrow\sigma$. This could have been derived from the axiom

$$\mu\alpha.\sigma \approx \sigma[\alpha:=\mu\alpha.\sigma].$$

However, the following equation cannot be obtained from this axiom

$$\mu\alpha.\beta\rightarrow\alpha \approx \mu\alpha. \; \beta\rightarrow\beta\rightarrow\alpha.$$

Therefore the definition of $\approx$ is given using trees.

3.2.4. Definition.

(Start) $\Gamma \vdash x{:}\sigma$ for $(x{:}\sigma) \in \Gamma$

$(\to E) \quad \dfrac{\Gamma \vdash M : \sigma \to \tau \quad \Gamma \vdash N : \sigma}{\Gamma \vdash MN : \tau};$ $\qquad (\to I) \quad \dfrac{\Gamma, x{:}\sigma \;\vdash M : \tau}{\Gamma \vdash (\lambda x.M) : \sigma \to \tau};$

$(\approx) \quad \dfrac{\Gamma \vdash M : \sigma}{\Gamma \vdash M : \tau}, \quad \text{if } \sigma \approx \tau.$

3.2.5. Examples.

(i) Morris [1968]. Let $Y \equiv \lambda f. (\lambda x.f(xx))(\lambda x.f(xx))$. Then $\vdash_{\lambda\mu} Y : (\sigma \to \sigma) \to \sigma$ for all σ. Indeed, define $\tau = \mu\alpha.\alpha \to \sigma$, then $\tau \approx \tau \to \sigma$ and we can construct the following derivation.

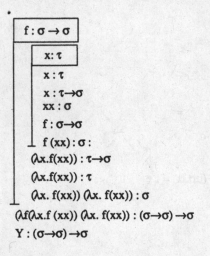

$(\lambda f(\lambda x.f\,(xx))\,(\lambda x.\,f(xx)) : (\sigma \to \sigma) \to \sigma$

$Y : (\sigma \to \sigma) \to \sigma$

(ii) Similarly, one shows $\vdash_{\lambda\mu} (\lambda x.xx)\,(\lambda x.xx) : \sigma.$

Properties of λμ-Curry

3.2.6 Theorem. The following properties hold for $\lambda\mu$.

(i)   CR.

(ii) SR.

(iii) SN fails, (Y can be typed).

(iv) $\Gamma \vdash M : \sigma$? is decidable (Cardone and Coppo [1990]).

(v) $\Gamma \vdash M : ?$ is computable (trivial, using $\mu\alpha.\alpha \to \alpha$).

Mendler [1987] has shown that there exists a restricted version of λμ-Church in which all typable terms are strongly normalizing, the restriction being that in $\mu\alpha.\sigma$ the variable α may not occur at negative positions in σ. This result probably holds for λμ-Curry as well.

Pragmatics of λμ-Curry

Recursive types occur in many programming languages, but usually in combination with simple type constructors like + (disjoint sum) and × (cartesian product) only. For example, given a unit type **1** and a type τ, one can form the type of lists over τ as

$$\mu\alpha.1 + \tau \times \alpha$$

and the type of binary trees over τ as

$$\mu\alpha.1 + \tau \times \tau \times \alpha.$$

Few programming languages allow combinations of μ in full generality. One of the first languages to do so was ALGOL 68 (Van Wijngaarden [1969]), where e.g. the 'mode declaration'

mode m = proc (m) m

corresponds to $\mu\alpha.\alpha\rightarrow\alpha$. An illuminating discussion on ALGOL 68 mode declarations and their relation to domain equations is presented in Lehmann [1977].

3.3. INTERSECTION TYPES

The system of lambda calculus with intersection types, notation λ∩, is taken from Barendregt, Coppo and Dezani [1983], which paper is based on earlier work of Coppo, Dezani, Sallé and Venneri. If in λ∩ one has M : σ and M : τ, then one has M : (σ∩τ). Moreover there is a universal type ω such that M : ω for all terms M. The operation ∩ induces a pre-ordering on types in which ω is the largest element.

Types and terms of λ∩

The terms of λ∩ are those of λ→, see definition 1.1.1.

3.3.1. Definition. The set of types of λ∩, notation T = Type (λ∩), is defined as follows

$$\mathbf{T} = V \mid C \mid T \rightarrow T \mid T \cap T.$$

One of the constants of C is selected and is called ω.

Assignment rules of λ∩- Curry

3.3.2. Definition (i) On T a relation ≤ is defined as follows

$$\sigma \leq \sigma;$$

$$\sigma \leq \omega; \qquad\qquad \omega \leq \omega \rightarrow \omega;$$

$$\sigma \cap \tau \leq \sigma; \qquad\qquad \sigma \cap \tau \leq \tau;$$

$$\frac{\sigma \leq \tau, \tau \leq \rho}{\sigma \leq \rho}; \qquad\qquad \frac{\sigma \leq \tau, \sigma \leq \rho}{\sigma \leq \tau \cap \rho};$$

$$(\sigma\rightarrow\rho) \cap (\sigma\rightarrow\tau) \leq \sigma \rightarrow (\rho \cap \tau);$$

$$\frac{\sigma \leq \sigma', \sigma \leq \tau'}{(\sigma' \to \tau) \leq (\sigma \to \tau')}.$$

(ii) $\sigma \sim \tau \Leftrightarrow \sigma \leq \tau$ and $\tau \leq \sigma$.

For example, one has $\omega \sim (\omega \to \omega)$ and $((\sigma \cap \sigma' \to \tau) \sim ((\sigma \to \tau) \cap (\sigma' \to \tau))$. We let $\cap$ bind stronger than $\to$, so one can write $\sigma \cap \sigma' \to \tau$ for $(\sigma \cap \sigma') \to \tau$.

3.3.3. Definition.

(Start) $\Gamma \vdash x : \sigma,$ for $(x:\sigma) \in \Gamma$;

(top) $\Gamma \vdash M : \omega$;

($\to$E) $\dfrac{\Gamma \vdash M : (\sigma \to \tau) \quad \Gamma \vdash N : \sigma}{\Gamma \vdash MN : \tau}$;   ($\to$I) $\dfrac{\Gamma, x:\sigma \vdash M : \tau}{\Gamma \vdash \lambda x.M : \sigma \to \tau}$;

($\cap$E) $\dfrac{\Gamma \vdash M : (\sigma \cap \tau)}{\Gamma \vdash M : \sigma, \; \Gamma \vdash M : \tau}$;   ($\cap$I) $\dfrac{\Gamma \vdash M : \sigma \quad \Gamma \vdash M : \tau}{\Gamma \vdash M : \sigma \cap \tau}$;

(sub) $\dfrac{\Gamma \vdash M : \sigma \quad \sigma \leq \tau}{\Gamma \vdash M : \tau}$.

3.3.4. Examples.

(i) $\vdash_{\lambda \cap} (\lambda x.xx) : (\sigma \cap (\sigma \to \tau) \to \tau)$;

(ii) $\vdash_{\lambda \cap} (\lambda x.xx)(\lambda x.xx) : \omega$;

(iii) $\vdash_{\lambda \cap} (\lambda xyz.xz \; (yz))(\lambda xy.x) : (\alpha \to \beta \to \beta)$.

In Van Bakel [1990] it is remarked that although the term in (iii) has a type in $\lambda \to$, it does not have the type $\alpha \to \beta \to \beta$ in that system.

Properties of $\lambda \cap$ Curry

The properties valid for $\lambda \cap$ are somewhat different from those for the other systems of implicitly typed lambda calculus.

3.3.5. Theorem. For $\lambda \cap$ the following properties hold.

(i)   CR.

(ii)   SR.

The stronger notion of Subject Conversion also holds, i.e. if $M =_\beta M'$ then

$$\Gamma \vdash_{\lambda \cap} M : \sigma \iff \Gamma \vdash_{\lambda \cap} M' : \sigma$$

(iii) SN fails, because every term has type ω.

(iv) $\Gamma \vdash M: \sigma$? is undecidable.

(v) $\Gamma \vdash M: ?$ holds trivially, because every term has type ω.

3.3.6. **Remark** (i) For the system $\lambda \cap^-$, obtained form $\lambda \cap$ by omitting rule (top), one has the following result of Van Bakel [1990]

$$SN (M) \Leftrightarrow \exists \Gamma \exists \sigma [\Gamma \vdash_{\lambda \cap^-} M : \sigma]$$

(ii) M has normal form $\Leftrightarrow$ $\exists \Gamma \exists \sigma [\Gamma \vdash M : \sigma$ and ω does not occur in σ],
see Barendregt et al. [1983].

Pragmatics of $\lambda \cap$

In $\lambda \cap$ intersection types are used for objects that have various types which are not structurally related. The same phenomenon occurs in many programming languages, where it is called 'overloading'. A well-known example is the use of the symbol + to denote both integer addition, real addition and string concatenation. In the intersection type discipline such a symbol can be given the type (**int→int**) $\cap$ (**real→real**) $\cap$ (**string→string**).

Recently new uses of intersection types have been suggested by Reynolds [1989] and Tennent [1989] in connection with ALGOL-like languages. The imperative features of such languages are accomodated by the introduction of so-called phrase types, such as

> **exp** [τ] for constructs producing a value of type τ
>
> **acc** [τ] for constructs accepting a value of type τ, such as the updating component of
> variables or result parameters of procedures. In denotational semantics these
> constructors are sometimes called 'l-values'.
>
> **var** [τ] for variables of type τ.

For example, in an assignment x : = 3, the left-hand side and right-hand side have phrase types **acc** [**int**] and **exp** [**int**], respectively.

Because in ALGOL-like languages a variables of type τ can both accept and produce a value of type τ, we need the coercions **var** [τ] $\leq$ **acc** [τ] and **var** [τ] $\leq$ **exp** [τ]. Using intersection types this can be achieved by defining

$$\textbf{var} \ [\tau] = \textbf{acc} \ [\tau] \cap \textbf{exp} \ [\tau].$$

Another phenomenon occuring in ALGOL-like languages is interference, e.g. when one command assigns to a variable that is evaluated or assigned to by an other command. In some cases this interference is undesirable, but in other cases it is very useful or even essential. What is needed are some syntactic constraints to control interference. It is possible to define these constraints using a variant of intersection types. For more details we refer to Reynolds [1989].

4. EXPLICIT TYPING

In this section several extensions of $\lambda\to$-Church will be considered. Three important extensions are $\lambda 2$-Church (second order lambda calculus), the sytstem $\lambda\underline{\omega}$ (weakly higher order lambda calculus) and the system λP (lambda calculus with dependent types). The intuition behind these extensions is the following. Types represent sets (spaces) of functions. Terms denote algorithms representing elements of these function spaces. Now there are four basic dependencies.

-   elements depend on elements;
-   elements depend on types;
-   types depend on types;
-   types depend on elements.

These four dependencies will be explained as the main features of respectively the systems $\lambda\to$, $\lambda 2$, $\lambda\underline{\omega}$ and λP.

Elements depending on elements are ubiquitous. A function f of two arguments on a set A may be used to form fxx for x in A. This fxx is an element depending on the element x. The mechanism of abstraction makes this dependency functional. One can form the function $g = \lambda x(:A).fxx$. This formation of functions is the main feature of all versions of the lambda calculus, in particular of $\lambda\to$. The other kind of dependencies will be described in subsections 4.1, 4.2 and 4.3 respectively. Subsection 4.4 gives a uniform treatment of the explicity typed systems.

4.1 ELEMENTS DEPENDING ON TYPES

In $\lambda\to$-Church one has

$$\vdash_{\lambda\to} (\lambda x{:}\alpha.x) : (\alpha\to\alpha). \tag{1}$$

If one writes $I_\sigma \equiv (\lambda x{:}\sigma.x)$, then I_σ is an element that depends on the type σ. The system $\lambda 2$ - Chuch makes this depending functional by deriving from (1)

$$\vdash_{\lambda 2} (\Lambda\alpha\lambda x{:}\alpha.x) : (\forall\alpha.(\alpha\to\alpha)).$$

Write $I_{poly} \equiv \Lambda\alpha. I_\alpha$. In order to obtain I_σ uniformly in σ from I_{poly}, a new reduction rule is introduced

$$I_{poly}\, \sigma \equiv (\Lambda\alpha.\, I_\alpha)\sigma \to I_\sigma. \tag{$\beta 2$}$$

In particular this implies that terms may be applied to types. In subsection 4.4 it will be seen that ($\beta 2$) can be considered as a particular case of ordinary β-reduction.

Types and terms of $\lambda 2$-Church.

4.1.1. **Definition.** (i) The set of types for $\lambda 2$-Church, notation $T = \text{Type}\,(\lambda 2)$, is the same as for the Curry version

$$T = V \mid C \mid T \to T \mid \forall VT.$$

(ii)   The set of pseudoterms for $\lambda 2$-Church, notation $\Lambda_T = \text{Term}(\lambda 2)$ is defined as follows.

$$\Lambda_T = V \mid C \mid \Lambda_T \Lambda_T \mid \Lambda_T T \mid \lambda V{:}T.\Lambda_T \mid \Lambda V.\Lambda_T.$$

(iii) On these pseudoterms Λ_T two notions of reduction are defined by

$$(\lambda x{:}\sigma.M)N \quad \rightarrow \quad M[x:=N], \qquad (\beta)$$

$$(\Lambda\alpha.M)\sigma \quad \rightarrow \quad M[\alpha:=\sigma]. \qquad (\beta_2)$$

4.1.2   Convention. $\Lambda\alpha\lambda x{:}\sigma\Lambda\beta.M$ stands for $\Lambda\alpha.(\lambda x{:}\sigma.(\Lambda\beta.(M)))$.

For example $(\Lambda\alpha\Lambda\beta\lambda x{:}\alpha\ \lambda y{:}\beta.x)(\gamma\rightarrow\gamma)(\forall\delta.\delta)ab$ is a pseudoterm that reduces in four $\beta\beta_2$-steps to a.

Assigment rules of $\lambda 2$- Church.

4.1.3.   Definition. $\Gamma \vdash_{\lambda 2} M{:}\sigma$ is defined by the following axiom and rules

$$(\text{Start}) \quad \Gamma \vdash x{:}\sigma, \quad \text{if } (x{:}\sigma)\in\Gamma;$$

$$(\rightarrow\text{E}) \quad \frac{\Gamma\vdash M:(\sigma\rightarrow\tau)\ \ \Gamma\vdash N:\sigma}{\Gamma\vdash MN:\tau}; \qquad (\rightarrow\text{I}) \quad \frac{\Gamma, x{:}\sigma\vdash M:\tau}{\Gamma\vdash(\lambda x.M):(\sigma\rightarrow\tau)};$$

$$(\forall\text{E}) \quad \frac{\Gamma\vdash M:\forall\alpha.\sigma}{\Gamma\vdash M\tau:\sigma\,[\alpha{:=}\tau]}; \qquad (\forall\text{I}) \quad \frac{\Gamma\vdash M:\sigma}{\Gamma\vdash(\Lambda\alpha.M):(\forall\alpha.\sigma)}, \text{ if } \alpha\notin FV(\Gamma).$$

4.1.4.   Examples. (i) $\vdash_{\lambda 2} (\Lambda\alpha\lambda x{:}\alpha.x):(\forall\alpha.\alpha\rightarrow\alpha).$

(ii) $\vdash_{\lambda 2} (\Lambda\alpha\ \Lambda\beta\ \lambda x{:}\alpha\ \lambda y{:}\beta.x):(\forall\alpha\forall\beta.\alpha\rightarrow\beta\rightarrow\alpha).$

(iii) $\vdash_{\lambda 2} (\Lambda\beta\ \lambda x{:}\bot.\ x(\bot\rightarrow\beta)x):(\forall\beta.\ \bot\rightarrow\beta),$ where $\bot\equiv\forall\alpha.\alpha.$

Properties of $\lambda 2$- Church

4.1.5   Theorem. The following properties are valid for $\lambda 2$ (see 2.1.5 for the meaning of the acronyms).

(i)   CR, for $\beta\beta_2$ - reduction on Λ_T.

(ii)   SR.

(iii)   SN.

(iv)   UT.

(v) $\Gamma\vdash M:\sigma$? is decidable.

(vi) $\Gamma\vdash M:?$ is computable.

Pragmatics of $\lambda 2$ - Church.

In Reynolds [1974] the system $\lambda 2$ was used to formalise various type-related concepts in programming languages, such as type definitions, abstract data types, and polymorphism. For example, an expression containing a type definition, like

type $t = \tau$ **in** e

can be represented by the $\lambda 2$- term $(\Lambda t.e)\ \tau$.

Many programming languages contain some form of abstract data type definition like

abstype t **with** x : σ (t) **is** τ **with** e₁ **in** e₂

which introduces an "abstract" type t with operations x : σ(t), together with a "representation" consisting of a "concrete" type τ and "concrete" operations e₁ of type σ (t). In λ2 such a construct can be modelled by the term

$$(\Lambda t \ (\lambda x{:}\sigma(t).\ e_2)) \ \tau \ e_1$$

In extensions of λ2 with so-called existential or Σ types it is even possible to consider the pair (τ, e₁) as a term of type Σt.σ(t), the type of representations of the abstract type. Thus representations become first-class citizens. For more information on this view of abstract data types we refer to Mitchell [1985], Cardelli [1985].

For an experimental language based on the Church version of λ2 and λμ, see Barendregt and van Leeuwen [1985]. That language (TALE) includes arrays and disjoint sums and its syntax and operational semantics are given in full detail.

The polymorphism provided by λ2-Church differs from that of λ2-Curry in the presence of explicit abstraction over type variables and application to type expressions. To illustrate the differences we rephrase the map example of section 2 in the system à la Church. The basis remains

null	:	$\forall\alpha.\ \text{list }\alpha\rightarrow\text{bool}$
nil	:	$\forall\alpha.\ \text{list }\alpha$
cons	:	$\forall\alpha.\ \alpha\rightarrow\text{list }\alpha\rightarrow\text{list }\alpha$
hd	:	$\forall\alpha.\ \text{list }\alpha\rightarrow\alpha$
tl	:	$\forall\alpha.\ \text{list }\alpha\rightarrow\text{list }\alpha$
if	:	$\forall\alpha.\ \text{bool}\rightarrow\alpha\rightarrow\alpha\rightarrow\alpha$

but the definition of map becomes

letrec map = (ΛαΛβ

. (λf : (α→β) λm : list α

. if list β

(null α m)

(nil β)

(cons β (f(hd α m)) (map α β f (tl α m)))

)

).

The differences with the Curry style will be clear. On the positive side, type inference is trivial. On the negative side, terms tend to become cluttered up with type information. For practical purposes one would like to have the best of both worlds, i.e. the conciseness provided by the Curry style and the simplicity of type inference provided by the Church style. Some partial solutions have been presented in McCracken

[1984], Boehm [1989], O'Toole 89 [1989], Pfenning [1988]. Although TALE is explicitly typed, type information may be left out in clearly defined cases when it can be reconstructed.

4.2. TYPE DEPENDENT TYPES

A natural example of a type depending on another type is $\alpha \to \alpha$ depending on α. In fact it is natural to define $f = \lambda \alpha \in T.\alpha \to \alpha$ such that $f(\alpha) = \alpha \to \alpha$. This will be possible in the system $\lambda \underline{\omega}$.

Another feature of $\lambda \underline{\omega}$ is that types are generated by the system itself and not in the informal metalanguage. There is a constant $*$ such that $\sigma : *$ correspondends to $\sigma \in T$. The informal statement

$$\alpha, \beta \in T \Rightarrow (\alpha \to \beta) \in T$$

now becomes the formal

$$\alpha : *, \beta : * \vdash (\alpha \to \beta) : *.$$

For the f above we then write $f \equiv \lambda \alpha : *. \alpha \to \alpha$. The question arises where this f lives. Neither on the level of the elements (of types), nor among the types. Therefore a new category K (of kinds) is introduced

$$K = * \mid K \to K.$$

That is $K = \{*, * \to *, * \to * \to *, ...\}$. A constant $\square$ will be introduced such that $k : \square$ corresponds to $k \in K$. If $\vdash k : \square$ and $\vdash F : k$, then F is called a *constructor* of kind k. We will see that $\vdash (\lambda \alpha : *. \alpha \to \alpha) : (* \to *)$, i.e. our f is a constructor of kind $* \to *$. Each element of T will be a constructor of kind $*$.

Types and terms of $\lambda \underline{\omega}$

Although types and terms of $\lambda \underline{\omega}$ can be kept separate, we will consider them as subsets of one general set T of pseudo expressions. This is a preparation to 4.3 and 4.4 in which it is essential that types and terms are being mixed.

4.2.1. Definition. (i) A set of pseudo expressions T is defined as follows.

$$T = V \mid C \mid T T \mid \lambda V : T . T \mid T \to T$$

(ii) Among the constants C two elements are selected and given the names $*$ and $\square$.

4.2.2. Notation. (i) x, y, z, ..., α, β, γ... range over V.

(ii) a, b, c,..., α, β, γ ...range over C.

Assigment rule of $\lambda \underline{\omega}$.

Because types and terms come from the same set T, the definition of statement is modified accordingly. Bases have to become linearly ordered. The reason is that in $\lambda \underline{\omega}$ one wants to derive

$$\alpha : *, x : \alpha \vdash x : \alpha$$

$$\alpha : * \vdash (\lambda x : \alpha . x) : (\alpha \to \alpha)$$

but not

$$x : \alpha, \alpha : * \vdash x : \alpha$$

$$x : \alpha \vdash (\lambda \alpha : *. x) : (* \to \alpha)$$

in which α occurs both free and bound.

4.2.3. Definition. (i) A *statement* of λω is if the form M : A with M, A ∈ $\mathcal{T}$.

(ii) A *context* is a finite linearly ordered set of statements with distinct variables as subjects. Γ, Δ,... range over contexts.

(iii) < > denotes the emtpy context. If Γ = < x_1:A_1,..., x_n:A_n> then

Γ, y:B = < x_1:A_1,..., $x_{n:An}$, y:B>.

4.2.4. Definition. The notion Γ⊢$_{λω}$ M : A is defined by the following axiom and rules. The letter s ranges over {∗, □}.

(Axiom) $$< > \vdash * : \square;$$

(Start) $$\frac{\Gamma \vdash A : s}{\Gamma, x : A \vdash x : A}, \text{ where x is fresh, i.e. not in } \Gamma \text{ or } A;$$

(Weakening) $$\frac{\Gamma \vdash B : C \quad \Gamma \vdash A : s}{\Gamma, x : A \vdash B : C}, \text{ where x is fresh};$$

(Type/ kind formation) $$\frac{\Gamma \vdash A : s \quad \Gamma \vdash B : s}{\Gamma \vdash (A \to B) : s};$$

(→E) $$\frac{\Gamma \vdash F : (A \to B) \quad \Gamma \vdash a : A}{\Gamma \vdash Fa : B};$$

(→I) $$\frac{\Gamma \vdash A : s, \quad \Gamma, x:A \vdash B : s \quad \Gamma, x:A \vdash b : B}{\Gamma \vdash (\lambda x:A.b) : (A \to B)};$$

(Conversion rule) $$\frac{\Gamma \vdash A : B \quad \Gamma \vdash B' : s}{\Gamma \vdash A : B'}, \text{ if } B =_\beta B'.$$

4.2.6. Examples. (i) α:∗, β:∗ ⊢$_{λω}$ (α→β) : ∗.

(ii) α:∗, β:∗, x:(α→β) ⊢$_{λω}$ x : (α→β).

(iii) α:∗, β:∗ ⊢$_{λω}$ (λx:(α→β) .x) : ((α→β) → (α→β)).

Write D ≡ λβ:∗. β→β. Then the following hold.

(iv) ⊢$_{λω}$ D : (∗→∗).

(v) α:∗ ⊢$_{λω}$ (λx:Dα .x) : D (Dα).

Properties of λω

4.2.7. Theorem. The following results hold for λω.

(i)   CR, for reduction on $\mathcal{T}$.

(ii)   SR.

(iii) SN, i.e. $\Gamma \vdash M : A \Rightarrow SN(M)\ \&\ SN(A)$.

(iv) UT, i.e. $\Gamma \vdash M : A\ \&\ \Gamma \vdash M : A' \Rightarrow A =_\beta A'$.

(v) $\Gamma \vdash M : A?$ is decidable.

(vi) $\Gamma \vdash M : ?$ is computable.

Pragmatics of $\lambda \underline{\omega}$

The relevance of $\lambda \underline{\omega}$ for programming languages is that the system permits computations with types and definitions of type constructors. Consider the following example.

4.2.8. Example.

If we assume constructor declarations

$$1 : * \qquad\qquad \text{int} : *$$
$$\times : * {\to} * {\to} * \qquad \text{bool} : *$$
$$+ : * {\to} * {\to} *$$

and recursive types of the form $\mu\alpha{:}*.\sigma$ similarly to section 3.2. we can from the type of integer lists as

$$\mu\beta{:}*.\ 1 + \text{int} \times \beta.$$

The 1 stands for the singleton type {nil}. Similarly for boolean lists we take

$$\mu\beta{:}*.\ 1 + \text{bool} \times \beta.$$

These two types can be obtained by applying a certain constructor of kind $* {\to} *$ to int and bool respectively, viz. the constructor

$$(\lambda\alpha{:}* \ \mu\beta{:}*\ .\ 1 + \alpha \times \beta) : * {\to} *.$$

Using a **let** definition mechanism for constructors, we can form the type of functions form integer lists to boolean lists as

$$\textbf{let } list = (\lambda\alpha{:}*\ \mu\beta{:}*\ .\ 1 + \alpha \times \beta)$$

$$\textbf{in } list\ int \to list\ bool$$

which is an abbreviation for

$$(\lambda list{:}*{\to}*.\ list\ int \to list\ bool)\ (\lambda\alpha{:}type\ \mu\beta{:}*.\ 1 + \alpha \times \beta)$$

where

$$(\lambda list{:}*{\to}*.\ list\ int \to list\ bool) : (* {\to} *) {\to} *$$

and which β-reduces to

$$(\lambda\alpha{:}*\mu\beta{:}*\ 1 + \alpha \times \beta)\ int \to (\lambda\alpha{:}*\mu\beta{:}*.\ 1 + \alpha \times \beta)\ bool$$

and subsequently to

$$(\mu\beta{:}\ *.1 + int \times \beta) \to (\mu\beta{:}\ *.1 + bool \times \beta).$$

The <u>let</u> -construction in the example above is of the form **let** $\alpha = \rho$ **in** σ which is an abbreviation for

$$(\lambda\alpha{:}k.\sigma)\rho$$

where σ and ρ are both constructors. In order to have the full benefit of the definition facility for constructors we also need

$$\text{let } \alpha = \rho \text{ in } M$$

which is an abbrevation for

$$(\lambda\alpha{:}k.M)\,\rho$$

where ρ is a constructor and M is a term. This construction is not well-formed in λω. It can be formed in the system λ2 in the special case that k ≡ *. The wish to form terms (λα:k .M) where k is an arbitrary kind leads to the system λω, which is the "union" of λω and λ2. The system λω will be defined in section 4.4.

4.3 ELEMENT DEPENDENT TYPES

An intuitive example of a type depending on an element is $A^n{\to}B$ with n∈ Int. In order to formalise the possibility of such "dependent types" in the system λP, the notion of kind is extended such that if A is a type and k is a kind, then A→k is a kind. In particular A→* is a kind. Then if f:A→* and a:A, one has fa : *. This fa is a dependent type.

Another idea important for a system with dependent types is the formation of cartesian products. Suppose that for each a:A a type B_a is given and that there is an element $b_a : B_a$. Then we may form the function $\lambda a{:}A.b_a$ which has as type the cartesian product $\Pi a{:}A.B_a$ of the B_a's. The formation of function spaces A→B can be seen as a particular instance of cartesian products. Indeed,

$$A{\to}B \equiv \Pi a{:}A.B \;(\equiv B^A \text{ informally})$$

provided that a does not occur (freely) in B. This is similar to the fact that a power of numbers is a constant product

$$\prod_{i=1}^{3} b_i = b_1 b_2 b_3 = b^3$$

provided that $b_1 = b_2 = b_3 = b$. Therefore the type constructor → can be left out in the presence of Π.

Types and terms of λP.

4.3.1 Definition. (i) The set of pseudo expressions of λP, notation $\mathcal{T}$, is defined as follows.

$$\mathcal{T} = V \mid C \mid \mathcal{T}\mathcal{T} \mid \lambda V{:}\mathcal{T}.\mathcal{T} \mid \Pi V{:}\mathcal{T}.\mathcal{T}$$

(ii) Among the constants C two elements are called * and □.

Assigment rules for λP

Statements and contexts are defined as for λω (statements are of the form M : A with M, A ∈ $\mathcal{T}$; contexts are finite linearly ordered sets of statements).

4.3.2. Definition. The notion $\Gamma \vdash_{\lambda P} M : A$ is defined by the following axiom and rules. Again the letter s ranges over {*, □ }.

(Axiom) $<> \vdash * : \square$;

(Start) $$\frac{\Gamma \vdash A : s}{\Gamma, x{:}A \vdash x : A}, \text{ where x is fresh;}$$

(Weakening) $$\frac{\Gamma \vdash B : C \quad \Gamma \vdash A : s}{\Gamma, x{:}A \vdash B : C}, \text{ where x is fresh;}$$

(Type/ kind formation) $$\frac{\Gamma \vdash A : * \quad \Gamma, x{:}A \vdash B : s}{\Gamma \vdash (\Pi x{:}A.B) : s};$$

($\rightarrow$I) $$\frac{\Gamma \vdash A : * \quad \Gamma, x{:}A \vdash B : s \quad \Gamma, x{:}A \vdash b : B}{\Gamma \vdash (\lambda x{:}A.b) : (\Pi x{:}A.B)};$$

($\rightarrow$E) $$\frac{\Gamma \vdash F : (\Pi x{:}A.B) \quad \Gamma \vdash a : A}{\Gamma \vdash Fa : B[x := a]};$$

(Conversion) $$\frac{\Gamma \vdash A : B \quad \Gamma \vdash B' : s}{\Gamma \vdash A : B'}, \text{ if } B =_\beta B'.$$

4.3.3. Examples. In λP the following hold.

(i) $A{:}* \vdash (A{\rightarrow}*) : \square.$

(ii) $A{:}*, P{:}(A{\rightarrow}*), a{:}A \vdash Pa : *.$

(iii) $A{:}*, P{:}(A{\rightarrow}*), a{:}A \vdash (Pa{\rightarrow}*) : \square.$

(iv) $A{:}*, P{:}(A{\rightarrow}*) \vdash (\Pi a{:}A. Pa{\rightarrow}*) : \square.$

(v) $A{:}*, P{:}(A{\rightarrow}*) \vdash (\lambda a{:}A \, \lambda p{:}Pa.p) : (\Pi a{:}A.Pa{\rightarrow}Pa).$

Properties of λP.

4.3.4. Theorem. The following results hold for λP.

(i)   CR, for reduction on $\mathcal{T}$.

(ii)   SR.

(iii) SN, i.e. $\Gamma \vdash M : A \Rightarrow$ SN(M) & SN(A).

(iv)   UT.

(v) $\Gamma \vdash M : A?$ is decidable.

(vi) $\Gamma \vdash M : ?$ is computable.

Pragmatics of λP

Systems like λP have been introduced by N.G. de Bruijn [1970], [1980] in order to represent mathematical theorems and their proofs. The method is as follows.

One assumes there is a set prop of propositions that is closed under implication. This is done by taking as context Γ_0 defined as

$$\text{prop} : *, \text{imp} : \text{prop} \to \text{prop} \to \text{prop}.$$

Write $\varphi \supset \psi$ for imp φ ψ. In order to express that a proposition is valid a T : prop $\to *$ is assumed and φ:prop is defined to be valid if Tφ is inhabited, i.e. M : Tφ for some M. Now in order to express that implication has the right properties, one assumes $\supset_e$ and $\supset_i$ such that

$$\supset_e \varphi \psi : T(\varphi \supset \psi) \to T\varphi \to T\psi.$$
$$\supset_i \varphi \psi : T\varphi \to T\psi \to T(\varphi \supset \psi).$$

So for the representation of implicational proposition logic one wants to work in context Γ_{prop} consisting of Γ_0 followed by

$$T : \text{prop} \to *$$
$$\supset_e : \Pi\varphi{:}\text{prop} \; \Pi \; \psi{:}\text{prop}. \; T(\varphi \supset \psi) \to T \varphi \to T\psi$$
$$\supset_i : \Pi\varphi{:}\text{prop} \; \Pi \; \psi{:}\text{prop}. \; (T\varphi \to T\psi) \to T(\varphi \supset \psi).$$

As an example we want to formulate that $\varphi \supset \varphi$ is valid for all propositions. The translation as type is $T(\varphi \supset \varphi)$ which indeed is inhabited

$$\Gamma_{prop} \vdash \lambda P \; (\supset_i \varphi\varphi \; (\lambda x{:}T\varphi.x)) : T(\varphi{\supset}\varphi).$$

(Note that since $\vdash T\varphi : *$ one has $\vdash (\lambda x{:}T\varphi.x) : (T\varphi \to T\varphi).$)

Having formalised many valid statements de Bruijn realised that it was rather tiresome to carry around the T. He therefore proposed to use $*$ itself for prop, the constructor $\to$ for $\supset$ and the identity for T. Then for $\supset_e \varphi \psi$ one can use

$$\lambda x{:}(\varphi \to \psi) \; \lambda y{:}\varphi.xy$$

and for $\supset_i \varphi \psi$

$$\lambda x{:}(\varphi \to \psi).x.$$

In this way the $\{\to, \forall\}$ fragment of (manysorted constructive) predicate logic can be interpreted too. A predicate P on a set (type) A can be represented as a P:A $\to *$ and for a:A one defines Pa to be valid if it is inhabited. Quantification $\forall x \in A.Px$ is translated as $\Pi x{:}A.Px$. Now a formula

$$\forall x \in A \; \forall y \in A.Pxy \to \forall x \in A \; Pxx$$

can be seen to be valid because its translation is inhabited

$$A{:}*, P{:}A{\to}* \; \vdash \; (\lambda z{:}(\Pi x{:}A \; \Pi y{:}A \; Pxy)\lambda x{:}A.zxx) : (\Pi x{:}A\Pi y{:}A.Pxy \to \Pi x{:}A.Pxx).$$

The system λP is given that name because predicate logic can be interpreted in it. The method interprets propositions (or formulas) as types and proofs as inhabiting terms and is the basis of several languages in the family AUTOMATH designed and implemented by de Bruijn and co-workers for the automatic verification of proofs. Similar projects inspired by AUTOMATH are described in Constable et al. [1986] (NUPRL), Harper et al. [1987] (LF) and Coquand et al. [1989] (calculus of constructions). The project LF uses the interpretation of formulas using T:prop $\to *$ like the original use in AUTOMATH.

4.4 GENERALIZED TYPE SYSTEMS

So far we have introduced four systems of typed lambda calculus à la Church, viz. $\lambda{\to}$, $\lambda 2$, $\lambda\underline{\omega}$ and λP. Although it may not seem so, there is a uniform way of describing these systems. We will define the notation 'generalised type system' (GTS) and show how the four systems in question are particular cases. The differentiation of systems is obtained by controlling which abstractions are allowed.

4.4.1. Definition. (i) The set of pseudo expressions of a GTS, notation $\mathcal{T}$

$$\mathcal{T} = V \mid C \mid \mathcal{T} \, \mathcal{T} \mid \lambda V{:}\mathcal{T}.\mathcal{T} \mid \Pi V{:}\mathcal{T}.\mathcal{T}$$

(ii) A *statement* of a GTS is of the form M : A with M, A$\in \mathcal{T}$. M is called the *subject* and A the *predicate*.

(iii) A *context* is a finite linearly ordered sequence of statements with as subjects distinct variables.

4.4.2. Definition. A *specification* of a GTS is a triple $\mathbf{S} = (S,A,R)$ such that

- $S \subseteq C$, the elements of S are called *sorts*

- A is a set of statements of the form c:s with c $\in$ C and s $\in$ S; the elements of A are called *axioms*.

- R is a set of pairs of the form (s_1, s_2) with s_1, $s_2 \in$ S; the elements of R are called *rules*.

4.4.3. Definition. Given a specification of a GTS $\mathbf{S}= (S,A,R)$, the corresponding GTS, notation $\lambda \mathbf{S}$, derives statements relative to a context Γ. The rules $(s_1, s_2) \in$ R determine which abstraction are allowed.

(Axiom) $<> \vdash c : s,$ if (c:s)$\in$ A ;

(Start) $\dfrac{\Gamma \vdash A : s}{\Gamma, x{:}A \vdash x : A}$, if s$\in$ S and x is fresh;

(Weakening) $\dfrac{\Gamma \vdash B : C \quad \Gamma \vdash A : s}{\Gamma, x{:}A \vdash B : C}$, if s$\in$ S and x is fresh;

(Π-elimination) $\dfrac{\Gamma \vdash F : (\Pi x{:}A.B) \quad \Gamma \vdash a : A}{\Gamma \vdash Fa : B[x:= a]}$;

(Π-formation) $\dfrac{\Gamma \vdash A : s_1 \quad \Gamma, x{:}A \vdash B : s_2}{\Gamma \vdash (\Pi x{\cdot}A.B) : s_2}$, if $(s_1, s_2)\in$ R;

(Π-introduction) $\dfrac{\Gamma \vdash A : s_1 \quad \Gamma, x{:}A \vdash B : s_2 \quad \Gamma, x{:}A \vdash b : B}{\Gamma \vdash (\lambda x{:}A.b) : (\Pi x{:}A.B)}$, if $(s_1, s_2)\in$ R;

$$\text{(Conversion)} \quad \frac{\Gamma \vdash A : B \quad \Gamma \vdash B' : s}{\Gamma \vdash A : B'}, \text{ if } s \in S \text{ and } B =_\beta B'.$$

4.4.4. Examples.

(i) Consider the following specification

$S = \{*, \square\}$

$A = \{*: \square\}$

$R = \{(*,*), (*, \square)\}$

Such a specification is written stylistically as

S	*, □
A	*: □
R	(*,*), (*, □)

This system $\lambda(S,A,R)$ is the same as λP.

(ii) Consider

S	*, □
A	*: □
R	(*,*), (□, □)

Then $\lambda(S,A,R)$ is $\lambda\underline{\omega}$.

4.4.5. Proposition.

(i) Consider the following specification

S	*, □
A	*: □
R	(*,*)

Then $\lambda(S,A,R)$ is in fact $\lambda\rightarrow$.

(ii) Consider the following specification.

S	*, □
A	*: □
R	(*,*), (□, *)

Then $\lambda(S,A,R)$ is $\lambda 2$.

Proof idea. (i) By induction on the generation of $\vdash$ it can be shown that if $\Gamma \vdash (\Pi x:A.B) : *$, then $x \notin FV(B)$. Therefore each $\Pi x:A.B$ is in fact $A \rightarrow B$.

(ii) Similarly. $\square$

By making variations in the GTS's introduced in 4.4.4. and 4.4.5. a natural cube of eight GTS's can be defined.

4.4.6. Definition (λ-cube). A set of eight GTS's will be defined. Each systems has as sorts S = {*, □} and as axioms A = {*: □}. As rules the systems have (*,*) plus one of the eight subsets of {(*, □), (□, *), (□, □)}. The following list gives the correspondence between systems and subsets; also alternative names of a system are given.

System	Rules besides (*,*)			Alternative names
λ→				simply typed lambda calculus
λ2	(□,*)			F, F_2
λω		(□,□)		
λω	(□,*)	(□,□)		Fω
λP			(*,□)	LF (logical framework)
λP2	(□,*)		(*,□)	
λPω		(□,□)	(*,□)	
λPω	(□,*)	(□,□)	(*,□)	λC; calculus of constructions

In the following picture of the λ-cube the edges → represent inclusion of systems.

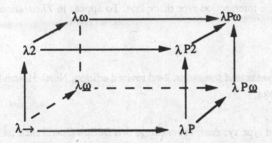

The λ-cube.

The systems λ→, λ2, λω and λP can be seen as spanning the λ-cube. E.g. λω is the union of λ2 and λω. The system λω = Fω was introduced in Girard [1972]. The system λPω is the calculus of constructions of Coquand and Huet [1988]. The λ-cube is introduced in Barendregt [1989] and is a finestructure of λPω. The notion of GTS is a generalisation of the λ-cube due indepently to Berardi and Terlouw (personal communication).

4.4.7. Theorem. All systems of the λ-cube enjoy the following properties.
   (i) CR.
   (ii) SR.
   (iii) SN.
   (iv) SN, i.e. Γ⊢M : A ⟹ SN(M) & SN(A).
   (v) UT, i.e. Γ⊢M: A & Γ⊢M : A' ⟹ A=A'.
   (vi) Γ⊢M : A? is decidable.

(vii) $\Gamma \vdash M : ?$ is computable.

There are also other interesting GTS's. For example

S	*
A	* : *
R	(*,*)

specifies the system $\lambda*$ in which every type is inhabited and not all legal terms are normalising. As remarked by H. Geuvers the following GTS

S	*, □, Δ
A	* : □, □ : Δ
R	(*,*), (□, *)

specifies λHOL, a GTS equivalent to higher order logic as in Church [1941]; the k in □ are used as sets. See Barendregt [1989], [1990] and Barendregt and Dekkers [199-] for more information on GTS's.

REFERENCES

Bakel, S. van.

[1990]   Complete restrictions of the intersection type discipline. To appear in *Theoretical Computer Science*.

Barendregt, H.P.

[1984]   *The lambda calculus, its syntax and semantics*, 2-nd revised edition, North Holland Publishing Company, Amsterdam, 1984.

[1989]   Introduction to generalised type systems, *Proceedings 3rd Italian Conference on Theoretical Computer Science*, (Eds. A. Bertoni e.a.), World Scientific, Singapore, 1-37.

[1990]   Functional programming and Lambda Calculus. To appear in *Handbook of Theoretical Computer Science*, (Ed. J. van Leeuwen), North Holland, Amsterdam.

[199-]   Lambda calculi with types. To appear in: *Handbook of Logic in Computer Science*, (Eds. S. Abramsky, D. Gabbai and T. Maibaum), Oxford University Press, Oxford.

Barendregt, H.P., Coppo, M, Dezani-Ciancaglini, M.

[1983]   A filter lambda model and the completeness of type assignment, *Journal of Symbolic Logic*, 48, 4, 931-940.

Barendregt, H.P. and M. van Leeuwen

[1985]   Functional programming and the language TALE, in: Lecture Notes in Computer Science 224, Springer, Berlin, 122-208.

Barendregt, H.P., Dekkers, W.
[199-]   Typed lambda calculi, syntax and semantics, to appear.

Boehm, H.J.
[1989]   Type inference in the Presence of Type abstraction, in: *SIGPLAN 89 Conference on Programming Languages Design and Implementation*, Portland, Oregon 1989.

Burstall, R., MacQueen, D., Sanella, D.
[1980]   *HOPE: An experimental applicative language*, report CSR-62-80, Edinburgh University.

Cardelli, L., Wegner, P.
[1985]   On understanding types, data abstraction, and polymorphism, *Computing Surveys* 17, 4, 471-522.

Cardone, F., Coppo, M.
[1990]   Type inference with recursive types: Syntax and semantics. To appear in *Information and Computation*.

Church, A.
[1941]   A formalisation of the simple theory of types, *Journal of Symbolic Logic* 5, 56-68.

[1941a]   *The calculi of lambda conversion*, Princeton University Press; Reprinted 1963 by University Microfilms Inc., Ann Arbor, Michigan, USA.

Constable, R.L. et al.
[1986]   *Implementing mathematics with the nuprl proof development system*, Prentice-Hall Inc., Englewood Cliffs, New Jersey.

Coquand, T. and G. Huet
[1988]   The calculus of constructions, *Information and Computation 76*, 95-120.

Coquand, T. et al.
[1989]   *The calculus of constructions, documentation and usersguide, version 4.10*, INRIA, Rocquencourt, France.

Curry, H.B.
[1934]   Functionality in combinatory logic, *Proc. Nat. Acad. Science USA* 20, 584-590.

Damas, L.
[1982]   Principal type schemes for functional programming, *Proceedings of the 9th ACM-POPL*, 207-212.

Girard, J.-Y.

[1972]   *Interprétation fonctionelle et élimination des coupures dans l'arithmétique d'ordre superieur.*
           Ph.D. Thesis, Université Paris VII.

Gordon, M.J.C., Milner, R., Wadsworth, C.

[1979]   A mechanical logic of computation. Edinburgh LCF, *Lecture Notes in Computer Science 78*,
           Springer.

Harper, R., MacQueen, D., Milner, R.

[1986]   *Standard ML*, Report ECS-LFCS-86-2, Edinburgh University.

Harper, R., F. Honsell and G. Plotkin,

[1987]   A framework for defining logics, *Proceedings second Symp. Logic in Computer Science*
           (Ithaca, N. Y.), IEEE, Washington DC, 194 - 204.

Hindley, J.R.

[1969]   The principal type-scheme of an object in combinatory logic, *Trans. Am. Math. Soc.* 146, 29-
           60.

Kfoury, A.J., Tiuryn, J., Uryczyn, P.

[1988]   A proper extension of ML with an effective type assigment, *Proceedings of the 15th ACM,
           POPL.*

Kfoury, A.J., Tiuryn, J., Uryczyn, P.

[1989]   Computational consequences and partial solutions of a generalized unification problem.
           Proceedings of the 4th IEEE - LICS, 98-105.

Lehmann, D.J.

[1977]   Modes in ALGOL Y. *Proceedings 5th Annual I.I.I. conference,* may 1977, Guidel, France,
           Published by INRIA, 1977.

McCracken, N.D.

[1984]   The typechecking of programs with implicit type structure, Semantics of data types, (Eds. G.
           Kahn e.a.), *Lecture Notes in Computer Science 173*, Springer, 301-315.

MacQueen, D., Plotkin, G., Sethi, R.

[1986]   An ideal model for recursive polymorphic types, *Information and control* 71, 95-130.

Mendler, N.P.

[1987]   Inductive types and type constraints in second-order lambda calculus, *Proceedings of the 2nd
           symposium of LICS.*

Milner, R.

[1978]   A theory of type polymorphism in programming, *Journal of Comp. Syst. Sci.*, 17, 348-375.

Morris, J.H.

[1968]   *Lambda calculus models of programming languages*, MAC-TR-57, Project MAC, MIT, Cambridge, Massachussets.

Mycroft, A.

[1984]   Polymorphic type schemes for functional programs, *Proceedings of the 9th ACM POPL*.

O'Toole, J.W., Gifford, D.K.

[1989]   Type reconstruction with first-class polymorphic values *SIGPLAN 89 Conference on Programming Languages Design and Implementation*, Portland, Oregon 1989.

Pfenning, F.

[1988]   Partial polymorphic type inference and higher-order unification, *Proceedings of the ACM LISP and Functional Programming Conference*.

Reynolds, J.C.

[1974]   Towards a theory of type structure, in: *Proc. of the Colloque sur la Programmation*, Paris, Lecture Notes in Computer Science 19, Springer, 408 - 425.

[1985]   Three approaches to type structure, in: *Mathematical Foundations of Software Development* (Eds. Ehring e.a.), Lecture Notes in Computer Science 185, Springer, Berlin, 97-138.

[1989]   Synctactic control of interference, part 2.

Tennent, R.D.

[1989]   Elementary data structures in ALGOL-like languages. *Science of Computer Programming* 13 (1989/90), 73-110.

Turner, D.

[1985]   Miranda, a non-strict functional language with polymorphic types, in: *Functional programming languages and computer architecture*, Nancy, Lecture Notes in Computer Science 201, Springer, Berlin, 1-16.

Wand, M.

[1987]   A simple algorithm and proof for type inference, *Fundamenta Informaticae X*, 115-122.

Wijngaarden, van, A. Mailloux, B, Peck, J.E.L., Koster, C.H.A.

[1969]   Report on the algorithmic language ALGOL 68, *Num. Math. 14*, 79-218.

Symbolic Finite Differencing - Part I

Robert Paige [1]

Computer Science Department
New York University/ Courant Institute
New York, NY 10012

ABSTRACT

Programming practice is limited by labor costs such as implementation design, program development, debugging, and maintenance (including evolution and integration). Because resource utilization is often difficult to predict precisely, the economics of software developement also depends on the risk of the implementation failing to meet its performance requirements. Consequently, complex algorithms are frequently avoided in large systems - even in optimizing compilers, where run-time performance of the compiled code is so important.

Our aim is to overcome some of these limitations by means of a transformational programming tool that facilitates implementation of complex algorithms with guaranteed worst-case asymptotic time and space. RAPTS, a working prototype of such a tool is scheduled to be demonstrated at ESOP '90.

This paper is in two parts. In part I we specify a general finite differencing framework that unifies aspects of compiler and programming methodologies, and is the basis for one of the three main transformations implemented in RAPTS. In Part II we illustrate how the transformational methodology underlying RAPTS can be used to improve the implementation of its own finite differencing transformation. Improved reduction in strength models and algorithms for conventional languages are produced as an outgrowth of this discussion.

1. Introduction.

Finite Differencing is an old and very useful mathematical idea that can speed up computation by replacing repeated costly calculations by more efficient incremental counterparts. Suppose we have a costly computation $f(x_1,...,x_n)$ in a program region R of high execution frequency. Then if we can maintain equality $E = f(x_1,...,x_n)$ as an invariant within R (at all points where $f(x_1,...,x_n)$ needs to be computed) by executing inexpensive modifications to E whenever any parameter x_i $i=1,...,n$ is modified, then we can replace all occurrences of $f(x_1,...,x_n)$ in R by the stored value E. This idea is well established in compiler methodology, where it underlies the classical method of strength reduction (see Cocke et. al.[3, 8, 9]). It also plays a major role in programming methodology, for which see Dijkstra[12], Earley[14-16], and Gries[24].

In this paper we seek to extend and unify the finite differencing technology found in low level compilers under a single framework, which generalizes the abstract invariant found in Paige[37].

1 This work is partly based on research supported by the Office of Naval Research under Contract No. N00014-87-K-0461.

We introduce several successively more general definitions of Finite Differencing program transformations. The most general of these transformations is used to derive efficient algorithms to implement each of these. This work overcomes several conceptual and algorithmic shortcomings in current strength reduction methods for conventional optimizing compilers. We also show how certain major aspects of high level programming are susceptible to automation.

The paper is organized as follows. The remainder of this section sketches a brief history of finite differencing. This is followed by preliminary notations and assumptions. The next section presents a comprehensive language independent specification of symbolic finite differencing in the form of a conditional rewrite system. In part II of this paper we present a taxonomy of restricted finite differencing problems and algorithmic solutions. The presentation makes use of set theoretic finite differencing to derive these solutions.

1.1. History

Finite Differencing has special historical significance in Computer Science. Henry Goldstine traced the idea back to Henry Briggs, a 16th century mathematician who, faced with the formidable limitations imposed on the speed with which he could perform manual calculations, discovered the technique of finite differencing to evaluate successive polynomial values using difference polynomials[22].

Briggs was a skilled 'calculator', whose task was to compute a d-th degree polynomial $p(x)$ at points $x_0 + i \times \Delta$, $i=1,...$ for some constant Δ. Letting $p_0(x) = p(x)$, he recognized that each polynomial $p_i(x) = p_{i-1}(x+\Delta) - p_{i-1}(x)$ has degree less than or equal to $d-i$ and that $p_d(x)$ is a constant, possibly 0. Moreover, simple rearrangement of the preceding formulas led Briggs to calculate each successive polynomial value $p(x_0 + i \times \Delta)$ using only d sums instead of the d sums and d products required by Horner's Rule. Briggs's method produced the following calculations:

```
x := x_0
compute t_i := p_i(x) for i=0,1,...,d
Repeat
    print t_0
    compute t_i := t_i + t_{i+1} for i=0,...d-1
    x := x+Δ
```

(It is believed that the special case of finite differencing for linear polynomials was known to the Phoenicians in antiquity [28].) The preceding code maintains equalities $t_i = p_i(x)$ for $i=0,...,d$ as invariants at the point where the polynomial value $p(x)$ needs to be printed. Consequently, the costly repeated calculation of $p(x)$ is made redundant and can be avoided by simply retrieving the stored value t_0. These invariants are established by *de novo* calculations (using, say, Horner's Rule) on entry to the loop, and are reestablished by incremental updates to t_i, $i=0,...,d$ when they are spoiled by the modification to x inside the loop.

Several hundred years later Babbage proposed to conserve manual labor further and improve reliability of polynomial tabulation by having a special purpose computer, his Analytic Difference Engine, execute the main loop of Briggs's algorithm after its registers would be supplied with initial values for t_i $i=0,...,d$. As Goldstine points out, finite differencing was the main idea underlying digital computers up through World War II, when such computers were used to produce gunnery tables [23].

However, Briggs's finite difference method embodies ideas extending well beyond the context in which he applied it. These ideas are of central importance to both compiler and programming methodologies. The essence of Briggs's idea underlies the classical method of strength reduction[2, 8, 9, 30, 44], a Fortran optimization that speeds up code by recognizing and maintaining arithmetic invariants. An extensive discussion of the method appears in Cocke and Schwartz [9], where it seems to be regarded as the most important machine independent optimization, generalizing redundant code elimination, constant propagation, and code motion. However, as we shall see, the method presented in Cocke and Schwartz is impractical for polynomials of degree greater than one.

Extending finite differencing to set theoretic expressions was initiated by Jay Earley [16], and developed by Fong et. al. [18-20], and Paige, et. al. [33-35, 37]. Proposals for implementation designs as high level compiler optimizations are due to Fong [19], Paige[34, 37], Rosen[41], and Tarjan [47].

The finite differencing idea has also been developed in the implementation of programming language environments, principally in attribute evaluation and reevaluation. Since the semantic rules in an attribute grammar are invariants defined with respect to an underlying grammar, various techniques to establish and maintain these invariants relative to modifications to syntactic units in the parse tree have been developed. Of particular importance is the elegant attribute reevaluation algorithm of Reps, et. al. [39], the incremental method of handling aggregate attributes of Hoover and Teitelbaum [26], and the coupling of database relations to an attribute grammar by Horwitz and Teitelbaum [27]. Aiming for a general tool to develop incremental software, Yellin and Strom developed a stream-like language called INC with a compiler that automatically generates provably efficient incremental programs from nonincremental specifications[53]. Their language includes relational algebra augmented with transitive closure, arithmetic, and abstract data types such as fixed length tuples and bags There are also a large number of heuristic approaches to the formidable task of incremental program optimization, which, while related to differencing, in their goals, have only achieved advantages in performance for limited special cases. One of the more general of these approaches has been suggested by Marlowe and Ryder[31].

The other area of systems where differencing plays an important direct role is in database concrete view maintenance and its application to integrity control. Here we mention the work of Bernstein et. al. [5], Koenig and Paige[29, 36], and Roussopoulis[42]. Differencing has also been critical in fixed point calculations needed to process recursive database queries efficiently (see for example, Bancilhon[4] or Whang and Navathe[51]). More general methods of integrating differencing with efficient fixed point calculations are found in Cai and Paige[6, 7].

The principle of maintaining invariants in order to make costly operations redundant was elucidated by Dijkstra[12], Gries[24], and many others as essential to the design of efficient algorithms. However, their approaches used sweeping aesthetic principles to choose invariants instead of formal criteria based on syntactic analysis of the program being designed. Although the idea has been mainly developed for imperative languages, it seems to have generic relevance to a variety of programming styles, including logic programming (see Petorossi[38] and Sacca and Zaniolo[43]; a similiarity with 'semi-naive evaluation' is noted by Ullman[49]) and functional programming (see Meertens[32] and Smith[46]).

2. Notations and Conventions

2.1. Language

Although we will formulate finite differencing independent of any specific language, the ideas will be illustrated for imperative languages using a wide spectrum of dictions from the familiar arithmetic notations in Algol and Fortran to the finite set, map, and tuple expressions of SETL[45]. With a few exceptions to be described, we will use set theoretic expressions that conform to universally accepted mathematical notations.

One such exception is the overloaded cardinality operator #s, which denotes the number of elements in a set or tuple s. Another is the choice operation ⇒ s, which denotes an arbitrary element selected from the set s. If s is empty, then the value of ⇒s is undefined. Of particular importance is the SETL set former $\{x \in s \mid k(x)\}$, which denotes the set of elements in a set or tuple s satisfying predicate k(x). An example of a slightly more general set former is $\{(x+y)^2 : x \in s, y \in t \mid odd(x+y)\}$, which denotes the set of squares of odd sums x+y, where $x \in s$ and $y \in t$. A map f is a finite set of ordered pairs with domain $\{x: [x,y] \in f\}$ and range $\{y: [x,y] \in f\}$. Thus, a map can be a single-valued function or a multi-valued binary relation. The function retrieval term f(x) denotes the value of function f at domain point x. If x does not belong to the domain of f or if f contains two or more different pairs with first component value x, then f(x) is undefined. We use the image set notation $f\{x\}$ to denote the set $\{y: [u,y] \in f \mid u = x\}$. If s is a set, then the extended image set f[s] denotes the set $\{y: [x,y] \in f \mid x \in s\}$. Tuple formers resemble set formers except that square brackets are used instead of curly brackets. For example, [sal(x): x ∈ dept] is a tuple listing the salaries (with repetitions allowed) of all members of the set dept.

Adding an element x to a set s is denoted by s with:= x. If x is undefined, then s is unchanged, and if s is initially undefined, it will be assigned $\{x\}$. To delete an element x from s, we use the notation s less:= x. Assignments of the form x op:= y abbreviate x := x op y. We use the for-loop control structure

    (for x ∈ s)
        block(x)
    end

to execute block (a sequence of statements) for each value x belonging to s. If s is a set, then we execute block for each value of x without repetition and in any order. If s is a tuple, then block is executed for every component value of s from the first to the last component. In either case, iteration proceeds through the initial value of s on entry to the loop (as through a copy of s, and cannot be affected by modifications to s within block).

2.2. Assumptions

The main goal, to be discussed last, is to apply finite differencing to program regions generated by transformation from high level functional specifications. In this context information about control flow, frequency of execution, and a great deal more useful information about these regions are supplied by the same transformations generating these regions. However, in order to make connections with existing compiler techniques in which control flow analysis is a required prerequisite for any code motion (see Cocke and Schwartz[9], Fong[19], Allen, Cocke, and Kennedy[3], Rosen[41], and Tarjan[47]), we can make a few simplifying assumptions. We assume that programs are single entry region of high execution frequency in which each expression is executed with roughly the same frequency and statements can be executed in any order. Essentially the same assumptions are found in the classical papers on strength reduction, e.g. Cocke and Kennedy[8].

We also assume expressions are side-affect free and behave like functions. Issues of safety and numerical precision are also regarded as orthogonal to the discussion here. Thus we assume arbitrary precision arithmetic.

3. Finite Differencing Framework

It is useful to formulate Finite Differencing in a general language-independent way that treats issues of correctness and efficiency separately. This section is entirely concerned with the correctness of a finite differencing framework that generalizes the earlier frameworks of Paige and Koenig[33] and Paige[37]. Part II of this paper presents efficient solutions.

There are three broad objectives in improving programs by Finite Differencing - (1) syntactic recognition of computational bottlenecks appearing within a program P; (2) choosing invariants whose maintenance inside P allows these bottlenecks to be removed; and (3) scheduling how collections of invariants can be maintained in P. To achieve these objectives we need to provide a syntactic characterization of bottlenecks (including the program contexts in which they may be avoided) and invariants (and the program contexts in which they can be usefully maintained). That is, we need to recognize a language of bottlenecks generated by composition and parameter substitution from elementary forms; we also need to apply a finite difference calculus to schedule code that maintains collections of possibly interacting invariants so that these bottlenecks can be removed.

Just a few informal examples of Finite Differencing indicate the wide range of applications that are possible. For a simplest example consider a product x×c appearing in the array access formula to be computed repeatedly in a program loop, where c is constant and x is a loop index variable modified only by fixed increments. Such a product can be replaced by less expensive successive additions. If the language has polynomial datatypes, then whenever a polynomial is used for tabulation, we can apply Briggs's method directly. The expense of database queries in an environment supporting a limited number of primitive update operations can be mitigated by maintaining appropriate invariants with dynamic indexes. A naive specification of Dijkstra's shortest path algorithm[13], in which the greedy computation of a local minimum is made explicit, can be implemented efficiently using the Fibonacci Heap of Fredman and Tarjan[21]. Both John Cocke and Ralph Wachter have observed the importance of Finite Differencing in implementing spreadsheets efficiently[10, 50].

3.1. Individual Invariants

In our Finite Differencing framework bottlenecks are restricted to program expressions that are *a priori* expensive, side-effect free, and functional. These expressions are single syntactic units recognizable using tree pattern matching. Examples are products (which are more expensive than sums) and set formers $\{x \in s \mid k(x)\}$ (which are costlier than computing predicate $k(x)$ only once).

However, local analysis is not sufficient to determine which invariants, if any, are best suited to remove a bottleneck. This choice depends on a careful global analysis of the way variables are modified in the environment containing the bottleneck. The analysis should determine with reasonable assurance whether Finite Differencing would actually improve code; that is, whether the cumulative cost of maintaining invariants is less than the cost of computing the original computational bottlenecks.

To appreciate the difficulty of 'fitting' invariants to bottlenecks, let us look at a few illustrative examples. We know it is profitable to maintain an invariant $e = x \times c$ to avoid computing a product x×c in a program region R (of high execution frequency) in which c is a region constant and x is only incremented and decremented by constants. However, if a product x × d can also be assigned to x within R, then differencing might not pay.

Sometimes it is resourceful to use the same invariant to remove different bottlenecks. For example, consider two set formers $\{x \in s \mid f(x) = q1\}$ and $\{y \in s \mid f(y) = q2\}$ inside a program region R where set s undergoes element addition and deletion, finite function f undergoes indexed assignments $f(x) := z$, and expressions q1 and q2 involve only free variables (i.e., variables not bound to their respective set formers) that can undergo arbitrary change. Then within R we can efficiently maintain the following index/invariant:

$$e = \{[f(w), w]: w \in s\}$$

and replace the expensive set formers by more efficient retrievals $e\{q1\}$ and $e\{q2\}$ respectively. However, if instead of the preceding two set formers, R contained set former $\{x \in s \mid f(x) = c\}$, where c is a region constant, then no index is necessary. It suffices to maintain equality

$$e = \{x \in s \mid f(x) = c\}$$

as an invariant, and replace occurrences of the set former by the stored value e.

For different dynamic environments we may also choose different invariants to remove the same bottleneck. Consider operation min/s, which denotes the smallest element of a set s. If s is only modified by assignment to the empty set and element addition, then an oblivious implementation of invariant e = min/s in O(1) time and space is possible to avoid the linear time search through s. However, in a dynamic environment where min/s is deleted from s, we only know how to use a more expensive heap implementation.

An 'expert' system is needed to choose the 'most specific' invariant suited to a bottleneck and its dynamic environment. Recognizing the most specific invariants for handling expression min/{min/f{x}: x in domain f} (which denotes the minimum of minima) is at the heart of Floyd's single source shortest path algorithm[17]. Within an abstract form of the algorithm f{x} is either augmented by a new value or is set to empty if min/f{x} is a minimum of minima. (This is the classical deletmin operation applied to the domain of f.) By using the oblivious implementation for each of the minima $E1(x) = min/f\{x\}$ and the heap implementation for the outermost minimum, we obtain an asymptotic space compression over a naive implementation.

A fully general specification of Finite Differencing requires sophisticated pattern matching, in which patterns, incorporating properties obtained from global analysis, can be partially ordered by a subsumption relation. For this purpose we use *nonlinear* patterns.

Definition: The set of nonlinear patterns consists of variables, constants, and any term $f(p_1, \cdots, p_k)$ where f is a function symbol of arity k and $p_1, \cdots, p_k$ are patterns. Linear patterns are nonlinear ones in which no pattern variable occurs more than once. Nonlinear pattern matching is defined as follows:

Definition: Pattern p_1 is said to *subsume* (i.e., be more general than) pattern p_2, denoted by $p_1 \geq p_2$, iff either (i) p_1 is a variable, or (ii) p_1 is $f(x_1, \cdots, x_k)$, p_2 is $f(y_1, \cdots, y_k)$, $x_i \geq y_i$ for $i = 1, \cdots, k$, and every occurrence of the same pattern variable in p_1 should match equal patterns in p_2. Relation $\geq$ is called the subsumption relation.

Patterns can also include special variables that match two extreme cases - (1) region constant expressions, and (2) expressions whose variables undergo unrestricted modification. We call these second kind of expressions *discontinuities*; the pattern variables that match them are called discontinuity parameters. By convention, if q is a discontinuity parameter, v matches any variable undergoing prescribed modification, c matches any region constant, and d is a specific constant, we order them $q > v > c > d$.

Once a collection of invariants is determined, the partial difference calculus based on Paige[37] can be used to schedule how they are maintained. Within this calculus invariants are restricted to the following general form:

(1) $\exists\, y1 \in f(x1,...,xn),\, \exists\, y2 \in y1,... \exists\, yk \in yk\text{-}1 \mid yk = E$

where f is an n-variate function, which is set valued when $k > 0$. In its simplest form when k=0, formula (1) reduces to an equality $E = f(x1,...,xn)$. Such an invariant is maintained in a program region R by establishing it on entry to R, and by updating E at each point in R when any of the parameters xi i=1,...,n is modified. Whenever invariant (1) can be maintained at each point in R where expression $\Rightarrow \cdots \Rightarrow f(x1,...,xn)$ (k applications of arbitrary choice from set f(x1,...,xn)) occurs, such occurrences are redundant and can be replaced by E. Invariant (1) may also imply certain other critical identities that support the correctness of other fruitful code replacements.

More formally, let $E :=: I(x1,...,xn)$ denote a particular invariant (1) to be maintained and exploited in a program region R, where x1,...,xn are the *input* parameters, and E is the *output* parameter. Here, I represents the abstract form of invariant (belonging to a library of such forms) being instantiated in R; parameters x1,...,xn are program variables, region constants, or discontinuity parameters, and E represents a new program variable uniquely associated with (1). When the parameters x1,...,xn are understood or are irrelevant, it is sometimes convenient to use the output variable E to stand for invariant (1). We call (1) the *Defining Invariant* and associate with it one or more rewrite rules, ei -> ei' i=1,...,k, where ei and ei' are patterns matching side-effect free expressions that behave like functions. Expressions e1,...,ek are called *replaceable terms*, and e1',...,en' are called *replacing terms*. In a program region where E is maintained each program expression that ei matches will be replaced by ei' i=1,...,k. We require that

(i)   at any program point where invariant (1) holds, replacement of ei by ei' must preserve program meaning, i=1,,...,k;

(ii)   for i=1,...,k each replaceable term ei may depend on parameters x1,...,xn, but not E, whereas ei' must involve E and may also involve x1,...,xn;

(iii)   there must be one distinguished rule e -> e', called the *binding rule*, in which e involves all of the parameters x1,...,xn; within this rule e is called the *binding term*;

(iv)   no two different replaceable terms can match the same program expression;

(v)   repeated reduction should terminate.

We also associate with invariant (1) code that should be executed in order to reestablish (1) (by updating E) when it is falsified at program points where any program variables among the parameters x1,...,xn is modified. This code is called partial difference code. Suppose that (1) holds just prior to a modification dx to a variable x on which (1) depends. Let B1 and B2 be two possibly empty code blocks such that

(i)   B1 and B2 only modify E and variables local to these blocks;

(ii)   If invariant (1) holds on entry to B1, then it holds at each point where any of its replaceable terms appear within B1, B2, and dx.

(iii)   The Hoare Formula $\{E :=: I(x1,...,xn)\}$ B1 dx B2 $\{E :=: I(x1,...,xn)\}$ is satisfied.

Then we say that B1 and B2 are *pre-* and *post-difference* code blocks of E with respect to modification dx and are denoted by ∂-E<dx> and ∂+E<dx> respectively. Note that all occurrences of x within ∂-E<dx> refer to the old value of x and that all occurrences of x within ∂+E<dx> refer to the new value of x.

Difference rules are specified in terms of modification patterns dxi for any of the parameters xi i=1,...,n that are program variables. Pattern dxi can involve any of the input parameters x1,...,xn (but not E) and additional patterns that match program expressions. For the difference rules to be well-defined, no two different modification patterns can match the same modification within a program.

Also associated with (1) is code that establishes the defining invariant on entry to the region where it is maintained.

In the simplest application of finite differencing, where a single invariant E :=: I(x1,...,xn) is maintained in a code region R, we transform R by,

(i)   inserting code to establish E on entry to R,

(ii)   replacing each modification dx in R to any variable x on which E depends by ∂-E<dx> dx ∂+E<dx>, and

(ii)   performing repeated *reductions* proceeding bottom-up within R, in which every occurrence of a replaceable term ei within R and within the difference code introduced in the previous step is replaced by an occurrence of ei', i=1,...,k

If we assume that E holds on entry to R, then the insertion of difference code makes all occurrences of ei inside R replaceable by ei'. The formal correctness proof found in[33] (and which follows directly from the definition of the invariant - and especially from the obvious fact that the difference code for E relative to any modification to a variable on which E does not depend is empty) extends to this more general framework. Apart from the code that establishes E on entry to R, the new program region formed from R by steps (ii) and (iii) above is called the *Differential* of E with respect to R, and is denoted by ∂E<R>. As was noted in[33] the differential operator is linear with respect to sequential code blocks; i.e., ∂E<Q:R> = ∂E<Q>;∂E<R>.

Before going on to describe the remaining aspects of the partial difference calculus, it is useful to look more closely at invariants using illustrative examples. Consider once again the invariant E :=: heap(s), which maintains set s as a 2-heap [52], implemented with vector E; let min/s -> E(1) be the binding rewrite rule. The difference code for E with respect to the delete-min operation s less:= min/s is the well-known 'siftdown' code[1]. However, it is incorrect to make siftdown the pre-difference ∂-E<s less:=min/s> with an empty post-difference, because the occurrence of replaceable term min/s within the delete-min operation would not be redundant. An empty pre-difference with siftdown as the post-difference is correct.

Next, consider an invariant E = {x ∈ t | f(x) ∈ s} with binding rule {x ∈ t | f(x) ∈ s} -> E and pre-difference rule

$$\partial E<s \cup:= \Delta> = E \cup:= \{x \in t \mid f(x) \in \Delta\}$$

where the post-difference is empty, and Δ is a pattern that matches any set valued expression. Unfortunately, the code implied by ∂E<s ∪:= {x ∈ t | f(x) ∈ s}> without performing any reductions is

$$E \cup := \{x \in t \mid f(x) \in \{y \in t \mid f(y) \in s\}\}$$
$$s \cup := \{x \in t \mid f(x) \in s\}$$

and the invariant only holds at the first of two occurrences of the replaceable term. Unlike the heap example, this time switching the pre-difference and post-difference code would not be correct. One solution is to precondition the program before finite differencing so that sets are only modified in terms of element additions and deletions. Then instead of the previous difference rule we would use

$$\partial\text{-}E{<}s := x{>} = (\text{for } y \in \{u \in t \mid f(u) = x\})$$
$$E \text{ with}{:=} y$$
$$\text{end}$$

where x is a pattern that matches any variable or region constant.

One last example illustrates how maintenance of one invariant may require repeated reduction to remove nested bottlenecks. Consider the invariant $e = \{[f(x),x] : x \in s\}$ to be used in removing the following costly expression:

$$\{y \in s \mid f(y) = \{w \in s \mid f(w) = q\}\}$$

where q involves only free variables (of these two set formers) that can undergo arbitrary modification. Application of the differential results in two applications of the rewrite rule $\{x \in s \mid f(x) = q'\} \rightarrow e\{q'\}$ to reduce the costly program expression to $e\{e\{q\}\}$. In this example q' is a discontinuity parameter matching any expression not containing the bound variable of the set former. Thus, if the program expression q involved y, then only only the inner set former would be reduced. Likewise if q involved w but not y, then only the outer set former would be reduced. Note that this example does not violate the rule against a replaceable term involving the output parameter e; here the replaceable term involves q', which matches e.

Of course, the condition that reductions terminate is important. Such termination is guaranteed if we can ensure that reductions simplify code by reducing the number of 'expensive' operations. Instead of providing a restricted rewrite rule syntax that guarantees termination, we prefer a more flexibile approach, which requires a separate termination proof for each finite differencing instance.

So far we have focussed on recognizing bottlenecks removable by a single invariant in isolation. However, when more than one invariant is needed, the possible interactions that arise between them complicate the process of recognizing bottlenecks, selecting invariants, and scheduling the code that maintains these invariants. The next few subsections investigate these interactions.

3.2. Sets of Invariants

The algorithms to recognize bottlenecks and to choose and maintain invariants make use of a library of invariant specifications. Within this library invariants are distinguished by the binding term together with the dynamic environment (i.e., the set of modifications contained in the difference rules). Invariants are also partially ordered by subsumption as follows. Let E1 and E2 be two invariants with dynamic environments D1 and D2, and binding terms t1 and t2 respectively. Then E1 subsumes E2 if t1 subsumes t2 and forall modifications d2 in D2, there exists a pattern d1 in D1 such that d1 subsumes d2. In order to select invariants deterministically, we require that no two incomparable invariants in the library can both subsume the same invariant (not necessarily in the library). (This condition is adapted from Hoffmann and O'Donnell's simple pattern forest condition[25].)

Bottlenecks are recognized and invariants are chosen by matching the binding terms (which involve all the input parameters of their invariants) to the program P from innermost to outermost expression of P. As a side effect, matching binds the parameters of the selected invariant E :=: $I(x1,...,xn)$ to program entities $y1,...,yn$. The Invariant is chosen only if it contains difference code with respect to every modification in P to a variable on which the invariant depends. If this invariant has not been previously selected, then output parameter E is bound to a new program variable not occurring in P. In case more than one invariant matches, we choose the most specific one. In case one bottleneck is properly enclosed in another, we process the innermost one first. Bottlenenecks occurring within assignment statements have highest priority, since simplification of the dynamic environment of P may increase opportunities for removing other bottlenecks, and may also lead to generally simpler difference code.

In order to determine all the invariants in advance (before their maintenance is scheduled), we partly simulate the reductions and difference code insertions that would be done to maintain each prospective invariant. Thus, for the recognition phase to terminate with a finite collection of invariants, we need to ensure that the rewriting system arising from the set of possibly interacting invariants terminates. By keeping track of all invariants and recognizing redundant invariants (i.e., when to use the same invariant for different bottlenecks) as the analysis proceeds bottom-up, we can keep the number of invariants down and guarantee the following crucial correctness condition: that the dependency graph, formed by drawing edges from invariants to the program variables on which they depend, is a dag.

Although termination proofs are left outside the finite differencing framework, it is worthwhile to mention several possible causes of nontermination. Nontermination can result from an invariant containing rewrite rules involving discontinuity parameters q, such as q -> e'. Also, unbridled use of identity invariants E = x can lead to runaway renaming of variables.

There is one special case, where automatic detection of a nonterminating condition is desirable. We assume that an expression $f(x1,...,xn)$ is an unremovable bottleneck, if it appears on the right-hand-side of an assignment, whose left-hand-side can be traced in a forward data-flow direction to any of the variables $x1,...,xn$. The preceding condition is called an *occurs* check after a similar condition that determines that a set of term equations cannot be unified[40].

Suppose we tried to maintain invariant E = x×c to remove the product appearing in assignment x := x×c. Then the post-difference code E := E × c would just generate a new product. To remove this new product, we would generate yet another product, and so forth.

In order to make the current definitions precise and also realistic, we need to resolve three remaining issues . According to the definition of Invariant, it is possible for the replaceable terms in the nonbinding rewrite rules of two or more different invariants to match the same program expression. In this case only one of the rewrite rules will be chosen arbitrarily for reduction. This form of nondeterminism is desirable in order to exploit the global effect of several invariants. It also captures the classical technique of Linear Test Replacement in our more general framework[44].

For a simple example of Linear Test Replacement, consider two invariants e1 = x × c1 and e2 = x × c2, where c1 and c2 are distinct region constants, and x is modified by increments x +:= 1. The binding rewrite rules are x×c1 -> e1 and x×c2 -> e2, but the nonbinding rules are x > c3 -> e1 > c3×c1 and x > c3 -> e2 > c3×c2, where c3 is a region constant. Clearly, only one of these nonbinding rules can be chosen for reduction.

In Linear Test Replacement the nonbinding reduction is only performed if the variable x is rendered useless; i.e., its value is not referenced in any control structure, and it does not contribute either directly or indirectly to program output. Thus, as a practical matter, it is important to consider reductions conditionally based on the global effect of maintaining several invariants. In this case, it is based on whether or not variable x would be made useless.

It is worth mentioning two other examples where useless variable analysis determines whether an invariant can be used at all. Consider a variable x and region constants c and d occurring in a program region R. It is profitable to use invariant $E = x \times c$ to remove a product $x \times c$ in R, where x is modified by $x := x \times d$, if the difference code

$$\partial E < x := x \times d > = E := E \times d,$$

makes x useless in R. The number of products is reduced by one. Of course, if x is not made useless, then finite differencing will degrade performance. The same argument can be made for the greedier goal of eliminating a sum $x + c$ in a region where x can be modfied by $x +:= d$. This second example can be found in several papers on reduction in strength (e.g., Lowry and Medlock[30]).

For completeness we also require that any collection of invariants include an implicit rule for detection and removal of any region constant expression, both in the original code and in any difference code introduced. In the last example products $c3 \times c1$ and $c3 \times c2$, introduced by nonbinding reductions, are region constants since c1, c2, and c3 are.

Determining all of the invariants before scheduling how to maintain them allows us to integrate such global cleanup optimizations as useless code elimination, constant folding, redundant and useless code elimination with finite differencing more efficiently than if cleanup came after scheduling. By folding global analysis of useless code together with analysis of invariants we can use efficient local processing to predict which invariants do not have to be maintained. Such information can also serve as a condition for choosing other invariants. More generally, advanced knowledge about the final maintenance code contributes to efficient scheduling, especially in allowing the same invariant (and not redundant copies) to be used for preventing different occurrences of bottlenecks.

Following Paige and Koenig[33] and Paige[37], the task of scheduling the difference code for invariants can be solved by extending the definitions of difference code and the differential within a partial difference calculus. Consider n invariants to be maintained in a program region R, in which each invariant Ej, j=1,...,n can depend only on underlying program variables x1,...,xm and Ei, i=1,...j-1. Then the difference code and differentials for single invariants can be combined algebraically to obtain differentials and difference code for all of the invariants collectively. The collective differential of E1,...,En with respect to R is denoted by $\partial\{E1,...,En\}<R>$. The collective pre- and post-difference code blocks with respect to a modification dx to a variable x are denoted by $\partial-\{E1,...,En\}<dx>$ and $\partial+\{E1,...,En\}<dx>$ respectively. A chain rule is used to derive the code for collective differentials and difference blocks based on the simpler rules for single invariants.

But before stating the chain rule it is useful to illustrate three different kinds of interactions between invariants. We consider the following four basic kinds of interaction:

(i)   when two distinct invariants share the same variable as an input parameter, it is called *horizontal* interaction;

(ii)   when an output variable of one invariant E1 is an input variable of another invariant E2, it is called *vertical* interaction, and we say that E2 depends on E1;

(iii) When the dynamic program environment is modified by an invariant E that reduces the right-hand-side of an assignment statement, it is called *dynamic* interaction, and we say that E is *dynamic*;

(iv) when the difference code of one invariant E1 with respect to a change dx to variable x contains a replaccable term e for another invariant E2, it is called *supporting* interaction, and we say that E1 *supports* E2 with respect to dx.

For these four cases and for the general rules to be presented, we show how to carefully order the code that maintains a collection of invariants correctly and efficiently without having to perform potentially costly copy operations.

3.3. Horizontal and Vertical Interaction

When sets of invariants are limited to horizontal and vertical interaction with no dynamic or supporting interaction, then the process of recognizing bottlenecks (by matching the binding terms and dynamic environments of invariants) and scheduling difference code is greatly simplified. All such bottlenecks are detected within the program region R being analyzed (in a bottom-up pass), and none are introduced within the difference code of invariants. In the absence of dynamic interaction, the dynamic environment is stable. Also, performing reductions is straightforward with tie breaking between nonbinding rewrite rules by arbitrary selection. All of these properties make termination proofs easy.

First consider the easiest case, where the only form of interaction is horizontal. Let E1 :=: I1(x) and E2 :=: I2(x) be two invariants that depend on a common argument x but do not depend on each other. Suppose that these two invariants are falsified by a modification dx to x. Suppose also that the pre-difference code for E1 (respectively E2) with respect to dx contains no occurrences of replaceable terms of E2 (respectively E1). Then the collective pre- and post-difference code is,

$$\partial\text{-}\{E1,E2\}<dx> = \partial\text{-}E1<dx>\ \partial\text{-}E2<dx>$$
or
$$\partial\text{-}E2<dx>\ \partial\text{-}E1<dx>$$

$$\partial\text{+}\{E1,E2\}<dx> = \partial\text{+}E1<dx>\ \partial\text{+}E2<dx>$$
or
$$\partial\text{+}E2<dx>\ \partial\text{+}E1<dx>$$

For example, consider the defining invariants E1 = [sal(x): x ∈ s] and E2 = #s, and the modification s with:= z. In taking the differential of E1 and E2 relative to a program region R, the difference code insertion and the obvious binding rules [sal(x): x ∈ s] -> E1 and #s -> E2 would be carried out in a straightforward way.

A more unusual example is that of the two defining invariants E1 = [[f(x),x]: x ∈ s] and E2 = {[g(x),x]: x ∈ s} with binding rules {x ∈ s | f(x) = q1} -> E1{q1} and {x ∈ s | g(x) = q2} -> E1{q2}, where q1 and q2 are discontinuity parameters. Difference code insertion relative to element additions to and deletions from s and indexed assignments to f and g are straightforward. However, this example illustrates reductions being performed in different orders within the same program region. Program expression {x ∈ s | f(x) = {y ∈ s | g(y) = u+v}} is reduced to E1{E2{u+v}}, while expression {x ∈ s | g(x) = {y ∈ s | f(y) = u+v}} is reduced to E2{E1{u+v}}.

Clearly, this poses no problem for bottom-up reduction, and a generalized form of pre-difference, post-difference, and differential for collections of invariants is easy.

Let us now permit vertical as well as horizontal interaction. Suppose that one invariant E1 :=: f(E2) depends on another invariant E2 :=: g(x) and perhaps also on x. Then we must form the difference of E1 with respect to the difference of E2 with respect to changes in x, as the following collective difference rule indicates:

$$\partial\text{-}\{E1,E2\}<dx> = \partial E1<\partial\text{-}E2<dx>>$$
$$\partial\text{-}E1<dx>$$

$$\partial\text{+}\{E1,E2\}<dx> = \partial\text{+}E1<dx>$$
$$\partial E1<\partial\text{+}E2<dx>>$$

Exchanging E1 and E2 in the code just above would be incorrect, since E2 would not be reestablished relative to any modification to E1 occurring in the difference code for E1 with respect to dx.

The two equalities E1 = #E2 and E2 = {x ∈ s | k(s)} and the modification s with:= z exemplify this kind of interaction. Note also, that when set E2 is augmented, then E1 is incremented without making any reference to E2. Consequently, E1 is not needed to maintain E2. If it is not needed for any other purpose, it can be eliminated.

As was observed in[34], vertical interaction can make invariants and the code that maintains them useless. However, that reference applied global useless code elimination to remove useless invariants after they were maintained in a program. Here, however, we want to integrate useless invariant analysis with finite differencing to make this analysis more efficient and to make differencing more powerful. In general the output parameter E of an invariant is useless if it is the input variable to some other invariant and,

(i) no difference code for any invariant (that depends on E) with respect to E makes reference to E;

(ii) all occurrences of E introduced by reductions are eliminated by further reductions due to other invariants

(iii) no reference to E introduced within its own difference code is part of a control structure and can determine whether or not any useful statements are executed.

For example, in a program region R where n is incremented by 1 repeatedly, we can remove the nest of bottlenecks in the naive compound growth formula $P \times (1 + r)^n$ using the three invariants: $t1 = 1 + r$, $t2 = t1^n$, and $t3 = P \times t2$. Invariant t2 is useless, because it is not referenced by the difference code maintaining t3.

Next consider an interesting special case when a new invariant is formed from an old one by parameter substitution in which the same parameter appears more than once. How do we maintain invariant

(4) $E :=: f(x,x,...,x,xm+1,...,xn)$

with respect to a modification dx to the variable x (occurring m times)? An easy answer is to replace (4) with m - 1 copies of x using invariants $Ei = x$, $i=1,...,m-1$ and $E' :=: f(x,E1,...,Em-1,xm+1,...,xn)$. However, more space efficient methods, requiring no more than one copy (and sometimes no copies) of x, were presented in [37]. The idea is to first consider the difference rules for the related function (formed from (4) by replacing the m occurrences of x by new variables x1,...,xm, each containing the value of x)

(4') $E' = f(x1,...,xn)$

with respect to successive modifications dxi i=1,...,m, each just the same as dx. Then we can sometimes distribute this difference code both before and after the modification dx in such a way that all occurrences of xi, i=1,...,m within the difference code placed before dx refers only to the old value of x (before it is changed), and all such occurrences in the difference code place after dx refers to the new value of x.

For example, consider the cross product s × s of set s, when the library of invariants only contains an invariant $E = t \times q$ with difference rules

    ∂-E<t with:= a> = (for y ∈ q) E with:= [a,y]
      and
    ∂-E<q with:= a> = (for y ∈ t) E with:= [y,a]

Rearrangement of the preceding difference code around a single modification to s leads to the following correct difference code for s × s:

    (for y ∈ s) E with:= [a,y]
    s with:= a
    (for y ∈ s) E with:= [y,a]

Various papers on Fortran strength reduction (e.g., Allen, et. al.[3]) discuss handling product i × i as a special case. The reader should refer to[37] for details of the general method.

We conclude this subsection with a simple chain rule that extends the previous definitions of pre- and post-difference code and differentials from single invariants to collections. Suppose we have a set {E1,...,En} of invariants whose dependency graph forms a dag and contains only horizontal and vertical interactions. Then the collective differential of {E1,...,En} relative to a program region R, denoted by ∂{E1,...,En}<R> is a new code block formed from R by taking the following two steps:

(i)   for each modification dx occurring within R, pick some E1 that does not depend on any of the output variables E2,...,En, and replace dx by ∂{E2,...,En}<∂E1<dx>>;

(ii)   perform repeated reductions associated with each of the invariants E1,..,En throughout the rest of B.

If the conditions of step (ii) above hold, then the collective pre- and post-difference code blocks are:

    ∂-{E1,...,En}<dx> = ∂{E2,...,En}<∂-E1<dx>>
                ∂-{E2,...,En}<dx>

    ∂+{E1,...,En}<dx> = ∂+{E2,...,En}<dx>
                ∂{E2,...,En}<∂+E1<dx>>

Once again we can adapt the chain rule proof from[33] to this slightly different setting. The recursive step (i) always terminates.

3.4. Dynamic and Supporting Invariants

Allowing dynamic interaction alters analysis for invariants significantly and changes the logic of the chain rule from the last subsection. Allowing maintenance of one invariant to introduce new bottlenecks whose removal would require new invariants to be maintained (as in Briggs's algorithm) complicates both the selection and scheduling of invariants. Since now invariants can be selected based on matching binding terms occurring within the difference code as well as in the original program text, proving a reasonable finite bound on the number of invariants selected can be a problem.

Let us first consider dynamic interaction. Suppose we want to remove the sum contained in the assignment $j := i + c$ using invariant $E1 = i + c$ in a program region R. Then because of the 'occurs check' condition, for $i + c$ to be removable, no modification to i occurring in R can depend on j either directly or indirectly. (Recall our conservative flow assumptions that any statement can be executed after any other statement.) Further, we know that any other invariant $E2 = f(j)$ cannot be used to remove an occurrence of expression $f(j)$ on the right-hand-side of an assignment to any variable on which i depends either directly or indirectly.

The preceding observation leads to a general rule for analyzing invariants. Let S be the set of all expressions matched by binding terms of invariants and occurring in assignments. Then S must contain an expression $f(x1,...,xn)$, involving variables $x1,...,xn$, with the following property. No other expression belonging to S can occur within any assignment to a variable on which any of the variables $x1,...,xn$ depend, either directly or indirectly. We call $f(x1,...,xn)$ *minimal*, and observe that S can be partially ordered. Thus, to handle dynamic interaction properly, invariant analysis must be modified to first examine assignment statements in topological order starting from minimal expressions. After that the remaining expressions can be examined bottom-up.

With dynamic interaction we modify the recursive step of the chain rule in the preceding subsection in the following way. Let dx be a modification to a variable x. To compute the differential $\partial\{E1,...,En\}<dx>$ we perform the following steps:

(i) first perform repeated reductions within dx using any of the invariants that do not depend on x;

(ii) take the differential $\partial\{Ei,...,En\}<dx'>$ (as in the preceding subsection) of the remaining invariants $Ei,...,En$ with respect to the new modification dx' resulting from step (i).

Finally, consider supporting interaction. Suppose that the difference code of one invariant $E1 = g(x)$ with respect to a change dx to variable x contains the binding term $f(x)$ of another invariant $E2 = f(x)$; i.e., invariant E2 supports invariant E1 with respect to dx. Suppose also that E1 does not support E2 with respect to dx or with respect to any modifications to E1 in the difference code for E1 with respect to dx. Finally, suppose that E1 does not depend on E2. In this case the differential of E2 with respect to the pre-difference block $\partial\text{-}E1<dx>$ (respectively postdifference $\partial\text{+}E1<dx>$) will replace occurrences of $f(x)$ involving the old value of x (respectively new value of x) appearing in these blocks by occurrences of E2. The correct collective difference code is,

$$\partial\text{-}\{E2,E1\}<dx> = \partial E2<\partial\text{-}E1<dx>>$$
$$\partial\text{-}E2<dx>$$

$$\partial\text{+}\{E2,E1\}<dx> = \partial\text{+}E2<dx>$$
$$\partial E2<\partial\text{+}E1<dx>>$$

Observe that the collection of reference counts embodied in the equalities $E2(w) = \#[x \in t \mid x = w]$ supports the equality $E1 = \{x: x \in t\}$ with respect to the modification t with:= z. For this example, t is a tuple, t with:= z concatenates z to the end of t, $E1$ stores the set of values in tuple t, and expression $[x \in t \mid x = w]$ forms a new tuple containing all the elements of t with value w.

To appreciate the preceding conditions consider two invariants $E1 = f1(x)$ and $E2 = f2(x)$, which both depend on the same variable x. Let dx be an assignment to x, and let $\partial+E1\langle x \rangle$ and $\partial+E2\langle x \rangle$ be empty. If $\partial-E2\langle x \rangle$ contains an occurrence of $f1(x)$, then it will not be redundant within the differential

$$\partial\{E2,E1\}\langle x \rangle = \partial-E1\langle x \rangle$$
$$\partial-E2\langle x \rangle$$
$$dx$$

because this occurrence involves the old value of x; but $E1$, being just modified, reflects the new value of x.

Briggs's method extends the preceding idea further. In order to tabulate a d-th degree polynomial $p(x)$, he used $d+1$ invariants, $t = p(x)$, $t1 = p1(x)$, $t2 = p2(x),...,td = pd$, where $t1$ supports t with respect to a change dx in x, and $ti+1$ supports ti with respect to dx $i= 1,...,d-1$. Since none of the difference code for $t1,...,td$ contains occurrences of $p(x)$, we can guess that the correct differential is

$$\partial\{t,t1,...,td\}\langle dx \rangle = \partial\{t1,...,td\}\langle \partial t \langle dx \rangle \rangle$$

Continuing to unwind the differential is straightforward.

It is interesting to examine some arithmetic examples that have inspired traditional strength reduction. Consider invariants for sums $E1 = x + c$, where c is a constant, and for products $E2 = x \times y$. Relevant difference rules include:

$$\partial-E1\langle x +:= y \rangle = E1 +:= y$$
$$\partial-E2\langle x +:= z \rangle = E2 +:= z \times y$$

Note that the difference code for $E1$ makes no reference to x, so is capable of making x useless. Note also, that the difference code for $E2$ is worthwhile only if it can be supported by an invariant $E3 = z \times y$.

It turns out that these invariants for sums and products can reduce all products in a d-th degree polynomial $p(x)$ programmed using Horner's rule in a loop where x is incremented by a constant. A similar observation has been made before by Cocke and Schwartz[9] and Allen, Cocke, and Kennedy[3]. What has not been said is that the result does not reproduce Briggs's method, but produces over d! sums and temporaries. Cleanup improves matters by only small constant factors.

The reason is this. A d-th degree polynomial written out using Horner's Rule requires d invariants to remove the visible products. But each of these invariants must be supported by other products occurring in difference code but not directly in the polynomial. To count the number of invariants and also the number of operations in the collective difference code, it is useful to consider the degree of each argument of a product $E = T \times Q$ for each invariant E. Let $temps(i,j)$ be one plus the number of invariants that either directly or indirectly support an invariant $E = T \times Q$, where T has degree i and Q has degree j. For our example, note that one of the arguments is always x, which has degree 1, or is a constant, which has degree 0.

It is easy to see that

temps(0,0) = 1,
temps(1,0) = 2,
temps(0,i) = 1 + i temps(0,i-1), and
temps(1,i) = 1 + temps(0,i) + i temps(1,i - 1)

The total number of invariants generated is,

$$\sum_{i=0}^{d} temps(1,i) = \Theta(d!)$$

The total number of operations is comparable. In Part II of this paper we give a simple transformation integrated with the chain rule to recover Briggs's method exactly.

One last example is about detecting all region constant expressions in a parse tree, where free(x) maps each expression node x to the set of free parameters on which x depends; RC is the set of nodes that are constant denotations, and RCV is the set of variable nodes that are region constants. Then the set of nodes corresponding to region constant expressions is specified by

lfp n. {x ∈ domain free | free(x) ⊆ n ∪ RCV ∪ RC}

which is the least fixed point of the set former relative to parameter n. The fixed point can be computed by the following code:

```
n := {}
( while ∃ x ∈ {y ∈ domain free | #(free(y) - (RCV ∪ RC ∪ n)) = 0})
    n with:= x
end
```

which follows from an easy fixed point argument[7, 11, 48]. Bottom-up analysis of the costly computation at the top of the while-loop determines the following six invariants,

```
e1 = RCV ∪ RC
e2 = e1 ∪ n
e3 = {[y,w] ∈ free | w ∉ e2}
e4(y) = #e3{y}
e5 = free⁻¹
e6 = {y ∈ domain free | e4(y) = 0}
```

where e5 supports e3 relative to element additions to e2. Further analysis determines that e1 is a region constant, e2 and e3 are useless invariants, and the result of the chain rule is the expected linear time code.

Consider the general case of n invariants, Ei i=1,...,n. We say that E1 is *minimal* with respect to invariants {E1,...,En} and a modification dx if

(i)   E1 does not depend on any of the variables Ei, i=2,...,n; and

(ii)   E1 does not support Ei, i=2,...,n with respect to dx;

Then the collective differential ∂{E1,...,En}<R> is a new code block formed from R by,

(i)   first performing reductions within dx from all those invariants that do not depend on x;

(ii)   next replacing each modification dx occurring within R by ∂{E2,...,En}<∂E1<dx>> where E1 is minimal with respect to Ei, i=1,..,n and dx;

(iii) finally, perform repeated reductions associated with each of the invariants E1,..,En throughout the rest of B.

4. Postscript

Part II of this paper presents a taxonomy of finite differencing problems and solutions based on the framework discussed in Part I. In particular finite differencing is divided into linear differencing in which invariants can only depend on one variable. Within this category is one-level linear differencing in which reductions are highly simplified and only horizontal interaction of invariants are permitted. This class corresponds to early reduction in strength[44].

In multi-level linear differencing all interactions are allowed. We present a one-pass linear randomized time algorithm that improves on the classical strength reduction algorithms of[8, 9, 30]. We then consider two aspects of nonlinear differencing, where invariants can depend on more than one variable. First we present an efficient algorithm supporting a variety of arithmetic identities. Next, nonlinear finite differencing is discussed from a transformational perspective. That is, we consider a very high level, declaration free, strongly typed, functional problem specification language implemented in RAPTS. Typings and universal sets are inferred from problem specifications. Further analysis to compile efficient data structures that implement sets and maps is obtained by transformations that are both guided by earlier analysis and also propagate modified semantic information for use by later transformations. Three successive transformations - fixed point iteration, set theoretic finite differencing, and data structure selection compile the specification language into C. In this context, we discuss the finite differencing phase of the high level compiler. Set theoretic finite differencing is also used to derive major pieces of the algorithms presented.

References

1. Aho, A., Hopcroft, J., and Ullman, J., *Design and Analysis of Computer Algorithms*, Addison-Wesley, 1974.

2. Allen, F. E., "Program Optimization," *Annual Review of Automatic Programming*, vol. 5, pp. 239-307, 1969.

3. Allen, F. E., Cocke, J., and Kennedy, K., "Reduction of Operator Strength," in *Program Flow Analysis*, ed. Muchnick, S. and Jones, N., pp. 79-101, Prentice Hall, 1981.

4. Bancilhon, F., "Naive Evaluation of Recursively defined Relations," in *On Knowledge-Base Management Systems*, ed. Mylopoulos, J, pp. 165-178, 1985.

5. Bernstein, P., Blaustein, B., and Clarke, E., "Fast Maintenance of Semantic Integrity Assertions Using Redundant Aggregate Data," in *Proceedings 6th International Conference on VLDB*, pp. 126-136, Montreal, Canada, October, 1980.

6. Cai, J. and Paige, R., "Binding Performance at Language Design Time," in *ACM POPL*, pp. 85 - 97, Jan, 1987.

7. Cai, J. and Paige, R., "Program Derivation by Fixed Point Computation," *Science of Computer Programming*, vol. 11, pp. 197-261, 1988/89.

8. Cocke, J. and Kennedy, K., "An Algorithm for Reduction of Operator Strength," *CACM*, vol. 20, no. 11, pp. 850-856, Nov., 1977.

9. Cocke, J. and Schwartz, J. T., *Programming Languages and Their Compilers*, Lecture Notes, CIMS, New York University, 1969.

10. Cocke, J., *private communication, 1986.*

11. Cousot, P. and Cousot, R., "Constructive versions of Tarski's fixed point theorems," *Pacific J. Math.*, vol. 82, no. 1, pp. 43-57, 1979.

12. Dijkstra, E. W., *A Discipline of Programming*, Prentice-Hall, 1976.

13. Dijkstra, E. W., "A note on two problems in connexion with graphs," *Numer. Math.*, vol. 1, no. 5, pp. 269-271, 1959.

14. Earley, J., "Toward an Understanding of Data Structures," *CACM*, vol. 14, no. 10, pp. 617-627, Oct. 1971.

15. Earley, J., "High Level Operations in Automatic Programming," in *Proc. Symp. on Very High Level Langs.*, vol. 9, Sigplan Notices, Apr, 1974.

16. Earley, J., "High Level Iterators and a Method for Automatically Designing Data Structure Representation," *J of Computer Languages*, vol. 1, no. 4, pp. 321-342, 1976.

17. Floyd, R., "Algorithm 97: shortest path," *CACM*, vol. 5, no. 6, p. 345, 1962.

18. Fong, A. and Ullman, J., "Induction Variables in Very High Level Languages," in *Proceedings Third ACM Symposium on Principles of Programming Languages*, pp. 104-112, Jan, 1976.

19. Fong, A., "Elimination of Common Subexpressions in Very High Level Languages," in *Proceedings Fourth ACM Symposium on Principles of Programming Languages*, pp. 48-57, Jan, 1977.

20. Fong, A., "Inductively Computable Constructs in Very High Level Languages," in *Proceedings Sixth ACM Symposium on Principles of Programming Languages*, pp. 21-28, Jan, 1979.

21. Fredman, M. and Tarjan, R., "Fibonacci Heaps and Their Uses in Improved Network Optimization Algorithms," in *25th Annual Symp. on FOCS*, pp. 338 - 346, Oct., 1984.

22. Goldstine, H., *A History of Numerical Analysis*, Springer-Verlag, New York, 1977.

23. Goldstine, H., *The Computer from Pascal to Von Neumann*, Princeton University Press, Princeton, New Jersey, 1972.

24. Gries, D., *The Science of Programming*, Springer Verlag, 1981.

25. Hoffmann, C. and O'Donnell, J., "Pattern Matching in Trees," *JACM*, vol. 29, no. 1, pp. 68-95, Jan, 1982.

26. Hoover, R. and Teitelbaum, T., "Efficient Incremental Evaluation of Aggregate Values in Attribute Grammars," in *Proc. Symp. on Compiler Construction*, pp. 39-50, 1986.

27. Horwitz, S. and Teitelbaum, T., "Generating Editing Environments Based on Relations and Attributes," *ACM TOPLAS*, vol. 8, no. 4, pp. 577-608, Oct. 1986.

28. Knorr, W., *private communication, 1982.*

29. Koenig, S. and Paige, R., "A Transformational Framework for the Automatic Control of Derived Data," in *Proceedings 7th International Conference on VLDB*, pp. 306-318, Sep, 1981.

30. Lowry, S. and Medlock, C., "Object Code Optimization," *CACM*, vol. 12, no. 1, pp. 13-22, Jan., 1969.

31. Marlowe, T. and Ryder, B., "An efficient hybrid algorithm for incremental dataflow analysis," in *17th Symp. ACM POPL*, 1990.

32. Meertens, L., "Algorithmics," in *Mathematics and Computer Science - Proc. CWI Symp. Nov. 1983*, ed. J. W. de Bakker, M. Hazewinkel and J.K. Lenstra, CWI Monographs Vol. I, North-Holland, 1986.

33. Paige, R. and Koenig, S., "Finite Differencing of Computable Expressions," *ACM TOPLAS*, vol. 4, no. 3, pp. 402-454, July, 1982.

34. Paige, R., *Formal Differentiation*, UMI Research Press, Ann Arbor, Mich, 1981.

35. Paige, R., "Transformational Programming -- Applications to Algorithms and Systems," in *Proceedings Tenth ACM Symposium on Principles of Programming Languages*, pp. 73-87, Jan, 1983.

36. Paige, R., "Applications of Finite Differencing to Database Integrity Control and Query/Transaction Optimization," in *Advances In Database Theory*, ed. Gallaire, H., Minker, J., and Nicolas, J.-M., vol. 2, pp. 171-210, Plenum Press, New York, Mar, 1984.

37. Paige, R., "Programming With Invariants," *IEEE Software*, vol. 3, no. 1, pp. 56-69, Jan, 1986.

38. Pettorossi, A. and Proietti, M., *The Automatic Construction of Logic Programs*, IFIPS WG2.1 TR 568 CHM-15, 1989.

39. Reps, T., Teitelbaum, T., and Demers, A., "Incremental Context-Dependent Analysis for Language-Based editors," *ACM TOPLAS*, vol. 5, no. 3, pp. 449-477, July, 1983.

40. Robinson, J. A., "A Machine Oriented Logic Based on the Resolution Principle," *JACM*, pp. 23-41, January, 1965.

41. Rosen, B. K., "Degrees of Availability," in *Program Flow Analysis*, ed. Muchnick, S., Jones, N., pp. 55-76, Prentice Hall, 1981.

42. Roussopoulos, N., *The Incremental Access Method of View Cache: Concept, Algorithm, and Cost Analysis*, Computer Science Technical Report Series UMIACS-TR-89-15, CS-TR-2193, Institute for Advanced Computer Studies, Department of Computer Science, University of Maryland, February, 1989.

43. Sacca, D. and Zaniolo, C., *Differential Fixpoint Methods and Stratification of Logic Programs*, MCC TR ACA-ST-032-88, 1988.

44. Samelson, K. and Bauer, F. L., "Sequential Formula Translation," *CACM*, vol. 3, no. 2, pp. 76-83, Feb, 1960.

45. Schwartz, J., Dewar, R., Dubinsky, D., and Schonberg, E., *Programming with Sets: An introduction to SETL*, Springer-Verlag, 1986.

46. Smith, D., "KIDS - A Knowledge-Based Software Development System," in *Proc. Workshop on Automating Software Design, AAAI-88*, pp. 129-136, Sept. 1988.

47. Tarjan, R., "A Unified Approach to Path Problems," *JACM*, vol. 28, no. 3, pp. 577-593, July, 1981.

48. Tarski, A., "A Lattice-Theoretical Fixpoint Theorem and its Application," *Pacific J. of Mathematics*, vol. 5, pp. 285-309, 1955.

49. Ullman, J., *Principles of Database and Knowledge-Base Systems, I,* Computer Science Press, 1988.

50. Wachter, R., *private communication, 1989.*

51. Whang, K. and Navathe, S., "An Extended Disjunctive Normal Form Approach for Processing Recursive Logic Queries in Loosely Coupled Environments," in *Proc. 13th Intl. Conf. on Very Large Data Bases*, pp. 275-287, Sept. 1987.

52. Williams, J. W. J., "Algorithm 232: Heapsort," *CACM*, vol. 7, no. 6, pp. 347-348, 1964.

53. Yellin, D. and Strom, R., *INC: A Language for Incremental Computations*, IBM Research Center/Yorktown Heights RC14375(#64375), 1989.

Implementation of an Interpreter for a Parallel Language in Centaur

Yves Bertot

INRIA, Sophia Antipolis

Route des Lucioles, 06565 Valbonne Cedex, France

Abstract

This paper presents the implementation of an interpreter for the parallel language ESTEREL in the CENTAUR system. The dynamic semantics of the language is described and completed with two modules providing a graphical visualization of the execution and a graphical execution controller. The problems of implementing a parallel language using natural semantics and of providing a visualization for a parallel language are especially addressed.

1. The Logical Kernel of the Interpreter

ESTEREL [esterel] is a language involving parallelism and broadcast signal communication used for the description of reactive systems, i.e., systems that react to successions of events [reactive]. The command system for an airplane or the man-machine interface [gfxobj] for an interactive system like CENTAUR are two examples of such reactive systems.

The interpreter described in this paper is based on a description of the *dynamic semantics* of ESTEREL written in natural semantics by the designers of the language [design]. We focus on the implementation of this dynamic semantics within CENTAUR [centaur], using the TYPOL formalism [typol].

We first give a short description of the language and the constructs it contains. Then we give an overview of the semantics' organization. Finally, we concentrate on the key points of the semantics: the use of a rewriting system to express parallelism in the execution of an ESTEREL program.

1.1. The ESTEREL Language

In [design], Berry and Gonthier give a schematic presentation of reactive systems. Such systems are composed of three layers:

- An *interface* with the environment, in charge of receiving input and producing output.
- A *reactive kernel* that contains the logic of the system. It decides the computations and outputs that must be generated in answer to inputs.
- A *data handling* layer that performs classical computations requested by the logical kernel.

ESTEREL is used to program the reactive kernel. It is not a full-fledged programming language but rather a program generator used to produce a reactive system written in Ada, C, or Le_Lisp[1]. The interface and data handling layer are specified in the host language. The data handling is integrated using abstract data type facilities.

---

[1] Ada is a trademark of the U. S. DoD, Le_Lisp is a trademark of INRIA.

The basic data manipulated in ESTEREL are signals. they correspond to stimuli that can be emitted and listened in the different parallel processes. Signals can carry additional values. Their communication is conceptually instantaneous and broadcasted. The basic constructs are the following instructions:

- **emit S** or **emit S(exp)**: emit the signal S or emit the signal S with the value of **exp**.
- **present S then** stat$_1$ **else** stat$_2$ **end**: execute stat$_1$ if S is present or stat$_2$ otherwise.
- **do stat watching S**: execute stat until the signal S appears.
- stat$_1$; stat$_2$: execute stat$_1$ and stat$_2$ in sequence, i.e, execute stat$_2$ only when stat$_1$ is terminated.
- stat$_1$ || stat$_2$: execute stat$_1$ and stat$_2$ in parallel.
- **X := exp**: assign the value of **exp** to the variable X. variables can be used in expressions as in any imperative language. They cannot be shared between parallel processes.

The basic concepts of the language are the synchrony hypothesis, parallelism, and broadcast signal communication. The synchrony hypothesis is based on the assumption that each reaction to an input is conceptually instantaneous. The reception of an input event and the emission of the corresponding reaction take place at the same time and define an ESTEREL *instant*.

The parallelism permits to enhance the modularity of the program. It gives an opportunity to design complicated reactive systems by breaking them down into simpler ones that communicate through broadcasted signals. When one of the processes wants to communicate a value, it only emits a signal. This signal is simultaneously received by whichever process is currently listening this channel.

Every correct ESTEREL program describes a relation between an infinite sequence of input events and an infinite sequence of reactions, each event being a collection of present signals, optionally carrying values. This relation can also be easily represented by a deterministic finite state automaton, receiving an input event, changing its state, and emitting the reaction. Naturally, the transition of an automaton is instantaneous. This justifies the synchrony hypothesis.

2. Natural Semantics

We use *natural semantics* to present the different aspects of a language in a unified manner. A natural semantics definition is an unordered collection of rules. A rule has two parts, a numerator and a denominator. Variables may occur in the numerator and the denominator. These variables allow a rule to be instantiated.

The numerator of a rule is again an unordered collection of formulae, the *premises*. The denominator is a single formula, the *conclusion*. Intuitively, if all premises hold, then the denominator holds. Formally, from proof-trees yielding the premises, we can derive a proof-tree yielding the conclusion.

The formulae may have several form depending on the meaning they are given by the programmer. A very frequent form is the *sequent* form. A sequent has two parts, and *antecedent* (on the left) and a consequent (on the right), and we use the turnstile symbol $\vdash$ to separate these parts. The consequent is a predicate. Predicates come in several forms indicated by various infix symbols. These infix symbols have no reserved meaning, they just help in memorizing what is being defined. The antecedent usually contains information on results that are assumed, whereas the consequent represents the information that is being described. For example, the formula:

$$\rho \vdash exp : \tau$$

expresses that in the context ρ (giving e.g. the types of identifiers) the expression *exp* has the type τ.

Some structure is introduced in the collection of rules. To this end, rules may be grouped into *sets*, with a given *name*. Formulae that are provable by a specific set of rules are usually denoted by placing the set's name on top of the turnstile ($\vdash$), as in the following example:

$$\text{eval} \\ \rho \vdash exp \to value$$

Natural semantics define a formalism that enables us to use a computer to reason about the semantics of a language. Typically, our unknown will be type values, execution states or generated code. There are many approaches to turn semantics definition into executable code. The one we use for this implementation of an interpreter is to compile rules into Prolog code, taking advantage of similarity of Prolog variables and variables in inference rules. Roughly speaking, the conclusion of a rule maps to a clause head, and the premises to the body. Distinct forms of formulae map to distinct Prolog predicates. An equation is turned into a Prolog goal. Given an ESTEREL program and ESTEREL's dynamic semantics, the interpretation of the program can be obtained by executing the corresponding Prolog goal. The compiler is provided by the CENTAUR system. The fact that we use Prolog to execute the dynamic semantics will appear in section 3 dealing with the control of the execution.

2.1. *The Dynamic Semantics of* ESTEREL

The data manipulated by the dynamic semantics are the executed program, the memory environment, and an input/output handler. During the interpretation, the program and the memory evolve to take into account the effects of execution. Any communication with the outer world is performed through the input/output handler. This handler permits a symbolic linking of the interpreter with an interface.

2.1.1. *The Main Loop*

Due to the synchrony hypothesis, any reaction to an input event is supposed to be instantaneous, thus defining an ESTEREL *instant*. The main body of the execution is a loop where each pass corresponds to one instant. This loop consists of four phases:

1. reception of an event.
2. computation of a reaction to the event.
3. emission of the computed reaction.
4. preparation of the program for the next instant.

In most cases, this loop is infinite since ESTEREL programs usually describe systems that run indefinitely (they define a relation between infinite sequences of inputs and outputs). However, some programs do not run indefinitely, they are detected in the second phase. For such programs, the interpreter stops at the end of the third phase, after having emitted the last reaction. A program whose execution is finished satisfies a property called *termination*.

Receiving a new event only provokes a modification of the memory. For this phase, the interpreter provides a communication with the outer world using an interface implemented in the Lisp part of the system. This interface uses graphical objects.

During the second phase, the dynamic semantics performs a normalization of the executed program and the memory in a rewriting system. The modification of the memory is the elaboration of the output reaction, while the modification of the program is the computation of a new state. This second phase is called the *normalization* or *execution* phase. We describe this phase more precisely in the next section.

The next phase is the communication of the computed reaction to the outer world. The meaningful data are the values of the global signals found in the memory. The interpreter also provides an interface using graphical objects for this phase.

The fourth phase finishes the computation of the new state. Three operations must be done:

1. Clean the values of local signals, so that they are not yet emitted for the following instant.
2. Set up the different temporal guards that appear in ESTEREL constructs. Conditionals triggered by the presence of signals in the coming instant are introduced in the program.
3. Perform some clean-up in the rewritten program, for example prune the parts where execution can no longer occur.

These operations are done by a simple tree traversal that performs yet another rewriting. This step is called an expansion step. The resulting program is ready for a new normalization. The computation for the next instant can proceed as soon as a new input event arrives.

2.1.2. *The Normalization Phase*

The normalization phase uses a rewriting system to express the evolution of the memory and the computation performed during the execution. Each elementary rewriting corresponds to the execution of an elementary operation. After a rewriting, the computation continues with the resulting object program, also called the *resumption*, until no further rewriting is possible.

Thus, the normalization function is based on two partial functions, the *execution* function and the *termination* function. The execution function performs the rewritings. It takes as arguments the memory and the program and returns the memory and the program modified by one elementary rewriting, when such a rewriting is possible. The *termination* function detects programs in normal form, it takes as argument only a program and returns a value only when no further rewriting is possible. Thus, there exist no program for which both the execution function and the termination function have a value. However, there exist programs for which neither of these functions is defined. Such programs are erroneous; the corresponding error is called a *causal loop*.

Besides detecting the programs in normal form, the termination function computes whether the object program satisfies the **termination** property or not. As we already explained, this property controls the termination of the main loop of the interpreter. We also see later that the termination property helps to define the behavior of the **sequence** construct. The termination function is defined in the set **terminated**.

2.1.3. *The Execution Function*

The execution function is one of the two partial functions used in the normalization phase. This function expresses how the memory is modified, how the control is performed, and how the executed instruction is removed when an elementary operation is performed. This function is defined in the TYPOL set **exec** and is represented by judgements of the following form:

$$\textbf{exec}$$
$$mem \vdash stat \Rightarrow stat', mem'$$

The terms *stat* and *mem* are given as arguments, *stat* is an ESTEREL program to execute and *mem* is the memory describing the values of the free variables appearing in *stat*. The terms *stat'* and *mem'* are returned by the function, they are the rewritten program and the modified memory.

We take a closer look at some rules from this set.
- Execution of an **assignment** statement. Let us consider the rule for the **assignment** statement:

$$\frac{\overset{\text{eval}}{mem(\rho,\sigma) \vdash exp \rightarrow val} \qquad update(\rho, x, val, \rho')}{\underset{mem(\rho,\sigma) \vdash x := exp \Rightarrow \text{nothing}, mem(\rho',\sigma)}{\text{exec}}}$$

The memory is divided in two parts for the variable memory and the signal memory. The execution of an **assignment** statement provokes a modification of the variable memory ρ into ρ'. The resumption is the blank statement **nothing**.
- Execution of the **present** statement. Here, we give one of the rules for the **present** statement:

$$\frac{\text{sig\_presence}(\sigma, S, +,)}{\underset{mem(\rho,\sigma) \vdash \text{if } exp \text{ then } stat_1 \text{ else } stat_2 \Rightarrow stat_1, mem(\rho,\sigma)}{\text{exec}}}$$

If the signal S is present (denoted by $+$), then the execution of this conditional corresponds to the execution of the first branch, with the same memory. This rule (in fact, not only this one) shows how a **present** statement alters the control flow of the execution.
- Execution of the **watching** statement. The watching statement is one of the ESTEREL constructs that implement temporal guards, i.e., constructs that allow the apparition of a signal to limit the time taken by operations. Let us consider the rule that defines its behavior:

$$\frac{\overset{\text{exec}}{mem \vdash stat \Rightarrow stat', mem'}}{\underset{mem \vdash \text{do } stat \text{ watching } S \Rightarrow \text{do } stat' \text{ watching } S, mem'}{\text{exec}}}$$

This rule shows that the "one step" execution of some ESTEREL constructs can be expressed directly from the execution of a subpart. It appears that the **watching** construct has no effect on the execution within an instant. In fact, the real behavior of this statement is described in the expansion phase (phase 4 of the main loop), by the rule:

$$\frac{\overset{\text{expanse}}{\vdash stat \rightarrow stat'}}{\underset{\vdash \text{do } stat \text{ watching } S \rightarrow \text{present } S \text{ else do } stat' \text{ watching } S}{\text{expanse}}}$$

This means that in the coming instant, the expansion of the instruction $stat$ will be executed only if S is not present.
Execution of the **sequence**. The **sequence** construct has a behavior that ensures that the tail of a sequence is always executed after the beginning

is finished. One first expresses that executing a sequence is executing its beginning with the following rule:

$$\frac{\text{exec} \atop mem \vdash stat_1 \Rightarrow stat_1', mem'}{\text{exec} \atop mem \vdash stat_1; stat_2 \Rightarrow stat_1'; stat_2, mem'}$$

Then one expresses that the tail can be executed if the head verifies the termination property:

$$\frac{\begin{array}{cc} \text{terminated} & \text{exec} \\ \vdash stat_1 \rightarrow \text{true}, \emptyset_{traps} & mem \vdash stat_2 \Rightarrow stat_2', mem' \end{array}}{\text{exec} \atop mem \vdash stat_1; stat_2 \Rightarrow stat_2', mem'}$$

- Execution of the **parallel**. In a way the execution of the **parallel** construct is very similar to the execution of the **sequence**. However, it is not necessary to wait until the head has been completely executed to execute the tail. No preference is given to either way and the two rules for the head and the tail are symmetric, and similar to the first rule of the **sequence**.

$$\frac{\text{exec} \atop mem \vdash stat_1 \Rightarrow stat_1', mem'}{\text{exec} \atop mem \vdash stat_1 \| stat_2 \Rightarrow stat_1' \| stat_2, mem'}$$

$$\frac{\text{exec} \atop mem \vdash stat_2 \Rightarrow stat_2', mem'}{\text{exec} \atop mem \vdash stat_1 \| stat_2 \Rightarrow stat_1 \| stat_2', mem'}$$

These two rules do not exclude each other. Each time a **parallel** construct is executed both rules can apply. Thus, the execution is not deterministic. The parallelism in the ESTEREL language comes directly from this nondeterminism in the interleaving of the elementary steps. The parallelism found in ESTEREL has the same properties as the parallelism that one can find in β-reduction for the λ-calculus.

Note that the execution of statements like **nothing** or **halt** is not defined. On the contrary, the termination function is defined for such statements. Rewriting a statement in **nothing** is virtually removing this statement from the program.

3. Tools for Visualizing Execution

The purpose of an execution visualization tool is to animate the program during the interpretation, using different colors or typefaces to express the current state of execution as in figure 1. Visualizing enhances debugging by helping the programmer to detect places where the execution behaves differently from expected.

Visualizing contains three problems. The first problem is to track correspondences between the resumptions of the rewritings and the original program, which is actually displayed on the screen. To solve this problem we use *multi-occurrences* as described in the next section. The second problem is to detect in the resumption the expression that are worth emphasizing in the program for the current state of execution. This problem can be solved systematically from the dynamic semantics. The third problem is to transform the computed data in an actual display of the program. This problem is easily solved using the *selection* machinery of CENTAUR [paths] and will not be described in this paper.

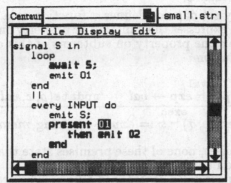

Figure 1   Examples of execution points (in bold face) and of a signal
blocked in read access (in reverse video)

3.1.   *Subject Tracking*

We use *occurrences* and *multi-occurrences* to designate sub-expressions of a tree. Occurrences are strings of navigation commands that enable us to express the position of an expression in the tree. Multi-occurrences are used when one want to express that an expression is not a sub-expression of the tree, but that it shares sub-expressions with this tree. The expressions that are emphasized in figure 1 are designated with multi-occurrences. During the rewritings in the dynamic semantics the expressions are given multi-occurrences. When a term t_1 with the multi-occurrence m_1 is rewritten in a term t_2, one computes a multi-occurrence m_2 to go with t_2 that expresses what sub-expressions of t_2 come from t_1.

example: if t_1 is rewritten in t_2 where these terms have the following values:
$$t_1 = \textbf{present S then emit O end; emit P}$$
$$t_2 = \textbf{emit O; emit P}$$
then the multi-occurrence m_2 associated with t_2 will have the following value:

$$m_2 = u[s(s(m_1, 1), 2), s(m_1, 2)]$$

where m_1 is the multi-occurrence associated with t_1, to express that the first son of t_2 is a sub-expression of m_1 and give its place in m_1 and do the same for its second son.

In a rule, the variable *subject* gives the multi-occurrence associated to the expression that appears to the right of the turnstile ($\vdash$) in the conclusion of the rule. Using this feature we can define a **subject** function that returns the multi-occurrence associated to any expression. This rule is defined using the following axiom:

$$\textbf{subject}$$
$$\vdash exp \longrightarrow subject$$

3.2.   *Execution Observation*

Now, we describe how we detect the interesting expressions (and the corresponding multi-occurrences) in the resumption of the rewritings. This work is performed at two moments. The first one is between each call to the execution function, in the normalization phase. The second one is during the expansion phase. The observation is performed by two functions that return multi-occurrences. We show that the description of these functions can be systematically derived from the dynamic semantics.

3.2.1. *Generalized Axioms*

In TYPOL, every set of rules defines a function or a property. A *generalized axiom* is a rule which expresses this function or property on a construct without any recursive call for the same property on subterms of this construct. The following rule is a generalized axiom:

$$\frac{\overset{\text{eval}}{\rho, \sigma \vdash exp \rightarrow val} \qquad \text{update}(\rho, x, val, \rho')}{\overset{\text{exec}}{mem(\rho, \sigma) \vdash x := exp \Rightarrow \texttt{nothing}, mem(\rho', \sigma)}}$$

Although it has premises, none of these premises state that the execution function is recursively called on a subterm.

The following rule is not a generalized axiom. The premise states that one has to execute an elementary rewriting in the body of the loop construct to execute an elementary rewriting in the entire construct:

$$\frac{\overset{\text{exec}}{mem \vdash stat \Rightarrow stat', mem'}}{\overset{\text{exec}}{mem \vdash \texttt{loop } stat \texttt{ end} \Rightarrow stat'; \texttt{loop } stat \texttt{ end}, mem'}}$$

The generalized axioms are the rules that express a property on the constructs that are elementary relative to this property. We shall say that the rules that are not generalized axioms are *recursive* rules.

3.2.2. *Observation of the Normalization Phase*

We have explained above that every rewriting that appears in the normalization phase corresponds to an elementary execution step. When stepping the execution we want to show the exact situation of the instructions that will be reduced in all the possible elementary steps. These points correspond to the expressions where a generalized axiom could be applied in any possible application of the execution function.

We also want to show the exact situation of all the points where no rewriting is possible. this gives a symmetric notion of *elementary execution suspensions*. These points correspond to the expression where a generalized axiom of the termination function expresses that the execution is suspended. At last, we want to express the temporary blocking of execution that come from a synchronization discipline on the access to signals.

With these three notions, we have a criterion to apply on the dynamic semantics that enables us to derive a TYPOL function that computes the corresponding sets of multi-occurrences. This resulting function is named the *front* function, it is described by judgements of the following type:

$$\overset{\text{front}}{sigs \vdash stat \rightarrow triple(set_1, set_2, set_3)}$$

The first parameter, *sigs*, is the set of all the signals which can still be emitted in the same instant — this set is used to detect the temporary blockings coming from the synchronization. The expression *stat* is the statement that describes the state of execution. The returned triple contains three sets of multi-occurrences designating sub-expressions of the program. The first component set_1 designates the instructions where an elementary step of execution can occur next, set_2 designates the expressions where the execution is blocked on synchronization, set_3 designates the points where the execution is suspended.

If we find a place where a generalized axiom from the set **exec** can be applied, the corresponding expression should be designated as an elementary execution step. The following rules are two generalized axioms from this set:

$$\frac{\overset{\text{eval}}{\rho, \sigma \vdash exp \rightarrow val} \quad \text{update}(\rho, x, val, \rho')}{\underset{mem(\rho, \sigma) \vdash x := exp \Rightarrow \text{nothing}, mem(\rho', \sigma)}{\text{exec}}}$$

$$\frac{\overset{\text{eval}}{\rho, \sigma \vdash exp \rightarrow \text{true}}}{\underset{mem(\rho, \sigma) \vdash \text{if } exp \text{ then } stat1 \text{ else } stat2 \text{ end} \Rightarrow stat1, mem(\rho, \sigma)}{\text{exec}}}$$

To these two rules correspond two axioms in the set **front**:

$$\overset{\text{front}}{sigs \vdash x := exp \rightarrow triple(\{subject\}, \emptyset, \emptyset)}$$

$$\overset{\text{front}}{sigs \vdash \text{if } exp \text{ then } stat1 \text{ else } stat2 \text{ end} \rightarrow triple(\{subject\}, \emptyset, \emptyset)}$$

These rules state that the expressions affected by the elementary executions are designated by multi-occurrences appearing in the triple's first set.

If we find a place where a generalized axiom from the set defining the termination function can be applied and expresses that the execution is suspended, we must express this in the front function. The following rule from the set **terminated** is an example of this case:

$$\overset{\text{terminated}}{\vdash \text{halt} \rightarrow \text{false}, \emptyset_{traps}}$$

The corresponding **front** axiom is as follows:

$$\overset{\text{front}}{sigs \vdash \text{halt} \rightarrow triple(\emptyset, \emptyset, \{subject\})}$$

Here the corresponding multi-occurrence is kept in the triple's third set.

Execution and termination are symmetric; recursive rules of the set **exec** correspond to recursive rules of the set **terminated**. We provide corresponding recursive rules for the set **front** too. These rules express that all the interesting expression found in a construct where a recursive of the execution function applies are the execution points that can be found in the subparts where a recursive call is possible. For example, we have two rules for the **parallel** construct in the set **exec**, they express that the execution can proceed in either branch:

$$\frac{\overset{\text{exec}}{mem \vdash stat_1 \Rightarrow stat_1', mem'}}{\underset{mem \vdash stat_1 \| stat_2 \Rightarrow stat_1' \| stat_2, mem'}{\text{exec}}}$$

$$\frac{\overset{\textbf{exec}}{mem \vdash stat_2 \Rightarrow stat'_2, mem'}}{\underset{\textbf{exec}}{mem \vdash stat_1 \| stat_2 \Rightarrow stat_1 \| stat'_2, mem'}}$$

The front function replaces the non-determinism of the execution function by an actual representation of the parallelism, by showing all the instructions that could be executed:

$$\frac{\overset{\textbf{front}}{sigs \vdash stat_1 \to triple(set_1, set'_1, set''_1)} \quad \overset{\textbf{front}}{sigs \vdash stat_2 \to triple(set_2, set'_2, set''_2)}}{\underset{\textbf{front}}{sigs \vdash stat_1 \| stat_2 \to triple(set_1 \cup set_2, set'_1 \cup set'_2, set''_1 \cup set''_2)}}$$

The synchronization discipline in ESTEREL expresses that all reading access to a signal (corresponding, e.g., to the instruction **present**) must be performed after all writing access (corresponding to the instruction **emit**). To see why a program fails to execute, we need to see when this discipline alters the execution. There exists a function, the *potential* function that approximates the signals that can still possibly be emitted from the current execution state in the current transition. The signal memory cells are marked using this information, thus permitting to forbid any reading access when necessary. The function that enforces this discipline is the function that permits to read in the signal memory: **sig_presence**. A systematic way to detect the places where the access discipline alters the execution is to detect the execution rules that perform a call to this function:

$$\frac{sig\_presence(\sigma, s, +, Value)}{\underset{\textbf{exec}}{mem(\rho, \sigma) \vdash \textbf{present } s \textbf{ then } stat_1 \textbf{ else } stat_2 \textbf{ end} \Rightarrow stat_1, mem(\rho, \sigma)}}$$

$$\frac{sig\_presence(\sigma, s, -, Value)}{\underset{\textbf{exec}}{mem(\rho, \sigma) \vdash \textbf{present } s \textbf{ then } stat_1 \textbf{ else } stat_2 \textbf{ end} \Rightarrow stat_2, mem(\rho, \sigma)}}$$

In the front function, we use directly the result of the potential function to know whether the **sig_presence** function will block the execution or not.

$$\frac{s \in sigs \qquad \overset{\textbf{subject}}{\vdash s \to s\_subject}}{\underset{\textbf{front}}{sigs \vdash \textbf{present } s \textbf{ then } stat_1 \textbf{ else } stat_2 \textbf{ end} \to triple(\{subject\}, \{s\_subject\}, \emptyset)}}$$

$$\frac{s \notin sigs}{\underset{\textbf{front}}{sigs \vdash \textbf{present } s \textbf{ then } stat_1 \textbf{ else } stat_2 \textbf{ end} \to triple(\{subject\}, \emptyset, \emptyset)}}$$

The call to **sig_presence** are always part of an generalized axiom for the execution. Thus, the expression that are detected as blocking the execution are always subparts of an expression detected as a possible elementary execution step.

3.2.3. *Observation of the Expansion Step*

The expansion step is not a normalization and we are not interested in the same phenomena. Here the rules of interest are not generalized axioms. The interesting rules are the rules where a **present** construct has been introduced for a temporal guard. The rule for the **watching** construct is one such rule:

$$\frac{\text{expanse} \atop \vdash stat \to stat'}{\text{expanse} \atop \vdash \text{do } stat \text{ watching } S \to \text{present } S \text{ else do } stat' \text{ watching } S}$$

The tool for the observation of the expansion step is defined in the set **show_xpans**. This set contains the following rule for the **watching** construct:

$$\frac{\text{show\_xpans} \qquad \text{subject} \atop \vdash stat \to set \qquad \vdash S \to position}{\text{show\_xpans} \atop \vdash \text{do } stat \text{ watching } S \to set \cup \{position\}}$$

The introduction of a **present** construct corresponds to the raising of a temporal guard. We designate the signal on which the guard is raised.

The set **show_xpans** is designed to traverse exactly the part of the tree which is traversed by the set **expanse**. Thus, any rule from the set **expanse** containing a recursive call to the expansion function has a corresponding one in the set **show_xpans** that contains a recursive call to the expansion observation. This can also be done systematically.

4. Tools for Execution Control

A good debugger must also provide a way to execute slowly a program so that the programmer can observe precisely the key parts of his program. Ideally the programmer must be able to command the speed of execution at any time. A generic control is already given for the execution of TYPOL itself. It is possible to customize this generic control tool to give a control better suited to the ESTEREL execution model.

The controller is actually a finite state automaton, written in the ESTEREL language itself. It receives messages from all parts of the system, such as *this rule has been applied*, or *this button has been depressed*. The generic tool provides facilities to design a specific automaton for a language.

The basic events attached to the application of rules are of four kinds:
1. *Try*. A rule is tried in the computation.
2. *Prove*. The application of a rule has been proved.
3. *Back*. A new try is done for a rule.
4. *Fail*. The application of a rule has failed, i.e., this rule does not apply.

These events describe the computation as it is done in the Prolog interpreter. When a rule is applied it is possible to know the applied rule and the multi-occurrence designating the data it is applied on. This information helps to control the execution. For example, the multi-occurrence designating the subject data can be used to detect break-points in the program, although it is not done in this version of the interpreter. The output of this generic debugger is a collection of messages, such as *make this button appear* sent to the interface part of the system, or *continue the execution* sent to the logical kernel, i.e., the Prolog interpreter.

With this controller, we attach operations to certain points of the execution. For example, one says *When this rule is applied, flush the input event* (the external part of the input/output communication is performed this way); one can even have conditional operations, like *at this point, if there is a breakpoint on the subject of the rule, prompt the user for a command*. The control of the execution is designed on top of the dynamic semantics, whose design is completely independent. One only needs to choose in the dynamic semantics the points where a control has to be added and to design the operations attached to this control, using all the data available in the computation.

For the ESTEREL interpreter we selected two points in the execution:
- The end of an instant.
- The execution of one rewriting in the normalization phase, i.e., the execution of an elementary instruction.

The first point is attached to the event *Prove* for the rule of the set **normal** that expresses the end of the normalization phase. The second point is attached to the event *Try* for the rule of the same set that expresses that a rewriting will be performed. The execution can then be broken down into steps, going from one of these points to another one. The interpreter provides a tool to express different commands such as:
- Execute the next elementary instruction and stop (command **Instruction**).
- Execute the next instant and stop (command **Instant**).

The generic controller provides other commands, that we keep in our controller:
- Abort as soon as possible (command **Abort**).
- Stop as soon as possible (command **Break**).
- Go without caring about instants or elementary executions or any similar event (command **Go**).

All these commands are grouped in a command box where some options appear only when the controller prompts the user for an order. The options *Break* and *Abort* are always available.

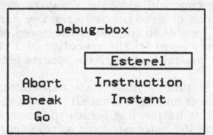

Figure 2 The controller's command box

5. Further Developments

This interpreter is a first step toward a complete debugger for the parallel language ESTEREL. Earlier experiments like [ml] only dealt with sequential languages. The treatment of parallelism introduces a new style of specification, making extensive use of rewriting to describe dynamic semantics. We have shown that this new style of specification iss still within the scope of natural semantics.

We have also shown that visualizing the execution state requires non-trivial computations. We have sketched a methodology to extract from the dynamic semantics a tool that helps visualizing execution. However, this methodology was a first attempt at solving this kind of problem and we have only provided an *ad hoc* treatment for this particular language. Regardless, the existence of a stated and well understood criterion of observation entitles us to claim that the shown information is relevant.

Visualizing is one of many debugging tools that track a correspondence between the executed program and the term that represents the execution state. Other such tools would, for example, allow to set *breakpoints* in the program so that the execution stops when *reaching* such points, or to access the value of local variables during the execution. In these examples, one must find the expressions that inherit the breakpoints in the current execution state or the expressions that represent the local variables.

The CENTAUR system proves to be a good choice of a tool box for the development of an application like this interpreter. The semantics definition is kept in a pure form, free of implementation details. It is therefore easy to maintain and to check for correctness. The design of the man-machine interface is eased by the graphical tools which are already provided by the system. The result is an application which is easy to integrate in a more complete environment, including a type-checker and a compiler, since such tools can also be developed in the system.

Bibliography

[centaur] P. BORRAS ET AL., "CENTAUR: the system", *Proceedings of the ACM SIGSOFT'88: Third Symposium on Software Development Environments*, November 1988, Boston, USA. (Also appears as *INRIA Research Report no. 777.*)

[design] G. BERRY, G. GONTHIER, "The ESTEREL Synchronous Programming Language: Design, Semantics, Implementation", *INRIA Research Report no. 842 (1988)*. To appear in *Science of Computer Programming*.

[esterel] G. BERRY, L. COSSERAT, "The synchronous Programming Language ES-TEREL and its Mathematical Semantics", *Seminar on Concurrency*, Springer Verlag LNCS 197, (1984).

[gfxobj] D. CLÉMENT, J. INCERPI, "Specifying the Behavior of Graphical Objects Using ESTEREL", *Proceedings of TAPSOFT'89 Colloquium on Current Issues in Programming Languages*, March 1989, Barcelona. (Also appears as *INRIA Research Report no. 836.*)

[ml] D. CLEMENT, J. DESPEYROUX, T. DESPEYROUX, G. KAHN, "A Simple Applicative Language: Mini-ML", *Proceedings of the 1986 ACM Conference on Lisp and Functional Programming*, August 1986, Cambridge Massachusetts.

[natural semantics] G. KAHN, "Natural Semantics", *Programming of Future Generation Computers*, K. Fuchi, M. Nivat (Editors), Elsevier Science Publishers B.V. (North-Holland), 1988. (Also appears as *INRIA Research Report no. 601 (1987).*)

[paths] D. CLÉMENT, L. HASCOËT, "Centaur Paths: a structure to designate subtrees" *in Centaur 0.9 Documentation, Vol II, June 1989*.

[reactive] D. HAREL, A PNUELI, "On the development of Reactive Systems: Logic and Models of Concurrent Systems", *Proceedings of NATO Advanced Study Institute on Logics and Models for Verification and Specification of Concurrent Systems*, NATO ASI Series F, vol. 13, Springer Verlag, (1985)

[typol] T. DESPEYROUX, "Typol, a formalism to implement Natural Semantics", *INRIA Technical Report no. 94, (1988)*.

Automatic Autoprojection of Higher Order Recursive Equations

Anders Bondorf

DIKU, University of Copenhagen*

Universitetsparken 1, DK-2100 Copenhagen Ø, Denmark

e-mail: anders@diku.dk

Abstract

Autoprojection, or self-applicable partial evaluation, has been implemented for first order functional languages for some years now. This paper describes an approach to treat a *higher order* subset of the Scheme language. The system has been implemented as an extension to the existing autoprojector *Similix* [Bondorf & Danvy 90] that treats a first order Scheme subset. To our knowledge, our system is the first fully automatic and implemented autoprojector for a higher order language.

Given a source program and some, but not all of its inputs, partial evaluation produces a residual program. When applied to the rest of the inputs, the residual program yields the same result as the source program would when applied to all inputs. One important application of autoprojection is semantics directed compiler generation: given a denotational, interpretive specification of a programming language, it is possible automatically to generate a stand-alone compiler by self-applying the partial evaluator.

Efficient autoprojection is known to require *binding time analysing* source programs to be partially evaluated. Binding time analysis establishes in advance which parts of the source program that can be evaluated during partial evaluation and which parts that cannot. We describe a new automatic binding time analysis for higher order programs written in the Scheme subset. The analysis requires no type information. It is based on a *closure analysis* [Sestoft 88b], which for any application point finds the set of lambda abstractions that can possibly be applied at that point. The binding time analysis has the interesting property that no structured binding time values are needed.

Since our language is higher order, interpreters written in a higher order style can be partially evaluated. To exemplify this, we present and partially evaluate three versions of an interpreter for a lambda calculus language: one written in direct style, one written in continuation passing style, and one implementing normal order reduction. The two latter are heavily based on higher order programming.

Keywords

Partial evaluation, self-application, binding time analysis, semantics directed compiler generation.

1. Introduction

Partial evaluation is a program transformation that *specializes* programs: given a source program and a part of its input (the *static* input), a partial evaluator generates a *residual* program. When applied to the remaining input (the *dynamic* input), the residual program yields the same result as the source program would when applied to all of the input. *Autoprojection* is a synonym for *self-applicable* partial evaluation, that is, specialization of the partial evaluator itself. It was established in the seventies that autoprojection can be used for automatic semantics directed compiler generation: specializ-

* This work was carried out while the author was staying at the University of Dortmund, Lehrstuhl Informatik V, Postfach 50 05 00, D-4600 Dortmund 50, Federal Republic of Germany. The work was partly supported by the Danish Research Academy.

ing a partial evaluator with static input being (the text of) an *interpreter* for some programming language S yields a *compiler* for S [Futamura 71] [Ershov 77] [Turchin 80]. Specializing the partial evaluator with static input being (the text of) the partial evaluator itself even yields a compiler generator (automatic compiler generator generation!).

The first successfully implemented autoprojector was *Mix* [Jones, Sestoft, & Søndergaard 85]. The language treated by Mix was a subset of statically scoped first order pure Lisp, and Mix was able to generate compilers out of interpreters written in this language. The experiment showed that autoprojection was possible in practice; an automatic version of Mix was developed later [Jones, Sestoft, & Søndergaard 89]. Since then, autoprojectors for several languages have been implemented: for a subset of Turchin's Refal language [Romanenko 88], for an imperative flowchart language [Gomard & Jones 89], for pattern matching based programs in the form of restricted term rewriting systems [Bondorf 89], and for first order functional languages with global variables [Bondorf & Danvy 90].

1.1 Autoprojecting higher order languages

The first autoprojector for a *higher order* functional language is (to our knowledge) *Lambda-mix* [Gomard 89] [JonGomBonDanMog 90]. Lambda-mix treats the untyped call-by-value lambda calculus. The system is surprisingly simple and easy to understand; even the generated compilers are small and readable (which is quite uncommon for compilers generated by autoprojectors!). However, a strong limitation in Lambda-mix is that static parameters of recursive functions *must* be induction variables [Aho, Sethi, & Ullman 86]; non-inductive variables are always dynamic. Lambda-mix thus does not *specialize* (recursive) calls to equal functions with equal patterns of static argument values (known as *polyvariant* program specialization [Bulyonkov 84]). Specialization is a kind of *folding* and thus gives *sharing* of functions in residual programs. Since Lambda-mix does not specialize calls, it does not perform well for some applications. For instance, when using partial evaluation to generate string pattern matchers

[Consel & Danvy 89], non-inductive recursive static variables are used.

In this paper we describe an implemented automatic autoprojector, *Similix-2*, that handles a higher order subset of the Scheme language [Rees & Clinger 86], essentially weakly (dynamically) typed, statically scoped, call-by-value recursive equations with lambda abstractions and applications. Similix-2 uses polyvariant program specialization and is, to our knowledge, the first fully automated and implemented autoprojector for a higher order language (Lambda-mix requires handwritten binding time annotations; an automatic version has been developed later [Gomard 90]).

Similix-2 has been developed and implemented by extending *Similix* [Bondorf & Danvy 90], an existing autoprojector for a first order Scheme subset. Similix-2 therefore has a number of features that have been inherited from Similix: side-effecting operations on global variables (such as i/o operations) are treated in a semantically correct way; primitives are user specified (as introduced in [Consel 88]), i.e. there is no fixed set of primitives; residual programs never duplicate computations (cf. *call duplication* [Sestoft 88a]); residual programs do not terminate more often than source programs; call unfolding is controlled automatically (by a simple strategy based on detecting *dynamic conditionals*). This paper does not cover these aspects which all come from Similix; we refer to [Bondorf & Danvy 90] (and to [Bondorf 90]).

Treating higher order languages opens new perspectives for using autoprojection for semantics directed compiler generation: Similix-2 treats interpreters written in continuation passing style and interpreters that implement (weak head) normal order reduction (outside-in, call-by-name) by "thunks" of the form $(\lambda \ () \ E)$. We exemplify this by specializing such interpreters. To our knowledge, this is the first time autoprojection has been used to generate compilers from interpreters of that kind.

1.2 Outline

The rest of the paper is organized as follows. Section 2 gives some background and introduces the main issues of this paper. In section 3, we present an interpreter for a lambda calculus language "Λ". The interpreter serves as an example of a higher order program; when it is specialized, programs in the Λ-language are in effect compiled. The sections 4 and 5 contain the technical part: we develop/describe two pre-analyses needed for partial evaluation of higher order programs; both analyses are presented formally in a compositional denotational semantics style. In section 6, we exemplify partial evaluation of higher order programs: the Λ-interpreter is specialized, and we also specialize two other Λ-interpreters: one written in continuation passing style and one implementing normal order reduction. The performance of the system is shown in section 7. Section 8 is a discussion, and in section 9 we conclude and sketch some open problems.

1.3 Prerequisites

Some knowledge about partial evaluation is required, e.g. as presented in [Jones, Sestoft, & Søndergaard 85] or [Jones, Sestoft, & Søndergaard 89].

2. Background and Issues

2.1 Preprocessing

An essential component of an autoprojector is the *preprocessor*. Preprocessing is performed *before* program specialization; its purpose is to add *annotations* (attributes) to the source program [Jones, Sestoft, & Søndergaard 85]. The annotations guide the program specializer (which actually produces the residual program) in various ways: they tell whether variables are bound to static or dynamic values, whether operations such as + or if can be reduced away during program specialization, and whether certain expressions (function calls, let-expressions) should be *unfolded*. Annotations relieve the specializer from taking decisions depending on the static input to the program being specialized, and this gives major improvements, especially when the specializer is self-applied [Bondorf, Jones, Mogensen, & Sestoft 90] (the essential reason: the static input to the program with respect to which the specializer is being specialized is not available). Without using annotations, the generated compilers would become unnecessarily general and hence large (in code size)

and slow. All autoprojectors we know of use preprocessing and annotations.

The central preprocessing phase is *binding time analysis* [Jones, Sestoft, Søndergaard 89]. Binding time analysis is an *approximative* analysis that *abstractly interprets* the program over a binding time domain, in the simplest case the two-point lattice $Static \sqsubseteq Dynamic$. *Static* is to be interpreted as "definitely static", i.e. it abstracts values that are available (*known*) at program specialization time. *Dynamic* means "possibly non-static" and abstracts values that are possibly not available (*unknown*) at program specialization time. Variables and operations are then classified according to their binding times. As a simple example, the operation + in the expression (+ x 1) is static (*eliminable, compile time*) if x is classified $Static$, and it is dynamic (*residual, run time*) if x is classified $Dynamic$. Static operations are evaluated during program specialization whereas residual code is generated for the dynamic ones. Static operations correspond to the overlined ones of [Nielson & Nielson 88], dynamic operations to the underlined ones.

2.2 Binding time analysing higher order programs

Nielson and Nielson have described an automatic binding time analysis for a *higher order* functional language [Nielson & Nielson 88]. Their analysis treats the *typed* lambda calculus. Mogensen has described an analysis for a polymorphically typed higher order functional language where programs are written in curried named combinator form [Mogensen 89b]. In these two papers, no autoprojector is developed; only binding time analysis is addressed. An automatic binding time analysis for Lambda-mix has been developed recently [Gomard 90].

The difficult point in binding time analysing higher order programs is to associate lambda abstractions with applications. If a program e.g. contains the application (x y), and if x during (partial) evaluation may be bound to (the value of) some abstraction, say (λ (z) (+ z 3)), occurring elsewhere in the program, then the binding time value of y influences the one of z. If, for instance, y is classified $Dynamic$, then z cannot be $Static$. On the other hand, if x can never possibly be bound to (the value of) (λ (z) (+ z 3)), then

73

it is unnecessarily conservative to let y influence z. The — not very useful — conservative extreme would be to assume that *any* abstraction might be applied at *any* application point.

For first order languages, the control flow is easy to follow from the program syntax. But for higher order programs, the control is difficult to trace: how does one deduce from the program text that y influences z? Nielson & Nielson use a *type inferencing* scheme (using the type information in the program); from the expression (x y), it would identify that x had type *Dynamic* → ... (since y is *Dynamic*), and eventually this type would be unified (using least upper bounds) with the type of (λ (z) (+ z 3)). Its type is Z → ..., where Z is the type of z. Unifying the types implies $Z \sqsupseteq Dynamic$, i.e. z's binding time value is at least *Dynamic*. Mogensen describes binding time values for function types as a kind of abstract closures: an abstract closure consists of the name of the combinator and the binding time values of the free variables. A rather complex recursion detection machinery based on the type information is used to avoid generating infinite abstract closures.

In this paper we present a different approach based on a variant of Sestoft's *closure analysis* [Sestoft 88b] [Sestoft 89]: a closure analysis is first performed, then the binding time analysis is performed:

bt-annotations = bt-analyse(P, cl-analyse(P))

For each application point in the program, the closure analysis collects the set of lambda abstractions that for any evaluation of the program possibly may be applied at that point — for instance that x above may be bound to (the value of) (λ (z) (+ z 3)). The analysis addresses *any* possible evaluation, not a particular one, so it must necessarily be approximative: it can give a *safe* description which, however, may be too conservative (cf. the conservative extreme mentioned above).

Using the information computed by the closure analysis, the binding time analysis immediately knows which formal parameters to lambda expressions that may be affected by an application (for instance that z depends on y). In this approach, binding time analysis is relatively simple to express; in particular, no *structured* binding time values (such as *Dynamic* → *Dynamic*) are needed.

Termination of the binding time analysis is easily guaranteed: the binding time description is changed monotonically, and the set of binding time values is trivially finite since there are no structured values.

2.3 Programming language

Similix-2 processes higher order recursive equations. The language is an extension of the one treated by Similix [Bondorf & Danvy 90]: lambda abstractions and applications have been added to the allowed expression forms. As for Similix, programs follow the syntax of Scheme and are thus directly executable in a Scheme environment.

A source program is expressed by a set of user defined procedures and a set of user defined operators. A Scheme procedure corresponds to a *function* in references such as [Jones, Sestoft, & Søndergaard 89]. Procedures are treated intensionally, whereas operators are treated extensionally. The partial evaluator knows the internal code of procedures. In contrast, an operator is a primitive operation: the partial evaluator never worries about the internal operations performed by a primitive operator. It can only do two things with a primitive operation: either evaluate the operation or suspend it generating residual code.

Every expression is identified by a unique *label*. The labels are (of course!) not part of the concrete syntax of a program, but they are important in the abstract syntax. The BNF of the abstract syntax of programs is given below. Except for the labels, this abstract syntax is identical to the concrete one.

Abstract syntax of the Scheme subset treated by Similix-2

```
Pr ∈ Program,   PD ∈ Definition,
F ∈ FileName,
L-E ∈ LabeledExpression,
L ∈ Label,   E ∈ Expression,
C ∈ Constant,   V ∈ Variable,
O ∈ OperatorName,   P ∈ ProcedureName

Pr ::= (loadt F)* (load F)* PD+
PD ::= (define (P V*) L-E)
L-E ::= L E
E ::= C | V | (if L-E₁ L-E₂ L-E₃)
```

```
| (let ((V L-E₁)) L-E₂)
| (O L-E*) | (P L-E*)
| (λ (v*) L-E₁) | (L-E₀ L-E*)
```

Notation: program texts and names of syntactic domains are written in this font. We write λ instead of lambda in program texts.

The primitive operators are defined in external files referred to by the loadt expressions. Definitions from other files can be reused using load. An expression is a constant (boolean, number, string, or quoted construction), a variable, a conditional, a let-expression (unary for simplicity), a primitive operation, a procedure call, a lambda abstraction, or an application; the latter two forms make the language higher order. The order of evaluation is applicative (strict, call-by-value, inside-out), and arguments are evaluated in an unspecified order.

We note that let-expressions are *not* considered syntactic sugar for applications of (higher order) lambda abstractions: this would not be beneficial since let-expressions are first order and thus simpler to deal with. Procedure calls are treated in another way than higher order applications; the two forms are therefore distinguished syntactically. Both procedure calls and higher order applications are, in turn, distinguished from applications of primitive operators. The distinctions are made during parsing. To keep the language simple, there is no letrec (nor any rec); recursion is expressed using named procedures.

Program input is assumed to be first order (ground, i.e. constants). The reason is that higher order values are treated intensionally in the partial evaluation process; the internal representation of functional values depends on the text of the program being partially evaluated.

2.4 Syntactic extensions

A number of built-in syntactic extensions are treated by Similix. We mention one which is used in the examples later: cond. It is expanded into nested if expressions. The system also treats user defined syntactic extensions following the syntax of [Kohlbecker 86] (only a subset of Kohlbecker's language is treated).

3. A sample interpreter

In this section we present a language Λ and an interpreter for Λ written in Scheme. Λ is a statically scoped lambda calculus language with unary abstractions and applications, constants, binary primitive operations, a conditional, and a recursive "let". A program is an expression following this (abstract) syntax:

Abstract syntax of Λ

```
E ∈ Expr,  C ∈ Const,
V ∈ Var,  B ∈ Binop

E ::= C | V | (B E₁ E₂) | (if E₁ E₂ E₃)
    | (λ V E) | (letrec V E₁ E₂) | (E₁ E₂)
```

A program takes one input value, which initially is bound to all variables (for simplicity). For an example, this program computes the factorial function:

Factorial program written in Λ

```
(letrec f
  (λ x (if (= x 0) 1 (* x (f (- x 1)))))
  (f input))
```

The (arbitrary) variable name input is used to refer to the input value.

3.1 Denotational semantics

The denotational semantics of the language is specified below. We use the notation from [Schmidt 86]; the conditional is written _ → _ [] _, and [v ↦ w]r is shorthand for λv1.v=v1 → w [] r(v1).

Denotational semantics of Λ

Semantic domains:

w ∈ Value, r ∈ Environment = Var → Value

Valuation functions:

run: Expr → Value → Value

run$[\![E]\!]$w = $E[\![E]\!]$ λv.w

E: Expr → Environment → Value

$E[\![c]\!]$r = $c[\![c]\!]$

$E[\![v]\!]$r = r($[\![v]\!]$)

$E[\![$ (B E_1 E_2) $]\!]$r = $B[\![B]\!]$ ($E[\![E_1]\!]$r) ($E[\![E_2]\!]$r)

$E[\![$ (if E_1 E_2 E_3) $]\!]$r =
$E[\![E_1]\!]$r → $E[\![E_2]\!]$r $[\!]$ $E[\![E_3]\!]$r

$E[\![$ (λ V E) $]\!]$r = λw.$E[\![E]\!][[\![v]\!]↦$w]r

$E[\![$ (letrec V E_1 E_2) $]\!]$r =
$E[\![E_2]\!]$ $fix(λr1.[[\![v]\!]↦E[\![E_1]\!]$r1]r)

$E[\![$ (E_1 E_2) $]\!]$r = ($E[\![E_1]\!]$r) ($E[\![E_2]\!]$r)

C: Const → Value *unspecified*

B: Binop → Value → Value → Value *unspecified*

No type checking is performed; this would require injection tags on values and has been omitted for simplicity.

3.2 Interpreter text

Because Scheme uses strict evaluation, it is straightforward to convert the denotational semantics into a Scheme program — an interpreter — if all functions are considered strict in all arguments. This of course defines a strict semantics of the interpreted language. In section 6.3, we show an interpreter that defines a non-strict semantics.

To translate the semantics into Scheme, we first uncurry the functions run, E, and B; this is simple since the functions already are used in an uncurried way. Uncurrying is advantageous from a readability point of view ((f x y) contra ((f x) y)), and it also sometimes gives better specialization (more about this in section 8.2).

We now give the interpreter text. C is just the identity function and has been omitted.

Direct style Λ interpreter written in Scheme

```
(loadt "scheme.adt")
(loadt "lam-int.adt")
(load "lam-aux.sim")

(define (run E w)
  (_E E (λ (V) w)))                          ;0
```

```
(define (_E E r)
  (cond
    ((isCst? E)
     (cst-C E))
    ((isVar? E)
     (r (var-V E)))                          ;p
    ((isBinop? E)
     (ext (binop-B E)
          (_E (binop-E1 E) r)
          (_E (binop-E2 E) r)))
    ((isIf? E)
     (if (_E (if-E1 E) r)
         (_E (if-E2 E) r)
         (_E (if-E3 E) r)))
    ((isLambda? E)
     (λ (w)                                  ;2
        (_E (lambda-E E)
            (upd (lambda-V E) w r))))         ;1,q
    ((isLetrec? E)
     (_E (letrec-E2 E)
         (fix (lambda (r1)                    ;4
                (upd (letrec-V E)             ;3,r
                     (_E (letrec-E1 E) r1)
                     r)))))
    ((isApply? E)
     ((_E (apply-E1 E) r)                     ;s
      (_E (apply-E2 E) r)))
    (else
     (error '_E "unknown form: ~s" E))))
(define (fix f)
  (λ (x) ((f (fix f)) x)))                    ;5,t,u
```

The comments (0-5 and p-u) are used for reference later (section 4.5).

Syntax accessors (such as letrec-E1), syntax predicates (such as isLambda?), and ext have been defined as primitive operations in the file "lam-int.adt". The standard Scheme primitives equal? and error are defined in "scheme.adt". The file "lam-aux.sim" defines environment updating as a syntactic extension:

Environment updating

```
(extend-syntax (upd)
  ((upd V w r)
   (λ (V1)
     (if (equal? V V1)
         w
         (r V1)))))
```

3.3 Analysing the interpreter

Partially evaluating the interpreter with static program input (run's E parameter) and dynamic data input (run's w parameter) in effect compiles Λ-programs into Scheme (since Similix generates residual code in Scheme).

What can be expected from binding time analysing the interpreter? Λ is statically scoped, so e.g. environment operations should be classified eliminable: they can be performed at partial evaluation time (compile time). For instance, the analysis should detect that r is statically available in the expression (r (var-V E)), and hence the application of the environment should be classified eliminable.

On the other hand, the expression A = ((_E (apply-E1 E) r) (_E (apply-E2 E) r)) clearly is a *run time* application, so we would expect it to be classified residual. That is, if the interpreted program contains an expression E satisfying (isApply? E), then we expect (a residual/compiled version of) A to occur in the specialized interpreter, i.e. in the target program.

4. Closure analysis

In this section, we give a formal presentation of the closure analysis. The purpose of the analysis is for any application point to collect the set of possible (values of) lambda abstractions that may be applied at that point.

The analysis originates from one developed by Sestoft (for the purpose of globalizing variables in higher order programs) for untyped higher order programs in curried named combinator form [Sestoft 88b] [Sestoft 89]. Our analysis is basically an extended version of Sestoft's, adapted to our concrete language. The extension is that we handle *multi-applications*, that is, our lambda abstractions are n-ary, not just unary (Sestoft also mentions this possible extension).

We describe the analysis in a different and more implementation suitable way than Sestoft's. Our approach is based on the idea of continuously updating global mappings: traversing a program expression does not result in a "value", but in updated global mappings. Using this method, the program text need only be traversed once for each fixed point iteration. This gives a relatively simple description (only one function traversing syntax), and it also naturally leads to an efficient implementation. A global mapping corresponds to what is called a *cache* in [Hudak & Young 88]: it associates every expression in the program with a value (this explains the need for expression labels in the abstract syntax).

4.1 Semantic domains and functions

We define some semantic domains and various utility functions used by the closure analysis. First, we need some (injective) functions for converting from syntactic to semantic domains:

L: Label $\rightarrow$ Label

V: Variable $\rightarrow$ Variable

P: ProcedureName $\rightarrow$ Label

P associates a procedure name with the label of the procedure body. The semantic domains are defined like this:

Index = $\{1, 2, \ldots\}$

$k \in$ Label = *unspecified*

$v \in$ Variable = Label $\times$ Index

Formal parameters to a procedure P are identified as $(k, 1)$, $(k, 2)$, etc., where $k = P[\![P]\!]$. Formal parameters to a lambda expression with body expression with label L are identified similarly ($k = L[\![L]\!]$). Note that these identifications are unique. The formal parameter v of a let-expression is associated with some arbitrary unique value v.

A *closure* abstracts the value of a lambda expression and is identified by the label of the *body* of the (lambda) expression. The closure analysis computes two mappings, μ_{cl} and ρ_{cl}, the first one binding labels and the second one binding variables. For every expression, μ_{cl} thus collects the set of closures that the expression may possibly evaluate to (during any possible program execution); for every variable, ρ_{cl} collects the set of closures that the variable may possibly be bound to. The codomain of both mappings is the powerset of closures (with the usual subset inclusion ordering):

Closure = Label

$c \in$ ClSet = $\wp$(Closure)

$\mu_{cl} \in$ ClMap = Label $\rightarrow$ ClSet

$\rho_{cl} \in$ ClEnv = Variable $\rightarrow$ ClSet

Maps and environments are updated by corresponding monotonic update functions. Map updating is performed by the function upd (which should not be confused with the upd in the Λ-interpreter):

upd: Label → ClSet → ClMap → ClMap

$\text{upd } k \ c \ \mu_{cl} = \mu_{cl} \sqcup [k \mapsto c] \perp_{ClMap}$

Environment updating has functionality

Variable → ClSet → ClEnv → ClEnv

and is defined in a similar way. For readability, we uniformly refer to all updating functions simply as upd; the functionality is clear from the context. The least upper bounds on functions and cartesian products are defined pointwise:

$\mu_{cl} \sqcup \mu'_{cl} = \lambda k \ . \ \mu_{cl}(k) \sqcup \mu'_{cl}(k)$

$(\mu_{cl}, \rho_{cl}) \sqcup (\mu'_{cl}, \rho'_{cl}) = (\mu_{cl} \sqcup \mu'_{cl}, \rho_{cl} \sqcup \rho'_{cl})$

Finally, we need a function for checking the arity of a closure:

arity: Closure → {0, 1, 2, ...}

4.2 The analysis

We now give the closure analysis rules. Given a set of procedure definitions, the function Cl computes the two mappings μ_{cl} and ρ_{cl}. The mappings are computed as simultaneous fixed points. Initially, all labels and all variables are mapped onto the empty closure set (since the input to a program is first order and thus contains no closures).

Explicit quantification of indices is avoided when clear from the context; primitive operators and procedures may be nullary in which case the index i ranges over the empty set. A *case* expression is used for syntax dispatching.

Closure analysis

Cl: Definition$^+$ → ClMap × ClEnv

$\text{Cl}[\![\text{(define (...) } L_1 E_1 \text{) ... (define (...) } L_n E_n \text{)}]\!] = fix(\lambda(\mu_{cl}, \rho_{cl}) \ . \ \bigsqcup_i \text{cl}[\![L_i E_i]\!] \mu_{cl} \rho_{cl})$

cl: LabeledExpression → ClMap → ClEnv → ClMap × ClEnv

$\text{cl}[\![L \ E]\!] \mu_{cl} \rho_{cl} = $
$\quad let \ k = L[\![L]\!] \ in$
$\quad \quad case \ [\![E]\!] \ of$

$\quad \quad [\![c]\!]: (\text{upd } k \ \{\} \ \mu_{cl}, \rho_{cl})$

$\quad \quad [\![v]\!]: (\text{upd } k \ \rho_{cl}(v[\![v]\!]) \ \mu_{cl}, \rho_{cl})$

$\quad \quad [\![(\text{if } L_1 E_1 \ L_2 E_2 \ L_3 E_3)]\!]: let \ (\mu'_{cl}, \rho'_{cl}) = \bigsqcup_i \text{cl}[\![L_i E_i]\!] \mu_{cl} \rho_{cl} \ in$
$\quad \quad \quad (\text{upd } k \ (\mu'_{cl}(L[\![L_2]\!]) \sqcup \mu'_{cl}(L[\![L_3]\!])) \ \mu'_{cl}, \rho'_{cl})$

$\quad \quad [\![(\text{let } ((V \ L_1 E_1)) \ L_2 E_2)]\!]: let \ (\mu'_{cl}, \rho'_{cl}) = \bigsqcup_i \text{cl}[\![L_i E_i]\!] \mu_{cl} \rho_{cl} \ in$
$\quad \quad \quad (\text{upd } k \ \mu'_{cl}(L[\![L_2]\!]) \ \mu'_{cl}, \text{upd } v[\![v]\!] \ \mu'_{cl}(L[\![L_1]\!]) \ \rho'_{cl})$

$\quad \quad [\![(O \ L_1 E_1 \ ... \ L_n E_n)]\!]: let \ (\mu'_{cl}, \rho'_{cl}) = (\mu_{cl}, \rho_{cl}) \sqcup \bigsqcup_i \text{cl}[\![L_i E_i]\!] \mu_{cl} \rho_{cl} \ in$
$\quad \quad \quad (\text{upd } k \ (\bigsqcup_i \mu'_{cl}(L[\![L_i]\!])) \ \mu'_{cl}, \rho'_{cl})$

$\quad \quad [\![(P \ L_1 E_1 \ ... \ L_n E_n)]\!]: let \ (\mu'_{cl}, \rho'_{cl}) = (\mu_{cl}, \rho_{cl}) \sqcup \bigsqcup_i \text{cl}[\![L_i E_i]\!] \mu_{cl} \rho_{cl} \ in$
$\quad \quad \quad (\text{upd } k \ \mu'_{cl}(P[\![P]\!]) \ \mu'_{cl}, \rho'_{cl} \sqcup \bigsqcup_i (\text{upd } (P[\![P]\!], i) \ \mu'_{cl}(L[\![L_i]\!]) \ \rho'_{cl}))$

$\quad \quad [\![(\lambda \ (V_1 \ ... \ V_n) \ T_1 E_1)]\!]: let \ (\mu'_{cl}, \rho'_{cl}) = \text{cl}[\![L_1 E_1]\!] \mu_{cl} \rho_{cl} \ in$
$\quad \quad \quad (\text{upd } k \ \{L[\![L_1]\!]\} \ \mu'_{cl}, \rho'_{cl})$

$\quad \quad [\![(L_0 E_0 \ L_1 E_1 \ ... \ L_n E_n)]\!]: let \ (\mu'_{cl}, \rho'_{cl}) = \bigsqcup_i \text{cl}[\![L_i E_i]\!] \mu_{cl} \rho_{cl} \ in$
$\quad \quad let \ c = \{k' \ | \ k' \in \mu'_{cl}(L[\![L_0]\!]) \wedge arity(k')=n\} \ in$
$\quad \quad \quad (\text{upd } k \ (\bigsqcup_{k' \in c} \mu'_{cl}(k')) \ \mu'_{cl}, \rho'_{cl} \sqcup \bigsqcup_{i \geq 1, k' \in c} (\text{upd } (k', i) \ \mu'_{cl}(L[\![L_i]\!]) \ \rho'_{cl}))$

$\quad end$

The rules for constants, variables, conditionals, and let-expressions are straightforward. For primitive operations, note that a closure occurring in an argument may possibly be returned, but no new closures may be introduced. For procedure calls, a closure returned by the procedure body may be returned; care must taken to account for the influence on the formal parameters of the procedure. Both for primitive operations and for procedure calls, it is taken into account that n may be 0 (therefore the term "$(\mu_{cl}, \rho_{cl}) \sqcup$"). A lambda abstraction is the "source" of closures; note that (as mentioned earlier) the closure is identified by the label of the body.

The rule for applications is the most complex one. First, the set c of lambda abstractions that E_0 may evaluate to is found. Then μ_{cl} is updated: the application (E) may evaluate to a closure being the result of evaluating the *body* of any of the lambda abstractions in the set c. Lambda abstractions are identified by the body labels, so μ'_{cl} is simply applied to the elements (k') in c. Finally, ρ_{cl} is updated: E influences the formal parameters of all lambda abstractions, which E_0 may evaluate to. The i'th parameter is influenced by E_i.

4.3 Finiteness

For any given program, there is a finite number of closure sets. The mappings μ_{cl} and ρ_{cl} are updated monotonically, so they can only be updated a finite number of times. Fixed point iteration will therefore stabilize after a finite number of iterations. An implementation of the analysis is thus guaranteed to terminate.

4.4 Implementation issues

In the description, the subexpressions of a compound expression are processed in a parallel way. This simplifies the description, but sequential processing is better from an implementation point of view. Sequential processing means that there is always only *one* active copy of μ_{cl} as well as of ρ_{cl}; the mappings are *single-threaded* [Schmidt 85] and can therefore be implemented as global variables which are updated destructively.

In practice, the mappings are not kept as separate variables, but the information is kept as *attributes* (annotations) in the abstract syntax. This

means that expression labels are not actually needed.

4.5 Application to the sample interpreter

We end the description of the closure analysis by showing what it gives when applied to the sample interpreter.

The lambda abstractions are referred to by a number (0 to 5), the application points by a letter (p to u); see the comments in the interpreter text. Each use of upd is macro expanded into an expression containing a lambda abstraction ((λ (V1) ...)) and an application ((r V1)). t identifies the application of f to (fix f), u the application of (f (fix f)) to x. The closure analysis gives the following possible abstractions at the application points:

$$p, q, r: 0, 1, 5 \qquad s: 2 \qquad t: 4 \qquad u: 3$$

We see that at environment application points, p, q, and r, the environment closures 0, 1, and 5 (but not closure 3!) are the (only) possibilities. Closure 2, which implements lambda abstraction in the interpreted language, is the only one which may be applied at application point s; s implements application in the interpreted language. The only closure that the functional f may be bound to at point t is closure 4 that maps environments to environments. Finally, an "unrolled" recursive environment at point u can only be closure 3.

5. Binding time analysis

This section describes the binding time analysis that assigns a binding time value to all variables and all expressions (labels). The binding time uses the information collected in closure analysis.

5.1 The binding time domain

The binding time domain is a four value lattice:

$$b \in \text{BtValue} = (\{\bot, S, CL, D\}, \sqsubseteq)$$

The partial ordering is given by

S approximates ordinary first order static values (constants), CL approximates closure values, and D approximates dynamic values (residual code expressions). The value $\perp$ is needed because S and CL are incomparable. S corresponds to *Static* in a standard binding time analysis for first order programs, D to *Dynamic*.

At program specialization time, a *closure* is generated for CL annotated lambda expressions: a closure contains an identification of the lambda expression and values for its free variables. Closures are always eventually (beta) reduced away during program specialization, and CL is thus used for eliminable lambda expressions. For D annotated lambda expressions, a residual lambda expression (residual code) is generated. The lambda expression is thus suspended: no beta reduction is performed. The body of the residual lambda expression is a residual version of the body of the source lambda expression.

Let us consider an example:

```
((if (p x) (λ (y) y) (λ (z) (cdr z))) 1)
```

If the result of the test is static, i.e. the binding time value of (the label of) the expression (p x) is S, then the conditional expression always reduces to one of its branches. Consequently, beta reduction can always be performed during program specialization: it is safe to classify the two lambda expressions eliminable (CL). If, however, the test is dynamic, then residual code is generated for the conditional expression and beta reduction is not possible. The two lambda expressions are therefore annotated residual (D). We note that we do not consider more "exotic" (post-)reductions on residual code; for this particular example, the reduction $((if\ E_0\ E_1\ E_2)\ E_3) \Rightarrow (if\ E_0\ (E_1\ E_3)\ (E_2\ E_3))$ would in fact enable beta reduction in case of a dynamic test.

5.2 Annotating lambda expressions

It is clearly desirable to classify eliminable as many lambda expressions as possible: this gives a more reduced residual program. On the other hand, a closure value must never be used in a context that makes it part of a residual code piece: residual code consists of expressions, not values internal to the program specializer. Therefore, if (the value of) a lambda expression may be used in such a context,

it must be annotated residual. Otherwise it can safely be classified eliminable. (We note that one could imagine a program specializer that always generates a closure when processing a lambda expression (as proposed in [Mogensen 89a]). The specializer should then convert the closure into an expression if used in a residual code context. The method requires tagging and (re-)traversing residual values to find the closures. This is undesirable, especially for self-application.)

The value of a lambda expression E_λ may occur as part of a residual code piece in the following cases: (1) Some expression E has binding time value D (i.e. the result of specializing E is expected to be a residual code piece) and E may *itself* — according to the closure analysis — evaluate to (the value of) E_λ. (2) Some non-procedure call compound expression is suspended (a residual version of the expression is generated) and has an *argument* expression that may evaluate to (the value of) E_λ. (3) The body of the program's goal procedure (fixed for any particular program specialization) may evaluate to (the value of) E_λ. In these three cases, E_λ must be classified residual.

Case (1) implies that whenever an expression gets binding time value D, then all lambda expressions that E may evaluate to should be raised to be classified residual. Case (3) is needed because residual code is always generated for the body of the goal procedure, regardless of its binding time value. The point in case (2) is that suspending an operation requires generating residual versions of the argument expressions. Procedure calls are an exception: in the residual version of a suspended procedure call, the procedure name has been *specialized* with respect to the static arguments (this is the point in polyvariant program specialization). Closures are *partially static structures* [Mogensen 88] containing static and dynamic subparts; the dynamic parts become arguments to the residual procedure call. For the other compound expressions, some simplification is possible. A case analysis shows that case (1) covers case (2) for conditionals, let-expressions, and primitive operations. Conditionals are suspended in case of a dynamic test and let-expressions are possibly suspended in case of a dynamic actual parameter expression. The point now is that if any *other* argument expression, which because of the suspension gets "caught" in a residual code context (conditions: the "then" and "else" branches; let-expressions: the body; primitive operations: any argument expression), may return a closure, then the closure analysis rules imply that the whole expression may return the same closure. Hence, the closure is "captured" by case (1) since the whole compound expression has binding time value D.

Binding time values for *formal parameters* of eliminable lambda expressions depend on the binding time values of the argument expressions at any relevant application point. The relevant application points are those where the lambda expression may possibly be applied (computed by the closure analysis). In the example from section 5.1, there is only one such point, and y and z get the same binding time value as 1. In general, least upper bounding over all relevant application points is needed. Lambda expressions annotated residual are not beta reduced, and so the formal parameters all become dynamic.

One might think of introducing a binding time value S-or-CL lying above S and CL, but below D. This makes sense since Scheme is dynamically typed. Introducing S-or-CL gives additional precision in the description, but the program specializer is burdened in two ways: first, any value of the S-or-CL type needs to be tagged as either an S-value or a CL-value; second, the program specializer needs to type check such values. This is avoided by letting $S \sqcup CL = D$.

5.3 Domains and functions

The binding time value of an expression $(\texttt{O } \texttt{L-E}_1 \ ... \ \texttt{L-E}_n)$ is typically $\sqcup_i$(the binding time value of $\texttt{L-E}_i) \sqcup S$. Treating primitive operations working on higher order structures (such as Scheme's `procedure?`) introduces complications since the program specializer represents closures in its own way; this problem is inherent to the very idea of treating higher order operations intensionally. By least upper bounding the arguments with S, any primitive operation on a closure becomes dynamic whereby the problem is avoided (since no reduction takes place at partial evaluation time).

It is possible for the user to define a more conservative binding time function for primitive operations than the one above. This is for instance useful for *generalizing* [Turchin 86], i.e. forcing a static value to become dynamic (sometimes needed for ensuring termination of program specialization). The binding time value of a primitive application is therefore defined via a function o:

$$o: \texttt{OperatorName} \rightarrow \text{BtValue}^* \rightarrow \text{BtValue}$$

In practice, a binding time function is user defined for each primitive [Bondorf & Danvy 90].

The binding time analysis computes two mappings:

$$\mu_{bt} \in \text{BtMap} = \text{Label} \rightarrow \text{BtValue}$$
$$\rho_{bt} \in \text{BtEnv} = \text{Variable} \rightarrow \text{BtValue}$$

These are dual to the closure mappings μ_{cl} and ρ_{cl}, and they are updated in a similar way.

The closure analysis identifies a closure by the label of the body of the lambda expression. The binding time value of a lambda abstraction will be assigned to the label of the lambda expression itself (the body has its own binding time value), so we introduce the function k2k:

$$\text{k2k: Label} \rightarrow \text{Label}$$

Given the label of the body of a lambda expression, k2k returns the label of the lambda expression itself.

Given the label of an expression, the following function raises the annotations of the set of lambda expressions, which that expression may return:

$$\text{raise: Label} \rightarrow \text{BtMap} \rightarrow \text{BtEnv} \rightarrow \text{BtMap} \times \text{BtEnv}$$

raise k μ_{bt} ρ_{bt} =

$\sqcup_{k' \in \mu_{cl}(k)}(\text{upd k2k}(k') \ D \ \mu_{bt},$

$\qquad \sqcup_{i \in \{1...\text{arity}(k')\}}(\text{upd } (k', i) \ D \ \rho_{bt}))$

$\sqcup \ (\mu_{bt}, \rho_{bt})$

Note that the formal parameters of the lambda expressions are also raised (ρ_{bt} is updated).

5.4 The analysis

We now give the binding time analysis rules. Given a set of procedure definitions, a label identifying the body of the goal procedure, and an initial binding time description ρ_{bt}^{input}, the program is binding time analysed by propagating binding time values through the program.

Binding time analysis

Bt: $\texttt{Definition}^+ \rightarrow \text{Label} \rightarrow \text{BtEnv} \rightarrow \text{BtMap} \times \text{BtEnv}$

$Bt[\![(\texttt{define} \ (...) \ L_1 E_1) \ ... \ (\texttt{define} \ (...) \ L_n E_n)]\!] k_{goal} \rho_{bt}^{input} =$

$\quad fix(\lambda(\mu_{bt}, \rho_{bt}) \cdot (\mu_{bt}^{init}, \rho_{bt}^{init}) \sqcup \bigsqcup_i bt[\![L_i E_i]\!] \mu_{bt} \rho_{bt}) \ where \ (\mu_{bt}^{init}, \rho_{bt}^{init}) = raise^3 \ k_{goal} \perp_{BtMap} \rho_{bt}^{input}$

bt: $\texttt{LabeledExpression} \rightarrow \text{BtMap} \rightarrow \text{BtEnv} \rightarrow \text{BtMap} \times \text{BtEnv}$

$bt[\![L \ E]\!] \mu_{bt} \rho_{bt} =$

$\quad let \ k = L[\![L]\!] \ in \ \mu_{bt}^o(k) = D \rightarrow raise^1 \ k \ \mu_{bt}^o \ \rho_{bt}^o \ [\!] \ (\mu_{bt}^o, \rho_{bt}^o)$

$\quad \quad where \ (\mu_{bt}^o, \rho_{bt}^o) =$

$\quad \quad case \ [\![E]\!] \ of$

$\quad \quad \quad [\![c]\!]: (upd \ k \ S \ \mu_{bt}, \rho_{bt})$

$\quad \quad \quad [\![v]\!]: (upd \ k \ \rho_{bt}(v[\![v]\!]) \ \mu_{bt}, \rho_{bt})$

$\quad \quad \quad [\![(\texttt{if} \ L_1 E_1 \ L_2 E_2 \ L_3 E_3)]\!]: let \ (\mu_{bt}', \rho_{bt}') = \bigsqcup_i bt[\![L_i E_i]\!] \mu_{bt} \rho_{bt} \ in \ let \ b_i = \mu_{bt}'(L[\![L_i]\!]) \ in$
$\quad \quad \quad (upd \ k \ (b_1 = D \rightarrow D \ [\!] \ b_2 \sqcup b_3) \ \mu_{bt}', \rho_{bt}')$

$\quad \quad \quad [\![(\texttt{let} \ ((\texttt{V} \ L_1 E_1)) \ L_2 E_2)]\!]: let \ (\mu_{bt}', \rho_{bt}') = \bigsqcup_i bt[\![L_i E_i]\!] \mu_{bt} \rho_{bt} \ in \ let \ b_i = \mu_{bt}'(L[\![L_i]\!]) \ in$
$\quad \quad \quad (upd \ k \ (b_1 = D \rightarrow D \ [\!] \ b_2) \ \mu_{bt}', upd \ v[\![v]\!] \ b_1 \ \rho_{bt}')$

$\quad \quad \quad [\![(\texttt{O} \ L_1 E_1 \ ... \ L_n E_n)]\!]: let \ (\mu_{bt}', \rho_{bt}') = (\mu_{bt}, \rho_{bt}) \sqcup \bigsqcup_i bt[\![L_i E_i]\!] \mu_{bt} \rho_{bt} \ in \ let \ b_i = \mu_{bt}'(L[\![L_i]\!]) \ in$
$\quad \quad \quad (upd \ k \ (o[\![o]\!][b_1, \ ..., \ b_n]) \ \mu_{bt}', \rho_{bt}')$

$\quad \quad \quad [\![(\texttt{P} \ L_1 E_1 \ ... \ L_n E_n)]\!]: let \ (\mu_{bt}', \rho_{bt}') = (\mu_{bt}, \rho_{bt}) \sqcup \bigsqcup_i bt[\![L_i E_i]\!] \mu_{bt} \rho_{bt} \ in \ let \ b_i = \mu_{bt}'(L[\![L_i]\!]) \ in$
$\quad \quad \quad (upd \ k \ (some \ b_i = D \rightarrow D \ [\!] \ \mu_{bt}'(P[\![P]\!])) \ \mu_{bt}', \rho_{bt}' \sqcup \bigsqcup_i (upd \ (P[\![P]\!], i) \ b_i \ \rho_{bt}'))$

$\quad \quad \quad [\![(\lambda \ (v_1 \ ... \ v_n) \ L_1 E_1)]\!]: let \ (\mu_{bt}', \rho_{bt}') = bt[\![L_1 E_1]\!] \mu_{bt} \rho_{bt} \ in$
$\quad \quad \quad \mu_{bt}''(k) = D \rightarrow raise^2 \ L[\![L_1]\!] \ \mu_{bt}' \ \rho_{bt}' \ [\!] \ (\mu_{bt}'', \rho_{bt}') \ where \ \mu_{bt}'' = upd \ k \ CL \ \mu_{bt}'$

$\quad \quad \quad [\![(L_0 E_0 \ L_1 E_1 \ ... \ L_n E_n)]\!]: let \ (\mu_{bt}', \rho_{bt}') = \bigsqcup_i bt[\![L_i E_i]\!] \mu_{bt} \rho_{bt} \ in \ let \ b_i = \mu_{bt}'(L[\![L_i]\!]) \ in$
$\quad \quad \quad let \ c = \{k' \ | \ k' \in \mu_{cl}'(L[\![L_0]\!]) \wedge arity(k') = n\} \ in$
$\quad \quad \quad \mu_{bt}''(L[\![L_0]\!]) = D \rightarrow (\mu_{bt}'', \rho_{bt}'') \sqcup \bigsqcup_{i \geq 1} (raise^2 \ L[\![L_i]\!] \ \mu_{bt}' \ \rho_{bt}'') \ [\!] \ (\mu_{bt}'', \rho_{bt}'')$
$\quad \quad \quad where \ \mu_{bt}'' = upd \ k \ (some \ b_i = D \rightarrow D \ [\!] \ \bigsqcup_{k' \in c} \mu_{bt}'(k')) \ \mu_{bt}'$
$\quad \quad \quad \quad \rho_{bt}'' = \rho_{bt}' \sqcup \bigsqcup_{i \geq 1, k' \in c} (upd \ (k', i) \ \mu_{bt}'(L[\![L_i]\!])) \ \rho_{bt}')$

$\quad end$

The applications of the function raise have been superscripted; the numbers refer to the cases (1)-(3) that cause lambda annotations to be raised (section 5.2).

5.5 Finiteness

There is a finite number of binding time values. Since the mappings μ_{bt} and ρ_{bt} are only updated monotonically, they can only be updated a finite number of times. Fixed point iteration will therefore stabilize after a finite number of iterations.

5.6 Application to the sample interpreter

When applied to the sample interpreter with static program input and dynamic data input, the binding time analysis correctly annotates the lambda abstractions for environment processing, 0, 1, 3, 4, and 5, as eliminable. Dually, the applications p, q, r, t, and u, become eliminable: the expression to be applied in all cases gets binding time value CL. The lambda expression 2 and the application s become residual.

The formal parameters to the lambda expressions 0, 1, 3, and 5 are all static (S). The parameter of abstraction 4 is a closure (CL), but this is only what one could expect: the parameter is an environment. Finally, the parameter of abstraction 2 is dynamic (D).

6. Results

In this section we use Similix-2 to specialize the direct style Λ-interpreter and two other Λ-interpreters: one written in continuation passing style and one implementing normal order reduction.

6.1 Direct style

Specializing the sample interpreter with respect to the factorial Λ-program yields the following Scheme target program:

Machine produced factorial target program, generated from direct style Λ-interpreter

```
(loadt "scheme.adt")
(loadt "lam-int.adt")
(define (run-0 w) ((_E-1 w) w))
(define (_E-1 r)
  (λ (w)
    (if (ext '= w 0)
        1
        (ext '*
             w
             ((_E-1 r) (ext '- w 1))))))
```

For readability, we have "cheated" by renaming some of the machine generated names (but this is a trivial conversion).

run-0 is the name of the goal procedure in the target program, i.e. run-0 computes the factorial function. We observe that the interpretation level has almost been completely removed: the interpreter's syntax analysis and environment operations have been performed. Only run time operations are left, with a small overhead due to the ext encodings. When computing factorial of 10, it is around 14 times faster to run the target program than to interpret the source program (see the next section on performance).

Recursion is expressed by the procedure _E-1. The redundant variable r corresponds to the input

variable in the factorial Λ-program: it is not actually referred to inside the recursive body of the letrec, but it is accessible, and this is reflected in the target program.

The target program can be generated either by directly specializing the Λ-interpreter with respect to the factorial program or by first generating a stand-alone compiler (using self-application) and then applying it to the factorial program.

6.2 Continuation passing style

The interpreter below can be derived from a continuation semantics for Λ. Continuations are strict and map values into values:

Continuation passing style Λ-interpreter

```
(loadt "scheme.adt")
(loadt "lam-int.adt")
(load "lam-aux.sim")
(extend-syntax (eta-convert)
  ((eta-convert c) (lambda (w) (c w))))
(extend-syntax (c-id)
  ((c-id) (λ (w) w)))
(define (run E w)
  (_E E (λ (V) w) (c-id)))
(define (_E E r c)
  (cond
   ((isCst? E)
    (c (cst-C E)))
   ((isVar? E)
    (c (r (var-V E))))
   ((isBinop? E)
    (_E (binop-E1 E)
        r
        (λ (w1)
          (_E (binop-E2 E)
              r
              (λ (w2)
                (c (ext (binop-B E)
                        w1
                        w2))))))))
   ((isIf? E)
    (_E (if-E1 E)
        r
        (λ (w1)
          (if w1
              (_E (if-E2 E) r c)
              (_E (if-E3 E) r c)))))
   ((isLambda? E)
    (c (λ (w1 c1)
         (_E (lambda-E E)
             (upd (lambda-V E) w1 r)
             (eta-convert c1)))))
   ((isLetrec? E)
    (_E (letrec-E2 E)
        (fix (λ (r1)
               (upd (letrec-V E)
```

```
                  (_E (letrec-E1 E)
                      r1
                      (c-id))
                  r)))
          c))
  ((isApply? E)
   (_E (apply-E1 E)
       r
       (λ (w1)
         (_E (apply-E2 E)
             r
             (λ (w2)
               (w1
                w2
                (eta-convert c)))))))
  (else
   (error '_E "unknown form: ~s" E))))

(define (fix f) (λ (x) ((f (fix f)) x)))
```

Binding time analysis (with static program and dynamic data input) classifies the environments eliminable (*CL*). The lambda expression (λ (w1 c1) ...) is classified residual (just as the corresponding lambda expression in the direct style interpreter was), and therefore the formal parameter continuation c1 also becomes residual (*D*). The eta-conversions are then inserted to achieve that the binding time analysis classifies _E's continuation parameter c eliminable rather than residual. This implies that the program specializer will beta reduce continuation applications at partial evaluation time, thus giving better, more reduced target programs.

The following target program is generated when specializing the interpreter with respect to the factorial program:

Machine produced factorial target program, generated from continuation style Λ-interpreter

```
(loadt "scheme.adt")
(loadt "lam-int.adt")

(define (run-0 w)
  ((_E-1 w) w (λ (w) w)))

(define (_E-1 r)
  (λ (w1 c1)
    (if (ext '= w1 0)
        (c1 1)
        ((_E-1 r)
         (ext '- w1 1)
         (λ (w) (c1 (ext '* w1 w)))))))
```

The target program is written in continuation passing style since the interpreter was.

6.3 Normal order reduction

The third interpreter is a variant of the direct style one, but it implements normal order reduction semantics. Normal order reduction is achieved by suspending the evaluation of arguments to applications. Instead of keeping values in environments, we thus now keep thunks of the form (λ () ...).

Normal order reduction Λ-interpreter

```
(loadt "scheme.adt")
(loadt "lam-int.adt")
(load "lam-aux.sim")

(extend-syntax (my-delay)
  ((my-delay w) (lambda () w)))

(extend-syntax (my-force)
  ((my-force w-delayed) (w-delayed)))

(define (run E w)
  (_E E (lambda (V) (my-delay w))))

(define (_E E r)
  (cond
    ((isCst? E)
     (cst-C E))
    ((isVar? E)
     (my-force (r (var-V E))))
    ((isBinop? E)
     (ext (binop-B E)
          (_E (binop-E1 E) r)
          (_E (binop-E2 E) r)))
    ((isIf? E)
     (if (_E (if-E1 E) r)
         (_E (if-E2 E) r)
         (_E (if-E3 E) r)))
    ((isLambda? E)
     (lambda (w)
       (_E (lambda-E E)
           (upd (lambda-V E) w r))))
    ((isLetrec? E)
     (_E (letrec-E2 E)
         (fix (lambda (r1)
                (upd (letrec-V E)
                     (my-delay
                       (_E (letrec-E1 E) r1))
                     r)))))
    ((isApply? E)
     ((_E (apply-E1 E) r)
      (my-delay (_E (apply-E2 E) r))))
    (else
     (error '_E "unknown form: ~s" E))))

(define (fix f) (λ (x) ((f (fix f)) x)))
```

Note that primitive operations are still call-by-value; only applications of lambda abstractions are call-by-name.

The following program produces a list of the first *n* even numbers. The function `evens-from` produces an infinite list of even numbers starting from a given number. Since `lazy-cons` is a lambda expression, the evaluation of its arguments is suspended and therefore calls to `evens-from` do not loop. Using a call-by-value interpreter, any call to `evens-from` would loop.

Even number program written in normal order Λ

```
((λ lazy-cons
  ((λ lazy-car
    ((λ lazy-cdr

      (letrec first-n
        (λ n (λ l
          (if (= n 0)
              '()
              (cons
                (lazy-car l)
                ((first-n (- n 1))
                 (lazy-cdr l))))))))
      (letrec evens-from
        (λ n
          ((lazy-cons n)
           (evens-from (+ n 2))))
        ((first-n input)              ;main
         (evens-from 0))))))
    (λ x (x (λ a (λ d d)))))))
  (λ x (x (λ a (λ d a))))))
(λ x (λ y (λ z ((z x) y))))))
```

The Λ-language has no let-expressions and only unary lambda expressions, so the program looks somewhat clumsy.

Specializing the normal order interpreter with respect to the even number program yields a target program in which syntax analysis and environment operations have all been performed. The program contains lots of thunks and is rather hard to read (we do not include it here). It is, however, quite efficient: running the target program is around 25 times faster than interpreting.

This example nicely shows the effect of partial evaluation: Scheme is call-by-value, so to achieve call-by-name evaluation, one would need to insert thunks everywhere by hand. This is complex, so instead one can write an interpreter for a call-by-name language. However, running the interpreter gives a siginificant interpretation overhead. But using partial evaluation, programs in the call-by-name language are compiled into efficient Scheme code (which is eventually itself compiled).

7. Performance

This section contains some benchmarks for Similix-2. The tables below show the speedups achieved by partial evaluation. Each table has four columns. The first one describes the result computed by the job in the second column. The third column shows the run time, the fourth column the speedup.

For simplicity, we identify programs with the functions they compute. Following the tradition, the program specializer is referred to as mix, the compiler generator as cogen. Binding time annotated (preprocessed) programs have the superscript "ann". The run time figures are in CPU seconds with one or two decimals; they exclude time for garbage collection (typically 0 to 40% additional time), but include postprocessing. The speedup ratios have been computed using more decimals than the ones given here; in some cases, the time has been computed by performing 10 successive runs and then dividing. The system is implemented in Chez Scheme [Dybvig 87] version 2.0.3, and the figures are for a Sun 3/160.

For the direct and continuation style examples, the source Λ-program is the factorial program; the figures are for 100 computations of factorial of 10. For the normal order example, the even number program is used; the figures are for 10 computations of "evens" of 20.

output	run	time/s	speedup
result	int(source, data)	5·7	14·3
	target(data)	0·40	
target	mix(int^{ann}, source)	0·53	7·8
	comp(source)	0·07	
comp	mix(mix^{ann}, int^{ann})	11·5	2·9
	cogen(int^{ann})	4·0	

Direct style Λ-interpreter

output	run	time/s	speedup
result	int(source, data)	6·1	17·1
	target(data)	0·36	
target	mix(int^{ann}, source)	1·2	7·8
	comp(source)	0·15	
comp	mix(mix^{ann}, int^{ann})	49·8	2·3
	cogen(int^{ann})	21·9	

Continuation passing style Λ-interpreter

output	run	time/s	speedup
result	int(source, data)	35·0	25·7
	target(data)	1·4	
target	mix(int^{ann}, source)	6·0	5·4
	comp(source)	1·1	
comp	mix(mix^{ann}, int^{ann})	16·3	3·2
	cogen(int^{ann})	5·1	

Normal order reduction Λ-interpreter

output	run	time/s	speedup
cogen	mix(mix^{ann}, mix^{ann})	82·3	3·0
	cogen(mix^{ann})	27·6	

Compiler generator

The first table shows that running the factorial target program is around 14 times faster than interpreting the factorial source program. Compiling by the stand-alone compiler is 8 times faster than by specializing the interpreter; this shows that the partial evaluator really is effectively self-applicable. Finally, generating the compiler by the mix-generated compiler generator cogen is 3 times faster than by specializing mix. The second and third tables are similar. The last table shows that generating cogen by running cogen is 3 times faster than by specializing mix.

Here are some additional figures: it takes 2-4 seconds to preprocess an interpreter (includes closure and binding time analyses); preprocessing mix takes around 19 seconds. The size of mix is 2.5K cells (measured as the number of "cons" cells needed to represent the program as a list), cogen 13.9K cells, the interpreters 0.18K-0.26K cells, and the compilers 1.9K-7.6K cells. For mix, this gives an expansion factor of 5.5 (13.9/2.5), for the interpreters factors in the range 10-29.

The figures all in all compare well to similar published benchmarks for first order languages [Jones, Sestoft, & Søndergaard 89] [Bondorf & Danvy 90] [Consel 89], and also to those of Lambda-mix [Gomard 89].

8. Discussion

Partial evaluation is no panacea: some programs specialize well, but others do not. Program generators in general take some specification as input; in the case of partial evaluation, the specification is a program. The quality of a program generated by any program generator depends on the quality of the specification. For partial evaluation, the quality of the residual program depends on the quality of the source program supplied to the partial evaluator.

The "quality" of a source program does not necessarily mean its clarity or efficiency. It often happens that less efficient and/or less clear programs lead to better (more efficient, more clear) residual programs.

8.1 Exploiting static information

Programs have to be expressed carefully not to lose static information. A simple example: suppose x and y are static and z dynamic. Then (+ (+ x y) z) specializes better than (+ x (+ y z)): in the former case, the inner + is reduced, but in the latter no reduction takes place.

8.2 Currying

It was mentioned earlier (section 3.2) that uncurrying functions sometimes gives better specialization. When binding time analysing a curried expression such as E = (λ (x) (λ (y) (+ (+ y y) x))), the binding time analysis might annotate x dynamic and y static. That is, a dynamic argument is supplied before a static argument. During program specialization, an application of E like ((E "code") 3) could be beta reduced to the residual code piece (+ 6 "code").

However, to avoid that procedure call unfolding and beta reduction of higher order applications *duplicates* or *discards* dynamic actual argument expressions, let-expressions are *inserted* for all formal parameters in source programs before preprocessing [Bondorf & Danvy 90]. The expression which is actually binding time analysed is therefore not E, but the semantically equivalent

```
(λ (x) (let ((x x)) (λ (y) (let ((y y))
   (+ (+ y y) x)))))
```

Since x is dynamic, the result of the body of the outer lambda expression becomes dynamic. The (value of the) inner lambda expression is a possible result of evaluating this body, and therefore the inner lambda expression becomes annotated residual. Hence, its parameter y becomes dynamic whereby static information is lost. It thus never happens that dynamic arguments are supplied before static arguments. This confirms the intuition in [Nielson & Nielson 88]: "early bindings before late bindings".

If a curried expression is always applied to all its arguments simultaneously, then it is advantageous to use an uncurried version. In the uncurried version, the binding time values of the parameters do not influence each other. Uncurrying thus prevents a possible loss of static information.

9. Conclusion and open problems

We have presented an approach to treat a higher order subset of Scheme in autoprojection. We have implemented the ideas by extending the existing Similix autoprojector. To our knowledge, our system is the first fully automated and implemented autoprojector for a higher order language. We have presented a binding time analysis based on a closure analysis. The domain of binding time values is finite and no structured binding time values are needed.

We have shown examples of interpreters from which target programs and stand-alone compilers were generated. Because the language is higher order, we are able to treat continuation passing style interpreters and interpreters that use "thunks" to implement normal order reduction.

Several problems remain open. In the line of compiler generation, the system should be applied to bigger, more realistic examples. It would also be interesting to experiment with interpreters for real lazy (i.e. call-by-need rather than call-by-name) languages; we have made some promising experiments in this direction.

The autoprojector itself could also be improved. One problem is that the binding time analysis is

monovariant, i.e. it only generates one binding time annotated version of each procedure. If a procedure is called with different binding time patterns, then the least upper bound is taken. This implies a possible loss of static information at program specialization time. It is not clear how to extend the closure analysis based binding time analysis to a polyvariant one.

Acknowledgements

This work has been carried out within the Similix project, a joint work of Olivier Danvy and the author. I am most grateful to Olivier for his many comments and proposals. Many other people have contributed in various ways; thanks to Lars Ole Andersen, Hans Dybkjær, Frank Frauendorf, Harald Ganzinger, Carsten K. Gomard, Neil D. Jones, Jesper Jørgensen, Karoline Malmkjær, Torben Mogensen, Peter Sestoft, and Jörg Süggel.

References

[Aho, Sethi, & Ullman 86] Alfred V. Aho, Ravi Sethi, and Jeffrey D. Ullman: *Compilers: Principles, Techniques and Tools*, Addison-Wesley 1986.

[Bjørner, Ershov, & Jones 88] Dines Bjørner, Andrei P. Ershov, and Neil D. Jones (eds.): *Partial Evaluation and Mixed Computation*, Gl. Avernæs, Denmark, October 1987, North-Holland 1988.

[Bondorf 89] Anders Bondorf: *A self-applicable partial evaluator for term rewriting systems*, TAPSOFT'89, Proceedings of the International Joint Conference on Theory and Practice of Software Development, J. Diaz and F. Orejas (eds.), Barcelona, Spain, Lecture Notes in Computer Science No 352 pp 81-96, Springer-Verlag 1989.

[Bondorf 90] Ph.D. thesis (forthcoming), DIKU, University of Copenhagen, Denmark.

[Bondorf & Danvy 90] Anders Bondorf and Olivier Danvy: *Automatic autoprojection of recursive equations with global variables and abstract data types*, Technical Report No 90-4, DIKU, University of Copenhagen, Denmark.

[Bondorf, Jones, Mogensen, & Sestoft 90] Anders Bondorf, Neil D. Jones, Torben Æ. Mogensen, and Peter Sestoft: *Binding time analysis and the taming of self-application*, submitted for publication, DIKU, University of Copenhagen, Denmark.

[Bulyonkov 84] Mikhail A. Bulyonkov: *Polyvariant mixed computation for analyzer programs*, Acta Informatica 21 pp 473-484, 1984.

[Consel 88] Charles Consel: *New insights into partial evaluation: the SCHISM experiment*, ESOP'88 (ed. Harald Ganzinger), Nancy, France, Lecture Notes in Computer Science No 300 pp 236-247, Springer-Verlag 1988.

[Consel 89] Charles Consel: *Analyse de programmes, Evaluation partielle et Génération de compilateurs*, Ph.D. thesis, LITP, University of Paris 6, France 1989.

[Consel & Danvy 89] Charles Consel and Olivier Danvy: *Partial evaluation of pattern matching in strings*, Information Processing Letters 30, No 2 pp 79-86, 1989.

[Dybvig 87] R. Kent Dybvig: *The SCHEME Programming Language*, Prentice-Hall, New Jersey 1987.

[Ershov 77] Andrei P. Ershov: *On the partial computation principle*, Information Processing Letters 6, No 2 pp 38-41, April 1977.

[Futamura 71] Yoshihiko Futamura: *Partial evaluation of computing process — an approach to a compiler-compiler*, Systems, Computers, Controls 2, 5, 45-50, 1971.

[Gomard 89] Carsten K. Gomard: *Higher Order Partial Evaluation — HOPE for the Lambda Calculus*, Master's thesis, DIKU student report 89-9-11, University of Copenhagen, 1989.

[Gomard 90] Carsten K. Gomard: *Partial Type Inference for Untyped Functional Programs*, submitted for publication, DIKU, University of Copenhagen, 1989.

[Gomard & Jones 89] Carsten K. Gomard and Neil D. Jones: *Compiler generation by partial evaluation*, Information Processing '89. Proceedings of the 11th IFIP World Computer Congress, G. X. Ritter (ed.), pp 1139-1144, North-Holland, 1989.

[Hudak & Young 88] Paul Hudak and Jonathan Young: *A collecting interpretation of expressions (without power-domains)*, Proceedings of the Fifteenth Annual ACM SIGACT-SIGPLAN Symposium on Principles of Programming Languages pp 107-118, San Diego, California, January 1988.

[JonGomBonDanMog 90] Neil D. Jones, Carsten K. Gomard, Anders Bondorf, Olivier Danvy, and Torben Æ. Mogensen: *A self-applicable partial evaluator for the lambda calculus*, IEEE Computer Society 1990 International Conference on Computer Languages, 1990.

[Jones, Sestoft, & Søndergaard 85] Neil D. Jones, Peter Sestoft, and Harald Søndergaard: *An experiment in partial evaluation: the generation of a compiler generator*, Rewriting Techniques and Applications (ed. J.-P. Jouannaud), Dijon, France, Lecture Notes in Computer Science No 202 pp 124-140, Springer-Verlag 1985.

[Jones, Sestoft, & Søndergaard 89] Neil D. Jones, Peter Sestoft, and Harald Søndergaard: *MIX: a self-applicable partial evaluator for experiments in compiler generation*, International Journal LISP and Symbolic Computation 2, 1, pp 9-50, 1989

[Kohlbecker 86] Eugene E. Kohlbecker: *Syntactic Extensions in the Programming Language Lisp*, Ph.D. thesis, Indiana University, Bloomington 1986.

[Mogensen 88] Torben Æ. Mogensen: *Partially static structures in a self-applicable partial evaluator*, pp 325-347 of [Bjørner, Ershov, & Jones 88].

[Mogensen 89a] Torben Æ. Mogensen: *Binding Time Aspects of Partial Evaluation*, Ph.D. thesis, DIKU, University of Copenhagen, Denmark 1989.

[Mogensen 89b] Torben Æ. Mogensen: *Binding time analysis for polymorphically typed higher order languages*, TAPSOFT'89, Proceedings of the International Joint Conference on Theory and Practice of Software Development, J. Diaz and F. Orejas (eds.), Barcelona, Spain, Lecture Notes in Computer Science No 352 pp 298-312, Springer-Verlag 1989.

[Nielson & Nielson 88] Hanne R. Nielson and Flemming Nielson: *Automatic binding time analysis for a typed λ-calculus*, Proceedings of the Fifteenth Annual ACM SIGACT-SIGPLAN Symposium on Principles of Programming Languages pp 98-106, San Diego, Calinfornia, January 1988.

[Rees & Clinger 86] Jonathan Rees and William Clinger (eds.): *Revised³ Report on the Algorithmic Language Scheme*, Sigplan Notices 21, 12, pp 37-79, December 1986.

[Romanenko 88] Sergei A. Romanenko: *A compiler generator produced by a self-applicable specialiser can have a surprisingly natural and understandable structure*, pp 445-463 of [Bjørner, Ershov, & Jones 88].

[Schmidt 85] David A. Schmidt: *Detecting global variables in denotational specifications*, ACM Transactions on Programming Languages and Systems 7, No 2 pp 299-310, April 1985.

[Schmidt 86] David A. Schmidt: *Denotational Semantics, a Methodology for Language Development*, Allyn and Bacon, Boston 1986.

[Sestoft 88a] Peter Sestoft: *Automatic call unfolding in a partial evaluator*, pp 485-506 of [Bjørner, Ershov, & Jones 88].

[Sestoft 88b] Peter Sestoft: *Replacing Function Parameters by Global Variables*, Master's thesis, DIKU student report 88-7-2, University of Copenhagen, 1988.

[Sestoft 89] Peter Sestoft: *Replacing function parameters by global variables*, Proceedings of the Fourth International Conference on Functional Programming and Computer Architecture, London, UK, pp 39-53, ACM Press, September 1989.

[Turchin 80] Valentin F. Turchin: *Semantic definitions in Refal and the automatic production of compilers*, Proceedings of the Workshop on Semantics-Directed Compiler Generation, Neil D. Jones (ed.), Århus, Denmark, Lecture Notes in Computer Science No 94 pp 441-474, Springer-Verlag 1980.

[Turchin 86] Valentin F. Turchin: *The concept of a supercompiler*, ACM Transactions on Programming Languages and Systems 8, No 3 pp 292-325, July 1986.

From Interpreting to Compiling Binding Times [*]

Charles Consel [†]   &   Olivier Danvy [‡]

Abstract

The key to realistic self-applicable partial evaluation is to analyze binding times in the source program, *i.e.*, whether the result of partially evaluating a source expression is static or dynamic, given a static/dynamic division of the input. Source programs are specialized with respect to the static part of their input. When a source expression depends on the concrete result of specializing another expression, the binding time of this other expression is first interpreted. A safe approximation of these abstract values is computed by binding time analysis.

This paper points out that this value-based information can be compiled into control-based directives driving the specializer as to what to do for each expression – instead of how to use the result of partially evaluating an expression. This compilation is achieved by a non-standard interpretation of the specialization semantics, based on the observation that a source expression is either reduced or rebuilt. The result is an action trees isomorphic to the abstract syntax tree of the source program. This approach suggests to reorganize the specializer so that it is driven first by the action tree and then by the abstract syntax tree – instead of performing first a syntax analysis and then interpreting binding times.

Some subtrees imply the corresponding expressions to be completely reduced or completely rebuilt. These expressions are completely evaluated or reproduced verbatim. This suggests to refine the specializer so that it evaluates, reduces, rebuilds, or reproduces source expressions. This also suggests a more radical implementation.

By pruning the source program based on its action trees, we extract combinators for each subtree that should be evaluated completely or reproduced verbatim. By implementing these combinators as runtime operators, we prune the text of the partial evaluator that was dedicated to evaluating or reproducing source expressions using symbolic interpretation. Because source programs are smaller, they can be specialized faster. Because half of the specializer disappears, it is smaller and faster too. For these compound reasons self-application performs better.

As a result, more processing is shifted away from the actual specializer. A pleasing symmetry appears in the actual specialization process. Its significance, *e.g.*, in the structure of compilers generated by self-application, remains to be explored.

Keywords: partial evaluation, self-application, actions, combinators.

---

[*]Extended abstract.

[†]Yale University (consel-charles@cs.yale.edu). This work was done jointly at University of Paris 6 under a MRES grant and at Yale under the Darpa grant N00014-88-K-0573.

[‡]This work has been carried out during a visit to the Computer Science Department of Indiana University, in the fall of 1989 (danvy@iuvax.cs.indiana.edu).

Introduction

Partial evaluation is a program transformation specializing a program with respect to a static part of its input. For self-application purposes, binding times in the source program are analyzed prior to the actual specialization. A binding time analysis automatically computes the binding time values (static or dynamic) of each expression in the source program with respect to an abstraction of its input: the arguments that are available are declared static and the others are dynamic. The result of binding time analysis is a collection of binding time trees isomorphic to the source abstract syntax trees (one for each procedure). Then the source program and the binding time trees are processed by the specializer together with concrete values. Specializing a source expression is achieved by first determining its syntactic category and then interpreting the binding time value of its sub-components as the result of their specialization is needed.

The point of this paper is that this interpretation of binding time values can be lifted from the specializer. Let us illustrate this through an example. Figure 1 displays a (first-order) program written in Scheme [Rees & Clinger 86] that computes the function concatenating two lists.

Our goal is to specialize procedure **append** with respect to its second argument. The result of preprocessing (which includes parsing and binding time analysis) is displayed in figure 2.

At the top, the program is parsed. Below, the binding time tree is reproduced. It is isomorphic to the corresponding syntax tree: the node corresponding to a dynamic identifier is (d), and to a static identifier is (s). In general, the first component of a binding time tree is the binding time value of the expression, and the rest (if any) are the binding time trees of the corresponding sub-expressions.

Because its induction variable is dynamic in this example, procedure **append** is a specialization point. This means that all the calls to **append** will give rise to specializing **append** with respect to the value of its second argument. Also, the dynamic parameter **x** need not be renamed during specialization, while the binding of **y** will be unfolded.

Let us specialize procedure **append** with respect to its second argument whose value is (3 4 5). The result is displayed in figure 3.

Let us analyze each step of the specialization. Because **append** is a specialization point, it gives rise to generating a residual procedure, named

```
(define append    ;;; List(A) * List(A) -> List(A)
  (lambda (x y)
    (if (null? x)
        y
        (cons (car x)
              (append (cdr x)
                      y)))))
```

Figure 1: Tagged concatenation of lists (source program)

```
(
  (append
   (*lambda-sp (x y) [i u]
     (*if (*app null? (*ide x))
          (*ide y)
          (*app cons (*app car (*ide x))
                     (*app append (*app cdr (*ide x))
                                  (*ide y))))))
)
(
  (append
   (s d)
   (d (d (d))
      (s)
      (d (d (d)) (d (d (d))
                     (s)))))
)
```

Figure 2: Parsed and binding time analyzed source program
append is a specialization point (lambda-sp). Its first parameter is dynamic
and left identical. Its second parameter is unfoldable. This is indicated by
the tags [i u].

append-0, which is a version of append specialized with respect to the static value (3 4 5). In a symbolic environment where x is bound to the residual identifier x and y is bound to the value (3 4 5) represented by '(3 4 5), we are ready to interpret the body of append symbolically.

It is a conditional expression. This requires to interpret the test expression in the same environment, which in turn needs interpreting the identifier (*ide x). The result is the residual identifier x. Because the binding time value of the argument of null? is dynamic, the application is rebuilt and the result of specializing the test part is (null? x). Because the binding time value of the test is dynamic, specializing the conditional expression will yield a residual conditional expression whose test part is (null? x), and whose consequent and alternative parts are the result of specializing the source consequent and alternative parts.

Identifier (*ide y) is bound in the environment. Its interpretation yields '(3 4 5).

Interpreting (*app cons ... ...) needs interpreting both arguments. Interpreting the first needs interpreting (*ide x). Because its binding time value is dynamic, the car operation cannot be folded and the application is rebuilt instead. The arguments of the call to append are interpreted similarly. The results are two residual expressions. Because their static projection (i.e., the pattern of static values in these arguments) coincides with the original one, we build a residual call to append-0. This call has only one argument because append-0 is a unary procedure. At this point we return two residual expressions as actual arguments of the application (*app cons ... ...). Because the binding time values of the two arguments are dynamic, the application is rebuilt.

Then the conditional expression is rebuilt, which concludes specializing procedure append.

To summarize: partial evaluation is staged in two phases – preprocessing and specialization. Binding time information has been collected during preprocessing. Decisions as to how to treat the program are taken during specialization, i.e., which expression should be reduced, which should be rebuilt. This staging has been pioneered in [Jones et al. 89]. The remaining overhead (e.g., interpreting the binding time informations) is removed by self-applying the specializer.

However, aside from self-application, something basic can be done: given the program and the binding time tree, we can infer which actions the specializer will be performing. The basic action of a specializer is to reduce or rebuild a source expression. Let us build an *action tree* isomorphic to the binding time tree and tagged with the two directives *Rd* (for reduce) and *Rb* (for rebuild). The result is displayed in figure 4.

We can see this action tree as providing directives to the specializer.

Our next observation is that the specializer can do better than, *e.g.*, reproducing large pieces of source program by symbolic interpretation. This suggests to introduce a directive *Id* at the root of each action subtree expressing that the source program should be rebuilt verbatim. Symmetrically, expressions that should be reduced completely can be handled by introducing a directive *Ev*. The new action tree is displayed in figure 5.

Now we may wonder why the specializer, whose basic tasks are to reduce and rebuild source expressions, and to coordinate these actions, should have the burden of evaluating or reproducing source expressions. There are faster ways to evaluate Scheme expressions – *e.g.*, by compiling them using a regular Scheme compiler. Similarly, there are faster ways to implement the identity function.

So let us prune the action tree by extracting *Ev*- and *Id*-combinators from the source program. The append example is too simple for giving rise to actually defining interesting combinators, but in an interpreter, many combinators arise naturally, *e.g.*, *Ev*-combinators for scope resolution and *Id*-combinators for store management. As a result, source programs are physically smaller. They can be expected to be specialized faster, besides the fact that there is no interpretation overhead anymore.

To conclude: by abstracting the various treatments of the specializer for each syntactic construct, we have deduced four basic actions: *Ev, Rd, Rb* and *Id*. *Rd* expresses that the corresponding syntactic construct will be reduced. *Ev* is a particular case of *Rd*: it denotes an expression that may be fully evaluated because it is completely static. Symmetrically, *Rb* indicates that the corresponding syntactic construct will be rebuilt. *Id* is a particular case of *Rb*: it denotes an expression that may be reproduced textually because it is completely dynamic. In the case of both *Rd* and *Rb*, subexpressions still have to be processed.

Introducing combinators has three major effects: (1) because both *Ev*-combinators and *Id*-combinators are treated more efficiently than by sym-

```
        (define append-0    ;;; List(Num) -> List(Num)
          (lambda (x)
            (if (null? x)
                '(3 4 5)
                (cons (car x)
                      (append-0 (cdr x))))))
```

Figure 3: Residual program corresponding to specializing **append** with respect to (3 4 5)

```
(
  (append
   (rb rd)
   (rb (rb (rb))
       (rd)
       (rb (rb (rb)) (rb (rb (rb))
                          (rd)))))
)
```

Figure 4: Action tree of procedure **append**

```
(
  (append
   (id ev)
   (rb (id (id))
       (ev)
       (rb (id (id)) (rb (id (id))
                          (ev)))))
)
```

Figure 5: Action tree of procedure **append** with *Ev*- and *Id*-directives

bolic interpretation, specialization is faster; (2) because these combinators are no more a part of the actual source program, the specializer has less data to process; (3) because self-application is a particular case of specialization, it benefits from points (1) and (2).

It is interesting to notice that these combinators capture both *purely static* and *purely dynamic* semantics of the source program. The remaining actions are the essence of specialization: reducing and rebuilding expressions, and managing control.

This paper is organized as follows. Section 1 describes the conventional specialization of source programs after binding time analysis. Section 2 presents a semantics-based derivation of action trees. Section 3 describes how to specialize source programs given their action trees. Section 4 investigates how to prune action trees and define combinators for specialization. Section 5 draws some assessments. Section 6 compares this approach with related work. Finally this work is put in perspective.

1 Specializing Programs using Binding Time Trees

This section discusses the kernel of a self-applicable specializer. As generally agreed in the partial evaluation community, all realistic self-applicable specializers (*i.e.*, stand-alone and producing non-trivial compilers from interpreters) are based on some analysis of the binding times of the program [Bondorf *et al.* 88]. Interestingly enough, front-end strategies diverge widely (regarding generalizing, automatizing, polyvariance, partially static structures, computation duplication, *etc.*). Still they all converge when it comes to the actual specialization.

No decisions are taken as to how to specialize the program. However, to ensure termination and avoid code duplication, decisions as to how to treat procedure calls and let expressions are taken prior to the actual specialization. These decisions are represented with *annotations*.

Still there are computational evidences and reasons behind them to go further than the standard binding time-based specializer.

1.1 The language: first-order recursive equations

Source and residual programs are collections of recursive definitions for first-order Scheme procedures. Scheme expressions are constants, variables, conditional expressions, uncurried applications of procedures and operators, and let blocks. The reduction order is call by value.

An expression and its associated binding time tree are related as follows: the expression is paired with a binding time value that specifies whether specializing the expression will yield a static value or a residual expression.

1.2 Binding time trees

The concept of binding time here is generalized from the traditional binding time of an *identifier* (compile time, link time, run time, *etc.*) to the binding time of an *expression*. The motivation is that during partial evaluation, an expression will be reduced if it depends solely on the static part of the input, or rebuilt if it depends on the rest of the input. This point is captured by the generalization of binding times from identifiers to expressions. As a consequence it is possible to know whether the result of partially evaluating any expression will yield a static value or a residual expression, independently of the concrete result of partially evaluating this expression. Binding time analysis produces a safe approximation of this information.

For example, the specializer does not need the actual result of partially evaluating the test part of a conditional expression to decide whether it can solve the test and reduce the expression to one of its alternatives, or whether it needs to build a residual conditional expression. Again, this is important for self-application purposes since it makes it possible to avoid processing both parts of the specializer that handle reducing and rebuilding a conditional expression. This makes self-application faster and residual programs smaller.

1.3 An example: conditional expressions

As pointed out in the introduction, specialization occurs in a context. For example, all the sub-expressions of a static expression are evaluated. For another example, all the sub-expressions of a completely dynamic expression will be reproduced verbatim. For a last example, a conditional expression may be reduced if its test part is static, or rebuilt if it is dynamic. In the former case, the consequent and the alternative are specialized in the same context as the conditional expression.

Next section describes how we can build action trees by using a nonstandard interpretation of the present semantics. These action trees represent further exploitation of the results of binding time analysis.

2 Semantics-Based Derivation of Action Trees

This section describes how to derive action trees from the specialization semantics. We have factorized it and defined a non-standard interpretation [Jones & Nielsen 89] generating action trees. We have instantiated the domain of residual programs to be the domain of action trees, and have provided a set of combinators to generate these trees. The result is a semantics-directed specification for deducing action trees from source programs and binding time trees.

2.1 The set of actions

In the factorization, there are two combinators for each syntactic construct. One captures the action of reducing the syntactic construct; the other represents the action of rebuilding the syntactic construct. Let us call these two actions respectively Rd and Rb.

This set of actions may be refined. Indeed Rd and Rb include respectively purely static expressions and purely dynamic expressions. Therefore, using this set, a specializer would interpret a purely static expression symbolically and would rebuild a purely dynamic expression. As an optimization, we enrich the set of actions with Ev, that denotes a purely static expression, and Id, that denotes a purely dynamic expression. Because the actions are more precise, the specializer may perform more accurate treatments, and thus be more efficient.

2.2 The action trees interpretation

Action trees are built using a non-standard interpretation of the factorized semantics: instead of residual expressions, we want to build action trees isomorphic to the binding time trees. This derivation is not detailed in this extended abstract. Instead, we give a set of simplified rules that capture the interpretation, in figure 6 and in appendix.

These rules are simplified because they only specify the action associated to each expression. Also, they do not account for the accumulation of trees.

Constant expressions are either evaluated or left identical according to their binding time value. Static and dynamic identifiers denote an action.

$$\rho \vdash [\![(\texttt{*cst C})]\!]\, s : Ev \qquad \rho \vdash [\![(\texttt{*cst C})]\!]\, d : Id$$

$$\rho \vdash [\![(\texttt{*ide I})]\!]\, s : \rho I \qquad \rho \vdash [\![(\texttt{*ide I})]\!]\, d : \rho I$$

$$\frac{\rho \vdash [\![\texttt{E-1}]\!]\, s : Ev \qquad \rho \vdash [\![\texttt{E-2}]\!]\, b_2 : Ev \qquad \rho \vdash [\![\texttt{E-3}]\!]\, b_3 : Ev}{\rho \vdash [\![(\texttt{*if E-1 E-2 E-3})]\!]\,(s, b_2, b_3) : Ev}$$

$$\frac{\rho \vdash [\![\texttt{E-1}]\!]\, s : a_1 \qquad \rho \vdash [\![\texttt{E-2}]\!]\, b_2 : a_2 \qquad \rho \vdash [\![\texttt{E-3}]\!]\, b_3 : a_3}{\rho \vdash [\![(\texttt{*if E-1 E-2 E-3})]\!]\,(s, b_2, b_3) : Rd}$$

$$\frac{\rho \vdash [\![\texttt{E-1}]\!]\, d : Id \qquad \rho \vdash [\![\texttt{E-2}]\!]\, b_2 : Id \qquad \rho \vdash [\![\texttt{E-3}]\!]\, b_3 : Id}{\rho \vdash [\![(\texttt{*if E-1 E-2 E-3})]\!]\,(d, b_2, b_3) : Id}$$

$$\frac{\rho \vdash [\![\texttt{E-1}]\!]\, d : a_1 \qquad \rho \vdash [\![\texttt{E-2}]\!]\, b_2 : a_2 \qquad \rho \vdash [\![\texttt{E-3}]\!]\, b_3 : a_3}{\rho \vdash [\![(\texttt{*if E-1 E-2 E-3})]\!]\,(d, b_2, b_3) : Rb}$$

$$\frac{\rho \vdash [\![\texttt{E-1}]\!]\, s : Ev \qquad \ldots \qquad \rho \vdash [\![\texttt{E-m}]\!]\, s : Ev}{\rho \vdash [\![(\texttt{*app op E-1}\ldots\texttt{E-m})]\!]\,(s, \ldots, s) : Ev}$$

$$\frac{\rho \vdash [\![\texttt{E-1}]\!]\, b_1 : Id \qquad \ldots \qquad \rho \vdash [\![\texttt{E-m}]\!]\, b_m : Id}{\rho \vdash [\![(\texttt{*app op E-1}\ldots\texttt{E-m})]\!]\,(b_1, \ldots, b_m) : Id}$$

$$\frac{\rho \vdash [\![\texttt{E-1}]\!]\, b_1 : a_1 \qquad \ldots \qquad \rho \vdash [\![\texttt{E-m}]\!]\, b_m : a_m}{\rho \vdash [\![(\texttt{*app op E-1}\ldots\texttt{E-m})]\!]\,(b_1, \ldots, b_m) : Rb}$$

$$\frac{\rho \vdash [\![\texttt{E-1}]\!]\, b_1 : Ev \qquad \ldots \qquad \rho \vdash [\![\texttt{E-n}]\!]\, b_n : Ev}{\rho \vdash [\![(\texttt{*app up E-1}\ldots\texttt{E-n})]\!]\,(b_1, \ldots, b_n) : Ev}$$

$$\frac{\rho \vdash [\![\texttt{E-1}]\!]\, b_1 : a_1 \qquad \ldots \qquad \rho \vdash [\![\texttt{E-n}]\!]\, b_n : a_n}{\rho \vdash [\![(\texttt{*app up E-1}\ldots\texttt{E-n})]\!]\,(b_1, \ldots, b_n) : Rd}$$

$$\frac{\rho \vdash [\![\texttt{E-1}]\!]\, b_1 : Id \qquad \ldots \qquad \rho \vdash [\![\texttt{E-n}]\!]\, b_n : Id}{\rho \vdash [\![(\texttt{*app sp E-1}\ldots\texttt{E-n})]\!]\,(b_1, \ldots, b_n) : Id}$$

$$\frac{\rho \vdash [\![\texttt{E-1}]\!]\, b_1 : a_1 \qquad \ldots \qquad \rho \vdash [\![\texttt{E-n}]\!]\, b_n : a_n}{\rho \vdash [\![(\texttt{*app sp E-1}\ldots\texttt{E-n})]\!]\,(b_1, \ldots, b_n) : Rb}$$

Figure 6: Inference rules for deducing actions
In the rules for application, op, up, and sp denote the names of an operator, an unfoldable procedure, and a specialization point, respectively.

In general all syntactic constructs that would be reduced are either Ev if all their components are Ev, or Rd; and all syntactic constructs that would be rebuilt are either Id if all their components are Id, or Rb.

3 Specializing Programs using Action Trees

This section discusses the structure of a specializer driven by action trees. Our set of actions abstracts the treatment of a specializer processing binding time trees. Therefore this treatment will be part of the new specializer processing action trees. The major difference concerns the decision as to which action to apply – since this decision has already been taken. Thus specialization essentially amounts to dispatching on the action.

As a result, the specializer is structured in four parts, evaluating, reducing, rebuilding, or reproducing each syntactic construct. Next step is to introduce the combinators for Ev and Id-expressions.

4 Defining Combinators for Specialization

Two out of the four specialization contexts entail a treatment that is completely independent from specialization: in a context Ev, source expressions are merely evaluated; in a context Id, expressions are merely reproduced. As computer scientists we have better ways than symbolic interpretation to evaluate or to reproduce constant Scheme expressions:

- we can run the Ev-expressions using the underlying Scheme processor;

- we could invoke the identity function on Id-expressions.

Using the underlying Scheme processor is faster by an order of magnitude, since we can compile the Ev-expressions instead of interpret them symbolically. It is not the rôle of a partial evaluator to mimic an evaluator by symbolic interpretation.

Nothing can beat the identity function, speedwise. It is not the rôle either of a partial evaluator to mimic the identity function by symbolic interpretation.

These observations suggest to extract the expressions annotated with these actions and to transform them into *combinators*. The idea is that both

Ev- and *Id*-combinators can be considered as primitive operations by the specializer.

Extracting *Ev-* and *Id*-combinators from a source program using its action trees is straightforward. Free variables are collected and abstracted. The corresponding definitions are added as static operators (*i.e.*, primitive procedures) or as residual procedures in the residual program.

Once *Ev-* and *Id*-combinators have been extracted from a source program, what remains is the essence of this program with respect to its partial input. It is also the essence of specialization: reduction and reconstruction of source expressions, and their management.

Because *Ev*-expressions are encapsulated in combinators, they are now treated as a call to a primitive and executed by the underlying machine. Because *Id*-expressions are encapsulated in combinators, a call to an *Id*-combinator is simply frozen. As a consequence, the specializer does not have to treat actions *Ev* and *Id*. To avoid multiplying trivial combinators, the treatment of some syntactic constructs survives: this concerns constants, variables, and calls to an operator.

5 Assessments

This section investigates various consequences of having observed and introduced action trees in the process of specialization and combinators in source programs.

5.1 Source programs

Because source programs are smaller, once they are pruned, they are faster to specialize. It is hard to characterize the average improvement, but experience confirms that pruning *Ev-* and *Id*-subtrees increases the speed of specialization.

5.2 Self-application

Still the classical question may be raised: is this self-applicable? To this question there is an immediate answer: it is self-applicable *a fortiori* because compiling binding times goes beyond binding time analysis, by exploiting binding time information further and moving static computation away from the specialization process. Because self-application is only a particular case of specialisation, the technique applies to self-application as well.

5.3 Combinators Rd and Rb?

One could imagine collecting Rd- and Rb-combinators as well. This would lead to fragment the process of specialization in even smaller units: each reduction and reconstruction would be handled by dedicated combinators, and specialization would be reduced to coordinating and combining these operations.

However is it worth it? A dedicated specializer (*i.e.*, the result of specializing a regular, Mix-like, specializer with respect to a source program) precisely offers this. As a matter of fact, all the Ev-, Rd-, Rb-, and Id-combinators can be identified in the text of the dedicated specializer – under unfolded form.

This observation again stresses the problem of granularity in semantics-based program manipulation. Aiming at exploiting binding time information further, we have succeeded to implement a new binding time shift in a self-applicable partial evaluator, by reorganizing and simplifying the basic steps of specialization. Because this has been achieved through a semantics-based derivation, it is not surprising that the result is the same in the end. However, intensionally the development is significant because it has been achieved without resorting to self-application. Source programs have become smaller and faster to specialize.

5.4 Purely static and purely dynamic semantics

Extracting Ev- and Id-combinators amounts to defining the purely static semantics of the source program as well as its purely dynamic semantics. We are now exploring what are the extensional meaning and the computational counterpart of these in, *e.g.*, the interpretive specification of a programming language, and their impact in the corresponding compilers obtained by self-application [Consel & Danvy 90].

5.5 On the purely dynamic semantics of specialization

During specialization, dynamic identifiers denote residual expressions, where potentially free variables occur. Among rebuilt expressions there may be binding declarations, *e.g.*, let expressions or residual lambda-expressions. This potentially yields name clashes that are usually avoided by systematically renaming residual variables.

Unfortunately this renaming impedes the purely dynamic semantics of specialization, since it is carried even for completely dynamic subexpressions – where there just cannot be any name clash, and thus no variable need to be renamed.

This problem is addressed and solved in [Danvy 89]. The practical consequence concerns the abstract syntax of source programs, where formal parameters are now qualified by a tag, as in figure 2. Each tag expresses whether the corresponding binding should be unfolded or whether it should be left residual; and if it is to be residual, whether the variable needs to be renamed.

5.6 An instruction set for specialization

We conjecture that the combinators we succeeded to extract from a source program hint at the existence of an instruction set in an architecture for specialization. This could be the basis for an algebra of specialization. We are currently investigating this issue.

5.7 An experiment: the generation of a linear string matcher

In [Consel & Danvy 89], we illustrated how the Knuth, Morris & Pratt linear matching algorithm could be derived from a naive, quadratic matching program by binding times analysis, staging, and specialization. Running both versions of the specializer (*i.e.*, the binding time-based version and the action-based one) shows an order-of-magnitude improvement of specialization when the static string is repetitive. This is due to the fact that in one case, matching the pattern (statically) against itself is interpreted whereas it is compiled in the other case.

5.8 Generality and extensibility of the approach

Compiling binding times is a general strategy because it does not rely on particular binding time analyses: action trees are solely generated from binding time information. This approach is extensible because the set of actions is extensible: the actions reflect the specialization process. Traditionally, when one wants to strenghten partial evaluation, *e.g.*, to handle higher order functions or partially static structures, both the binding time analysis and the specializer have to be extended. The binding time analysis has to collect new information for the additional elements. The specializer has to be modified to treat these additional elements according to the binding time information. In our approach, we can extract additional actions from the specializer for capturing the new aspects of the specialization process. This has successfully been done when extending Schism to handle higher order functions and partially static structures, as reported in [Consel 90].

6 Comparison with Related Work

6.1 Binding time analysis

Binding time analysis is commonly agreed to be the necessary tool for realistic self-application. The problem with it is that it is too general: from [Jones & Muchnick 78] to [Nielsen & Nielsen 88], there is more in binding time analysis than self-applicable partial evaluation.

In this paper we argue that the information collected by the binding time analysis (namely: the binding time trees) can be exploited further, and that this exploitation can be dedicated to the process of specialization. We introduce action trees as characterizing specialization more precisely. Action trees are built by interpreting the binding time trees, which is done once and for all.

6.2 Actions in MIX

In Mix, a program is annotated with specialization actions after the binding time analysis. A set of two actions is used: eliminable and residual [Sestoft 86]. They respectively denote an expression whose syntactic construct will be statically reduced and an expression whose syntactic construct will be residual. Because nothing distinguishes a purely static expression from a purely dynamic one, both are interpreted symbolically.

6.3 Semantics-based compiler generation

Due to its self-application properties, partial evaluation has interesting applications to semantics-directed compiler generation. The point is that self-applying the specializer with respect to the interpretive specification of a programming language yields a residual program having the functionality of a compiler. Correspondingly, the intensional Curry program obtained by specializing the specializer with respect to itself has the functionality of a compiler generator. Because we extract combinators from source specifications automatically, our generated compilers extract combinators as well.

In Mitchell Wand's framework and Peter Mosses's Action Semantics, a great emphasis is put on extracting or designing combinators. In contrast, our set of combinators is automatically abstracted during partial evaluation according to the binding times of the source program. Not surprisingly, considering that the goal is to specialize programs, such combinators are not as general as those found in Action Semantics. However they add up to automatizing the derivation of compilers and machine architectures from interpretive specifications.

Conclusions and Issues

Compiling binding times in a self-applicable partial evaluator goes beyond the effect of self-application and contributes to improving it too.

Extracting combinators captures the purely static and purely dynamic semantics of source programs.

Combining both provides two basic items abstracting structures from semantic specifications: in the case of an interpreter, self-application provides the compiling algorithm, and our combinators provide the instruction set of the corresponding machines, both for the compilation and the runtime program. The *Ev*-combinators are the instruction set for the compiler, and the *Id*-combinators are a part of the dynamic semantics.

Background and Acknowledgements

Actions were coined in [Consel 89] and implemented in Schism, a self-applicable partial evaluator for a dialect of Scheme. Then the second author observed that action trees and the corresponding specializer could be derived using a non-standard interpretation of the binding time-based specializer. Action trees have been successfully extended to tackle higher order functions and partially static structures [Consel 90].

Thanks go to Karoline Malmkjær, Siau Cheng Khoo, and Carolyn Talcott for commenting earlier versions of this paper.

References

[Bondorf et al. 88] Anders Bondorf, Neil D. Jones, Torben Æ. Mogensen, Peter Sestoft: *Binding Time Analysis and the Taming of Self-Application*, to appear in TOPLAS, DIKU, University of Copenhagen, Denmark (1988)

[Consel & Danvy 89] Charles Consel, Olivier Danvy: *Partial Evaluation of Pattern Matching in Strings*, Information Processing Letters, Vol. 30, No 2 pp 79-86 (1989)

[Consel 89] Charles Consel: *Analyse de Programme, Evaluation Partielle, et Génération de Compilateurs*, PhD thesis, University of Paris VI, Paris, France (June 1989)

[Consel 90] Charles Consel: *Higher Order Partial Evaluation with Data Structures*, Working paper, Computer Science Department, Yale University, New Haven, Connecticut (January 1990)

[Consel & Danvy 90] Charles Consel, Olivier Danvy: *Static and Dynamic Semantics Processing*, Technical Report 761, Computer Science Department, Yale University, New Haven, Connecticut (November 1989)

[Danvy 89] Olivier Danvy: *Avoiding Name Clashes during Self-Applicable Partial Evaluation*, Working paper, Computer Science Department, Indiana University, Bloomington, Indiana (fall 1989)

[Jones & Muchnick 78] Neil D. Jones, Steven S. Muchnick: *TEMPO: A Unified Treatment of Binding Time Parameter Passing Concepts in Programming Languages*, G. Goos & J. Hartmanis (eds.), Lecture Notes in Computer Science No 66, Springer-Verlag (1978)

[Jones et al. 89] Neil D. Jones, Peter Sestoft, Harald Søndergaard: *MIX: a Self-Applicable Partial Evaluator for Experiments in Compiler Generation*, Vol. 2, No 1 pp 9-50 of the International Journal LISP and Symbolic Computation (1989)

[Jones & Nielsen 89] Neil D. Jones, Flemming Nielsen: *Abstract Interpretation: a Semantics-Based Tool for Program Analysis*, to appear in the Handbook of Logic and Computer Science, University of Copenhagen and Aarhus University, Denmark (1989)

[Nielsen & Nielsen 88] Flemming Nielsen, Hanne R. Nielsen: *Automatic Binding Time Analysis for a Typed Lambda-Calculus*, proceedings of the ACM Symposium on Principles of Programming Languages pp 98-106 (1988)

[Rees & Clinger 86] Jonathan Rees, William Clinger (eds.): *Revised³ Report on the Algorithmic Language Scheme*, Sigplan Notices, Vol. 21, No 12 pp 37-79 (December 1986)

[Sestoft 86] Peter Sestoft: *The Structure of a Self-Applicable Partial Evaluator*, pp 236-256 of *Programs as Data Objects*, Harald Ganzinger and Neil D. Jones (eds.), Lecture Notes in Computer Science No 217, Springer-Verlag (1986)

[Wand 82] Mitchell Wand: *Semantics-Directed Machine Architecture*, proceedings of the ACM Symposium on Principles of Programming Languages pp 234-241 (1982)

A Inference rules for deducing actions (continued)

$$\frac{\rho \vdash [\![E\text{-}1]\!]\, b_1 : Ev \ldots \rho \vdash [\![E\text{-}k]\!]\, b_k : Ev \quad [I\text{-}1 \mapsto Ev, \ldots, I\text{-}k \mapsto Ev]\rho \vdash [\![E]\!]\, b : Ev}{\rho \vdash [\![(\texttt{*let [u} \ldots]\ (I\text{-}1 \ldots)\ (E\text{-}1 \ldots)\ E)]\!]\,((b_1, \ldots, b_k), b) : Ev}$$

$$\frac{\rho \vdash [\![E\text{-}1]\!]\, b_1 : a_1 \ldots \rho \vdash [\![E\text{-}k]\!]\, b_k : a_k \quad [I\text{-}1 \mapsto a_1, \ldots, I\text{-}k \mapsto a_k]\rho \vdash [\![E]\!]\, b : a}{\rho \vdash [\![(\texttt{*let [u} \ldots]\ (I\text{-}1 \ldots)\ (E\text{-}1 \ldots)\ E)]\!]\,((b_1, \ldots, b_k), b) : Rd}$$

$$\frac{\rho \vdash [\![E\text{-}1]\!]\, b_1 : Id \ldots \rho \vdash [\![E\text{-}k]\!]\, b_k : Id \quad [I\text{-}1 \mapsto Id, \ldots, I\text{-}k \mapsto Id]\rho \vdash [\![E]\!]\, b : Id}{\rho \vdash [\![(\texttt{*let [i} \ldots]\ (I\text{-}1 \ldots)\ (E\text{-}1 \ldots)\ E)]\!]\,((b_1, \ldots, b_k), b) : Id}$$

$$\frac{\ldots \rho \vdash [\![E\text{-}x]\!]\, b_x : a_x \ldots \rho \vdash [\![E\text{-}y]\!]\, b_y : a_y \ldots \rho \vdash [\![E\text{-}z]\!]\, b_z : a_z \ldots}{[\ldots, I\text{-}x \mapsto a_x, \ldots, I\text{-}y \mapsto a_y, \ldots, I\text{-}z \mapsto a_z, \ldots]\rho \vdash [\![E]\!]\, b : a}$$
$$\frac{}{\rho \vdash (\texttt{*let [} \ldots \texttt{u} \ldots \texttt{i} \ldots \texttt{r} \ldots]\ (\ldots I\text{-}x \ldots I\text{-}y, \ldots I\text{-}z \ldots)\ (\ldots E\text{-}x \ldots E\text{-}y \ldots E\text{-}z \ldots)\ E),}{((b_1, \ldots, b_x, \ldots, b_y, \ldots, b_z, \ldots, b_k), b) : Rb}$$

Implementing Finite-domain Constraint Logic Programming on Top of a PROLOG-System with Delay-mechanism

Danny De Schreye[*], Dirk Pollet, Johan Ronsyn, Maurice Bruynooghe[**]
Department of Computer Science, Katholieke Universiteit Leuven
Celestijnenlaan 200A, 3030 Heverlee, Belgium.

Abstract. In the past few years, an extensive amount of empirical evidence has proved the practical value of finite-domain constraint logic programming (CLP). Using special CLP-systems, many constraint satisfaction applications have been programmed very quickly and the resulting programs have a good performance. In this paper, we show how to implement a finite-domain CLP on top of a PROLOG-system equipped with a delay mechanism. The advantages are that the language features are easy to implement, the overhead caused both to the underlying PROLOG-system and to the CLP-environment itself are small and that the system is relatively portable.

1. Introduction

The pioneering work of A.Colmerauer on PROLOG II [Colmerauer 82] and PROLOG III [Colmerauer 87], the theory developed by J.Jaffar and J.L. Lassez [Jaffar & Lassez 87] and the development of systems such as CHIP [Dincbas et al 88b] and CLP(R) [Jaffar & Michaylov 87] have established the importance of constraint logic programming. The CHIP-system, using finite domain, is an elegant and powerful tool for dealing with a large class of scheduling problems. The many applications, (e.g. [Dincbas et al 88a], [Graf et al 89], [Van Hentenryck 89]), provide empirical evidence for the fact that with finite-domain CLP, a programmer can quickly solve complex constraint problems and obtain a high run-time efficiency at the same time. The underlying paradigm is that a programmer declaratively formulates the constraints of the problem at hand in a generate-and-test-like manner, and that the execution mechanism of the CLP-environment applies various efficient constraint satisfaction techniques (e.g. forward checking, looking ahead, first-fail principle) to solve this set of constraints. Therefore, an efficient run-time behaviour is obtained in combination with a low development time.

CLP differs from classical constraint problem solving (CPS) techniques in that it does not rely on the construction and manipulation of a dependency graph. However, by enforcing an advanced control regime on the coroutined activation of the given generators and constraints, it can simulate the effect of various relaxation algorithms which are used in CPS to simplify and solve the dependency graph. In this sense, CLP can be considered as a CPS-shell. We refer to the comments of P.Van Hentenreyck at [Dechter 89] for a more elaborated position on this point.

The main problems with applying finite-domain CLP to solve concrete scheduling (or CPS) problems are of a pragmatic nature. The CHIP-system is still not available on the software market. Also, as far as we know, none of the commercial PROLOG-manufacturers have developed an extension to their product to include CLP.

On the other hand, scheduling problems continue to form a source of expenses, in

* supported by the Belgian I.W.O.N.L.-I.R.S.I.A. under contract number 5203.
** supported by the Belgian National Fund for Scientific Research.

the form of management-and production-bottle-necks, in many companies. Thus, the demand for a good (elegant and efficient) CPS-shell is very high. This is why we are currently faced with an urgent need for alternative implementations of (finite-domain) CLP.

There are several approaches for building such an implementation. One is to take an existing PROLOG and to extend its execution model, as it was done in CHIP. This is a good approach, but it is also a very difficult one, requiring a deep understanding of the WAM-architecture.

In [De Schreye & Bruynooghe 89] we present a different approach. The starting point is the observation that the main differences between a simple generate-and-test program and a logically equivalent (computing the same answer substitutions for the top-level query) forward checking program are that:

1. The forward checking program generates by selecting values from predefined (finite) domains.

2. In the naive program, constraints act as passive tests, while in the forward checking program they actively reduce the size of the search space (by eliminating values from the domains).

3. In the naive program, all calls to generators precede the constraints. In the forward checking program, the activation of the generators and the constraints is interleaved using a special control rule.

Based on these observations, the implementation proposed in [De Schreye & Bruynooghe 89] consists of two components: a logic component and a control component. The logic component is encoded in a set of library predicates, written in PROLOG. They support the specification of new (finite) domains, they assign copies of these domains to the domain-variables and they redefine the built-in constraints, so that they can act actively on the domains. The control component delays the generators and activates the constraints as soon as all but one of their domain-variables have obtained a value.

In [De Schreye & Bruynooghe 89] we used the program transformation technique *Compiling Control* (see [Bruynooghe et al 89]) to compile the control component. In this way, we obtain a standard PROLOG program, imitating the forward checking execution, by starting from a generate-and-test program and a set of library predicates. For simple constraint problems, such as the N-queens problem and the five-houses puzzle, our results were comparable to those obtained with the CHIP-system. However, for real-world, large size constraint problems, the transformation phase becomes computationally very expensive. The reason is that the control compilation requires a complete (abstract) analysis of the behaviour of the given program under the new control rule. Also, the framework was not very flexible, in the sense that extensions, such as looking ahead, the first-fail principle and optimization techniques, caused various problems and therefore where not included.

In this paper we describe how a delay mechanism can be used to replace the control compilation. We show how the framework of [De Schreye & Bruynooghe 89] can be reformulated using the delay-declarations (WHEN-declarations) of NU-Prolog [Thom & Zobel 88]. We also extend the framework to include support for first-order looking-ahead and two versions of the first-fail principle (in addition to the forward checking). A general optimization procedure was also included in the original version of this paper, but it is omitted because of space restrictions (details are available from the authors). We believe that on the basis of our treatment, the reader should be able to program his own (finite-domain) CLP-environment on top of PROLOG (provided that the PROLOG-system includes a delay-mechanism, which is the case for several systems, such as NU-Prolog, Sicstus, Prolog II).

2. The integration of domains

In this section we introduce some basic library predicates that support the generation of candidate solutions to a given problem, by selecting values from predefined domains. The important thing about them, is that the programmer is not confronted with the task of explicitly manipulating these domains. The predicates in this section are simplified versions of the ones we will propose (later in the paper) for the final environment. Some of the material in this section was already introduced in [De Schreye & Bruynooghe 89]. We recall it here, to make the paper self-contained.

In addition to a redefinition of all the built-in-constraints (an example is given at the end of the section), we introduce two library predicates: create_domain/3, which is used to construct a prototype of a finite domain, and select_from_domain/2, which is used to assign a value (from a domain) to a domain-variable. In Box 1, we give an example of how these library predicates are used in an application. The example is the N-queens problem. We follow the syntax of NU-Prolog (see [Thom & Zobel 88]) throughout the paper.

```
?- forward(test/3).

queens(N,Q):- create_domain(queens,gendom(D,N),D),
                    gen(N,Q), safe(Q).
gendom([],0).
gendom([N|D], N):- N>0, M is N-1, gendom(D,M).
gen(0,[]).
gen(N,[H|T]):- N>0, M is N-1, select_from_domain(queens,H), gen(M,T).
safe([]).
safe([X]).
safe([X,Y| Z]):- n-attack(X,1,[Y|Z]), safe([Y|Z]).
n_attack(X,T,[]).
n_attack(X,T,[Y|Z]):-  test(X,T,Y), S is T+1, n_attack(X,S,Z).
test(X,T,Y):-  Y \= X, Y \= X+T, Y \= X-T.
```
Box 1: The N-queens program.

Notice how this program resembles the usual generate-and-test formulation for the N-queens problem. The differences are: it includes a call to the library predicate create-domain/3 to create the finite domain [1,2,...,N], the usual call to permute, generating a permutation of the list [1,2,...,N], is replaced by a call to the predicate gen/2, which on its turn calls the library predicate select_from_domain/2 to instantiate each domain-variable, and there is a declaration "?- forward(test/3)" specifying that all the built-in constraints in the definition of test/3 should be executed with a forward checking algorithm. All other predicates are identical to the usual formulation. The way in which the program manipulates the domain is hidden in the definition of the two library predicates, given in Box 2.

The first two arguments of the predicate create_domain/3 are input. The first is an atom, which serves as a unique identifier for the defined domain. The second argument is a procedure call, which either computes a list D (the third argument) of all objects in the domain, or it is equal to true, in which case the list of domain-values, D, is given as input to the third argument. The reason for these alternatives is that the domain may or may not be dependent on certain of the problems input parameters (e.g. the number of queens, N).

```
create_domain(Id,Proc,D):-  call(Proc), real_create(D,D1),
                                 retractall( dom(Id,_)), assert( dom(Id,D1)).
real_create([],[]).
real_create([H|T],[(H,_)|TD]):-  real_create(T,TD).


select_from_domain(Id, (&,Id,X,Xdom)):-  dom(Id,Xdom), member( (X,1), Xdom).
member(X,[X|_]).
member(X,[H|T]):-  member(X,T).
```
Box 2: Initial form of the library predicates[1].

The procedure create_domain/3 first calls the procedure Proc. After the successful completion of Proc, the third argument of create_domain/3 contains the domain-list, D. Then, the auxiliary procedure, real_create/2 changes the representation of the domain, and finally, this new representation, D1, is asserted as dom(Id,D1).

The new domain representation is a list of pairs, each consisting of a domain-value and a fresh variable (e.g. the domain [1,2,3] is represented as [(1,_), (2,_), (3,_)]). The reason why we use this partially instantiated representation is that we can now eliminate a value from the domain by merely instantiating the free variable associated with it to some reserved symbol (say 0). Thus, the list [(1,_), (2,0), (3,_)] represents the domain [1,3].

The procedure select_from_domain/2 picks up a copy of the domain identified by its first (input) argument, Id. Then, it does not associate a simple domain-value to its second (output) argument (which corresponds to the domain-variable in the call), but instead, it instantiates the domain-variable to a 4-tuple. This 4-tuple consists of a tag, &, identifying the variable as a domain-variable from that point on, the identification-atom of the domain, a fresh variable and a copy of the domain. Finally, the non-deterministic member/2-call picks a value from the domain (the next value which does not have a 0 associated to it) and assigns it to the fresh variable.

With these two predicates - and a proper redefinition of the \=-constraint -, obtaining a forward checking program has turned into a control problem. Indeed, if we partially execute a call to the select_from_domain/2-predicate, but we delay the corresponding call to member/2, then we have assigned a copy of the domain to the domain-variable, but we have postponed the actual assignment of a value. Using an appropriate redefinition of \=/2 (see below), we can now actively remove values from the domain of that variable. After this elimination of domain-elements, the call to member/2 is reactivated and the variable obtains its value from the reduced domain.

Clearly, the programmer must specify which predicates should be solved using a forward checking algorithm. He expresses this information in terms of declarations (e.g. the ?- forward(test/3) declaration for N-queens). The effect of such a declaration is that, in a preprocessing phase, the users program is transformed into a program in which every

1) The compound structures (&,Id,X,Xdom) and (X,1) in these definitions make use of a special PRO-LOG-notation. In PROLOG, (a,b,c) is short for ','(a, ','(b,c)) , where the single quotes distinguish between the two uses for the symbol ",".

call to a built-in-constraint in the definition of test/3 (or every call to the predicate itself, in the case of a declaration concerning a built-in-constraint, e.g. ?- forward(\=/2)) is replaced by the corresponding call to the forwardly redefined built-in. In our example, we get the new definition for test/3 of Box 3.

The definition for the forward version of \=/2, namely for\=/2, deals with a large number of cases. Some of the clauses (relevant for our example) are also shown in Box 3. The will refine this definition in the next sections.

```
test(X,T,Y):-  for\=(X,Y), for\=(Y,X+T), for\=(Y,X-T).
for\= ( (&,_,X,_), (&,_,Y,_) ):-
               ground(X), ground(Y), !, X <>Y.
for\= ( (&,_,X,_), (&,_,Y,DY) ):-
               ground(X), !, real_for\= (DY, X).
for\= ( (&,_,X,DX), (&,_,Y,_) ):-
               ground(Y), !, real_for\= (DX, Y).
for\=( (&,_,X,_), (&,_,Y,_) + T):-
               T <> (&,_,_,_),
               ground(X), ground(Y), !, X <> Y+T.
for\=( (&,_,X,_), (&,_,Y,DY) + T):-
               T <> (&,_,_,_),
               ground(X), !, S is X-T, real_for\=(DY,S).
...
real_for\= ([], _).
real_for\= ([(X,Y)|T],S):-  ( X=S, !, Y=0  ;  real_for\= (T,S) ) .
```
Box 3: The forward redefinition of \=/2.

We conclude with some comments on the special form of the values that are assigned to the domain-variables by the select_from_domain/2-predicate. The tag-field, &, identifies a variable as a domain-variable. Such an identification is important, because a number of built-in predicates will have an undesired behaviour if we can not capture (and redefine) the case of a domain-variable occurring as one of the arguments in the call. As an example, it is clear that the effect of calls such as write(X) or X=3 will have an unexpected behaviour if X is a domain-variable. These predicates need to be redefined. For write/1 we could define:

    new_write(X):-   X = (&,_,Y,_), !, write(Y).
    new_write(X):-   write(X).

and replace every call to write/1 in the users program by a corresponding call to new_write/1 in the preprocessing phase. Similarly, we can deal with the =/2 predicate.

Clearly, redefining the built-in predicates does not take care of problems caused by user-defined predicates which act directly on the domain-variables. For instance, if the domain consists of pairs (month(Nr1), year(Nr2)), then the user should not define a predicate

    get_year((month(_), year(X)), X) .

and make a call to it with a domain-variable as its argument. This will fail, because of the new structure (the 4-tuple) assigned to the variable. Again, this can be solved in the preprocessing phase. All implicit unifications in the heads of clauses can be transformed to equivalent explicit unifications in the body of the clauses (normalization). In the example, we get the new clause:

    get_year(X, Y):-   X = (month(_), year(Z)), Z = Y.

Then, the appropriate redefinition of =/2 will deal with the unification of a domain-variable and a non-domain-variable (or constant).

A more simple solution is that the programmer should at least be aware of the type of representation used for the domain-variables, and that - in those cases where he needs access to a substructure of an actual domain-value - he should write his program accordingly.

The second component of the 4-tuple, the identifier of the domain, will not be mentioned any further in the remainder of the paper. It is included to make the forward redefinition of certain built-in constraints more efficient. For instance, =/2 renamed as for=/2 includes the clause:

for= ((&, Id, X, DX), (&, Id, Y, DY)):-   !, X=Y, DX = DY.

If the Id's for X and Y are not equal, then much more complicated actions need to be taken.

3. The integration of the control

In [De Schreye & Bruynooghe 89], the logic described in boxes 1,2 and 3 (in the version obtained after the preprocessing phase) is used as input to a program transformation system (Compiling Control, see [Bruynooghe et al 89]). The second input to the transformation system is a specification of the new computation rule described above. The transformation synthesizes a new PROLOG-program that behaves, under the standard computation rule of PROLOG, as the old program behaves under the new rule.

We now discuss the problem of enforcing the appropriate control on the given (extended) generate-and-test program, by using delay-predicates. We use the WHEN-declarations of NU-Prolog (see [Thom & Zobel 88]).

Essentially, the control that we want to obtain is the following. Calls to member/2 must be delayed for as long as there are constraints available which can be forwardly executed. A constraint C(X1,...,Xn) is forwardly executable if all but one of its domain-variable-arguments are instantiated. Every constraint is delayed until it is forwardly executable.

We are now faced with a technical problem. As far as we know, it is impossible to formulate a WHEN-declaration on the member/2-predicate, which initially delays every call to the predicate and reactivates them as soon as all the constraints have been generated, but none of them is forwardly executable.

However, a simple way to achieve this control, is to place the member/2-calls behind all the constraints in the initial program and to formulate WHEN-declarations on the constraints (but not on the member/2-predicate). This corresponds to the methodology for using WAIT-declarations proposed in [Naish 86]: tests must be placed before generators and tests are delayed until they are sufficiently instantiated.

To achieve this in our framework, it is necessary to adapt the library-predicate select_from_domain/2. We replace it by two new predicates: one to assign domains to domain-variables: assign_domain/2, and one to instantiate the variables (essentially the member/2-calls): instantiate/1.

For the N-queens problem, this leads to the new program-structure of Box 4 (which forms the final basis of the framework we propose). The definition of the library predicates is given in Box 5.

The predicate assign_domain/2 is identical to select_from_domain/2, except for the call to member/2, which was omitted. Instantiate/1 consumes a list of domain-variables

```
?- forward(test/3).

queens(N,Q):-   create_domain(queens, gendom(D,N), D),
                generators([ gen(N,Q)], V),
                safe( Q),
                instantiate( V).
gen(0,[]).
gen(N,[H|T]):-  N>0, M is N-1, assign_domain(queens, H), gen(M,T).
gendom/2, safe/1, n_attack/3 and test/3 : as in Box 1.
```
Box 4: Final version for the N-queens program.

```
create_domain/3 : as in Box 2.

assign_domain(Id, (&, Id, X, D)):-   dom(Id, D).
instantiate([]).
instantiate([(&,_,X,D)|T]):-   member( (X,1), D), instantiate(T).
generators([], []).
generators([Proc|T],V):-   solve_accumulate(Proc, [], V1),
                              generators(T,V2), append(V1,V2,V).
solve_accumulate(true, V, V).
solve_accumulate( (A, B), Acc, V):-   solve_accumulate(A, Acc, V1),
                                       solve_accumulate(B, V1, V).
solve_accumulate(assign_domain(Id,X), Acc, V):-  !, call( assign_domain(Id,X)),
                                                   append(Acc, [X], V).
solve_accumulate( A, V, V):-  builtin(A), !, call(A).
solve_accumulate( A, Acc, V):-  clause(A, B), solve_accumulate(B, Acc, V).
```
Box 5: The library predicates.

and assigns a value to each of them. The list of domain-variables is produced by the predicate generators/2. This predicate has a double function: it calls a list of user-defined generator-predicates and it accumulates a list of all the domain-variables created by these generators. To do this, it makes use of the solve_accumulate/2-predicate, which defines a PROLOG-meta-interpreter. Only, this meta-interpreter accumulates in his second argument the list of all domain-variables generated so far.

To make the code more readable, we included calls to append/3 in the various procedures. These can be eliminated and replaced by accumulating parameters. Also, we defined the solve_accumulate/3-predicate as a variant of the vanilla-interpreter. In order to deal with full PROLOG, it should be redefined as a variant of a complete PROLOG-meta-interpreter.

Finally, there is the control component itself. This is formulated at the level of the (forward redefinitions of the) constraints. The forward definition of each built-in constraint, forC(X1,...,Xn), is accompanied by a WHEN-declaration. The declarations delay each call to the constraint, if less than n-1 of its domain-variable-arguments are instantiated.

This raises a problem, since it is not clear at compile-time, which arguments of a given built-in-constraint will correspond to domain-variables in the users program and which will not. Therefore, on the highest level in the forward definition of each constraint, we make a case study. It distinguishes between different patterns in the call, on the basis of the presence of domain-variables. Some examples in the case of \=/2 are:

```
for\= (X,Y+Z):-   X= (&,_,_,_), Y = (&,_,_,_), Z = (&,_,_,_), !,
                      for\=ddplusd(X,Y,Z).
for\= (X,Y+Z):-   X= (&,_,_,_), Y = (&,_,_,_), !,
                      for\=ddplusa(X,Y,Z).
...
```

Then, accompanying each definition of the more specialized constraints, for\=ddplusd , for\=ddplusa, ..., we have a WHEN-declaration. As an example, we have:

```
for\=ddplusd( (_,_,X,_), (_,_,Y,_), (_,_,Z,_) )
        WHEN  (ground(X) and ground(Y)) or
              (ground(X) and ground(Z)) or
              (ground(Y) and ground(Z))
```

4. Extending the framework

In this section we briefly discuss the following extensions: first-order looking ahead and two versions of the first-fail principle.

4.1 First-order looking-ahead

It is generally believed (see [Dechter 89]) that for most applications, higher order looking-ahead does not pay off. Forward checking seems an ideal combination in view of the trade-off between actively reducing the size of the search-space and avoiding too much overhead. However, for some problems, first-order looking-ahead may still be a sensible alternative.

Assume that we have a program including a call $X < Y+Z$, where X,Y and Z are domain-variables, and that the programmer wants the constraint to be dealt with by a first-order looking-ahead algorithm. To achieve this, he adds the declaration:

```
?- look-ahead(</2).
```

As a result, the call is transformed to look<(X,Y+Z) by the preprocessor. One of the clauses (the one dealing with the case where X,Y and Z are domain-variables) defining this predicate in the library is given in Box 6.

```
look<ddplusd(X,Y,Z):-  min_value(X,Xmin),
                       max_value(Y,Ymax),
                       max_value(Z,Zmax),
                       Xbound is Ymax+Zmax,
                       Ybound is Xmin-Zmax,
                       Zbound is Xmin-Ymax,
                       restrict_domain(X, </2, Xbound),
                       restrict_domain(Y, >/2, Ybound),
                       restrict_domain(Z, >/2, Zbound),
                       for<ddplusd(X,Y,Z).
```
Box 6: Part of the first-order looking-ahead definition for </2.

Here, min_value(X,Xmin) succeeds if Xmin is the minimal value of the domain of X. The predicate-call restrict_domain(A, Constraint/2, Value) restricts the domain of the domain-variable A to all values X, such that Constraint(X, Value) holds. Finally, for<ddplusd/3 is the forward checking predicate for $X < Y+Z$, given that X,Y and Z are domain-variables.

4.2 The first-fail principle

According to the first-fail principle, it is more efficient to have a failing constraint very early in the search. In finite-domain CLP, this principle translates to: if we are going to instantiate a domain-variable, then we should first select the variable which is most strongly constrained. This on its turn can be reformulated using two concrete conditions:

1. Select the variable with the smallest domain,
2. Select the variable that occurs in the largest number of constraints.

Implementing these two rules in our environment is particularly easy, because each generate-and-test block in the users program ends with a call to instantiate(V), where V is the list of all the domain-variables.

Now assume that instead of instantiating the domain-variables with 4-tuples, we use 5-tuples of the form (&, Id, Length, X, Domain) - to deal with the smallest domain principle - or even 6-tuples, (&, Id, Length, Constraints, X, Domain), - to deal with both the first-fail principles.

The new variables, Length and Constraints, are open ended lists. The last ground member of the list Length is an integer representing the current length of the domain. Similarly, the last ground member of the list Constraints is an integer representing the number of constraints containing the considered domain-variable.

With this information available, the instantiate/1-predicate can be redefined to select (and instantiate) the domain-variable with the smallest domain, as in Box 7. Here, select_on_Length(V, X, V1) succeeds if X is a member of V having a minimal value for its Length-variable and V1 is the list obtained by removing X from V.

Similarly, we can perform a selection on the basis of the number of constraints which contain the domain-variable, or, we could combine the two first-fail principles into new selection/instantiation-predicate instantiate_L_C/1. In this case, we would first compute the sublist of all domain-variables with a minimal domain-length and then select one of them occurring in a minimal number of constraints.

```
create_domain_L(Id, Proc, D):-  call(Proc), real_create_L(D,D1,0,Length),
                                  retractall(dom(_,_,_)),assert(dom(Id,D1,Lenght)).
real_create_L([], [], L, L).
real_create_L([H|T], [(H,_)| TD], N, L):-   M is N+1, real_create_L(T, TD, M, L).
assign_domain_L(Id, (&,Id, L, X, D) ):-  dom(Id, D, L).
instantiate_L([]):-  !.
instantiate_L(V):-  select_on_Length(V, X, V1), X= (_,_,_,Y,D),
                      member( (Y,1), D), instantiate_L( V1).
generators/2 : as in Box 5.
```
Box 7: Version of the library predicates supporting first-fail on domain-size.

For each domain-variable, the values of its Length-(and Constraints-)variable are initialized in a new version of the real_create/2-predicate, and updated in (new) forward versions of the built-in-constraints. While the real_create_L/2-predicate of Box 7 creates the new representation of the domain, it also counts the initial length of the domain and asserts it, along with the new representation. Clearly, it the case of the second first-fail principle, the initial value for Constraints is always 0. Later on, whenever a forward version of a constraint eliminates a value from the domain of some domain-variable (see the definition of real_for\=/2 in Box 3 for an example), it must now update the Length-variable at the same time.

Some additional optimizations can be carried through here. For instance, if the constraint computes a new length 0 for a domain-variable, then the constraint should fail. Also, if it computes a length equal to 1, then it can instantiate the domain-variable itself to its only remaining value. This may lead to a quicker reactivation of some of the other delayed constraints.

Updating the Constraints-variables is also performed in the redefined constraints. As an example, assume that we have a constraint X = Y, where X and Y are domain-variables, that there is a user-defined predicate cons/n including the call X = Y in its definition and that there is a declaration ?- forward(cons/n). The definition of for=dd/2 (without first-fail) is:

```
?- for=dd((_,_,X,_), (_,_,Y,_)) WHEN ground(X) or ground(Y)
for=dd( (&,Id,X,DX), (&,Id,Y,DY)):-   !, X=Y, DX = DY.
for=dd( (_,_,X1,_), Y):- ground(X1), !, Y = (_,_,Y1,_),
                             Y1 = X1, restrict_domain( Y, =/2, X1).
for=dd( X, (_,_,Y1,_)):-  ground(Y1), !, X = (_,_,X1,_),
                             X1 = Y1, restrict_domain( X, =/2, Y1).
```

where the predicate restrict_domain/3 is the one mentioned in Box 6. The corresponding forward definition of =/2, named for=dd_C/2, which also updates the Constraints-variable of both the domain-variables occurring in the arguments of the call is given in Box 8.

```
for=dd_C(X,Y):-  constraints_plus_one([X,Y]),
                 real_for=dd_C(X,Y).
?- real_for=dd_C( (_,_,_,X,_), (_,_,_,Y,_) ) WHEN ground(X) or ground(Y)

real_for=dd(X,Y):-  for=dd_clauses(X,Y),
                    constraints_minus_one([X,Y]).
for=dd_clauses( (&,Id,_,X,DX), (&,Id,_,Y,DY)):-   !, X=Y, DX = DY.
for=dd_clauses( (_,_,_,X1,_), Y):- ground(X1), !, Y = (_,_,_,Y1,_),
                             Y1 = X1, restrict_domain( Y, =/2, X1).
for=dd_clauses( X, (_,_,_,Y1,_)):-  ground(Y1), !, X = (_,_,_,X1,_),
                             X1 = Y1, restrict_domain( X, =/2, Y1).
```

Box 8: Forward version of =/2 updating the Constraints-variables.

Here, the predicates constraints_plus_one/1 and constraints_minus_one/1 update the value of the Constraints-variable of each domain-variable in their list-argument in the obvious way. Also, for=dd_clauses/2 is identical to for=dd/2, except that the WHEN-declaration is omitted.

It should be clear that the use of the various first-fail mechanisms produces a lot of overhead. The programmer must decide whether the first-fail principle should be included or not. To express his choice, he can use various declarations. Namely:

```
?- first_fail_L.    , or:
?- first_fail_L_C.
```

in addition to a declaration for each constraint cons/n occurring in his program:

```
?- forward(cons/n).    , or:
?- look_ahead(cons/n).
```

This implies that there will be three different definitions for the library predicates real_create/2, assign_domain/2 and instantiate/1. One acts on 4-tuples, one on 5- and one on 6-tuples. Depending on the declarations, the appropriate definitions are loaded by the preprocessor. For each constraint, there are 9 different definitions: one for every combination of one of the options: no first-fail (default), first_fail_L and first_fail_L_C, with one of the options: ordinary execution (default - these will however take special care in handling domain-variables), forward execution and looking-ahead.

Discussion

We have described a PROLOG-implementation of finite-domain CLP. It makes use of a delay-mechanism, the WHEN-declarations of NU-Prolog. Based on our description, we believe that it should be easy for an experienced PROLOG-programmer to implement his own CLP-environment. On the other hand, the described implementation does not alter the underlying PROLOG-system in any way. Therefore, it does not cause overhead for programs which make no use of the CLP-environment. Also, the implementation is based on library predicates, not on a meta-interpreter (although the generators are executed under meta-interpretation). Thus, in general, we avoid the overhead of an extra layer of interpretation. Finally, it is usually not hard to define one delay-mechanism in terms of another. Since most PROLOG-systems will probably include a delay-facility in the near future, this makes our system relatively portable.

We developed various applications within the environment. Both typical test-examples, such as the N-queens problem and the five-houses puzzle, and real scheduling problems were successfully implemented. Below, we give a table with a comparison of different execution-times for computing the first solution to the N-queens problem. The comparison includes four programs: the simple generate-and-test program, a coroutining version of this program, the forward checking program of Box 4 and the forward checking program using first-fail on the length of the domains. The experiment was performed with NU-Prolog (and our environment) on a SUN3/280.

N	G & T	Corout.	For. Check.	For.Check.+F.F.
4	0.02	0.01	0.14	0.40
10	156.00	0.83	3.03	4.52
16	-	171.38	4.85	5.08

Table 1: Execution times for the first N-queens solution.

One of our more realistic experiments was the implementation of a program for the computation of a schedule for the nursing staff of a division in the university hospital of Leuven. The division includes 23 nurses. The schedule is made for a period of one month. Some of the nurses requests can not always be fulfilled. They are encoded into functions which must be optimized. Also, night-shifts and weekend-work can usually not be totally equally distributed within the given period of one month. Therefore, information of schedules for the previous months is kept in a database. Using this information, the distribution of the night-shifts and weekends are also performed by optimizing certain functions.

Computing an optimal schedule for one month takes the program approximately (depending on the actual constraints for that month) 2 minutes and 30 seconds. It takes a head-nurse more than one week to make a (less optimal) schedule by hand.

Clearly, there are many improvements that can be made to the implementation described in this paper. It was not our aim to present the ultimate efficient techniques, but to give a conceptual overview of a working design. A lot of search included in the implementation of the first-fail principle (scanning lists) can certainly be reduced by using more clever search-strategies. Several other refinements are possible as well.

Finally, on the level of the concepts, several improvements are desirable. The most important one is the use of hierarchies of constraints, as proposed in [Borning et al 89].

This provides a more elegant approach to the problem of optimizing a solution. Our further work will therefore focus on both types of improvements, in addition to some further experiments with large size applications.

References

[Borning et al 89] A.Borning, M.Maher, A.Martindale, M.Wilson, Constraint Hierarchies and Logic Programming, in Proc. of the Sixth International Conference on Logic Programming, eds. G.Levi and M.Martelli, 1989, pp.:149-164.

[Bruynooghe et al 89] M.Bruynooghe, D.De Schreye, B.Krekels, Compiling Control, J.Logic Programming, 1989 (6), pp.: 135-162.

[Colmerauer 82] A.Colmerauer, PROLOG II: Manuel de reference et modele theorique, Technical Report, GIA - Faculte de Science de Luminy, 1982.

[Colmerauer 87] A.Colmerauer, Opening the Prolog III Universe, BYTE Magazine, 12(9), 1987, pp.: 177-182.

[Dechter 89] R.Dechter, ed., Proc. Workshop on Constraint Problem Solving, IJCAI89, Detroit, 1989.

[De Schreye & Bruynooghe 89] D.De Schreye, M.Bruynooghe, The Compilation of Forward Checking Regimes through Meta-interpretation and Transformation, Proc. Workshop on Meta-programming in Logic Programming, MIT-Press, 1989.

[Dincbas et al 88a] M.Dincbas, H.Simonis, P.Van Hentenryck, Solving a Cutting-Stock Problem in Constraint Logic Programming, in Proc. of the 5th International Conference on Logic Programming, 1988, pp.: 42-58.

[Dincbas et al 88b] M.Dincbas, P.Van Hentenryck, H.Simonis, A.Aggoun, T.Graf, F.Bertheir, The Constraint Logic Programming Language CHIP, in Proc of FGCS88, 1988, pp.: 693-702.

[Graf et al 89] T.Graf, P.Van Hentenryck, C.Pradelles, L.Zimmer, Simulation of Hybrid Circuits in Constraint Logic Programming, in Proc. of IJCAI89, 1989, pp.:72-77.

[Jaffar & Lassez 87] J.Jaffar, J-L.Lassez, Constraint Logic Programming, in Proc. 14th ACM Principles of Programming Languages Conference, Munich, 1987.

[Jaffar & Michaylov 87] J.Jaffar, S.Michaylov, Methodology and implementation of a CLP System, in Proc. of the 4th International Conference on Logic Programming, 1987, pp.: 196-218.

[Naish 86] L.Naish, Negation and Control in Prolog, LNCS 238, Springer-Verlag, 1986.

[Thom & Zobel 88] J.Thom, J.Zobel, NU-Prolog Reference Manual, Version 1.3, Technical Report 86/10, Machine Intelligence Project, Computer Science Department, University of Melbourne, 1988.

[Van Hentenryck 89] P.Van Hentenryck, Constraint Satisfaction in Logic Programming, Logic Programming Series, MIT-Press, Cambridge, 1989.

Type Inference for Action Semantics

Susan Even* and David A. Schmidt[†]
Computing and Information Sciences Dept.
Kansas State University, Manhattan, KS 66506 USA
schmidt@cis.ksu.edu

1. Introduction

In a series of papers [11,12,13,14,15,25,26], Mosses and Watt define *action semantics*, a metalanguage for high level, domain-independent formulation of denotational semantics definitions. Action semantics was designed to support readability, abstraction, modularity, and modifiability of language definitions [13,15].

In our recent work [5], we studied a combinator-based version of action semantics. We developed a typing system for actions based on *types* and *kinds*. The types within a kind are partially ordered to reflect subtyping. We then defined a category-sorted algebra model [18,20] for the system where actions are natural transformations over interpretation functors (which map the type names and their ordering to predomains and coercion functions). Thus, an action is a family of continuous functions that behave consistently with respect to the subtyping relation. Coercion functions— even nonembeddings— disappear.

The typing system and its interpretation support an ML-style type inference algorithm for action expressions. Type inference must respect the subtyping laws, so we encounter the problems discovered by Mitchell [10], Fuh and Mishra [6], and Wand [24] regarding constraints sets. But action notation and its model are formulated so that the major problems regarding constraints are "restricted away." In particular, the monotonic behavior of actions with respect to the subtyping ordering keeps the cardinality of constraints sets small and makes constraints on record types unnecessary, even in the presence of record union and concatenation operations.

This paper presents our variant of action semantics and its typing system. We give the type inference algorithms, state properties that action semantics expressions satisfy, give soundness and completeness properties and explain why they hold for type inference on action semantics expressions. We also present a small example.

2. Action Semantics

In our version of action semantics, actions are combinators that operate upon *facets* (also called *kinds*) [11,14]. A facet is a collection of types; for example, the *functional facet* is the kind of all types that can be used as temporary values ("transient information" [14]) in a computation. The types int, bool, real, bool×real, and so on, belong to the functional facet. The other facet studied in this paper is the *declarative facet*, which contains types of identifier, value binding ("scoped information"). The types in this facet are record types [3,19]. Two other facets, the *imperative facet* and the *communicative facet* [14], are omitted for brevity's sake.

The types in a facet are partially ordered to reflect subtyping relationships [2,18,19]. For example, the type int is a subtype of the type real, written int≤real [3,19]. Values of type int may be used in any context in which a real may appear. Figure 1 lists the types in the functional and declarative facets and their orderings. We use ns ("nonsense") to stand for an undefined type. Call ns the

---
* Partially supported by ONR Grant N-00014-88-K0455.   † Partially supported by NSF Grant CCR-8822378.

Figure 1

Functional facet: Types are *Proper-functional-type* $\cup$ { ns }, where:

$t \in$ *Proper-functional-type*
$p \in$ *Primitive-type*

$$t ::= p \mid t_1 \rightarrow t_2 \mid t_1 \times t_2$$
$$p ::= \textbf{int} \mid \textbf{real} \mid \textbf{bool} \mid \cdots$$

The ordering is the smallest reflexive, transitive ordering such that:

$\textbf{int} \leq \textbf{real}$, etc., on the primitive-types
$t \leq \textbf{ns}$ for all t
$t_1 \rightarrow t_2 \leq t_1' \rightarrow t_2'$ iff $t_1' \leq t_1$ and $t_2 \leq t_2'$
$t_1 \times t_2 \leq t_1' \times t_2'$ iff $t_1 \leq t_1'$ and $t_2 \leq t_2'$

Declarative facet: Types are *Proper-declarative-type* $\cup$ { ns }, where:

$d \in$ *Proper-declarative-type*

$$d ::= \{ i{:}\, t_i \}_{i \in I} \mid \{ i{:}\, t_i \}_{i \in I \, \text{exactly}}$$
where I is a finite set of identifiers

The ordering is the smallest reflexive, transitive ordering such that:

$d \leq \textbf{ns}$ for all d
$\{ i{:}\, t_i \}_{i \in I} \leq \{ j{:}\, t_j' \}_{j \in J}$ iff $J \subseteq I$ and for all $j \in J$, $t_j \leq t_j'$
$\{ i{:}\, t_i \}_{i \in I \, \text{exactly}} \leq \{ i{:}\, t_i \}_{i \in I}$
$\{ i{:}\, t_i \}_{i \in I \, \text{exactly}} \leq \{ i{:}\, t_i' \}_{i \in I \, \text{exactly}}$ iff for all $i \in I$, $t_i \leq t_i'$

---

improper type; all other types are *proper types*.

The types for records deserve closer scrutiny. It is customary to read the type $\{ i{:}\, t_i \}_{i \in I}$ as the type of records that have *at least* bindings of type t_i for identifiers $i \in I$ (but may have additional bindings) [1,3] and the type $\{ i{:}\, t_i \}_{i \in I \, \text{exactly}}$ as the type of records that have bindings for *exactly* the identifiers in I and no others. But the key to understanding the two forms of record type is the subtyping ordering on them: the $\{ i{:}\, t_i \}_{i \in I}$-types use the "inheritance subtyping" of [3], whereas the $\{ i{:}\, t_i \}_{i \in I \, \text{exactly}}$-types do not. We have found good use for the two forms of record types: some actions operate well under inheritance subtyping and some simply do not. We can accommodate both.

Figure 2 gives the interpretations for the proper types. Note that we naively interpret the types $\{ i{:}\, t_i \}_{i \in I}$ and $\{ i{:}\, t_i \}_{i \in I \, \text{exactly}}$ the same way! This is surprising in light of the previous paragraph, but we wish to emphasize that the subtyping ordering is the crucial feature of records. The ordering is interpreted into coercion functions on the interpreted types. Since the coercions need not be mere embeddings [18], we may well be concerned about the computational overhead in using them. But we will soon see that coercions are never explicitly or implicitly inserted in action expressions.

The improper type, ns, is interpreted as the singleton set; a coercion into ns is the constant function.

The interpretation of the types and subtyping relation is formalized as a functor from the partial ordering of type names, treated as a category, into the category **Pdom** of predomains [18,20].

Actions are mappings whose domains and codomains are facets. We call the domain of an action its *source*, and its codomain its *target*. For example, we write $copy: F \rightarrow F$ to state that the source and target of action *copy* are the functional facet ("*F*"). (The declarative facet will be represented by a "*D*".) Since a facet contains many types, actions are polymorphic mappings on the predomains that

Figure 2

$A_F[\![\text{int}]\!] = \mathbb{Z}$

$A_F[\![\text{real}]\!] = \mathbb{Q}$

$A_F[\![\text{bool}]\!] = \mathbb{B}$

...

$A_F[\![t_1 \to t_2]\!] = A_F[\![t_1]\!] \to A_F[\![t_2]\!]$

$A_F[\![t_1 \times t_2]\!] = A_F[\![t_1]\!] \times A_F[\![t_2]\!]$

$A_F[\![\text{int} \leq \text{real}]\!] = \lambda n.\, n$

$A_F[\![t_1 \to t_2 \leq t_1' \to t_2']\!] = \lambda f.\, A_F[\![t_2 \leq t_2']\!] \circ f \circ A_F[\![t_1' \leq t_1]\!]$

$A_F[\![t_1 \times t_2 \leq t_1' \times t_2']\!] = A_F[\![t_1 \leq t_1']\!] \times A_F[\![t_2 \leq t_2']\!]$

$A_D[\![\{\, i{:}\, t_i \,\}_{i \in I}]\!] = \prod_{i \in I} A_F[\![t_i]\!]$

$A_D[\![\{\, i{:}\, t_i \,\}_{i \in I \text{ exactly}}]\!] = \prod_{i \in I} A_F[\![t_i]\!]$

$A_D[\![\{\, i{:}\, t_i \,\}_{i \in I} \leq \{\, j{:}\, t_j' \,\}_{j \in J}]\!] = \lambda r.\, \prod_{j \in J} A_F[\![t_j \leq t_j']\!](r \downarrow j)$

$A_D[\![\{\, i{:}\, t_i \,\}_{i \in I \text{ exactly}} \leq \{\, i{:}\, t_i \,\}_{i \in I}]\!] = \lambda r.\, r$

$A_D\{\, i{:}\, t_i \,\}_{i \in I \text{ exactly}} \leq \{\, i{:}\, t_i' \,\}_{i \in I \text{ exactly}} = \lambda r.\, \prod_{i \in I} A_F[\![t_i \leq t_i']\!](r \downarrow i)$

---

the types denote. Each action a has a monotonic *typing function* T_a that describes its behavior on argument types. For example, *copy* is the identity mapping on the functional facet, so its typing function is $T_{copy} = (\lambda t{:}F.\, t)$, which states that *copy* maps an argument of type t to an answer of type t. The meaning of *copy* is the family of identity functions $\{\lambda v{:}t.\, v\}_{t \in F}$, which we represent by $\lambda t{:}F.\lambda v{:}t.\, v$.

Actions exist for all the fundamental operations of programming languages: value passing, arithmetic, binding creation and lookup, storage allocation and updating, and so on [11,13,15]. Figure 3 presents a minimal subset of primitive actions that is representative of action sets for modelling statically typed languages. We have already seen *copy*; *succ* increments arguments from int and real and is undefined on nonnumbers; *put v* emits value v as its result; *pass* is the identity mapping for the declarative facet; *bind i* emits a declarative facet record that holds exactly the one binding of identifier i to the argument received by the action; *find i* retrieves from its declarative record argument the binding to i; *forget$_D$* takes arguments from the two facets and outputs the one from the functional facet; *freeze$_{i_a}a$* passes its declarative record argument to action a and converts the resulting action, which awaits a functional facet value, into a functional facet value itself and outputs it; and *eval* applies a function to an argument.

The third column of Figure 3 states that an action $a{:}K_1 \to K_2$ is a family of mappings $\{f_k{:}k \to T_a(k)\}_{k \in K_1}$ that behave *naturally*, that is, it respects the subtyping ordering:

$$
\begin{array}{ccc}
& a(k) & \\
A_F[\![k]\!] & \longrightarrow & A_F[\![T_a(k)]\!] \\
A_F[\![k \leq k']\!] \downarrow & & \downarrow A_F[\![T_a(k) \leq T_a(k')]\!] \\
& a(k') & \\
A_F[\![k']\!] & \longrightarrow & A_F[\![T_a(k')]\!]
\end{array}
$$

Figure 3

action	kinding	typing function	meaning
copy	$F \dashrightarrow F$	$\lambda t{:}F.\, t$	$\lambda t{:}F.\lambda v{:}t.\, v$
succ	$F \dashrightarrow F$	$\lambda t{:}F.\, if\ t{\leq}real\ then\ t\ else\ ns$	$\lambda t{\leq}real.\lambda v{:}t.\, v{+}1$
put(v:t_0)	$D \dashrightarrow F$	$\lambda d{:}D.\, t_0$	$\lambda d{:}D.\lambda r{:}d.\, v$
pass	$D \dashrightarrow D$	$\lambda d{:}D.\, d$	$\lambda d{:}D.\lambda r{:}d.\, r$
bind i	$F \dashrightarrow D$	$\lambda t{:}F.\, \{\, i{:}t\, \}_{exactly}$	$\lambda t{:}F.\lambda v{:}t.\, \{\, i{=}v\, \}$
find i	$D \dashrightarrow F$	$\lambda d{:}D.\ if\ i{:}t\ appears\ in\ d$ $then\ t\ else\ ns$	$\lambda d{:}D.\lambda r{:}d.\, r{\downarrow}i$
forget_D	$D{\times}F \dashrightarrow F$	$\lambda(d, t).\, t$	$\lambda(d, t){:}D{\times}F.\lambda(r, v){:}d{\times}t.\, v$
freeze_{i_0}a	$D \dashrightarrow F$	$\lambda d{:}D.\, t_0 \to T_a(d, t_0)$	$\lambda d{:}D.\lambda r{:}d.\lambda v{:}t_0.\, a(d, t_0)(r, v)$
	where T_a is the typing function for $a{:}D{\times}F \dashrightarrow F$		
eval	$F \dashrightarrow F$	$\lambda t{:}F.\ if\ t{=}(t_1{\to}t_2){\times}t_3\ and\ t_3{\leq}t_1$ $then\ t_2\ else\ ns$	$\lambda t{\leq}((t_1 \to t_2){\times}t_3).\lambda(f, v){:}t.\, f(v)$

(note: all typing functions and meanings are "ns-strict": for action a, $T_a(ns) = ns$ and $a(ns) = \lambda().0.$)

where $k, k' \in K_1$ and $k{\leq}k'$. Thus, an action a is a *natural transformation* from the functor A_F to the functor $A_F \circ T_a$ [18,20].

Modelling actions as natural transformations has several important consequences. The first is that coercion functions— even nonembedding coercions— need not be inserted into a composite natural transformation. The commutativity property, shown above, of a natural transformation guarantees that the answer produced by a composite natural transformation from an argument *must* be unique regardless of what coercions (if any) are applied to the argument, the answer, or the intermediate values produced by components of the composite natural transformation. So, we don't use coercions.

The second consequence is that the interpretation of a record type $\{\, i{:}t_i\, \}_{i\in I}$ is not critical. The essence of inheritance typing is expressed in the subtyping ordering and the respect that a natural transformation has for the ordering. An argument of type $\{\, i{:}t_i\, \}_{i\in I\,exactly}$ *must* be treated consistently by a natural transformation as if it also belonged to those record types $\{\, j{:}t_j'\, \}_{j\in J}$, such that $J{\subseteq}I$, $t_j{\leq}t_j'$, $j \in J$. But as the previous paragraph noted, the argument need never be coerced into $\{\, j{:}t_j'\, \}_{j\in J}$. At first glance, none of the actions in Figure 3 appear to exploit inheritance typing. But actions like *find i* are forced to have uniform structure because of it. Also, there exist actions analogous to $freeze_{i_0}a$ and *eval* that operate on the declarative facet and make crucial use of inheritance typing.

Finally, the modelling of actions as natural transformations prevents self-application. This justifies the definition of the action $freeze_{i_0}a$. For an argument $d_0 \in D$, $freeze_{i_0}a$ must output action a bound to d_0. But this is impossible, for such a result would be an action (natural transformation) of kinding $F \dashrightarrow F$. So, the output must be the functional facet value $a(d_0, t_0)$, a function of type $t_0 \to T_a(d_0, t_0)$, instead. The *eval* action, which activates $a(d_0, t_0)$, exploits the subtyping ordering to recover (some of) the polymorphism in a.

We study three forms of action composition: $a;a'$, sequential composition; $a*a'$, parallel composition; and $\triangleright a$, a restricted concatenation composition. Figure 4 shows the flow of arguments directed by the compositions.

The composition $a_1;a_2$ represents sequential composition: arguments to $a_1;a_2$ are given to a_1, which produces results that are given to a_2. The results produced by a_2 are the results for the composed action. The target of a_1 must equal the source of a_2. For example, *copy;succ* accepts a functional facet value that is passed sequentially from *copy* to *succ*, and the output is the incremented value.

Figure 4

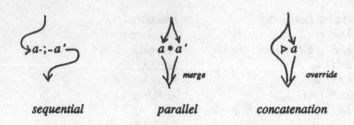

sequential	*parallel*	*concatenation*

The composition $a_1 * a_2$ represents parallel composition: arguments to $a_1 * a_2$ are given to both a_1 and a_2, each of which produces its own results. The results are *merged* to produce the results for the composed action. (In the functional facet, merging is tupling; in the declarative facet, merging is record union.) The sources of a_1 and a_2 must be identical. For example, *copy* * *succ* accepts an argument, which is given to both *copy* and *succ*. The two results— the value and its successor— are merged into a pair. As another example, the declarative record argument to (*put* 3; *bind A*) * (*find C*; *bind B*) is given to the two operands of *. The left operand ignores the record, emitting a binding of A to 3. The right operand finds the binding to C and uses it to make a binding to B. The bindings to A and B are unioned into one declarative record.

The composition $\triangleright a$ represents concatenation composition: the declarative record argument to the action is given to a, and a's output, which is another declarative record, is concatenated to the original record, overriding bindings in the original argument. For example, $\triangleright$ (*find A*; *bind B*) accepts a record, which is used to make a binding of B to A's value. The binding to B is concatenated to the original bindings. (The form of concatenation composition given here is a restricted version of the binary composition $a \triangleright a'$, where the outputs of the two actions are concatenated. Thus, the unary form is really *pass* $\triangleright a$, which explains why we treat $\triangleright a$ as a "composition.")

Figure 5 lists the compositions. The typing function T_{union} limits record union so that only records with "exactly" types (i.e., types of form $\{ i: t_i \}_{i \in I \text{ exactly}}$) can be unioned. One way of understanding this restriction is that the record union operation can not union together two records with extra, "hidden" fields. (The union of a record of type $\{ A:\textbf{bool} \}$ to one of type $\{ B:\textbf{int} \}$ might fail because the first record might have a hidden B-binding that clashes with the B-binding in the second record.) But another way of understanding the restriction is that the record union operation simply does not behave well with inheritance subtyping. (A union of a record with just an A-binding to one with just a B-binding will succeed, but a union of a record with A- and B-bindings to one with a B-binding fails, even though the record with A- and B-bindings has a type that is a subtype of records with just A-bindings.) A similar problem arises with record concatenation, and T_{concat} handles it in a similar way.

Figure 6 shows a sample language definition in action semantics.

3. Type Inference of Action Expressions

We might translate a source program through the semantics definition of Figure 6 and then type check the action semantics expression. For example, the typing scheme $\{ A:present(\theta) \} \alpha \rightarrow \theta$ *if* $\theta \leq real$ is the best typing scheme for the expression $\text{E}[\![B=2:\textbf{int} \text{ in } \textbf{add} A B]\!] = a_0: D \rightarrow F$, where:

Figure 5

for $a: K_1 \rightarrow K_2$ and $a': K_1' \rightarrow K_2'$

action	kinding	typing function	meaning
$a ; a'$	$K_1 \rightarrow K_2'$ if $K_2 = K_1'$	$T_{a'} \circ T_a$	$\lambda k : K_1 . a'(T_a(k)) \circ a(k)$
$a * a'$	$K_1 \rightarrow F$ if $K_1 = K_1'$ and $K_2 = K_2' = F$	$\lambda k : K_1 . T_a(k) \times T_{a'}(k)$	$\lambda k : K_1 . \lambda v : k . (a(k)(v), a'(k)(v))$
	$K_1 \rightarrow D$ if $K_1 = K_1'$ and $K_2 = K_2' = D$	$\lambda k : K_1 . T_{union}(T_a(k), T_{a'}(k))$	$\lambda k : K_1 . \lambda v : k . union(a(k)(v), a'(k)(v))$
$\triangleright a$	$D \rightarrow D$ if $K_1 = K_2 = D$	$\lambda d : D . T_{concat}(d, T_a(d))$	$\lambda d : D . \lambda r : d . concat(r, a(d)(r))$
	$F \times D \rightarrow D$ if $K_1 = F \times D$ and $K_2 = D$	$\lambda(t, d) : F \times D . T_{concat}(d, T_a(t, d))$	$\lambda(t, d) : F \times D . \lambda(v, r) : t \times d . concat(r, a(t, d)(v, r))$

where:

$T_{union}(d_1, d_2) =$ if $(d_1 = \{ i : t_i \}_{i \in I}$ exactly and $d_2 = \{ j : t_j \}_{j \in J}$ exactly and $I \cap J = \emptyset)$
        then $\{ i : t_i \}_{i \in I} @ \{ j : t_j \}_{j \in J}$ exactly $else$ ns

$T_{concat}(d_1, d_2) =$ if $(d_2 = \{ i : t_i \}_{i \in I}$ exactly$)$ then $d_2 @ (d_1 \setminus I)$ $else$ ns

@ is "append" and \ is "set subtraction"

Figure 6

$D:$ Declaration $\rightarrow (D \rightarrow D)$
     $D[\![D_1 \text{ and } D_2]\!] = D[\![D_1]\!] * D[\![D_2]\!]$
     $D[\![I = E]\!] = E[\![E]\!] ; bind\, I$

$E:$ Expression $\rightarrow (D \rightarrow F)$
     $E[\![D \text{ in } E]\!] = (\triangleright D[\![D]\!]) ; E[\![E]\!]$
     $E[\![N : t]\!] = put\, (N : t)$
     $E[\![op\, E_1\, E_2]\!] = (E[\![E_1]\!] * E[\![E_2]\!]) ; op$
     $E[\![I]\!] = find\, I$
     $E[\![\text{lambda } I : t . E]\!] = freeze_t ((\triangleright (forget_D ; bind\, I)) ; E[\![E]\!])$
     $E[\![E_1\, E_2]\!] = (E[\![E_1]\!] * E[\![E_2]\!]) ; eval$

$a_0 = (\triangleright (put\, (2 : int) : bind\, R)) ; (find\, A * find\, B) ; add$

in the sense that every typing $d_0 \rightarrow t_0$ that results from a ground substitution into the typing scheme conforms with the typing function: $T_{a_0}(d_0) = t_0$. Also, for any type $d_0 \neq$ ns such that $T_{a_0}(d_0) = t_0 \neq$ ns, there exists a ground substitution into the scheme that yields the typing $d_0 \rightarrow t_0$. If such properties hold, we say that the typing scheme is *sound* and *complete*, respectively. In [5], we showed the proof of soundness and completeness of a method of type inference for action semantics expressions. In this section, we give the algorithms that implement the method.

Polymorphic type inference originated with ML [9] and was extended for subtypes by Mitchell [10]; implementations were undertaken by Fuh and Mishra [6,7]. Subtyping was represented by a set of *constraints* of the form $\tau_1 \leq \tau_2$, where τ_1 and τ_2 represent typing schemes. Problems arose: subtyping constraints crept in at every function application, so even small programs had typing schemes whose constraint sets were unmanageable [7]. Also, checking satisfiability of constraints was not easy [6,16]. Cardelli [1], Cardelli and Wegner [3], Cardelli and Mitchell [2], Stansifer [22], Wand [24], Jategaonker and Mitchell [8], and Remy [17] studied subtyping of record types. In particular, Wand [24] noted the need for a complex constraint on the typing scheme for the record concatenation operation.

The type inference algorithm in this paper handles subtypes, records, and record concatenation and union operations yet avoids large constraint sets and constraints on records. Since action semantics is built on a model where actions are natural transformations, few constraints are needed to obtain soundness and completeness properties for type inference. Since the action semantics notation is more constrained than that studied by Wand, constraints on record concatenation and union are avoided. Thus, we achieve the goal of simple, ML-style type inference for a notation with subtypes and records.

We now give the syntax of typing schemes for actions. A typing scheme has the form:

$$S_1 \xrightarrow{\cdot} S_2 \ \text{if} \ C$$

where:

$S \in$ *Typing-scheme*

$C \in$ *Constraint*

$v \in$ *Functional-facet-scheme*

$d \in$ *Declarative-facet-scheme*

$f \in$ *Field-scheme*

$S ::= v \mid d$

$v ::= \textbf{int} \mid \textbf{real} \mid \cdots \mid v_1 \times v_2 \mid v_1 \rightarrow v_2 \mid \theta$

$d ::= \{ i{:}f_i \}_{i \in I} \alpha \mid \{ i{:}f_i \}_{i \in I} \text{exactly} \mid \{ i{:}f_i \}_{i \in I} \alpha_{\text{exactly}}$

$f ::= absent \mid present(v) \mid \Delta$

$C ::= v_1 \leq v_2 \mid C_1 \ and \ C_2 \mid true$

Placeholders ("variables") are represented by θ, Δ, and α. θ is a variable for an arbitrary proper type in the functional facet. Δ is a *field variable* [17, 24]; the phrase $i{:}\Delta$ represents unknown status about the presence or absence of identifier i (and its type) in a record type. α is a *row variable* [17,24]; the scheme $\{ i{:}f_i \}_{i \in I} \alpha$ represents unknown status about all identifiers $j \notin I$ in the record type. For example, the scheme $\{ A{:}present(\theta) ; B{:}\Delta ; C{:}absent \} \alpha_{\text{exactly}}$ represents the family of record types that have an A-field, might (or might not) have a B-field, definitely do not have a C-field, might (or might not) have other fields beyond A, B, and C, and finally, have no hidden fields. Field and row variables are used for "bookkeeping" during type inference; their use leads to simple definitions of unification and inference for record operations. As in Tofte [23], Remy [17], and Wand [24], we assume that a row variable α, as appearing in $\{ i{:}f_i \}_{i \in I} \alpha$, has as its "domain of use" I. That is, α can be instantiated only with fields whose labels are not in I.

We use the usual notion of substitution [21] and use U to stand for an arbitrary substitution. A specific substitution is written $[j \mapsto S_j]_{j \in J}$. The function *unify*: *Typing-scheme*×*Typing-scheme* → *Substitution* does first-order unification [21].

Figure 7 gives the type schemes for the actions in Figure 3, and Figure 8 gives the typing schemes for the compositions. Type inference for sequential composition depends on the unification of the target scheme for action a and the source scheme of action a'. (Note that the constraints of the two action's schemes must be satisfied, else the composition defines a "nonsense" mapping.) ML-style unification is used for unification of nonrecord typing schemes. When record schemes are unified, a simplified version of Tofte's unification algorithm is employed [23]. Its definition is given in Figure 9. (For example, the unification of $\{ A{:}\Delta_1 ; C{:}absent \} \alpha$ to

Figure 7

action	scheme
$put\ (n{:}t_0)$	$\{\ \}\alpha \rightarrow t_0$
$succ$	$\theta \rightarrow \theta\ \ if\ \theta{\leq}real$
$pass$	$\{\ \}\alpha \rightarrow \{\ \}\alpha$
$bind\ i$	$\theta \rightarrow \{\ i{:}present(\theta)\ \}_{\mathbf{exactly}}$
$find\ i$	$\{\ i{:}present(\theta)\ \}\alpha \rightarrow \theta$
$forget_D$	$\{\ \}\alpha \times \theta \rightarrow \theta$
$freeze_{t_0}(a)$	let $\ d \times v_1 \rightarrow v_2\ if\ C\ \ $ be the scheme for a let $\ U = unify(t_0, v_1)$ in if $is\text{-}sat(U(C))$ then $U(d) \rightarrow (t_0 \rightarrow U(v_2))\ if\ U(C)$ else $failure$ $\qquad\qquad$ ($is\text{-}sat$ checks the satisfiability of a set of constraints [6,16].)
$eval$	$(\theta_1 \rightarrow \theta_2) \times \theta_3 \rightarrow \theta_2\ \ if\ \theta_3{\leq}\theta_1$

Figure 8

let the scheme for action a be $S_1 \rightarrow S_2\ if\ C$
and the scheme for action a' be $S_1' \rightarrow S_2'\ if\ C'$

action	typing scheme
$a\,;a'$	if $U = unify(S_2, S_1') \neq failure$ $\qquad$ and $is\text{-}sat(U(C\ and\ C'))$ $\qquad$ then $U(S_1) \rightarrow U(S_2')\ if\ U(C\ and\ C')$ $\qquad$ else $failure$
$a * a'$	if $U = unify(S_1, S_1') \neq failure$ $\qquad$ and $U', S' = S_{merge}(U(S_2), U(S_2')) \neq failure$ $\qquad$ and $is\text{-}sat(U' \circ U(C\ and\ C'))$ $\qquad$ then $U' \circ U(S_1) \rightarrow S'\ if\ U' \circ U(C\ and\ C')$ $\qquad$ else $failure$
$\triangleright a$	if $U, S = S_{concat}(declarative\text{-}facet\text{-}scheme\text{-}in(S_1), S_2) \neq failure$ $\qquad$ and $is\text{-}sat(U(C))$ $\qquad$ then $U(S_1) \rightarrow S\ if\ U(C)$ $\qquad$ else $failure$

Figure 9

---

unify-record: *Declarative-facet-scheme*×*Declarative-facet-scheme*→ *Substitution*

unify-record$(d_1, d_2)=$
    let $I=$*fields-in*$(d_1)\cup$*fields-in*(d_2)
    let $U_1, d_1'=$*extend-record-with-new-fields*$(I\backslash$*fields-in*$(d_1), d_1)$
    let $U_2, d_2'=$*extend-record-with-new-fields*$(I\backslash$*fields-in*$(d_2), d_2)$
    let $\{$ *fields*$_1$ $\}$*row*$_1=d_1'$
    let $\{$ *fields*$_2$ $\}$*row*$_2=d_2'$
    let $U_3=$*unify-row-variables*$($*row*$_1,$ *row*$_2)$
    let $U_4=$*unify-fields*$($*fields*$_1,$*fields*$_2)$
    in $U_4 \circ U_3 \circ U_2 \circ U_1$

where:

extend-record-with-new-fields$(J,\{ i{:}f_i \}_{i\in I\text{ exactly}})=[]$, $\{ i{:}f_i \}_{i\in I}@\{ j{:}absent \}_{j\in J\text{exactly}}$
extend-record-with-new-fields$(J,\{ i{:}f_i \}_{i\in I}\alpha)=[\alpha\mapsto \{ j{:}\Delta_j \}_{j\in J}\gamma]$, $\{ i{:}f_i \}_{i\in I}@\{ j{:}\Delta_j \}_{j\in J}\gamma$
extend-record-with-new-fields$(J,\{ i{:}f_i \}_{i\in I}\alpha_{\text{exactly}})=[\alpha\mapsto \{ j{:}\Delta_j \}_{j\in J}\gamma]$, $\{ i{:}f_i \}_{i\in I}@\{ j{:}\Delta_j \}_{j\in J}\gamma_{\text{exactly}}$
    (assume variables Δ_j and γ are newly generated)

unify-row-variables$(_{\text{exactly}}, _{\text{exactly}})=[]$
unify-row-variables$(\alpha, _{\text{exactly}})=[\alpha\mapsto \{$ $\}_{\text{exactly}}]$
unify-row-variables$(\alpha, \beta)=[\alpha\mapsto \gamma][\beta\mapsto \gamma]$
unify-row-variables$(\alpha, \beta_{\text{exactly}})=[\alpha\mapsto \gamma_{\text{exactly}}][\beta\mapsto \gamma]$
unify-row-variables$(\alpha_{\text{exactly}}, _{\text{exactly}})=[\alpha\mapsto \{$ $\}]$
unify-row-variables$(\alpha_{\text{exactly}}, \beta_{\text{exactly}})=[\alpha\mapsto \gamma][\beta\mapsto \gamma]$
    (assume variable γ is newly generated)
(the operation is commutative)

unify-fields$(d_1, d_2)=$
    if $d_1=d_2=\{$ $\}$ then $[]$
    else let $\{ i{:}f_1 \}@d_1'=d_1$
         let $\{ i{:}f_2 \}@d_2'=d_2$
         let $U_1=$*unify*(f_1,f_2)
         let $U_2=$*unify-fields*$(U_1(d_1'), U_1(d_2'))$
         in $U_2 \circ U_1$

$\{ A{:}present(\theta_2){:} B{:}present(bool) \}_{\text{exactly}}$ is the substitution: $[\alpha\mapsto \{ B{:}\Delta_2 \}\beta]$ $[\beta\mapsto \{$ $\}_{\text{exactly}}]$ $[\Delta_1\mapsto present(\theta_2)]$ $[\Delta_2\mapsto present(bool)]$, which produces the scheme:
$\{ A{:}present(\theta_2){;} B{:}present(bool){;} C{:}absent \}_{\text{exactly}}$, which is equivalent to:
$\{ A{:}present(\theta_2){;} B{:}present(bool) \}_{\text{exactly}}$.

    Parallel composition depends on the inference defined by S_{merge}. See Figure 10. When merging functional facet values, ordinary tupling occurs, so a product type is inferred. When merging declarative records, the records are unioned if they have no fields in common. The type inference must verify that the types of the two records have no fields in common and both record type schemes are "exactly." The key to keeping the inference simple is the omission of some of the cases in functions *resolve-row-variables* and *resolve-fields*. The omitted cases create complex record constraints for unioning typing schemes like $\{ \cdots \}\alpha$ to $\{ \cdots \}\beta$ or unioning $\{ A{:}\Delta_1 \}_{\text{exactly}}$ to $\{ A{:}\Delta_2 \}_{\text{exactly}}$ [24]. We will show that the typing schemes for action expressions have properties that make the omitted cases impossible in our system.

Figure 10

S_{merge}: *Typing-scheme×Typing-scheme → Substitution×Typing-scheme*

$S_{merge}(v_1, v_2) = [], v_1 \times v_2$

$S_{merge}(d_1, d_2) =$
    let $I = fields\text{-}in(d_1) \cup fields\text{-}in(d_2)$
    let $U_1, d_1' = extend\text{-}record\text{-}with\text{-}new\text{-}fields(I \backslash fields\text{-}in(d_1), d_1)$
    let $U_2, d_2' = extend\text{-}record\text{-}with\text{-}new\text{-}fields(I \backslash fields\text{-}in(d_2), d_2)$
    let $U_3, d = S_{union}(d_1', d_2')$
    in $U_3 \circ U_2 \circ U_1, d$

where:

$S_{union}(\{fields_1\}row_1, \{fields_2\}row_2) =$
    let $U_1, row = resolve\text{-}row\text{-}vars(row_1, row_2)$
    let $U_2, fields = resolve\text{-}fields(fields_1, fields_2)$
    in $U_2 \circ U_1, \{fields\}row$

where:

    $resolve\text{-}row\text{-}vars(\textbf{exactly, exactly}) = [], \textbf{exactly}$
    $resolve\text{-}row\text{-}vars(\alpha_{\textbf{exactly}}, \textbf{exactly}) = [], \alpha_{\textbf{exactly}}$
    $resolve\text{-}row\text{-}vars(\alpha, \textbf{exactly}) = [\alpha \mapsto \beta_{\textbf{exactly}}], \beta_{\textbf{exactly}}$
    $resolve\text{-}row\text{-}vars(\alpha, \alpha) = [\alpha \mapsto \{\ \}_{\textbf{exactly}}], \textbf{exactly}$
    $resolve\text{-}row\text{-}vars(\alpha_{\textbf{exactly}}, \alpha_{\textbf{exactly}}) = [\alpha \mapsto \{\ \}], \textbf{exactly}$
    $resolve\text{-}row\text{-}vars(\alpha\textit{[exactly]}, \beta\textit{[exactly]}) =$ do not appear in our system
        (the italic brackets enclose optional phrases)
    (the operation is commutative)

$resolve\text{-}fields(d_1, d_2) =$
    if $d_1 = d_2 = \{\ \}$ then $[], \{\ \}$
    else let $\{i{:}f_1\}@d_1' = d_1$
        let $\{i{:}f_2\}@d_2' = d_2$
        let $U_1, f' = cases\ (f_1, f_2)\ of$
               $(absent, f)$ or $(f, absent)$: $[], f$
               (Δ, Δ): $[\Delta \mapsto absent], absent$
               $(\Delta, present(v))$ or $(present(v), \Delta)$: $[\Delta \mapsto absent], present(v)$
               $(present(v), present(v'))$: *failure*
               (Δ, Δ'): does not appear in our system
        let $U_2, d = resolve\text{-}fields(U_1(d_1'), U_1(d_2'))$
        in $U_2 \circ U_1, \{i{:}f'\}@d$

Concatenation composition depends on the inference defined by S_{concat}. See Figure 11. $S_{concat}(d_1, d_2)$ requires that d_2 has an "exactly" typing (cf. Figure 5). Problems arise when row and field variables appear in d_2, because unknown bindings are overriding existing ones. Fortunately, action semantics expressions have the property that any row and field variables in d_2's typing scheme must be present in d_1's, which represents the harmless case where an unknown binding is overriding itself. The omitted cases in Figure 11 never arise.

Despite the omitted cases, the definitions in Figures 10 and 11 are well-defined for the restricted actions we use. There are two crucial properties: a scheme $S \rightarrow T$ *if* C has the α-*preserved* property

Figure 11

S_{concat}: *Declarative-facet-scheme*×*Declarative-facet-scheme*
        → *Substitution*×*Declarative-facet-scheme*

$S_{concat}(d_1, d_2) =$
    let $I = \textit{fields-in}(d_1) \cup \textit{fields-in}(d_2)$
    let $U_1, d_1' = \textit{extend-record-with-new-fields}(I \backslash \textit{fields-in}(d_1), d_1)$
    let $U_2, d_2' = \textit{extend-record-with-new-fields}(I \backslash \textit{fields-in}(d_2), d_2)$
    let $\{\textit{fields}_1\} row_1 = d_1'$
    let $\{\textit{fields}_2\} row_2 = d_2'$
    let $U_3, row = \textit{override-row-vars}(row_1, row_2)$
    let $\textit{fields} = \textit{override-fields}(\textit{fields}_1, \textit{fields}_2)$
    in $U_3 \circ U_2 \circ U_1, \{\textit{fields}\} row$

where
    $\textit{override-row-vars}(row_1, \text{\scriptsize exactly}) = [], row_1$
    $\textit{override-row-vars}(\alpha_{\text{exactly}}, \alpha_{\text{exactly}}) = [], \alpha_{\text{exactly}}$
    $\textit{override-row-vars}(\alpha, \alpha) = [\alpha \mapsto \beta_{\text{exactly}}], \beta_{\text{exactly}}$
    $\textit{override-row-vars}(\textit{all other cases}) = $ do not appear in our system

$\textit{override-fields}(d_1, d_2) =$
    if $d_1 = d_2 = \{\}$ then $\{\}$
    else let $\{i : f_1\} @ d_1' = d_1$
        let $\{i : f_2\} @ d_2' = d_2$
        let $f' = \textit{cases}(f_1, f_2)$ of
               $(f, \textit{absent}) : f$
               $(f, \textit{present}(v))) : \textit{present}(v)$
               $(\Delta, \Delta) : \Delta$
               (Δ, Δ') or $(\textit{absent}, \Delta)$ or $(\textit{present}(v), \Delta)$: do not appear in our system
        let $d = \textit{override-fields}(d_1', d_2')$
        in $\{i : f'\} @ d$

---

if, whenever T is a declarative facet scheme containing a row variable α, then S is a declarative facet scheme containing the same α, and it has the Δ-*preserved* property if, whenever T is a declarative facet scheme containing a record field $i : \Delta$, then S is a declarative facet scheme containing the same $i : \Delta$.

Proposition: *Let* $a_i : S_i \overset{.}{\to} S_i'$ *if* C_i, $i \in 1..2$; *let* $U = \textit{unify}(S_1, S_2) \neq \textit{failure}$; *let* $U(a_i) = U(S_i) \overset{.}{\to} U(S_i')$ *if* $U(C_i)$. *If* a_1 *and* a_2 *have the* α-*preserved and* Δ-*preserved properties for all row variables* α *and field variables* Δ, *then so have* $U(a_1)$ *and* $U(a_2)$.

Proof: All row and field variables are created by substitution into row variables. The result follows from the α-preserved property. $\square$

Consider the inference for $a_1 * a_2$, where $a_i : d_i \overset{.}{\to} d_i'$ if C_i, $i \in 1..2$. Assume that the schemes have the α- and Δ-preserved properties. The type inference unifies d_1 with d_2 (giving substitution U), forcing the row and field variables to be the same in $U(d_1)$ and $U(d_2)$. If $U(d_i')$ has a row variable, by the Proposition, it is in $U(d_i)$ as well. So, if both $U(d_1')$ and $U(d_2')$ have row variables, they must be identical, implying that the two arguments to S_{union} have the same row variables— the omitted cases in Figure 10 never arise. A similar result holds for field variables in $U(d_1')$ and $U(d_2')$.

For inference on $\triangleright a$, if a's scheme $d \dotrightarrow d'$ if C has the α- and Δ-preserved properties, then the row and field variables in d' will be present in d. The omitted cases in Figure 11 never arise.

We now consider soundness and completeness. Say that a substitution into a typing scheme is a *ground substitution* if no variables remain after the substitution is applied to the scheme. A ground substitution maps a typing-scheme into a type. An instantiated scheme such as $\{ A\text{:}absent\text{; } B\text{:}present(\text{bool}) \}_{exactly}$ is read as the type $\{ B\text{:}bool \}_{exactly}$, that is, "absent" fields are dropped when the record is "exactly." When a ground substitution yields an instantiated scheme like $\{ A\text{:}absent \}$, that is, an "absent" field in a "non-exactly" record, we disallow the substitution, since the instantiated scheme has no interpretation in our typing system. (But such a type is legal in [2].)

Definition: A typing-scheme $S_1 \dotrightarrow S_2$ if C is *sound for action* $a\text{:} K_1 \dotrightarrow K_2$ iff for all $k \in K_1$, for all ground substitutions U, $U(S_1) = k \neq \text{ns}$, and $U(C)$ holds true imply $T_a(k) = U(S_2)$.

The typing-scheme is *complete for action* a iff for all $k \in K_1$, $T_a(k) \neq \text{ns}$ implies there exists a ground substitution U such that $U(S_1) = k$ and $U(C)$ holds true.

In an earlier paper [5], we showed that the typing schemes in Figure 7 and the type inference in Figure 8 give sound and complete typing schemes for action semantics expressions. A key to the results is that the typing functions T_a are monotonic with respect to the subtyping ordering. Thus, the domain of a typing function is a down-closed set in the underlying partial ordering of types.

This structural property of domains of typing functions gives an advantage for type inference: it reduces the size of constraint sets, because the typing schemes naturally represent down-closed sets. Further, composition of actions introduces no new constraints into the constraints set of the typing scheme for the composed action, since the typing functions (which describe the behavior of natural transformations) *must* compose. Constraints appear only when the domain of an action must be further restricted (e.g., *succ*). In contrast, in the Mitchell/Fuh&Mishra system [6,7,8,10] constraints represent coercion functions. For example, the identity mapping has the scheme: $\theta_1 \rightarrow \theta_2$ if $\theta_1 \leq \theta_2$, and the composition of $a\text{:} \theta_1 \rightarrow \theta_2$ with $a'\text{:} \theta_1' \rightarrow \theta_2'$ generates the constraint $\theta_2 \leq \theta_1'$.

4. An Example

We now give an example of type inference. Consider this program in the language in Figure 6:

$F = (\text{lambda } C\text{:real. div } C \text{ } B) \text{ and } A = 3\text{:int in } F \text{ } A$

The action semantics denotation of the program is a_7, where:

$a_7 = (\triangleright a_5) \text{ ; } a_6$

$a_6 = \text{E}[\![F \text{ } A]\!] = (\text{find } F * \text{find } A) \text{ ; } \text{eval}$

$a_5 = \text{D}[\![F = (\text{lambda } C \text{:real. div } C \text{ } B) \text{ and } A = 3\text{:int}]\!] = a_4 * a_1$

$a_4 = \text{D}[\![F = \text{lambda } C \text{:real. div } C \text{ } B]\!] = a_3 \text{ ; } \text{bind } F$

$a_3 = \text{E}[\![\text{lambda } C \text{:real. div } C \text{ } B]\!] = \text{freeze}_{real}((\triangleright (\text{forget}_D \text{ ; } \text{bind } C)) \text{ ; } a_2)$

$a_2 = \text{E}[\![\text{div } C \text{ } B]\!] = (\text{find } C * \text{find } B) \text{ ; } \text{div}$

$a_1 = \text{D}[\![A = 3\text{:int}]\!] = \text{put } (3\text{:int}) \text{ ; } \text{bind } A$

We will write $a \in S_1 \dotrightarrow S_2$ if C to denote that a has the indicated typing scheme.

Type inference for a_1:

$\text{put}(3\text{:int}) \in \{ \text{ } \} \alpha_1 \dotrightarrow \text{int}$

$\text{bind } A \in \theta_1 \dotrightarrow \{ A \text{:}present(\theta_1) \}_{exactly}$

$(put(3:\text{int}) ; bind\,A) \in \{\ \}\alpha_1 \dot{\rightarrow} \{A:present(\text{int})\}_{\textbf{exactly}}$
and $U = [\theta_1 \mapsto \text{int}]$

Type inference for a_2:

$find\,C \in \{C:present(\theta_2)\}\alpha_2 \dot{\rightarrow} \theta_2$

$find\,B \in \{B:present(\theta_3)\}\alpha_3 \dot{\rightarrow} \theta_3$

$(find\,C * find\,B) \in \{C:present(\theta_2), B:present(\theta_3)\}\alpha_4 \dot{\rightarrow} \theta_2 \times \theta_3$
and $U = [\alpha_2 \mapsto \{B:present(\theta_3)\}\alpha_4][\alpha_3 \mapsto \{C:present(\theta_2)\}\alpha_4]$

$div \in \theta_4 \times \theta_5 \dot{\rightarrow} \textbf{real}$ if $\theta_4 \leq \textbf{real}$ and $\theta_5 \leq \textbf{real}$

$(find\,C * find\,B) ; div \in \{C:present(\theta_6), B:present(\theta_7)\}\alpha_4 \dot{\rightarrow} \textbf{real}$ if $\theta_6 \leq \textbf{real}$ and $\theta_7 \leq \textbf{real}$
and $U = [\theta_4 \mapsto \theta_6][\theta_2 \mapsto \theta_6][\theta_5 \mapsto \theta_7][\theta_3 \mapsto \theta_7]$

Type inference for a_3:

$forget_D \in \{\ \}\alpha_5 \times \theta_8 \dot{\rightarrow} \theta_8$

$bind\,C \in \theta_9 \dot{\rightarrow} \{C:present(\theta_9)\}_{\textbf{exactly}}$

$(forget_D ; bind\,C) \in \{\ \}\alpha_5 \times \theta_{10} \dot{\rightarrow} \{C:present(\theta_{10})\}_{\textbf{exactly}}$
and $U = [\theta_8 \mapsto \theta_{10}][\theta_9 \mapsto \theta_{10}]$

$\triangleright (forget_D ; bind\,C) \in \{C:\Delta_1\}\alpha_6 \times \theta_{10} \dot{\rightarrow} \{C:present(\theta_{10})\}\alpha_6$
and $U = [\alpha_5 \mapsto \{C:\Delta_1\}\alpha_6]$

$a_2 \in \{C:present(\theta_6), B:present(\theta_7)\}\alpha_4 \dot{\rightarrow} \textbf{real}$ if $\theta_6 \leq \textbf{real}$ and $\theta_7 \leq \textbf{real}$

$(\triangleright (forget_D ; bind\,C)) ; a_2 \in \{B:present(\theta_7), C:\Delta_1\}\alpha_7 \times \theta_{11} \dot{\rightarrow} \textbf{real}$ if $\theta_{11} \leq \textbf{real}$ and $\theta_7 \leq \textbf{real}$
and $U = [\theta_{10} \mapsto \theta_{11}][\theta_6 \mapsto \theta_{11}][\alpha_6 \mapsto \{B:present(\theta_7)\}\alpha_7][\alpha_4 \mapsto \alpha_7]$

$(freeze_{\textbf{real}}((\triangleright (forget_D ; bind\,C)) ; a_2)) \in$
$\{B:present(\theta_7), C:\Delta_1\}\alpha_7 \dot{\rightarrow} (\textbf{real} \rightarrow \textbf{real})$ if $\theta_7 \leq \textbf{real}$
and $U = [\theta_{11} \mapsto \textbf{real}]$

$U(\theta_{11} \leq \textbf{real}) = \textbf{real} \leq \textbf{real} = true$

Type inference for a_4:

$a_3 \in \{B:present(\theta_7), C:\Delta_1\}\alpha_7 \dot{\rightarrow} (\textbf{real} \rightarrow \textbf{real})$ if $\theta_7 \leq \textbf{real}$

$bind\,F \in \theta_{12} \dot{\rightarrow} \{F:present(\theta_{12})\}_{\textbf{exactly}}$

$a_3 ; bind\,F \in \{B:present(\theta_7), C:\Delta_1\}\alpha_7 \dot{\rightarrow} \{F:present(\textbf{real} \rightarrow \textbf{real})\}_{\textbf{exactly}}$ if $\theta_7 \leq \textbf{real}$
and $U = [\theta_{12} \mapsto (\textbf{real} \rightarrow \textbf{real})]$

Type inference for a_5:

$a_1 \in \{\ \}\alpha_1 \dot{\rightarrow} \{A:present(\text{int})\}_{\textbf{exactly}}$

$a_4 \in \{B:present(\theta_7), C:\Delta_1\}\alpha_7 \dot{\rightarrow} \{F:present(\textbf{real} \rightarrow \textbf{real})\}_{\textbf{exactly}}$ if $\theta_7 \leq \textbf{real}$

$a_4 * a_1 \in \{B:present(\theta_7), C:\Delta_1\}\alpha_8 \dot{\rightarrow} \{A:present(\text{int}), F:present(\textbf{real} \rightarrow \textbf{real})\}_{\textbf{exactly}}$
if $\theta_7 \leq \textbf{real}$
and $U = [\alpha_1 \mapsto \{B:present(\theta_7), C:\Delta_1\}\alpha_8][\alpha_7 \mapsto \alpha_8]$

Type inference for a_6:

$find\,F \in \{F:present(\theta_{13})\}\alpha_9 \dot{\rightarrow} \theta_{13}$

$find\,A \in \{A:present(\theta_{14})\}\alpha_{10} \dot{\rightarrow} \theta_{14}$

$find\,F * find\,A \in \{F:present(\theta_{13}), A:present(\theta_{14})\}\alpha_{11} \dot{\rightarrow} \theta_{13} \times \theta_{14}$
and $U = [\alpha_9 \mapsto \{A:present(\theta_{14})\}\alpha_{11}][\alpha_{10} \mapsto \{F:present(\theta_{13})\}\alpha_{11}]$

$eval \in (\theta_{15} \rightarrow \theta_{16}) \times \theta_{17} \dot{\rightarrow} \theta_{16}$ if $\theta_{17} \leq \theta_{15}$

$(find F * find A); eval \in \{F :present(\theta_{15} \rightarrow \theta_{16}), A :present(\theta_{18})\}\alpha_{11} \dashrightarrow \theta_{16}$ if $\theta_{18} \leq \theta_{15}$
  and $U = [\theta_{13} \mapsto (\theta_{15} \rightarrow \theta_{16})][\theta_{14} \mapsto \theta_{18}][\theta_{17} \mapsto \theta_{18}]$

Type inference for a_7:

$a_5 \in \{B :present(\theta_7), C :\Delta_1\}\alpha_8 \rightarrow \{A :present(int), F :present(real \rightarrow real)\}_{exactly}$ if $\theta_7 \leq real$
$\triangleright a_5 \in \{B :present(\theta_7), C :\Delta_1, A :\Delta_2, F :\Delta_3\}\alpha_{12}$
  $\dashrightarrow \{B :present(\theta_7), A :present(int), F :present(real \rightarrow real), C :\Delta_1\}\alpha_{12}$
    if $\theta_7 \leq real$
    and $U = [\alpha_8 \mapsto \{A :\Delta_2, F :\Delta_3\}\alpha_{12}]$
$a_6 \in \{F :present(\theta_{15} \rightarrow \theta_{16}), A :present(\theta_{18})\}\alpha_{11} \dashrightarrow \theta_{16}$ if $\theta_{18} \leq \theta_{15}$
$(\triangleright a_5); a_6 \in \{B :present(\theta_7), C :\Delta_1, A :\Delta_2, F :\Delta_3\}\alpha_{13} \dashrightarrow real$ if $\theta_7 \leq real$
    and $U = [\alpha_{11} \mapsto \{B :present(\theta_7), C :\Delta_1\}\alpha_{13}][\theta_{15} \mapsto real][\theta_{16} \mapsto real][\theta_{18} \mapsto int][\alpha_{12} \mapsto \alpha_{13}]$
$U (\theta_{18} \leq \theta_{15}) = int \leq real = true$

So, the typing scheme is:

$\{B :present(\theta_7), C :\Delta_1, A :\Delta_2, F :\Delta_3\}\alpha_{13} \dashrightarrow real$ if $\theta_7 \leq real$

The field variables in the scheme's source are just "little row variables;" since neither they nor the row variable α_{13} appear in the scheme's target or constraints, we compress them into:

$\{B :present(\theta_7)\}\alpha' \dashrightarrow real$ if $\theta_7 \leq real$

The compression of field variables with row variables can (and should) also be undertaken in the intermediate steps above, but we chose not to do so, in order that the inference steps matched the definitions in Figures 7-11.

The scheme for the program tells us that the program requires a declarative record argument that has a binding of B to a value with a subtype of **real** so that the program can produce a **real**-typed answer. By the soundness and completeness properties, the scheme describes all the well-defined behaviors of the program. Thus, the scheme is useful for program analysis and code improvement.

5. Conclusion

We have shown how to perform type inference for action semantics expressions in a fashion that avoids large constraint sets and constraints on record types for record union and concatenation operations. We have implemented the type inference algorithm as well as an interpreter for action semantics [4].

Although constraints on record types are unnecessary for record union and concatenation, they appear in the typing schemes for the *freeze* and *eval* actions for the declarative facet. (The actions are used to model definition and invocation of statically scoped procedures.) We have extended the type inference algorithm in this paper to handle constraints on records.

The subset of action semantics presented in this paper is appropriate for statically typed languages. Of course, full action semantics can give semantics to dynamically typed languages as well. We model dynamic typing with an additional type called **dynamic** and the subtyping constraint $t \leq$ **dynamic** for all proper functional types t. Type inference with dynamic types has a problem: the "occurs check" [6], which is used to detect that a constraint like $\theta \times int \leq \theta$ is unsatisfiable, can not be relied upon, since $[\theta \mapsto$ **dynamic**$]$ is a satisfiable substitution. The occurs check also fails for type inference on records that can contain as components other records and functions on records. We have extended the type inference algorithm to handle these problems, and we plan to present the results in the near future.

Acknowledgements: David Watt and Peter Mosses contributed many helpful comments, and Tim Ramsey provided word processing expertise.

References

[1] Cardelli, L. A semantics of multiple inheritance. In *LNCS 173: Semantics of Data Types*, G. Kahn, et. al., eds., Springer, Berlin, 1984, pp. 51-68.

[2] Cardelli, L., and Mitchell, J. Records and subtypes. Proc. of 5th Conf. on Mathematical Foundations of Programming Semantics, New Orleans, LA, 1989, Springer LNCS, to appear.

[3] Cardelli, L., and Wegner, P. On understanding types, data abstraction, and polymorphism. *Computing Surveys* 17-4 (1985) 471-522.

[4] Even, S. An implementation of action semantics. M.S. report, Computer Science Dept., Iowa State Univ., Ames, Iowa, 1987.

[5] Even, S., and Schmidt, D.A. Category-sorted algebra-based action semantics. Proc. Conf. on Algebraic Methodology and Software Technology, Iowa City, IA, May 1989. To appear in *Theoretical Computer Science*.

[6] Fuh, Y.-C., and Mishra, P. Type inference with subtypes. In *LNCS 300: ESOP '88*, H. Ganzinger, ed., Springer, Berlin, 1988, pp, 94-114.

[7] _____. Polymorphic type inference: closing the theory-practice gap. In *LNCS 351: TAPSOFT 89*, J. Diaz and F. Orejas, eds. Springer, Berlin, 1989.

[8] Jategaonkar, L., and Mitchell, J. ML with extended pattern matching and subtypes. Proc. 1988 ACM Conf. on LISP and Functional Programming, Snowbird, Utah, July 1988, pp. 198-211.

[9] Milner, R. A theory of type polymorphism in programming. *J. of Computer and System Sci.* 17 (1983) 267-310.

[10] Mitchell, J. Coercion and type inference. Proc. 11th ACM Symp. on Prin. of Prog. Lang., Salt Lake City, Utah, 1984, pp. 175-186.

[11] Mosses, P. Abstract semantic algebras! In *Formal Description of Programming Concepts II*, D. Bjoerner, ed., North-Holland, Amsterdam, 1983, pp. 45-72.

[12] ___. A basic abstract semantic algebra. In *LNCS 173: Semantics of data types*, Springer, Berlin, 1984, pp. 87-108.

[13] ___. The modularity of action semantics. To appear in *SDF Benchmark Series in Computational Linguistics- Workshop II*, MIT Press, Cambridge.

[14] ___. Unified algebras and action semantics. In *LNCS 349: STACS89*, B. Monien, R. Cori, eds., Springer, Berlin, 1989.

[15] ___ and Watt, D. The use of action semantics. In *Formal Description of Programming Concepts III*, North-Holland, Amsterdam, 1987.

[16] Ohori, A., and Buneman, P. Type inference in a database programming language. Proc. 1988 ACM Conf. on LISP and Functional Programming, Snowbird, Utah, 1988, pp.174-183.

[17] Remy, Didier. Typechecking records and variants in a natural extension of ML. In *Proc. 16th ACM Symp. on Principles of Prog. Languages*, Austin, Texas, 1989, pp. 77-88.

[18] Reynolds, J. Using category theory to design implicit conversions and generic operators. In *LNCS 94: Semantics-Directed Compiler Generation*, N. Jones, ed. Springer, 1980, pp. 211-258.

[19] ___. The essence of Algol. In *Algorithmic Languages*, J. deBakker and J.C. vanVliet, eds., Noth-Holland, Amsterdam, 1981, pp. 345-372.

[20] ___. Semantics as a design tool. Course lecture notes, Computer Science Dept., Carnegie-Mellon Univ., Pittsburgh, PA, 1988.

[21] Robinson, J.A. A machine-oriented logic based on the resolution principle. *J. ACM* 12-1 (1965) 23-41.

[22] Stansifer, R. Type inference with subtypes. Proc. 15th ACM Symp. on Prin. of Prog. Lang., San Diego, CA, 1988, pp. 88-97.

[23] Tofte, M. Operational semantics and polymorphic type inference. Ph.D. thesis, Computer Science Dept., Edinburgh Univ., Edinburgh, Scotland, 1988.

[24] Wand, M. Type inference for record concatenation and multiple inheritance. Proc. 4th Symp. Logic in Computer Science, Asilomar, CA, 1989, IEEE Press.

[25] Watt, D. Executable semantic descriptions. *Software: Practice and Experience*, 16 (1986) 13-43.

[26] ___. An action semantics of standard ML. In *LNCS 298: Mathematical Foundations of Programming Semantics*, M. Main, et. al., eds., Springer, Berlin, 1987, pp. 572-598.

On the Expressive Power of Programming Languages

Matthias Felleisen*
Department of Computer Science
Rice University
Houston, TX 77251-1892

Abstract

The literature on programming languages contains an abundance of informal claims on the relative expressive power of programming languages, but there is no framework for formalizing such statements nor for deriving interesting consequences. As a first step in this direction, we develop a formal notion of expressiveness and investigate its properties. To demonstrate the theory's closeness to published intuitions on expressiveness, we analyze the expressive power of several extensions of functional languages. Based on these results, we believe that our system correctly captures many of the informal ideas on expressiveness, and that it constitutes a good basis for further research in this direction.

1 Comparing Programming Languages

The literature on programming languages contains an abundance of informal claims on the relative expressive power of programming languages and on the expressibility or non-expressibility of programming constructs with respect to programming languages. Unfortunately, programming language theory does not provide a formal framework for specifying and verifying such statements. This lack makes it impossible to draw any firm conclusions from these claims or to use them for an objective comparison of programming languages.

Landin [10] was the first to propose the development of a formal framework for comparing programming languages. He studied the relationship among programming constructs

---

*Supported in part by NSF and Darpa

and began to classify some as "essential" and some as "syntactic sugar." Others, most notably Reynolds [17, 18] and Steele and Sussman [19], followed Landin's example. They informally analyzed the expressiveness of imperative extensions of higher-order functional languages and initiated a study of "core" languages. The crucial idea behind the separation of language features is summarized in the remark of Sussman and Steele [19] that there are simple, "syntactically local" translations into applicative languages for many common programming constructs, but that some, notably escape expressions and assignments, involve complex reformulations of large fractions of programs.

The informal approach of Landin and others suggests that a facility is expressible if every usage instance is replaceable by a behaviorally equivalent instantiation of an expression schema. The two key concepts in this idea are *expression schema* and *behavioral equivalence*. These are well-known and widely studied concepts in programming language theory, and are easily adaptable as the basis of a formal definition of expressibility. A first analysis of this definition shows that it supports many informal judgements in the programming language literature. We therefore believe that it correctly formalizes the informal ideas and that it constitutes a basis for further research.

In the following sections, we propose a formal model of expressibility and expressiveness, investigate some of its properties, and analyze the expressive powers of several extensions of functional languages. First, we introduce our formal framework of expressiveness based on the notion of expressibility. Second, we study the expressiveness of an idealized version of Scheme [20] and verify the informal expressibility claims of Steele and Sussman [19] behind the Scheme language design. Finally, we compare our ideas to the study of definability in mathematical logic and put our work in perspective.

2 A Formal Theory of Expressiveness

Since Landin's informal ideas about essential and non-essential language features form the basis of our formal framework of expressibility, we begin our investigation with some typical and widely accepted examples of "syntactic sugar." Consider a goto-free, Algol-like language that has a **while**-loop construct but lacks a **repeat**-loop. Clearly, few programmers would consider this a loss since the **repeat**-construct is roughly equivalent to the **while**-construct. More precisely, for all statements s and expressions e

(**repeat** s **until** e) *is expressible as* (s; **while** $\neg e$ **do** s).

When an instance of the *expressed* (left-hand) side is needed, the appropriate instantiation of the *expressing* (right-hand) side will perform the same operations. Moreover, a *simple* preprocessor could translate a program with **repeat**-statements into a program with the equivalent **while**-programs.

In a dynamically-typed, functional language the **let**-expression is another prototypical example of "syntactic sugar." If a functional language has first-class procedures, the lexical declaration of a variable binding in the form of a **let**-expression is an abbreviation of the immediate application of an anonymous procedure to the initial value:

(**let** x **be** v **in** e) *is expressible as* (**apply** (**procedure** x e) v).

Similarly, functional languages can also realize if-expressions and the truth values through functional combinators [1:133]. In a *lazy* setting, selector procedures can express

$$\textbf{true } as \textbf{ (procedure } (x\ y)\ x),$$

$$\textbf{false } as \textbf{ (procedure } (x\ y)\ y),$$

and, based on this, an if-construct as an application of the test expression to the two branches:

$$(\textbf{if } tst\ thn\ els)\ is\ expressible\ as\ (\textbf{apply } tst\ thn\ els).$$

Although the let- and if-examples are similar, they also reveal some of the typical vagueness in informal expressibility claims. For practical purposes, the implementations of if, true, and false suffice. If a program produces an answer, it is possible to replace the *expressed* phrases with the *expressing* construction without effect on the final result. But, if the subexpression *tst* of an if-expression does not evaluate to a boolean value, a built-in if-construct may signal an error or diverge whereas the *expressing* phrases may return a proper value. In short, the *expressing* phrases may yield results in more situations than the built-in, *expressed* constructs. Still, both expressibility statements are widely accepted claims and deserve consideration.

The essence of simple statements about "syntactic sugar" relationships is a set of three formal properties. First, the *expressing* phrase is only constructed with facilities in a restricted sublanguage. Second, it is constructed without analysis of the subphrases of the *expressed* phrase. Third, replacing the instances of an *expressed* phrase in a program by the corresponding instances of the *expressing* phrases has no effect on the behavior of terminating programs, but may transform a previously diverging program into a converging one. A formal framework of expressibility must account for these ideas with precise definitions.

For our purposes, a programming language is a set of syntactic phrases with a semantics. A program is a phrase whose behavior we can observe by submitting it to an evaluator, which may or may not produce an answer for a given program.

Definition 2.1. (*Programming Language*) A *programming language* $\mathcal{L}$ consists of

- a set of $\mathcal{L}$-phrases, which is a set of freely generated abstract syntax trees (or *terms*), based on a possibly infinite number of function symbols $\mathsf{F}, \mathsf{F}_1, \ldots$ with arity $a, a_1, \ldots$;

- a set of $\mathcal{L}$-programs, which is a non-empty subset of the set of phrases; and

- an operational semantics, which is a partial computable function, $eval_{\mathcal{L}}$, from the set of $\mathcal{L}$-programs to an unspecified set of $\mathcal{L}$-answers:

$$eval_{\mathcal{L}} : \mathcal{L}\text{-programs} \rightarrow \mathcal{L}\text{-answers}.$$

The function symbols, including the 0-ary symbols, are referred to as *programming constructs* or *facilities*.

Note. The set of phrases is (the universe of) a *many-sorted*, freely generated term algebra. For simplicity, we ignore the many-sortedness of the abstract syntax. Moreover, in our examples we often use concrete syntax for readability. ∎

Our prototypical example of a programming language is based on the language Λ of the pure λ-calculus [1]. In order to compare the expressiveness of call-by-value and call-by-name procedures later in this section, we extend Λ with a new constructor, λ_v, and rename λ to λ_n. That is, the phrases are generated from a set of variables $\{x, y, z, \ldots\}$ (0-ary constructors) and three binary constructors: $\lambda_v : variable \times term \longrightarrow term$ (call-by-value abstraction), $\lambda_n : variable \times term \longrightarrow term$ (call-by-name abstraction) and $\cdot : term \times term \longrightarrow term$ (juxtaposition):

$$e ::= x \mid (\lambda_v x.e) \mid (\lambda_n x.e) \mid (ee)$$

where e ranges over terms and x over variables. The constructors λ_v and λ_n bind their variable arguments in their term arguments; if all variables in a Λ-term are bound, we say the term is closed. The set of Λ-programs is the set of closed terms. Λ-answers are λ-abstractions; we also refer to them as Λ-*values* and let v range over this set. We adopt the usual λ-calculus conventions about the concrete syntax of Λ-terms [1].

The operational semantics of Λ is based on the β- and β_v-reduction schemas and the standard reduction function [1, 16]. The reduction schemas denote relations on the term language. Their definitions are as follows:[1]

$$(\lambda_n x.e)e' \longrightarrow e[x/e'] \qquad (e' \text{ is arbitrary}) \qquad (\beta)$$

$$(\lambda_v x.e)v \longrightarrow e[x/v] \qquad (v \text{ is a value}). \qquad (\beta_v)$$

An evaluation proceeds by reducing the leftmost-outermost occurrences of reducible expressions (redexes) outside of abstractions until no more such redexes exist. More precisely, if the tree is a redex, the redex is contracted and the evaluation process starts over with the new program. Otherwise, if the left part of the application is a call-by-value abstraction, the search for a redex continues with the right part; if it is not, it concentrates on the left part. The evaluation process terminates after producing an answer, i.e., an abstraction. By summarizing the standard reduction process into a function from Λ-programs to Λ-answers, we obtain the operational evaluation function.

A sublanguage is a programming language without certain programming constructs. The programs in the sublanguage must have the same behavior as in the full language.

Definition 2.2. (*Sublanguage*) A programming language $\mathcal{L} \setminus \{F_1, \ldots, F_n\}$ is a *sublanguage* of a language $\mathcal{L}$ if

- the F_i's are constructors of $\mathcal{L}$'s phrase language,

---

[1]$e_1[x/e_2]$ is e_1 with all free x substituted by e_2, possibly with some of the bound variables in e_1 renamed to avoid name clashes. More formally, for the definition of the operational semantics we consider the quotient of Λ under α-equivalence.

- the set of $\mathcal{L} \setminus \{F_1, \ldots, F_n\}$-phrases is the subset of $\mathcal{L}$-phrases that do not contain any constructs in $\{F_1, \ldots, F_n\}$,

- the set of $\mathcal{L} \setminus \{F_1, \ldots, F_n\}$-programs is the subset of $\mathcal{L}$-programs that do not contain any constructs in $\{F_1, \ldots, F_n\}$, and

- the semantics of $\mathcal{L} \setminus \{F_1, \ldots, F_n\}$ is a restriction of $\mathcal{L}$'s semantics, i.e., for all $\mathcal{L} \setminus \{F_1, \ldots, F_n\}$-programs e, $eval_{\mathcal{L}\setminus\{F_1,\ldots,F_n\}}(e) = eval_{\mathcal{L}}(e)$.

We sometimes refer to $\mathcal{L}$ as a *language extension* of $\mathcal{L} \setminus \{F_1, \ldots, F_n\}$.

Every language is obviously a sublanguage of itself. In our running example, the sublanguage Λ_n is Λ without λ_v-abstractions, Λ_v is Λ without call-by-name abstractions:

$$\Lambda_n = \Lambda \setminus \lambda_v; \quad \Lambda_v = \Lambda \setminus \lambda_n.$$

A restriction of the above evaluation process to Λ_v-terms and Λ_n-terms yields call-by-value and call-by-name semantics, respectively.

Next we can turn to the relationship between *expressed* and *expressing* phrases in an "is expressible as"-relation. The syntactic aspect of the relationship is that the abbreviated expression is only generated from a restricted set of syntactic constructors, and that the translations of the subexpressions of the *expressed* phrase occur as subexpressions of the *expressing* phrase. The restriction of a language to a sublanguage takes care of the former condition; the latter condition is satisfiable by considering *parameterized* phrases, i.e., phrases containing meta-variables, and instantiations of such phrases.

Definition 2.3. (*Syntactic Abstraction*) The set of *syntactic abstractions* over a programming language $\mathcal{L}$ is the set of freely generated trees based on $\mathcal{L}$'s constructors and an infinite number of additional 0-ary constructors called *meta-variables* $(\alpha, \alpha_1, \ldots)$. We denote syntactic abstractions with $M(\alpha_1, \ldots, \alpha_n)$. If $M(\alpha_1, \ldots, \alpha_n)$ is a syntactic abstraction and $e_1, \ldots, e_n$ are phrases in $\mathcal{L}$, then the *instance* $M(e_1, \ldots, e_n)$ is a phrase in $\mathcal{L}$ that is like $M(\alpha_1, \ldots, \alpha_n)$ except at occurrences of α_i where it contains the phrase e_i:

- if $M(\alpha_1, \ldots, \alpha_n) = \alpha_i$ then $M(e_1, \ldots, e_n) = e_i$, and

- if $M(\alpha_1, \ldots, \alpha_n) = F(M_1(\alpha_1, \ldots, \alpha_n), \ldots, M_a(\alpha_1, \ldots, \alpha_n))$ for some F with arity a then $M(e_1, \ldots, e_n) = F(M_1(e_1, \ldots, e_n), \ldots, M_a(e_1, \ldots, e_n))$.

Note. Algebraically a syntactic abstraction $M(\alpha_1, \ldots, \alpha_n)$ is a (sorted) *polynomial* over the free term algebra with the variables $\alpha_1, \ldots, \alpha_n$. An instantiation of a syntactic extension is an application of the function to appropriate arguments. In the terminology of equational algebraic specifications, syntactic abstractions are known as *derived operators* [6]. In Lisp-like languages, syntactic abstractions are realized as *macros* [9]; logical frameworks know them as *notational abbreviations* [7]. ∎

In the framework of our example language Λ,

$$M(\alpha_1, \alpha_2, \alpha_3) = (\lambda_n \alpha_1 . \alpha_2)\alpha_3$$

is a syntactic abstraction over Λ. The expression $(\lambda_n x.x)y$ is the instance $M(x, x, y)$.

The semantic aspect of the relationship between *expressed* and *expressing* phrases is that the replacement of the former by the latter in arbitrary programs has no effect on the program behavior. To capture this idea, we need to formalize an expansion of a program from a language into a sublanguage according to a set of syntactic abstractions.

Definition 2.4. (*Syntactic Expansion*) Let $\mathcal{L}' = \mathcal{L} \setminus \{F_1, \ldots, F_n\}$ be a sublanguage of $\mathcal{L}$. A *syntactic environment* ρ (over $\mathcal{L}'$ for $\mathcal{L}$) is a finite map from the syntactic constructors $F_1, \ldots, F_n$ to syntactic abstractions. A *syntactic expansion* $[\![\cdot]\!]_\rho$ from $\mathcal{L}$ to $\mathcal{L}'$ relative to the syntactic environment ρ maps $\mathcal{L}$-phrases to $\mathcal{L}'$-phrases as follows:

- if $F \notin Dom(\rho)$ then $[\![F(e_1, \ldots, e_a)]\!]_\rho = F([\![e_1]\!]_\rho, \ldots, [\![e_a]\!]_\rho)$

- if $\rho(F) = M(\alpha_1, \ldots, \alpha_a)$ then $[\![F(e_1, \ldots, e_a)]\!]_\rho = M([\![e_1]\!]_\rho, \ldots, [\![e_a]\!]_\rho)$.

At this point, everything is in place for the definition of a formal notion of expressibility. A language can express a set of constructs if there are syntactic abstractions that can replace occurrences of the old constructs without effect on the program's behavior. Given this, we must only agree on the behavioral characteristics of programs that we would like to observe. In order to avoid overly restrictive assumptions about the set of programming languages, we follow a minimalistic approach and observe the termination behavior of programs.[2]

Definition 2.5. (*Expressibility*) Let $\mathcal{L} \setminus \{F_1, \ldots, F_n\}$ be a sublanguage of $\mathcal{L}$ and let $\mathcal{L}$ be a sublanguage of $\mathcal{L}'$. The programming language $\mathcal{L} \setminus \{F_1, \ldots, F_n\}$ *can express the syntactic facilities* $\{F_1, \ldots, F_n\}$ *with respect to* $\mathcal{L}'$ if for every F_j there is a syntactic abstraction M_j such that for all $\mathcal{L}$-programs p,

$$eval_{\mathcal{L}}(p) \text{ is defined if and only if } eval_{\mathcal{L}}([\![p]\!]_\rho) \text{ is defined}$$

where $\rho = \{(F_j, M_j) \mid 1 \leq j \leq n\}$.

$\mathcal{L} \setminus \{F_1, \ldots, F_n\}$ can **weakly** express the syntactic facilities F_j with respect to $\mathcal{L}'$ if there are syntactic abstractions M_j such that for all $\mathcal{L}$-programs p,

$$eval_{\mathcal{L}}(p) \text{ is defined implies } eval_{\mathcal{L}}([\![p]\!]_\rho) \text{ is defined}$$

where $\rho = \{(F_j, M_j) \mid 1 \leq j \leq n\}$.

The qualifying clause "with respect to" is omitted whenever the language universe is obvious from the context. If $\mathcal{L} \setminus \{F_1, \ldots, F_n\}$ can express F because of the syntactic abstraction M, we sometimes say that M expresses F when $\mathcal{L} \setminus \{F_1, \ldots, F_n\}$ and $\mathcal{L}'$ are understood.

The terminology "weakly expressible" reflects our belief that *any* differences in behavior should be noted as a failure of complete expressibility. The definition is also consistent with the fact that expressibility implies weak expressibility.

---

[2]This restriction only excludes *total* programming languages from further consideration. But, by omitting any references to the characteristics of results, it is possible to consider a broad variety of programming languages, e.g., languages with or without basic, observable data.

Proposition 2.6 *If $\mathcal{L}$ can express* F, *then* $\mathcal{L}$ *can* **weakly** *express* F.

An alternative understanding of the expressibility relation is that the *expressing* phrase and the *expressed* phrase are interchangeable *in all programs*. This relation between phrases is widely studied in semantics and is known as *operational* or *observational equivalence* [12, 15, 16]. For a formal definition of this relation, we must first establish the auxiliary notion of a context.

Definition 2.7. (*Context*) An $\mathcal{L}$-*program context for a phrase e* is a unary syntactic abstraction, $C(\alpha)$, such that $C(e)$ is an $\mathcal{L}$-program.

The syntactic abstraction

$$C_0(\alpha) = (\lambda_n xy.\alpha)(\lambda_n x.x)\Omega, \text{ where } \Omega = (\lambda_n x.xx)(\lambda_n x.xx)$$

is a program context for all expressions whose free variables are among x and y.

In order to establish a relation to the above definition of expressibility, our definition of operational equivalence only compares the termination behavior of programs.

Definition 2.8. (*Operational Equivalence*) Let $\mathcal{L}$ be a programming language and let $eval_{\mathcal{L}}$ be its operational semantics. The $\mathcal{L}$-terms e_1 and e_2 are *operationally equivalent*, $e_1 \cong_{\mathcal{L}} e_2$, if there are $\mathcal{L}$-program contexts for both e_1 and e_2, and if for all such contexts $C(\alpha)$, $eval_{\mathcal{L}}$ is defined on $C(e_2)$ if and only if it is defined on $C(e_1)$.

With the above program context C_0, it is possible, for example, to differentiate the phrases x and y. Since Ω diverges, the program $C_0(x) = (\lambda_n xy.x)(\lambda_n x.x)\Omega$ terminates whereas $C_0(y) = (\lambda_n xy.y)(\lambda_n x.x)\Omega$ diverges.

Based on the idea that an expressing phrase must be operationally equivalent to an expressed phrase, we can now establish our first major meta-theorem on expressibility: If a programming construct fundamentally alters the operational equivalence relation of the extended language, it is impossible to express the additional construct in the restricted sublanguage.

Theorem 2.9 *Let* $\mathcal{L}_0 = \mathcal{L}_1 \setminus \{F_1, \ldots, F_n\}$ *be a sublanguage of* $\mathcal{L}_1$, *and let* $\mathcal{L}_1$ *be a sublanguage of* $\mathcal{L}$. *Let* $\cong_0$ *and* $\cong_1$ *be the operational equivalence relations, respectively.*

(*i*) *If the operational equivalence relation of* $\mathcal{L}_1$ *does not conservatively extend the operational equivalence relation of* $\mathcal{L}_0$, *i.e.,* $\cong_0 \not\subseteq \cong_1$, *then* $\mathcal{L}_0$ *cannot express the facilities* $F_1, \ldots, F_n$ *with respect to* $\mathcal{L}$.

(*ii*) *The converse of* (*i*) *does not hold. That is, there are cases where* $\mathcal{L}_0$ *cannot express a facility* F *even though the operational equivalence relation of* $\mathcal{L}_1$ *is a conservative extension of the operational equivalence relation of* $\mathcal{L}_0$, *i.e.* $\cong_0 \subseteq \cong_1$.

Proof. (*i*) The non-conservativeness of the extension implies that there are two terms e and e' in $\mathcal{L}_0$ such that $e \cong_0 e'$ but $e \not\cong_1 e'$. Given the theorem's assumption, the operational equivalence relation for $\mathcal{L}_1$ can only distinguish e from e' through a context built with some $F \in \{F_1, \ldots, F_n\}$. To prove this auxiliary claim, assume the contrary. Then there is a program context $C(\alpha)$ for e and e' over $\mathcal{L}_1$ such that $C(\alpha)$ does not contain any constructors in $\{F_1, \ldots, F_n\}$, and such that (without loss of generality) $eval_1$ produces an answer for $C(e)$ but not for $C(e')$. Since neither e nor e' nor C contain any constructor in $\{F_1, \ldots, F_n\}$, $C(e)$ and $C(e')$ are $\mathcal{L}_0$-programs. By the definition of a sublanguage, $eval_0(C(e))$ is defined because $eval_1(C(e))$ is defined and $eval_0(C(e'))$ is undefined because $eval_1(C(e'))$ is undefined. Consequently, $eval_0$ is defined on $C(e)$ but not on $C(e')$, which contradicts the assumption that $e \cong_0 e'$. We have thus proved the auxiliary claim.

Now, assume contrary to the claim in the theorem that $\mathcal{L}_0$ can express $F_1, \ldots, F_n$. Hence, there is a syntactic environment ρ that maps each F_i to some syntactic abstraction M_i. Let $C(\alpha)$ be a context over $\mathcal{L}_1$ that can differentiate the two terms e and e' based on some $F, \ldots \in \{F_1, \ldots, F_n\}$. Let us say that $eval_1$ produces an answer for $C(e)$ but not for $C(e')$. By the definition of expressibility, $C(e)$ and $C(e')$ have counterparts in $\mathcal{L}_0$, $p = [\![C(e)]\!]_\rho$ and $p' = [\![C(e')]\!]_\rho$, that have the same termination behavior:

$$eval_1(p) \text{ is defined because } eval_1(C(e)) \text{ is defined}$$

and

$$eval_1(p') \text{ is undefined because } eval_1(C(e')) \text{ is undefined.}$$

By construction, the programs p and p' can only differ in a finite number of occurrences of e and e', respectively. From this fact and the assumption that $e \cong_0 e'$, we can immediately derive that p and p' have the same termination behavior in $\mathcal{L}_0$, i.e.,

$$eval_0(p) \text{ is defined if and only if } eval_0(p') \text{ is defined.}$$

But this implies that

$$eval_1(p) \text{ is defined if and only if } eval_1(p') \text{ is defined}$$

because $\mathcal{L}_0$ is a sublanguage of $\mathcal{L}_1$. Since this conclusion contradicts the above fact that p converges and p' diverges, we have proved our claim.

(ii) A simple example can be constructed by merging two disjoint languages such that a program in the combined language is either in one or the other language. The extension of the operational equivalence relation is conservative and the features in the added language are in general not expressible.

One particular example of this kind is the simply typed λ-calculus, whose types are either base types or arrow types. Because of the type system, it is impossible to define the typical *cons*, *car*, and *cdr* functions for pairs of elements of arbitrary types. Hence this simply-typed language cannot express these pairing functions. On the other hand, also due to the type system of the language, the new functions cannot be bound to free variables in phrases of the sublanguage, which implies that the pairing functions cannot be used to distinguish phrases in the simply typed language. It follows that pairing type constructors and functions increase the expressive power without destroying operational equivalences of the underlying language. ∎

Based on this first meta-theorem on expressibility, we can now easily show that the sublanguage Λ_v is not strong enough to express call-by-name abstraction, and that Λ_n is not strong enough to express call-by-value abstraction. However, Λ_n can **weakly** express λ_v since call-by-name abstractions are applicable to both proper values and undefined expressions.

Proposition 2.10 Λ *extends both* Λ_v *and* Λ_n.

(*i*) Λ_v *cannot express* λ_n *with respect to* Λ.

(*ii*) Λ_n *cannot express* λ_v *with respect to* Λ.

(*iii*) Λ_n *can* **weakly** *express* λ_v *with respect to* Λ.

Proof. (*i*) Consider the expressions $\lambda_v f.f(\lambda_v x.x)\Omega$ and $\lambda_v f.\Omega$ where Ω is the call-by-value variant of our prototypical infinite loop. In the pure call-by-value setting, the two are operationally equivalent

$$\lambda_v f.f(\lambda_v x.x)\Omega \cong_{\Lambda_v} \lambda_v f.\Omega.$$

Both abstractions are values; upon application to an arbitrary value, both of them diverge. But, in the extended language Λ, we can differentiate the two with the context

$$C(\alpha) = \alpha(\lambda_v x.(\lambda_n y.x)).$$

The context applies a phrase to a function that returns the value of the first argument after absorbing the second argument without evaluating it. Hence, $C(\lambda_v f.f(\lambda_v x.x)\Omega)$ terminates while $C(\lambda_v f.\Omega)$ diverges, and the extension of Λ_v to Λ is non-conservative with respect to operational equivalence. By Theorem 2.9, λ_n is not expressible.

(*ii*) There are two proofs for part (*ii*). The first is another application of the preceding meta-theorem and is derived from a closely related theorem by Ong [13: Thm. 4.1.1].[3] The second—related to but discovered independently of the first—provides some operational understanding for the reasons why Λ_n cannot express λ_v-abstractions. We only present the second one.

A simple consequence of the operational semantics for Λ_n is that a subterm e of a program $C(e)$ can only affect the evaluation if it occurs in a leftmost-outermost position in some term of the evaluation sequence, *i.e.*,

$$C(e) \longrightarrow^* eq_1 \ldots q_n,$$

for some arbitrary $q_1, \ldots, q_n$, $n \geq 0$ [15]. When this happens, we say the term becomes *active*.

Suppose a syntactic abstraction $S(x, e_1)$ over Λ_n could express $\lambda_v x.e_1$. To show that this is impossible, we prove that $S(x, e_1)e_2$ cannot be operationally equivalent to $(\lambda_v x.e_1)e_2$

---

[3]Gordon Plotkin pointed out Abramsky's and Ong's work on the lazy λ-calculus, which provided the ideas for the first proof and corrected a mistake in an early draft of this report.

for arbitrary e_1 and e_2. Clearly, $\mathbf{S}(x, e_1)$ must be a value (or must reduce to a value). Let $\lambda_n y.p$ be this value. It follows that

$$\mathbf{S}(x, e_1)e_2 \longrightarrow^* (\lambda_n y.p)e_2 \longrightarrow p[y/e_2].$$

Since $\mathbf{S}$ is defined without knowledge of e_1 and e_2, the evaluation of $p[y/e_2]$ proceeds independently of e_2 until e_2 becomes active. Consequently, we must distinguish two cases. First, the evaluation of $p[y/e_2]$ may never activate e_2. This is impossible because e_2 in the call-by-value program is evaluated and can thus cause divergence. Second, the evaluation of $p[y/e_2]$ activates e_2 for a first time, that is,

$$p[y/e_2] \longrightarrow^* e_2 q_1 \ldots q_n.$$

Since the evaluation was thus far independent of e_2, e_2 is arbitrary and must hold for an arbitrary choice. So, let

$$e_2 = \mathbf{YK} = (\lambda_n f.(\lambda_n x.f(xx))(\lambda_n x.f(xx)))(\lambda_n xy.x).$$

But then the reduction sequence for the expression $\mathbf{S}(x, e_1)e_2$ ends in

$$\mathbf{YK} q_1 \ldots q_n \longrightarrow^+ \lambda_n d.\mathbf{YK},$$

which is independent of whether x is free in e_1 or not. If x is not free in e_1, however, the program $(\lambda_v x.e_1)(\mathbf{YK})$ reduces to the evaluation of e_1:

$$(\lambda_v x.e_1)(\mathbf{YK}) \longrightarrow (\lambda_v x.e_1)(\lambda_n d.(\mathbf{YK})) \longrightarrow e_1.$$

Substituting the diverging term Ω for e_1 leads to the desired contradiction. Since there are no other cases, this proves the second claim.

(*iii*) Clearly, $\lambda_v x.e$ operationally approximates $\lambda_n x.e$ and, hence, $\mathbf{M} = \lambda_n \alpha_1.\alpha_2$ can weakly express λ_v . ∎

Proposition 2.10 provides two examples of pairs of *universal* programming languages that we can differentiate according to our expressiveness criterion. The third part of this proposition also shows that the above meta-theorem on expressibility does *not* carry over to weak expressibility. Even in the case of a language extension that is non-conservative with respect to the operational equivalence or approximation relation, the restricted language may already be able to express the new facilities in a weak sense. Call-by-value procedures and Λ_n provide the prototypical example.

Theorem 2.9 (cont'd) *Let* $\mathcal{L}_0$, $\mathcal{L}_1$, $\cong_0$ *and* $\cong_1$ *be as above.*

(*iii*) *Part* (*i*) *does not hold for* **weak** *expressibility. That is, there are cases where* $\mathcal{L}_0$ *can* **weakly** *express* $\mathsf{F}_1, \ldots, \mathsf{F}_n$ *relative to* $\mathcal{L}_1$ *even though the extended operational approximation relation does not subsume the restricted one, i.e.,* $\cong_0 \not\subseteq \cong_1$.

The definition of an expressibility relationship also leads to a natural measure of expressive power between programming languages. A programming language is less expressive than another if the latter can express all the facilities the former can express in a given language universe.

Definition 2.11. (*Expressiveness*) Let $\mathcal{L}_0$ and $\mathcal{L}_1$ be sublanguages of $\mathcal{L}$. The language $\mathcal{L}_0$ *is less expressive than* $\mathcal{L}_1$ *with respect to* $\mathcal{L}$ if $\mathcal{L}_1$ can express all sets of facilities with respect to $\mathcal{L}$ that $\mathcal{L}_0$ can express with respect to $\mathcal{L}$.

Expressiveness is a pre-order on sublanguages in a given language framework.

Theorem 2.12 *The less-expressive-than relation is a pre-order in its first two arguments.*

(*i*) $\mathcal{L}_0$ *is less expressive than* $\mathcal{L}_0$ *with respect to to* $\mathcal{L}$.

(*ii*) *If* $\mathcal{L}_0$ *is less expressive than* $\mathcal{L}_1$ *with respect to* $\mathcal{L}$ *and* $\mathcal{L}_1$ *is less expressive than* $\mathcal{L}_2$ *with respect to* $\mathcal{L}$, *then* $\mathcal{L}_0$ *is less expressive than* $\mathcal{L}_2$ *with respect to* $\mathcal{L}$.

Based on the definitions of expressibility and expressiveness, we can now analyze the expressiveness hierarchy in more practical languages. In the next section, we study an idealized version of Scheme as a concrete example of this kind, thus providing further insight into our general framework.

Syntax

$$
\begin{array}{llll}
v & ::= & 0 \mid 1 \mid -1 \mid 2 \mid -2 \mid \ldots & \text{(numerals)} \\
  &   & \mid \text{zero?} \mid \text{add}_1 \mid \text{sub}_1 \mid + \mid - & \text{(numeric functions)} \\
  &   & \mid (\textbf{lambda}\ (x \ldots)\ e) & \text{(abstractions)} \\
e & ::= & v & \text{(values)} \\
  &   & \mid x & \text{(variables)} \\
  &   & \mid (e\ e \ldots) & \text{(applications)}
\end{array}
$$

Semantics

$$
(f a \ldots) \longrightarrow \delta(f, a, \ldots) \quad \text{for zero?}, \text{add}_1, \ldots
$$
$$
((\textbf{lambda}\ (x_1 \ldots x_n)\ e)\ v_1 \ldots v_n) \longrightarrow e[x_1/v_1] \ldots [x_n/v_n]
$$

Constant Interpretation

$$
\begin{array}{lllll}
\delta(\text{add}_1, n) & = & n+1 & \delta(+, n, m) & = & n+m & \delta(\text{zero?}, 0) & = & (\textbf{lambda}\ (x\ y)\ x) \\
\delta(\text{sub}_1, n) & = & n-1 & \delta(-, n, m) & = & n-m & \delta(\text{zero?}, n) & = & (\textbf{lambda}\ (x\ y)\ y) \\
& & & & & & & & \text{for } n \neq 0
\end{array}
$$

FIGURE 1: *Pure Scheme*

---

3 The Structure of *Idealized Scheme*

Pure Scheme [3, 4, 5] is an extension of the simple call-by-value language Λ_v that includes multi-ary procedures and algebraic constants. There are basic constants and functional constants; the latter operate on constants and closed abstractions. We assume that the semantics of constants is given through an interpretation δ from functional constants and closed values to closed values. Typically, the constants include integers, characters, booleans, and some appropriate functions. Initially, we only include integers and a minimal set of functions. Figure 1 contains the complete specification of *Pure Scheme*. The semantics is given via reduction rules, which are applied in the standard reduction order defined in the preceding section; the extended evaluation function is undefined for a program when the evaluation of the program gets stuck because of the application of a constant symbol to a λ-expression, the application of a numeral to a value, or the application of a constant function to a value for which δ is undefined.

The main characteristic of *Idealized Scheme* is the extension of the functional core language *Pure Scheme* with imperative facilities and type predicates:

- predicate constants for determining the type of a value,

- branching expressions for the local manipulation of control,

- control expressions for the non-local manipulation of control, and

- assignment statements for the manipulation of state variables.

The extensions are motivated by the belief that imperative facilities and type predicates add to the expressive power of the language [19, 20]. In this section, we demonstrate how to formulate these beliefs in our formal expressiveness framework and how to relate the extensions to the core language.

The addition of type predicates to *Pure Scheme* is simple. For extending *Pure Scheme* with a predicate like int?, it suffices to extend the interpretation function δ with the clauses

$$\delta(\text{int?}, n) = (\text{lambda } (x\ y)\ x)$$
$$\delta(\text{int?}, (\text{lambda } (x \ldots)\ e)) = (\text{lambda } (x\ y)\ y)$$

We refer to the extended language as $PS(\text{int?})$. With int?, programs in the extended language can now effectively test the type of a value, which is impossible in *Pure Scheme*.

Theorem 3.1 *Pure Scheme cannot express* int? *with respect to* $PS(\text{int?})$.

Proof Sketch. The claim is another consequence of Theorem 2.9. In *Pure Scheme*, we have:

$$\begin{array}{l}
(((p\ 1)\ (\text{lambda } () \\
\quad (((p\ (\text{lambda } ()\ \Omega)) \\
\quad\quad (\text{lambda } ()\ 2) \\
\quad\quad (\text{lambda } () \\
\quad\quad\quad (((p\ 2) \\
\quad\quad\quad\quad (\text{lambda } ()\ 1) \\
\quad\quad\quad\quad (\text{lambda } ()\ \Omega))))))) \\
\quad (\text{lambda } ()\ \Omega)))
\end{array}
\cong_{ps}
\begin{array}{l}
(((p\ 1)\ (\text{lambda } () \\
\quad (((p\ (\text{lambda } ()\ \Omega)) \\
\quad\quad (\text{lambda } ()\ 2) \\
\quad\quad (\text{lambda } ()\ \Omega)))) \\
\quad (\text{lambda } ()\ \Omega)))
\end{array}$$

In the extended language, however, p could be bound to the predicate int?, which would distinguish the two expressions operationally. ∎

The programming language world knows two types of local branching statements for languages like *Pure Scheme*: the truth-value based if-construct and the Lisp-style if-construct that distinguishes one special value from all others. The semantics of the former relies on the presence of two distinct values: true and false, or 0 and 1. The following two reduction rules characterize the behavior of truth-value based if:

$$(\text{if } 0 \; e_t \; e_f) \longrightarrow e_t \qquad\qquad (\text{if.true})$$

$$(\text{if } 1 \; e_t \; e_f) \longrightarrow e_f. \qquad\qquad (\text{if.false})$$

If the test value in an if-expression is neither 0 nor 1, the evaluation of the program is undefined. We refer to the extended language as $PS(\text{if})$.

Clearly, *Pure Scheme* can express such a simple if.

Theorem 3.2 *Pure Scheme can express truth-value based* if *with respect to* $PS(\text{if})$.

Proof Sketch. Consider the syntactic abstraction:

$$(\text{if } e \; e_1 \; e_2) \;=\; (((\text{zero? } e)$$
$$\qquad\qquad (\text{lambda } () \; e_1)$$
$$\qquad\qquad (\text{lambda } () \; (((\text{zero? } (\text{sub}_1 \; e)) \; (\text{lambda } () \; e_2) \; (\text{lambda } () \; \Omega))))))$$

It is easy to show that this abstraction is operationally equivalent to if. ∎

Note. (i) The trick of *freezing* the evaluation of expressions through vacuous **lambda**-abstraction was already known to Landin and Burge [10], but, clearly, it is impossible to express typed if without 0-ary abstraction in a call-by-value framework.

(ii) The preceding theorem crucially depends on the specification that values other than 0 and 1 in the test position of the if construct render the program undefined. ∎

The Lisp-style if assumes that there is *one* distinct value for *false*, in Lisp usually called nil, and *all other values* represent *true*. With 0 serving as nil, the reduction rules differ accordingly from (if.true) and (if.false):

$$(\text{if } v \; e_t \; e_f) \longrightarrow e_t \text{ for } v \neq 0 \qquad\qquad (\text{if.v})$$

$$(\text{if } 0 \; e_t \; e_f) \longrightarrow e_f. \qquad\qquad (\text{if.nil})$$

Theorem 3.2 (cont'd) *Pure Scheme cannot express* if *with respect to* $PS(\text{Lisp-if})$.

Proof Sketch. Obviously Lisp-style if is equivalent—in our formal sense—to the addition of a **total** functional constant null? for distinguishing 0 from all other values. By Theorem 3.1 it follows that Lisp-if is not expressible. ∎

A more interesting question about expressiveness arises in the context of non-local control abstractions. *Idealized Scheme* has the operation call-with-current-continuation, abbreviated **call/cc**, which applies its sub-expression to an abstraction of the current control state. In analogy to denotational semantics, the Scheme-terminology for this abstraction is *continuation*. Figure 2 specifies the syntax and a simple reduction semantics of $PS(\textbf{call/cc})$, an extended version of *Pure Scheme* with this control facility. The reduction semantics forms the basis of a simple equational calculus for **call/cc** and continuations, and permits a simple, algebra-like reasoning in the presence of control operations [4, 5].

Additional Syntax

$$e \ ::= \ \ldots \mid (\textbf{call/cc } e) \qquad (\textit{continuation captures})$$

Evaluation Contexts

$$E ::= \alpha \mid (v\ E) \mid (E\ e)$$

Additional Semantics

$$
\begin{aligned}
E[(\textbf{call/cc } e)] &\longrightarrow (\textbf{call/cc } (\textbf{lambda } (k) \\
&\qquad E[e \ (\textbf{lambda } (x) \ (k \ E[x]))]))) \\
(\textbf{call/cc } (\textbf{lambda } (k) \ E[(k\ e)])) &\longrightarrow (\textbf{call/cc } (\textbf{lambda } (k) \ e)) \\
(\textbf{call/cc } (\textbf{lambda } (k) \ (\textbf{call/cc } e))) &\longrightarrow (\textbf{call/cc } (\textbf{lambda } (k) \ (e \ k))) \\
(\textbf{call/cc } (\textbf{lambda } (k) \ e)) &\longrightarrow e, \text{ if } k \notin e
\end{aligned}
$$

FIGURE 2: *Pure Scheme* with control

Theorem 3.3 *Pure Scheme cannot express* **call/cc** *relative to* $PS(\textbf{call/cc})$.

Proof Sketch. The theorem is a consequence of Theorem 2.9, i.e., the addition of **call/cc** invalidates operational equivalences in the extended language. A typical example[4] is the operational equivalence

$$(\textbf{lambda } (f) \ ((f\ 0)\ \Omega)) \cong_{ps} (\textbf{lambda } (f) \ \Omega).$$

As pointed out in the proof of Proposition 2.10(i), these two procedures are equivalent in a functional setting because both diverge when applied to a value. When we add **call/cc**, however, we can construct the context $(\textbf{call/cc } \alpha)$, which can differentiate between the two expressions. Whereas the composition of the first expression with this context evaluates to 0:

$$(\textbf{call/cc } (\textbf{lambda } (f) \ ((f\ 0)\ \Omega))) = (\textbf{call/cc } (\textbf{lambda } (f) \ 0)) = 0$$

the second expression diverges in the same context:

$$(\textbf{call/cc } (\textbf{lambda } (f) \ \Omega)) = \Omega. \qquad \blacksquare$$

The final addition to *Pure Scheme* is the **set!**-construct, Scheme's form of assignment statement. Like in a traditional Algol-like programming language, the **set!**-expression destructively alters a binding of an identifier to a value. A simple reduction semantics for $PS(\textbf{set!})$, *Pure Scheme* with **set!** and **letrec** (for recursive declarations of assignable variables with initial values), is given in Figure 3. Again, this semantics is the basis for an equational calculus for reasoning about operational equivalences in $PS(\textbf{set!})$ [3, 4].

---

[4]This example is a folklore example in the theoretical "continuation" community, but it was also used by Meyer and Riecke to argue the "unreasonableness" of continuations [11].

Additional Syntax

$$e ::= \ldots \mid (\textbf{set!}\ x\ e) \qquad\qquad (assignments)$$
$$\mid (\textbf{letrec}\ ([x\ v]\ldots)\ e) \qquad (recursive\ definitions)$$

Evaluation Contexts

$$E ::= \alpha \mid (v\ E) \mid (E\ e) \mid (\textbf{set!}\ x\ E)$$

Additional Semantics

$$((\textbf{lambda}\ (x\ldots)\ e)\ v\ldots) \longrightarrow (\textbf{letrec}\ ([x\ v]\ldots)\ e),\ \text{instead of } \beta_v$$
$$(\textbf{letrec}\ (\ldots[x\ v]\ldots)\ e) \longrightarrow (\textbf{letrec}\ (\ldots[x\ v]\ldots)\ e[x/v])$$
$$\text{if } x \text{ is not assignable in } e$$
$$\text{and doesn't occur in the defined values}$$
$$(\textbf{letrec}\ (\ldots[x\ v]\ldots)\ E[x]) \longrightarrow (\textbf{letrec}\ (\ldots[x\ v]\ldots)\ E[v])$$
$$(\textbf{letrec}\ (\ldots[x\ u]\ldots)\ E[\textbf{set!}\ x\ v]) \longrightarrow (\textbf{letrec}\ (\ldots[x\ v]\ldots)\ E[v])$$
$$(\textbf{letrec}\ ([x\ v]\ldots)\ E[(\textbf{letrec}\ ([y\ u]\ldots)\ e)]) \longrightarrow (\textbf{letrec}\ ([x\ v]\ldots[y\ u]\ldots)\ E[e])$$

FIGURE 3: *Pure Scheme* with state

Theorem 3.4 *Pure Scheme cannot express* **set!** *with respect to PS(*set!*).*

Proof Sketch. Consider the expression

$$((\textbf{lambda}\ (d)\ (f\ 0))\ (f\ 0)),$$

which contains the same subexpression twice. Clearly, in a functional language like *Pure Scheme* the two subexpressions $(f\ 0)$ return the same value, if any, and, given that the value of the first subexpression is discarded, the expression is operationally equivalent to

$$(f\ 0).$$

In the extended language, this is no longer true. Consider the context

$$C(\alpha) = (\textbf{letrec}\ (f\ (\textbf{lambda}\ (x)\ (\textbf{set!}\ f\ (\textbf{lambda}\ (x)\ \Omega))))\ \alpha),$$

which declares a procedure f. Upon the first application, the procedure modifies the declaration so that a second invocation leads to divergence. Consequently, an expression with a single use of the function converges, but an expression with two uses diverges. The verification of these claims with the reduction semantics is straightforward. ∎

At this point we do not know whether the above results hold in the framework of weak expressiveness. We conjecture that they carry over but lack a proof of this statement.

4 Related Work

Kleene's study of definitional extensions in mathematical logic [8, 21] is the most closely related work. A formal system S is a definitional extension of a formal system S' if, roughly, the (provable) formulas of S can be translated into (provable) formulas of S' with a map that is homomorphic with respect to the logical operations and the constructors in S'. This is clearly analogous to our notion of expressibility when we replace provability with termination. Thus, the concept of an expressible programming construct directly corresponds to Kleene's notion of eliminable symbols and postulates [8:§74; 21:I.2].

Williams [22] considers a whole spectrum of formalization techniques for semantic conventions in formal systems. His work starts with ideas of applicative and definitional extensions of logics but also considers techniques that are more relevant in computational settings, e.g. compilation and interpretation. The goal of Williams's research is a comparison of the formalization techniques and not a study of the expressiveness of programming languages. Some of his results may be relevant for future extensions of our work.

Comparative schematology was an early but quite different attempt at measuring the relative expressive power of programming languages: see Chandra and Manna's report [2] for an example. Schematology studies programming languages with a fixed operational semantics for a simple set of control constructs, e.g. **while**-loop programs or recursion equations, and with uninterpreted constant and function symbols. In the absence of arithmetic, it is possible to decide certain questions about such uninterpreted program schemas. Moreover, it makes sense to compare the set of functions that are computable when data structures like stacks, arrays, queues, or general equality are added. In the presence of arithmetic, the approach can no longer compare the expressive power of programming languages since everything can be encoded. Also, given that many modern languages contain higher-order (procedural) data for control structure purposes, we find this approach unsuited for the comparison of realistic languages.

A secondary piece of related work is the study of the full abstraction property of mathematical models [13, 15] and the representability of functions in λ-calculi [1]. In many cases, the natural denotational model of a programming language contains too many elements so that operationally equivalent phrases have different mathematical meanings. Since it is relatively easy to reverse-engineer a programming language from a model, the equality relation of models without the full abstraction property directly corresponds to the operational equivalence of a language extension. As a consequence, such models naturally lead to the discovery of non-expressible programming constructs. Still, the study of full abstraction does not provide true insight into the expressive power of languages. On one hand, the discovery of new facilities directly depends on the choice of model. For example, whereas a direct model of Λ_n requires a facility for exploiting deterministic parallelism, a continuation model leads to operations on the continuation of an expression (in addition to parallel constructs). On the other hand, by Theorem 2.9 we also know that a non-conservative extension of the operational equivalence relation is only a *sufficient* but not a *necessary* condition for the non-expressibility of a programming construct. In short, research on full abstraction is a valuable contribution to—see Proposition 2.10—but not a replacement of the study of expressiveness.

5 Towards a Formal Programming Language Design Space

In the preceding sections we have developed a formal framework for comparing the expressive power of programming languages. An analysis of its properties and an application of the framework to an idealized version of Scheme have demonstrated how close the formal notions are to the intuitive ideas in the literature. In particular, we have shown that an increase in expressive power may destroy semantic properties of the core language (Theorem 2.9), but we also conjecture that more expressive languages make programs more concise.

The current framework is only a first step towards a formal programming language design space. The crucial idea behind our development is the restriction of the translation process from an extended language to a smaller language. We believe that there may be an entire spectrum of feasible restrictions that yield interesting, alternative notions of expressiveness, and that these alternatives deserve exploration. Moreover, we have not yet tackled the problem of deriving properties from expressiveness claims but expect to do so in the future. In the long run, we hope that some theory of language expressiveness develops into a formal theory of the programming language design space.

Acknowledgement. Dan Friedman directed my attention to the idea of expressiveness by insisting that an understanding of new programming constructs in terms of procedures or macro implementations is superior to an implementation based on interpreters. Conversations with Bruce Duba and Mitchell Wand clarified my understanding of the problem. Bob Harper pointed out the relationship to logic, which ultimately led to the current formalization. Hans Boehm, Robert Cartwright, Dan Friedman, Robert Hieb, John Lamping, and Mitchell Wand suggested many improvements in the presentation of the material. Finally, comments by members of the POPL'88 committee, and by the anonymous referees of ESOP'90 pointed out weaknesses in previous drafts.

6 References

1. BARENDREGT, H.P. *The Lambda Calculus: Its Syntax and Semantics.* Revised edition. Studies in Logic and the Foundations of Mathematics 103. North-Holland, Amsterdam, 1984.

2. CHANDRA, A.K. AND Z. MANNA. The power of programming features. *Journal of Computer Languages* (Pergamon Press) 1, 1975, 219–232.

3. FELLEISEN, M. AND D.P. FRIEDMAN. A syntactic theory of sequential state. *Theor. Comput. Sci.* 69(3), 1989, 243–287. Preliminary version in: *Proc. 14th ACM Symposium on Principles of Programming Languages,* 1987, 314-325.

4. FELLEISEN, M. AND R. HIEB. The revised report on the syntactic theories of sequential control and state. Technical Report 100, Rice University, June 1989.

5. FELLEISEN, M., D.P. FRIEDMAN, E. KOHLBECKER, AND B. DUBA. A syntactic theory of sequential control. *Theor. Comput. Sci.* 52(3), 1987, 205–237. Preliminary version in: *Proc. Symposium on Logic in Computer Science,* 1986, 131–141.

6. GOGUEN, J., J. THATCHER, AND E. WAGNER. An initial algebra approach to the specification, correctness, and implementation of abstract data types. In *Current Trends in Programming Methodology* IV, edited by R. Yeh. Prentice-Hall, Englewood Cliffs, New Jersey, 1979, 80–149.

7. GRIFFIN, T. Notational definition—A formal account. In *Proc. Symposium on Logic in Computer Science*, 1988, 372–383.

8. KLEENE, S. C. *Introduction to Metamathematics*, Van Nostrand, New York, 1952.

9. KOHLBECKER, E. *Syntactic Extensions in the Programming Language Lisp.* Ph.D. dissertation, Indiana University, 1986.

10. LANDIN, P.J. The next 700 programming languages. *Commun. ACM* 9(3), 1966, 157–166.

11. MEYER, A.R. AND J.R. RIECKE. Continuations may be unreasonable. In *Proc. 1988 Conference on Lisp and Functional Programming*, 1988, 63–71.

12. MORRIS, J.H. *Lambda-Calculus Models of Programming Languages.* Ph.D. dissertation, MIT, 1968.

13. ONG, L C.-H. Fully abstract models of the lazy lambda-calculus. In *Proc. 29th Symposium on Foundation of Computer Science*, 1988, 368–376.

14. PATERSON, M.S. AND C.E. HEWITT. Comparative schematology. In *Conf. Rec. ACM Conference on Concurrent Systems and Parallel Computation*, 1970, 119–127.

15. PLOTKIN, G.D. LCF considered as a programming language. *Theor. Comput. Sci.* 5, 1977, 223–255.

16. PLOTKIN, G.D. Call-by-name, call-by-value, and the λ-calculus. *Theor. Comput. Sci.* 1, 1975, 125–159.

17. REYNOLDS, J.C. GEDANKEN—A simple typeless language based on the principle of completeness and the reference concept. *Commun. ACM* 13(5), 1970, 308–319.

18. REYNOLDS, J.C. The essence of Algol. In *Algorithmic Languages*, edited by de Bakker and van Vliet. North-Holland, Amsterdam, 1981, 345–372.

19. STEELE, G.L., JR. AND G.J. SUSSMAN. Lambda: The ultimate imperative. Memo 353, MIT AI Lab, 1976.

20. SUSSMAN, G.J. AND G.L. STEELE JR. Scheme: An interpreter for extended lambda calculus. Memo 349, MIT AI Lab, 1975.

21. TROELSTRA, A. S. *Metamathematical Investigation of Intuitionistic Arithmetic and Analysis.* Lecture Notes in Mathematics 344. Springer-Verlag, Berlin, 1973.

22. WILLIAMS, J.G. On the formalization of semantic conventions. Draft version: September 1988. To appear in *Journal of Symbolic logic*, 1990.

Higher Order Escape Analysis:
Optimizing Stack Allocation in Functional Program Implementations[1]

Benjamin Goldberg and Young Gil Park

Department of Computer Science[2]
Courant Institute of Mathematical Sciences
New York University

Abstract.

In this paper, we present a method for optimizing the allocation of closures in memory. This method is based on *escape analysis*, an application of abstraction interpretation to higher order functional languages. Escape analysis determines, at compile time, if any arguments to a function have a greater lifetime than the function call itself. Such arguments, especially if they are closures, must be allocated in the heap rather than in the stack. In most implementations, however, stack allocation of closures is preferable due to the lower cost of allocation and reclamation. Therefore, we use escape analysis to determine when arguments can be stack allocated safely.

In the past, first order escape analysis has been used in optimizing LISP compilers, and has been described in various data-flow analysis frameworks for a language with complex types. The analysis described here, being higher order, provides more accurate escape information, although for a very simple higher order functional language.

1. Introduction

Higher order functions are an important part of functional languages. They have generally been seen, however, as having a high implementation overhead. Two reasons for this view are that 1) they force an implementation to use a heap to store closures, and 2) programs using higher order functions are particularly difficult to analyze for optimization purposes.

The need for heap allocation arises when parameters and locally defined objects within a function outlive a call to that function. For example, in the following program fragment

```
let f x y z = x + y + z
    g a b = f b a
in  g 1 2
```

a closure representing the partial application of **f** during the execution of **g** will outlive the call to **g**. Thus, the closure containing the parameters a and b will have to be heap allocated. In this case, the partial application of **f**, along with g's parameters a and b, are said to *escape* from the call to g.

Notice that in the following program fragment

```
let f x y z = x + y + z
    h x = x 3
    g a b = h (f b a)
in  g 1 2
```

the closure representing the partial application of **f** does not escape from **g**. In this case, the closure and pa-

---

1. This research was supported in part by a National Science Foundation Research Initiation Award, CCR-8909634.
2. Address: 251 Mercer St., New York, NY 10012. Email: goldberg@cs.nyu.edu, park@cs.nyu.edu.

$c \in Con$ constants

$x \in Id$ identifiers

$e \in Exp$ expressions, defined by

$$e ::= \; c \mid x \mid e_1 \, e_2 \mid e_1 \to e_2, e_3 \mid e_1 + e_2 \mid e_1 = e_2 \mid \lambda x. \, e \mid$$

$$\text{let } x_1 = e_1; \ldots; x_n = e_n \text{ in } e$$

Figure 1. The syntax of nml

---

rameters can be allocated in g's activation record on the stack. *Escape analysis* is a compile time analysis that determines whether an object, such as a closure or a parameter, needs to be heap allocated.

In this paper we assume that stack allocation is less expensive than heap allocation, although we recognize that there are safety issues (such as stack overflow, etc.) that are important (see [Chase88]). There are also persuasive arguments in favor of heap allocation. In the Standard ML compiler [AM87], all closures are allocated in the heap. It appears that with a large amount of memory and a sophisticated garbage collection strategy, the overhead of garbage collection is quite small. However, on most current systems (and especially in distributed systems where garbage collection is more expensive), stack allocation of closures is preferable.

A simple escape analysis was used in the Orbit compiler for Scheme [Kranz88]. It is a first order escape analysis in which the following program could not be analyzed accurately.

```
let f a b = a + b
    g h a b = h b a
in  g f 1 2
```

because h is an unknown function (i.e. a function bound to a formal parameter) in the body of g. Orbit's escape analysis assumes that any argument to an unknown function will escape from that function. Thus, it will assume that both a and b escape from the call to h inside of g, and therefore escape from g. In fact, neither a nor b escape from g.

Another analysis, called lifetime analysis [RM88], was developed to compute, if possible, the relative lifetimes of dynamically allocated objects in a first order language with structures and recursive types (such as trees). Escape analysis is a particular instance of lifetime analysis in which the lifetime of a function's activation record is compared to the objects defined inside the function. Other analyses for optimizing storage allocation were proposed in [JM76], [MJ81], [Schwartz75], [Barth77], and [Chase87].

In the following sections, we present an analysis that, using abstract interpretation ([CC77],[Mycroft81]), gives escape information in the presence of higher order functions (although we do not deal with structures and recursive types). Higher order abstract interpretation has been mainly used for strictness analysis ([BHA85],[HY86]), although other higher order analyses have been developed (such as sharing analysis [Goldberg87]). Our use of abstraction interpretation differs from that of Mycroft, and is similar to that of Hudak and Young, because we form an abstraction of a nonstandard semantics, rather than the standard semantics, of our programming language.

2. A Simple Higher Order Functional Language

For this discussion a very simple higher order monomorphically typed strict functional language, *nml* (for *not much* of a *language*), will suffice. The syntax of the language is given in figure 1, although we omit the type declarations. The standard semantic domains of nml are as follows:

D, the standard domain of values,

$Env: Id \to D$, the domain of environments,

$$E[\![\,c\,]\!] \; Env = c, \text{ for each constant } c \in Con$$
$$E[\![\,x\,]\!] \; Env = Env[\![\,x\,]\!], \text{ for each identifier } x \in Id$$
$$E[\![\,e_1 + e_2\,]\!] \; Env = (E[\![\,e_1\,]\!] \; Env) + (E[\![\,e_2\,]\!] \; Env)$$
$$E[\![\,e_1 = e_2\,]\!] \; Env = (E[\![\,e_1\,]\!] \; Env = E[\![\,e_2\,]\!] \; Env)$$
$$E[\![\,e_1 \; e_2\,]\!] \; Env = (E[\![\,e_1\,]\!] \; Env) \; (E[\![\,e_2\,]\!] \; Env)$$
$$E[\![\,e_1 \rightarrow e_2, e_3\,]\!] \; Env = E[\![\,e_1\,]\!] \; Env \rightarrow E[\![\,e_2\,]\!] \; Env, \; E[\![\,e_3\,]\!] \; Env$$
$$E[\![\,\lambda x.e\,]\!] \; Env = \lambda y.E[\![\,e\,]\!] \; Env[y/x]$$
$$E[\![\, \text{let } x_1 = e_1; \ldots; x_n = e_n \text{ in } e\,]\!] \; Env = E[\![\,e\,]\!] \; Env'$$
$$\text{where } Env' = [(E[\![\,e_1\,]\!] \; Env')/x_1, \ldots, (E[\![\,e_n\,]\!] \; Env')/x_n]$$

Figure 2. The standard semantics of nml

$E: Exp \rightarrow Env \rightarrow D$, the semantic function for expressions.
The standard semantic function E is defined in figure 2. For notational convenience, all syntactic objects are printed in boldface type, including all nml identifiers. Variables referring to syntactic objects are printed in boldface italic type. Semantic variables are printed in non-bold italic type.

3. An Exact Escape Semantics

In this section, we describe a nonstandard semantics for nml such that the result of a function call indicates whether a particular parameter escapes. The escape semantic domains are defined as follows:

$D_e^{int} = D_e^{bool} = \ldots = 2 \times \{err\}$, where 2 is the two element domain ordered by $0 \leq 1$,

$D_e^{T_1 \rightarrow T_2} = 2 \times (D_e^{T_1} \rightarrow D_e^{T_2})$, for any types T_1 and T_2,

$D_e = \sum_T D_e^T$,

$Env_e = Id \rightarrow D_e$, the domain of escape environments.
The semantic function is
$$E_e: Exp \rightarrow Env_e \rightarrow D_e$$
and is defined in figure 3.

Under these semantics, the value of an expression is a pair whose first element is a boolean (0 or 1) that

$$E_e[\![\,c\,]\!] \; Env = \; <0, err> \text{, for any constant } c$$
$$E_e[\![\,x\,]\!] \; Env = Env[\![\,x\,]\!]$$
$$E_e[\![\,e_1 + e_2\,]\!] \; Env = \; <0, err>, \text{ likewise for the other arithmetic operators}$$
$$E_e[\![\,e_1 \; e_2\,]\!] \; Env = (E_e[\![\,e_1\,]\!] \; Env)_{(2)} \; (E_e[\![\,e_2\,]\!] \; Env)$$
$$E_e[\![\,e_1 \rightarrow e_2, e_3\,]\!] \; Env = Oracle \; [\![\,e_1\,]\!] \rightarrow E_e \; [\![\,e_2\,]\!] \; Env, E_e \; [\![\,e_3\,]\!] \; Env$$
$$E_e[\![\,\lambda x.e\,]\!] \; Env = \; < v, \lambda y. \, E_e[\![\,e\,]\!] \; Env[y/x] >$$
$$\text{where } v = \bigvee_{z \in F} (Env[\![\,z\,]\!])_{(1)}, \text{ and } F \text{ is the set of free variables in } (\lambda x.e)$$
$$E_e[\![\, \text{let } x_1 = e_1; \ldots; x_n = e_n \text{ in } e\,]\!] \; Env = E_e[\![\,e\,]\!] \; Env'$$
$$\text{where } Env' = [(E_e[\![\,e_1\,]\!] \; Env')/x_1, \ldots, (E_e[\![\,e_n\,]\!] \; Env')/x_n]$$

Figure 3. The exact escape semantics of nml

indicates whether a particular parameter escapes, and whose second element is a function that captures the higher order behavior of the expression. *err* denotes a non-function value.

Given an $x \in D_e$ we use the notation $x_{(1)}$ and $x_{(2)}$ to refer to the first and second elements of x, respectively. The domain D_e is partially ordered in the standard way:

$$\forall \, x,y \in D_e, x \leq y \text{ iff } x_{(1)} \leq y_{(1)} \text{ and } x_{(2)} \leq y_{(2)}$$

For each type $T = T_1 \to T_2$, there is a bottom element $\perp_T$ of D_e defined as follows:

$$\perp_T = \, < 0, \, \lambda x. \perp_{T_2}>$$

For each primitive type T, $\perp_T = \, < 0, err>$.

In order to return the actual escape value of each expression, we must be able to determine which branch of a conditional would be evaluated at run-time. The only way to do this would be to embed the standard semantics within the escape semantics. For convenience, we instead resort to an oracle to choose the appropriate branch of the conditional.

Given an nml function f, its meaning under the escape semantics will be a pair $<f_{(1)}, f_{(2)}>$. We then use $f_{(2)}$ to determine if a particular argument in a call to f escapes. Suppose, for example, we want to know, given the function application $(f \, x)$, if x escapes. To do so, we let $<x_{(1)}, x_{(2)}>$ be the value of x under that escape semantics and let $y = f_{(2)} <1, x_{(2)}>$. If $y_{(1)} = 1$ then x escapes in the standard semantics, otherwise x does not. Section 6 gives a detailed description of how the escape semantics is used.

4. The Abstract Escape Semantics

We now present an abstraction of the exact escape semantics that allows an approximation of the exact escape behavior to be found at compile time. The semantic domains are essentially identical to those of the exact escape semantics:

$$D_{ae}^{int} = D_{ae}^{bool} = \ldots = 2 \times \{err\},$$

$$D_{ae}^{T_1 \to T_2} = 2 \times (D_{ae}^{T_1} \to D_{ae}^{T_2}),$$

$$D_{ae} = \sum_T D_{ae}^T \, ,$$

$$Env_{ae} = Id \to D_{ae}.$$

The semantic function

$$E_{ae} : Exp \to Env_{ae} \to D_{ae}$$

is defined in figure 4. The difference between the exact and the abstract semantics lies in the handling of the conditional. Rather than referring to the standard semantics (as denoted by the oracle) the conditional is handled by taking the least upper bound of the escape values of the two branches.

5. Termination

In our abstract escape semantics, a function may be expressed recursively and is thus defined as the least fixpoint of the corresponding functional. That is, for the function

$$f = F(f)$$

where f is of type T and F is a functional (corresponding to the body of f), the meaning of f is defined to be the least function satisfying the above equation. Domain theory tells us that the least fixpoint f can be found as follows:

$$f = \lim_{i \to \infty} F^i (\perp_T)$$

where $F^0(x) = x$ and $F^i(x) = F(F^{i-1}(x))$.

$$E_{ae}[\![c]\!]\ Env\ =\ <0,\ err>$$

$$E_{ae}[\![x]\!]\ Env\ =\ Env[\![x]\!]$$

$$E_{ae}[\![e_1 + e_2]\!]\ Env\ =\ <0,\ err>,\ \text{likewise for the other arithmetic operators}$$

$$E_{ae}[\![e_1\ e_2]\!]\ Env\ =\ (E_{ae}[\![e_1]\!]\ Env)_{(2)}\ (E_{ae}[\![e_2]\!]\ Env)$$

$$E_{ae}[\![e_1 \rightarrow e_2, e_3]\!]\ Env\ =\ (E_{ae}\ [\![e_2]\!]\ Env) \sqcup (E_{ae}\ [\![e_3]\!]\ Env)$$

$$E_{ae}[\![\lambda x.e]\!]\ Env\ =\ <v,\ \lambda y.\ E_{ae}[\![e]\!]\ Env[y/x] >$$

where $v = \bigvee\limits_{z \in F} (Env[\![z]\!])_{(1)}$, and F is the set of free variables in $(\lambda x.e)$

$$E_{ae}[\![\ \text{let } x_1 = e_1;\ \ldots;\ x_n = e_n \text{ in } e]\!]\ Env\ =\ E_{ae}[\![e]\!]\ Env'$$

where $Env' = [(E_{ae}[\![e_1]\!]\ Env')/x_1, \ldots, (E_e[\![e_n]\!]\ Env')/x_n]$

Figure 4. The abstract escape semantics of nml

To ensure that our analysis terminates, we must show that a fixpoint is reached in finite time. That is, for all functions defined according to the above equation, there must exist some j such that

$$F^k(\bot_T) = F^j(\bot_T)$$

for all $k > j$.

A simple way of showing that there exists such a j is to show that every functional F must be monotonic and that the fixpoint iteration is performed over a finite domain (using the technique described in [BHA85]).

Every functional is composed of the monotonic operation $\vee$ (logical *or*) and the least upper bound operator (as defined in figure 4) and is thus monotonic. Furthermore, each subdomain $D_{ae}{}^T$ is finite since $D_{ae}{}^{T_0}$ is finite for each primitive type T_0 (**int**, **bool**, etc.) and $D_{ae}{}^{T_1 \rightarrow T_2}$ is finite whenever $D_{ae}{}^{T_1}$ and $D_{ae}{}^{T_2}$ are finite. When finding the least fixpoint of a function of type T we need only search over the subdomain $D_{ae}{}^T$. Thus, the least fixpoint can be computed in a finite number of iterations. Figure 5 contains an example of fixpoint finding.

6. Using the Abstract Functions

In this section, we describe how the abstract functions are used to detect the escape properties of the corresponding functions in an nml program.

6.1. Global Escape Analysis

Using a global escape analysis, we find escape information about each nml function f that holds true for every possible application of f. To do so, we apply the corresponding abstract function to arguments that cause the greatest escapement possible. For each type T, we define the abstract function R^T that corresponds to an nml function from which every argument escapes.

$$R^T = \lambda z_1. <z_{1(1)}, \lambda z_2. <z_{1(1)} \vee z_{2(1)}, \ldots, \lambda z_m. < \bigvee\limits_{p=1}^{m} z_{p(1)}, err> \ldots >>$$

where m is the number of arguments that a function of type T can take (before returning a primitive value).

Given an identifier f bound to a function of n arguments in some environment Env, $G_i(f, Env)$ returns 1 if the ith parameter could escape and 0 otherwise. G_i is defined as follows:

$$G_i(f, Env) = (E_{ae}\ [\![(f\ x_1 \ldots\ x_n)]\!]\ Env[y_1/x_1, \ldots, y_n/x_n])_{(1)}$$

where for all $j \leq n, j \neq i$,

Consider the following nml function definition (of type $int \rightarrow int \rightarrow int$, for example):

$f = \lambda x. \lambda y. (x=0) \rightarrow y, f (x-1) y$

Using the definitions in figure 4, the corresponding function in D_{ae} is described by:

$$f = <0, \lambda x. <x_{(1)}, \lambda y. E_{ae}[\![(x=0) \rightarrow y, f (x-1) y]\!] [x/x, y/y, f/f]>>$$

$$= <0, \lambda x. <x_{(1)}, \lambda y, y \sqcup (f_{(2)} <0, err>_{(2)} y)>>$$

Therefore f is the least fixpoint of the functional F defined by

$$F = \lambda f. <0, \lambda x. <x_{(1)}, \lambda y. y \sqcup (f_{(2)} <0, err>_{(2)} y)>>$$

The least fixpoint is found by the following fixpoint iteration:

$$f^0 = F(\perp_{int \rightarrow int \rightarrow int}) = <0, \lambda x. <x_{(1)}, \lambda y. y \sqcup (\perp_{int \rightarrow int \rightarrow int(2)} <0, err>_{(2)} y)>>$$

$$= <0, \lambda x. <x_{(1)}, \lambda y. y \sqcup \perp_{int \rightarrow int(2)} y>>$$

$$= <0, \lambda x. <x_{(1)}, \lambda y. y \sqcup \perp_{int}>>$$

$$= <0, \lambda x. <x_{(1)}, \lambda y. y>>$$

$$f^1 = F(f^0) = <0, \lambda x. <x_{(1)}, \lambda y. y \sqcup ((\lambda x. <x_{(1)}, \lambda y. y>) <0, err>_{(2)} y))>>$$

$$= <0, \lambda x. <x_{(1)}, \lambda y. y \sqcup (\lambda y. y) y))>>$$

$$= <0, \lambda x. <x_{(1)}, \lambda y. y)>>$$

Since $f^0 = f^1 = F(f^0)$, a fixpoint has been found, thus $f = <0, \lambda x. <x_{(1)}, \lambda y. y)>>$

This means that when f is applied to two arguments, only the second argument may escape.

Figure 5. An example of fixpoint finding

$$y_j = <0, R^{T_j}>$$

where T_j is the type of x_j and

$$y_i = <1, R^{T_i}>.$$

Since each $y_{j(2)}$ is a function from which every argument escapes, and since the abstract function for f is monotonic, $G_i(f, Env)$ provides the worst case behavior with respect to the escapement of f's ith argument.

6.2. Local Escape Analysis

Generally, we would like to know if an argument escapes from a particular call to a function f. This depends on the values of the arguments of that call. We define the function L_i such that $L_i(f, e_1,..., e_n, Env)$ returns 1 if the ith argument of $(f e_1 ... e_n)$ might escape, 0 otherwise. The environment Env must be an environment mapping the free identifiers within e_1 through e_n to elements of D_{ae}. The function L_i is defined as follows

$$L_i(f, e_1,..., e_n, Env) = (E_{ae} [\![(f x_1 ... x_n)]\!] Env[y/x_j])_{(1)} \quad (1)$$

where, for all $j \leq n, j \neq i$,

$$y_j = <0, (E_{ae} [\![e_j]\!] Env)_{(2)}>$$

and

$$y_i = <1, (E_{ae} [\![e_i]\!] Env)_{(2)}>.$$

$Env = [f/f, h/h, p/p, q/q, g/g]$, where

$f \quad = <0, \lambda x. <x_{(1)}, \ \lambda y. \ E_{ae} \ [\![\ x+y]\!] \ Env[x/x,y/y]>>$

$\quad = <0, \lambda x. <x_{(1)}, \ \lambda y. \ <0, err>>>$

$p \quad = q = <0, \ \lambda b. \ <0, err>>$

$h \quad = <0, \lambda a. \ E_{ae} \ [\![\ (a=0) \rightarrow p, q]\!] \ Env[a/a]>$

$\quad = <0, \lambda a. \ p \sqcup q>$

$\quad = <0, \lambda a. \ <0, \ \lambda b. \ <0, err>>>$

$g \quad = <0, \lambda m. <m_{(1)}, \ \lambda n. \ E_{ae} \ [\![\ m \ n]\!] \ Env[m/m,n/n]>>$

$\quad = <0, \lambda m. <m_{(1)}, \ \lambda n. \ m_{(2)} \ n>>$

Figure 6. Abstract Escape Functions

7. Examples

Consider the following nml program:

```
let f = λx. λy. x+y;
    h = λa. (a=0) → p, q;
    p = λb. b+1;
    q = λb. b-1;
    g = λm. λn. m n;
in  ... (g f 4) ... (g h 4) ...
```

Figure 6 shows the corresponding abstract escape functions. Our aim to is analyze the escape properties of g, both globally and locally.

7.1. A Global Escape Analysis Example

To find the global (i.e. worst case) escape property of g, we apply the global analysis function G_i described in section 6.1 to the abstract function g and the environment Env shown in figure 6. We assume g is of type $(int \rightarrow int \rightarrow int) \rightarrow int \rightarrow int \rightarrow int$.

$$G_1(g, Env) = (E_{ae} \ [\![(g \ x_1 \ x2)]\!] \ Env[y_1/x_1, y_2/x_2])_{(1)}$$

where $y_1 = <1, \lambda z_1. <z_{1(1)}, \ \lambda z_2. \ <z_{1(1)} \vee z_{2(1)}, err>>>$ and $y_2 = <0, err>$.

Thus

$$G_1(g, Env) = ((g_{(2)} \ y_1)_{(2)} \ y_2)_{(1)}$$
$$= (((\lambda m. \ <m_{(1)}, \ \lambda n. \ m_{(2)} \ n>) \ y_1)_{(2)} \ y_2)_{(1)}$$
$$= ((\lambda z_1. \ <z_{1(1)}, \ \lambda z_2. \ <z_{1(1)} \vee z_{2(1)}, err>>) \ <0,err>)_{(1)}$$
$$= 0$$

indicating that g's first parameter can never escape.

$$G_2(g, Env) = (E_{ae} \ [\![(g \ x_1 \ x2)]\!] \ Env[y_1/x_1, y_2/x_2])_{(1)}$$

where $y_1 = <0, \lambda z_1. <z_{1(1)}, \ \lambda z_2. \ <z_{1(1)} \vee z_{2(1)}, err>>>$ and $y_2 = <1,err>$.

Thus

$$G_2(g, Env) = ((g_{(2)} \ y_1)_{(2)} \ y_2)_{(1)}$$
$$= (((\lambda m. \ <m_{(1)}, \ \lambda n. \ m_{(2)} \ n>) \ y_1)_{(2)} \ y_2)_{(1)}$$
$$= ((\lambda z_1. \ <z_{1(1)}, \ \lambda z_2. \ <z_{1(1)} \vee z_{2(1)}, err>>) \ <1,err>)_{(1)}$$
$$= 1$$

indicating that the first parameter to g might escape in some situations.

7.2. A Local Escape Analysis Example

To find what arguments escape from the each application of g in the program, we use the local analysis function L_i described in section 6.2. Since we know from the global analysis of g that its first parameter can never escape, we only need to test if the second parameter escapes (using L_2). For the expression (g f 4),

$$L_2(g, f, 4, Env) = (E_{ae} [\![(g\ x_1\ x_2)]\!]\ Env[<0, f_{(2)}>/x_1, <1, err>/x_2])_{(1)}$$
$$= ((g_{(2)} <0, f_{(2)}>)_{(2)} <1, err>)_{(1)}$$
$$= (((\lambda m.\ <m_{(1)},\ \lambda n.\ m_{(2)}\ n>) <0, \lambda x.\ <x_{(1)},\ \lambda y.\ <0, err>>>)_{(2)} <1, err>)_{(1)}$$
$$= ((\lambda x.\ <x_{(1)},\ \lambda y.\ <0, err>>>)_{(2)} <1, err>)_{(1)}$$
$$= 1.$$

This indicates that the second argument to g escapes. For the expression (g h 4),

$$L_2(g, h, 4, Env) = (E_{ae} [\![(g\ x_1\ x_2)]\!]\ Env[<0, h_{(2)}>/x_1, <1, err>/x_2])_{(1)}$$
$$= ((g_{(2)} <0, h_{(2)}>)_{(2)} <1, err>)_{(1)}$$
$$= (((\lambda m.\ <m_{(1)},\ \lambda n.\ m_{(2)}\ n>) <0, \lambda a.\ <0,\ \lambda b.\ <0, err>>>)_{(2)} <1, err>)_{(1)}$$
$$= ((\lambda a.\ <0,\ \lambda b.\ <0, err>>)_{(2)} <1, err>)_{(1)}$$
$$= 0.$$

This indicates that no argument to g escapes (even though the result is a partial application).

8. Escape Analysis on Lists

We have not yet discussed escape analysis in the presence of the list operators **cons**, **car**, and **cdr**. We extend the abstract semantic function E_{ae} as follows:

$$E_{ae}[\![\text{cons}]\!]\ Env\ =\ <0, \lambda a.\ <a_{(1)},\ \lambda b.<a_{(1)} \vee b_{(1)},\ err>>>$$
$$E_{ae}[\![\text{cdr}]\!]\ Env\ =\ <0, \lambda x.\ <x_{(1)}, err>>$$
$$E_{ae}[\![\text{car}]\!]\ Env\ =\ <0, R^T>$$

where T is the type of the elements of the list to which **car** is being applied and R^T is defined in section 6.1. In other words, once an object has been placed on a list, we are unable to determine when it is removed. This means that if some head or tail of a list escapes from a function then all of the elements of the list are seen as escaping. In addition, the function value of the car of a list is seen as the maximally escaping function of that type. Admittedly, this is an unsatisfactory analysis on lists. We are working on an escape analysis that could be applied to lists in a manner similar to the way that strictness analysis was extended to lists [Wadler87].

9. Conclusions

We have taken an existing, useful optimization and used denotational semantics and abstract interpretation to apply it to higher order programming languages. We have yet to implement the analysis in a real compiler and thus it remains to be seen if the benefit of the analysis outweighs its cost (mainly fixpoint finding).

10. Acknowledgments

We would like to thank the National Science Foundation for funding this work. We would also like to thank our wives, Wendy Goldberg and Jihwa Park, for their support and encouragement. We also thank our children, Jonathan Goldberg and Grace Park, for providing pleasant distractions.

References

[AM87]
A. Appel and D.B. MacQueen. A standard ML compiler. In *Proceedings of the 1987 Conference on Functional Programming and Computer Architecture*. September, 1987.

[Barth77]
J.M. Barth. Shifting garbage collection overhead to compile time. *Communications of the ACM*, 20(7), July 1977.

[BHA85]
G.L. Burn, C.L. Hankin, and S. Abramsky. The theory of strictness analysis for higher order functions. In *Programs as Data Objects*, LNCS 217. Springer-Verlag. 1985

[CC77]
P. Cousot and R. Cousot. Abstract interpretation: A unified lattice model for static analysis of programs by construction or approximation of fixpoints. In *Proceedings of the 4th Annual ACM Symposium on Principles of Programming Languages*. January 1977.

[Chase87]
D.R. Chase. *Garbage Collection and Other Optimizations*. Ph.D. Thesis, Rice University. 1987

[Chase88]
D.R. Chase. Safety considerations for storage allocation optimizations. In *Proceedings of the SIGPLAN' 88 Conference on Programming Language Design and Implementation*. June, 1988.

[Goldberg87]
B. Goldberg. Detecting sharing of partial applications in functional programs. In *Proceedings of the 1987 Conference on Functional Programming and Computer Architecture*. September, 1987.

[HY86]
P. Hudak and J. Young. Higher-order strictness analysis for the untyped lambda calculus. In *Proceedings of the 13th Annual ACM Symposium on Principles of Programming Languages*. January, 1986.

[JM76]
N. Jones and S. Muchnick. Binding time optimization in programming languages: An approach to the design of an ideal language. In *Proceedings of the 3rd Annual ACM Symposium on Principles of Programming Languages*. January 1976.

[Kranz88]
D. Kranz. *ORBIT: An Optimizing Compiler for Scheme*. Ph.D. Thesis, Yale University, Department of Computer Science. May 1988.

[MJ81]
S. Muchnick and N. Jones, editors. *Flow Analysis and Optimization of LISP-like Structures*. Prentice-Hall, 1981.

[Mycroft81]
A. Mycroft. *Abstract Interpretation and Optimizing Transformations for Applicative Programs*. Ph.D. Thesis, University of Edinburgh. 1981.

[RM88]
C. Ruggieri and T.P. Murtagh. Lifetime analysis of dynamically allocated objects. *Proceedings of the 15th Annual ACM Symposium on Principles of Programming Languages*. January, 1988.

[Schwartz75]
J.T. Schwartz. Optimization of very high level languages - I. Value transmission and its corollaries. *Journal of Computer Languages*, 1:161-194, 1975.

[Wadler87]
P. Wadler, Strictness analysis on non-flat domains. In *Abstract Interpretation of Declarative Languages*. C. L. Hankin and S. Abramsky, editors. Ellis Horwood, 1987.

Development of Concurrent Systems by Incremental Transformation[1]

E. Pascal Gribomont

Philips Research Laboratory

avenue van Becelaere, 2

B - 1170 Brussels (Belgium)

Abstract. A formal development method for concurrent programs is proposed. It generalizes several variants of the stepwise refinement method often used in concurrency, in that not only atomicity refinements, but also arbitrary transformations, are taken into account. The method is illustrated by simple examples.

1 Introduction

It is now widely accepted that systems of concurrent processes are complex objects, which should be specified, designed and verified in a formal way. Much work has been devoted to this problem, and useful results have been obtained. Some of them are now briefly recalled, upon which our work is based.

Logics and related formalisms are adequate tools for the expression of properties of concurrent systems. They are also appropriate for proving these properties [38,28,34,35]. The design and the verification of concurrent systems are easier when appropriate abstract languages are used, for instance CSP [23,24], Action Systems [5] or UNITY [10]. The semantics of these languages and of the programs written in them can be formally stated. The notion of invariant, initially introduced for sequential programming, has proved very useful in parallel programming as well [1,38,43].

These formal tools (languages, logics and deduction systems) should be the foundation of a formal methodology of parallel programming [24,32,10]. The usual methodology for the design of concurrent systems relies on the notion of "stepwise refinement". Roughly speaking, this method consists in generating a sequence of systems, each of them being slightly more complicated and, hopefully, "better" than its predecessor. Many examples of concurrent systems developed by the stepwise refinement method (in fact, several variants of it) have appeared in the literature; some of them are [14,8,27,3,9]. It should be emphasized that this method seems to be quite general; it is not restricted to some languages or programming constructs.

In practice, the designer has first to discover a possible refinement, and then to establish that this refinement is valid. The first step is usually a creative one : the designer wants to transform the program in order to satisfy a stronger specification, or the same specification in a more efficient way. The designer has to identify some parts of the program which maybe should be replaced by new parts. The second step is to check whether an attempted refinement is acceptable or not. This can be done by producing an appropriate invariant of the refined version. It has been observed that an adequate "small" change in the system usually induces a "small" change in the invariant; the nature of this change is not identified easily and its expression depends on the language used to write the assertions.

Much work about the problem of stepwise refinement in concurrency has been and still is performed. The obtained results can be roughly classified in two categories. The papers of the first category contain examples of development. The authors introduce a sequence of versions of their programs, each of them with a proof, that is, an invariant. This kind of presentation allows the readers and the authors themselves to understand the subtleties of the problem and its proposed solution in an incremental way. An early example in this category is [14]; many examples presented in [10] are also based on the stepwise refinement method.

The second category contains more theoretical results about the notion of refinement itself. These results are usually about a particular but important kind of refinement, called the "atomicity refinement",

---

[1]Supported in part by the ESPRIT project ATES.

or the "sequential refinement". The notion of atomicity occurs in concurrent programming when the interleaving semantics is used, that is, when concurrency is modelled by non-determinism: a step of the computation consists in executing a statement of some arbitrarily chosen process of the system. In a "coarse-grained" system, a statement can be a rather big segment of program, involving the access to several variables; in a "fine-grained" system, a statement is a simple assignment or a simple test. A sequential refinement consists in "breaking" a statement into a sequence of more elementary statements; for instance, the double assignment $(x, y) := (y, x)$ is refined into the sequence $t := x; x := y; y := t$, where t is a new variable. An early work about refinements is [31]; more recent papers are [27,30,7].

From the theoretical point of view, it is rather easy to deal with sequential refinements. Suppose we have a program P whose invariance properties are established by some invariant I. If a process π of P contains some statement S, sequentially equivalent to $S_1; S_2$, one can attempt to split the statement S into the sequence formed by the more elementary statements S_1 and S_2. Due to possible interaction with other processes, the program P' obtained by such a transformation is not always correct with respect to the specifications of P. A simple method to evaluate the impact of the refinement on the semantics of the program is as follows. Let R be the predicate which is false when the control of the execution of π is between the statements S_1 and S_2 (that means that the next statement executed by π will be S_2) and true otherwise. If a formula J exists such that the formula $I' =_{def} [(R \Rightarrow I) \wedge (\neg R \Rightarrow J)]$ is an invariant of the refined version P', then the specified invariance properties of P, summarized in the invariant I, are preserved in the refined program P' (except maybe in "transient" states, when R is false). On the contrary, when no adequate J can be found, the semantics of P' deeply differs from the semantics of P, and the refinement is likely to be incorrect. This method and the strategy for finding J, when it exists, have been presented and illustrated in detail in [18,19].

In practice, sequential refinement is not sufficient, since new variables are introduced in a very restricted way. Especially, this kind of refinement disallows the strengthening and the weakening of the guards of the statements, and modifying guards is often used in practice during the design of concurrent systems. More general transformations, involving for instance the unrestricted introduction of new variables, may induce substantial changes in the computation, if the guards of some statements of the program are made dependent on the value of the new variables.

The purpose of this paper is to generalize the method recalled above to the general case of arbitrary transformations. The main problem is the choice of a "refinement formula" R; this choice is evident for sequential refinements, but not for more general transformations. On the contrary, when the formula R has been chosen, the determination of an adequate J (when there is one) can be done in the same way for a sequential refinement or for an arbitrary transformation.

The paper goes on as follows. The formal tools needed to explain and apply the method are presented in Section 2; the method for finding R and J is presented in Section 3 and illustrated in Sections 4 and 5. Section 6 is a conclusion.

2 Formal tools

In this section, we first introduce briefly our programming notation, called FCS (for Formal Concurrent System), with a simple example. This example will also show that sequential refinements are not sufficient in practice: more general transformations are needed, even in the development of elementary concurrent systems. Afterwards, the Hoare logic for FCS is introduced, together with the notions of weakest liberal precondition and strongest liberal postcondition.

2.1 A programming notation

The programming notation FCS is elementary and best explained by an example. Here is first a graphical presentation of a toy algorithm.

This is a simple scheme for mutual exclusion. P and Q are cyclic processes sharing the variable T (for "Turn"). A process, say P, can perform internal computation (not involving the shared variable T) either in its non-critical state p_0 or in its critical state p_c. As, at every time, at most one process

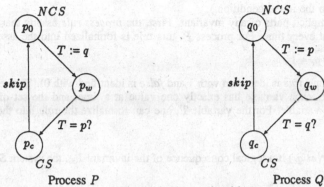

Figure 1: A toy algorithm

can execute its critical section (CS), the shared variable is used to implement the mutual exclusion; when, for instance, process Q is in its critical section, then process P must be delayed, in its waiting state p_w. Classical *place predicates* will be used; for instance, the formula $(at\ p_w \wedge at\ q_c)$ is true when process P is in its waiting state and process Q is in its critical state. The mutual exclusion is modelled by the formula

$$\neg (at\ p_c \wedge at\ q_c).$$

The equivalent FCS, called S_{00}, is simply a lexical version of the graphical representation:

$$\mathcal{P} = \{P, Q\}, \quad \text{where } P = \{p_0, p_w, p_c\} \text{ and } Q = \{q_0, q_w, q_c\};$$
$$\mathcal{M} = \{T : \{p, q\}\};$$
$$\mathcal{T} = \{ (p_0, T := q, p_w), \qquad\qquad (q_0, T := p, q_w),$$
$$(p_w, T = p \longrightarrow skip, p_c), \quad (q_w, T = q \longrightarrow skip, q_c),$$
$$(p_c, skip, p_0), \qquad\qquad (q_c, skip, q_0)\}.$$

An FCS has three components. First, the *set of (formal) processes* $\mathcal{P}$, second, the *memory* $\mathcal{M}$ and, third, the *set of transitions* $\mathcal{T}$. Processes are disjoint non-empty sets of *labels*; the memory is a finite set of typed program variables. A *transition* is an expression like $\tau = (O, G \longrightarrow A, E)$, where O is the *origin* (or *entry point*), E is the *extremity* (or *exit point*) and $G \longrightarrow A$ is the *guarded (multiple) assignment* of the transition. An axiomatic semantics for FCS is given in the next paragraph. Let us simply mention here that a step of computation consists in executing an arbitrary executable transition (if there is one). The transition τ is *executable* when the formula $cond(\tau) =_{def} (at\ O \wedge G)$ is true; after the execution of τ, $at\ E$ is true. A formula I is an *invariant* of an FCS if each transition τ respects I: if τ is executed from a state satisfying I (and $cond(\tau)$), then the resulting state also satisfies I. An *initial condition* A may be specified for an FCS; it means that only computations whose first state satisfies A are considered. If an FCS is introduced with an invariant, this invariant is also the initial condition, unless stated otherwise.

Comments. Every transition of the system S_{00} involves a single process (either P or Q). Some systems can contain transitions involving several processes; in this case, the origin and the extremity contains a label of each involved process.

We are not interested in the internal computation performed by the processes; as a consequence, it is not modelled in the formal concurrent system S_{00}.

With self-explaining notation, a useful invariant of the system is

$$I_{00} =_{def} \quad (at\ p_w \Rightarrow (T = q \vee at\ q_w)) \wedge (at\ q_w \Rightarrow (T = p \vee at\ p_w))$$
$$\wedge (at\ p_c \Rightarrow T = p) \wedge (at\ q_c \Rightarrow T = q).$$

(The invariant I_{00} is also the initial condition.)

Let us emphasize two implicit parts of any invariant. First, the *process rule* asserts that each process is at exactly one place at every time. For process P, this rule is formalized into the assertion

$$at\ p_0 + at\ p_w + at\ p_c = 1$$

(with the usual convention: *true* is identified with 1 and *false* is identified with 0). The second implicit part is the *variable rule*: each variable has exactly one value at a time, and the set of the possible values is the *type* of the variable. For the variable T, one can formalize the rule into the assertion

$$T = p \lor T = q.$$

As the formula $\neg(at\ p_c \land at\ q_c)$ is a logical consequence of the invariant I_{00}, the system S_{00} guarantees mutual exclusion.

Some useful pieces of notation are introduced now.

If $L = \ell_1 \cdots \ell_n$ is a sequence (or a set) of labels belonging to distinct processes $P_1, \ldots, P_n$ of some system S, then $at\ L$ stands for $(at\ \ell_1 \land \cdots \land at\ \ell_n)$. If B is a formula, then $B[at\ L]$ is obtained by "making $at\ L$ true" in formula B; more formally, $B[at\ L]$ is obtained by replacing each place predicate $at\ k$ occurring in B by $true$ when $k \in \{\ell_1, \ldots, \ell_n\}$, by $false$ when $k \in (P_1 \cup \cdots \cup P_n) \setminus \{\ell_1, \ldots, \ell_n\}$, by $at\ k$ (no change) when $k \notin (P_1 \cup \cdots \cup P_n)$.

Notice that the formulas $(B \land at\ L)$ and $(B[at\ L] \land at\ L)$ are always equivalent.

Here is an example, about the system S_{00} introduced in the previous section. If B is I_{00}, then $B[at\ p_w]$ is obtained by replacing in B the formulas $at\ p_0$, $at\ p_w$ and $at\ p_c$ by *false*, *true* and *false*, respectively. The result is $[(T = q \lor at\ q_w) \land (at\ q_c \Rightarrow T = q)]$, reducing into $(T = q \lor at\ q_w)$. Similarly, $B[at\ p_w q_c]$ is obtained by replacing, in $B[at\ p_w]$, the place predicates $at\ q_0$ and $at\ q_w$ by *false*, and $at\ q_c$ by *true*; the result is $T = q$.

2.2 Hoare logic for FCS

In the previous paragraph, the invariant I_{00} of the system S_{00} has been introduced without proof; let us now introduce the Hoare deduction system [22,2] for proving that some formula is an invariant of some FCS. The deduction system also provides an axiomatic semantics for the language FCS.

The following elements are fixed throughout this paragraph:

- An FCS $S = (\mathcal{P}, \mathcal{M}, \mathcal{T})$.

- A family of processes $\{P_1, \ldots, P_n\} \subset \mathcal{P}$.

- A family of transitions $T_0 \subset \mathcal{T}$.

- Labels $\ell_i, m_i \in P_i$, for all i ($\ell_i = m_i$ is allowed).

- A transition $\tau = (L, C \longrightarrow A, M) \in \mathcal{T}$, where C and A are respectively a guard and an assignment; L and M stand for $\ell_1 \cdots \ell_n$ and $m_1 \cdots m_n$, respectively. (Only the case $n = 1$ has appeared in the example S_{00}.)

- P and Q are assertions, that is, logical formulas interpreted on the states of S.

Hoare's logic is adapted to FCS by the following rules.

$$\{P\}\ C \longrightarrow A\ \{Q\} \quad =_{def} \quad \{P \land C\}\ A\ \{Q\}, \tag{1}$$

$$\{P\}\ (L,\ C \longrightarrow A,\ M)\ \{Q\} \quad =_{def} \quad \{P[at\ L]\}\ C \longrightarrow A\ \{Q[at\ M]\}, \tag{2}$$

$$\{P\}\ T_0\ \{Q\} \quad =_{def} \quad \bigwedge_{\tau \in T_0} [\{P\}\ \tau\ \{Q\}]. \tag{3}$$

These rules model the execution mechanism of FCS.

The first rule expresses the semantics of the guarded assignment $C \longrightarrow A$; it is equivalent to A when C is true; otherwise, it cannot be executed (as a consequence, the triple $\{\neg C\}\, C \longrightarrow A\,\{Q\}$ is vacuously true).

The second rule expresses the semantics of the transition; it can be executed only when $(at\ L \wedge C)$ is true and leads to a state where $at\ M$ is true.

The third rule is not mandatory; it is introduced as an abbreviation.

As an example, we will prove that the invariant I_{00} is respected by the transition $\tau = (p_0,\ T := q\,,\ p_w)$. Due to rule (2), the triple $\{I_{00}\}\,\tau\,\{I_{00}\}$ reduces to the triple $\{I_{00}[at\ p_0]\}\, T := q\, \{I_{00}[at\ p_w]\}$. The precondition is evaluated in

$$(at\ q_w \Rightarrow T = p) \wedge (at\ q_c \Rightarrow T = q),$$

whereas the postcondition is evaluated in

$$(T = q \vee at\ q_w) \wedge (at\ q_c \Rightarrow T = q).$$

The classical Hoare axiom for the assignment is

$$\{P\}\, x := e\, \{Q\} \iff (P \Rightarrow Q[x/e]);$$

it allows to further reduce the triple to the implication

$$[(at\ q_w \Rightarrow T = p) \wedge (at\ q_c \Rightarrow T = q)] \Rightarrow [(q = q \vee at\ q_w) \wedge (at\ q_c \Rightarrow q = q)],$$

which is a tautology.

2.3 Programming calculus

The liberal version of Dijkstra's programming calculus is adapted to the language FCS as follows.

$$wlp[(C \longrightarrow A);\ Q] \quad =_{def} \quad (C \Rightarrow wlp[A;\ Q]), \tag{4}$$

$$slp[P;\ (C \longrightarrow A)] \quad =_{def} \quad slp[(P \wedge C);\ A], \tag{5}$$

$$wlp[(L,\ C \longrightarrow A,\ M);\ Q] \quad =_{def} \quad at\ L \Rightarrow wlp[(C \longrightarrow A);\ Q[at\ M]], \tag{6}$$

$$slp[P;\ (L,\ C \longrightarrow A,\ M)] \quad =_{def} \quad slp[P[at\ L];\ (C \longrightarrow A)] \wedge at\ M, \tag{7}$$

$$wlp[T;\ Q] \quad =_{def} \quad \bigwedge_{\tau \in T} wlp[\tau;\ Q], \tag{8}$$

$$slp[P;\ T] \quad =_{def} \quad \bigvee_{\tau \in T} slp[P;\ \tau]. \tag{9}$$

The predicate transformers wlp and slp are strongly related to Hoare's logic; their extensions have been defined in such a way that the three formulas

$$\{P\}\, X\, \{Q\}, \quad P \Rightarrow wlp[X;\ Q], \quad slp[P;\ X] \Rightarrow Q$$

are equivalent not only when X is an assignment, but also when it is a guarded assignment, a transition or a set of transitions. The first formula is used when P and Q are both known or both unknown. The second formula is used when only Q is known and the third one is used when only P is known. *Comment.* Let us emphasize the difference between wp [13], and wlp [11]:

$$wlp[(C \longrightarrow A);\ Q] \quad \equiv \quad C \Rightarrow wlp[A;Q],$$

$$wp[\text{if } C \longrightarrow A \text{ fi};\ Q] \quad \equiv \quad C \wedge wp[A;Q].$$

3 A methodology of incremental transformation

In this section, we introduce a notion of refinement that is general enough to allow any kind of program transformation. Afterwards, we show how the effect of such a transformation on the semantics of the refined system can be formalized. The method generalizes the results presented in [18,19].

3.1 Examples and definitions

Various kinds of transformations usually referred to as "refinements" are now illustrated with the elementary system S_{00}. This example provides a useful guideline towards an appropriate definition of the concept of refinement. It formalizes the original development of Peterson's algorithm given in [39].

The system S_{00} has an obvious drawback: it enforces the processes to access their critical section strictly in turn. This is too restrictive: we would like to allow one process to proceed when the other is in its non-critical section. Otherwise stated, the guards $T = p$ and $T = q$ should be weakened into the guards $(at\ q_0 \vee T = p)$ and $(at\ p_0 \vee T = q)$, respectively.

As place predicates are not considered as program variables in FCS, this transformation is (syntactically) disallowed. However, nothing prevents the introduction of new variables, for recording the truthvalues of $at\ p_0$ and $at\ q_0$. Such variables are called *secondary variables* because their values are fully determined by the values of already existing, *primary* objects (variables and place predicates); on the contrary, the values of the primary variables do not depend on the values of the secondary variables. As a consequence, the impact of the introduction of secondary variables on the invariant I of the system is trivial: if a secondary variable x is introduced, then the invariant becomes $I' =_{def} (I \wedge P(x))$, where $P(x)$ describes the value of x in terms of primary objects.

Let us introduce boolean variables inP and inQ to record the values of the place predicates $at\ p_0$ and $at\ q_0$. More precisely, we define $inP =_{def} \neg at\ p_0$ and $inQ =_{def} \neg at\ q_0$. This leads to the system S_{11} given below.

$$\mathcal{P} = \{P, Q\}, \quad \text{where } P = \{p_0, p_w, p_c\} \text{ and } Q = \{q_0, q_w, q_c\};$$
$$\mathcal{M} = \{T : \{p, q\}, inP : bool, inQ : bool\};$$
$$\mathcal{T} = \{(p_0, (inP, T) := (true, q), p_w), \quad (q_0, (inQ, T) := (true, p), q_w),$$
$$(p_w, T = p \longrightarrow skip, p_c), \quad (q_w, T = q \longrightarrow skip, q_c),$$
$$(p_c, inP := false, p_0), \quad (q_c, inQ := false, q_0)\}.$$

Obviously, the invariant I_{11} associated with the system S_{11} will be

$$I_{11} =_{def} [I_{00} \wedge (at\ p_0 \equiv \neg inP) \wedge (at\ q_0 \equiv \neg inQ)].$$

Now, we would like to weaken the guards $T = p$ and $T = q$ into $(\neg inQ \vee T = p)$ and $(\neg inP \vee T = q)$, respectively. This will lead to the refined system S_{22}, but an invariant I_{22} has to be discovered for it. Let us note that this transformation is less trivial than the previous one; in particular, the new invariant I_{22} is not bound to be $(I_{11} \wedge F)$ for some formula F. A method for discovering I_{22} is explained in the sequel.

As S_{22} contains double assignments, sequential refinements should be attempted. However, such transformations require that new "intermediate" labels are introduced first. In fact, two new labels p_i and q_i are introduced in P and Q respectively; this leads to the refined system S_{33} and to a refined invariant I_{33} for it. As no transition evokes the new labels, the new invariant will be

$$I_{33} =_{def} (I_{22} \wedge \neg at\ p_i \wedge \neg at\ q_i).$$

As a last step, the sequential refinements themselves can be attempted; for instance, the transition

$$(p_0, (inP, T) := (true, q), p_w)$$

will be replaced either by the transitions

$(p_0, inP := true, p_i)$,

$(p_i, T := q, p_w)$,

or by the transitions

$(p_0, T := q, p_i)$,

$(p_i, inP := true, p_w)$,

A similar replacement will be done for the transition

$(q_0, (inQ, T) := (true, p), q_w)$.

These transformations will lead to the refined system S_{44} and, hopefully, to an appropriate invariant I_{44} for this system. (I_{44} will be appropriate if the formula $\neg(at p_c \wedge at q_c)$ is still a logical consequence of it.) Once again, the derivation of I_{44} from I_{33} is not trivial; especially, the way the assignments about inP (or inQ) and T are ordered may be important.

As a conclusion, we see that two very different kinds of refinements must be performed. First, the refinements from S_{00} to S_{11} and from S_{22} to S_{33} are rather trivial. The role of these transformations is simply to introduce new objects (secondary variables or labels), in order to prepare more substantial and less trivial refinements. For this reason, they are called *preliminary refinements*. Their main characteristic is that they respect the invariant of the system; with self-explaining notation, we have the relation

$$I_{new} \equiv (I_{old} \wedge F),$$

where the formula F describes the new objects. No specific methodology is needed to deal with such transformations; they are also called *non-semantical refinements*, since they do not alter the invariant (that is, the semantics) of the system.

On the other hand, the refinements from S_{11} to S_{22} and from S_{33} to S_{44} are not trivial. They involve the introduction of no new object, but some transitions are replaced by new ones. In order not to rule out any kind of program transformation, no restriction is placed on the nature of the new transitions, except that they must be syntactically acceptable; as a consequence, they cannot evoke undefined labels and variables.[2] As such transformations are likely to alter deeply the invariant (the semantics) of the system, they are called *semantical refinements*. The *sequential refinement* (or *atomicity refinement*) is the most elementary case of semantical refinement.

3.2 Sequential refinement

The purpose of this paper is to evaluate the impact on the invariant of any kind of semantical refinement but, as the particular case of sequential refinement has already been studied [7,18], it is helpful to recall it first.

A sequential refinement S' of an FCS S is obtained by replacing a transition $\tau = (\ell, C \longrightarrow A, m)$ of S by two transitions $\tau' = (\ell, C' \longrightarrow A', n)$ and $\tau'' = (n, C'' \longrightarrow A'', m)$, where τ' and τ'' satisfy the following compatibility conditions. First, n is a new label; one can suppose that it has been introduced by a preliminary refinement, and that the invariant of the system S is $(I \wedge \neg at\, n)$. Second, for all assertions P and Q, if the triple $\{P\} \tau \{Q\}$ is true, then there exists an assertion R such that the triples $\{P\} \tau' \{R\}$ and $\{R\} \tau'' \{Q\}$ are also true. The second condition can be rewritten as

$$wlp[\tau; Q] \Rightarrow wlp[\tau'; wlp[\tau''; Q]], \text{ for all } Q.$$

---

[2]If new labels and variables are needed, preliminary refinements must be performed first to introduce them.

Comment. The definition of a sequential refinement given here agrees with the formal notion of refinement introduced in [6,36,37]. This notion is convenient in the framework of sequential programming but, as already mentioned, insufficient in the framework of parallel programming.

We briefly recall the method for dealing with sequential refinements. (More details are given in [18] and will be given, for the general case, in the next paragraph.) A definition is introduced first. A *transient state* of the sequentially refined system S' is a state where the place predicate *at n* is true (n is the new label). It is considered that a sequential refinement is acceptable, or valid, when the invariant of the initial system S remains true throughout the computations of the refined system S', except maybe in transient states. This is the case if and only if an assertion J exists such that

$$I' =_{def} [(\neg at\ n \Rightarrow I) \wedge (at\ n \Rightarrow J)]$$

is an invariant of the system S'. As a consequence, to validate a refinement means to discover an adequate J. Such a J is a solution of the constraint

$$\{(\neg at\ n \Rightarrow I) \wedge (at\ n \Rightarrow J)\}\ T'\ \{(\neg at\ n \Rightarrow I) \wedge (at\ n \Rightarrow J)\}, \tag{10}$$

where $T' = (T \setminus \{\tau\}) \cup \{\tau', \tau''\}$ is the set of transitions of the refined system S'. It is helpful to decompose this constraint into four parts, depending on the fact that *at n* can be true or false in the precondition or in the postcondition. The four resulting constraints are listed below.

$$\begin{aligned}
&\{\neg at\ n \wedge I\}\ T'\ \{\neg at\ n \Rightarrow I\}, \\
&\{\neg at\ n \wedge I\}\ T'\ \{at\ n \Rightarrow J\}, \\
&\{at\ n \wedge J\}\ T'\ \{\neg at\ n \Rightarrow I\}, \\
&\{at\ n \wedge J\}\ T'\ \{at\ n \Rightarrow J\}.
\end{aligned} \tag{11}$$

The first constraint is easy to check, since J does not occur in it. The second and the third constraints are rewritten respectively into

$$\begin{aligned}
&(slp[(\neg at\ n \wedge I);\ T'] \wedge at\ n) \Rightarrow J, \\
&J \Rightarrow (at\ n \Rightarrow wlp[T';\ (\neg at\ n \Rightarrow I)]),
\end{aligned}$$

and give respectively a strongest possible choice and a weakest possible choice for J.[3] Last, the fourth constraint contains two occurrences of J; as a consequence, it cannot be solved easily. The proposed strategy is to repeatedly select "candidates" in the set of formulas determined by the *slp*- and *wlp*-constraints, and to use the fourth constraint as an acceptance/rejection filter.

3.3 The general case

Our purpose is to identify the semantical consequences of the replacement of a transition by an arbitrary set of new transitions. The starting point is the constraints (10,11). The conditions $\neg at\ n$ and $at\ n$ have no longer any meaning here; they are replaced respectively by a *refinement condition* R and its negation $\neg R$. The problem is to determine an appropriate refinement condition. Our guideline for doing that will be to simplify the constraints as much as possible; we suppose that a refinement condition R has been chosen, and we look for the properties of R inducing simplification of the constraints. As a starting point, the invariant of the refined system S' is

$$I' \equiv [(R \Rightarrow I) \wedge (\neg R \Rightarrow J)].$$

In practice, the invariant I is the conjunction of several assertions. All of them are true when R is true, but some of them are false when R is false. This suggests a decomposition like $I =_{def} (I^- \wedge I^+)$, where the invariant I^- contains only non-altered assertions, whereas the formula I^+ may contain altered ones. More formally, we have $\{I\}\ T'\ \{I^-\}$, and even $\{I^-\}\ T'\ \{I^-\}$, but we have not $\{I\}\ T'\ \{I^+\}$. This decomposition suggests to rewrite

---

[3] A further simplification is possible: T' can be replaced by τ' in the *slp*-constraint, and by τ'' in the *wlp*-constraint. Let us also mention that it is sufficient to find $J[at\ n]$.

$$I' \equiv [I^- \wedge (R \Rightarrow I^+) \wedge (\neg R \Rightarrow K)], \tag{12}$$

for appropriate I^- and I^+; formulas R and K are still unknown. (Note that J is $(I^- \wedge K)$.) If I is the conjunction $(I_1 \wedge \cdots \wedge I_n)$, it is convenient to evaluate first $\{I\}\, T' \setminus T\, \{I_j\}$, for $j = 1, \ldots, n$: the conjunction I^0 of the I_j's for which the triple is true is a good approximation of I^-. More often than not, I^0 is an invariant, so $I^- =_{def} I^0$ is appropriate. It is also convenient to choose $R =_{def} I^+$, for obtaining a simplified form of formula (12), that is:

$$I' \equiv [I^- \wedge (I^+ \vee K)]. \tag{13}$$

In order to discover K, the constraint

$$\{I'\}\, T'\, \{I'\}$$

will be made explicit and simplified. We first observe that I^- is true in every relevant state; it is therefore convenient to discard any state not satisfying I^-. Formally, this means that I^- is taken as an additional axiom of the deduction system. The constraint is rewritten into

$$\{I^+ \vee K\}\, T'\, \{I^+ \vee K\}.$$

The set T' of the transitions of the refined system S' can be partitioned into the set $T' \cap T$ of old transitions and the set $T' \setminus T$ of new transitions. Furthermore, we distinguish the case where I^+ is true in the precondition and the case where K is true in the precondition. The constraint is therefore split into the set of constraints listed below.

$$\{I^+\}\, T' \cap T\, \{I^+ \vee K\},$$
$$\{K\}\, T' \cap T\, \{I^+ \vee K\},$$
$$\{I^+\}\, T' \setminus T\, \{I^+ \vee K\},$$
$$\{K\}\, T' \setminus T\, \{I^+ \vee K\}.$$

As I^+ is respected by old transitions, a further reduction leads to

$$\{I^+\}\, T' \setminus T\, \{I^+ \vee K\},$$
$$\{K\}\, T'\, \{I^+ \vee K\}. \tag{14}$$

As K occurs in the definition (13) of I' only in the term $(I^+ \vee K)$, it is not a real restriction to add the constraint $(K \Rightarrow \neg I^+)$. As a consequence, K must be stronger than formula $\neg I^+$ whereas, on the other hand, the first constraint of (14) asserts that $(I^+ \vee K)$ must be weaker than the formula $slp[I^+; T' \setminus T]$.

The set C of appropriate choices for K is therefore a subset of

$$C_0 =_{def} \{X \ : \ [(K_U \Rightarrow X) \wedge (X \Rightarrow K_D)]\},$$

where

$$K_U =_{def} \neg I^+ \wedge slp[I^+; T' \setminus T],$$
$$K_D =_{def} \neg I^+. \tag{15}$$

The determination of the whole set C is usually intractable but, fortunately, we are satisfied with a single element of it. Furthermore, practice shows that, when an appropriate K exists, the formula K_U often turns out to be acceptable. If it is not, the strategy proposed for the sequential refinement still holds in the general case: repeatedly select "candidates" inside C_0 and test them against the second constraint of (14); any candidate satisfying this test can be accepted.

4 A worked-out elementary example

In this section, the system S_{11} introduced in paragraph 3.1 is incrementally transformed into Peterson's algorithm.

4.1 Weakening a guard

The first step is to refine the system S_{11} (§ 3.1) by weakening the guard $T = p$ into the guard $(\neg inQ \lor T = p)$. This will lead to the system S_{21}. In order to simplify the notation, we rename S_{11} into S and S_{21} into S'. The latter is obtained from the former by replacing the transition

$$\tau : (p_w, \ T = p \longrightarrow skip, \ p_c),$$

by the transition

$$\tau' : (p_w, \ \neg inQ \lor T = p \longrightarrow skip, \ p_c).$$

The invariant I of the system S is

$$(at \ p_w \Rightarrow (T = q \ \lor \ at \ q_w)) \land (at \ q_w \Rightarrow (T = p \ \lor \ at \ p_w))$$
$$\land \ (at \ p_c \Rightarrow T = p) \land (at \ q_c \Rightarrow T = q)$$
$$\land \ (at \ p_0 \equiv \neg inP) \land (at \ q_0 \equiv \neg inQ);$$

The triple $\{I\} T' \{A\}$ is checked for each assertion A; this leads to the decomposition $I = (I^- \land I^+)$, where

$$I^- : \ (at \ p_w \Rightarrow (T = q \ \lor \ at \ q_w)) \land (at \ q_w \Rightarrow (T = p \ \lor \ at \ p_w)) \land$$
$$(at \ q_c \Rightarrow T = q) \land (at \ p_0 \equiv \neg inP) \land (at \ q_0 \equiv \neg inQ),$$

$$I^+ : \ (at \ p_c \Rightarrow T = p).$$

Formula I^- is easily checked to be an invariant of the refined system (but, obviously, this invariant does not ensure mutual exclusion). Definitions (15) give rise to

$$K_D = \neg I^+$$
$$= (at \ p_c \land T = q),$$

$$K_U = \neg I^+ \land slp[I^+; T' \setminus T]$$
$$= \neg I^+ \land slp[I^+; (p_w, \neg inQ \lor T = p \longrightarrow skip, p_c)])$$
$$= (at \ p_c \land T = q) \land [at \ p_c \land (\neg inQ \lor T = p)]$$
$$= at \ p_c \land T = q \land \neg inQ.$$

The "candidate set" for K is

$$\mathcal{K}_0 = \{X : [(at \ p_c \land T = q \land \neg inQ) \Rightarrow X] \land [X \Rightarrow (at \ p_c \land T = q)]\}.$$

We tentatively select $K =_{def} K_U$ and check that the triple $\{K\} T' \{I^+ \lor K\}$ holds (recall that, in the present context, I^- is assumed to be true in all states). The formula $I^+ \lor K$ reduces to $(at \ p_c \Rightarrow (T = p \lor \neg inQ))$. The formula $I' =_{def} [I^- \land (I^+ \lor K)]$ can be simplified into

$$I_{21} =_{def} \ (at \ p_w \Rightarrow (T = q \ \lor \ at \ q_w)) \land (at \ q_w \Rightarrow (T = p \ \lor \ at \ p_w))$$
$$\land \ (at \ p_c \Rightarrow (T = p \lor \neg inQ)) \land (at \ q_c \Rightarrow T = q)$$
$$\land \ (at \ p_0 \equiv \neg inP) \land (at \ q_0 \equiv \neg inQ).$$

It is straightforward to check that the formula

$$I_{21} \Rightarrow \neg(at \ p_c \land at \ q_c)$$

is valid; as a consequence, the refinement preserves the mutual exclusion.

A similar work leads to the system S_{22} and the invariant

$$I_{22} =_{def} \ (at \ p_w \Rightarrow (T = q \ \lor \ at \ q_w)) \land (at \ q_w \Rightarrow (T = p \ \lor \ at \ p_w))$$
$$\land \ (at \ p_c \Rightarrow (T = p \lor \neg inQ)) \land (at \ q_c \Rightarrow (T = q \lor \neg inP))$$
$$\land \ (at \ p_0 \equiv \neg inP) \land (at \ q_0 \equiv \neg inQ).$$

4.2 Sequential decomposition

We consider now a sequential refinement. The initial version is $S =_{def} S_{33}$ and the refined version $S' =_{def} S_{43}$ is obtained by replacing the transition

$$\tau : \quad (p_0, (inP, T) := (true, q), \ p_w),$$

by the transitions

$$\tau' : \quad (p_0, \ inP := true, \ p_i),$$
$$\tau'' : \quad (p_i, \ T := q, \ p_w).$$

As usual, the invariant $I =_{def} I_{33}$ is split into

$$I^- : \quad (at \ p_w \Rightarrow (T = q \ \lor \ at \ q_w)) \land (at \ q_w \Rightarrow (T = p \ \lor \ at \ p_w)) \land$$
$$(at \ p_c \Rightarrow (T = p \ \lor \ \neg inQ)) \land$$
$$(at \ p_0 \equiv \neg inP) \land (at \ q_0 \equiv \neg inQ) \land \neg at \ q_i,$$
$$I^+ : \quad (at \ q_c \Rightarrow (T = q \ \lor \ \neg inP)) \land \neg at \ p_i.$$

Formulas K_D and K_U are easily computed; once again, the fact that I^- is always true in relevant states (it is an invariant of I_{43}) induces some simplification. The results are

$$K_D = \neg I^+$$
$$= (at \ q_c \land T = p \land inP) \ \lor \ at \ p_i,$$
$$K_U = \neg I^+ \land slp[I^+; \ T' \setminus T]$$
$$= (\neg I^+ \land slp[I^+; \ (p_0 \to p_i)]) \ \lor \ (\neg I^+ \land slp[I^+; \ (p_i \to p_w)])$$
$$= (\neg I^+ \land at \ p_i \land slp[I^+[at \ p_0]; \ inP := true]) \ \lor \ (\neg I^+ \land at \ p_w \land slp[I^+[at \ p_i]; \ T := q])$$
$$= (at \ p_i \land slp[true; \ inP := true]) \ \lor \ (at \ q_c \land T = p \land inP \land at \ p_w \land slp[false; \ T := q])$$
$$= (at \ p_i \land inP) \ \lor \ false$$
$$= (at \ p_i \land \neg at \ p_0)$$
$$= at \ p_i.$$

We have to select a K within the set

$$\mathcal{K}_0 = \{ X : [at \ p_i \Rightarrow X] \land [X \Rightarrow ((at \ q_c \land T = p \land inP) \ \lor \ at \ p_i)] \}.$$

Once again, $K = K_U$ is an appropriate choice, such that $\{K\} t \{I^+ \lor K\}$ holds for each transition t of the refined system. The formula $(I^+ \lor K)$ reduces to $[(at \ q_c \Rightarrow (T = q \ \lor \ \neg inP)) \ \lor \ at \ p_i]$, and further to $[at \ q_c \Rightarrow (T = q \ \lor \ \neg inP \ \lor \ at \ p_i)]$. The formula $I' =_{def} [I^- \land (I^+ \lor K)]$ is

$$I_{43} =_{def} \quad (at \ p_w \Rightarrow (T = q \ \lor \ at \ q_w)) \land (at \ q_w \Rightarrow (T = p \ \lor \ at \ p_w))$$
$$\land \ (at \ p_c \Rightarrow (T = p \ \lor \ \neg inQ)) \land (at \ q_c \Rightarrow (T = q \ \lor \ \neg inP \ \lor \ at \ p_i))$$
$$\land \ (at \ p_0 \equiv \neg inP) \land (at \ q_0 \equiv \neg inQ)$$
$$\land \ \neg at \ q_i.$$

A similar sequential refinement leads to S_{44}; an invariant of this system is

$$I_{44} =_{def} \quad (at \ p_w \Rightarrow (T = q \ \lor \ at \ q_w)) \land (at \ q_w \Rightarrow (T = p \ \lor \ at \ p_w))$$
$$\land \ (at \ p_c \Rightarrow (T = p \ \lor \ \neg inQ \ \lor \ at \ q_i))$$
$$\land \ (at \ q_c \Rightarrow (T = q \ \lor \ \neg inP \ \lor \ at \ p_i))$$
$$\land \ (at \ p_0 = \neg inP) \land (at \ q_0 \equiv \neg inQ),$$

and the mutual exclusion is still satisfied.

Comments. In [18,19], we proposed a slightly different technique; for the first sequential refinement, we could have chosen $R =_{def} \neg at \ p_i$ instead of $R =_{def} I^+$. One can check that both choices lead to the same refined invariant I_{43}.

One can also check that reverting the order in the sequential refinement, that is, replacing the transition

$$\tau : \quad (p_0, (inP, T) := (true, q), p_w),$$

by the transitions

$$\mu' : \quad (p_0, T := q, p_i),$$
$$\mu'' : \quad (p_i, inP := true, p_w),$$

leads to an unsatisfactory version (see [39,15,17]).

5 Development of a data transfer protocol

Even the development of small to medium-sized systems involves rather many steps but most of them reduce to routine symbolic manipulation. The interesting, non trivial steps are concerned with the specific algorithmic idea(s) of the system in development.

We address in this section the development of a variant of Stenning's data transfer protocol [42]. In order to keep the presentation within a short size, only the crucial step of the design will be considered (see [20] for the complete development).

5.1 The initial version

A data transfer protocol must ensure reliable transmission of information from a station to another. The problem is that transmission channels are not safe: they can lose, corrupt, duplicate and reorder messages. It is assumed that any corruption is detected by the receiving station, which simply discards corrupted messages. The sequence of data is to be transmitted without loss, alteration, duplication or permutation.

The information to be sent along is represented by a sequence $X =_{def} (X[n] : n = 1, 2, \ldots)$ of messages, whereas a similar sequence Y records the already (and correctly) transmitted part of X. A simple transmission strategy is as follows. The sending station repeatedly transmits a message $X[n]$. The receiving station discards corrupted copies of $X[n]$ until a correct copy is received; then, "acknowlegments" are repeatedly sent back to the sending station. Upon receiving such an acknowledgment, the sending station can begin to send copies of the next message $X[n + 1]$.

Our initial version will implement this elementary strategy, at a rather abstract level: first, no process is introduced (like in UNITY [10], a formal concurrent system can be represented by a set of global actions) and, second, the (unreliable) channels are supposed to be synchronous. Three counters are used. The sequence $X[1 : LA]$ has been successfully transmitted and acknowledged ("LA" means "Last Acknowledged"); the sequence $X[1 : LR]$ has been correctly received ("LR" means "Last Received") and the sequence $X[1 : HS]$ has been transmitted ("HS" means "Highest Sent"). As a consequence of the transmission stategy, the relation $LA \leq LR \leq HS \leq LA + 1$ is maintained. Here is the formal representation of the initial system $S_0 = (\mathcal{P}_0, \mathcal{M}_0, \mathcal{T}_0)$.

$$\mathcal{P}_0 = \emptyset;$$

$$\mathcal{M}_0 = \{LA, LR, HS : nat; \ X, Y : array[nat] \ of \ string\};$$

$$\mathcal{T}_0 = \{ 1. \ (LA = HS \ \longrightarrow \ (HS, Y[HS + 1]) := (HS + 1, X[HS + 1])),$$
$$2. \ (LA = HS \ \longrightarrow \ HS := HS + 1),$$
$$3. \ (LA < HS \ \longrightarrow \ Y[HS] := X[HS]),$$
$$4. \ (LA < HS \ \longrightarrow \ skip),$$
$$5. \ (Y[LR + 1] \neq NIL \ \longrightarrow \ (LA, LR) := (LA + 1, LR + 1)),$$
$$6. \ (Y[LR + 1] \neq NIL \ \longrightarrow \ LR := LR + 1),$$
$$7. \ (Y[LR + 1] = NIL \ \longrightarrow \ LA := LR),$$
$$8. \ (Y[LR + 1] = NIL \ \longrightarrow \ skip) \}.$$

The invariant is

$$I_0 =_{def} \quad (LA \le LR \le HS \le LA+1) \land$$
$$\forall s\, (Y[s] \in \{X[s], NIL\}) \land$$
$$\forall s\, (1 \le s \le LR \Rightarrow Y[s] = X[s]) \land$$
$$\forall s\, (HS < s \Rightarrow Y[s] = NIL),$$

and simply expresses the strategy informally introduced above. Any state satisfying I_0 is an adequate initial state; the standard initial state is characterized by

$$C_0 =_{def} \quad LA = LR = HS = 0 \land \forall s\, (0 < s \Rightarrow Y[s] = NIL)).$$

Transitions 1 and 2 model message transmission. When message $X[HS]$ has been acknowledged, message $X[HS+1]$ can be transmitted; this transmission can succeed (transition 1) or fail (transition 2). The value NIL is a "dummy" value; it models the initial empty value of elements of the recording sequence Y, and also any corrupted value. As a result, unsuccessful transmission is simply modelled by *skip*.

If message $X[HS]$ has not been acknowledged within some delay (this delay is not modelled here), it has to be transmitted again, and retransmission can succeed (transition 3) or fail (transition 4).

When a new, uncorrupted message arrives, it is acknowledged; the transmission of the acknowledgment can succeed (transition 5) or fail (transition 6). The acknowledgment corresponding to some message is sent repeatedly, until the next message arrives. The acknowledgment retransmission can succeed (transition 7) or fail (transition 8).

5.2 Correctness of the initial version

The invariant expresses that, at every time, the prefix $X[1 : LR]$ of the sequence has been correctly transmitted; it is also clear that the counters LA, LR and HS cannot decrease. These properties are the interesting invariance properties of the system. Although we are mainly concerned by invariance properties, let us also mention an interesting liveness property of the system : the counters increase, provided that some fairness requirements are satisfied. This property is formally specified and proved in [20]; only a graphical proof outline is given here (Fig. 2), with the following notation :

$$A_n : \quad LA = LR = HS = n,$$
$$B_n : \quad LA = LR = n \land HS = n+1 \land Y[HS] = X[HS],$$
$$C_n : \quad LA = LR = n \land HS = n+1 \land Y[HS] = NIL,$$
$$D_n : \quad LA = n \land LR = HS = n+1.$$

The self loops in Fig. 2 correspond to useless moves, whereas the other arcs correspond to useful moves. Fairness requirements are that self looping cannot last forever. These requirements can be informally expressed as follows.

The receiver cannot delay the sender forever,   (loop A),
The sender cannot delay the receiver forever,   (loop B),
The transmission channel cannot fail forever,   (loop C),
The acknowledgment channel cannot fail forever,   (loop D).

5.3 Stenning's window principle

The next step will be the implementation of Stenning's technique. For now, the transmitter may be ahead of the receiver, but only by one message. The synchrony between the transmitter and the receiver can be decreased by allowing a "window" of already sent but still unacknowledged messages. Let $W \ge 1$ be the finite maximal size of the window. Notice that the candidates for retransmission are no longer $X[HS]$ only, but each $X[r]$ such that $LA < r \le HS$. All the messages belonging to this

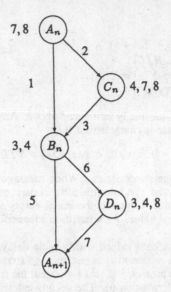

Figure 2: Graphical proof outline

window will be retransmitted after some delay. (In our model, the delay is left unspecified; any finite delay is acceptable, as far as only correctness is concerned.) A preliminary refinement is needed to introduce a window index r; that leads to the system S_1, with invariant $I_1 = I_0$. The window principle is now introduced by a semantical refinement. The set of transitions of the resulting system S_2 is

$$T_2 = \{ 1. \quad (HS - LA < W \longrightarrow (HS, Y[HS+1]) := (HS+1, X[HS+1])),$$
$$2. \quad (HS - LA < W \longrightarrow HS := HS+1),$$
$$3. \quad (LA < r \le HS \longrightarrow (Y[r], r) := (X[r], r+1)),$$
$$4. \quad (LA < r \le HS \longrightarrow r := r+1),$$
$$5. \quad (\neg(LA < r \le HS) \longrightarrow r := LA+1),$$
$$6. \quad (Y[LR+1] \ne NIL \longrightarrow (LA, LR) := (LA+1, LR+1)),$$
$$7. \quad (Y[LR+1] \ne NIL \longrightarrow LR := LR+1),$$
$$8. \quad (Y[LR+1] = NIL \longrightarrow LA := LR),$$
$$9. \quad (Y[LR+1] = NIL \longrightarrow skip)\}.$$

Transitions 1 and 2 correspond to first message transmission, transition 3, 4 and 5 implement message retransmission, transitions 6 and 7 correspond to message reception and acknowledgment, and transitions 8 and 9 implement acknowledgment retransmission.

As usual, some parts of the initial invariant are respected by the new transitions but others are not; this gives rise to the decomposition $I_1 =_{def} (I^- \wedge I^+)$, where

$$I^- =_{def} \quad (LA \le LR \le HS) \wedge$$
$$\forall s (Y[s] \in \{X[s], NIL\}) \wedge$$
$$\forall s (1 \le s \le LR \Rightarrow Y[s] = X[s]) \wedge$$
$$\forall s (HS < s \Rightarrow Y[s] = NIL),$$

$$I^+ =_{def} \quad HS \le LA + 1.$$

Formulas K_D and K_U are determined as follows.

$$K_D \equiv \neg I^+$$
$$\equiv HS > LA + 1.$$

$$K_U \equiv \neg I^+ \wedge slp[I^+; T' \setminus T]$$
$$\equiv HS > LA + 1 \wedge slp[HS \leq LA + 1; \{1, 2, 3, 4, 5\}]$$
$$\equiv HS > LA + 1 \wedge (slp[HS \leq LA + 1; \{1, 2\}] \vee slp[HS \leq LA + 1; \{3, 4, 5\}])$$
$$\equiv HS > LA + 1 \wedge (HS \leq LA + 2 \wedge HS \leq LA + W \vee HS \leq LA + 1)$$
$$\equiv HS = LA + 2 \wedge HS \leq LA + W.$$

(In this computation, I^- is assumed to be true and only relevant variables have been considered.) The choice $K =_{def} K_U$ is too strong but, as K_U is a conjunction, it is natural to try one of the conjunct. An adequate choice is $(I^+ \vee K) =_{def} HS \leq LA + W$. The resulting invariant is

$$I_2 =_{def} \quad (LA \leq LR \leq HS \leq LA + W) \wedge$$
$$\forall s (Y[s] \in \{X[s], NIL\}) \wedge$$
$$\forall s (1 \leq s \leq LR \Rightarrow Y[s] = X[s]) \wedge$$
$$\forall s (HS < s \Rightarrow Y[s] = NIL).$$

The correctness proof given for S_0 is easily adapted to S_2.

6 Related work and further work

The abstract programming language used in this paper is based on the classical notion of a transition system, frequently used in parallel programming (see e.g. [25,33]). Our variant has been obtained by adding labels to the formalism presented in [41]. The adaptation of Hoare logic to this language is similar in spirit to the adaptations for concurrency presented in [26,28] (although some technical differences exist). The rules (3) comes from [16].

The stepwise refinement approach has been widely used in parallel programming. Early contributions are mainly concerned with the refinement of the grain of parallelism [14]; [27] introduces the concept of a state function, which connects the invariant of the refined version with the invariant of the initial version. This concept can lead to concise proofs, but the discovery of appropriate state functions is not always trivial.

In this paper, a (semantical) refinement is the replacement of an old transition by a set of new transitions. This definition is too general, since any transformation can be achieved by a sequence of such replacements. However, the distinction between a refinement and a general transformation is somewhat arbitrary; several authors have demonstrated that many non-trivial transformations of concurrent systems can be considered as refinements [43,4,9]. The notion of refinement deserves further theoretical study.

Mainly invariance properties have been considered in this paper. Temporal logic has been used to specify and prove other kinds of program properties [34,35]. We have observed that when a refined version maintains a liveness property, the proof of this property is easily adapted, but this is not a general result. A refinement method taking into account the liveness properties has been proposed in [7], but it is restricted to atomicity refinements. Another weakness of the method proposed here is that it is sound but not complete [12]. More precisely, if the invariant of the refined version does not imply some wanted invariance property, one cannot deduce that this property does not hold. From the theoretical point of view, completeness can be achieved by using predicate transformers like the "weakest safe invariant" introduced in [43], or the "weakest invariant" introduced in [29]. The problem is that these predicate transformers are not easily computed. However, this approach seems interesting for finite state systems since, in this case, weakest and strongest invariants can be computed in a mechanical way.

References

[1] E.A. ASHCROFT and Z. MANNA, "Formalization of Properties of Parallel Programs", Machine Intelligence, 6, pp. 17-41, 1970

[2] K.R. APT, "Ten years of Hoare logic", ACM Toplas, 3, pp. 431-483, 1981

[3] K.R. APT, "Correctness Proofs of Distributed Termination Algorithms", ACM Toplas, 8, pp. 388-405, 1986

[4] R.J.R. BACK and R. KURKI-SUONIO, "Decentralization of Process Nets with Centralized Control", Proc. 2nd ACM Symp. on Principles of Distributed Computing, pp. 131-142, 1983

[5] R.J.R. BACK and R. KURKI-SUONIO, "Distributed Cooperation with Action Systems", ACM Toplas, 10, pp. 513-554, 1988

[6] R.J.R. BACK, "A Calculus of Refinements for Program Derivations", Acta Informatica, 25, pp. 593-624, 1988

[7] R.J.R. BACK, "A Method for Refining Atomicity in Parallel Algorithms", LNCS, 366, pp. 199-216, 1989

[8] E. BEST, "A Note on the Proof of a Concurrent Program", IPL, 9, pp. 103-104, 1979

[9] M. CHANDY and J. MISRA, "An Example of Stepwise Refinement of Distributed Programs: Quiescence Detection", ACM Toplas, 8, pp. 326-343, 1986

[10] M. CHANDY and J. MISRA, "Parallel Program Design: A Foundation", Addison-Wesley, 1988

[11] J. de BAKKER, "Mathematical theory of program correctness", Prentice-Hall, 1980

[12] J.W. de BAKKER and L.G.L.T. MEERTENS, "On the completeness of the inductive assertion method", JCSS, 11, pp. 323-357, 1975

[13] E.W. DIJKSTRA, "A discipline of programming", Prentice Hall, New Jersey, 1976

[14] E.W. DIJKSTRA and al., "On-the-Fly Garbage Collection: An Exercise in Cooperation", CACM, 21, pp. 966-975, 1978

[15] E.W. DIJKSTRA, "An assertional proof of a program by G.L. Peterson", EWD 779, 1981

[16] R. GERTH, "Transition logic", Proc. 16th ACM Symp. on Theory of Computing, pp. 39-50, 1984

[17] E.P. GRIBOMONT, "Synthesis of parallel programs invariants", LNCS, 186, pp. 325-338, 1985

[18] E.P. GRIBOMONT, "Development of concurrent programs : an example" LNCS, 352, pp. 210-224, 1989

[19] E.P. GRIBOMONT, "Stepwise refinement and concurrency : a small exercise" LNCS, 375, pp. 219-238, 1989

[20] E.P. GRIBOMONT, "Stenning's protocol", in "Formal methods for parallel programming", Internal report, 1989

[21] D. GRIES, "The Science of Programming", Springer-Verlag, Berlin, 1981

[22] C.A.R. HOARE, "An axiomatic basis for computer programming", CACM, 12, pp. 576-583, 1969

[23] C.A.R. HOARE, "Communicating Sequential Processes", CACM, 21, pp. 666-677, 1978

[24] C.A.R. HOARE, "Communicating Sequential Processes", Prentice-Hall, 1985

[25] R.M. KELLER, "Formal Verification of Parallel Programs", CACM, 19, pp. 371-384, 1976

[26] L. LAMPORT, "The 'Hoare Logic' of Concurrent Programs", Acta Informatica, 14, pp. 21-37, 1980

[27] L. LAMPORT, "An Assertional Correctness Proof of a Distributed Algorithm", SCP, 2, pp. 175-206, 1983

[28] L. LAMPORT and F.B. SCHNEIDER, "The 'Hoare Logic' of CSP, and All That", ACM Toplas, 6, pp. 281-296, 1984

[29] L. LAMPORT, "win and sin: Predicate Transformers for Concurrency", DEC SRC Report 17, 1987

[30] L. LAMPORT, "A Theorem on Atomicity in Distributed Algorithms", DEC SRC Report 28, 1988

[31] R.J. LIPTON, "Reduction: a method of proving properties of parallel programs", CACM, 18, pp. 717-721, 1975

[32] N.A. LYNCH and M.R. TUTTLE, "Hierarchical Correctness Proofs for Distributed Algorithms", Proc. 6th ACM Symp. on Principles of Distributed Computing, pp. 137-151, 1987

[33] Z. MANNA and A. PNUELI, "How to cook a temporal proof system for your pet language", Proc. 10th ACM Symp. on Principles of Programming Languages, pp. 141-154, 1983

[34] Z. MANNA and A. PNUELI, "Adequate proof principles for invariance and liveness properties of concurrent programs", SCP, 4, pp. 257-289, 1984

[35] Z. MANNA and A. PNUELI, "Specification and verification of concurrent programs by ∀-automata", Proc. 14th ACM Symp. on Principles of Programming Languages, pp. 1-12, 1987

[36] C. MORGAN, "The Specification Statement", ACM Toplas, 10, pp. 403-419, 1988

[37] J.M. MORRIS, "A theoretical basis for stepwise refinement and the programming calculus", SCP, 9, pp. 287-306, 1987

[38] S. OWICKI and D. GRIES, "An Axiomatic Proof Technique for Parallel Programs", Acta Informatica, 6, pp. 319-340, 1976

[39] G.L. PETERSON, "Myths about the mutual exclusion problem", IPL, 12, pp. 115-116, 1981

[40] R.D. SCHLICHTING and F.D. SCHNEIDER, "Using Message Passing for Distributed Programming: Proof Rules and Disciplines", ACM Toplas, 6, pp. 402-431, 1984

[41] J. SIFAKIS, "A unified approach for studying the properties of transition systems", TCS, 18, pp. 227-259, 1982

[42] N.V. STENNING, "A data transfer protocol", Computer Networks, 1, pp. 99-110, 1976

[43] A. van LAMSWEERDE and M. SINTZOFF, "Formal derivation of strongly correct concurrent programs", Acta Informatica, 12, pp. 1-31, 1979

Set Domains

Reinhold Heckmann

FB 10 – Informatik

Universität des Saarlandes

6600 Saarbrücken

Bundesrepublik Deutschland

email: heckmann@cs.uni-sb.de

Abstract

Set domains are intended to give semantics to a data type of sets together with a wide range of useful set operations. The classical power domain constructions are shown to be inappropriate for this purpose. Lower and upper domain do not support quantification, whereas Plotkin's domain does not contain the empty set. This is an immense defect, since the empty set is not only interesting in its own, but is also needed to define operations such as filtering a set through a predicate. Two constructions, the *big* and the *small set domain*, are proposed that support the desired set operations. The big domain is bounded complete, whereas the small one only respects Plotkin's SFP-property. Both constructions are free with respect to suitable algebraic theories.

1 Introduction

Following the Scott-Strachey approach [12] to the semantics of programming languages, the various types occurring in a functional programming language are associated with corresponding domains of semantic entities. For instance, tuple or record types and functional types correspond to product and exponentiation of domains respectively. Originally, there was no domain construction corresponding to set types over a given ground type.

In 1976, Plotkin [8] proposed a power domain construction, analogous to power set forming, to describe the semantics of non-deterministic programming languages. Because his construction goes beyond the category of bounded complete (Scott) domains, Plotkin proposed the larger category of *SFP-domains* that is closed under his construction. A short time later, Smyth [9] introduced a simpler construction, the upper or Smyth power domain, that respects bounded completeness. In [10], a third power domain construction occurs, the lower power domain, that completes the triumvirate of classical power domain constructions.

For a lazy functional programming language, we want to introduce an abstract data type of sets with some primitive operations that allow to derive a wide range of useful other operations, including some of higher order. As outlined in section 3, the set data type should support union, filtering a set through a predicate, and checking whether a predicate holds for some or all elements of a set (quantification). The semantics of the set data type should be given by means of a suitable 'set domain' construction.

In section 4, we check whether some of the classical power domains could serve as set domain, i.e. satisfy the specification given in section 3. All three power domains have an important defect: they do not contain a representation of the empty set. The empty set is not only interesting in its own. Its lack also makes important operations, such as filtering a set through a predicate, impossible to define. Adjoining the empty set to lower and upper power domain is simple, but both of them support quantification in a half-hearted manner: they only say 'yes', never 'no', or vice versa. Plotkin's power domain better supports quantification, but there is no simple way to extend it by the empty set.

Thus, we look for new constructions. The fact that lower and upper domain support opposite halves of quantification suggests to combine them to their product after extension by the empty set. Certain conditions make stand out two subsets of this product, the small and the big set domain which support all operations we want to have. The small domain is a subset of the big one, and it still contains isomorphic images of the three classical power domains. The big set domain introduced in section 5 is bounded complete, hence it is useful in the context of Scott domains. Similar to Plotkin's domain, the construction of the small set domain described in section 6 leads out of the scope of Scott domains, but respects Plotkin's SFP-property.

All members of the base of the small set domain may be built up by finite applications of our primitive set operations. This is not true for the big domain. An equality on sets may be derived from the primitive set operations and a given equality on the ground domain. If the given equality is the greatest continuous equality on the ground domain, then the set equality is again the greatest continuous one on the small set domain (see section 7). This again is not true for the big one.

Starting from problems in data base theory, Buneman et al. [1] also proposed to combine lower and upper power domain to a so-called sandwich power domain. In contrast to me, they left off the empty set and did not investigate their construction in detail.

Gunter investigated the logic of the classical power domains [2]. By extending the logic of Plotkin's domain in a natural way, he developed a so-called mixed power domain. It is a subset from our small set domain, but inherits from Plotkin's domain the lack of the empty set. In the last few months, Gunter further developed the theory of the mixed power domain [3,4]. In particular, he added the empty set and arrived exactly at what we call the small set domain. In parallel independent work, Gunter and I developed the notion of a mix algebra and showed that the small set domain is a free construction w.r.t. the mix theory (see section 8). I found the additional result that the big set domain is also a free construction w.r.t. an algebraic theory which however is less natural than the mix theory (see section 9).

2 Domain-theoretic background

We start off with the necessary domain-theoretic background. We only give definitions and facts. For proofs, we refer to the literature or to an elaborated version of this paper [5].

A *poset* (partially ordered set) $(P, \leq)$ is a set P together with a reflexive, antisymmetric, and transitive relation '$\leq$'. When there is no risk of confusion, we identify the poset $\mathbf{P} = (P, \leq)$ with its carrier P. We refer to the standard notions of minimal and maximal elements, upper and lower bounds, bounded subsets, least upper bound (lub) denoted by '$\sqcup$', greatest lower bound (glb), directed set, directed complete poset (dcpo), monotonic and continuous function.[1] Two points x and y are consistent – $x \uparrow y$ – if they have a common upper bound.

A set $A \subseteq \mathbf{P}$ is a *lower* set iff with any point a in A, all points *below* a belong to A. It is an *upper* set iff with any point a in A, all points *above* a belong to A. It is *convex*, iff with any points a and c in A, all points *between* a and c belong to A. For $A \subseteq \mathbf{P}$, let $\downarrow A = \{y \in \mathbf{P} \mid \exists x \in A : x \geq y\}$ be the lower closure of A, and $\uparrow A = \{y \in \mathbf{P} \mid \exists x \in A : x \leq y\}$ the upper closure. $\downarrow A$ is the least lower superset of A, and $\uparrow A$ the least upper one. We use the abbreviations $\downarrow x = \downarrow\{x\}$ etc.

A point a in a directed complete poset $\mathbf{P}$ is *isolated* (or: *finite*), iff for all directed sets $D \subseteq \mathbf{P}$ with $a \leq \sqcup D$, there is an element d in D such that $a \leq d$. The set of all isolated points of $\mathbf{P}$ is called $\mathbf{P}^0$. We use the name 'isolated' in order to avoid the name conflict with finite sets. Nevertheless, finite sets of isolated (finite) elements are called *bifinite*. A directed complete poset $\mathbf{P}$ is *algebraic*, iff every point of $\mathbf{P}$ is the lub of a directed set of isolated points. The set $\mathbf{P}^0$ of all isolated points of $\mathbf{P}$ is called the *base*. A *domain* is an algebraic poset whose base is countable, and which contains a least element $\bot$. The *iso-lower closure* $\Downarrow A$ of a subset A of an algebraic dcpo $\mathbf{P}$ is the set of all isolated points below some member of A, i.e. $\Downarrow A = \downarrow A \cap \mathbf{P}^0$. If $\Downarrow A$ equals A, i.e. if A is a lower subset of the base, then A is called *iso-lower* set.

A domain has property M [6,8], if for any bifinite set E, there is a finite set F of upper bounds of E with the property, that there is a member of F below every upper bound of E. Generally, there exist different finite sets F with this property for a given bifinite set E. Among those, there is a least one w.r.t. set inclusion. It is bifinite and consists of the *minimal upper bounds (mubs)* of E. A domain has property SFP [8], if it has property M, and every bifinite set E has a bifinite superset G that is closed w.r.t. mubs of subsets. A thorough discussion of these properties may be found in [6]. A domain is bounded complete if every bounded subset has a lub, or equivalently if every two bounded isolated points have a lub. It is complete if every subset has a lub.

Thus, a hierarchy of domains is introduced. Complete domains are bounded complete, the latter have property SFP, and SFP implies M. Membership in these domain classes is preserved by sum and product. Exponentiation, i.e. forming the space of continuous functions, only preserves (bounded) completeness and SFP, but neither M nor the property to be a plain domain [11].

The Lawson topology

In this section, we introduce the Lawson topology [7,8] for a fixed underlying M-domain $\mathbf{D}$. The closed sets of this topology have many pleasing mathematical properties. They may be used to define the classical power domains.

Following Plotkin [8], we define the Lawson topology[2] by its sub-basis: the collection of all cones $\uparrow a$ for isolated a and of their complements. The topological closure of a set A is denoted by $\overline{A}$. It is the least closed superset of A. All finite sets are closed. The Lawson topology is homeomorphic to a compact [7] metric [5] space.

The set $\mathcal{C}D$ of Lawson closed sets of a given M-domain $\mathbf{D}$ forms a complete domain when ordered by '$\supseteq$' [5]. Its isolated points are the sets being both closed and open. All lubs exist, lub is intersection, glb is set union followed by closure, the least element is $\mathbf{D}$, and the greatest one is $\emptyset$. The useful mathematical properties of closed sets are summarized in the following theorem [5]:

---

[1]w.r.t. directed sets, not ascending sequences.
[2]called Cantor topology by Plotkin

Theorem 2.1 (Operations in the Lawson domain)

For domains **D**, **X**, and **Y**, the following operations are continuous:

Union:	$\cup : C\mathbf{D} \times C\mathbf{D} \to C\mathbf{D}$
Intersection:	$\cap : C\mathbf{D} \times C\mathbf{D} \to C\mathbf{D}$
Upper cone:	$\uparrow : \mathbf{D} \to C\mathbf{D}$
Upper closure:	$\uparrow : C\mathbf{D} \to C\mathbf{D}$
Lower closure:	$\downarrow : C\mathbf{D} \to C\mathbf{D}$
Product:	$\times : C\mathbf{X} \times C\mathbf{Y} \to C(\mathbf{X} \times \mathbf{Y})$
Extension:	$ext : (\mathbf{X} \to C\mathbf{Y}) \to (C\mathbf{X} \to C\mathbf{Y})$ with $ext\, f\, A = \bigcup_{a \in A} fa$

Note that a lot of information is contained in this theorem, e.g. 'if A is closed, then $\downarrow A$ and $\uparrow A$ are closed', '$\uparrow(\bigcap_{A \in D} A) = \bigcap_{A \in D} \uparrow A$ for all directed collections D', 'if A is closed and f is continuous and produces only closed sets, then $\bigcup_{a \in A} fa$ is closed' etc.

3 Specification of set domains

3.1 Introduction

In this section, we state the properties we expect from a set domain construction. It is a trial to formalize some intuitive requirements, and hence, it might seem a bit vague. However, in sections 5 and 6, we rigorously construct the big and the small set domain and show later that they both meet the specification. This also implies that the given specification is not exact enough to describe a unique domain construction. Besides small and big set domain, there might be further constructions which meet the specification.

Assume an M-domain **D**, the ground domain, is given. We want to specify a domain $S\mathbf{D}$ of sets over **D** that supports a broad collection of set operations. The set domains over different ground domains **X** and **Y** are not independent, because some set operations involve both $S\mathbf{X}$ and $S\mathbf{Y}$. Thus, we should speak of a set domain construction $\mathbf{D} \mapsto S\mathbf{D}$ instead of speaking of a single set domain. For the sake of brevity, we often omit the word 'construction' hoping that the reader nevertheless understands what we mean. The symbol 'S' is to be understood as generic; we denote the small set domain (construction) by 'σ' and the big one by 'Σ' in the later parts of this article.

To have more freedom in their construction, we do not require that set domains really consist of sets. We call the elements of a set domain *formal* sets in contrast to the actual, mathematical sets. Naturally, there is some relation between formal and actual sets as outlined below.

The operations on formal sets usually differ from the corresponding mathematical operations on actual sets. Thus, a distinction is needed. We adopt the convention to mark the formal set operations by means of additional horizontal or vertical bars.

3.2 Empty set and finite union

As a first requirement, we want the set domain $S\mathbf{D}$ to contain a formal empty set and a formal set union.

Definition 3.1 (CAIN domains and linear maps)

A *CAIN poset* $(\mathbf{P}, \cup, \bar{\emptyset})$ is a poset **P** together with a monotonic map $\cup : \mathbf{P} \times \mathbf{P} \to \mathbf{P}$ being Commutative, Associative, and Idempotent (i.e. $A \cup A$ for all $A \in \mathbf{P}$), and an element $\bar{\emptyset}$ of **P** which is the Neutral element of ' $\cup$ '.

A *CAIN domain* $(\mathbf{P}, \cup, \bar{\emptyset})$ is a CAIN poset where $\mathbf{P}$ is a domain and $\cup$ is continuous.

A map $f : X \to Y$ between CAIN posets is *linear* iff it is a homomorphism w.r.t. the CAIN theory, i.e. $f\bar{\emptyset}_X = \bar{\emptyset}_Y$ and $f(A \cup B) = fA \cup fB$ hold. $\qquad\square$

As usual in algebra, we identify CAIN posets with their carrier. If X is an arbitrary domain and Y is a CAIN domain, then the function space $X \to Y$ becomes a CAIN domain in a natural way by defining $\bar{\emptyset} = \lambda x. \bar{\emptyset}_Y$ and $f \cup g = \lambda x. fx \cup gx$.

Returning to set domains, our first requirement for the set domain is that it be a CAIN domain.

3.3 Singleton sets

As a next requirement, there should be a function which maps elements into singleton sets. We require this function $\{\!|.|\!\} : D \to SD$, $x \mapsto \{\!|x|\!\}$ not only to be continuous, but also to be injective, i.e. $x \neq y$ has to imply $\{\!|x|\!\} \neq \{\!|y|\!\}$. An additional condition is that the empty set is not a singleton, i.e. $\{\!|x|\!\} \neq \bar{\emptyset}$ for all $x \in D$.

As we shall see, the singleton map for the big and also the small set domain are even embeddings, i.e. $x \leq y$ iff $\{\!|x|\!\} \leq \{\!|y|\!\}$ holds. However, we do not require this for general set domains explicitly.

By means of the operations $\bar{\emptyset}$ and $\cup$, we may extend $\{\!|.|\!\}$ to finite subsets of the ground domain thus relating actual with formal sets:

$$\{\!|x_1, \ldots, x_n|\!\} = \begin{cases} \{\!|x_1|\!\} \cup \cdots \cup \{\!|x_n|\!\} & \text{if } n > 0 \\ \bar{\emptyset} & \text{if } n = 0 \end{cases}$$

3.4 Function extension

Next, we require that functions defined on elements of the ground domain may be raised to functions defined on formal sets. More precise, we want a continuous second order functional $ext : (X \to SY) \to (SX \to SY)$ for every two domains X and Y. For every continuous map $f : X \to SY$, the extended map $ext\, f$ should be linear and extend f properly to sets, i.e. $ext\, f\, \{\!|x|\!\} = fx$ has to hold. These axioms imply $ext\, f\, \{\!|x_1, \ldots, x_n|\!\} = fx_1 \cup \cdots \cup fx_n$ for $n > 0$. Furthermore, we want ext to be linear in its functional argument, i.e. $ext\, (\lambda x. fx \cup gx)\, S = (ext\, f\, S) \cup (ext\, g\, S)$.

Given the ext functional as a primitive operator of a set data type allows us to derive many other useful operations. Some examples are given now:

- $map : (X \to Y) \to (SX \to SY)$
  defined by $\quad map\, f\, A = ext\, (\lambda x. \{\!|fx|\!\})\, A \quad$ or equivalently $\quad map\, f = ext\, (\{\!|.|\!\} \circ f)$
  $map\, f$ is a linear map between SX and SY with $map\, f\, \{\!|x_1, \ldots, x_n|\!\} = \{\!|fx_1, \ldots, fx_n|\!\}$.

- $union : S(SD) \to SD \quad$ defined by $\quad union = ext\, (\lambda x. x)$
  It is a linear map with the property $union\, \{\!|S_1, \ldots, S_n|\!\} = S_1 \cup \cdots \cup S_n$ for $n > 0$, i.e. it is a formal 'big union'.

- $\_ \bar{\times} \_ : SX \times SY \to S(X \times Y)$
  defined by using ext twice: $\quad A \bar{\times} B = ext\, (\lambda a.\, ext\, (\lambda b.\, \{\!|(a, b)|\!\})\, B)\, A$
  Using the two-fold linearity of ext in its functional and its set argument, one obtains $\{\!|x_1, \ldots, x_n|\!\} \bar{\times} \{\!|y_1, \ldots, y_m|\!\} = \{\!|(x_i, y_j) \mid 1 \leq i \leq n, 1 \leq j \leq m|\!\}$ using an obvious notation analogous to ZF notation for actual sets. Hence, ' $\bar{\times}$ ' denotes a formal Cartesian product.

3.5 Existential quantification

As further operations, we want some set theoretic predicates. In order to derive them, formal sets must somehow be related with Booleans. In doing so, we introduce the Boolean poset $\mathbf{B} = \{\bot, \mathsf{T}, \mathsf{F}\}$ ordered by $\bot \leq \mathsf{T}$ and $\bot \leq \mathsf{F}$. We turn it into a CAIN domain by letting $\bar{\emptyset}$ be F. The CAIN axioms then enforce $\mathsf{F} \mathbin{\bar{\cup}} \mathsf{F} = \mathsf{F}$ and $\mathsf{F} \mathbin{\bar{\cup}} \mathsf{T} = \mathsf{T} \mathbin{\bar{\cup}} \mathsf{F} = \mathsf{T} \mathbin{\bar{\cup}} \mathsf{T} = \mathsf{T}$, i.e. formal union is disjunction. Concerning $\bot$, the equations $\mathsf{F} \mathbin{\bar{\cup}} \bot = \bot \mathbin{\bar{\cup}} \mathsf{F} = \bot \mathbin{\bar{\cup}} \bot = \bot$ have to hold. However, the CAIN axioms don't fix the values of $\mathsf{T} \mathbin{\bar{\cup}} \bot$ and $\bot \mathbin{\bar{\cup}} \mathsf{T}$ except they have to be equal and cannot be F. Thus, there are two choices: the strict disjunction where the result is $\bot$, and parallel disjunction where the result is T. We arbitrarily choose the latter because it is more defined. Henceforth, $\mathbf{B}$ is always understood as CAIN domain equipped with 'parallel or' denoted by '$\vee$'. Sometimes, we also use 'parallel and' denoted by '$\wedge$'. As indicated above, the space of predicates $\mathbf{D} \to \mathbf{B}$ also becomes a CAIN domain by raising disjunction to predicates, i.e. with operations $p \vee q = \lambda x.\, p\,x \vee q\,x$ and $\underline{\mathsf{F}} = \lambda x.\, \mathsf{F}$.

After these preliminaries, we can now state our next requirement for the generic set domain. There has to be a functional for existential quantification which, given a predicate, tells whether some element of a given formal set satisfies it. Quantification is specified analogously to functional extension.[3]

For every domain $\mathbf{D}$, there should be a continuous second order functional $exists : (\mathbf{D} \to \mathbf{B}) \to (\mathcal{S}\mathbf{D} \to \mathbf{B})$ such that for every continuous predicate $p : \mathbf{D} \to \mathbf{B}$, there is a linear predicate $exists\ p$ extending p properly to sets, i.e. $exists\ p\ \{\!|x|\!\} = p\,x$ has to hold. These axioms imply $exists\ p\ \{\!|x_1, \ldots, x_n|\!\} = p\,x_1 \vee \cdots \vee p\,x_n$ for $n > 0$. In addition, we require $exists$ to be also linear in its functional argument.

Given the $exists$ functional as a primitive operator of a set data type allows us to derive many other useful predicates, e.g.

- $forall : (\mathbf{D} \to \mathbf{B}) \to (\mathcal{S}\mathbf{D} \to \mathbf{B})$ defined by $forall\ p\ S = \neg(exists\ (\lambda x.\, \neg(p\,x))\ S)$
  This implies $forall\ p\ \{\!|x_1, \ldots, x_n|\!\} = p\,x_1 \wedge \cdots \wedge p\,x_n$ for $n > 0$.

- $empty : \mathcal{S}\mathbf{D} \to \mathbf{B}$ defined by $empty\ S = \neg(exists\ (\lambda x.\, \mathsf{T})\ S) = forall\ (\lambda x.\, \mathsf{F})\ S$
  Hence, we obtain $empty\ \{\!|x_1, \ldots, x_n|\!\} = \begin{cases} \mathsf{T} & \text{if } n = 0 \\ \mathsf{F} & \text{if } n > 0 \end{cases}$

For the tests of containment, inclusion, and set equality, we need a given continuous equality '$==$' on the ground domain.

- $\_\ in\ \_ :$ $\mathbf{D} \times \mathcal{S}\mathbf{D} \to \mathbf{B}$ $x\ in\ B = exists\ (\lambda b.\, x == b)\ B$
- $\_\ \bar{\subseteq}\ \_ :$ $\mathcal{S}\mathbf{D} \times \mathcal{S}\mathbf{D} \to \mathbf{B}$ $A \bar{\subseteq} B = forall\ (\lambda a.\, a\ in\ B)\ A$
- $\_ == \_ :$ $\mathcal{S}\mathbf{D} \times \mathcal{S}\mathbf{D} \to \mathbf{B}$ $(A == B) = (A \bar{\subseteq} B) \wedge (B \bar{\subseteq} A)$

We consider this equality check a bit closer in section 7.

3.6 Filtering a set through a predicate

We finally want to provide an operation that filters a set through a given predicate. The operation $filter : (\mathbf{D} \to \mathbf{B}) \to (\mathcal{S}\mathbf{D} \to \mathcal{S}\mathbf{D})$ should be linear in its set argument as well as in its predicate argument and operate on singletons as one expects.

---

[3]Later, we shall see that for the two set domains, quantification is a special instance of extension.

$$filter\ p\ (A \cup B) = (filter\ p\ A) \cup (filter\ p\ B) \qquad filter\ (p \vee q)\ A = (filter\ p\ A) \cup (filter\ q\ A)$$

$$filter\ p\ \bar{\emptyset} = filter\ \underline{\mathsf{F}}\ S = \bar{\emptyset} \qquad\qquad filter\ p\ \{|x|\} = \begin{cases} \{|x|\} & \text{if } px = \mathsf{T} \\ \bar{\emptyset} & \text{if } px = \mathsf{F} \end{cases}$$

Instead of requiring the existence of an operation satisfying these axioms, we derive it from a simpler one using *ext*: $\qquad filter\ p\ S = ext\ (\lambda x.\ x\ when\ (px))\ S$

where $\_\ when\ \_ : \mathbf{D} \times \mathbf{B} \to S\mathbf{D}$ is an operation which models the effect of *filter* on singletons. Hence, $x\ when\ \mathsf{T} = \{|x|\}$ and $x\ when\ \mathsf{F} = \bar{\emptyset}$ must hold. With these axioms for '*when*', one obtains linearity of *filter* in the set argument and its correct behavior for singletons. For linearity of *filter* in the predicate, one needs the additional axiom $x\ when\ (a \vee b) = (x\ when\ a) \cup (x\ when\ b)$, i.e. linearity of '*when*' in its Boolean argument.

Instead of requiring now the existence of an operation '*when*' with these axioms, we go one step further and define it by means of an even simpler operation. In order to define '*when*', only $x\ when \perp$ has to be fixed, because the values for T and F are already given by the *when*-axioms above. We define

$$x\ when\ b = \begin{cases} \{|x|\} & \text{if } b = \mathsf{T} \\ \{|x?|\} & \text{if } b = \perp \\ \{||\} & \text{if } b = \mathsf{F} \end{cases}$$

using a new operation $\{|.?|\} : \mathbf{D} \to S\mathbf{D}, x \mapsto \{|x?|\}$. For monotonicity of '*when*', the new operation must satisfy the laws $\{|x?|\} \leq \{|x|\}$ and $\{|x?|\} \leq \{||\} = \bar{\emptyset}$. For linearity of '*when*', one additionally needs $\{|x|\} \cup \{|x?|\} = \{|x|\}$.

The question mark was chosen as symbol, because $\{|x?|\}$ intuitively denotes a set where the membership of x in it is questionable. As the computation proceeds, the membership might either be validated ($\{|x?|\} \leq \{|x|\}$) or refuted ($\{|x?|\} \leq \{||\}$). Extending our formal set notation in an obvious way, one obtains for instance the formal set $\{|1?, 2, 3|\} = \{|1?|\} \cup \{|2|\} \cup \{|3|\}$ which surely contains 2 and 3 and might also contain 1, but no other number. Hence, formal sets differ from actual sets of mathematics in that they may contain doubtful members which are neither proved to be inside nor outside. The last axiom of the previous paragraph reads $\{|x?, x|\} = \{|x|\}$, i.e. sure membership overrides doubtful membership.

3.7 Summary

Our list of requirements for a general set domain construction is now complete. We list the required operations and their axioms again for later reference:

- $\_\ \cup\ \_ : S\mathbf{D} \times S\mathbf{D} \to S\mathbf{D}$ commutative, associative, and idempotent with unit $\bar{\emptyset}$;
- $\{|.|\} : \mathbf{D} \to S\mathbf{D}$ injective and never returning $\bar{\emptyset}$;
- $ext : (\mathbf{X} \to S\mathbf{Y}) \to (S\mathbf{X} \to S\mathbf{Y})$ linear in both arguments and satisfying $ext\ f\ \{|x|\} = fx$;
- $exists\ .\ (\mathbf{X} \to \mathbf{B}) \to (S\mathbf{X} \to \mathbf{B})$ linear in both arguments and satisfying $exists\ p\ \{|x|\} = px$;
- $\{|.?|\} : \mathbf{D} \to S\mathbf{D}$ satisfying the axioms $\{|x?|\} \leq \{|x|\}$ and $\{|x?|\} \leq \bar{\emptyset}$ and $\{|x|\} \cup \{|x?|\} = \{|x|\}$.

One might additionally want to have an operation creating a 'universal set' over any ground domain, i.e. a set containing all members of the ground domain. We think that this operation would have a higher level of conceptual complexity than the operations listed above that only allow for constructing sets from given sets or creating small sets (empty set and singletons) from scratch. For the same reasons, there is no operation of complement – the complement of the empty set would be the universal set – and no big intersection – the intersection over the empty set is the universal set.

For lists, there is another useful higher order operation called *fold* or *reduce* that takes a binary operation and combines the list items by this operation. Since the items of a set do not appear in a fixed order, the binary operation must be commutative and associative in order to make its *fold* be well defined. Therefore, we don't propose a general *fold* operation, but only some special instance of it: big union is a folded union.

4 The classical power domains

In this section, we show that the three classical power domain constructions fail to meet the complete specification above. In the section thereafter, we then present our set domains.

4.1 The lower power domain

We start with the lower or Hoare power domain $\mathcal{L}\mathbf{D}$. It may be defined as the set of all iso-lower subsets of $\mathbf{D}$ ordered by inclusion '$\subseteq$'. An isomorphic representation would be the set of Lawson closed lower subsets[4] of $\mathbf{D}$ ordered by inclusion, but the approach using iso-lower sets is technically simpler for our purposes.

Usually, the empty set is omitted from the domain, although it is a perfect iso-lower resp. closed lower set. Adding it poses no difficulty; it becomes the least element of the power domain.

$\mathcal{L}\mathbf{D}$ is a complete domain. Lubs and glbs are given by set union and intersection respectively. The least element is the empty set, and the greatest one is the set of all isolated points $\mathbf{D}^0$. The isolated sets in $\mathcal{L}\mathbf{D}$ are the sets $\Downarrow E$ where E is bifinite.

We now browse through the various topics of the specification and investigate to what extent they are satisfied.

- $\bar{\emptyset} = \emptyset$ and $A \cup B = A \cup B$ These operations obviously satisfy the CAIN axioms.

- $\{\!|x|\!\} = \Downarrow x$ is a continuous embedding. Because of $x \in \Downarrow x$, the result is never empty.

Combining these operations, one obtains $\{\!|x_1, \ldots, x_n|\!\} = \Downarrow\{x_1, \ldots, x_n\}$.

- $ext\, f\, A = \bigcup_{a \in A} fa$ One easily verifies that it is continuous and linear in both arguments and that $\bigcup_{a \in \Downarrow x} fa = fx$ holds.

Now, we derive the *map* functional and the big union from *ext*.

- $map\, f\, A = ext\, (\lambda x.\, \{\!|fx|\!\})\, A = \bigcup_{a \in A} \Downarrow(fa) = \Downarrow(fA)$

- $union\, A = ext\, (\lambda x.\, x)\, A = \bigcup_{a \in A} a$

- $A \bar{\times} B = ext\, (\lambda a.\, ext\, (\lambda b.\, \{\!|(a, b)|\!\})\, B)\, A$

  $= \bigcup_{a \in A} \bigcup_{b \in B} \Downarrow\{(a, b)\} = \bigcup_{c \in A \times B} \Downarrow\{c\} = \Downarrow(A \times B) = A \times B$

The very last equation holds, because the product of iso-lower sets is again an iso-lower set.

Next, we consider the operation of doubtful membership. Since $\{\!|x?|\!\} \leq \bar{\emptyset} = \emptyset$ has to hold, and $\emptyset$ is the least element of the domain, there is no other choice than

- $\{\!|x?|\!\} = \emptyset$

---

[4]These are the closed sets of the Scott topology

- $x \ when \ b = \begin{cases} \Downarrow x & \text{if } b = \mathsf{T} \\ \emptyset & \text{if } b = \bot \text{ or } = \mathsf{F} \end{cases}$

- $filter \ p \ A \ = \ ext \ (\lambda a.\ a \ when \ (p\,a))\ A \ = \ \bigcup_{a \in A}(a \ when \ (p\,a))$

$$= \ \bigcup \{\Downarrow a \mid a \in P,\ pa = \mathsf{T}\} \ = \ \Downarrow \{a \in P \mid pa = \mathsf{T}\}$$

In contrast to the operations above, there is no existential quantification which meets the specification. To show this, we consider the lower power domain $\mathcal{L}1$ over the one-point-domain $1 = \{\bullet\}$. It consists of two points: $\emptyset$ and $\{\bullet\}$, with $\emptyset \le \{\bullet\}$. Now let p be the predicate assigning T to $\bullet$. Then $exists \ p \ \emptyset = \mathsf{F}$ and $exists \ p \ \{\bullet\} = \mathsf{T}$ should hold in contradiction to monotonicity.

Summarizing, we see that the lower power domain is able to give quite naturally meaning to the operations '$\bar{\emptyset}$', '$\bar{\cup}$', 'ext', '$union$', and '$\bar{\times}$'. But all operations using predicates can only use one part of the predicate, and operations returning Booleans are only able to return one Boolean or $\bot$. Thus, the lower power domain in some sense only gives half of the necessary semantic information.

In the course of the computation of a set, the sets in the lower power domain always increase. No element can disappear during a computation, but there might appear new elements at any time, even if the set was empty before. Thus, the sets of this power domain seem to give a lower bound on the final result of computations. In fact, a formal set L approximates an actual set S, iff $L \le \Downarrow S$, i.e. L contains all elements which are known to be below some member of the actual set to be approximated.

This interpretation lets the $exists$ predicate only telling T or $\bot$, never F. Once an element with a required property was detected in a set, it cannot disappear later on, and we know there is a member of the actual set above it which must also satisfy the property due to monotonicity. Thus, the answer is T. Conversely, if no element was found satisfying a predicate, only $\bot$ can be returned, since such an element might appear later.

For the same reasons, $x \ when \ \bot = \{x?\}$ is empty. As long as the condition is not evaluated, we cannot be sure whether there is any element in the outcoming set.

4.2 The upper or Smyth power domain

Now we turn to the upper power domain first proposed by Smyth [9]. The upper power domain $\mathcal{U}\mathbf{D}$ over a domain $\mathbf{D}$ consists of the Lawson closed upper sets of $\mathbf{D}$ ordered by containment '$\supseteq$'. This poset is a complete domain, even if the ground domain is not; the ground domain only needs to be an M-domain. Its isolated sets are the sets $\uparrow E$, where E is bifinite. The lub coincides with set intersection[5]. Its least element is the whole domain $\mathbf{D}$, and its greatest one is $\emptyset$.

Smyth originally did not include the empty set in his power domain, although it is a perfect closed upper set. Furthermore, it is isolated, because it is the upper closure of the bifinite set $\emptyset$.

Now, we investigate to what extent the upper power domain satisfies the specification of the big set domain.

- $\bar{\emptyset} = \emptyset$ and $P \bar{\cup} Q = P \cup Q$ obviously satisfy the specification.

- $\{x\} = \uparrow x$ is continuous and an injective embedding. It is never empty.

Combining these operations, one obtains $\{x_1, \ldots, x_n\} = \uparrow \{x_1, \ldots, x_n\}$.

- $ext \ f \ A = \bigcup_{a \in A} fa$ is well defined and continuous by theorem 2.1. It is not difficult to show that this operation satisfies its specification.

---

[5]but glb is not identical with set union.

Now, we derive some set theoretic functions from ext.

- $map\ f\ A = ext\ (\lambda x.\ \{\!|fx|\!\})\ A = \bigcup_{a \in A} \uparrow(fa) = \uparrow(fA)$
- $union\ A = ext\ (\lambda x.\ x)\ A = \bigcup_{a \in A} a$
- $A \bar{\times} B = ext\ (\lambda a.\ ext\ (\lambda b.\ \{\!|(a,b)|\!\})\ B)\ A$
  $= \bigcup_{a \in A} \bigcup_{b \in B} \uparrow\{(a,b)\} = \bigcup_{p \in A \times B} \uparrow\{p\} = \uparrow(A \times B) = A \times B$

The very last equation holds, because the product of upper sets is again an upper set.

Next, we consider the doubtful singletons. $\{\!|x?|\!\} \leq \bar{\emptyset} = \emptyset$ holds automatically, because $\emptyset$ is the greatest element. Then, $\{\!|x?|\!\} \leq \{\!|x|\!\}$ has to hold which is satisfied by the simplest possible choice

- $\{\!|x?|\!\} = \{\!|x|\!\} = \uparrow\dot{x}$
- $x\ when\ b = \begin{cases} \{\!|x|\!\} & \text{if } b = \mathsf{T} \text{ or } = \bot \\ \emptyset & \text{if } b = \mathsf{F} \end{cases}$
- $filter\ p\ A = ext\ (\lambda a.\ a\ when\ (p\,a))\ A = \bigcup_{a \in A}(a\ when\ (p\,a))$
  $= \bigcup\{\uparrow a \mid a \in A,\ pa \neq \mathsf{F}\} = \uparrow\{a \in A \mid pa \neq \mathsf{F}\}$

As with the lower power domain, there is no existential quantification satisfying the requirements. Consider the domain $\mathcal{U}1$. It consists of two points: $\emptyset$ and $\{\bullet\}$, with $\{\bullet\} \leq \emptyset$. If p is a predicate mapping $\bullet$ to T, then $exists\ p\ \{\bullet\} = \mathsf{T}$ and $exists\ p\ \emptyset = \mathsf{F}$ should hold contradicting monotonicity.

During a computation, the sets in the Smyth power domain always shrink. Every element might disappear, even until the empty set, but it is impossible that new elements appear. Thus, the sets of this power domain give an upper bound on the final result of computations; they contain elements that are suspected to be in the final result. A member U of the upper power domain approximates an actual set S iff $S \subseteq U$.

According to this interpretation, $x\ when\ \bot$ equals $\{\!|x|\!\}$. Before the condition is not evaluated, x might be in the final result and cannot yet be dropped. For the same reasons, the $exists$ predicate can only return F or $\bot$, never T. If there is no element in the Smyth set satisfying the predicate, $exists$ may safely return F, since there is no possibility that such an element appears somehow. On the other hand, the answer must be $\bot$, if an element satisfying the predicate was found, because this element might disappear later on.

Summarizing, we see that the Smyth power domain gives only one half of the desired semantic information. Fortunately, its semantic properties are dual to those of the lower power domain, such that we may hope to get the full information by combining the two power domains. We try this in the next section after having briefly considered the remaining construction.

4.3 The convex or Plotkin power domain

Given a domain $\mathbf{D}$, sets of points of $\mathbf{D}$ might be ordered by the so-called Egli-Milner ordering. $A \leq B$ holds, if for all a in A, there is b in B with $a \leq b$, and also for all b in B, there is a in A with $a \leq b$. This ordering is reflexive and transitive, but not antisymmetric. Restriction to convex sets makes the Egli-Milner ordering antisymmetric. Thus, the Lawson closed convex sets form a poset when ordered by Egli-Milner. We call it extended Plotkin domain $\mathcal{P}'\mathbf{D}$ since it contains the empty set in contrast to Plotkin's original construction. It would be an M-domain, if it had a least element. It does not have a least element because of the empty set which is totally unrelated with any other set.

The Plotkin power domain $\mathcal{P}D$ over $\mathbf{D}$ consists of the *non-empty* closed convex subsets of $\mathbf{D}$ ordered by the Egli-Milner ordering. This 'power domain' is in fact a domain (in the sense of Plotkin). The singleton $\{\bot\}$ is the least element.

The Plotkin power domain over the one-point-domain $\mathbf{1}$ has exactly one member: the set $\{\bullet\}$. On the other hand, there should be at least two formal sets – $\bar{\emptyset}$ and $\{\!|\bullet|\!\}$. This makes Plotkin's construction inappropriate for our purposes. Using the extended Plotkin domain instead, one might choose $\bar{\emptyset} = \emptyset$ and $\{\!|\bullet|\!\} = \{\bullet\}$, but then it is impossible to define $\{\!|\bullet?|\!\}$ properly. A solution could be to put the empty set artificially above $\{\bot\}$, or to add a new artificial least element. We did not follow these approaches further because the algebraic properties of the pure Plotkin domain are messed up by such artificial supplements.

5 The big set domain

In this section, we present the big set domain as combination of lower and upper power domain that is well suited for our purposes.

A member A of the big set domain is represented as pair (A^L, A^U)[6] consisting of an iso-lower set A^L and a Smyth set A^U. According to our interpretation of the lower and upper power domain, A approximates an actual set S, if all members a of A^L may surely be extended to an element s of S above a, and there are no members of S outside A^U. Formally, this is written $A^L \subseteq \Downarrow S$ and $S \subseteq A^U$. This implies that $A^L \subseteq \Downarrow A^U$ should hold. Pairs satisfying this condition are called *legal*. Legal pairs are also called *sandwiches* following Buneman [1], because they approximate an actual set S from both sides.

Definition 5.1   The big set domain $\Sigma\mathbf{D}$ over an M-domain $\mathbf{D}$ has carrier

$\{(A^L, A^U) \mid$ (1) A^L is an iso-lower set of $\mathbf{D}$

(2) A^U is an upper closed set, i.e. a Smyth set

(3) $A^L \subseteq \Downarrow A^U$ $\}$

The elements are ordered by

$(A^L, A^U) \leq (B^L, B^U)$ iff $A^L \subseteq B^L$ and $A^U \supseteq B^U$

i.e. the order is inherited from $\mathcal{L}\mathbf{D} \times \mathcal{U}\mathbf{D}$.   □

Theorem 5.2
$\Sigma\mathbf{D}$ is a Scott domain. $(\emptyset, \mathbf{D})$ is its least element. If it exists, the lub of a family $(A_i)_{i\in I}$ is $(\bigcup_{i\in I} A_i^L, \bigcap_{i\in I} A_i^U)$. Isolated points are all pairs $(\Downarrow E, \uparrow F)$ where E and F are bifinite and $E \subseteq \Downarrow\uparrow F$ holds. The projections $\pi^L : \Sigma\mathbf{D} \to \mathcal{L}\mathbf{D}$ and $\pi^U : \Sigma\mathbf{D} \to \mathcal{U}\mathbf{D}$ are both continuous.   □

Note that $\Sigma\mathbf{D}$ is bounded complete, even if the ground domain $\mathbf{D}$ is not.

The big set domain is a sub-domain of the product $\mathcal{L}\mathbf{D} \times \mathcal{U}\mathbf{D}$ of lower and upper power domain. Because all pairs below a legal pair are also legal, the highest parts of the product are cut off by the condition of legality. Especially, this removes the top element of the product and causes the existence of many maximal elements.

When we consider the set operations, we can use our knowledge of the operations in the lower and upper domain. Most operations are simple combinations, only in case of inclusion and equality, a synergetic effect occurs.

---

[6]Buneman and also Gunter write the pairs the other way round, i.e. the upper set to the left.

In the sequel, we adopt some conventions. The operations of the lower power domain are indexed by L. For instance, ext_L denotes its extension. Similarly, the upper operations are indexed by U. If A is a sandwich, then $A = (A^L, A^U)$, and similarly, $B = (B^L, B^U)$ etc. If f is a function from somewhere to $\Sigma\mathbf{D}$, then $f^L = \pi^L \circ f : \ldots \to \mathcal{L}\mathbf{D}$, and analogously $f^U = \pi^U \circ f : \ldots \to \mathcal{U}\mathbf{D}$.

Continuity and correctness of the combined functions follow from those of the participants. For the basic operations, legality of the results must be shown. Naturally, this is not necessary for the derived operations.

- $\bar{\emptyset} = (\bar{\emptyset}^L, \bar{\emptyset}^U) = (\emptyset, \emptyset)$ This is a sandwich, since $\emptyset \subseteq \Downarrow\emptyset$.

- $P \,\bar{\cup}\, Q = (P^L \,\bar{\cup}_L\, Q^L, P^U \,\bar{\cup}_U\, Q^U) = (P^L \cup Q^L, P^U \cup Q^U)$
  The result is legal, since $P^L \cup Q^L \subseteq \Downarrow P^U \cup \Downarrow Q^U = \Downarrow(P^U \cup Q^U)$.

- $\{\!|x|\!\} = (\{\!|x|\!\}_L, \{\!|x|\!\}_U) = (\Downarrow x, \uparrow x)$ For all x, $\Downarrow x \subseteq \Downarrow\uparrow x$ holds as required.

- $ext\ f\ A = (ext_L\ f^L\ A^L, ext_U\ f^U\ A^U) = (\bigcup_{a \in A^L} (fa)^L, \bigcup_{a \in A^U} (fa)^U)$
  To prove that the result is legal, let $y \in \bigcup_{a \in A^L} (fa)^L$. Then there is $x \in A^L$ such that $y \in (fx)^L$. Since A is legal, $x \in A^L \subseteq \Downarrow A^U$ holds, i.e. there is $x' \in A^U$ with $x \leq x'$. Then

$$
\begin{aligned}
y \in (fx)^L &\subseteq (fx')^L && \text{by monotonicity of } f \\
&\subseteq \Downarrow(fx')^U && \text{since } fx' \text{ is legal} \\
&\subseteq \Downarrow \bigcup_{a \in A^U} (fa)^U
\end{aligned}
$$

The equations for the derived operations *map*, *union*, and formal product may be computed from the definition of *ext*. They turn out to be free combinations of the corresponding lower and upper operations, for instance $P \,\bar{\times}\, Q = (P^L \times Q^L, P^U \times Q^U)$.

Existential quantification may be derived from functional extension. The big set domain $\Sigma 1$ over the one-point-domain consists of the legal pairs of iso-lower and Smyth sets of 1. There are four pairs: $(\emptyset, \emptyset)$, $(\emptyset, \{\bullet\})$, $(\{\bullet\}, \emptyset)$, and $(\{\bullet\}, \{\bullet\})$. The third in this enumeration is illegal. Hence, three sandwiches remain. Their order is depicted in the following diagram:

$$\bar{\emptyset} = (\emptyset, \emptyset) \qquad\qquad (\{\bullet\}, \{\bullet\}) = \{\!|\bullet|\!\}$$
$$\diagdown \quad \diagup$$
$$(\emptyset, \{\bullet\})$$

Thus, this domain is isomorphic to the Boolean domain. By relating $\bar{\emptyset}$ with F, and $\{\!|\bullet|\!\}$ with T we obtain the two mappings *mkbool* and *mkset*. They are even linear, i.e. CAIN isomorphisms between $(\Sigma 1, \,\bar{\cup}\,, \bar{\emptyset})$ and $(\mathbf{B}, \vee, \mathsf{F})$.

- The predicate *exists* may be built using *mkbool* and *mkset*:

  $exists\ p = mkbool \circ (ext\ (mkset \circ p))$

  This function obviously meets its specification. Some formal manipulation gives the result

  $$
  exists\ p\ A = \begin{cases} \mathsf{T} & \text{if } \exists u \in A^L : pu = \mathsf{T} \\ \mathsf{F} & \text{if } \forall v \in A^U : pv = \mathsf{F} \\ \perp & \text{otherwise} \end{cases}
  $$

  i.e. this predicate may return every Boolean, and it looks at both parts of the argument predicate.

- $forall\ p\ A = \neg(exists\ (\lambda a.\ \neg(p\,a))\ A) = \begin{cases} \mathsf{F} & \text{if } \exists u \in A^L : pu = \mathsf{F} \\ \mathsf{T} & \text{if } \forall v \in A^U : pv = \mathsf{T} \\ \perp & \text{otherwise} \end{cases}$

- $empty\ A = forall\ (\lambda a.\ \mathsf{F})\ A = \begin{cases} \mathsf{F} & \text{if } A^L \neq \emptyset \\ \mathsf{T} & \text{if } A^U = \emptyset \text{ (then } A^L \text{ must be empty, too)} \\ \bot & \text{if } A^L = \emptyset \text{ and } A^U \neq \emptyset \end{cases}$

The remaining predicates are considered more closely in section 7. We finally consider the operations leading to *filter*.

- $\{|x?|\} = (\{|x?|\}_L, \{|x?|\}_U) = (\emptyset, \uparrow x)$

The result is always legal, and the operation satisfies its axioms.

- $filter\ p\ A\ =\ ext\ (\lambda a.\ a\ when\ (pa))\ A\ =\ (filter_L\ p\ A^L,\ filter_U\ p\ A^U)$
  $=\ (\Downarrow\{a \in A^L \mid pa = \mathsf{T}\},\ \uparrow\{a \in A^U \mid pa \neq \mathsf{F}\})$

As the operations show, we were successful in finding a set domain that is an almost free combination of the lower and upper power domain, and thus, can answer both 'yes' and 'no'. But we are not able to construct all isolated sandwiches by means of the basic operations, because there are too much. In the next section, we strengthen the condition of legality in order to exclude some sandwiches.

6 The small set domain

Now, we identify a subset of the big set domain that exactly comprises those sandwiches that are obtained by the set operations and lubs of directed collections.

The big set domain as defined in the previous section consists of pairs $A = (A^L, A^U)$ where A^L is an iso-lower set, A^U is a Smyth set, and $A^L \subseteq \Downarrow A^U$ holds.

The singleton operation $\{|x|\} = (\Downarrow x, \uparrow x)$ produces sandwiches, where the lower and the upper part touch each other in the point x. Intuitively, such touching points are preserved by union ' $\cup$ ', and also by *map f* due to the continuity of f. Thus, it seems that all points of A^L may be raised into a touching point, or more formally, $A^L \subseteq \Downarrow(touch\ set)$.

The set of all touching points between A^L and A^U is the intersection of A^U with the closure of A^L. Thus, we finally reach at the condition $A^L \subseteq \Downarrow(\overline{A^L} \cap A^U)$. Here, the Lawson closure may be replaced by the directed closure, i.e. the set of all lubs of directed sets in A^L. Since $\Downarrow(\overline{A^L} \cap A^U)$ is a subset of $\Downarrow A^U$, the condition is indeed stronger than the condition of legality.

The condition is a bit unhandy, since it involves a closure and two occurrences of A^L. Fortunately, there is a much simpler, but equivalent condition which is used in the following definition:

Definition 6.1 The small set domain σD over an M-domain D has carrier
$\{(A^L, A^U) \mid A^U$ is a Smyth set and there is a subset A^M of A^U with $A^L = \Downarrow A^M\}$
Its order is inherited from ΣD. The sandwiches in σD are called *tight*. □

The small set domain is isomorphic to the mixed power domain with empty set defined by Gunter [3,4]. The restriction of tightness makes the sandwiches less dependent on very low points like $\bot$, since A^L is uniquely determined by a subset of A^U. Informally, one can say that only those parts of A^L lying within A^U are important, whereas the lower parts of A^L don't play any role.

The small set domain is still big enough for our purposes:

Theorem 6.2
All results of the operations $\bar{\emptyset}$, $\{|.|\}$, $\{|.?|\}$, and *mkset* are tight. If A and B are tight, then $A \cup B$ is, too. If f generates tight sandwiches for all arguments, and A is tight, then $ext\ f\ A$ is tight. The least sandwich $(\emptyset, D)$ is tight. Lubs of directed collections of tight sandwiches are tight. □

The theorem shows that σD is big enough to allow all set operations we wanted to have. Additionally, it claims that the bottom element of ΣD is also in σD and that directed lubs in ΣD remain valid in σD. Thus, the poset σD is directed complete and has a least element. In the following, we consider further mathematical properties of the small set domain.

Lower and upper power domain are easily embedded by means of the mappings $L \mapsto (L, \mathbf{D})$ and $U \mapsto (\emptyset, U)$. Plotkin's power domain, even with the extension by the empty set, is isomorphically embedded into the small set domain by the function φ with $\varphi S = (\Downarrow S, \uparrow S)$. Its image is characterized by the additional condition $A^U \subseteq \uparrow (\overline{A^L} \cap A^U)$.

For every general sandwich S, there is a member of the extended Plotkin power domain P such that $\varphi P \geq S$. Since φP is a tight sandwich, the maximal points of the two set domains and of the extended Plotkin power domain embedded by φ are all the same. The isolated maximal points are exactly the images (by φ) of finite sets of isolated maximal elements.

The small set domain σD is not necessarily bounded complete, even in the case of bounded complete ground domain $\mathbf{D}$. An example may be obtained from Plotkin's example for his power domain over pairs of Booleans by means of the embedding φ. The sets of Plotkin's example are consistent, but have no lub in his domain. One has to show that they don't have a lub in the greater setting of the small set domain after embedding. Naturally, they do have a lub in the big set domain because it is bounded complete. However, this lub is not tight.

Big and small set domain over the one-point domain coincide. Over the Booleans, the big set domain has 17 elements, whereas the small one only has 14. The three sandwiches not being tight are $(\{\bot\}, \{\mathsf{T}\})$, $(\{\bot\}, \{\mathsf{F}\})$, and $(\{\bot\}, \{\mathsf{T}, \mathsf{F}\})$. Plotkin's domain has 7 elements in this case. Now, we state that the small set 'domain' is in fact a domain in the sense of Plotkin:

Theorem 6.3
The poset σD is an M-domain.[7] Its isolated points are the sandwiches $(\Downarrow E, \uparrow F)$ where E and F are bifinite and E is a subset of $\uparrow F$. If $\mathbf{D}$ is an SFP-domain, then σD is an SFP-domain, too. $\square$
This theorem may be proved by explicitly computing the mubs of bifinite sets.

We already showed that all set operations are possible in the small set domain σD. We now demonstrate that they are enough to construct all domain elements.

Theorem 6.4
All isolated points of the small set domain may be constructed by a finite number of applications of the operations $\bar{\emptyset}$, $\cup$, $\{\!|.|\!\}$, and $\{\!|.?|\!\}$ applied to isolated points of the ground domain. $\square$

Since the small power domain is algebraic, an arbitrary sandwich in it may be obtained by the same operations plus directed lubs.

Proof: Let $P = (\Downarrow E, \uparrow F)$ be an isolated point of the small set domain. This means E and F are bifinite, and $E \subseteq \uparrow F$. Let $E = \{e_1, \ldots, e_r\}$. Since $E \subseteq \uparrow F$, for each point e_k in E, there is a point f_k in F below. Let $F' = \{f_1, \ldots, f_r\}$, and $G = F \setminus F'$ the remainder of F, $G = \{g_1, \ldots, g_s\}$. With these notations, we claim

$$P = \{\!|e_1, \ldots, e_r|\!\} \cup \{\!|f_1, \ldots, f_r|\!\} \cup \{\!|g_1?, \ldots, g_s?|\!\}$$

By executing the singleton operations and some of the unions, the big expression above reduces to $(\Downarrow E, \uparrow E) \cup (\Downarrow F', \uparrow F') \cup (\emptyset, \uparrow G) = (\Downarrow E \cup \Downarrow F', \uparrow E \cup \uparrow F' \cup \uparrow G)$. We may further compute $\uparrow F' \cup \uparrow G = \uparrow (F' \cup G) = \uparrow F$. $E \subseteq \uparrow F$ implies $\uparrow E \subseteq \uparrow F$, whence the second component of the pair simplifies to $\uparrow F$. Remember for any f_k in F', there is a point e_k in E above, whence $\Downarrow F' \subseteq \Downarrow E$. Therefore, the left component becomes $\Downarrow E$. Thus, we finally obtain $(\Downarrow E, \uparrow F) = P$. $\square$

---

[7] Remember that σD was only defined for M-domains $\mathbf{D}$.

7 Set equality

A continuous equality for a given domain $\mathbf{D}$ is a continuous mapping $Eq : \mathbf{D} \times \mathbf{D} \to \mathbf{B}$ such that $Eq\,(x, y) = \mathsf{T}$ implies $x = y$, and $Eq\,(x, y) = \mathsf{F}$ implies $x \neq y$. The mathematical equality '$=$' in $\mathbf{D}$ is not a continuous equality since it is not even monotonic.

There is a continuous equality for every domain, namely $\lambda(x, y).\bot$. Among all the continuous equalities, there is a greatest one, that is the function defined by

$$(x == y) = \begin{cases} \mathsf{T} & \text{if } x \text{ and } y \text{ are identical, maximal, isolated points} \\ \mathsf{F} & \text{if } x \not{\uparrow} y, \text{ i.e. } x \text{ and } y \text{ are not consistent} \\ \bot & \text{otherwise} \end{cases}$$

From the basic set operations and a continuous equality in the ground domain, we derived an equality operation for formal sets in section 3. If the greatest continuous equality of the ground domain is used, the derived equality in the small set domain is again the greatest continuous equality, i.e. it can be used once more to construct the greatest continuous equality for sets of sets etc. For the big set domain, the derived equality is *not* the greatest continuous one. Its 'positive' part is as required: it returns T, iff the argument sets are identical maximal isolated points. Its 'negative' part however is too small: there are inconsistent sandwiches, where the constructed equality returns $\bot$ instead of F.

For instance, consider the big set domain over the Booleans. The sandwiches $A = (\{\bot\}, \{\mathsf{T}\})$ and $B = (\{\bot\}, \{\mathsf{F}\})$ are inconsistent, because their formal lub in the free product of lower and upper power domain, namely $(\{\bot\}, \emptyset)$, is not legal. Intuitively, A describes non-empty sets that at most contain T, and B describes non-empty sets that at most contain F. Using the set equality derived in section 3, $(A == B)$ evaluates to $\bot$. Both A and B are not tight, such that this example does not matter for the small set domain.

8 The small set domain as a free construction

For given algebraic theory $\mathcal{T}$, a $\mathcal{T}$-algebra $\mathbf{F}$ is free over a generating object $\mathbf{X}$, if there is an embedding $\iota : \mathbf{X} \hookrightarrow \mathbf{F}$ such that for every $\mathcal{T}$-algebra $\mathbf{Y}$ and every map $f : \mathbf{X} \to \mathbf{Y}$ there is a unique $\mathcal{T}$-homomorphism $\bar{f} : \mathbf{F} \to \mathbf{Y}$ which extends f, i.e. $\bar{f} \circ \iota = f$. A free construction $\mathcal{F}$ w.r.t. $\mathcal{T}$ is a map that attaches to every generator $\mathbf{X}$ a free $\mathcal{T}$-algebra $\mathcal{F}\mathbf{X}$ over $\mathbf{X}$.

In the context of domain theory, all objects and algebras have to be (SFP)-domains, and all mappings have to be continuous. Since every monotonic mapping from a domain base $\mathbf{X}^0$ to a domain $\mathbf{Y}$ may be uniquely extended to a continuous mapping from $\mathbf{X}$ to $\mathbf{Y}$, one needs to consider posets and monotonic functions only. Such algebras are called monotonic algebras.

The classical power domains are free construction w.r.t. suitable algebraic theories: Plotkin's power domain extended by the empty set is free for the CAIN theory, the lower one for the OAIN theory with additional axiom $A \leq A \,\bar{\cup}\, B$, and the upper one for the CAIN theory with additionally $A \cup B \leq B$.

The small set domain is a free construction for the *mix theory* as Gunter [3,4] and I independently found out. The mix theory is a CAIN theory enriched by an additional unary operation '?'.[8] This operation is the extension of the operation of doubtful singleton, $\{\!\{.?\}\!\}$, from elements to formal sets. $A?$ is built from A by discarding all secure memberships and only retaining the

---

[8]denoted by $\square$ by Gunter

doubtful ones, e.g. $\{|1?, 2|\}? = \{|1?, 2?|\}$. Its axioms are derived from what we required for $\{|.?|\}$ in section 3 together with linearity. In the following definition, we give – in contrast to Gunter – a minimal set of axioms, i.e. for each of the four axioms, there is a monotonic algebra satisfying all axioms except the given one.

Definition 8.1 (Mix algebras)

A (monotonic) mix algebra $(\mathbf{P}, \mathbin{\bar\cup}, \bar{\emptyset}, \_?)$ is a CAIN poset $(\mathbf{P}, \mathbin{\bar\cup}, \bar{\emptyset})$ with an additional monotonic operation $\_? : \mathbf{P} \to \mathbf{P}$ satisfying the following 4 axioms[9]

$(A1)\quad A? \le \bar{\emptyset} \qquad (A2)\quad A? \le A$

$(A3)\quad A \mathbin{\bar\cup} A? \ge A \qquad (A4)\quad (A \mathbin{\bar\cup} B)? \le A? \mathbin{\bar\cup} B?$

A mapping f between two mix algebras is a mix homomorphism iff it is monotonic and linear and additionally satisfies $f(A?) = (fA)?$. For a mix domain, the underlying poset has to be a domain and all operations must be continuous. □

One may easily check out that small as well as big set domain become mix domains by defining $(A^L, A^U)? = (\emptyset, A^U)$. The Boolean domain is a mix domain isomorphic to $\sigma 1 = \Sigma 1$ with $\bar{\emptyset} = \mathsf{F}$, $\mathbin{\bar\cup}$ being parallel disjunction, and $\mathsf{F}? = \mathsf{F}$ and $\mathsf{T}? = \bot? = \bot$.

The mix theory as defined above allows for deriving some theorems which hold in all mix algebras. Among those, there is (A3) and (A4) with equality. We now present the most important of these theorems with their proofs which end up in a characterization of mix homomorphisms. Gunter did not do so in his publications as far as I know them.

$(T1)\quad A \mathbin{\bar\cup} B? \le A \qquad$ since $A \mathbin{\bar\cup} B? \overset{A1}{\le} A \mathbin{\bar\cup} \bar{\emptyset} \overset{N}{=} A$

$(T2)\quad A \mathbin{\bar\cup} A? = A \qquad$ by (A3) and (T1)

$(T3)\quad \bar{\emptyset}? = \bar{\emptyset} \qquad$ since $\bar{\emptyset} \overset{T2}{=} \bar{\emptyset} \mathbin{\bar\cup} \bar{\emptyset}? \overset{N}{=} \bar{\emptyset}?$

$(T4)\quad A?? = A? \qquad$ since $A?? \overset{A2}{\le} A? \overset{T2}{=} A? \mathbin{\bar\cup} A?? \overset{T1}{\le} A??$

$(T5)\quad A? = A$ iff $A \le \bar{\emptyset}$

$\qquad$ Proof: '$\Rightarrow$' $A \overset{lhs}{=} A? \overset{A1}{\le} \bar{\emptyset} \qquad$ '$\Leftarrow$' $A? \overset{A2}{\le} A \overset{T2}{=} A \mathbin{\bar\cup} A? \overset{rhs}{\le} \bar{\emptyset} \mathbin{\bar\cup} A? \overset{N}{=} A?$

$(T6)\quad X \le \bar{\emptyset}$ and $X \le A$ iff $X \le A? \qquad$ i.e. $A?$ is the greatest lower bound of $\bar{\emptyset}$ and A.

$\qquad$ Proof: '$\Rightarrow$' $X \le \bar{\emptyset}$ implies $X = X?$ by (T5). $X \le A$ implies $X? \le A?$ by monotonicity of '?'. Together, $X \le A?$ follows. $\qquad$ '$\Leftarrow$' by (A1) and (A2).

$(T7)\quad (A \mathbin{\bar\cup} B)? = A? \mathbin{\bar\cup} B?$

$\qquad$ Proof: '$\le$' is (A4). '$\ge$' is deduced by (T6) from $A? \mathbin{\bar\cup} B? \le \bar{\emptyset}$ (by (A1) and (N)) and $A? \mathbin{\bar\cup} B? \le A \mathbin{\bar\cup} B$ (by (A2)).

$(T8)\quad$ The three statements $A \le A \mathbin{\bar\cup} B$ and $A? \le B?$ and $A? \le B$ are equivalent.

$\qquad$ Proof: $(1) \Rightarrow (2)$: $A? \overset{1}{\le} (A \mathbin{\bar\cup} B)? \overset{T7}{=} A? \mathbin{\bar\cup} B? \overset{T1}{\le} B?$

$\qquad\qquad (2) \Rightarrow (3)$: $A? \overset{2}{\le} B? \overset{A2}{\le} B$

$\qquad\qquad (3) \Rightarrow (1)$: $A \overset{T2}{=} A \mathbin{\bar\cup} A? \overset{3}{\le} A \mathbin{\bar\cup} B$

$(T9)\quad X \le \bar{\emptyset}$ and $X \le A$ and $A \mathbin{\bar\cup} X \ge A$ iff $X = A?$

$\qquad$ Proof: '$\Leftarrow$' is immediate by (A1), (A2), and (A3).

$\qquad$ '$\Rightarrow$': $X \le \bar{\emptyset}$ and $X \le A$ imply $X \le A?$ by (T6). $A \mathbin{\bar\cup} X \ge A$ implies $A? \le X$ by (T8).

Gunter defined mix algebras by an axiom system consisting of (T7), (T4), (T2), (A2), and (T1). Because (T1) implies (A1) by choosing $A = \bar{\emptyset}$ and (T2) implies (A3) and (T7) implies (A4), his mix theory is equivalent with ours.

---

[9]Here and in the sequel, all axioms and theorems are implicitly universally quantified over $\mathbf{P}$.

(T9) is a particularly interesting theorem. It implies that the operation '?' is uniquely determined in a given mix algebra, i.e. for given CAIN poset, there is at most one choice for the operation '?' to turn it into a mix algebra. Another important consequence is the following theorem which cannot be found in Gunter's publications [2,3,4].

Theorem 8.2

A monotonic linear mapping between two mix algebras is automatically a mix homomorphism. □

Proof: Let $f : \mathbf{X} \to \mathbf{Y}$ be a monotonic linear map between the two mix algebras $\mathbf{X}$ and $\mathbf{Y}$. Then for all $A \in \mathbf{X}$, $A? \leq \bar{\emptyset}$ and $A? \leq A$ and $A \cup A? \geq A$ imply $f(A?) \leq \bar{\emptyset}$ and $f(A?) \leq fA$ and $fA \cup f(A?) \geq fA$ respectively. By (T9), $f(A?) = (fA)?$ follows. □

Finally, one can show that the small set domain is free for the mix algebra:

Theorem 8.3

For every domain $\mathbf{D}$, the small set domain $\sigma\mathbf{D}$ is a mix domain. For every arbitrary mix domain $\mathbf{Y}$ and every continuous map $f : \mathbf{D} \to \mathbf{Y}$, there is a unique linear continuous map $\bar{f} : \sigma\mathbf{D} \to \mathbf{Y}$ with $\bar{f}\{|x|\} = fx$. $\bar{f}$ is a mix homomorphism. □

A proof of a similar theorem may be found in [3]. Our theorem follows from it by applying Theorem 8.2.

Corollary 8.4

For every continuous map $f : \mathbf{X} \to \sigma\mathbf{Y}$, there is a unique linear continuous extension $\bar{f} : \sigma\mathbf{X} \to \sigma\mathbf{Y}$ with $\bar{f} \circ \{|.|\} = f$. It is explicitly given by $\bar{f} = ext\, f$ where ext is defined as in section 5. □

Theorem 8.3 and (T9) imply together that the functions ext, $exists$, and '$\{|.?|\}$' as defined in section 5 are the only ones that satisfy the respective specifications in case of the small set domain.

9 The big set domain as a free construction

In Gunter's papers, the freedom of the big set domain is an open question. I found out that it is also a free construction, but w.r.t. an algebraic theory that is less natural than the mix theory since it involves a partial operation with a strange meaning. The problem is that all reasonable operations on sandwiches seem to preserve tightness.

The solution is to use an operation that marries sandwiches to each other i.e. (A^L, A^U) ⊚ $(B^L, B^U) = (A^L, B^U)$. A problem is that the partners may not harmonize such that the marriage is not durable. This means that ' ⊚ ' is a partial operation only. The exact definition for the big set domain is

$$(A^L, A^U) ⊚ (B^L, B^U) = \begin{cases} (A^L, B^U) & \text{if } A^L \subseteq \Downarrow B^U \\ undefined & \text{otherwise} \end{cases}$$

' ⊚ ' becomes a total continuous operation if '*undefined*' is added to the big set domain as an artificial top element. This is done in the following definition which enumerates the axioms of a sandwich algebra.

Definition 9.1 (Sandwich algebras)

A (monotonic) sandwich algebra $(\mathbf{P}, \cup, \bar{\emptyset}, ⊚)$ is a CAIN poset $(\mathbf{P}, \cup, \bar{\emptyset})$ with an additional monotonic operation $\_ ⊚ \_ : \mathbf{P} \times \mathbf{P} \to \mathbf{P} \cup \{undefined\}$ where $x \leq undefined$ for all $x \in \mathbf{P}$ satisfying the following 4 axioms

(A1) $A ⊚ A = A$ (A2) $A ⊚ B \leq (A \cup A') ⊚ B$ (A3) $A ⊚ B \geq A ⊚ (B \cup B')$

(A4) If $A ⊚ B$ and $A' ⊚ B'$ are defined, then $(A \cup A') ⊚ (B \cup B') = (A ⊚ B) \cup (A' ⊚ B')$

A mapping f between two sandwich algebras is a sandwich homomorphism iff it is monotonic and linear and additionally satisfies $f(A \otimes B) = (fA) \otimes (fB)$ whenever $A \otimes B$ is defined, i.e. in P. For a sandwich domain, the underlying poset has to be a domain and all operations must be continuous. □

One may easily verify that the big set domain becomes a sandwich domain by defining '$\otimes$' as indicated above. The Boolean domain is a sandwich domain with $\bar{\emptyset} = \mathsf{F}$ and $\cup$ being parallel disjunction since it is isomorphic to $\Sigma 1$.

As for the mix theory, some theorems may be derived from the axioms.

(T1) If $A \otimes B$ and $A \otimes B'$ are defined, then $A \otimes (B \cup B') = (A \otimes B) \cup (A \otimes B')$
Proof: let $A' = A$ in (A4) and apply (I).

(T2) If $A \otimes B$ and $A' \otimes B$ are defined, then $(A \cup A') \otimes B = (A \otimes B) \cup (A' \otimes B)$
Proof: let $B' = B$ in (A4) and apply (I).

(T3) If $A \otimes B$ is defined, then $(A \cup B) \otimes B = (A \otimes B) \cup B$ and $A \otimes (A \cup B) = A \cup (A \otimes B)$.
Proof: the first equation by (T2) and (A1), the second one by (T1) and (A1).

(T4) $A \otimes B$ and B are both $\leq (A \cup B) \otimes B$.
Proof: $B = B \otimes B$ by (A1), then apply (A2) in both cases.

(T5) $A \otimes (A \cup B) \leq$ both of A and $A \otimes B$.
Proof: $A = A \otimes A$ by (A1), then apply (A3) in both cases.

(T6) $\bar{\emptyset} \otimes B \leq B$ since $\bar{\emptyset} \otimes B \overset{T4}{\leq} (\bar{\emptyset} \cup B) \otimes B \overset{N}{=} B \otimes B \overset{A1}{=} B$

(T7) $\bar{\emptyset} \otimes B \leq \bar{\emptyset}$ since $\bar{\emptyset} \otimes B \overset{N}{=} \bar{\emptyset} \otimes (\bar{\emptyset} \cup B) \overset{T5}{\leq} \bar{\emptyset}$

(T8) Every sandwich algebra is a mix algebra by the definition $B? = \bar{\emptyset} \otimes B$.
Proof: (T6) means $B? \leq B$ and (T7) means $B? \leq \bar{\emptyset}$. These inequations also show that $B?$ is defined for all B. (T3) implies $B? \cup B = (\bar{\emptyset} \otimes B) \cup B = (\bar{\emptyset} \cup B) \otimes B = B$ by (N) and (A1). (T1) gives $(A \cup B)? = A? \cup B?$.

(T9) $A \leq A \cup B$ iff $\bar{\emptyset} \otimes A \leq \bar{\emptyset} \otimes B$ iff for all C: $C \otimes A \leq C \otimes B$.
Proof: '(1) $\Rightarrow$ (3)': $C \otimes A \overset{1}{\leq} C \otimes (A \cup B) \overset{A3}{\leq} C \otimes B$
(3) obviously implies (2), and (2) implies (1) by (T8) and theorem (T8) of the mix theory.

(T10) $A \cup B \leq B$ iff for all C: $A \otimes C \leq B \otimes C$.
Proof: '$\Rightarrow$': $A \otimes C \overset{A2}{\leq} (A \cup B) \otimes C \overset{lhs}{\leq} B \otimes C$
'$\Leftarrow$': $A \cup B \overset{A1}{=} (A \cup B) \otimes (A \cup B) \overset{T2}{=} (A \otimes (A \cup B)) \cup (B \otimes (A \cup B))$. (T2) is applicable since both marriages to the right are defined due to (T5) viz. $A \otimes (A \cup B) \leq A$ and $B \otimes (A \cup B) \leq B$. The precondition with $C = A \cup B$ may be applied to the last term resulting in $(B \otimes (A \cup B)) \cup (B \otimes (A \cup B)) \overset{I}{=} B \otimes (A \cup B) \overset{T5}{\leq} B$.

(T11) $A \leq A \cup B \geq B$ iff for all C: $C \otimes A = C \otimes B$.
This is deduced directly from (T9). We call A and B in this case upper equivalent and write $A \approx_U B$. This relation obviously is an equivalence relation. For the big set domain, one can show $A \approx_U B$ iff $A^U = B^U$, hence the name.

(T12) $A \geq A \cup B \leq B$ iff for all C: $A \otimes C = B \otimes C$.
This is deduced directly from (T10). We call A and B in this case lower equivalent and write $A \approx_L B$. For the big set domain, one can show $A \approx_L B$ iff $A^L = B^L$, hence the name.

(T13) If $A \otimes B$ is defined, then it is in the intersection of the lower class of A and the upper class of B, i.e. $A \approx_L A \otimes B \approx_U B$.
Proof: The lower equivalence by (T3) and (T5), and the upper one by (T3) and (T4).

(T14) For given A and B, there is an X such that $A \approx_L X \approx_U B$ iff $A \oplus B$ is defined. In this case, $A \oplus B = X$ holds. $A \oplus B$ is undefined iff there is no such X.

Proof: If $A \oplus B$ is defined, there is such an X by (T13). Conversely, assume such an X. Note that (T11) and (T12) hold no matter whether the married couples involving 'C' are defined or not. Hence, $A \oplus B \overset{T12}{=} X \oplus B \overset{T11}{=} X \oplus X \overset{A1}{=} X$, i.e. $A \oplus B$ is defined and equals X.

Similar to mix algebras, (T14) implies that the operation '$\oplus$' is uniquely determined in a given sandwich algebra, i.e. for given CAIN poset, there is at most one choice for the operation '$\oplus$' to turn it into a sandwich algebra. Another important consequence is the following theorem:

Theorem 9.2   A monotonic linear mapping between two sandwich algebras is automatically a sandwich homomorphism. □

Proof: Let $f : \mathbf{X} \to \mathbf{Y}$ be a monotonic linear map between the two sandwich algebras $\mathbf{X}$ and $\mathbf{Y}$. Let A and B be members of $\mathbf{X}$ such that $A \oplus B$ is defined. Then $A \approx_L A \oplus B \approx_U B$ holds by (T13). Using the equivalence of $S \approx_L T$ with $S \geq S \cup T \leq T$ and of $S \approx_U T$ with $S \leq S \cup T \geq T$, one obtains by monotonicity and linearity of f the relations $fA \approx_L f(A \oplus B) \approx_U fB$. (T14) then implies $fA \oplus fB = f(A \oplus B)$. □

Finally, one can show that the big set domain is free for the sandwich algebra:

Theorem 9.3   For every domain $\mathbf{D}$, the big set domain $\Sigma \mathbf{D}$ is a sandwich domain. For every arbitrary sandwich domain $\mathbf{Y}$ and every continuous map $f : \mathbf{D} \to \mathbf{Y}$, there is a unique linear continuous map $\bar{f} : \Sigma \mathbf{D} \to \mathbf{Y}$ with $\bar{f}\{\!|x|\!\} = fx$. $\bar{f}$ is a sandwich homomorphism. □

Sketch of proof: For a bifinite actual set $E \subseteq \mathbf{D}$, we define $f'E = \bigcup_{e \in E} fe$. The isolated sandwiches are given by $(\Downarrow E, \uparrow F)$ with $E \subseteq \Downarrow \uparrow F$. We define for them $\bar{f}(\Downarrow E, \uparrow F) = f'E \oplus f'F$. Then one has to show that this mapping is well defined, i.e. independent from the actual choice of E and F, and that the married couple on the right hand side is always defined. Next $\bar{f}$ is shown to be monotonic and linear. Then it may be extended to the whole domain $\Sigma \mathbf{D}$ to a continuous linear map. Uniqueness is shown by using the fact $(\Downarrow E, \uparrow F) = (\Downarrow E, \uparrow E) \oplus (\Downarrow F, \uparrow F) = \{\!|e \mid e \in E|\!\} \oplus \{\!|y \mid y \in F|\!\}$ and theorem 9.2. □

Corollary 9.4

For every continuous map $f : \mathbf{X} \to \Sigma \mathbf{Y}$, there is a unique linear continuous extension $\bar{f} : \Sigma \mathbf{X} \to \Sigma \mathbf{Y}$ with $\bar{f} \circ \{\!|.|\!\} = f$. It is explicitly given by $\bar{f} = ext\, f$ where ext is defined as in section 5. □

It is particularly nice because it neither mentions sandwich theory nor marrying, i.e. it is independent from this partial and semantically dubious operation.

The corollary, (T8) and (T14) imply together that the functions ext, $exists$, and '$\{\!|.?|\!\}$' as defined in section 5 are the only ones that satisfy the respective specifications in case of the big set domain.

10   Conclusion

In order to describe the semantics of a set type with given operations, we proposed two set domains whose construction is identical with the sandwich [1] and the mixed power domain with empty set [3,4]. The big set domain is useful in the context of bounded complete (Scott) domains, whereas the small one is suitable in the setting of SFP (Plotkin) domains. Besides not being bounded complete, the mathematical properties of the small domain are superior to those of the big one, because all its isolated points may be constructed by means of the supported set operations, and the greatest continuous equality of the ground domain easily carries over to it.

Both constructions produce free domains with respect to suitable algebraic theories where the theory of the small set domain is more natural than that of the big one. The freedom results allow for deducing that our primitive operations *ext*, *exists*, and doubtful singleton are uniquely determined by their specification if the underlying set domain with empty set, union, and singleton is given.

The discussion of the set operations they support sheds some light upon the informational content of the various domains. We worked out a more formal characterization of the domains by the behavior of existential quantification. It induces an isomorphism between the big set domain ΣD and the space of linear continuous second order predicates $(D \rightarrow B) \overset{lin}{\rightarrow} B$ – linear w.r.t. parallel disjunction. Since all other power domains are subdomains of the big set domain, they all correspond to sets of linear second order predicates which may be characterized by additional logical constraints.[10]

Acknowledgements

I am most grateful to Fritz Müller for his hints to the literature, many fruitful discussions, and the suggestion to investigate existential quantification on the set domains. Helmut Seidl also was always ready for discussions and read some drafts, and Reinhard Wilhelm made valuable proposals to improve the quality of a first draft. I also wish to thank the ESOP referee who suggested to investigate the question of freedom of the two set domains.

References

[1] Buneman, P., Davidson, S.B., Watters, A.: A semantics for Complex Objects and Approximate Queries: Extended Abstract, Internal Report MS-CIS-87-99, University of Pennsylvania, (Oct. 1988). Also in 7th ACM Principles of Database Systems.

[2] Gunter, C.A.: A Logical Interpretation of Powerdomains, Internal Report without number and date, University of Pennsylvania, before Sept. 1989

[3] Gunter, C.A.: The Mixed Powerdomain, Internal Report MS-CIS-89-77, Logic & Computation 18, University of Pennsylvania, (Dec. 1989)

[4] Gunter, C.A.: Relating Total and Partial Correctness Interpretations of Non-Deterministic Programs, In: P. Hudak, ed.: Principles of Programming Languages (POPL '90), ACM, (1990), 306-319

[5] Heckmann, R.: Set Domains, Ph.D. Thesis, Universität des Saarlandes, to appear

[6] Jung, A.: Cartesian Closed Categories of Domains, Ph.D. Thesis, FB Mathematik, Technische Hochschule Darmstadt, (1988)

[7] Lawson, J.D.: The Versatile Continuous Order, in: Main, M., Melton, A., Mislove, M., Schmidt, D., eds: Mathematical foundations of programming language semantics, 1987, Lecture Notes in Computer Science 298, (1988)

[8] Plotkin, G.D.: A powerdomain Construction, SIAM J. Comput., Vol. 5, No. 3, (1976), 452-487

[9] Smyth, M.B.: Power Domains, Journal of Computer and System Sciences 16, (1978), 23-36

[10] Smyth, M.B.: Power Domains and Predicate Transformers: A Topological View, ICALP 83, in: J. Diaz, ed.: Lecture Notes in Computer Science 154, Springer, (1983), 662-676

[11] Smyth, M.B.: The Largest Cartesian Closed Category of Domains, Theoretical Computer Science 27, (1983), 109-119

[12] Stoy, J.E.: Denotational Semantics: The Scott-Strachey Approach to Programming Language Theory, M.I.T. Press, (1977)

---

[10]These results were submitted to LICS'90, but there was no notification of (non-)acceptance yet.

Resolution and Type Theory

Leen Helmink

Philips Research Laboratories
P.O. Box 80.000, 5600 JA Eindhoven, the Netherlands

Abstract.
In this paper, an inference mechanism is proposed for proof construction in Constructive Type Theory. An interactive system that implements this method has been developed.

Key words. Type Theory, Calculus of Constructions, Typed Lambda Calculus, Natural Deduction.

1 Introduction

A method is presented to perform unification based top down proof construction for Constructive Type Theory, thus offering a well-founded, elegant and powerful underlying formalism for a proof development system. It combines the advantages of Horn clause resolution and higher order natural deduction style theorem proving. No theoretical contribution to Constructive Type Theory is claimed. The method is demonstrated for the Calculus of Constructions [Co85], but is applicable to other variants of type theory as well, e.g. systems in the families of AUTOMATH [Br73][Da80], Martin-Löf [Ma84], LF [Ha87], Elf [Pf89]. A full derivation example is included.

The problem addressed in this paper is to construct an object in a given context, given its type. This amounts to higher order theorem proving. This paper demonstrates that this construction problem can be handled by Horn clause resolution, provided that the set of available Horn clauses is continuously adapted to the context in which the proof is conducted. This rests on a mechanism that provides a simple clausal interpretation for the assumptions in a context. The method is not complete, due to the expressive power of type theory. Although the provided inference steps suggest certain search strategies (*tactics*), these issues are outside the scope of this paper. A proof environment based on the method, named *Constructor*, has been developed within Esprit project 1222: 'Genesis' [He88][He89]. Experiments with this system demonstrate the power and efficiency of the method.

2 Constructive Type Theory (CTT)

We assume familiarity with Constructive Type Theory [Br73][Co85][Cq85][Fo83][Hu87], a variant of the *propositions as types* paradigm. This section describes the particular system of interest. We shall use a system developed by Coquand, a version of the Calculus of Constructions. It must be emphasized that this is just one of the possible variants for which the presented proof construction method is applicable.

2.1 Terms

The syntactic formation rules for the terms in the system are defined as:

- constant, viz. one of {*prop, type, kind*}.
- variable, denoted by an identifier.
- $\lambda[x{:}A].B$, typed abstraction, where A and B are terms, and x a variable.
- $\Pi[x{:}A].B$, generalized Cartesian product of types B indexed over x of type A, where A and B are terms, and x a variable. [1]
- $(A\ B)$, application, where A and B are terms (function and argument). [2]

A *typing* is a construction of the form $[t{:}T]$, where t and T are terms. The intuition behind this is that T is the type of t. Types may have types themselves, and we will refer to such expressions as domains. Four levels of expressions are distinguished in the hierarchy of types: 0-, 1-, 2-, and 3-expressions, where n-expressions serve as types of $(n+1)$-expressions ($n = 0, 1, 2$). There is only one 0-expression: the constant 'supertype' *kind*. We introduce two predefined constants as primitive 1-expressions (kinds) of the system: the kind *type*, the set containing all 'plain' types (2-expressions), and the kind *prop*, that plays an identical role and is treated similarly, but which is inhabited by propositions (2-expressions) [3]. The level of 3-expressions contains objects and proofs.

2.2 Correctness

A *context* is a list of assumptions, introducing variables with their type. A context is of the form:

$$[x_1{:}A_1],...,[x_n{:}A_n] \quad (n{\geq}0)$$

No variable may be declared more than once in a context. Moreover, the free variables occurring in A_i must have been declared earlier in the context, i.e. $\mathcal{FV}(A_i) \subseteq \{x_1,...,x_{i-1}\}$, where $\mathcal{FV}(A)$ stands for the set of variables occurring free in A. Apart from assumptions, contexts may contain *definitions*. A definition introduces a variable as an abbreviation for an arbitrary correct expression. A definition is of the form $[c \equiv a{:}A]$, where c is a fresh identifier, and establishes that c abbreviates the term a of type A.

We will use Γ as a metavariable over contexts. Well-formedness of a context Γ will be denoted *well-formed*(Γ). We will write $\Gamma, [x{:}A]$ to denote the context Γ extended with the assumption $[x{:}A]$, and Γ_1, Γ_2 for the concatenation of contexts Γ_1 and Γ_2. The symbol 'Ø' represents the empty context. We will write $E \in \Gamma$ to denote that E is a member of context Γ. A *sequent* is an expression of the form $\Gamma \vdash [a{:}A]$, denoting that $[a{:}A]$ is a correct typing in the well-formed context Γ. The predicate $constant(x)$ denotes that x is one of the constants *type, prop* or *kind*. We will write $B[a/x]$ to denote substitution of the term a for the free occurrences of the variable x in the expression B. We will write '$=_{\beta\delta}$' to denote the transitive reflexive closure of β- and δ-reduction. β-reduction corresponds to the usual notion in typed lambda-calculus, and δ-reduction denotes local expansion of definitions that have been introduced in the context. Note that both β- and δ-reduction are context-dependent. We assume α-conversion whenever necessary and all equality is modulo α-conversion. This can be achieved by using De Bruijn indices [Br72] or Barendregt's variable convention [Ba81].

---

[1]In type theory, typed abstraction is often denoted $[x{:}A]B$, while typed product is denoted $(x{:}A)B$ or $\{x{:}A\}B$.

[2]Application associates to the left, so we will write (a b c) for ((a b) c).

[3]In many versions of this system, *type* and *prop* are identified (usually denoted '$*$' or '*Type*'). Here we will explicitly distinguish between them to avoid possible confusion. This is however not essential to the formalism.

Well-formedness of contexts and correct typing of terms is inductively defined as:

[0] *well-formed*($\emptyset$)

[1a] If *well-formed*(Γ) then $\Gamma \vdash [type:kind]$

[1b] If *well-formed*(Γ) then $\Gamma \vdash [prop:kind]$

[2a] If $\Gamma \vdash [A:K]$ and *constant*(K) then *well-formed*($\Gamma, [x:A]$)

[2b] If $\Gamma \vdash [a:A]$ then *well-formed*($\Gamma, [c \equiv a:A]$)

[3a] If *well-formed*(Γ) and $[x:A] \in \Gamma$, then $\Gamma \vdash [x:A]$

[3b] If *well-formed*(Γ) and $[c \equiv a:A] \in \Gamma$, then $\Gamma \vdash [c:A]$

[4] If $\Gamma, [x:A] \vdash [b:B]$ then $\Gamma \vdash [\lambda[x:A].b : \Pi[x:A].B]$

[5] If $\Gamma, [x:A] \vdash [B:K]$ and *constant*(K) then $\Gamma \vdash [\Pi[x:A].B:K]$

[6] If $\Gamma \vdash [a:A]$ and $\Gamma \vdash [b : \Pi[x:A].B]$ then $\Gamma \vdash [(b\ a):B[a/x]]$

[7] If $\Gamma \vdash [a:A]$ and $\Gamma \vdash [B:K]$ and *constant*(K) and $A =_{\beta\delta} B$ then $\Gamma \vdash [a:B]$

Details and properties of the described system can be found in [Co85][Cq85][Ha89][Hu87][Ju86].

2.3 Interpretation and Use

If, for a dependent product type $\Pi[x:A].B$, x does not occur free in B ($x \notin \mathcal{FV}(B)$), the type simplifies, as usual, to the ordinary *function type* $A \to B$. In case $A:prop$, A is considered a proposition and a typing $[a:A]$ is interpreted as: a is a proof for A, i.e. a proposition plays the role of the type of its proofs. This means that a proposition is considered valid if and only if it is inhabited. The system described contains intuitionistic higher order predicate logic. For example, if $B:prop$, then $\Pi[x:A].B$ can be interpreted as the universally quantified proposition $\forall x:A.B$. If x does not occur free in B and $A:prop$ and $B:prop$, then $\Pi[x:A].B$ can be interpreted as the intuitionistic implication $A \Rightarrow B$. The Calculus of Constructions formalism thus provides a definition language that can be and has been used to formalize and mechanically verify many parts of mathematics. Texts in this language are written in the form of *theories* (*books* in AUTOMATH terminology). Theories are CTT contexts. For a field of interest, assumptions allow the axiomization of the primitive notions, whereas the definitions allow abbreviation of derived notions like lemmas.

3 CTT Proof Construction Method

It is a well-known fact, that correctness of sequents $\Gamma \vdash [t:T]$ (t has type T in context Γ) in Constructive Type Theory and related systems is decidable, even feasibly decidable, and several proof checkers exist that mechanically determine correctness for given CTT theories [Ju76], [Da80], [Co85]. For a proof construction system, the objective is not to verify whether a given object has a certain given type, but, for a given type, to attempt construction of an inhabitant of this type. More precisely: given a context (theory) Γ and a type A, the objective is to construct an object p such that $\Gamma \vdash [p:A]$. For propositions, this corresponds to finding a proof object.

The central problem with goal directed proof construction in Constructive Type Theory is that direct backward chaining with the correctness rules of section 2.2 is hardly possible. Therefore, the approach is to extract from the given formalization a sound set of derived rules, that do allow easy backward inference. These derived rules then serve as the primitive proof steps of the system.

In the method, CTT sequents will be derived using Horn clause resolution. In goal directed proving, the idea is to start off with a goal to be proven, and to replace goals by appropriate subgoals by resolution with inference rules [Ro65]. Horn clause inference rules consist of a (possibly empty) set of antecedents $S_1...S_k$ and one conclusion S. Horn clauses will be denoted: $S \Leftarrow S_1...S_k$. In the method, antecedents and conclusions will all be CTT sequents. Sequents may contain logical variables over CTT terms. To avoid confusion with CTT variables, we will denote logical variables by identifiers prefixed will a '♯' symbol. Logical variables are considered to be universally quantified over clauses. A term is grounded if it does not contain logical variables. A context will be called grounded if it contains grounded terms only. The meaning of a Horn clause is that *if* instantiations for the logical variables can be found, such that the antecedent sequents are correct, *then* the associated consequent is a correct sequent. A Horn clause will be considered *valid* if its meaning is correct with respect to the correctness rules of CTT. Unification determines how two rules can be combined into derivations. A derivation for a sequent is either a Horn clause concluding that sequent, or it is a derivation where an antecedent sequent S_i is replaced by the antecedents of a Horn clause concluding S_i', after unifying S_i and S_i'. If no antecedents are left in a derivation, the derivation is complete and serves as a justification for the correctness of its conclusion sequent. Derivations correspond to derived Horn clauses and have the same interpretation.

The queries considered consist of one goal of the form $\Gamma \vdash [♯P{:}A]$, where Γ must be a grounded, well-formed context, A must be a grounded, correct domain, and $♯P$ is a logical variable. For a given query S, the derivation process starts with the trivial derivation '$S \Leftarrow S$', which is obviously valid. The objective is to transform this derivation by resolution with valid Horn clauses, until the derivation '$S' \Leftarrow$' is reached. S' is then a correct instance of S.

Derivations and Horn clauses will be of the form: $\Gamma \vdash [p{:}A] \Leftarrow \Gamma_1 \vdash [p_1{:}A_1] ... \Gamma_n \vdash [p_n{:}A_n]$. The following invariant properties will hold for all derivations (but not necessarily for Horn clauses):

1. all contexts Γ and $\Gamma_1 ... \Gamma_n$ will be grounded and well-formed.
2. $\Gamma \subseteq \Gamma_1 , ... , \Gamma \subseteq \Gamma_n$.
3. for any logical variable $♯P$ occurring in the type field A_i of a subgoal $\Gamma_i \vdash [p_i{:}A_i]$, $♯P \in \{p_1...p_{i-1}\}$. If an object field p_i of a subgoal $\Gamma_i \vdash [p_i{:}A_i]$ is not a logical variable, then for any logical variable $♯P$ occurring in p_i, $♯P \in \{p_1...p_{i-1}\}$.
4. for any logical variable $♯P$ occurring in the object field p of the conclusion $\Gamma \vdash [p{:}A]$, $♯P \in \{p_1...p_n\}$.

The first property reflects the fact that construction always takes place within a known context. The second property states that contexts can be extended during backward proving. The third property ensures that logical variables are 'introduced before use'. The fourth property guarantees that the conclusion of a derivation will be grounded when all subgoals have been solved (the type field A of a derivation conclusion is grounded from the start). For our queries $\Gamma \vdash [♯P{:}A]$ this implies that an object $♯P$ of the requested type A has been constructed. Note that the trivial derivations that correspond to our queries of interest have all the required properties.

It turns out that we can avoid a problem that usually arises with inference rules over sequents, viz. unification over contexts. The reason for this is that in contrast to general purpose higher order theorem provers as presented in e.g. [Pa86], [Pa89] and [Fe88], the method inferences at the object level, not at the meta level. This is possible because the method is specialized for type theory only; It is not a generic inference method over arbitrary sequents. Contexts will be treated in a special way, and it is sufficient to unify over typings. Our goals, that denote CTT sequents, will be regarded as tuples with a typing and a context.

For the method to work, it is necessary that contexts occurring in derivations are grounded, so that (1) we do not unify over contexts at all, and (2) we can extract the necessary object level horn clauses directly from contexts. The exact consequences of this restriction will be alluded later.

In the subsequent sections, valid Horn clauses will be derived. These Horn clauses will not violate the given invariant property for derivations. Some of the Horn clauses correspond directly to correctness rules for type theory and are of interest to all subgoals in a derivation. The problem is that no suitable Horn clause can be given for the application rule (rule 6), on account of the substitution. A solution for this problem is presented, that rests on a mechanism to provide a direct clausal interpretation for the assumptions in a context. The Horn clauses thus obtained cover derivation steps that can construct the necessary application terms. This is the crux of the method. For any given subgoal $\Gamma_i \vdash [p_i:A_i]$, this mechanism, when applied to the context Γ_i, allows derivation of a set of valid Horn clauses that are candidates for resolution on this particular subgoal. A proposal for this mechanism was first suggested by [Ah85].

3.1 Kinds rule

The *kinds* rule (rule 1) is directly equivalent to the valid Horn clauses:

$$\Gamma \vdash [type : kind] \Leftarrow .$$
$$\Gamma \vdash [prop : kind] \Leftarrow .$$

For any subgoal $\Gamma_i \vdash [p_i:A_i]$, such a rule applies if $[p_i:A_i]$ unifies with $[type:kind]$ or $[prop:kind]$. Γ is not treated as a logical variable. Because contexts in our derivations are always grounded and well-formed, the well-formedness check on Γ_i (required in rule 1) is needless.

3.2 Lambda abstraction rule

The lambda abstraction rule (rule 4) corresponds to the valid Horn clause:

$$\Gamma \vdash [\lambda[x{:}\sharp A].\sharp B : \Pi[x{:}\sharp A].\sharp T] \Leftarrow \Gamma, [x{:}\sharp A] \vdash [\sharp B{:}\sharp T].$$

The typing of a goal of the form $\Gamma_i \vdash [P : \Pi[x{:}A].T]$ may be unified with the typing in the conclusion of this rule, unifying P with $\lambda[x{:}\sharp A].\sharp B$ and resulting in the new stripped subgoal $[\sharp B{:}\sharp T]$, to be solved in the context Γ_i extended with the typing $[x{:}\sharp A]$. Γ does not play the role of a logical variable. To ensure that this new context is grounded and well-formed, the restriction is imposed that A must be grounded and correct domain, thus preventing logical variables over domains to be introduced in the context. For example, this rule can not be used to find a proof for an implication $\sharp A \Rightarrow B$, because this would introduce an unknown assumption $[p{:}\sharp A]$ in the context.

3.3 Pi abstraction rule

The pi abstraction rule (rule 5) corresponds to the valid Horn clause:

$$\Gamma \vdash [\Pi[x{:}\sharp A].\sharp B : \sharp K] \Leftarrow \Gamma, [x{:}\sharp A] \vdash [\sharp B{:}\sharp K].$$

For goals of the form $\Gamma_i \vdash [\Pi[x{:}A].B : K]$, application of this rule results, after unification of typings, in a stripped subgoal $[B{:}K]$, to be solved in the context Γ_i extended with the typing $[x{:}A]$. K must be a constant. Though this check has to be postponed if K is not grounded, it can be demonstrated that this need never occur, and K must be either *type* or *prop*. To ensure that the new context is grounded and well-formed, again the restriction is imposed that A must be a grounded and correct domain. For example, this prevents using this rule on a goal $\Gamma_i \vdash [\sharp P{:}prop]$.

3.4 Derived Clauses

The application rule (rule 6) cannot be translated directly to a valid Horn clause, on account of the substitution. A solution is offered, for which the following theorem is essential:

Correctness of a sequent of the form

$$\Gamma \vdash [C : \Pi[x_1{:}A_1] \dots \Pi[x_n{:}A_n].B]$$

is equivalent to the validity of the Horn clause:

$$\Gamma, \Gamma' \vdash [(C \, \sharp x_1 \dots \sharp x_n) : B[\sharp x_1/x_1, ..., \sharp x_n/x_n]] \Leftarrow \Gamma, \Gamma' \vdash [\sharp x_1{:}A_1]$$
$$\Gamma, \Gamma' \vdash [\sharp x_2{:}A_2[\sharp x_1/x_1]]$$
$$\dots$$
$$\Gamma, \Gamma' \vdash [\sharp x_n{:}A_n[\sharp x_1/x_1, ..., \sharp x_{n-1}/x_{n-1}]].$$

where $\sharp x_1 \dots \sharp x_n$ are the logical variables of the Horn clause. The context Γ, Γ' denotes any well-formed context extension of Γ. Note that all possible occurrences of the CTT variables x_i have been replaced by corresponding logical variables $\sharp x_i$. For a complete proof of this theorem the reader is referred to [He88]. For n=0, the set of premises is empty and the application in the consequent simplifies to the object C. The selection rule (rule 3a and 3b) justifies that the theorem is in particular applicable to all introductions and definitions occurring in any well-formed context Γ, i.e.

For all CTT variables c, if

$$[c : \Pi[x_1{:}A_1] \dots \Pi[x_n{:}A_n].B] \in \Gamma \quad \text{or} \quad [c \equiv C : \Pi[x_1{:}A_1] \dots \Pi[x_n{:}A_n].B] \in \Gamma$$

this theorem guarantees that:

$$\Gamma \vdash [(c \, \sharp x_1 \dots \sharp x_n) : B[\sharp x_1/x_1, ..., \sharp x_n/x_n]] \Leftarrow \Gamma \vdash [\sharp x_1{:}A_1]$$
$$\Gamma \vdash [\sharp x_2{:}A_2[\sharp x_1/x_1]]$$
$$\dots$$
$$\Gamma \vdash [\sharp x_n{:}A_n[\sharp x_1/x_1, ..., \sharp x_{n-1}/x_{n-1}]].$$

This result is now used to interpret the introductions and definitions in a context in this clausal form. The idea is to 'unfold' the top level Π-abstractions for context elements to clauses. For a goal $\Gamma_i \vdash [p_i{:}A_i]$, all clauses thus obtained from the grounded context Γ_i are available as valid Horn clauses for resolution on this goal. Note that resolving a goal with such a Horn clause does not affect the associated context, i.e. all subgoals that arise are to be solved in the original context Γ_i. Although for a given context element of type $\Pi[x_1{:}A_1] \dots \Pi[x_n{:}A_n].B$ (where B is not itself a Π-abstraction) the theorem gives $n + 1$ different valid Horn clauses, it is sufficient to provide the completely unfolded clause with n antecedents. The small price to pay is that the resulting proofs may contain η-redexes. If desired, these can be reduced immediately. See also section 5.

3.5   Unification and Type Conversion

Unification determines whether a clause is applicable in a given situation. Unification will also handle the type conversion rule (rule 7), dealing with equality of types. It is important to observe that it is sufficient to provide unification over typings, not over contexts (although context information is of course relevant for β- and δ-reductions during unification). Unifying typings $[P{:}A]$ and $[P'{:}A']$ can be achieved by unifying the objects P and P' and subsequently unifying the types A and A'. For types, the unification is with respect to β- and δ-equality. Although β-equality for objects is not explicit in the correctness rules, it is also desirable to identify β- (and δ-) equivalent terms. This is justified by the closure under reduction property, and corresponds to proof normalization [Co85][Da80][Ha87]. Because we unfold derived clauses completely, it is desirable to augment object unification with outermost η-equality, to ensure reachability of objects in η-normal form. Unification for expressions in typed λ-calculus with respect to α, β and possibly η-conversion requires complete higher order unification. This problem has a possibly infinite set of solutions and is known to be semidecidable, in the sense that if two terms do not unify, search algorithms for unifiers may diverge [Hu75]. [Hu75] also gives an algorithm that can be used for implementations of the method. Sound approximations for higher order unification may also be used, although this affects completeness, of course.

4   Completeness

An interesting question is whether the method is complete in the sense that a top down derivation can be constructed for all correct inhabitants (modulo object conversion) of a given type (checking is complete). Note that completeness is of course determined by the completeness of the higher-order unification procedure. But what exactly are the consequences of the restriction that we impose on the context, viz. that it is always grounded?

We already saw that our queries of interest are not affected by the restriction. Now consider the effect of the restriction during the inferencing process. It should be clear that only the lambda rule and the pi rule are affected by the restriction, as they may extend a context during resolution.

For issues related to completeness (at least in a non-deterministic sense), the following observation is important: due to the third invariant property on derivations, we only need to consider goals where the type field of the conclusion is grounded, because any logical variable $\sharp P$ occurring there can be instantiated by first solving the associated goal where $\sharp P$ is introduced. This implies that the partiality of the lambda-abstraction rule poses no fundamental restrictions, because it can be circumvented by postponing resolution on the goal in question. It is clear that the restriction on the applicability of the pi-abstraction rule poses real limitations: it explicitly restricts querying for arbitrary 2-expressions, i.e. it refuses to enumerate all Π-abstracted propositions or types. The expressive power of CTT is such, that it does allow the construction of proofs that involve e.g. induction loading, where a stronger proposition is sought to construct a proof for a weaker one. Top down construction of such proofs is unattainable in general. The limitations imposed on the pi abstraction rule are related to this fundamental problem.

Thus, the method as presented is not complete. The restriction affects construction of propositions and types. Since it is possible to enumerate all propositions (or types), the method can be made complete by replacing the pi rule by an enumerator algorithm, in those places where construction is desired.

5 Derivation Example

As an example, consider the following correct theory Γ_0:

$[nat : type]$,
$[0 : nat]$,
$[s : \Pi[x{:}nat].\ nat]$,
$[< : \Pi[x{:}nat].\ \Pi[y{:}nat].\ prop]$,
$[axiom1 : \Pi[x{:}nat].\ (<\ x\ (s\ x))]$,
$[trans : \Pi[x{:}nat].\ \Pi[y{:}nat].\ \Pi[z{:}nat].$
$\qquad \Pi[p{:}(<\ x\ y)].\ \Pi[q{:}(<\ y\ z)].\ (<\ x\ z)]$,
$[ind : \Pi\ [p : \Pi[x{:}nat].\ prop].$
$\qquad \Pi\ [g : (p\ 0)].$
$\qquad \Pi\ [h : \Pi[n{:}nat].\ \Pi[hyp{:}(p\ n)].\ (p\ (s\ n))].$
$\qquad \Pi\ [z : nat].\ (p\ z)]$,
$[pred1 \equiv \lambda[x{:}nat].\ (<\ 0\ (s\ x)) : \Pi[x{:}nat].\ prop]$

To elucidate the method, a top down derivation is now presented for the theorem $\forall y{:}nat.\ (pred1\ y)$, i.e. a proof object $\sharp P$ is sought, such that $\Gamma_0 \vdash [\sharp P : \Pi[y{:}nat].\ (pred1\ y)]$. The associated trivial derivation for the query is:

$$\Gamma_0 \vdash [\sharp P : \Pi[y{:}nat].\ (pred1\ y)] \Leftarrow \Gamma_0 \vdash [\sharp P : \Pi[y{:}nat].\ (pred1\ y)].$$

The Horn clauses available for resolution are:

$$\Gamma \vdash [\lambda[x{:}\sharp A].\sharp B : \Pi[x{:}\sharp A].\sharp T] \Leftarrow \Gamma, [x{:}\sharp A] \vdash [\sharp B{:}\sharp T].$$
$$\Gamma \vdash [\Pi[x{:}\sharp A].\sharp B : \sharp K] \Leftarrow \Gamma, [x{:}\sharp A] \vdash [\sharp B{:}\sharp K].$$

viz. the lambda abstraction rule and the pi abstraction rule (the kinds rule is of no relevance to this example). These Horn clauses are always available for goals. For a given goal, they are extended with Horn clauses that can be obtained from the unfolded context elements of the goal. For the antecedent in the given trivial derivation this means:

$[nat : type] \Leftarrow .$
$[0 : nat] \Leftarrow .$
$[(s\ \sharp X) : nat] \Leftarrow [\sharp X : nat].$
$[(<\ \sharp X\ \sharp Y) : prop] \Leftarrow [\sharp X : nat]\ [\sharp Y : nat].$
$[(axiom1\ \sharp X) : (<\ \sharp X\ (s\ \sharp X))] \Leftarrow [\sharp X : nat].$
$[(trans\ \sharp X\ \sharp Y\ \sharp Z\ \sharp P\ \sharp Q) : (<\ \sharp X\ \sharp Z)] \Leftarrow [\sharp X{:}nat]\ [\sharp Y{:}nat]\ [\sharp Z{:}nat]$
$\qquad\qquad\qquad\qquad\qquad\qquad\qquad [\sharp P{:}(<\ \sharp X\ \sharp Y)]\ [\sharp Q{:}(<\ \sharp Y\ \sharp Z)].$
$[(ind\ \sharp P\ \sharp G\ \sharp H\ \sharp Z) : (\sharp P\ \sharp Z)] \Leftarrow [\sharp P : \Pi[x{:}nat].\ prop]\ [\sharp G : (\sharp P\ 0)]$
$\qquad\qquad\qquad\qquad\qquad\qquad\quad [\sharp H : \Pi[n{:}nat].\ \Pi[hyp{:}(\sharp P\ n)].\ (\sharp P\ (s\ n))]\ [\sharp Z : nat].$
$[(pred1\ \sharp X) : prop] \Leftarrow [\sharp X : nat].$

where Γ_0 has been omitted from the sequents. Similar clauses can be constructed for extensions of Γ_0. The only rule applicable to our derivation is the lambda abstraction rule. Resolution gives:

$$\Gamma_0 \vdash [\sharp P : \Pi[y{:}nat].\ (pred1\ y)] \Leftarrow \Gamma_0, [y{:}nat] \vdash [\sharp P' : (pred1\ y)].$$

instantiating $\sharp P$ to $\lambda[y{:}nat].\sharp P'$. In the extended context of the subgoal, a derived clause for y ($[y{:}nat] \Leftarrow .$) is now available. Resolution with the induction clause (ind) from the context gives:

$$\Gamma_0 \vdash [\sharp P : \Pi[y{:}nat].(pred1\ y)] \Leftarrow \Gamma_0, [y{:}nat] \vdash [pred1 : \Pi[x{:}nat].\,prop]$$
$$\Gamma_0, [y{:}nat] \vdash [\sharp G : (pred1\ 0)]$$
$$\Gamma_0, [y{:}nat] \vdash [\sharp H : \Pi[n{:}nat].\,\Pi[hyp{:}(pred1\ n)].\,(pred1\ (s\ n))]$$
$$\Gamma_0, [y{:}nat] \vdash [y : nat].$$

instantiating $\sharp P'$ to $(ind\ \sharp P''\ \sharp G\ \sharp H\ \sharp Z)$, $\sharp P''$ to $pred1$, and $\sharp Z$ to y. Note that this requires higher order unification. The first subgoal is grounded and can be checked, but this goal can also be solved after resolution with the lambda abstraction rule, provided that the unification knows that $pred1$ is equivalent to $[x{:}nat](pred1\ x)$ (outermost η-equivalence). The last subgoal is solved directly with the Horn clause for y from the context. The derivation thus becomes:

$$\Gamma_0 \vdash [\sharp P : \Pi[y{:}nat].(pred1\ y)] \Leftarrow \Gamma_0, [y{:}nat] \vdash [\sharp G : (pred1\ 0)]$$
$$\Gamma_0, [y{:}nat] \vdash [\sharp H : \Pi[n{:}nat].\,\Pi[hyp{:}(pred1\ n)].\,(pred1\ (s\ n))].$$

The first subgoal resolves with the Horn clause for $axiom1$ from the context, instantiating $\sharp G$ to $(axiom1\ 0)$ and leaving $[0{:}nat]$ as trivial subgoal that can be resolved immediately. The remaining subgoal is stripped twice with the lambda abstraction rule. The derivation is now:

$$\Gamma_0 \vdash [\sharp P : \Pi[y{:}nat].\,(pred1\ y)] \Leftarrow \Gamma_1 \vdash [\sharp H' : (pred1\ (s\ n))].$$

instantiating $\sharp H$ to $\lambda[n{:}nat].\lambda[hyp{:}(pred1\ n)].\,\sharp H'$. Γ_1 stands for $\Gamma_0, [y{:}nat], [n{:}nat], [hyp{:}(pred1\ n)]$. The remaining proof obligation is now resolved with the context clause for transitivity ($trans$):

$$\Gamma_0 \vdash [\sharp P : \Pi[y{:}nat].\,(pred1\ y)] \Leftarrow \Gamma_1 \vdash [0 : nat]$$
$$\Gamma_1 \vdash [\sharp Y : nat]$$
$$\Gamma_1 \vdash [(s\ (s\ n)) : nat]$$
$$\Gamma_1 \vdash [\sharp P1 : (<\ 0\ \sharp Y)]$$
$$\Gamma_1 \vdash [\sharp Q : (<\ \sharp Y\ (s\ (s\ n)))].$$

instantiating $\sharp H'$ to $(trans\ 0\ \sharp Y\ (s\ (s\ n))\ \sharp P1\ \sharp Q)$. The first and third subgoal are eliminated with context clauses from Γ_1 for 0, s and n. Because these subgoals are grounded, this amounts to checking. Resolving the last subgoal with $axiom1$ instantiates $\sharp Q$ to $(axiom1\ n)$ and $\sharp Y$ to $(s\ n)$. The derivation has become:

$$\Gamma_0 \vdash [\sharp P : \Pi[y{:}nat].\,(pred1\ y)] \Leftarrow \Gamma_1 \vdash [(s\ n) : nat]$$
$$\Gamma_1 \vdash [\sharp P1 : (<\ 0\ (s\ n))]$$
$$\Gamma_1 \vdash [(s\ n) : nat].$$

The proof is completed with the context clauses for s, n and hyp. The complete proof $\sharp P$ is now:

$$\lambda[y{:}nat].\,(ind\ pred1$$
$$(axiom1\ 0)$$
$$\lambda[n{:}nat].\,\lambda[hyp{:}(pred1\ n)].\,(trans\ 0\ (s\ n)\ (s\ (s\ n))\ hyp\ (axiom1\ (s\ n)))$$
$$y)$$

Note that this proof is an η-redex. This is due to the fact that derived clauses are unfolded as far as possible here, thus constructing applications that are provided with the full number of arguments. If outermost η-conversion of objects is provided, the η-normal proof can also be derived.

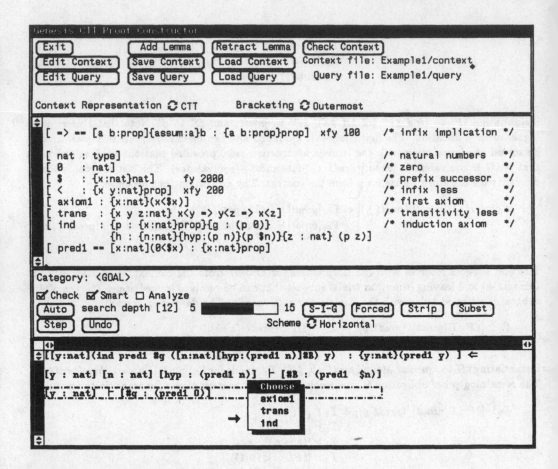

Figure 1: *Here, we are in the middle of an interactive session, solving the query from the example in the previous section. The second window contains the global context. For each goal, candidate clauses for resolution can be selected from a menu. The proof under construction is collected in the head of the derivation. Note the different local context extensions for the different subgoals.*

6 The *Constructor* Proof Environment

This section gives a short description of an interactive proof environment, named *Constructor*, that implements an inference machine based on the described method. The machine enforces correctness of proof construction in CTT. The mouse-based interface has been built using the *Genesis* system, the tool generator that resulted from Esprit project 1222. Details of the *Constructor* system can be found in [He88][He89]. Here, we will explain its most important features.

When using *Constructor*, there is always a global context present, which is the theory that formalizes a domain of interest. A proof editor is provided in which conjunctions of queries can be posed, and that admits application of correct proof steps. Queries are interpreted in the global context. Queries are typings of the form [*A*:*B*]. Figures 1 and 2 present some screen images of the system (for the syntax used in the figures see section 6.1).

Both interactive user-guided inference and automatic search are possible and may intermingle. In interactive mode the user may, for a selected goal, choose a clause from a menu with resolution candidates. Optionally, the system checks instantiated subgoals that may arise after resolution steps. Currently only one default search strategy or *tactic* (*tactical* in LCF terminology) is present for automatic search. It uses a consecutively bounded depth-first search strategy. The maximum search depth must be specified interactively. Alternative solutions are generated upon request. Facilities to 'undo' user or tactic choices are provided. The resolution method itself is used (by way of bootstrapping) for correctness checking of contexts and local context introductions. Completed derivations may be added to the global context as lemmas. To this end, they must be given a name and will be available for use in subsequent queries. It is possible to 'freeze' definitions, i.e. to hide their contents and treat them as axioms. In case of clash of variable names (α-clash), unique variable names are generated by numbering. Textual editing of theories and queries is provided in the environment itself.

The special handling of contexts can be implemented efficiently. For example, translation of context elements to clauses only needs to be done once, because the main theorem guarantees that clauses remain valid in extended contexts (this is due to the fact that CTT is monotonic). Verifying well-formedness of contexts can be done incrementally. Contexts can be shared amongst goals.

Apart from the application rule (rule 6) and the selection rule (rule 3), which are handled by the method proposed, the *Constructor* system is parameterized with respect to the correctness rules for type theory, i.e. the system can handle different versions and extensions of type theory. For example, it poses no problems to interpret various dialects of AUTOMATH [Br73][Da80].

6.1   Technical Details

In *Constructor*, typed abstraction is denoted $[x{:}A]B$, whereas typed product is denoted as $\{x{:}A\}B$. Multiple variable introductions are permitted, e.g. $[x\ y{:}A]B$ denotes $[x{:}A][y{:}A]B$. Variables and definitions that are introduced can be declared as fix operators, much like in a Prolog fashion. For example, '$[\ =>\ ==\ [a\ b{:}prop]\{p{:}a\}b : \{a\ b{:}prop\}prop]\ xfy\ 100$' declares '=>' (implication) as a right associative infix operator with priority level *100*. Application is treated as a left-associative infix operator. Bracketing is used in the usual way to over-rule priorities. Logical variables are prefixed with a '♯' symbol.

The built-in unification procedure implements a simple approximation of higher order unification with the following characteristics :

- *Higher Order Structural Matching*
  First order unification where logical variables for functors match structurally, e.g. '(♯F 0)' unifies with '(suc 0)' yielding unifier ♯F=suc.
- *Alpha conversion*
  The unification is modulo the name of bound variables, e.g. '[x:nat]x' equals '[y:nat]y'.
- *Beta conversion*
  The built in unification procedure will reduce β-redexes if necessary. To ensure that the reduction is always sound, a goal is added to demonstrate that the argument will have the required domain type, in the context in question.
- *Delta conversion*
  The built in unification procedure will do δ-reduction on definitions if necessary, i.e. it may expand abbreviating names.

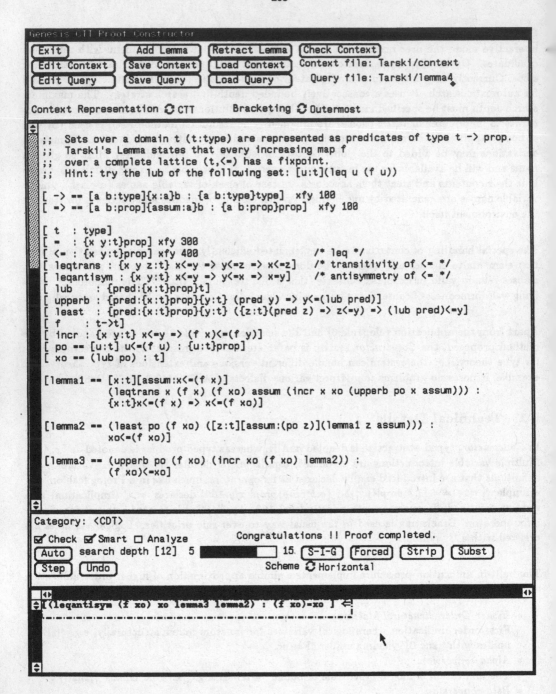

```
Genesis CTT Proof Constructor
[Exit]            [Add Lemma]     [Retract Lemma] [Check Context]
[Edit Context]    [Save Context]  [Load Context]  Context file: Tarski/context
[Edit Query]      [Save Query]    [Load Query]     Query file: Tarski/lemma4

Context Representation  ⟳ CTT       Bracketing  ⟳ Outermost

;;  Sets over a domain t (t:type) are represented as predicates of type t -> prop.
;;  Tarski's Lemma states that every increasing map f
;;  over a complete lattice (t,<=) has a fixpoint.
;;  Hint: try the lub of the following set: [u:t](leq u (f u))

[ -> == [a b:type]{x:a}b : {a b:type}type] xfy 100
[ => == [a b:prop]{assum:a}b : {a b:prop}prop] xfy 100

[ t   : type]
[ =  : {x y:t}prop] xfy 300
[ <= : {x y:t}prop] xfy 400                   /* leq */
[ leqtrans : {x y z:t} x<=y => y<=z => x<=z]   /* transitivity of <= */
[ leqantisym : {x y:t} x<=y => y<=x => x=y]    /* antisymmetry of <= */
[ lub   : {pred:{x:t}prop}t]
[ upperb : {pred:{x:t}prop}{y:t} (pred y) => y<=(lub pred)]
[ least : {pred:{x:t}prop}{y:t} ({z:t}(pred z) => z<=y) => (lub pred)<=y]
[ f      : t->t]
[ incr : {x y:t} x<=y => (f x)<=(f y)]
[ po == [u:t] u<=(f u) : {u:t}prop]
[ xo == (lub po) : t]

[lemma1 == [x:t][assum:x<=(f x)]
           (leqtrans x (f x) (f xo) assum (incr x xo (upperb po x assum))) :
           {x:t}x<=(f x) => x<=(f xo)]

[lemma2 == (least po (f xo) ([z:t][assum:(po z)](lemma1 z assum))) :
           xo<=(f xo)]

[lemma3 == (upperb po (f xo) (incr xo (f xo) lemma2)) :
           (f xo)<=xo]
```

```
Category: <CDT>
☑ Check  ☑ Smart  ☐ Analyze      Congratulations !! Proof completed.
[Auto]  search depth [12] 5 ▮▮▮▮▮▮▮▮▯▯ 15. [S-I-G] [Forced] [Strip] [Subst]
[Step] [Undo]                    Scheme ⟳ Horizontal
```

```
[(leqantisym (f xo) xo lemma3 lemma2) : (f xo)=xo ] ⟸
```

Figure 2: *Proving Tarski's Lemma [Hu87]. After automatically proving* lemma1, lemma2 *and* lemma3 *first, the fixed point property for the witness is proven correct (bottom window). Note that the proof of* lemma2 *is not in η-normal form. The search strategy confirms that the proofs given by Huet [Hu87] are indeed the shortest proofs.*

The unification also recognizes outermost η-equality for objects, so that it can use the lambda abstraction rule to verify given application objects where the functor has not been provided with the full number of arguments. This can be regarded as the inverse operation of 'unfolding' Π-abstractions to clauses. The implemented unification procedure will always yield at most one unifier. If complicated higher order unification is required, two options are available: (1) provide appropriate auxiliary definitions to obtain the desired result (cf. *pred1* in the derivation example) (2) Interactively substitute a template of the desired proof object by hand. Checking objects (also those that can not be constructed by the unification) is always possible, because all relevant terms are known then.

The *Constructor* system automatically proves the example from the previous section within seconds. As another example, the system can construct the proof for Tarski's Lemma [Hu87] [4] , a famous example from constructive mathematics, by first proving the lemmas as proposed in [Hu87], and adding those to the context. In fact, on SUN 4 workstations, the system only needs the second of the three lemmas used in [Hu87] to find the complete proof. See also figure 2.

The performance of the system is good. On SUN 4 workstations, the system performs on an average 4000 unifications every second (including possible β and δ-reductions). Currently, no clause compilation takes place. Automatic construction of the proofs shown in the figures runs in seconds.

The *Constructor* system is implemented in Common Lisp. If we disregard the interface, it consists of 1800 lines of code. User licences for the *Constructor* system can be obtained at no cost. The system runs on SUN 3/4 workstations with 8+ Megabytes of memory. A full Sun Common Lisp Licence is required. A version without the window interface is also available and runs on any Common Lisp.

7 Related Systems

The *Nuprl* system ([Co86]) offers an interesting and impressive interactive proof development environment that is based on Martin-Löf's Type Theory [Ma84]. It is a significant improvement over the LCF proof system ([Go79]) that strongly influenced it. There is an inconvenience in the Nuprl system that may have been overcome by the method proposed in this document. The problem referred to is that proof construction in Nuprl is not based on unification based clausal resolution. The inference rules are the correctness rules for the underlying type theory, and implications in a context can not be used directly as derived rules to resolve goals. Defining a new rule requires a detailed knowledge of the system and the programming language ML. As unification is not directly available, derivation of new hypotheses by instantiating others is often demanded, i.e. variables need to be given that could have been calculated. Tactics in Nuprl are written in the meta language ML. Because unification based resolution with hypotheses is not provided, writing tactics is difficult. Automated theorem proving has not yet been accomplished with Nuprl ([Co86], p.13).

One of the most powerful existing proof systems is *Isabelle* [Pa86][Pa89]. Comparison to this system is difficult, because Isabelle is a generic theorem prover, whereas the proof method proposed here is dedicated to only one single proof formalism, viz. CTT. The same remark can be made for a comparision to the work of Miller on theorem provers [Fe88].

---

[4]Actually, Huet uses a different version of the Calculus of Constructions where [*type:kind*] and [*prop:type*], but this is not essential to the example.

8 Discussion

The method presented combines the advantages of resolution inference with the power of type theory.

Because proof construction is not decidable, strategic information has to be provided by users, either in the form of interactive choices, or in the form of algorithms (tactics). Resolution inference allows easy writing of tactics. The method presented may have potential to be used as a logic programming language, that includes all the essential features of e.g. Prolog, but that also provides typing, higher order facilities and the use of local assumptions, thereby creating the possibility to handle queries containing universal quantification or implication (much like λProlog [Na88]). Note that the resulting derivations are in a natural deduction style.

As a meta language, the CTT formalism is suitable to specify logical systems. The method presented makes the object level inference rules of a logic directly available for resolution instead of just the underlying correctness rules of CTT, thus offering the appropriate inference level. The abbreviation mechanism provides the possibility for hiding and the use of derived lemmas.

The requirement that contexts are always grounded in derivations is essential to the method, because it avoids the problem of unification over contexts and prevents the undesired generation of new axioms, while permitting extraction of necessary derived Horn clauses. It has been demonstrated that the consequences of this restriction are directly related to a fundamental problem in higher order theorem proving, and a solution is offered if completeness is desired.

It should be noted that proofs constructed by the method are in β-normal form, aside from definitions. In other words, the proofs constructed are cut-free. The proofs are not guaranteed in η-normal form, unless outermost η-reduction on objects is provided.

Actual implementations of proof systems can efficiently handle many issues. A version of such a proof system, *Constructor*, automatically constructed many non-trivial proofs.

Acknowledgements

The author owes much gratitude to Jan Bergstra, Loe Feijs, Bert Jutting, Ton Kalker, Frank van der Linden and Rob Wieringa for numerous suggestions and corrections. Special thanks are due to René Ahn, for essential contributions to this work, to Marcel van Tien, who implemented most of *Constructor*, and to Henk Barendregt, for many stimulating and clarifying discussions.

References

[Ah85] Ahn, R.M.C. *Some extensions to Prolog based on* AUTOMATH. Internal Philips technical note nr. 173/85, 1985.

[Ba81] Barendregt, H. *The Lambda-Calculus: Its Syntax and Semantics.* North-Holland, 1981.

[Br72] De Bruijn, N.G. *Lambda-Calculus Notation with Nameless Dummies, a Tool for Automatic Formula Manipulation, with Application to the Church-Rosser Theorem.* Indag. Math. 34, 5, pp 381-392, 1972.

[Br73] De Bruijn, N.G. *A survey of the project Automath.* In: *To H.B. Curry: Essays on Combinatory Logic, Lambda Calculus and Formalisms.* (Seldin & Hindley, Eds.), Academic Press, 1980.

[Co86] Constable, R.L. et al. *Implementing Mathematics with the Nuprl Proof Development System.* Prentice Hall, 1986.

[Co85] Coquand, T. *Une Theory des Constructions.* Thèse de troisième cycle, Université de Paris VII, 1985.

[Cq85] Coquand, T. & Huet, G.P. *Constructions: A Higher Order Proof System for Mechanizing Mathematics.* EUROCAL85, Linz, Springer-Verlag LNCS 203, 1985.

[Da80] van Daalen, D.T. *The Language Theory of Automath.* Ph. D. Dissertation, Eindhoven University of Technology, Dept of Mathematics, 1980.

[Fe88] Felty, A. & Miller, D.A. *Specifying Theorem Provers in a Higher-Order Logic Programming Language.* CADE-9, Argonne, pp 61-80, Springer-Verlag LNCS 310, 1988.

[Fo83] Fortune, S. et al. *The Expressiveness of Simple and Second-Order Type Structures.* J. ACM 30, 1 (Jan.), pp 151-185, 1983.

[Go79] Gordon, M.J., Milner, R. & Wadsworth, C.P. *Edingburgh LCF.* Springer-Verlag LNCS 78, 1979.

[Ha87] Harper, R., Honsell, F. & Plotkin, G. *A Framework for defining logics.* Second Annual Symposium on Logic in Computer Science, Ithaca, IEEE, pp. 194-204, 1987.

[Ha89] Harper, R. & Pollack, R. *Type Checking, Universe Polymorphism, and Typical Ambiguity in the Calculus of Constructions.* Tapsoft '89, Barcelona, Springer-Verlag LNCS 352, Volume 2, 1989.

[He88] Helmink, L. & Ahn, R. *Goal Directed Proof Construction in Type Theory.* Internal Philips technical note nr. 229/88, 1988. Also available as document 28.3 of Esprit project 1222: 'Genesis'.

[He89] Helmink, L. & Tien, M. van. *Genesis Constructive Logic Machine: User's Guide.* Available as document 28.5 of Esprit project 1222: 'Genesis'.

[Hu75] Huet, G.P. *A Unification Algorithm for Typed λ-calculus.* Theoret. Comput. Sci. Vol.1, pp. 27-57, 1975.

[Hu87] Huet, G.P. *Induction Principles Formalized in the Calculus of Constructions.* Tapsoft '87, Pisa, Springer-Verlag LNCS 250, Volume 1, 1987.

[Ju76] Jutting, L.S. *A Translation of Landau's "Grundlagen" in AUTOMATH.* Ph.D. Dissertation, Eindhoven University of Technology, Dept of Mathematics, 1976.

[Ju86] Jutting, L.S. *Normalization in Coquand's system.* Internal Philips technical note nr. 156/88, 1988.

[Ma84] Martin-Löf, P. *Intuitionistic Type Theory.* Bibliopolis, Napoli, 1984.

[Na88] Nadathur G. & Miller, D.A. *An overview of λProlog.* In: *Logic Programming: Proceedings of the Fifth International Conference and Symposium.* (Kowalski & Bowen, Eds.), MIT Press, Cambridge, Massachusetts, Volume 1, pp 820-827, August 1988.

[Pa86] Paulson, L.C. *Natural Deduction as Higher-Order Resolution.* J. Logic Programming 3, pp 237-258, 1986.

[Pa89] Paulson, L.C. *The Foundation of a Generic Theorem Prover.* J. Automated Reasoning 5, pp 363-379, 1989.

[Pf89] Pfenning, F. *Elf: a language for logic definition and verified meta-programming.* Fourth Annual Symposium on Logic in Computer Science, IEEE, pp 313-322, 1989.

[Ro65] Robinson, J.A. *A Machine Oriented Logic Based on the Resolution Principle.* J. ACM 12, 1 (Jan.), 23-49, 1965.

A Syntactic Theory of Transparent Parameterization

Stanley Jefferson *
Shinn-Der Lee †
Daniel P. Friedman ‡

Computer Science Department
Indiana University
Bloomington, Indiana 47405

Abstract

We present a calculus for Lamping's programming system of transparent and orthogonal parameterization. The calculus is shown to be consistent, to have a standardization procedure, and to correspond with an operational semantics obtained from the denotational semantics by viewing the semantic equations as state transition rules. Lamping's system is remarkable because it is small, having only four constructions, yet it can easily express a wide variety of parameterization mechanisms including lexical variables, dynamic variables, procedure calls, first-class environments, modules, and method lookup and inheritance mechanisms of object-oriented systems. Due to its orthogonal and transparent parameterization mechanisms, every object, including data and code, in Lamping's programming system can be parameterized, and a parameterized object can be manipulated as if it were a ground object. This blurs the distinction between data and code, allowing one to think of data as code and vice versa.

1 Introduction

Parameterization mechanisms in programming languages provide for the expression of potential dependencies of a program unit on the values of some parameters. Most languages incorporate different parameterization mechanisms for different circumstances. For instance, in a language such as Modula-2, the result of an expression depends on the values of its free variables, the result of a function application depends on the values of the arguments, and the behavior of a module depends on the behaviors of the modules it imports. Lamping [4,5] introduces a programming system, having only four

*Supported by the National Science Foundation under grant CCR 89-01919.
†Supported by the National Science Foundation under grant CCR 87-02117.
‡Supported by the National Science Foundation under grants CCR 87-02117 and CCR 89-01919, and by the Air Force Office of Scientific Research under grant AFOSR 89-0186.

constructions, that can easily express a wide variety of parameterization mechanisms
including lexical variables, dynamic variables, procedure calls, first-class environments,
modules, and objects, classes, method lookup and inheritance in object-oriented systems. Moreover, Lamping's programming system is capable of expressing recursion and
parallel let. It is small and simple, having only one more construction than that of the
λ-calculus, and it is computationally equivalent to the λ-calculus. The versatility of his
system is a consequence of its ability to express sets of bindings and to parameterize
over them, which in turn is a consequence of the transparency and orthogonality of its
parameterization mechanisms. Orthogonality allows any component of a construction
to be replaced by a parameter. Transparency allows the value of a parameter to pass
through a construction, making it accessible to the components of the construction.
Due to its orthogonal and transparent parameterization mechanisms, every object, including data and code, in Lamping's programming system can be parameterized, and a
parameterized object can be manipulated as if it were a ground object. This blurs the
distinction between data and code, allowing one to think of data as code and vice versa.

This paper presents a calculus for Lamping's system. The calculus is shown to be
consistent, to have a standardization procedure, and to correspond with an operational
semantics obtained from the denotational semantics by viewing the semantic equations
as state transition rules. Consistency and correspondence imply that the calculus and
the operational semantics produce the same unique result for every program that terminates with a ground constant; standardization provides a particular order of reduction
for determining that result. With Lamping's denotational definition, reasoning occurs
on the metalevel of domains and continuous functions. With our calculus, reasoning is
performed algebraically on a syntactic level. The calculus, thus, can serve as a symbolic
reasoning system.

The remainder of this paper is organized as follows. Section 2 is an informal overview
of Lamping's programming system, culminating with an object-oriented programming
example. Section 3 develops a calculus for the system. Section 4 gives an example of
reasoning with the calculus. Section 5 proves that the calculus is consistent and that it
has a standardization procedure. Section 6 reproduces Lamping's denotational semantics and gives the correspondence between the calculus and an operational semantics
obtained from the denotational semantics. Section 7 is the conclusion.

2   Overview

We now present the syntax of Lamping's system, followed by an informal description
of the semantics and several examples illustrating the capabilities of the system. The
reader familiar with denotational semantics may also want to refer to Lamping's denotational definition, reproduced in Figure 6.

The pure system has a core syntax consisting of four categories of expressions: variables, let expressions, supply expressions, and data expressions. Ground constants (*e.g.*,
true, false, $0, 1, \ldots$) and primitive operators (*e.g.*, $\land, \lor, \neg, +, -, *, /, \ldots$, if then else, $\ldots$)
may be added to the pure system. We consider a language Π whose syntax is displayed
in Figure 1. It is essentially the same as that given by Lamping except that we have
added a special constant ϵ which denotes an error value. The results of this paper could

Syntactic categories :

$$c \in \mathcal{C} = \{\epsilon, 0, 1, 2, \ldots\} \quad \text{(constants)}$$
$$x \in \mathcal{V} \quad \text{(variables)}$$
$$M, N \in \Pi \quad \text{(expressions)}$$

Abstract syntax :

$$
\begin{aligned}
M ::=\ & x \\
& |\ \text{let } x = M \text{ in } N \\
& |\ \text{supply } x = M \text{ to } N \\
& |\ \text{data } x : M \\
& |\ c \\
& |\ M + N
\end{aligned}
$$

Figure 1: Syntax of the language Π

be extended to a language with additional ground constants and primitive operators, but doing so would increase the length of the proofs and obscure the main ideas.

We adopt the following conventions: a, b, c are metavariables for $\mathcal{C}$; w, x, y are meta-variables for $\mathcal{V}$; uppercase $A, \ldots, Z$ denote Π-expressions; $\equiv$ denotes syntactic equivalence; and parentheses are used to resolve ambiguity.

From here on, we shall distinguish between the use of the terms *variable* and *parameter*: *variable* refers to syntax, while *parameter* refers to semantics. The system has two classes of parameters: lexically scoped *lexical parameters* and dynamically scoped *data parameters*. Lexical parameters are the same as those found in conventional lexically scoped languages. Data parameters are similar to conventional function parameters in that they provide an abstraction mechanism for expressions. Unlike function parameterization, data parameterization is a transparent abstraction mechanism. Depending on the context, an occurrence of a variable can denote either a lexical parameter or a data parameter.

The expression let $x = M$ in N specifies value M for lexical parameter x in expression N. The following expression, which evaluates $(x + y)$ at $x = 3$ and $y = 2$, yielding 5, demonstrates lexical parameterization:

$$
\begin{aligned}
&\text{let } x = 1 \text{ in} \\
&\text{let } y = 2 * x \text{ in} \\
&\text{let } x = 3 \text{ in} \\
&\quad (x + y)
\end{aligned}
$$

Data parameterization is notated by data $x : M$. It indicates a potential dependency of the expression M on the parameter x; any free occurrence of x in M is a place holder for a value to be supplied. Moreover, it declares x to be a data parameter. For example, data $x : (2 * x)$ is an expression which when supplied a value n for the data parameter x results in the value $2n$. The notation for supplying value M for data parameter x to expression N is supply $x = M$ to N. A supply expression is the only way to associate a value with a data parameter. In the next example, the expression on the left associates the data parameter x with 3 and evaluates to 6. It is equivalent to the expression on the right.

supply x = 3 to   let f = data x : (2 * x) in
   data x : (2 * x)   supply x = 3 to f

The following two expressions show the different handling of overriding by the two mechanisms:

let x = 1 in   supply x = 1 to
  let y = 2 * x in   let y = data x : (2 * x) in
    let x = 3 in   supply x = 3 to
       y   y

Although the third let overrides the first one in the expression on the left, the lexical parameter x in expression 2 * x is bound to 1. Therefore, the result is 2. The expression on the right has a result of 6, because the second supply overrides the first one and the value supplied for data parameter x is determined at the time when expression data x : (2 * x) is used.

The expression data x : (2 * x) in the previous example evaluates to a parameterized object. Transparency necessitates the explicit naming of data parameters when a parameterized object is "called."

Transparency has some interesting properties. First, data parameters can be supplied in any order. The following two expressions are equivalent:

supply x = 3 to   supply y = 4 to
  supply y = 4 to   supply x = 3 to
    data y : data x : (3 * x + 4 * y)   data y : data x : (3 * x + 4 * y)

Second, one supply matches multiple data:

let f = data x : (2 * x) in
  let g = data x : (x * x) in
    supply x = 3 to
      (f + g)

In this example, (f + g) is equivalent to (data x : (2 * x)) + (data x : (x * x)). The supply supplies 3 for the x's in (f + g). Consequently, the result is 15.

Since parameterization is transparent to all constructions, the supply distributes over the primitive operator + in the above example. That is, the following two expressions are equivalent:

supply x = 3 to   (supply x = 3 to data x : (2 * x))
  ((data x : (2 * x)) + (data x : (x * x)))   + (supply x = 3 to data x : (x * x))

It is, therefore, possible to write (f + g). In the λ-calculus, (f + g) would have to be expressed as $(\lambda x.(f\ x) + (g\ x))$, since parameterization is not transparent to the addition operator +.

$$\text{data } x_1, \ldots, x_n : M \equiv \text{data } x_1 : \ldots : \text{data } x_n : M$$

$$\text{supply } x_1 = M_1, \ldots, x_n = M_n \text{ to } N$$
$$\equiv \text{supply } x_1 = M_1 \text{ to } \ldots \text{ supply } x_n = M_n \text{ to } N$$

Figure 2: **Multiple data and supply**

Consider the expression

```
B ≡ data body :
      supply x  =  3 to
        supply y  =  4 to
          supply dist  =  √(data x : x)² + (data y : y)² to
            supply closer  =  (data dist : dist) <
                              (data point : supply body  =  (data dist : dist) to point) to
          body
```

which supplies values for the data parameters x, y, dist, and closer to the value denoted by body. This is essentially a parameterized set of bindings which can be made to affect the value supplied for body. For instance,

$$\text{supply body } = \text{data dist : dist to } B$$

retrieves the value $\sqrt{(\text{data x : x})^2 + (\text{data y : y})^2}$ bound to dist in the set of bindings B. To completely evaluate $\sqrt{(\text{data x : x})^2 + (\text{data y : y})^2}$, the values bound to x and y are retrieved from the set of bindings B. The result is, therefore, $\sqrt{3^2 + 4^2} = 5$.

We define some syntactic extensions, given by Lamping, for programming with sets of bindings. Figure 2 defines two syntactic extensions for versions of multiple data and supply. Figure 3 defines syntactic extensions for manipulating sets of bindings. The transmit operation makes the set of bindings M affect the expression N by supplying N as a value for the data parameter body to M. The o operation combines two sets of bindings M and N by making M affect the result of making N affect body. The key properties are

$$\text{transmit } \{x_1 = M_1, \ldots, x_n = M_n\} \text{ to } N$$
$$= \text{supply } x_1 = M_1, \ldots, x_n = M_n \text{ to } N$$

and

$$\{x_1 = M_1, \ldots, x_n = M_n\} \circ \{y_1 = N_1, \ldots, y_m = N_m\}$$
$$= \{x_1 = M_1, \ldots, x_n = M_n, y_1 = N_1, \ldots, y_m = N_m\}$$

provided that the data parameter body is reserved only for the definitions of sets of bindings.

To illustrate the use of the definitions, we rewrite the expression B from above:

```
B ≡ { x  =  3,
      y  =  4,
      dist  =  √(data x : x)² + (data y : y)²,
      closer  =  (data dist : dist) < (data point : transmit point to (data dist : dist)) }
```

$$\{x_1 = M_1, \ldots, x_n = M_n\}$$
$$\equiv \text{data body} : \text{supply } x_1 = M_1, \ldots, x_n = M_n \text{ to body}$$

$$\text{transmit } M \text{ to } N \equiv \text{supply body} = N \text{ to } M$$

$$M \circ N \equiv \text{data body} : \text{transmit } M \text{ to transmit } N \text{ to body}$$

Figure 3: Binding definitions

$$\text{class}(x_1, \ldots, x_n) \text{ is } M \equiv \text{data } x_1, \ldots, x_n : M$$

$$\text{subclass}(x_1, \ldots, x_n) \text{ of } M \text{ is } N \equiv M \circ \text{class}(x_1, \ldots, x_n) \text{ is } N$$

$$\text{with } x_1 = M_1, \ldots, x_n = M_n \text{ instantiate } N$$
$$\equiv \text{supply } x_1 = M_1, \ldots x_n, = M_n \text{ to } N$$

$$M.x \equiv \text{transmit } M \text{ to data } x : x \qquad \text{when } M \not\equiv \text{self}$$

$$\text{self}.x \equiv \text{data } x : x$$

Figure 4: Object-oriented programming definitions

The set of bindings B can be considered as an instance of a cartesian point class: x and y are coordinates of the point, dist is the distance of the point from the origin, and closer compares the distances of this point and another given point point.

In the remainder of this section we give an example illustrating object-oriented programming in Π. Figure 4 gives definitions that will be used in the object-oriented programming example. An instance is represented as a set of bindings. A class is a parameterized set of bindings. A subclass of a class is formed by combining the set of new bindings representing the subclass with the set of bindings representing the class. Supplying values for the parameters of a class yields an instance of that class. The expression $M.x$ denotes the value bound to x in instance M, and corresponds to sending the message x to M. In an instance, the keyword self refers to the instance itself.

Using the definitions of Figure 4, a class cpclass of cartesian points can be defined as:

```
cpclass ≡ class(a, b) is
            { x = a,
              y = b,
              dist = √((self.x)² + (self.y)²),
              closer = self.dist < (data point : point.dist) }
```

An instance, cp, of a cartesian point at coordinates (3, 4) can be defined by

$$cp \equiv \text{with a } = 3, \text{ b } = 4 \text{ instantiate cpclass}$$

Consider a subclass mpclass of cpclass that inherits all bindings of cpclass except that the distance is redefined as the Manhattan distance from the origin:

$$\text{dist } = \text{ self.x } + \text{ self.y}$$

As a result, the self.dist in the definition of closer should use the newly defined dist. The subclass mpclass can be defined as

$$\text{mpclass} \equiv \text{subclass () of cpclass is } \{\text{dist } = \text{ self.x } + \text{ self.y}\}$$

Since the new dist overrides the old one and closer uses the latest binding of dist, we get the desired behavior.

In summary, the expression

```
let cpclass = class(a, b) is
              { x = a,
                y = b,
                dist = √((self.x)² + (self.y)²),
                closer = self.dist < (data point : point.dist) } in
let mpclass = subclass () of cpclass is {dist = self.x + self.y} in
    let cp = with a = 3, b = 4 instantiate cpclass in
      let mp = with a = 3, b = 4 instantiate mpclass in
        supply point = mp to
        cp.closer
```

has a value of true since the distance of a cartesian point at coordinates (3, 4) is 5 and the distance of a Manhattan point at coordinates (3, 4) is 7. In section 4 we prove, using the calculus defined in section 3, that a Manhattan point at coordinates (3, 4) evaluates to 7 when sent the message dist.

3 A Calculus

In this section we give a calculus for the language Π. First, we define the notions of free lexical variables, free data variables, lexically closed expressions, programs, and substitution.

The notion of the set of free lexical variables of an expression M is an extension of the same notion in the λ-calculus. The set of *free lexical variables* of an expression M, denoted by $FLV(M)$, is defined inductively:

$$FLV(x) = \{x\},$$
$$FLV(\text{let } x = P \text{ in } Q) = (FLV(Q) - \{x\}) \cup FLV(P),$$
$$FLV(\text{supply } x = P \text{ to } Q) = FLV(P) \cup FLV(Q),$$
$$FLV(\text{data } x : P) = FLV(P) - \{x\},$$
$$FLV(c) = \emptyset,$$
$$FLV(P + Q) = FLV(P) \cup FLV(Q).$$

Similarly, the set of *free data variables* of an expression M, denoted by $FDV(M)$, is defined inductively:

$$FDV(x) = \emptyset,$$
$$FDV(\text{let } x = P \text{ in } Q) = FDV(P) \cup FDV(Q),$$
$$FDV(\text{supply } x = P \text{ to } Q) = (FDV(P) \cup FDV(Q)) - \{x\},$$
$$FDV(\text{data } x : P) = FDV(P) \cup \{x\},$$
$$FDV(c) = \emptyset,$$
$$FDV(P + Q) = FDV(P) \cup FDV(Q).$$

A *program* is an expression that does not have free lexical variables or free data variables. A lexically closed expression is an expression that does not have free lexical variables.

The *substitution* of lexically closed expression M for variable x in expression N, denoted by $N[x := M]$, is defined inductively according to the structure of N:

$$x[x := M] \equiv M,$$
$$y[x := M] \equiv y \quad \text{if } x \not\equiv y,$$
$$(\text{let } x = P \text{ in } Q)[x := M] \equiv \text{let } x = (P[x := M]) \text{ in } Q,$$
$$(\text{let } y = P \text{ in } Q)[x := M] \equiv \text{let } y = (P[x := M]) \text{ in } Q[x := M] \quad \text{if } x \not\equiv y,$$
$$(\text{supply } w = P \text{ to } Q)[x := M] \equiv \text{supply } w = (P[x := M]) \text{ to } Q[x := M],$$
$$(\text{data } x : P)[x := M] \equiv \text{data } x : P,$$
$$(\text{data } y : P)[x := M] \equiv \text{data } y : (P[x := M]) \quad \text{if } x \not\equiv y,$$
$$c[x := M] \equiv c,$$
$$(P + Q)[x := M] \equiv (P[x := M]) + (Q[x := M]).$$

Note that any free occurrence of the variable x in the body P of the expression data $x : P$ is a free data variable, and not a free lexical variable. Consequently, $(\text{data } x : P)[x := M] \equiv (\text{data } x : P)$.

The following definition gives the basic notion of reduction for our calculus:

Definition 3.1 (Basic π-Reduction) The *basic π-reduction* is

$$\pi = \pi_1 \cup \pi_2 \cup \pi_3 \cup \pi_4 \cup \pi_5 \cup \pi_6$$

where, with $FLV(M) = \emptyset$, (read $A \to B$ as a relation between redex A and its contractum B)

$\pi_1 : \qquad\qquad \text{let } x = M \text{ in } P \to P[x := M]$

$\pi_2 : \text{supply } x = M \text{ to data } x : P \to \text{supply } x = M \text{ to } P[x := M]$

$\pi_3 : \text{supply } y = M \text{ to data } x : P \to \text{data } x : \text{supply } y = M \text{ to } P \quad \text{if } x \not\equiv y$

$\pi_4 : \qquad\qquad \text{supply } x = M \text{ to } c \to c$

$\pi_5 : \quad \text{supply } x = M \text{ to } (P + Q) \to (\text{supply } x = M \text{ to } P) + (\text{supply } x = M \text{ to } Q)$

$\pi_6 : \qquad\qquad\qquad a + b \to c \quad \text{if } [a] + [b] = [c].$

Consider the expression supply $x = M$ to data $x : P$ in π_2. The data parameter x in P is supplied the lexically closed expression M. This can be done by substituting free x's in P by M. Since data parameters are dynamically scoped, the data parameter x might be needed in $P[x := M]$, so we must retain the supply in the contractum.

Consider the expression supply $y = M$ to data $x : P$ in π_3. The expression data $x : P$ is expecting a value for x. The supply, on the other hand, supplies a value for y. Thus, π_2 is not applicable. But transparent data parameterization requires that expression supply $y = M$ to data $x : P$ be equivalent to expression data $x :$ supply $y = M$ to P. Since M has no free lexical variables, there is no danger of turning any free lexical variable x in M into a free data variable. This basic π-reduction serves the purpose of moving the data outward in order to find a match with the closest supply that supplies a value for the data parameter x.

Reduction π_4 says that a constant does not depend on data parameters. Transparency requires that data parameters distribute over the primitive operator $+$; this is formalized in reduction π_5. The denotation of a constant symbol c is given by $[c]$. Reduction π_6 simulates the behavior of the primitive operator $+$ extended to be strict with respect to error.

Based on the basic π-reduction, we define one-step π-reduction, π-reduction, and π-equality in the usual way [1]:

(i) *One-step π-reduction*, denoted by $\to_\pi$, is the compatible closure of π:

$M \to N \Rightarrow M \to_\pi N,$

$M \to_\pi N \Rightarrow \text{let } x = M \text{ in } P \to_\pi \text{let } x = N \text{ in } P,$

$P \to_\pi Q \Rightarrow \text{let } x = M \text{ in } P \to_\pi \text{let } x = M \text{ in } Q,$

$M \to_\pi N \Rightarrow \text{supply } x = M \text{ to } P \to_\pi \text{supply } x = N \text{ to } P,$

$P \to_\pi Q \Rightarrow \text{supply } x = M \text{ to } P \to_\pi \text{supply } x = M \text{ to } Q,$

$M \to_\pi N \Rightarrow \text{data } x : M \to_\pi \text{data } x : N,$

$M \to_\pi N \Rightarrow M + P \to_\pi N + P,$

$P \to_\pi Q \Rightarrow M + P \to_\pi M + Q.$

(ii) *π-reduction*, denoted by $\twoheadrightarrow_\pi$, is the reflexive and transitive closure of $\to_\pi$.

$M \to_\pi N \Rightarrow M \twoheadrightarrow_\pi N,$

$M \twoheadrightarrow_\pi M,$

$M \twoheadrightarrow_\pi N, N \twoheadrightarrow_\pi P \Rightarrow M \twoheadrightarrow_\pi P.$

(iii) *π-equality (π-convertibility, π-calculus)*, denoted by $=_\pi$, is the least equivalence relation generated by $\twoheadrightarrow_\pi$.

$M \twoheadrightarrow_\pi N \Rightarrow M =_\pi N,$

$M =_\pi M,$

$M =_\pi N \Rightarrow N =_\pi M,$

$M =_\pi N, N =_\pi P \Rightarrow M =_\pi P.$

4 Reasoning with the Calculus

Using the calculus, we show that expression mp.dist, where mp is the Manhattan point

$$
\begin{aligned}
\{ \, &x \, = \, 3, \\
&y \, = \, 4, \\
&dist \, = \, self.x + self.y, \\
&closer \, = \, self.dist < (data\ point : point.dist)\},
\end{aligned}
$$

is equivalent to the constant expression 7:

mp.dist ≡ transmit mp to (data dist : dist)   *by definition*
    ≡ supply body = (data dist : dist) to
      data body :
        supply x = 3, y = 4 to
          supply dist = (data x : x) + (data y : y) to
            supply closer = (data dist : dist) < (data point : point.dist) to
            body   *by definition*
  →$_\pi$ supply body = (data dist : dist) to
      supply x = 3, y = 4 to
        supply dist = (data x : x) + (data y : y) to
          supply closer = (data dist : dist) < (data point : point.dist) to
          data dist : dist   *by π_2*
  →→$_\pi$ supply body = (data dist : dist) to
      supply x = 3, y = 4 to
        supply dist = (data x : x) + (data y : y) to
          supply closer = (data dist : dist) < (data point : point.dist) to
          (data x : x) + (data y: y)   *by π_3 and then π_2*

By a series of π_5 reductions, the above expression can be reduced to $M + N$ where subexpression M corresponds to (data x : x) and subexpression N corresponds to (data y : y). Subexpression M can be reduced to the constant expression 3:

M ≡ supply body = (data dist : dist) to
    supply x = 3, y = 4 to
      supply dist = (data x : x) + (data y : y) to
        supply closer = (data dist : dist) < (data point : point.dist) to
        (data x : x)
  →$_\pi$ supply body = (data dist : dist) to
    supply x = 3, y = 4 to
      supply dist = (data x : x) + (data y : y) to
        supply closer = (data dist : dist) < (data point : point.dist) to
        3   *by repeated π_3 and then π_2*

Then, by a series of five π_4 reductions, the above expression reduces to the constant expression 3.

Similarly, subexpression N reduces to the constant expression 4. Therefore, $M + N$ reduces to $3 + 4$, which reduces to 7 by π_6.

$(P1)\ M \underset{1}{\twoheadrightarrow} M$

$(P2)\ M \underset{1}{\twoheadrightarrow} M_1, N \underset{1}{\twoheadrightarrow} N_1, FLV(M) = \emptyset \Rightarrow \mathsf{let}\ x = M\ \mathsf{in}\ N \underset{1}{\twoheadrightarrow} \mathsf{let}\ x = M_1\ \mathsf{in}\ N_1$

$(P3)\ M \underset{1}{\twoheadrightarrow} M_1, N \underset{1}{\twoheadrightarrow} N_1, FLV(M) = \emptyset \Rightarrow \mathsf{supply}\ x = M\ \mathsf{to}\ N \underset{1}{\twoheadrightarrow} \mathsf{supply}\ x = M_1\ \mathsf{to}\ N_1$

$(P4)\ M \underset{1}{\twoheadrightarrow} M_1 \Rightarrow \mathsf{data}\ x : M \underset{1}{\twoheadrightarrow} \mathsf{data}\ x : M_1$

$(P5)\ M \underset{1}{\twoheadrightarrow} M_1, N \underset{1}{\twoheadrightarrow} N_1 \Rightarrow M + N \underset{1}{\twoheadrightarrow} M_1 + N_1$

$(P6)\ M \underset{1}{\twoheadrightarrow} M_1, N \underset{1}{\twoheadrightarrow} N_1, FLV(M) = \emptyset \Rightarrow \mathsf{let}\ x = M\ \mathsf{in}\ N \underset{1}{\twoheadrightarrow} N_1[x := M_1]$

$(P7)\ M \underset{1}{\twoheadrightarrow} M_1, N \underset{1}{\twoheadrightarrow} N_1, FLV(M) = \emptyset$
$\qquad \Rightarrow \mathsf{supply}\ x = M\ \mathsf{to}\ (\mathsf{data}\ x : N) \underset{1}{\twoheadrightarrow} \mathsf{supply}\ x = M_1\ \mathsf{to}\ N_1[x := M_1]$

$(P8)\ M \underset{1}{\twoheadrightarrow} M_1, N \underset{1}{\twoheadrightarrow} N_1, FLV(M) = \emptyset, y \not\equiv x$
$\qquad \Rightarrow \mathsf{supply}\ y = M\ \mathsf{to}\ (\mathsf{data}\ x : N) \underset{1}{\twoheadrightarrow} \mathsf{data}\ x : (\mathsf{supply}\ y = M_1\ \mathsf{to}\ N_1)$

$(P9)\ N \underset{1}{\twoheadrightarrow} c, FLV(M) = \emptyset \Rightarrow \mathsf{supply}\ x = M\ \mathsf{to}\ N \underset{1}{\twoheadrightarrow} c$

$(P10)\ M \underset{1}{\twoheadrightarrow} M_1, N \underset{1}{\twoheadrightarrow} N_1 + N_2, FLV(M) = \emptyset$
$\qquad \Rightarrow \mathsf{supply}\ x = M\ \mathsf{to}\ N \underset{1}{\twoheadrightarrow} (\mathsf{supply}\ x = M_1\ \mathsf{to}\ N_1) + (\mathsf{supply}\ x = M_1\ \mathsf{to}\ N_2)$

$(P11)\ M \underset{1}{\twoheadrightarrow} a, N \underset{1}{\twoheadrightarrow} b, [a] + [b] = [c] \Rightarrow M + N \underset{1}{\twoheadrightarrow} c$

Figure 5: **Parallel reductions**

5 Consistency and Standardization

Given a calculus, two immediate concerns are its consistency and its standardization procedure. Consistency is implied by a Church-Rosser theorem which shows the confluence of two reduction paths that proceed in two different directions from the same expression. It says that if a program has a result then the result is unique no matter what order of reduction we choose. The derivation in the previous section is meaningful only if the calculus is Church-Rosser. Standardization is a particular order of reduction that provides a semi-effective procedure for finding the result of a program. It says that if a program has a result then the result can be obtained by that particular order of reduction.

For the proof of the Church-Rosser theorem, we follow Tait-Martin-Löf's strategy for the corresponding work on the λ-calculus [1]. We define a parallel reduction which is a superset of the one-step π-reduction and a subset of the π-reduction. Thus, its reflexive and transitive closure is the π-reduction. Then, we show that this parallel reduction satisfies the diamond property. From this, we infer that its reflexive and transitive closure also satisfies the diamond property. Since the reflexive and transitive closure of the parallel reduction is the π-reduction, we have the π-reduction satisfying the diamond property also. Hence, the calculus is Church-Rosser.

The inductive definition of the parallel reduction from an expression A to an expression B, denoted by $A \underset{1}{\twoheadrightarrow} B$, is given in Figure 5. Parallel reductions can be classified into three categories. The first category parallel reduces an expression to itself. This is (P1). The second category parallel reduces an expression A to an expression B with B being derived from A by parallel reducing every top-level subexpression of A. Consequently, the top-level structure of B is the same as that of A. There are six classes of expressions in the language, but constants and variables can only reduce to themselves, so we have four classes left. They are dealt with in (P2)–(P5). The third category parallel reduces an expression A to an expression C with C being derived from A by parallel reducing A to an intermediate expression B, as in the second category, then applying a basic π-reduction to B to get C. Since there are six basic π-reductions, this category has six cases: (P6)–(P11).

Theorem 5.1 (Church-Rosser) π-reduction satisfies the diamond property. That is, if $M \twoheadrightarrow_\pi M_1$ and $M \twoheadrightarrow_\pi M_2$ then there is an M_3 such that $M_1 \twoheadrightarrow_\pi M_3$ and $M_2 \twoheadrightarrow_\pi M_3$.

Outline of proof : By an induction on the length of proof of $M \twoheadrightarrow_1 M_1$, we can show that $\twoheadrightarrow_1$ satisfies the diamond property. From that, by a simple diagram chase, we can show that $\twoheadrightarrow_1^*$ also satisfies the diamond property. Then, $\rightarrow_\pi \subset \twoheadrightarrow_1$ implies $\twoheadrightarrow_\pi = \rightarrow_\pi^* \subset \twoheadrightarrow_1^*$. Similarly, $\twoheadrightarrow_1 \subset \twoheadrightarrow_\pi$ implies $\twoheadrightarrow_1^* \subset \twoheadrightarrow_\pi^* = \twoheadrightarrow_\pi$. Therefore, $\twoheadrightarrow_1^* = \twoheadrightarrow_\pi$. Hence $\twoheadrightarrow_\pi$ satisfies the diamond property. $\square$

For the proof of the standardization theorem, we follow the strategies in [2,3,6]. We begin by defining the notion of outermost reduction. Informally, an outermost reduction always reduces an outermost redex.

Definition 5.2 (Evaluation Contexts) (i) An *evaluation context* $C[\,]$ is defined inductively:

- $[\,]$ is an evaluation context,

- if $FLV(M) = \emptyset$ and $C[\,]$ is an evaluation context then supply $x = M$ to $C[\,]$ is an evaluation context,

- if $C[\,]$ is an evaluation context then $C[\,] + M$ and $M + C[\,]$ are evaluation contexts.

(ii) If $C[\,]$ is an evaluation context and M is an expression then $C[M]$ denotes the result of replacing the $[\,]$ of $C[\,]$ by M.

Definition 5.3 (Outermost Reduction) *Outermost reduction*, denoted by $\mapsto_\pi$, is the least relation between Π-expressions such that whenever $M \mapsto_\pi N$, there is an evaluation context $C[\,]$ and a basic π-reduction $P \rightarrow Q$ with $M \equiv C[P]$ and $C[Q] \equiv N$.

Next, we allow a redex other than an outermost one to be reduced. But once a redex within an outermost redex is reduced, we can never go back to reduce the outermost redex. A sequence of expressions derived using this strategy is called a standard reduction sequence. With this, we can show that if $M \twoheadrightarrow_\pi N$ then there is a standard reduction sequence $P_1, \ldots, P_p$ such that $M = P_1$ and $P_p = N$.

Definition 5.4 (Standard Reduction Sequences) *Standard reduction sequences* (srs's) are defined inductively: if $M_1, \ldots, M_m$ and $N_1, \ldots, N_n$ are srs's then
- (S1) x is a srs,
- (S2) (let $x = M_1$ in N_1), ..., (let $x = M_1$ in N_n), ..., (let $x = M_m$ in N_n) is a srs,
- (S3) (supply $x = M_1$ to N_1), ..., (supply $x = M_1$ to N_n), ..., (supply $x = M_m$ to N_n) is a srs,
- (S4) (data $x : M_1$), ..., (data $x : M_m$) is a srs,

(S5) c is a srs,

(S6) $(M_1 + N_1), \ldots, (M_m + N_1), \ldots, (M_m + N_n)$ is a srs,

(S7) if $M_0 \mapsto_\pi M_1$ then $M_0, \ldots, M_m$ is a srs.

Theorem 5.5 (Standardization) $M \twoheadrightarrow_\pi N$ iff there is a srs $P_1, \ldots, P_p$ with $M \equiv P_1$ and $P_p \equiv N$.

Outline of proof : ($\Leftarrow$) Clearly if there is a srs $P_1, \ldots, P_p$ such that $M \equiv P_1$ and $P_p \equiv N$ then $M \twoheadrightarrow_\pi N$ is provable in the calculus.

($\Rightarrow$) If $A_0 \xrightarrow{}_1 A_1$ and $A_1, \ldots, A_n$ is a srs then, by a lexicographic induction on n, on the number of one-step π-reduction used in the proof of $A_0 \xrightarrow{}_1 A_1$, and on the structure of A_0, we can show that there is a srs $B_0, \ldots, B_m$ with $A_0 \equiv B_0$ and $B_m \equiv A_n$.

$M \twoheadrightarrow_\pi N$ implies there are expressions $M_1, \ldots, M_m$ such that $M \equiv M_1 \xrightarrow{} \cdots \xrightarrow{} M_m \equiv N$. From $M_{m-1} \xrightarrow{} M_m$ and M_m being a srs (any expression is a srs), we can find a srs $P_1, \ldots, P_p$ such that $M_{m-1} \equiv P_1$ and $P_p \equiv M_m$. From $M_{m-2} \xrightarrow{}_1 P_1$ and $P_1, \ldots, P_p$ being a srs, we can find a srs $Q_1, \ldots, Q_q$ such that $M_{m-2} \equiv Q_1$ and $Q_q \equiv P_p \equiv M_m$. Repeat this procedure from M_m back up to M_1 and we are done. □

If M is a program and $M \twoheadrightarrow_\pi c$ then the srs is a sequence of outermost reductions:

Corollary 5.6 Let M be a program. Then $M \twoheadrightarrow_\pi c$ iff $M \mapsto_\pi^* c$.

6   Operational Semantics and Correspondence

In order to relate the π-calculus to Lamping's denotational semantics, we prove that the calculus corresponds to an operational semantics that was informally derived from the denotational semantics. The correspondence states that the calculus and the operational semantics produce the same result for every program that terminates with a ground constant. This notion of correspondence is the same as in [2,3,6].

Lamping's denotational semantics is reproduced in Figure 6. The operational semantics, defined in Figure 7, is a simple state transition system. It is informally derived from the denotational semantics by viewing the equations of the denotational definition as state transition rules. A state is either a basic state or a compound state. A compound state is a pair of states σ_1 and σ_2 written as $(\sigma_1 + \sigma_2)$, and serves as a mechanism for evaluating addition expressions. A concrete environment represents an environment as an association list. The arid concrete environment, represented by Ω, binds every variable to the concrete parameterized object $<\epsilon, \Omega>$. A concrete parameterized object corresponds to a lexically closed expression.

Theorem 6.1 (Correspondence) Let M be a program. Then

$$\ll M, \Omega, \Omega \gg \vdash^* \ll c, \Omega, \Omega \gg \quad \text{iff} \quad M \mapsto_\pi^* c.$$

Outline of proof : ($\Rightarrow$) We show that each transition rule can be simulated by a sequence of standard reductions. With this and the standardization theorem, it is straightforward to show that the operational semantics can be simulated by the calculus.

($\Leftarrow$) First, by induction on the number of transition steps, we can show that for any state σ, if $\sigma \vdash^* \ll c, \Omega, \Omega \gg$ and $\sigma \vdash^* \sigma'$, then $\sigma' \vdash^* \ll c, \Omega, \Omega \gg$. Next, let $M_0, \ldots, M_m$ be

Semantic domains:

$$
\begin{aligned}
c &\in \mathcal{C} && \text{(constants)} \\
x &\in \mathcal{V} && \text{(variables)} \\
\rho, \delta &\in \mathcal{U} = \mathcal{V} \to \mathcal{O} && \text{(environments)} \\
\mathcal{O} &= \mathcal{U} \to \mathcal{C} && \text{(parameterized objects)}
\end{aligned}
$$

Valuation function: $\mathcal{M} : \Pi \to \mathcal{U} \to \mathcal{U} \to \mathcal{C}$:

$$
\begin{aligned}
\mathcal{M}\,[\![x]\!]\,\rho\,\delta &= \rho(x)\,\delta \\
\mathcal{M}\,[\![\text{let } x = M \text{ in } N]\!]\,\rho\,\delta &= \mathcal{M}\,[\![N]\!]\,(\rho[(\mathcal{M}\,[\![M]\!]\,\rho)/x])\,\delta \\
\mathcal{M}\,[\![\text{supply } x = M \text{ to } N]\!]\,\rho\,\delta &= \mathcal{M}\,[\![N]\!]\,\rho\,(\delta[(\mathcal{M}\,[\![M]\!]\,\rho)/x]) \\
\mathcal{M}\,[\![\text{data } x : M]\!]\,\rho\,\delta &= \mathcal{M}\,[\![M]\!]\,(\rho[\delta(x)/x])\,\delta \\
\mathcal{M}\,[\![c]\!]\,\rho\,\delta &= [\![c]\!] \\
\mathcal{M}\,[\![M + N]\!]\,\rho\,\delta &= (\mathcal{M}\,[\![M]\!]\,\rho\,\delta) + (\mathcal{M}\,[\![N]\!]\,\rho\,\delta)
\end{aligned}
$$

Figure 6: **Denotational Semantics of** Π

Data structures:

$$
\begin{aligned}
\omega &\in \mathcal{O} = \Pi \times \mathcal{U} && \text{(concrete parameterized objects)} \\
\rho, \delta &\in \mathcal{U} = \{\Omega\} + (\mathcal{U} \times \mathcal{V} \times \mathcal{O}) && \text{(concrete environments)} \\
\beta &\in \mathcal{B} = \Pi \times \mathcal{U} \times \mathcal{U} && \text{(basic states)} \\
\sigma &\in \mathcal{S} = \mathcal{B} + (\mathcal{S} \times \{+\} \times \mathcal{S}) && \text{(states)}
\end{aligned}
$$

Environment extension: $\bullet[\bullet \leftarrow \bullet] : \mathcal{U} \times \mathcal{V} \times \mathcal{O} \to \mathcal{U}$:

$$
\rho[x \leftarrow \omega] = (\rho, x, \omega).
$$

Environment lookup: $\mathsf{lookup}(\bullet, \bullet) : \mathcal{U} \times \mathcal{V} \to \mathcal{O}$:

$$
\begin{aligned}
\mathsf{lookup}(\Omega, x) &= {<}\epsilon, \Omega{>}, \\
\mathsf{lookup}(\rho[x \leftarrow \omega], x) &= \omega, \\
\mathsf{lookup}(\rho[y \leftarrow \omega], x) &= \mathsf{lookup}(\rho, x) \quad \text{if } x \not\equiv y,
\end{aligned}
$$

Transition rules: $\bullet \vdash \bullet : \mathcal{S} \to \mathcal{S}$:

$$
\begin{aligned}
\ll x, \rho, \delta \gg &\vdash \ll M, \rho', \delta \gg && \text{if } \mathsf{lookup}(\rho, x) = {<}M, \rho'{>} \\
\ll \text{let } x = M \text{ in } N, \rho, \delta \gg &\vdash \ll N, \rho[x \leftarrow {<}M, \rho{>}], \delta \gg \\
\ll \text{supply } x = M \text{ to } N, \rho, \delta \gg &\vdash \ll N, \rho, \delta[x \leftarrow {<}M, \rho{>}] \gg \\
\ll \text{data } x : M, \rho, \delta \gg &\vdash \ll M, \rho[x \leftarrow \mathsf{lookup}(\delta, x)], \delta \gg \\
\ll c, \rho, \delta \gg &\vdash \ll c, \Omega, \Omega \gg && \text{if } \rho \neq \Omega \ \text{ or } \ \delta \neq \Omega \\
\ll M + N, \rho, \delta \gg &\vdash (\ll M, \rho, \delta \gg + \ll N, \rho, \delta \gg) \\
(\ll a, \Omega, \Omega \gg + \ll b, \Omega, \Omega \gg) &\vdash \ll c, \Omega, \Omega \gg && \text{if } [\![a]\!] + [\![b]\!] = [\![c]\!] \\
\sigma_1 \vdash \sigma_2 &\Rightarrow (\sigma_1 + \sigma) \vdash (\sigma_2 + \sigma) \\
\sigma_1 \vdash \sigma_2 &\Rightarrow (\sigma + \sigma_1) \vdash (\sigma + \sigma_2)
\end{aligned}
$$

Convention: $\vdash^*$ denotes the reflexive and transitive closure of binary relation $\vdash$.

Figure 7: **Operational semantics of** Π

a sequence of expressions with $M \equiv M_0 \mapsto_\pi \cdots \mapsto_\pi M_m \equiv c$. For each i, we can show that there is a state σ such that $\ll M_{i-1}, \Omega, \Omega \gg \vdash^* \sigma$ and $\ll M_i, \Omega, \Omega \gg \vdash^* \sigma$. Now, if $\ll M_i, \Omega, \Omega \gg \vdash^* \ll c, \Omega, \Omega \gg$, then $\sigma \vdash^* \ll c, \Omega, \Omega \gg$ also. Hence, $\ll M_{i-1}, \Omega, \Omega \gg \vdash^* \sigma \vdash^* \ll c, \Omega, \Omega \gg$. With $\ll M_m, \Omega, \Omega \gg \equiv \ll c, \Omega, \Omega \gg$ as the basis, by an induction on m back up to 0, we have $\ll M, \Omega, \Omega \gg \equiv \ll M_0, \Omega, \Omega \gg \vdash^* \ll c, \Omega, \Omega \gg$. $\square$

7 Conclusion

Lamping's system of transparent parameterization provides a unified view of parameterization which can easily express a wide range of parameterization mechanisms. We have developed a calculus for this system. The calculus is consistent, has a standardization procedure, and corresponds to an operational semantics directly obtained from the denotational semantics. It provides a simple symbolic reasoning system for the language Π, which can be used to determine the result of a program and to prove the equivalence of programs. The calculus is small, having only three conversion rules for the core syntax. We believe the calculus provides additional insight into Lamping's system of parameterization. In particular, it clarifies the relationship between lexical substitution and data parameterization.

References

[1] H.P. Barendregt. *The Lambda Calculus: Its Syntax and Semantics*. North-Holland, second edition, 1984.

[2] Matthias Felleisen and Daniel P. Friedman. A syntactic theory of sequential state. *Theoretical Computer Science*, 69(3):243–287, 1989.

[3] Matthias Felleisen, Daniel P. Friedman, Eugene Kohlbecker, and Bruce Duba. A syntactic theory of sequential control. *Theoretical Computer Science*, 52(3):205–237, 1987.

[4] John O. Lamping. A unified system of parameterization for programming languages. In *1988 ACM Conference On Lisp and Functional Programming*, pages 316–326, July 1988.

[5] John O. Lamping. *A Unified System Of Parameterization For Programming Languages*. PhD thesis, Stanford University, April 1988.

[6] Gordon D. Plotkin. Call-by-name, call-by-value and the λ-calculus. *Theoretical computer Science*, 1:125–159, 1975.

[7] Joseph E. Stoy. *Denotational Semantics: The Scott-Strachey Approach to Programming Language Theory*. MIT Press, 1981.

A Backwards Analysis for Compile-time Garbage Collection

Thomas P. Jensen
DIKU
Univ. of Copenhagen
Universitetsparken 1
DK - 2100 Ø
Denmark

Torben Æ. Mogensen
DIKU
Univ. of Copenhagen
Universitetsparken 1
DK - 2100 Ø
Denmark

Abstract

This paper describes a context semantics that computes the exact number of uses of the value of an expression. This uses information about the actual value, obtained from the standard semantics of the language. The standard semantics is then abstracted away from the analysis to yield an approximating backwards analysis. It is shown how the results obtained can be used to transform a program into one that uses less dynamically alocated storage. The analysis is presented in terms of a first order functional language, and an extension to higher order functional languages is sketched.

1 Introduction

One of the major features of functional programming languages is that the programmer can concentrate on the declarative aspects of programs paying little attention to how the program is executed. While this has the advantage of producing programs that are easy to read and reason formally about, it may also lead to algorithms that are very time and space consuming. A lot of work has been done to design analyses that can detect such bad behaviour in order to transform programs into more efficient ones. This paper deals with the problem of minimizing the use of storage. There seem to be two different ideas to pursue here. Wadler [Wadler 84],[Wadler 85] has investigated how program transformation can be used to compose functions so as to decrease the amount of intermediate storage used. The work is based on the observation that most of the storage used is occupied by results of function calls which immediately are supplied to another function as arguments never to be used later. If we could compose the producing and consuming functions into one, it may be that we could avoid building the intermediate data structure in the first place. The other idea is to point out those places in the program where some part of storage becomes inaccessible. This allows us to return that part of storage to the storage manager or even to reuse directly. Such a method would in principle have to keep track of how many times the result of an expression is used in the remaining computation, so as to detect the last posibble use of a value. Determinig the exact usage count is undecidable so we must satisfy ourselves with approximations hereto. Mycroft [Mycroft 81] has developed an abstract interpretation to obtain these approximate reference counts. We suggest another analysis based on the work of Hughes [Hughes 88] which from information about usage of the result of an expression can derive information about usage of the results of the various subexpressions. The description of the usage of an expression is called the *context* of that expression. Eventually we will end up with contexts for all expressions in the program and this information will then be used to insert suitable instructions for freeing or reusing storage.

The paper is organized as follows: We start with a semantic definition of a small first order functional language. We then define the domain of contexts used for usage counting and give a context analysis, which exactly describes the context of a given expression in a program. The standard semantics is then abstracted out of the context analysis and the context domain is similarly reduced to yield precisely the information necessary for detecting reusable storage. We then show how to exploit the information obtained to produce programs with less storage use. Finally we show how the method can be extended to higher order languages.

2 A first order language and its semantics

As programming language we use a first order functional language written in combinator form. The syntax is as follows:

$$
\begin{aligned}
pgm \ ::=\ & exp \ \texttt{whererec} \\
& f_1\, x_{11} \ldots x_{1n} = exp_1 \\
& \vdots \\
& f_m\, x_{m1} \ldots x_{mn} = exp_m
\end{aligned}
$$

$$
\begin{aligned}
exp \ ::=\ & n \\
\mid\ & c \\
\mid\ & exp_1 :: exp_n \\
\mid\ & \texttt{case}\ exp_1\ \texttt{of atom?}(n){:}exp_2\ (n_1.n_2){:}exp_3 \\
\mid\ & \texttt{if}\ exp_1\ \texttt{then}\ exp_2\ \texttt{else}\ exp_3 \\
\mid\ & exp_1 = exp_2 \\
\mid\ & f_j(exp_1, \ldots, exp_n)
\end{aligned}
$$

where x_{ij}, n, n_1, n_2 belong to the syntactic domain of variables and c denotes an element of the domain of constants.

The expression $exp_1 :: exp_n$ constructs a pair consisting of the values of exp_1 and exp_2. Destructuring is performed by means of a caseexpression; if exp_1 evaluates to a pair (v_1, v_2) then exp_3 is evaluated with n_1 bound to v_1 and n_2 bound to v_2. If, on the other hand, exp_1 evaluates to an atomic value, then exp_2 is evaluated with n bound to that value.

The value domain *Value* consists of atomic values (such as booleans and integers) and structured values. We define

$$
\begin{aligned}
Basic &= Int + Bool + \ldots \\
Value &= Basic + (Value \times Value) \\
\rho : Env &= Var{\rightarrow}Value \\
\phi : Fun{\rightarrow}Value^n{\rightarrow}Value
\end{aligned}
$$

The semantics of the language is specified by the functions $\mathcal{E}$ and P with functionality

$$
\mathcal{E} : Exp{\rightarrow}Env{\rightarrow}Fenv{\rightarrow}Value \quad \text{and} \quad \mathcal{P} : Pgm{\rightarrow}Value
$$

They are defined in figure 1.

$$\begin{aligned}
\mathcal{E}[\![\,v\,]\!]\rho\phi &= \rho(v)\\
\mathcal{E}[\![\,c\,]\!]\rho\phi &= c\\
\mathcal{E}[\![\,exp_1 :: exp_2\,]\!]\rho &= (\mathcal{E}[\![\,exp_1\,]\!]\rho\phi, \mathcal{E}[\![\,exp_2\,]\!]\rho\phi)\\
\mathcal{E}[\![\,\textbf{case}\ exp_1\ \textbf{of} &= \textbf{let}\ v = \mathcal{E}[\![\,exp_1\,]\!]\rho\phi\ \textbf{in}\\
\qquad atom?(n) : exp_2 &\quad \textbf{if}\ inBasic(v)\ \textbf{then}\ \mathcal{E}[\![\,exp_2\,]\!]\rho[n \mapsto v]\phi\\
\qquad (n_1, n_2) : exp_3]\!]\rho\phi &\quad \textbf{else}\ \mathcal{E}[\![\,exp_3\,]\!]\rho[n_1 \mapsto v_1, n_2 \mapsto v_2]\phi\\
&\qquad \textbf{where}\ v = (v_1, v_2)\\
\mathcal{E}[\![\,\textbf{if}\ exp_1\ \textbf{then}\ exp_2\ \textbf{else}\ exp_3\,]\!]\rho\phi &= \textbf{let}\ v = \mathcal{E}[\![\,exp_1\,]\!]\rho\phi\ \textbf{in}\\
&\quad \textbf{if}\ v = \textbf{true}\ \textbf{then}\ \mathcal{E}[\![\,exp_2\,]\!]\rho\phi\\
&\quad \textbf{else}\ \mathcal{E}[\![\,exp_3\,]\!]\rho\phi\\
\mathcal{E}[\![\,exp_1 = exp_2\,]\!]\rho\phi &= \textbf{let}\ v_1 = \mathcal{E}[\![\,exp_1\,]\!]\rho\phi,\ v_2 = \mathcal{E}[\![\,exp_2\,]\!]\rho\phi\ \textbf{in}\\
&\quad \textbf{if}\ inBasic(v_1)\ \textbf{and}\ inBasic(v_2)\\
&\quad \textbf{then}\ v_1 = v_2\ \textbf{else}\ \bot\\
\mathcal{E}[\![\,f_j(exp_1, \ldots, exp_n)\,]\!]\rho\phi &= \textbf{let}\ v_1 = \mathcal{E}[\![\,exp_1\,]\!]\rho\phi,\\
&\qquad \vdots\\
&\quad v_n = \mathcal{E}[\![\,exp_n\,]\!]\rho\phi\\
&\quad \textbf{in}\\
&\quad \phi(f_j)(v_1, \ldots, v_n)\\
\mathcal{P}[\![\,exp\ \textbf{whererec} \ldots\,]\!]\rho_0 &= \mathcal{E}[\![\,exp\,]\!]\rho_0 fenv\\
\textbf{where}\ fenv &= fix(\lambda\phi.[f_j \mapsto \lambda y_{j1}\ldots.\lambda y_{jn}.\mathcal{E}[\![\,exp_j\,]\!][x_{ij} \mapsto y_{ij}]\phi])
\end{aligned}$$

Figure 1: Standard semanics

3 The context analysis

We now present the concept of a *context*. Contexts are used to describe how many times the value of an expression will be used in further computations. As we operate with structured values, our contexts must have a shape which enables us for any substructure of the value to tell how many times it will be used. This suggests the following domain of contexts, which we in the sequel shall denote by D :

$$D = \{\bot, 0, \text{ABSENT}\,\} \cup \{n(d_1, d_2) \mid n \in \mathcal{N}\ \text{and}\ d_1, d_2 \in D\,\}$$
where
$$\mathcal{N} = \{1, 2, 3, \ldots\}$$

where D is ordered as follows

$$\begin{aligned}
\bot &\sqsubseteq x \quad \forall x \in D\\
n_1(d_1, d_2) &\sqsubseteq n_2(d_1', d_2') \quad \text{if}\ n_1 = n_2,\ d_1 \sqsubseteq d_1'\ \text{and}\ d_2 \sqsubseteq d_2'
\end{aligned}$$

The elements in the domain have the following interpretation:

$\bot$ The undefined context. There is a conflict in how the value is going to be used, *i.e.*, it will be used both as an atomic and as a structured value.

ABSENT The value is not used in the remaining computation. This information tells us that we can safely omit to compute the value.

0 An atomic value is expected. Note that we do not count how many times a single atom is used. We are not concerned with reclamation of cells containing atomic values, as it is largely an implementation issue how such values are stored.

$n(d_1, d_2)$ The value must be a structure and the top-level cell is used n times. The substructures are used as described by d_1 and d_2.

When an expression is known to be used both in context α_1 and α_2, we need a means of combining these two contexts into one describing both α_1 and α_2. Following [Hughes 88] we define an operator, $\&$, which unifies two contexts into one representing all constraints present in the two. $\&$ obeys the following rules for all $\alpha \in D$:

$$
\begin{aligned}
\bot \,\&\, \alpha &= \bot \\
\text{ABSENT} \,\&\, \alpha &= \alpha \\
0 \,\&\, 0 &= 0 \\
0 \,\&\, n(d_1, d_2) &= \bot \\
n_1(d_1, d_2) \,\&\, n_2(d_1{}', d_2{}') &= n(d_1 \,\&\, d_1{}', d_2 \,\&\, d_2{}') \qquad \text{where } n = n_1 + n_2
\end{aligned}
$$

Together with the fact that $\&$ is commutative, this defines the $\&$ operator.

Still following [Hughes 88] we define an operator, $\to$, on contexts that preserve absence and contradiction in a context α:

$\alpha \to \beta$ is defined as follows:

$$
\begin{aligned}
\bot \to \beta &= \bot \\
\text{ABSENT} \to \beta &= \text{ABSENT} \\
\alpha \to \beta &= \beta \quad \text{otherwise}
\end{aligned}
$$

For example, if an expression is evaluated in context ABSENT then the value of the expression will not be used and so neither will the value of any variable occurring in the expression. Hence we must ensure that any absence or contradiction in the surrounding context is propagated to the subexpressions.

Starting from the standard semantics $\mathcal{E}$ we now develop an analysis which calculates the exact context of any variable occurring in an expression given the context of the whole expression. The analysis is defined by the function $\mathcal{C}$, which has the following type

$$\mathcal{C} : \text{Var} \to \text{Exp} \to \text{Env} \to \text{Fenv} \to D \to D$$

and is defined in figure 2.

The rules for the case-expression and the rule concerning function calls deserve an explanation: When evaluating a case-expression $\text{case} \, exp_1 \, \text{of atom?}(n) : exp_2 \, (n_1, n_2) : exp_3$ the value of exp_1 determines which one of the branches is chosen. Further it tells us what structure exp_1 is supposed to evaluate to, and hence provides input to the analysis of subexpression exp_2 or exp_3. So if exp_1 evaluates to an atomic value, we can conclude that the variable x will be used *both* when evaluating exp_1 to an atomic value *and* when evaluating exp_2 in the original context. We thus get the rule

$$\mathcal{C}x[\![exp_1]\!]\rho\,\phi\,0 \,\&\, \mathcal{C}x[\![exp_2]\!]\rho[n \mapsto v]\,\phi\,\delta$$

$$
\begin{aligned}
&Cx[\![e\ ]\!]\rho\,\phi\,\delta &=&\ \delta\to\text{ABSENT} &&\text{if x does not occur free in e}\\
&Cx[\![x\ ]\!]\rho\,\phi\,\delta &=&\ \delta\\
&Cx[\![exp_1 :: exp_2\ ]\!]\rho\,\phi\,\delta &=&\ \delta\to\textbf{case }\delta\textbf{ of}\\
&&&\quad 0:\bot\\
&&&\quad n(d_1,d_2): Cx[\![exp_1\ ]\!]\rho\,\phi\,d_1\ \&\ Cx[\![exp_2\ ]\!]\rho\,\phi\,d_2\\
&Cx[\![\textbf{case }exp_1\textbf{ of} &=&\ \delta\to\textbf{let }v=\mathcal{E}[\![exp_1\ ]\!]\rho\,\phi\textbf{ in}\\
&\quad \textbf{atom?}(n):exp_2 &&\quad\textbf{if }inBasic(v)\textbf{ then}\\
&\quad (n_1,n_2):exp_3]\!]\rho\,\phi\,\delta &&\qquad Cx[\![exp_1\ ]\!]\rho\,\phi\,0\ \&\ Cx[\![exp_2\ ]\!]\rho[n\mapsto v]\,\phi\,\delta\\
&&&\quad\textbf{else}\\
&&&\qquad Cx[\![exp_1\ ]\!]\rho\,\phi\,1(Cn_1[\![exp_3\ ]\!]\rho'\,\phi\,\delta, Cn_2[\![exp_3\ ]\!]\rho'\,\phi\,\delta)\ \&\\
&&&\qquad Cx[\![exp_3\ ]\!]\rho'\,\phi\,\delta\\
&&&\qquad\textbf{where }\rho'=[n_1\mapsto v_1, n_2\mapsto v_2]\text{ and }v=(v_1,v_2)\\
&Cx[\![\textbf{if }exp_1\textbf{ then }exp_2 &=&\ \delta\to\textbf{let }v=\mathcal{E}[\![exp_1\ ]\!]\rho\,\phi\textbf{ in}\\
&\quad \textbf{else }exp_3]\!]\rho\,\phi\,\delta &&\quad Cx[\![exp_1\ ]\!]\rho\,\phi\,0\ \&\\
&&&\quad (\textbf{if }v=\textbf{true then }Cx[\![exp_2\ ]\!]\rho\,\phi\,\delta\\
&&&\quad \textbf{else if }v=\textbf{false then }Cx[\![exp_3\ ]\!]\rho\,\phi\,\delta)\textbf{ else }\bot\\
&Cx[\![exp_1=exp_2\ ]\!]\rho\,\phi\,\delta &=&\ \delta\to Cx[\![exp_1\ ]\!]\rho\,\phi\,0\ \&\ Cx[\![exp_2\ ]\!]\rho\,\phi\,0\\
&Cx[\![f_j(exp_1,\ldots,exp_n)\ ]\!]\rho\,\phi\,\delta &=&\ Cx[\![exp_1\ ]\!]\rho\,(f_j\#1\,w\,\delta)\ \&\ \ldots\ \&\ Cx[\![exp_n\ ]\!]\rho\,(f_j\#n\,w\,\delta)\\
&&&\quad\textbf{where }w_i=\mathcal{E}[\![exp_i\ ]\!]\rho\,\phi\ ,\ w=(w_1,\ldots,w_n)\\
&&&\quad\text{and }f_j\#i\,w\,\delta=Cx_1[\![body_j]\!][x_{j1}\mapsto w_1,\ldots,x_{jn}\mapsto w_n]\,\delta
\end{aligned}
$$

Figure 2: Context Semantics

On the other hand, if exp_1 evaluates to a structured value (v_1,v_2), we evaluate exp_3 with the variables n_1 and n_2 bound to v_1 and v_2. So v_1 and v_2 are used according to how n_1 and n_2 are used when evaluating exp_3 in the original context. Furthermore, the topmost cell of (v_1,v_2) is used exactly once when exp_1 evaluates to a structured value. This explains the rule

$$
Cx[\![exp_1\ ]\!]\rho\,\phi\,1(Cn_1[\![exp_3\ ]\!]\rho'\,\phi\,\delta, Cn_2[\![exp_3\ ]\!]\rho'\,\phi\,\delta)\ \&\ Cx[\![exp_3\ ]\!]\rho'\,\phi\,\delta
$$
$$
\text{where }\rho'=\rho[n_1\mapsto v_1, n_2\mapsto v_2]
$$

Similarly, a function call in context δ means that the body of the function will be evaluated in context δ. From the body of the function and the context in which it is evaluated, we can deduce the context of each of the formal parameters of the function (expressed as a function $f_j\#i : Value^*\to D\to D$ for each formal parameter x_i). These contexts are the contexts in which the actual parameters are evaluated. The total usage of variable x is then the combination (by &) of its usages in the evaluation of each of the actual parameters, which explains the rule

$$
Cx[\![exp_1\ ]\!]\rho\,\phi\,(f_j\#1\,w\,\delta)\ \&\ \ldots\ \&\ Cx[\![exp_n\ ]\!]\rho\,\phi\,(f_j\#n\,w\,\delta)
$$

4 Approximations to the context analysis

Our analysis uses the standard semantics $\mathcal{E}$, which makes it unusable in a compiler. In search for an analysis that can be used at compile time we define an approximation to the context analysis C that does not use the standard semantics $\mathcal{E}$. Without $\mathcal{E}$ we are unable to tell which one of the branches in a **case** or **if** –expression is going to be evaluated, thus we shall have to take into account not one but many computation paths which means that our expressions do not appear in one but many contexts. This leads us to consider *sets of contexts*.

Given an ordering on a set $\mathcal{M}$, an ordering on the powerset $P(\mathcal{M})$ can be defined in several ways. We have chosen to work within the *Hoare* (or *lower*) power domain $\mathbf{P}_H(D)$ for reasons to become clear shortly. The Hoare powerdomain consists of all the *Scott-closed* subsets of D ordered by subset inclusion. A set M is Scott-closed if it is *downwards closed* w.r.t. the ordering on D and is closed w.r.t. limits of chains, *i.e.*, it has to satisfy the following two conditions:

1. $x \sqsubseteq y \wedge y \in \mathcal{M}$ implies $x \in \mathcal{M}$
2. $x_1, x_2, \ldots \in \mathcal{M} \wedge x_1 \sqsubseteq x_2 \sqsubseteq \ldots$ implies $\bigsqcup(x_i) \in \mathcal{M}$

The least element in $\mathbf{P}_H(D)$ is the set $\{\perp\}$ and the largest D itself. The Hoare powerdomain was chosen because we do not want contradictory contexts to affect the rest of the analysis. Had we chosen a powerdomain which is upwards closed, we would not have been able to say anything about expressions that could appear in a bottom context, as the upwards closure of $\perp$ is the entire domain.

The *Scott-closure* of a set $\mathcal{N}$ is the least Scott-closed set containing $\mathcal{N}$. The operator & defined on the context domain D is extended to work on $\mathbf{P}_H(D)$ by stipulating that for $\mathcal{M}, \mathcal{N} \in \mathbf{P}_H(D)$, $\mathcal{M} \& \mathcal{N}$ is the Scott-closure of the set obtained by pointwise application of the operator & to $\mathcal{M}$ and $\mathcal{N}$.

If we are only interested in whether a value is going to be used one or many times in the remaining computation, the $\mathbf{P}_H(D)$ domain is much too informative. We could do with a a domain where the structured values could be either $1(n_1, n_2)$ or $2(n_1, n_2)$, where the latter represents structures used two *or more* times. Seen from an implementation point of view this reduction in size of the domain will make the analysis more tractable to automation.

We consider the domain D' defined by:

$$D' = \{\text{ABS}, 0\} \cup \{1(d_1, d_2) \mid d_1, d_2 \in D'\} \cup \{2(d_1, d_2) \mid d_1, d_2 \in D'\}$$

We show that D' is an abstraction of $\mathbf{P}_H(D)$ by defining a concretization function $\gamma : D' \to \mathbf{P}_H(D)$ and taking as abstraction function $\alpha : \mathbf{P}_H(D) \to D'$ induced by γ: $\alpha(x) = \bigsqcup\{y \mid \gamma(y) \sqsubseteq x\}$. γ is defined by:

$$
\begin{aligned}
\gamma(\text{ABS}) &= \{\perp, \text{ABSENT}\} \\
\gamma(0) &= \{\perp, \text{ABSENT}, 0\} \\
\gamma(1(d_1, d_2)) &= \{\perp, \text{ABSENT}, 0\} \cup \\
&\quad \{1(d_1', d_2') \mid d_1' \in \gamma(d_1), d_2' \in \gamma(d_2)\} \\
\gamma(2(d_1, d_2)) &= \{\perp, \text{ABSENT}, 0\} \cup \\
&\quad \{n(d_1', d_2') \mid n \in \mathcal{N}, d_1' \in \gamma(d_1), d_2' \in \gamma(d_2)\}
\end{aligned}
$$

We extend the & operator to work on elements in the domain D' by carrying the computation to the powerdomain $\mathbf{P}_H(D)$ and taking the least element in D' that safely approximates (*i.e.*, is greater than) the result. $\&'$ has the following tabulation:

$$
\begin{aligned}
\text{ABS} \ \&' \ \delta &= \delta \\
0 \ \&' \ 0 &= 0 \\
0 \ \&' \ n(\delta_1, \delta_2) &= n(\delta_1, \delta_2) \quad n = 1, 2 \\
n_1(\delta_1, \delta_2) \ \&' \ n_2(\delta_1', \delta_2') &= 2(\delta_1 \ \&' \ \delta_1', \delta_2 \ \&' \ \delta_2')
\end{aligned}
$$

As all contexts contain contradiction and absence, the $\rightarrow$ operator degenerates to a requirement saying that if an expression is evaluated in context ABS then each variable occuring in the expression is used in context ABS .

The analysis is described by the function C' , which has functionality:

$$C' : Var \rightarrow Exp \rightarrow D' \rightarrow D'$$

It is shown in figure 3

$$
\begin{aligned}
C'\mathrm{x}[\![\mathrm{x}\,]\!]\alpha &= \alpha \\
C'\mathrm{x}[\![e\,]\!]\alpha &= \mathrm{ABS} \qquad \text{if x does not occur free in } e \\
C'\mathrm{x}[\![exp_1 :: exp_2\,]\!]\alpha &= \alpha \rightarrow \mathbf{case}\ \alpha\ \mathbf{of} \\
&\quad\ 0 : \mathrm{ABS} \\
&\quad\ n(\alpha_1, \alpha_2) : C'\mathrm{x}[\![exp_1\,]\!]\alpha_1\ \&'\ C'\mathrm{x}[\![exp_2\,]\!]\alpha_2 \\
C'\mathrm{x}[\![\mathbf{case}\ exp_1\ \mathbf{of} &= \alpha \rightarrow \mathbf{let}\ \bar\alpha = 1(C'n_1[\![exp_3\,]\!]\alpha, C'n_2[\![exp_3\,]\!]\alpha)\mathbf{in} \\
\quad \mathbf{atom?}(n) : exp_2 &\quad\ C'\mathrm{x}[\![exp_1\,]\!]0\ \&'\ C'\mathrm{x}[\![exp_2\,]\!]\alpha\ \sqcup \\
\quad (n_1, n_2) : exp_3]\!]\alpha &\quad\ C'\mathrm{x}[\![exp_1\,]\!]\bar\alpha\ \&'\ C'\mathrm{x}[\![exp_3\,]\!]\alpha \\
C'\mathrm{x}[\![\mathbf{if}\ exp_1\ \mathbf{then}\ exp_2 &= \alpha \rightarrow (C'\mathrm{x}[\![exp_1\,]\!]0\ \&'\ (C'\mathrm{x}[\![exp_2\,]\!]\alpha \sqcup C'\mathrm{x}[\![exp_3\,]\!]\alpha)) \\
\quad \mathbf{else}\ exp_3]\!]\alpha \\
C'\mathrm{x}[\![exp_1 = exp_2\,]\!]\delta &= \alpha \rightarrow (C'\mathrm{x}[\![exp_1\,]\!]0\ \&'\ C'\mathrm{x}[\![exp_2\,]\!]0) \\
C'\mathrm{x}[\![f_j(exp_1, \ldots, exp_n)\,]\!]\alpha &= C'\mathrm{x}[\![exp_1\,]\!](f_j\#1\ \alpha)\ \&'\ \ldots\ \&'\ C'\mathrm{x}[\![exp_n\,]\!](f_j\#n\ \alpha) \\
&\quad\ \text{where}\ f_j\#i\ \alpha = C\mathrm{x}_{ji}[\![body_j]\!]\alpha
\end{aligned}
$$

Figure 3: Abstract context semantics

5 Using a global environment and delayed unfolding

Although the domain D' has a very nice structure it still has infinite chains, *i.e.*, the usual iterative method for finding fixpoints will in general not terminate. In this section we describe another method based on approximations by grammars. The method was used for binding time analysis in [Mogensen 89] and a similar idea can also be found in [NDJones 81]. The general idea is to use a global environment that binds variables to their context and functions to the least upper bound of the contexts of the calls to them. This in itself will not ensure termination, but we can now represent the global environment by a grammar: each binding in the environment is represented by a production in the grammar. In a rule $N \rightarrow rhs$, the left hand side nonterminal N is the name of a function or variable and the right hand side rhs represents the context bound to that name. The right hand side of a production will contain the topmost "constructor" of the context, but use references to other nonterminals for the substructures. Since the operators $\&'$ and $\sqcup$ require the full depth of their argument contexts, evaluation of these would require complete unfolding of the grammar rules of their arguments. Therefore we only evaluate the topmost constructor of the result before we suspend the operations. We suspend the operators by letting them appear explicitly in the grammar rules, operating on nonterminals. We will use some algebraic properties of $\&'$ and $\sqcup$ to rewrite the right hand sides to normal form, thus making it easier to compare productions and thus detecting a fixed point.

When using a global environment we will replace the C' function with two functions: C'' will find the context of a variable in an expression given the context of the expression *and* the global environment. Q will update an environment with the contexts found in an expression given the context of the expression and the old environment. C'' will use the environment in some places instead of evaluating the contexts of some expressions, *e.g.*, , to find the contexts of argument expressions to a function call. The environment will have these bound to the formal parameter names of the function. The context found in the environment is the context found by assuming that the context of the function body is the combination (by $\sqcup$) of the contexts of *all* the calls to the function.

C'' and Q have the functionalities

$$C'' : Var \to Exp \to D' \to Cenv \to D'$$

$$Q : Exp \to D' \to Cenv \to Cenv$$

where

$$Cenv = (Var \cup Fun) \to D'$$

The definitions of the functions C'' and Q are given in figures 4 and 5. They are used to produce a fixed point context environment κ_{fix}:

$$\kappa_{fix} = fix\lambda\kappa.Q[\![exp_1]\!](\kappa'f_1)(\ldots Q[\![exp_n]\!](\kappa'f_n)\kappa')$$

where $\kappa' = \kappa[x_{11} \mapsto C''x_{11}[\![exp_1]\!](\kappa f_1)\kappa,\ldots x_{mn} \mapsto C''x_{mn}[\![exp_1]\!](\kappa f_m)\kappa]$

$C''x[\![x]\!]\alpha\kappa$	$= \alpha$	
$C''x[\![e]\!]\alpha\kappa$	$= $ ABS	if x does not occur free in e
$C''x[\![exp_1 :: exp_2]\!]\alpha\kappa$	$= \alpha \to$ **case** α **of**	
	$\quad 0 : $ ABS	
	$\quad n(\alpha_1, \alpha_2) : C''x[\![exp_1]\!]\alpha_1\kappa \,\&' \, C''x[\![exp_2]\!]\alpha_2\kappa$	
$C''x[\![$**case** exp_1 **of**	$= \alpha \to$ **let** $\bar{\alpha} = 1(\kappa\, n_1, \kappa\, n_2)$ **in**	
$\quad$ atom?$(n) : exp_2$	$\quad C''x[\![exp_1]\!]0\kappa \,\&' \, C''x[\![exp_2]\!]\alpha\kappa \,\sqcup$	
$\quad (n_1, n_2) : exp_3]\!]\alpha\kappa$	$\quad C''x[\![exp_1]\!]\bar{\alpha}\kappa \,\&' \, C''x[\![exp_3]\!]\alpha\kappa$	
$C''x[\![$**if** exp_1 **then** exp_2	$= \alpha \to (C''x[\![exp_1]\!]0\kappa \,\&' \, (C''x[\![exp_2]\!]\alpha\kappa \,\sqcup\, C''x[\![exp_3]\!]\alpha\kappa))$	
$\quad$ **else** $exp_3]\!]\alpha\kappa$		
$C''x[\![exp_1 = exp_2]\!]\alpha\kappa$	$= \alpha \to (C''x[\![exp_1]\!]0\kappa \,\&' \, C''x[\![exp_2]\!]0\kappa)$	
$C''x[\![f_j(exp_1,\ldots,exp_n)]\!]\alpha\kappa$	$= C''x[\![exp_1]\!](\kappa\, x_{j1}) \,\&' \, \ldots \,\&' \, C''x[\![exp_n]\!](\kappa\, x_{jn})$	

Figure 4: Abstract context semantics with global environment

This use of a global environment of contexts will make the result of the analysis less precise, as the contexts of the calls to a particular function are combined instead of treated separatedly. However, if the analysis is to be used in a compiler, separate treatment of different calls to the same function would require generating different versions of code for that function, one version for each different context.

As mentioned earlier, a global environment is in itself not enough to ensure termination. We can, however, now replace the environment by what amounts to a grammar: The identifiers in the environment are used as nonterminals, and each binding in the environment is represented

$$
\begin{aligned}
\mathcal{Q}[\![x\,]\!]\alpha\kappa &= \kappa \\
\mathcal{Q}[\![e\,]\!]\alpha\kappa &= \kappa \qquad \text{if } x \text{ does not occur free in } e \\
\mathcal{Q}[\![exp_1 :: exp_2\,]\!]\alpha\kappa &= \textbf{case } \alpha \textbf{ of} \\
&\qquad \text{ABS} : \kappa \\
&\qquad 0 : \kappa \\
&\qquad n(\alpha_1, \alpha_2) : \mathcal{Q}[\![exp_1\,]\!]\alpha_1(\mathcal{Q}[\![exp_2\,]\!]\alpha_2\kappa) \\
\mathcal{Q}[\![\textbf{case } exp_1 \textbf{ of} &= \textbf{let } \alpha_1 = C''n_1[\![exp_3\,]\!]\alpha\kappa\,, \alpha_2 = C''n_2[\![exp_3\,]\!]\alpha\kappa \textbf{ in} \\
\quad \textbf{atom?}(n) : exp_2 &\qquad \mathcal{Q}[\![exp_1\,]\!]1(\alpha_1, \alpha_2)(\mathcal{Q}[\![exp_2\,]\!]\alpha(\mathcal{Q}[\![exp_3\,]\!]\alpha\kappa')) \\
\quad (n_1, n_2) : exp_3]\!]\alpha\kappa &\qquad \textbf{where } \kappa' = \kappa[n_1 \mapsto \alpha_1, n_2 \mapsto \alpha_2] \\
\mathcal{Q}[\![\textbf{if } exp_1 \textbf{ then } exp_2 &= \mathcal{Q}[\![exp_1\,]\!]0(\mathcal{Q}[\![exp_2\,]\!]\alpha(\mathcal{Q}[\![exp_3\,]\!]\alpha\kappa)) \\
\quad \textbf{else } exp_3]\!]\alpha \\
\mathcal{Q}[\![exp_1 = exp_2\,]\!]\delta &= \mathcal{Q}[\![exp_1\,]\!]0(\mathcal{Q}[\![exp_2\,]\!]0\kappa) \\
\mathcal{Q}[\![f_j(exp_1, \ldots, exp_n)\,]\!]\alpha &= \mathcal{Q}[\![exp_1\,]\!](\kappa x_{j1})(\ldots \mathcal{Q}[\![exp_n\,]\!](\kappa x_{jn})\kappa[f_j \mapsto \alpha])
\end{aligned}
$$

Figure 5: Updating the global environment

by a production in the grammar. The grammar is not quite a tree-grammar: instead of an alternative-operator ($|$) we use the operators $\&'$ and $\sqcup$. What we get is thus actually a set of mutually recursive equations involving the constructors (ABS, 0, $1(\_,\_)$ and $2(\_,\_)$) in the abstract context domain the operators $\&'$ and $\sqcup$. In general, such a set of equations can not be considered a solution, as a fixed point iteration may be required to find the value of any variable. We thus require the equations to be *constructive*: The topmost constructor in the value of a variable are stated explicitly on the right hand side of the equation (production) for that variable, and the parameters of the constructor are given solely by $\&'$, $\sqcup$ and variables (nonterminals). This constructiveness of the equations is what makes us compare them with a grammar. Note that, whereas a production in a normal grammar produces a set of values, our type of grammar each nonterminal produce only a single value: the value of the corresponding variable in the least fixed point of the equations.

As the analysis using C'' and $\mathcal{Q}$ modifies an environment to produce a fixed point environment, we use functions C''' and $\mathcal{Q}'$ to modify a grammar to produce a fixed point grammar. The values that the fixed point grammar produces for a given nonterminal is the same value that the corresponding variable is bound to in the fixed point environment.

In order to recognize a fixed point, the productions are written in a normal form. As mentioned above, the topmost constructor is explicitly given, so that part is already in normal form. The remaining parts are stated as expressions using $\&'$ and $\sqcup$ on nonterminals. In order to rewrite such expressions to normal form we use algebraic properties of the operators:

$$
\begin{aligned}
x \sqcup x &= x & &\sqcup \text{ is absorptive} \\
x \sqcup y &= y \sqcup x & &\sqcup \text{ is commutative} \\
x \sqcup (y \sqcup z) &= (x \sqcup y) \sqcup z & &\sqcup \text{ is associative} \\
x \&' x \&' x &= x \&' x & &\&' \text{ is semi-absorptive} \\
x \&' y &= y \&' x & &\&' \text{ is commutative} \\
x \&' (y \&' z) &= (x \&' y) \&' z & &\&' \text{ is associative} \\
x \&' (y \sqcup z) &= (x \&' y) \sqcup (x \&' z) & &\&' \text{ distributes over } \sqcup \\
x \&' y \sqcup x &= x \&' y & &\&' \text{ is majoring}
\end{aligned}
$$

The commutativity, associativity and distributativity allows us to rewrite any expressions into a sum-of-products-of-nonterminals normal form, where $\sqcup$ takes the rôle of the addition operator, and $\&'$ the rôle of the multiplication operator. The semi-absorptivity of $\&'$ allows us to have each variable at most twice in any product and the absorptivity of $\sqcup$ allows us to have each product occurring at most once in a sum. Further reduction can be obtained by using the majorance of $\&'$. Note that the semi-apsorptivity and majorance of $\&'$ are properties of the *abstract* context domain; the *concrete* context domain does not have these properties. The semi-apsorptivity was obtained by combining all numbers greater than one into a single symbol ("2"). The majorance was obtained by combining $\perp$ and ABSENT into ABS , making this the least element of D' .

It is easy to see from this description, that there, given a finite set of nonterminals, there are only finitely many different reduced normal forms. Thus, given also a finite set of productions, a fixed point grammar can be found in finite time. While the semi-apsorptivity of $\&'$ is essential for keeping the normal forms finite, the majorance is just convenient for keeping them small. In fact, the first implementation of the analysis didn't use this property.

We define an *unfold* operation on sum-of-products normal forms with respect to a grammar: all nonterminals are expanded *once* according to the productions in the grammar, each yielding a constructor with sum-of-products as parameters. Using the definitions of $\&'$ and $\sqcup$ the resulting expression is reduced to a single constructor with sum-of-product parameters. As $\&'$ and $\sqcup$ are defined, they are immediately usable on terms of the "constructor with sum-of-products parameters" form, and we will use them as such in the definitions of C''' and Q' . For reasons of space, we only show the rules where they differ from C'' and Q . The definitions are found in figure 6. Note that it is only when constructing or decomposing values in the abstract context domain, that any changes occur. Note also that at the place where we build contexts, we have nonterminals (n_1, n_2) at hand. Were this not the case, we would have to annotate the expressions in question with nonterminals before starting the analysis.

$$
\begin{aligned}
C'''\mathrm{x}[\![exp_1 :: exp_2\,]\!]\alpha\kappa \;=\;& \alpha\rightarrow\textbf{case } \alpha \textbf{ of}\\
& 0 : \mathrm{ABS}\\
& n(\alpha_1, \alpha_2) : C'''\mathrm{x}[\![exp_1\,]\!](unfold\,\alpha_1\,\kappa)\kappa\ \&'\\
& \qquad\qquad\qquad C'''\mathrm{x}[\![exp_2\,]\!](unfold\,\alpha_2\,\kappa)\kappa\\[4pt]
C'''\mathrm{x}[\![\textbf{case } exp_1 \textbf{ of} \;=\;& \alpha\rightarrow\textbf{let } \bar{\alpha} = 1(n_1, n_2) \textbf{ in}\\
\quad \mathrm{atom?}(n) : exp_2 & \qquad C'''\mathrm{x}[\![exp_1\,]\!]0\kappa\ \&'\ C'''\mathrm{x}[\![exp_2\,]\!]\alpha\kappa\ \sqcup\\
\quad (n_1, n_2) : exp_3]\!]\alpha\kappa & \qquad C'''\mathrm{x}[\![exp_1\,]\!]\bar{\alpha}\kappa\ \&'\ C'''\mathrm{x}[\![exp_3\,]\!]\alpha\kappa\\[8pt]
Q'[\![exp_1 :: exp_2\,]\!]\alpha\kappa \;=\;& \textbf{case } \alpha \textbf{ of}\\
& \mathrm{ABS} : \kappa\\
& 0 : \kappa\\
& n(\alpha_1, \alpha_2) : Q'[\![exp_1\,]\!](unfold\,\alpha_1\,\kappa)(Q'[\![exp_2\,]\!](unfold\,\alpha_2\,\kappa)\kappa)\\[4pt]
Q'[\![\textbf{case } exp_1 \textbf{ of} \;=\;& \textbf{let } \alpha_1 = C'''n_1[\![exp_3\,]\!]\alpha\kappa\ , \alpha_2 = C'''n_2[\![exp_3\,]\!]\alpha\kappa \textbf{ in}\\
\quad \mathrm{atom?}(n) : exp_2 & \qquad Q'[\![exp_1\,]\!]1(n_1, n_2)(Q'[\![exp_2\,]\!]\alpha(Q'[\![exp_3\,]\!]\alpha\kappa'))\\
\quad (n_1, n_2) : exp_3]\!]\alpha\kappa & \qquad \textbf{where } \kappa' = \kappa[n_1 \mapsto \alpha_1, n_2 \mapsto \alpha_2]
\end{aligned}
$$

Figure 6: Modifications required for using grammars

6 Using the analysis

How can we exploit the information obtained *e.g.*, in an optimising compiler? There are several answers to that question and they should be measured against how complex they are to implement. The simplest would be just to return to the free-list those cells that are not used any more. A better (and more expensive) method is to keep a "compile-time free-list" containing those cells which are no longer used but still can be addressed by the variables in scope. Operations that request new store cells should then be replaced by operations that reuses the cells in this "free-list". For that purpose one has to extend the language with operators that destructively update cells like rplaca and rplacd in LISP. See [Mycroft 81] for more on this subject.

In this article we adopt a strategy for reusing cells that is facilitated by the fact that the only way of destructuring is by means of a case-expression. Assume that we by means of the context analysis can deduce that a certain ":: "-expression is evaluated in a context that is described by $1(n_1, n_2)$. Thus the topmost cell of the structure is going to be used only once in the future. Replace this :: with a $::_1$ which builds the cons-cell and place a tag on it saying this cell will only be used once. Now consider the case-expression.

```
case exp₁ of
    atom?(v) : exp₂
    (n₁,n₂)  : exp₃
```

If exp_1 evaluates to a tagged cons-cell (built by $::_1$) we can free the cons-cell as soon as we begin evaluation of exp_3. We might even change exp_3 to directly reuse the cons-cell if we could deduce that it always evaluates to a tagged cons-cell. We simply pick a :: -operation in exp_3 and replace it with an operation which overwrites and returns the cell instead of allocating a new cell. If this cons-expression appears in a context $1(n_1, n_2)$ we needn't even erase the tag. Note that to be sure we reclaim the cell, exactly one such modified :: -operation will have to be present in each possible evaluation path of exp_3.

The context analysis can be combined with an abstract interpretation that for any exp_1 in a case-expression determines whether the topmost constructor of any value it can take will be *always tagged, never tagged, possibly tagged* or *never a cons-cell*. This will make it possible to do some of the testing on tags at compile time rather than run time. In fact, it can be argued that the cost of testing for tags outweighs the benefit of being able to reclaim some of the cells. By using the combined context analysis / abstract interpretation, you can at compile time mark those case-expressions where you can *always* reclaim a cons-cell, and thus avoid run time tags altogether.

7 Extension to higher order languages

We now show how to extend our context analysis to higher order languages. This is usually considered a hard problem, but we shall see that the global environment method introduced in the section 5 is of use here.

We introduce higher order functions in the language by means of partial applications. We change the grammar for expressions in section 2 by replacing the production

$$exp ::= f_j(exp_1, \ldots, exp_n)$$

by the two rules:

$$exp ::= f_j$$

$$exp ::= exp_1 @ exp_2$$

This implies that expressions can evaluate to closures, where closures have the form $[f, v_1, \ldots, v_j]$ with arity$(f) > j$. Define an *abstract* closure to be a pair of the form (f, n) where f is the name of a function and n is a number recording the (insufficient) number of arguments f has been applied to. In order to modify our analysis to encompass these higher order constructs, we need a *closure analysis* like the one described in [Sestoft 89]. This analysis collects for every e_1 in an expression $e_1 @ e_2$ the set of possible abstract closures e_1 can evaluate to during the execution of the program. For an expression e_1 we denote this set by $K(e_1)$.

The context analysis C'', that uses the global environment, is modified as follows: We replace the rule for function call by the following two rules:

$$
\begin{aligned}
C''\mathrm{x}[\![f]\!]\alpha\kappa \quad &= \quad \mathrm{ABS} \\
C''\mathrm{x}[\![e_1 @ e_2]\!]\alpha\kappa \quad &= \quad C''\mathrm{x}[\![e_1]\!]0\,\&' \\
&\qquad C''\mathrm{x}[\![e_2]\!]((\kappa\,\mathrm{x}_{i_1 n_1'}) \sqcup \ldots \sqcup (\kappa\,\mathrm{x}_{i_m n_m'})) \\
&\qquad \text{where } K(e_1) = \{(f_{i_1}, n_1), \ldots, (f_{i_m}, n_m)\} \\
&\qquad \text{and } n_1' = n_1 + 1, \ldots, n_m' = n_m + 1
\end{aligned}
$$

Similarly, the rules for Q are modified as follows:

$$
\begin{aligned}
Q[\![f]\!]\alpha\kappa \quad &= \quad \kappa \\
Q[\![e_1 @ e_2]\!]\alpha\kappa \quad &= \quad \kappa[f_{a_1} \mapsto (\alpha \sqcup (\kappa\,f_{a_1})), \ldots, f_{a_k} \mapsto (\alpha \sqcup (\kappa\,f_{a_k}))] \\
&\qquad \text{where } \{f_{a_1}, \ldots, f_{a_k}\} = \\
&\qquad \{f_{i_j} \mid (f_{i_j}, n_j) \in K(e_1) \text{ and } f_{i_j} \text{ has } n_j + 1 \text{ parameters}\}
\end{aligned}
$$

Explanation: The value of e_1 will be used as a closure, *i.e.*, not a cons-cell, hence the context 0. If the value of e_1 can be described by the abstract closure (f, n) we can deduce that the value of e_2 will be bound to the $(n + 1)$'st formal parameter of f. The context of the value of e_2 is thus the same as that of this formal parameter, and the context of the formal parameter can be looked up in the environment. As we can only predict an approximating set of abstract closures for e_1 we need to take the least upper bound of the corresponding contexts. If a closure of the form (f, n) receives its last parameter (f has $n + 1$ parameters), the current context describes the context of a call to f, so we update the environment entry describing f.

As no contexts are built or decomposed in the above rules, the higher order analysis can be modified to use grammars in exactly the same way as the first order analysis.

8 Conclusion

We have devised a method capable of finding the context in which a given expression in a program is evaluated. This information is used to determine the number of references to the cons-cells we create during the execution of the program. This enables reuse of cons-cells which are never referenced more than once.

An implementation of the first order analysis shows that the method works well in practice. If there is a large number of identifiers in a program, the potential size of productions is enormous, but experiments with reasonably sized programs has not had such problems. A program containing 100 identifiers, thus giving a grammar with 100 nonterminals / productions, showed no more than 3 different nonterminals in any product and no more than 2 products in any reduced sum. For this program (a self-interpreter for the language used in this paper) the analysis was able to find the single cons-operation which would always have a maximum of one reference. (The other cons-operations either executes cons-operations in the interpreted program, or builds environments that can be used repeatedly).

The use of a global environment / grammar seems crucial to the extension of the analysis to higher order languages, as the context for the final invocation of a closure is needed to find the context of an argument to a partial application, and this is not available locally. It would be interesting to extend the higher order analysis to also count references to closures, so some of these can be reclaimed / overwritten upon application.

Note that, as the analysis is defined in terms of a semantics where the evaluation order is unspecified, the result is equally applicable to call-by-value and call-by-need languages.

References

[Hughes 88]   Hughes, R.J.M. Backwards Analysis of Functional Programs. In *Workshop on Partial Evaluation and Mixed Computation*. 1988.

[Mogensen 89] Mogensen, Torben Æ. *Binding Time Aspects of Partial Evaluation*. PhD thesis, DIKU, University of Copenhagen, 1989.

[Mycroft 81]   Mycroft, A. *Abstract Interpretation and Optimising Transformation for Applicative Programs*. PhD thesis, Univ. of Edinburgh, 1981.

[NDJones 81]   N.D. Jones, S.S. Muchnick. *Program Flow Analysis*. Prentice-Hall, 1981.

[Sestoft 89]   Sestoft, P. Replacing Function Parameters by Global Variables. In *Functional Programming Languages and Computer Architecture, London, September 89*. ACM Press and Addison-Wesley, 1989.

[Wadler 84]   Wadler, P. Listlessness is better than laziness: Lazy evaluation and compile-time garbage collection. In *Proceedings of the ACM symposium on LISP and Functional Programming*. 1984.

[Wadler 85]   Wadler, P. Listlessness is better tha laziness II: Composing listless functions. In *Proc. of the Workshop on Programs as Data Objects*. 1985.

Techniques for Improving Grammar Flow Analysis

(*Extended Abstract*)

Martin JOURDAN & Didier PARIGOT

INRIA*

Abstract

Grammar Flow Analysis (GFA) is a computation framework that can be applied to a large number of problems expressed on context-free grammars. In this framework, as was done on programs with Data Flow Analysis, those problems are split into a general resolution procedure and a set of specific propagation functions. This paper presents a number of improvement techniques that act on the resolution procedure, and hence apply to every GFA problem: grammar partitioning, non-terminals static ordering, weak stability and semantic stability. Practical experiments using circularity tests for attribute grammars will show the benefit of these improvements. This paper is a shortened version of [JoP90].

1 Introduction

In optimizing compilers, we have to statically infer run-time properties of programs, so that we can take advantage of this knowledge to generate better code. For instance, we may want to know whether the value of a given variable in an expression is statically predictable, so that we can use this constant value to generate better code (this is called *constant folding*). It turns out that many similar problems, when expressed formally, all reduce to solving a set of equations on the program graph; these equations relate pieces of information attached to immediately neighboring nodes, and edges are used to propagate this information. The basis of Data Flow Analysis (DFA) is that the method to solve these equations is independent from the semantics of the equations themselves, so that it is possible to devise a generic resolution procedure [CoC79]. This procedure is parametrized by the specific equations of the problem at hand. Any improvement of this generic resolution procedure will hence benefit to every DFA problem. The DFA framework has been universally acknowledged, and most of the problems dealing with static analysis of programs are expressed in terms of DFA [JoM81, ASU86].

Grammar Flow Analysis (GFA) is a technique recently introduced by Reinhard Wilhelm and Ulrich Möncke [MöW82, Mön87] that transports that theory to the computation

---

*Authors' address: INRIA, Domaine de Voluceau, Rocquencourt, BP 105, F-78153 LE CHESNAY Cedex, France. E-mail: {jourdan,parigot}@minos.inria.fr.

of properties of context-free grammars. GFA is performed on the grammar graph, whose nodes correspond either to non-terminals or productions, and whose edges are drawn according to the productions. Propagation functions are defined on productions, and carry some information that is attached to the non-terminals. According to the direction of these functions, we distinguish bottom-up and top-down GFA problems. In a bottom-up problem, the information attached to the LHS non-terminal of a production depends on the information attached to the non-terminals in the RHS. Examples of bottom-up problems are:

- computing the $First_k$ sets on a context-free grammar [ASU86, MöW82];

- computing the synthesized dependency graphs in an attribute grammar (AG) and testing it for circularity [Knu68, LoP75, DJL84, JoP88, DJL88];

- pre-computing the sets of matching patterns in the construction of a bottom-up tree pattern matcher [HoO82, Mön85].

In a top-down GFA problem, the information attached to a non-terminal in the RHS of a production depends on the information attached to the LHS non-terminal, but generally also on the previously computed results of an associated bottom-up problem, which are attached to the non-terminals in the RHS [Mön87]. Examples of these are:

- computing the $Follow_k$ sets on a context-free grammar, given the $First_k$ sets;

- computing the inherited dependency graphs in an AG, which depend on the synthesized ones;

- finding the sets of totally-ordered partitions in the construction of an l-ordered AG equivalent to a given non-circular AG [EnF82]; this computation also uses the synthesized dependency graphs.

Although bottom-up and top-down GFA problems are not symmetric in the same way as e.g. forward and backward DFA problems, they are solved by similar generic procedures.

In some cases, the complexity of a GFA problem can be reduced by computing only approximations of the exact solution [Mön87]. This subject will not be addressed in this abstract, but it is in the full report [JoP90].

As can be seen from the list of examples given above, GFA is a very general and useful technique for every kind of language processors. Thus, every improvement of the general resolution procedure will benefit to the whole broad domain of GFA. The issue of how to efficiently implement the general GFA resolution procedure was only briefly touched in the original papers [Mön87]. Conversely, much work has been done to efficiently solve a particular GFA problem, namely testing an AG for non-circularity. The purpose of this paper is to exhibit a number of more or less well-known techniques, originally devised for that specific purpose, that actually apply to the whole domain of GFA and can improve the resolution of *every* GFA problem. These techniques are:

- *grammar partitioning* [Che81], in which the grammar is decomposed into subgrammars according to the "derives from" relation, and the subgrammars are processed in an order derived from the quotient relation;

- *non-terminals static ordering* [Par85, JoP88], in which the same "derives from" relation is used to derive a near-optimal order for processing the non-terminals;

- *weak stability* [DJL84], which allows to skip the processing of non-terminals and productions that are known to derive only terminal trees;

- *semantic stability* [Par85, Che85, JoP88], which takes into account the "age" of each piece of information to avoid redundant computations.

The rest of the paper is organized as follows. Section 2 will present in an informal way the theory of Grammar Flow Analysis; in particular, a naive resolution algorithm will be given. Sections 3 to 6 will each be devoted to one of the four improvement techniques listed above, and the subsequent section discusses their combination. Section 8 briefly presents the results of a practical experiment using non-circularity tests for AGs as the test case, together with a short discussion thereof. The paper ends with some concluding remarks and the list of references. More details, examples and results can be found in [JoP90].

The improvements will be described in such a way that they are readily applicable to bottom-up GFA problems. Their transposition for top-down problems will generally not be detailed, but it is an easy exercise left to the interested reader (see also [JoP90]).

2 Bases of Grammar Flow Analysis

This section presents only briefly and informally the basic notions, data structures and algorithms involved in GFA. For a more comprehensive discussion see Möncke [Mön87]. The following formulation is borrowed and adapted from Möncke & Wilhelm [MöW82].

2.1 The grammar graph

Let $G = \langle N, T, P, Z \rangle$ be a context-free grammar, with N the set of non-terminals, T the set of terminals—which are irrelevant to GFA[1]—, P the set of productions and Z the start symbol. Each production will be of the form $p : X_0 \rightarrow X_1 X_2 \cdots X_{n_p}$, where n_p is the number of non-terminals in the RHS of p and the terminals are omitted. The occurrences of non-terminals in a production are numbered from left to right, $p[0] = X_0$ being the LHS one, and $p[i] = X_i$, $0 < i \leq n_p$, being the RHS ones.

The grammar graph is a directed graph $G = \langle V, E \rangle$ with set of vertices $V = N \cup P$ and set of edges E defined as follows:

$$\forall p \in P, \forall X \in N, (p, X) \in E \iff X = p[0]$$
$$\forall p \in P, \forall X \in N, (X, p) \in E \iff \exists i, 0 < i \leq n_p, X = p[i]$$

---

[1] They are indeed irrelevant to the GFA framework and resolution procedure, even if they are relevant to a particular problem, e.g. for *First*$_k$ and *Follow*$_k$.

2.2 GFA problems

A GFA problem is a triple $\langle \mathbf{L}, (\phi_p)_{p \in P}, (\psi_X)_{X \in N} \rangle$. The first component, $\mathbf{L}$, is the space of flow information; pieces of information are attached to non-terminals as $L_X \in \mathbf{L}$.[2]

The second component, $(\phi_p)_{p \in P}$, is a family of *information propagation functions*. For a bottom-up problem, and for each production p, there exists one propagation function $\phi_{p,0} : \mathbf{L}^{n_p} \mapsto \mathbf{L}$, which maps a tuple of elements of flow information $(L_{p[i]})_{0 < i \leq n_p}$ on the non-terminals in the RHS of production p into an element of information to be attached to the LHS non-terminal. For a top-down problem, and for each production p, there exists a list of propagation functions $\phi_{p,i} : \mathbf{L} \mapsto \mathbf{L}$ $(0 < i \leq n_p)$, which map an element of flow information on the LHS non-terminal of p into an element of information for $p[i]$, $0 < i \leq n_p$. Each of the $\phi_{p,0}$ and $\phi_{p,i}$ may use other information defined on the grammar, but assuming not to depend on the problem. In addition, in a top-down problem, the $\phi_{p,i}$ may use information on all the non-terminals of p that was previously computed for an associated bottom-up problem.

Lastly, $(\psi_X)_{X \in N}$ is a family of *information combination functions*, $\psi_X : \mathbf{L}^{|P_X|} \mapsto \mathbf{L}$ where

$$P_X = \begin{cases} \{p \in P \mid p[0] = X\} & \text{for a bottom-up problem} \\ \{p \in P \mid \exists i, 0 < i \leq n_p, p[i] = X\} & \text{for a top-down problem}^3 \end{cases}$$

P_X is thus the set of productions in which the information attached to X is to be computed, according to the direction of the problem at hand; then, ψ_X combines the elements of information computed on each of these productions into a single element to be attached to X. Note that the ψ_X must be commutative for the problem to be well-defined.

2.3 The solution of a GFA problem

The solution on grammar G of the DFA problem $\langle \mathbf{L}, (\phi_p)_{p \in P}, (\psi_X)_{X \in N} \rangle$ is a set $\{L_X\}_{X \in N}$, where $L_X \in \mathbf{L}$ for each X in N, of elements of information attached to each non-terminal, verifying one of the following equations:[4]

- for a bottom-up problem:

$$\forall X \in N, L_X = \psi_X[\phi_{p,0}[L_{p[i]}]_{0 < i \leq n_p}]_{p \in P_X} \qquad (1)$$

- for a top-down problem:

$$\forall X \in N, L_X = \psi_X[\phi_{p,i}(L_{p[0]})]_{p \in P_X, p[i]=X} \qquad (2)$$

These equations express that the solution is a combined fixed point of a set of functions, and can thus be computed by iteration over the grammar graph.

---

[2]For some problems there is actually one information space $\mathbf{L}_X$ per non-terminal X, but this does not change much the formulation.

[3]In that case, P_X is really a multiset since a same non-terminal may appear more than once in the RHS of some production.

[4]In these two equations, the notation $f[x_j]_{j \in S}$ stands for $f(x_{j_1}, x_{j_2}, \ldots, x_{j_k})$ if $S = \langle j_1, j_2, \ldots, j_k \rangle$.

```
Algorithm A₀ (G: grammar):
foreach X ∈ N do L_X ← ⊥ endfor;
repeat convergence ← true;
    foreach p ∈ P do
    let X = p[0];
    old ← L_X;
    L_X ← ψ'_X(φ_{p,0}(L_{p[1]}, L_{p[2]}, ..., L_{p[n_p]}), L_X)
    if L_X ≠ old then
        convergence ← false
    endif
    endfor
until convergence.
```

Figure 1: Naive GFA resolution algorithm

2.4 A naive resolution algorithm

In this section we present an algorithm to solve bottom-up DFA problems (the adaptation to top-down ones is obvious; it can be found in [JoP90]). We assume that the information space $\mathbf{L}$ is partially ordered with a bottom element $\perp$ and that a least fixed point is sought. We also assume that the combination functions ψ_X are *incremental*, i.e.,

$$\psi_X(\gamma_1, \gamma_2, \ldots, \gamma_{|P_X|}) = \psi'_X(\gamma_1, \psi'_X(\gamma_2, \cdots \psi'_X(\gamma_{|P_X|}, \perp) \cdots))$$

for some function ψ'_X. This condition is not absolutely necessary but we assume it holds to make the algorithm simpler. Also, all of these assumptions are verified by each of the GFA problems listed in section 1, because in those cases the information space is a set and the combination functions are the union function, which is incremental. The naive resolution algorithm is presented in Fig. 1.[5] It is naive in the sense that it is a simple derivation of the fixed point equation (1) and there exists no special order to process the non-terminals and the productions, i.e., the grammar graph is visited in a totally random order. The purpose of the improvements to be presented in the following sections is to determine a near-optimal order and to eliminate redundant computations, such that information is propagated faster along the graph and convergence is reached faster.

As a special but quite common case[6] we derive a version of this algorithm for problems in which the information space is structured as a set of sets, i.e., each L_X is itself a set, and in which the combination functions are the set-theoretic union. In this case, the propagation functions are more easily expressed in terms of individual elements of these sets. We hence assume that, for each production p, there exists an auxiliary function $\phi'_{p,0} : L_{p[1]} \times L_{p[2]} \times \cdots \times L_{p[n_p]} \mapsto L_{p[0]}$, which maps a tuple of information elements on the RHS non-terminals into an element of information for the LHS one. The whole propagation function is then defined as the set-theoretic generalization of $\phi'_{p,0}$, that is:

$$\phi_{p,0}(L_{p[1]}, L_{p[2]}, \ldots, L_{p[n_p]}) = \{\phi'_{p,0}(\gamma_1, \gamma_2, \ldots, \gamma_{n_p}) \mid \gamma_i \in L_{p[i]}, 0 < i \leq n_p\}$$

---

[5]The names of the algorithms are chosen to recall those of the practical experiment of section 8, which are themselves a subset of those used in the full report [JoP90].

[6]As an evidence, Möncke considers only this case in his reference paper on GFA [Mön87]. This is the case for instance of the $First_k$ and synthesized dependency graphs problems.

Algorithm A_3 (G: grammar):

init:	**foreach** $X \in N$ **do** $L_X \leftarrow \emptyset$ **endfor**;
iterate:	**repeat** convergence $\leftarrow$ true;
select-nt:	**foreach** $X \in N$ **do**
select-prod:	**foreach** $p \in P_X$ **do**
combine:	**foreach** $\gamma_1 \in L_{p[1]}, \ldots, \gamma_{n_p} \in L_{p[n_p]}$ **do**
compute:	$\gamma_0 \leftarrow \phi'_{p,0}(\gamma_1, \ldots, \gamma_{n_p})$;
test:	**if** $\gamma_0 \notin L_X$ **then**
increase:	$L_X \leftarrow L_X \cup \{\gamma_0\}$;
	convergence $\leftarrow$ **false**
	endif
	endfor
	endfor
	endfor
	until convergence.

Figure 2: Naive algorithm for set-based problems

The resulting algorithm is presented in Fig. 2.[7] Our improvements will be expressed on this latter algorithm, with the help of the labels attached to some of the statements. The transposition to the more general algorithm will not be given. The purpose of the improvements will be to reduce as much as possible the number of "compute" and "test" steps, which are assumed to be expensive[8] and hence dominate the running time.

3 Grammar Partitioning

As can be seen from the definition in section 2.2, the information flows exclusively along the edges of the grammar graph. It is thus natural, in order to have this information propagate faster, to take into account the structure of this graph, rather than picking non-terminals and productions at random. The first idea that comes to the mind is hence to partition the grammar graph into strongly connected components and process those components in the order defined by the quotient relation. Note that this technique was used right from the beginning in DFA, where the program is decomposed into a control flow graph of basic blocks, and blocks are processed from inner to outer [CoC79, JoM81].

The order in which productions are processed depends on the order in which non-terminals are processed; more precisely, each time a non-terminal is processed, all the productions of which it is the LHS symbol are processed (line labeled "select-prod" in Algorithm A_3). This must be so in order to ensure that when a non-terminal is referenced in the RHS of a production, the information attached to it is as complete as possible. We hence require, when computing the strongly connected components of the grammar graph, that every production vertex be in the same component as the vertex corresponding to

---

[7]Note that we already have decreased the random factor by subordinating the choice of the production to process to the choice of its LHS non-terminal.

[8]In non-circularity tests for AGs for instance, these steps involve the computation of a transitive closure and testing the membership of a (sometimes big) graph in a set of graphs.

Algorithm A_4 (G: grammar):
build the graphs Γ and Γ_0 from G;
apply algorithms for Sorting, Entry Points Priority, Other Symbols Priority;[a]
for $i \leftarrow 1$ **to** K **do**
    apply Algorithm A_0 or A_3 to subgrammar B_i;
    discard or store away the information attached to non-terminals of priority i
endfor.

---

[a]If necessary, more details on these algorithms can be found in the original works [Che81, DJL84] and in [JoP90].

Figure 3: GFA resolution algorithm using partitioning

its LHS non-terminal. We thus define the following auxiliary relation:

$$\forall X, Y \in N, X \,\Gamma\, Y \iff \exists p \in P, \exists i, 0 < i \le n_p, X = p[i] \wedge Y = p[0]$$

Γ is the "derives from" relation on non-terminals, and its graph is the same as the grammar graph in which the production vertices are merged with their LHS non-terminal vertices.

The strongly connected components of Γ define the subgrammars of G we are interested in. Moreover, if Γ_0 is the quotient relation associated with Γ, Γ_0 defines a partial order to be used for processing these subgrammars. Since by construction Γ_0 is acyclic, a simple topological sort will derive from it a total order. We hence denote the subgrammars as $B_1, B_2, \ldots, B_K$, where K is the total number of strongly connected components of G, so that B_i will be processed before B_{i+1} (note: $Z \in B_K$).

For reasons to be explained later, it is interesting to distinguish *entry points* and *output points*[9] of these subgrammars B:

$$\forall X \in B, X \in EP(B) \iff \exists Y \notin B, X \,\Gamma\, Y$$
$$\forall X \in B, X \in OP(B) \iff \exists Y \notin B, Y \,\Gamma\, X \vee \nexists Y \in N, Y \,\Gamma\, X$$

Entry points of a subgrammar are thus those non-terminals that derive from non-terminals in subgrammars to be processed later, and output points are those non-terminals that derive into non-terminals of subgrammars that have already been processed or derive only terminal productions. Output points will not be used before next section.

The order for processing subgrammars is used to assign a *priority* to each non-terminal, that is the rank of the stage after which that non-terminal will no longer be referenced. An entry point of a subgrammar will be assigned the priority (rank) of the last subgrammar that references it; other non-terminals will be assigned the priority of their own subgrammar. This notion of priority is useful to reduce the space consumption of the algorithm, because after stage i we can either store in secondary memory or discard completely—if the problem at hand allows it—the information attached to non-terminals of priority i. As will be shown in section 8, this technique is very effective. The resulting algorithm is presented in Fig. 3.

---

[9]As can be seen from the definitions, the names of "entry" and "output" points are hence rather misleading, because they are inconsistent with the direction of the edges in the grammar graph. We however keep them for the sake of compatibility with previous works [DJL84, JoP88].

For the top-down case, we must use the inverse of relation Γ and swap the roles of entry and output points. The strongly connected components will then be the same, but the processing order will be different; in that case, Z belongs to B_1.

4 Non-Terminals Static Ordering

Grammar partitioning uses the "derives from" relation to exhibit subgrammars and derive an optimal order for their processing; it however leaves unspecified the order for processing non-terminals and productions *inside* each subgrammar. The purpose of this section is to establish a near-optimal order for processing non-terminals. Since by definition each subgrammar is a strongly connected component for the "derives from" relation, the latter is not sufficient to define the processing order, i.e., it is impossible to find a total order compatible with Γ. Heuristics will help make the choice.

The first heuristic will be to order the non-terminals of a given subgrammar from output points to entry points; this order is indeed the "closest" to relation Γ. The core of the ordering algorithm is thus a topological sort based on relation Γ and starting with output points. The sort is however modified to solve three difficulties:

1. Since we want output points to be the starting point of the topological sort, we must first delete from $\Gamma|_B$ every edge whose tail (sink) is an output point, except those whose head (source) is also an output point. Note that each output point is the tail of at least one such "back edge", otherwise it would not belong to the subgrammar.

2. We then consider only output points and edges connecting two output points, and topologically order this subgraph. If this is not possible because of a cycle, we make an arbitrary choice in the cycle.

3. We then proceed to topologically sort the rest of the subgrammar. If a yet unbroken cycle shows up, we make an arbitrary choice in the cycle.

The resulting algorithm is completely detailed in Jourdan & Parigot [JoP88]. To integrate it in the complete GFA algorithm, we need to modify A_3 as follows:

- add a call to the non-terminals static ordering algorithm in line "init";
- use this order in line "select-nt".

As for the order in which to process productions in each P_X (line "select-prod"), none is better than any other because all the non-terminals in the RHS have been processed earlier in the current iteration (apart from back edges, but this is taken into account by the global convergence flag). We can only note that directly recursive productions should be processed after the others. The modified algorithm is not shown and left to the reader.

For top-down GFA, the basic idea is the same except that we use the inverse of Γ and that the roles of entry and output points are reversed. In this case the resulting order is not necessarily the inverse of the bottom-up order.

The advantages of this ordering is that, as expected, information propagates faster, as shown by the important reduction of the number of iterations (line "iterate") needed to reach convergence (see section 8).

Note that this technique is similar to an improvement of DFA called "reasonable node listing", however its efficiency is particularly important for GFA.

5 Weak Stability

Weak stability allows to skip recomputations of relations for non-terminals and/or productions that are known to generate only finite trees of height $\leq i$ and hence become "stable" after iteration i (line "iterate" in A_3). This is done as follows:

1. at the beginning of the algorithm (line "init"), no non-terminal or production is weakly stable;

2. after each iteration (end of loop "iterate"):

   (a) mark as weakly stable those productions that have only weakly stable non-terminals in their RHS;[10]

   (b) mark as weakly stable those non-terminals that derive only weakly stable productions;

3. in the course of an iteration, skip weakly stable non-terminals (line "select-nt") and productions (line "select-prod").

When used alone, this technique is not very efficient because it fails on every recursive non-terminal. However it is not totally useless, as shown in sections 7 and 8. An incremental variant of this technique is described in the full report [JoP90].

6 Semantic Stability

This improvement, called semantic stability,[11] aims at saving execution time by drastically reducing the number of redundant computations. It is based on the observation that, if the information used in the basic step of the algorithm (inner loop of A_0 or line labeled "compute" in A_3) is "old" enough to have been processed during an earlier iteration, then it is useless to process it again in the current iteration, which means that we may skip the basic step. Of course, doing so is correct only if the information space is partially ordered and if the propagation and combination functions are monotonic, i.e., if skipping a basic step with "old" parameters does not lose any information because that information is already present in the "old" value of L_X, where X is the non-terminal at hand. Note that the formulation of algorithm A_0 should be slightly modified to make this apparent. Note also that these conditions are not very constraining; in particular they are verified in every set-based GFA problem (see section 2.4).

Thus the basic idea of this improvement is to associate a "time-stamp" with each piece of information and run the basic step only if at least one such piece of information appearing in the RHS of the computation step is not "old" enough to have already been processed. In the special case of set-based GFA problems, this time-stamp can even be associated with each element of the sets attached to non-terminals, and tested in the combinations in which this element appears (line labeled "combine" in A_3). In that case, the new algorithm is as presented in Fig. 4.

---

[10]If partitioning is also used, non-terminals in already processed subgrammars are considered as weakly stable.

[11]because, as opposed to the previous ones, it does not take into account the syntactic information represented by the grammar graph.

```
                    Algorithm A₉ (G: grammar):
        init:       foreach X ∈ N do Lₓ ← ∅ endfor;
                    it ← 0;
     iterate:       repeat convergence ← true;
                        it ← it + 1;
   select-nt:           foreach X ∈ N do
 select-prod:               foreach p ∈ Pₓ do
     combine:                   foreach γ₁ ∈ L_{p[1]}, ..., γ_{n_p} ∈ L_{p[n_p]} do
  check-time:                       if ∃i, 0 < i ≤ n_p, time(γᵢ) ≥ max-time(it, p) then
     compute:                           γ₀ ← φ'_{p,0}(γ₁, ..., γ_{n_p});
        test:                           if γ₀ ∉ Lₓ then
    increase:                               time(γ₀) ← ⟨it, p⟩;
                                            Lₓ ← Lₓ ∪ {γ₀};
                                            convergence ← false
                                        endif
                                    endif
                                endfor
                            endfor
                        endfor
                    until convergence.
```

Figure 4: GFA resolution algorithm using semantic stability

The correctness of this algorithm strongly depends on the choice of the function "max-time". Assuming that the productions are numbered, we define the time-stamp of an element of information as the time when it was created, that is the ordered pair $\langle it, p \rangle$ where it is the number of the iteration and p the number of the production being processed. These pairs are lexicographically ordered.

A weak version of "max-time" is

$$\text{max-time}(it, p) = \langle it - 2, 0 \rangle$$

in which we forget about the production. Indeed, any element of information created during iteration $it - 2$ has been processed at latest during iteration $it - 1$ and processing it again during iteration it or later is redundant.

To achieve a finer condition, we must require that non-terminals and productions are always processed in the same order during each iteration (lines "select-nt" and "select-prod"). In this case, we can assume that the number of a production is the rank at which it is processed during an iteration, and the definition of "max-time" can be refined as:

$$\text{max-time}(it, p) = \begin{cases} \langle it - 1, p - 1 \rangle & \text{if } p \neq 1 \\ \langle it - 2, |P| \rangle & \text{if } p = 1 \end{cases}$$

because any element of information created at $\langle it, p \rangle$ can be used immediately during the rest of the iteration (i.e., at $\langle it, p' \rangle$ with $p' > p$) or during the first part of the next one (i.e., at $\langle it + 1, p' \rangle$ with $p' \leq p$) and thus becomes redundant after $\langle it + 1, p \rangle$.

The figures of section 8 will show that this simple idea is very effective.

7   Combination

All of the four previously presented improvements can be used alone or in combination.

The most effective technique is grammar partitioning. This is because it allows to tailor the number of iterations in each subgrammar to the "semantic complexity" of the GFA problem for this subgrammar, rather than having to process the whole grammar during a number of iterations that is in any case at least equal to the maximum number of iterations in each subgrammar. Furthermore it is the only improvement that reduces space consumption, because the results are produced and can be disposed of incrementally rather than in a single burst at the end.

Non-terminals static ordering reduces the number of iterations by ensuring as much as possible that all uses of some information occur after the time when it is computed. It can be used independently from partitioning by applying it to the whole grammar, the only entry point being the start symbol and the output points being the non-terminal deriving only terminal productions (if the grammar is assumed to be reduced). However its combination with partitioning is more effective since the advantages of the latter are fully retained: time is reduced because partitioning ensures that information on a subgrammar is completely computed before being used in other subgrammars, and space is reduced because we can forget about information attached to non-terminals that will no longer be referenced.

When used alone, weak stability is not very effective because it cannot act on recursive non-terminals. However, grammar partitioning offers more opportunities for weak stability, because non-terminals outside the subgrammar at hand are considered as weakly stable, even if they are recursive in their own subgrammar.

Syntax-based techniques reduce the number of basic computation steps by using static information (the shape of the grammar graph), whereas semantic stability aims at the same goal by using dynamic time-stamping techniques. One could thus think that the latter is subsumed by the former because, since information propagates faster, most of the basic steps are actually useful and cannot be eliminated by semantic stability. As the figures of section 8 will show, this is partly true, but it appears that the combination of both techniques is more effective than each of them taken separately; this is especially true when the semantic complexity of some (sub-) grammar is high, i.e., when the sets L_X contain many different elements.

8   Practical Results

To illustrate in practice the effects of our GFA improvement techniques, we have chosen the non-circularity test for AGs, because they fully illustrate the power of the GFA improvements.

8.1   Rough results

We have implemented several versions of the non-circularity test as part of the FNC-2 AG processing system [JoP89]. The various algorithms differ in which improvement technique(s) they use; they are detailed in Table 1. All of them use *covering* [LoP75,

	partitioning	ordering	weak stability	sem. stability
A_3				
A_4	•			
A_5		•		
A_6	•	•		
A_7			•	
A_8	•	•	•	
A_9				•
A_{10}	•	•	•	•

Table 1: Features of the various algorithms

	simproc	asm	pl1_c	pascal	simula
nt	10	58	139	115	126
pr	21	216	376	216	244
rhs_{max}	4	2	4	6	6
rhs_{ave}	1.14	0.46	1.07	1.18	1.13
att_{max}	8	10	16	15	17
att_{ave}	4.60	3.62	8.90	7.39	7.28
K	5	57	92	58	58
d_{max}	1	2	3	4	4
d_{ave}	1	1.07	1.04	1.20	1.10
tcl_{circ}	21	267	389	457	268

Table 2: Characteristics of the example AGs

DJL84], an approximation that strongly reduces the practical complexity of the non-circularity test.

These algorithms were tried on five practical AGs of increasing complexity. All of these AGs are non-circular. We will use the following notations:

- For each AG:

  nt number of non-terminals

  pr number of productions

  rhs_{max}, rhs_{ave} maximum and average number of non-terminals in the RHS of any production

  att_{max}, att_{ave} maximum and average number of attributes per non-terminal

  K number of syntactic equivalence classes (subgrammars)

  The characteristics of our five AGs are presented in Table 2.

- For each algorithm:

  d_{max}, d_{ave} maximum and average number of graphs in any L_X at the end of the computation[12]

---

[12]Because of covering, some L_X's might be temporarily larger than that in the course of the computation, if one newly created graph happens to cover two or more old graphs.

$R_{\max}$ maximum number of co-resident graphs at any time, i.e., $\max_{time}(\sum_{X \in N} |L_X|)$

tcl number of transitive closures (basic steps) computed

tcl_{circ} number of transitive closures computed for actually testing the non-circularity (see below)

Since the three figures $d_{\max}$, d_{ave} and tcl_{circ} characterize the results of the problem at hand, they have been "factored out" and also appear in Table 2.

- For algorithms not using partitioning:

it number of iterations over the whole grammar

- For algorithms using partitioning:

$it_{\max}$ maximum number of iterations over any subgrammar

it_{ave} same in weighted average, i.e., with obvious notations, $(\sum_{j=1}^{K} it_j \times pr_j)/pr$

Statistics gathered from the execution of the various algorithms are presented in Table 3.

The tcl_{circ} figure is related to the way we actually test the non-circularity. Briefly said, we do it globally in a final pass—over either the whole grammar, when partitioning is not used, or each subgrammar—after all the synthesized dependency graphs have been computed, rather than incrementally on every graph. More details can be found in the full report [JoP90]. Let us only note that tcl_{circ} is interesting on its own since, being the number of final graph combinations, it is a very good measure of the "semantic complexity" of the non-circularity problem for a given AG.

In the naive versions of the algorithm in which no special order is computed, the processing order (lines "select-nt" and "select-prod") is determined by the textual appearance in the grammar source file. Since practical grammars are generally presented in a top-down manner, using textual order is close to the worst case for bottom-up GFA problems!

When partitioning is used, the "useless" graphs (see section 3) are actually discarded rather than stored in secondary memory, and their space is reclaimed by a specialized garbage collector. The $R_{\max}$ figure is computed by this garbage collector.

8.2 Discussion

Algorithm A_4 uses only partitioning. The gains in time (i.e., in the number of basic steps executed) are already quite good, especially on AGs with simple syntactic structure (asm, $pl1\_c$). This is because information propagates faster, as shown by the decrease of the number of iterations ($it_{\max}(A_4) \leq it(A_3)$ and $it_{ave}(A_4) \ll it(A_3)$). The most important advantage of grammar partitioning is however the gains in space it allows to achieve: compare the $R_{\max}$ figures for A_4 w.r.t. A_3.

When non-terminals static ordering is used alone (A_5), it also makes information propagate faster; this is proved by the strong decrease of the number of iterations w.r.t. A_3. However it has no influence on space consumption. Comparing the results for A_4 and A_5 gives interesting insights on the way grammar partitioning and non-terminals static ordering act when used separately. Grammar partitioning is more effective on

		simproc	asm	pl1_c	pascal	simula
A_3	R_{max}	11	67	147	149	154
	it	7	8	15	21	19
	tcl	145	2,260	5,125	9,768	5,099
A_4	R_{max}	5	21	30	57	80
	it_{max}	4	3	13	21	14
	it_{ave}	3.10	1.12	4.31	7.16	8.29
	tcl	78	561	1,924	6,031	2,632
A_5	R_{max}	11	64	146	147	182
	it	4	3	9	9	7
	tcl	101	1,064	3,645	4,288	2,376
A_6	R_{max}	5	21	30	58	99
	it_{max}	4	3	6	8	7
	it_{ave}	2.76	1.08	2.37	3.41	4.30
	tcl	73	556	1,304	2,746	1,756
A_7	R_{max}	11	67	147	149	154
	it	7	8	15	21	19
	tcl	109	900	3,555	8,446	3,865
A_8	R_{max}	5	21	30	58	99
	it_{max}	4	3	6	8	7
	it_{ave}	2.76	1.08	2.37	3.41	4.30
	tcl	56	545	1,160	2,679	1,655
A_9	R_{max}	11	67	147	149	154
	it	7	8	15	21	19
	tcl	57	588	1,165	1,942	1,628
A_{10}	R_{max}	5	21	30	58	99
	it_{max}	4	3	6	8	7
	it_{ave}	2.76	1.08	2.37	3.41	4.30
	tcl	49	540	915	1,661	1,246

Table 3: Execution statistics

grammars with simple syntactic structure because it allows not to process again at each iteration a large share of simple subgrammars. However, for more complicated examples with "big" subgrammars (*pascal, simula*), the bad influence of randomly processing the non-terminals inside each subgrammar shows up again, which explains that non-terminals static ordering is more effective in these cases. Anyway, the real winner is the combination of both techniques (A_6), which gives better (and generally much better) results than each of them taken separately: there is a real synergy between these two improvements. The gains in space achieved by grammar partitioning alone are retained in its combination with non-terminals static ordering.

Weak stability used alone (A_7) has a perceptible influence only because the bare algorithm (A_3) is really bad and needs a lot of iterations to reach convergence; this is especially true when the grammar has many terminal productions (*asm*). When weak stability is used in combination with grammar partitioning and non-terminals static ordering (A_8), this influence is however less important, but nevertheless not negligible.

When comparing A_8 with A_3, we can see that the combination of all syntax-based improvements reaches its goal, which is to make information propagate faster, in a quite effective way. Furthermore space consumption is reduced by virtue of grammar partitioning.

Semantic stability used alone (A_9) is also a real winner: it performs roughly as well as the combination of syntax-based improvements (a little better for AGs with a high semantic complexity such as *pascal*, a little worse for AGs with a low syntactic complexity such as *asm*). However we must note that this is achieved at higher bookkeeping costs, and that semantic stability has no influence on space consumption (the R_{max} figures are the same for A_9 as for A_3).

Combining semantic stability with the syntax-based techniques is always profitable (compare A_{10} with A_8 on one hand and A_9 on the other hand). This means that neither the dynamic approach (semantic stability) nor the static one (syntax-based techniques) subsumes the other and, rather, that they complement each other.

All in all, the four techniques we have presented are quite effective in reducing the practical complexity of GFA problems. Comparing the results for A_{10} w.r.t. A_3 suffices to be convinced of that. To conclude the discussion on the benefits of our improvements, let us examine the processing of a "simple" subgrammar: we need at least one iteration to construct the graphs, another one to check that convergence is reached (this one may be suppressed by weak stability) and, in our scheme, a final one for actually testing the non-circularity. Thus, for a "simple" grammar, the total number of transitive closures should be of the order of three times the tcl_{circ} figure. With all our improvements we reach this behavior for our three simplest AGs, and we reach close to it for the two other ones. This is, in our opinion, an indication (but *not* a formal proof) that our improvements reach close to optimality.

9 Conclusion

This paper showed that Grammar Flow Analysis is an interesting computation framework for many classical problems dealing with grammars. It also showed that simple techniques could drastically improve the resolution of those problems and were able to reach close to optimality, while being easy to implement. Practical experiments show that problems that were believed to be intractable because of their computational cost—e.g. circularity tests for AGs—now become quite feasible in practice by using the improvement techniques we described. Furthermore, these techniques are so effective that we have used them in many stages in the FNC-2 system (SNC test, DNC test, OAG test, ...), which allows to cascade these stages while keeping a reasonable execution time (less than 80 seconds to build a complete optimized evaluator for our *pascal* AG).

While the basic techniques for implementing GFA are now well understood, there stays to discover new application fields. We believe that GFA and its efficient implementation will give a new boost to the use of grammars as a basic tool of computer science.

References

[ASU86] A. V. Aho, R. Sethi & J. D. Ullman, *Compilers: Principles, Techniques and Tools*, Addison Wesley, Reading, MA, 1986.

[Che81] K. S. Chebotar, "Some Modifications of Knuth's Algorithm for Verifying Cyclicity of Attribute Grammars," *Progr. and Computer Software* 7, 1 (Jan. 1981), 58–61.

[Che85] ———, private communication, 1985.

[CoC79] P. Cousot & R. Cousot, "Systematic Design of Program Analysis Frameworks," in *6th ACM Symp. on Principles of Progr. Languages*, San Antonio, TX, 269–282, Jan. 1979.

[DJL84] P. Deransart, M. Jourdan & B. Lorho, "Speeding up Circularity Tests for Attribute Grammars," *Acta Inform.* 21 (Dec. 1984), 375–391.

[DJL88] ———, *Attribute Grammars: Definitions, Systems and Bibliography*, Lect. Notes in Comp. Sci. #323, Springer-Verlag, New York–Heidelberg–Berlin, Aug. 1988.

[EnF82] J. Engelfriet & G. Filè, "Simple Multi-Visit Attribute Grammars," *J. Comput. System Sci.* 24, 3 (June 1982), 283–314.

[HoO82] C. M. Hoffmann & M. J. O'Donnell, "Pattern Matching in Trees," *J. ACM* 29, 1 (Jan. 1982), 68–95.

[JoM81] N. D. Jones & S. S. Muchnick, eds., *Program Flow Analysis: Theory and Applications*, Prentice-Hall, Englewood Cliffs, NJ, 1981.

[JoP88] M. Jourdan & D. Parigot, "More on Speeding up Circularity Tests for Attribute Grammars," rapport RR-828, INRIA, Rocquencourt, Apr. 1988.

[JoP89] ———, *The FNC-2 System User's Guide and Reference Manual* release 0.4, INRIA, Rocquencourt, Feb. 1989. This manual is periodically updated.

[JoP90] ———, "Techniques for Improving Grammar Flow Analysis," report to appear, INRIA, Rocquencourt, 1990.

[Knu68] D. E. Knuth, "Semantics of Context-free Languages," *Math. Systems Theory* 2, 2 (June 1968), 127–145. Correction: *Math. Systems Theory* 5, 1 (Mar. 1971), 95–96.

[LoP75] B. Lorho & C. Pair, "Algorithms for Checking Consistency of Attribute Grammars," in *Proving and Improving Programs*, Arc et Senans, G. Huet & G. Kahn, eds., 29–54, INRIA, Rocquencourt, July 1975.

[Mön85] U. Möncke, "Generierung von Systemen zur Transformation attributierter Operatorbäume: Komponenten des Systems und Mechanismen der Generierung," Diplomarbeit, Univ. des Saarlandes, Saarbrücken, 1985.

[Mön87] ———, "Grammar Flow Analysis," ESPRIT PROSPECTRA Project report S.1.3.-R-2.2, Univ. des Saarlandes, Saarbrücken, Mar. 1986, revised Jan. 1987. To appear in *ACM Trans. Progr. Languages and Systems*.

[MöW82] U. Möncke & R. Wilhelm, "Iterative Algorithms on Grammar Graphs," in *Conf. on Graphtheoretic Concepts in Computer Science (WG'82)*, Neunkirchen a.Br., H. J. Schneider & H. Göttler, eds., 177–194, Hanser Verlag, München, June 1982.

[Par85] D. Parigot, "Un système interactif de trace des circularités dans une grammaire attribuée et optimisation du test de circularité," rapport de DEA, Univ. de Paris-Sud, Orsay, Sept. 1985.

The Specificity Rule for Lazy Pattern-Matching in Ambiguous Term Rewrite Systems

Richard Kennaway
School of Information Systems, University of East Anglia
Norwich NR4 7TJ, U.K.

Abstract

Many functional languages based on term rewriting (such as Miranda[1] and ML) allow the programmer to write ambiguous rule systems, with the understanding that rules will be matched against a term in the order in which the rules are written, and that the pattern-matching of a rule against a term proceeds from left to right.

This gives a precise semantics to such ambiguous systems, but it has disadvantages. It depends on the textual ordering of the program, whereas the standard theory of term rewriting has no such concept. As a result, equational reasoning is not always valid for this semantics, defeating the primary virtue of functional languages. The semantics also fails to be fully lazy, in that sometimes a non-terminating computation will be performed on a term which has a normal form.

We define a rule, called *specificity*, for computation in ambiguous term rewrite systems. This rule (really a meta-rule) stipulates that a term rewrite rule of the system can only be used to reduce a term which matches it, if that term can never match any other rule of the system which is more specific than the given rule. One rule is more specific than another if the left-hand side of the first rule is a substitution instance of the second, and the reverse is not true. Specificity captures the intuition underlying the use of ambiguity in ML and Miranda, while also providing lazy pattern-matching.

A natural generalisation of the idea provides a semantics for Miranda's lawful types.

1. Introduction

Van voorwaarts naar achter, van links naar rechts...
From forward to back, from left to right...
— Dutch nursery rhyme

The elegance and usefulness of functional programming lie in the fact that a functional program can be read as a piece of mathematics. In many functional languages, a program consists of a set of type declarations defining some domains of values, a set of axioms asserting that certain of these values are equal, and a term; executing the program amounts to proving that term equal to some term which possesses a printable representation. Proving properties of such a functional program may be performed by equational reasoning using those same axioms (together with induction principles).

Functional programming languages in this style include SASL [20], KRC [21], Miranda [22,23], ML [10], Lazy ML [1], Hope [6], Hope+ [18], Clean [5], and most recently, Haskell [11]. However, closer inspection reveals that for all of these languages, the simple picture sketched above is not accurate. An example is provided by everyone's favorite toy functional program: the factorial.

Example 1.

$$\text{fac } 0 = 1 \qquad\qquad (1.1)$$
$$\text{fac } n = n * (\text{fac } (n-1)) \qquad\qquad (1.2)$$

---

[1] Miranda is a trademark of Research Software Ltd.

This is written in Miranda's syntax, but the point applies equally to the other languages mentioned. We assume that other rules are also present in the system to perform arithmetic. Here are the steps which a Miranda implementation performs to evaluate the expression (fac 2).

$$
\begin{array}{lll}
\text{fac 2} & \rightarrow\ 2*(\text{fac } (2-1)) & (1.2) \\
& \rightarrow\ 2*(\text{fac } 1) & (\text{arithmetic}) \\
& \rightarrow\ 2*(1*(\text{fac } (1-1))) & (1.2) \\
& \rightarrow\ 2*(1*(\text{fac } 0)) & (\text{arithmetic}) \\
& \rightarrow\ 2*(1*1) & (1.1) \\
& \rightarrow\ 2*1 & (\text{arithmetic}) \\
& \rightarrow\ 2 & (\text{arithmetic})
\end{array}
$$

But all is not as it appears. Consider the passage from $2*(\text{fac } (2-1))$ to $2*(\text{fac } 1)$. This was performed by invoking the arithmetic rule for $(2-1)$, replacing that expression by 1. However, if the rules are considered as a conventional term rewrite system, there is another possibility. We can apply rule (2) to the subterm $(\text{fac } (2-1))$, to obtain $2 * ((2-1) * (\text{fac } ((2-1)-1)))$. We could then apply the same rule to the subterm $(\text{fac } ((2-1)-1))$, obtaining $2 * ((2-1) * (((2-1)-1) * (\text{fac } (((2-1)-1)-1))))$. If we now decide to do the arithmetic, then after a few reductions we get $(2*(1*(0*(\text{fac } (-1)))))$. Depending on whether or not the rules for multiplication can rewrite a term $0*t$ to 0 without requiring t to be an integer, this term either reduces to 0, or cannot be reduced to any normal form.

Similarly, the term $(\text{fac } 0)$ is intended to be rewritten to 1 by rule 1.1, yet it matches both 1.1 and 1.2, and could be rewritten to $0*(\text{fac } (0-1))$ instead, which again will either rewrite to 0 or fail to terminate.

Thus the semantics of a program in Miranda, or any of the other languages mentioned above, is not simply the declarative semantics of a term rewrite system, but has an essential operational part: the reduction strategy which specifies which redex is to be reduced at each step. For lazy languages, such as Miranda, LML, and Haskell, the reduction strategy can be described as the following meta-rule. For the moment, we ignore Miranda's lawful types.

(1) The rules are to be matched against a term to be evaluated in the order in which they appear in the program.

(2) For each rule, the matching of its left hand side is performed from left to right, evaluating subterms as required by (3).

(3) If during pattern matching one attempts to match a constructor (i.e. a basic value or one of the tags of a user-defined type) in the pattern against a subterm whose principal function symbol is not a constructor, then the subterm is evaluated to constructor form before re-attempting the match. If the constructor form of the subterm has a different constructor than that appearing in the rule, the rule fails to match and the next rule is tried.

This "top-to-bottom left-to-right" pattern-matching strategy is common to Miranda, Lazy ML [LML], and Haskell. ML and Hope have "strict" semantics: all arguments to a function are evaluated before any pattern-matching is done. As a result, the order of pattern-matching within a rule has no effect on the semantics, but the order of rules is still significant. The above example behaves the same way in strict languages as it does in lazy languages. We are primarily interested in lazy semantics, and will not further discuss strict languages.

The functional programmer quickly becomes accustomed to this use of textual order, but it is not a trivial point. The presence of a particular strategy causes equational reasoning about the program to be not always valid. In the above example the problems stemmed from the ambiguity of the rule-systems.

However, the reduction strategy can cause problems even for regular (or, as it may shortly become known [Klo9?], *orthogonal*) rule-systems.

Example 2.

list ::= Nil | Cons num list		
f Nil Nil	= 1	(3.1)
f Nil (Cons x y)	= 2	(3.2)
f (Cons x y) z	= 3	(3.3)
g Nil Nil	= 1	(3.4)
g (Cons x y) Nil	= 2	(3.5)
g z (Cons x y)	= 3	(3.6)
c x y z	= x z y	(3.7)
loop	= loop	(3.8)

This rule-system is orthogonal, and even strongly sequential. Since g is just f, but taking the arguments in the opposite order, and c is the argument-switching combinator, we might expect c g = f to hold. But with Miranda's top-to-bottom, left-to-right evaluation strategy, we find that (f (Cons 1 Nil) loop) fails to match 3.1 and 3.2, matches rule 3.3, and is reduced to 3, but (c g (Cons 1 Nil) loop) reduces first to (g loop (Cons 1 Nil)), and then attempted matching against 3.4 invokes evaluation of loop, which fails to terminate. Thus even for well-behaved rule-systems, the built-in reduction strategy complicates proofs of properties of programs.

Top-to-bottom left-to-right pattern-matching is useful in allowing the programmer to write default rules without having to explicitly exclude from the default case all the previous cases. However, we have seen that it muddies the semantics. It also results in the ordering of the arguments to a function playing two different and conflicting roles: it directs the pattern-matching, but the programmer may also want the order of arguments to reflect their meaning, grouping related arguments together.

We will describe an alternative reduction strategy, called *specificity*, which will allow programmers to write "default" rules as in the factorial example, but without sacrificing equational reasoning. The meaning of such systems will be described by a transformation into another system which does not have such ambiguities, and to which equational reasoning is applicable.

2. Specificity

For orthogonal strongly sequential systems, Huet and Lévy showed a long time ago how to perform lazy pattern-matching independently of textual ordering [12]. They describe a reduction strategy for such systems which always selects a "needed" redex, i.e. one which must be reduced to reach the normal form of the whole term. They prove that this strategy always finds the normal form of any term which has one. Example 2 is such a system; the semantics given to it by their strategy satisfies c g = f, as desired.

We take that work for granted, and will describe a semantics for ambiguous rule-systems such as example 1, by translating them into orthogonal, strongly sequential systems, to which the Huet-Lévy strategy may then be applied.

Intuitively, the reason that the term (fac 0) should be considered to match the rule (1.1) and not (1.2) is that (1.1) is "more specific" than (1.2). If the programmer had intended (fac 0) to match (1.2), it was superfluous to write the rule (1.1). The reason that (fac (2−1)) should not be considered to match (1.2) is that the subterm (2−1) is capable of further evaluation which may, for all we know (without performing some sort of look-ahead) result in 0, causing rule (1.1) to match. Reduction of (fac (2−1)) should therefore be postponed pending further evaluation of the subterm (2−1). This is the basic idea of specificity.

A simple generalisation of this idea can also be used to give a semantics for Miranda's lawful types.

3. Definitions and notations

We assume familiarity with the basic concepts of term rewriting (see, e.g. [13,14]), and will only define our notations and the key concepts in our treatment of specificity. A term has the form $F(t_1,...,t_n)$, where $t_1,...,t_n$ ($n \geq 0$) are terms. A subterm of a term may be specified by an *address*, a finite sequence of positive integers, in an obvious way. Given a term $t = F(t_1,...,t_n)$ and an address $u = i \cdot v$ (i an integer, v an address), t/u is the term t_i/v. $\langle \rangle$ is the empty address; $t/\langle \rangle = t$. If u is an address of a subterm of t, $t[u:=t']$ is the term obtained by replacing that subterm of t by t'. An address u of t is *proper* if t/u is not a variable.

A *substitution* is a function σ from some finite set of variables to terms. $\sigma(t)$ is the result of replacing every occurrence of a variable x in t by $\sigma(x)$. An *address substitution* is a similar function defined on a finite set of addresses, and is applied to a term in the obvious way.

We write $t \leq_s t'$ if t' is a substitution instance of t. t and t' are *unifiable* if there is a t'' such that $t \leq_s t'' \geq_s t'$. We write $t \uparrow_s t'$.

These definitions extend to rewrite rules in the obvious way: if R_1 is $t_1 \rightarrow t'_1$ and R_2 is $t_2 \rightarrow t'_2$, then $R_1 \leq_s R_2$ iff for some substitution σ, $\sigma(t_1) = t_2$ and $\sigma(t'_1) = t'_2$.

A term is *linear* if no variable occurs more than once in it. A *closed* term is a term containing no variables. When dealing with linear terms, the identity of variables will often be unimportant. We may use the symbol • to indicate an occurrence of an unspecified variable, different from every other variable in the term, and ∙ to represent a tuple of distinct unspecified variables.

A *matching* of a term t into a term t' at address u of t' is a variable substitution σ such that $\sigma(t) = t'/u$. An address v of t' is *matched by* this matching if $u \leq v$, v/u is an address of t, and $t/(v/u)$ is not a variable.

3.1. Preorderings

We shall be defining several preorderings besides the $\leq_s$ defined above. For any preordering $\leq_x$, we define the associated relations. $\geq_x$, $<_x$, and $>_x$ in the obvious way. u_x is the least upper bound operator (defined up to equivalence in the preordering). We also define:

$$A \uparrow_x B \quad \Leftrightarrow \quad \exists C. \ (A \leq_x C) \wedge (B \leq_x C)$$
$$\Downarrow_x A \quad = \quad \text{the set of } \leq_x\text{-minimal members of the set A.}$$
$$\Uparrow_x A \quad = \quad \text{the set of } \leq_x\text{-maximal members of the set A.}$$

For example, $t \uparrow_s t'$ means that t and t' are unifiable; when this is so, $t u_s t'$ exists and is their most general unifier.

A *term rewrite system* (or *TRS*) is a triple $(\Sigma, \mathcal{R}, T)$, where Σ is a set of non-variable function symbols, $\mathcal{R}$ is a set of rewrite rules, and T is a set of terms over Σ which is closed under reduction by $\mathcal{R}$ and by the subterm relation. That is, if t is in T, all its subterms are in T, and if $\text{Red}(\mathcal{R})(t,t')$, then t' is in T. We may refer to a TRS by its rule-set $\mathcal{R}$, considering Σ and T to be fixed. The specification of a set of terms T as a part of the system allows us to uniformly treat typed systems, where not all terms that could be formed from the function symbols are legal.

3.2. Mismatches, conflicts and orthogonality

Given two open terms t and t', a *mismatch* of t and t' is an address u common to both terms, such that t/u and t'/u have different function symbols, neither being an identifier, and no proper initial segment of u has this property.

A rule R is *ambiguous with* a rule R' if R $\uparrow_{ls}$ R', and R $\neq$ R'. The relation is symmetric. Some special cases are of importance. Firstly, if R $\uparrow_s$ R' (that is, the most general substitutions σ and σ' such that σ*l*R = σ'*l*R' are such that also σrR = σrR'), then we say that R and R' are *weakly ambiguous*. Secondly, if *l*(R) $<_{ls}$ *l*(R'), then we say that R is *less specific than* R', and write R $<_{ls}$ R'. If R and R' are ambiguous, and neither is less specific than the other, we say that they *overlap*.

A rule R *obstructs* a rule R' *at* u if u is a nonempty proper address of *l*(R') and *l*(R')/u $\uparrow_s$ *l*(R).

Rules R and R' *conflict* if they are either ambiguous with each other or one obstructs the other. We call such conflicts respectively ambiguities and obstructions.

These various relations between rules, and examples thereof, are illustrated in the figure.

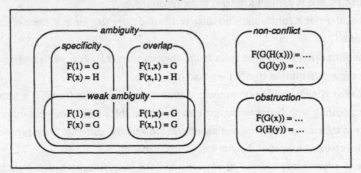

Note that it is possible for two rules to conflict with each other in more than one way. For example, rules F(F(x)) = ... and F(F(G(x))) = ... display both an obstruction and a specificity conflict with each other. In addition, F(F(x)) obstructs itself at the address 1.

A TRS is *orthogonal* if its rules are left-linear, and none of its rules conflict. A set of terms is *orthogonal* if a rule-system, in which each of the terms is the left hand side of one rule, is orthogonal. Note that orthogonality of a TRS is not quite the same as orthogonality of the set of its left-hand sides; the only difference is that if two or more rules have identical left hand sides the system will not be orthogonal, although the set of its left hand sides might be.

3.3. Applicative and functional TRSs

We call a TRS (Σ,𝓡,T) *applicative* if every symbol in Σ has arity 0, except for one symbol having arity 2, which we will denote by @, and call *application*, but is usually not written explicitly. Otherwise, the system is called *functional*. Some term rewrite languages only allow applicative systems to be defined. SASL and KRC are examples. In these languages, the application symbol is not explicitly represented in the syntax, but is implied by juxtaposition. This is also true of Miranda, when algebraic types are not being used. A term such as n * (fac (n−1)) will look like this when applications are written explicitly:

$$@((@(*,n),@(fac,@((@(-,n),1)))$$

It is clearer when written as a syntax tree:

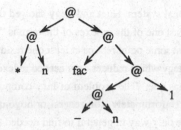

When quoting examples from Miranda, we shall follow its syntax, but when presenting "generic" examples, we follow the functional syntax, in which we would write the second factorial rule as Fac(n) = *(n,Fac(−(n,1))).

3.4. Operator-constructor systems and completeness

DEFINITION. An *operator symbol* of a TRS (F,𝑅,T) is a symbol which is the principal function symbol of the left-hand side of some rule of the system. A *constructor symbol* is a symbol which is not an operator. An *operator-constructor* system is one in which no operator appears as a sub-principal function symbol in the left hand side of any rule. A system is *complete for* a function symbol F if no closed normal form has F as its principal function symbol. A system is *complete* if it is complete for each of its operators. □

Applicative systems are in general not operator-constructor systems, as the application symbol appears in both principal and subprincipal positions in the left hand sides. However, they can be transformed into operator-constructor form. An example will show the general method.

An applicative rule:	S x y z = (x z) (y z)
With explicit application:	@(@(@(S, x), y), z) = @(@(x, z), @(y, z))
Transformed to op-con form:	@(S, x) = $S_1(x)$
	@($S_1(x)$, y) = $S_2(x, y)$
	@($S_2(x, y)$, z) = @(@(x, z), @(y, z))

In the transformed system, @ is an operator, and S, S_1, and S_2 are constructors.

Subject to some such transformation, Hope and ML programs are operator-constructor systems, as is Miranda, except for its lawful types (which we consider in section 7).

In Miranda, Hope, and ML, programs are, in effect, always complete. In Miranda, if one defines a function by Head(Cons(x, y)) = x, and tries to evaluate Head(Nil), a run-time error is detected and the program is terminated. We would say that a program which tries to evaluate Head(Nil) is not a program at all, any more than a syntactically erroneous program is.

Hope enforces completeness at compile-time: the programmer would be required to provide a rule to deal with Head(Nil).

ML would cause an exception to be raised on evaluating Head(Nil). This is not a run-time error, and is best described as saying that the compiler has automatically completed the programmer's incomplete rule set by causing Head to return an error value when the programmer's rules for Head do not match. (A formal semantics of ML exception handling along these lines is given in [9].)

3.5. Strong sequentiality

Strong sequentiality was defined by Huet and Lévy [12]. The definition is highly technical and there is not space to state it here. We shall briefly and informally describe the intuition behind the notion.

In an orthogonal system, Huet and Lévy showed that the any term having a normal form but not in normal form, at least one of the redexes of the term is "needed" — that is, every reduction of the term to normal form will at some point reduce at least one residual of that redex. They showed, furthermore, that any reduction strategy which reduces only needed redexes is normalising — it will find the normal form of any term which has one. The problem of lazy computation is thus reduced to the problem of finding needed redexes. Unfortunately, for general orthogonal systems, this is uncomputable. The reason is essentially that the only way in general to find needed redexes is to first reduce the term to normal form and see which steps of the reduction were in fact needed.

The problem is solved by seeking a stronger condition than orthogonality, which ignores the right-hand sides of the rules. Huet and Lévy showed that the following property of an orthogonal rule system $\mathcal{R}$ is decidable:

> for every term t having a n.f. but not in n.f., there exists a redex of t, such that for any rule-system having the same left-hand sides as $\mathcal{R}$, the redex is needed.

When $\mathcal{R}$ satisfies this condition, it is said to be *strongly sequential*. For such systems, there is also an algorithm for finding a needed redex in every term not in n.f. (Finding *all* the needed redexes of a term is still undecidable, however).

For orthogonal operator-constructor systems, the test for strong sequentiality is easily described. Take any linear, open term t, which is obtained from some left-hand side of $\mathcal{R}$ by replacing some subterms by new variables. Look at the set T of left-hand sides of $\mathcal{R}$ which are instances of t (N.B. not the reverse relation). Say that $\mathcal{R}$ is *strongly sequential at* t if T has the property that:

> if T has two or more members, then there is an address u of a variable occurrence
> in t such that every member of T instantiates u.

Then $\mathcal{R}$ is strongly sequential iff $\mathcal{R}$ is strongly sequential at every such term t. When this is the case, the addresses u found for such t encode a normalising reduction strategy for $\mathcal{R}$. But it would take us too far afield to describe this strategy.

Here is a well-known example of a non-strongly sequential rule system, known as "Berry's F" [4]:

Example 3.
$$F(x, 0, 1) = \ldots$$
$$F(1, x, 0) = \ldots$$
$$F(0, 1, x) = \ldots$$

This fails the above test, since all three rules are instances of F(a,b,c), yet neither a, nor b, nor c is instantiated by all three left-hand sides.

For example 2 of section 1, the terms which must be tested are f(x,y), f(Nil,x), f(x,Nil), f(x,Cons(y,z)), and similarly for g with the arguments reversed. In each of these terms, the occurrence of the variable x satisfies the condition. Thus the system is strongly sequential.

4. Specificity in operator-constructor systems

We can now formally define specificity. We deal first with a restricted class of TRSs.

4.1. DEFINITION. A TRS is *Type 0* if it is a complete, left-linear, operator-constructor system, and no two left-hand sides of $\mathcal{R}$ are identical (ignoring change of variable names). □

Programs in Miranda (without lawful types) and ML are Type 0 rewrite systems (except for the minor fact that they do not forbid rules having identical left-hand sides). Type 0 systems may be ambiguous, as demonstrated by the examples in section 1, but they do not contain obstructions.

Given a Type 0 rule-system $\mathcal{R}$, we define another system $\text{Spec}(\mathcal{R})$. The rules of $\text{Spec}(\mathcal{R})$ will be substitution instances of the rules of $\mathcal{R}$; thus the reduction relation of $\text{Spec}(\mathcal{R})$ will be a subrelation of the reduction relation of $\mathcal{R}$. As we wish to preserve the Type 0 property, the substitutions we apply to obtain the rules $\text{Spec}(\mathcal{R})$ will be constructor substitutions, i.e. substitutions whose range consists only of constructor terms.

Given certain further conditions on $\mathcal{R}$, $\text{Spec}(\mathcal{R})$ will be orthogonal and strongly sequential. We define $\text{Spec}(\mathcal{R})$ to be the meaning of "$\mathcal{R}$ with the specificity rule".

4.2. DEFINITION. Let $\mathcal{R}$ be a Type 0 TRS. $\text{Spec}(\mathcal{R})$ is the following rule-set:

$$\text{Spec}'(R,\mathcal{R}) = \{\ \sigma(R) \mid \sigma \text{ is a linear constructor substitution}$$
$$\wedge\ \forall R' \in \mathcal{R}.\ R' >_{ls} R \ \Rightarrow\ R' \text{ and } \sigma R \text{ are not ambiguous}\ \}$$
$$\text{Spec}'(\mathcal{R}) = \bigcup\{\ \text{Spec}'(R,\mathcal{R}) \mid R \in \mathcal{R}\ \}$$
$$\text{Spec}(\mathcal{R}) = \Downarrow_s(\text{Spec}'(\mathcal{R})) \qquad\qquad\qquad \square$$

This definition proceeds in two stages. First, for each R in $\mathcal{R}$ we define a set $\text{Spec}'(R,\mathcal{R})$ of instances of R, chosen so as not to be ambiguous with any rule of $\mathcal{R}$ more specific than R. Then we take the minimal members of all these (in general infinite) sets, with respect to the $\leq_s$ ordering (not the specificity ordering). This is $\text{Spec}(\mathcal{R})$. This second step serves merely to eliminate redundant rules — both $\text{Spec}'(\mathcal{R})$ and $\text{Spec}(\mathcal{R})$ have the same reduction relation. While either may be used as a definition of the semantics of specificity, $\text{Spec}(\mathcal{R})$ may also be used as a direct implementation.

The following basic properties of $\text{Spec}(\mathcal{R})$ are easily proved.

4.3. THEOREM. Let $\mathcal{R}$ be Type 0.

(1) The reduction relation generated by $\text{Spec}(\mathcal{R})$ is a subrelation of that generated by $\mathcal{R}$.

(2) A term is a normal form of $\text{Spec}(\mathcal{R})$ if and only if it is a normal form of $\mathcal{R}$.

(3) $\text{Spec}(\mathcal{R})$ is Type 0.

(4) If $\mathcal{R}$ contains no specificity conflicts then $\mathcal{R} = \text{Spec}(\mathcal{R})$. $\square$

From (1) and (2) it follows that any evaluation of a term to normal form in $\text{Spec}(\mathcal{R})$ can be performed in $\mathcal{R}$. The converse is of course not true — the purpose of $\text{Spec}(\mathcal{R})$ is to eliminate computations such as the example in which fac $1 = 0$.

5. Examples

We consider the effect of Spec on the examples of section 1.

Example 1.

fac 0 = 1	(1.1)
fac n:{INT−0} = n * (fac (n−1))	(1.2)

The notation x:{INT−0} is intended to schematically express the infinite set of rules obtained from fac n = ... by substituting any non-zero integer for n. This rule-system is orthogonal and strongly sequential.

Example 2. This example, being already orthogonal, is not changed by Spec. As it is strongly sequential, the Huet-Lévy reduction strategy maintains the validity of the equational reasoning leading to the conclusion that c g = f is valid. More precisely, for any term t, $(t\ (c\ g))$ has normal form t' iff $(t\ f)$ has normal form t'.

$\text{Spec}(\mathcal{R})$ is not always as well-behaved as this. Firstly, overlap ambiguities in $\mathcal{R}$ may persist into $\text{Spec}(\mathcal{R})$, as illustrated by "parallel or":

Example 4.   Or(True, x) = True

$$Or(x, True) = True$$
$$Or(x, y) = False$$

Assuming that the only constructors that can appear as arguments to Or are True and False, Spec transforms this to:

$$Or(True, x) = True$$
$$Or(x, True) = True$$
$$Or(False, False) = False$$

The ambiguity between the first two rules is unaffected by the transformation. There is nothing surprising about this. Specificity is not a magic wand which will eliminate all ambiguities from a system. It is only intended to deal with those ambiguities resulting from the use of "default" rules.

A second reason for non-orthogonality of $Spec(\mathcal{R})$ is more interesting. Here is another formulation of the Or function.

Example 5.
$$Or(x, y) = True$$
$$Or(False, False) = False$$

Assuming that Or takes boolean arguments, Spec gives:

$$Or(True, y) = True$$
$$Or(x, True) = True$$
$$Or(False, False) = False$$

The first two rules are ambiguous with each other. Looking at the original rule set, this is only to be expected. To refute the possibility that a term $Or(t,t')$ might match the rule $Or(False,False) = ...$, it is sufficient to either evaluate t far enough to discover that it is not False, or evaluate t' far enough to discover that it is not False. But it is not possible to tell in advance which should be evaluated. The specificity transformation cannot create sequentiality where none existed, but it makes the non-sequentiality of the original system explicit.

6. Conditions for orthogonality and strong sequentiality

To eliminate ambiguities from $Spec(\mathcal{R})$, we must make further restrictions on $\mathcal{R}$.

6.1. DEFINITION. Let $t \leq_s t'$. $[t,t']$ is the set of terms t'' such that $t \leq_s t'' \leq_s t'$. A set of this form is called an *interval*. The interval is *thin* if $\leq_s$ is a total ordering on its members. □

6.2. EXAMPLE. (i) $[F(\bullet,\bullet,\bullet), F(\bullet,G(\bullet,H(J(\bullet,\bullet))),\bullet)] = \{ F(\bullet,\bullet,\bullet), F(\bullet,G(\bullet,\bullet),\bullet), F(\bullet, G(\bullet, H(\bullet)),\bullet), F(\bullet,G(\bullet,H(J(\bullet,\bullet))),\bullet) \}$. This interval is thin.

(ii) $[F(\bullet,\bullet),F(0,1)] = \{ F(\bullet,\bullet), F(0,\bullet), F(\bullet,1), F(0,1) \}$. This interval is not thin.

6.3. DEFINITION. $\mathcal{R}$ is *Type 1* if

(i) $\mathcal{R}$ is Type 0.

(ii) If t and t' are left hand sides of $\mathcal{R}$, and $t \sqcup_s t'$ exists, then it is (up to renaming of variables) also a left hand side of $\mathcal{R}$. Briefly, we say that $l(\mathcal{R})$ is $\sqcup_s$-*closed*.

(iii) Let T and T' be two left hand sides of $\mathcal{R}$ such that $T \leq_s T'$ and the interval $[T,T']$ contains no other left-hand side of $\mathcal{R}$. Then the interval is thin. (We refer to this property by saying that $\mathcal{R}$ has *thin gaps*.) □

6.4. THEOREM. If $\mathcal{R}$ is Type 1 then $Spec(\mathcal{R})$ is orthogonal.

PROOF (OUTLINE). Condition (ii) rules out the situation of example 3, by ensuring that whenever two rules R_1 and R_2 of $\mathcal{R}$ overlap, every term to which they both apply is also matched by a rule R_3 more specific than both rules. This ensures that substitution instances of R_1 and R_2 which are not ambiguous with R_3 are not ambiguous with each other.

Condition (iii) rules out the situation of example 5, where there were two independent ways of instantiating a rule R_1 to make it unambiguous with R_2. $\square$

We next consider strong sequentiality of Spec($\mathcal{R}$). In fact, all that is needed to ensure strong sequentiality of Spec($\mathcal{R}$) is that the set of maximally specific members of R be strongly sequential.

6.5. DEFINITION. A rewrite system $\mathcal{R}$ is Type 2 if it is Type 1, and $\Uparrow_{ls}\mathcal{R}$ is strongly sequential. $\square$

6.6. THEOREM. If $\mathcal{R}$ is Type 2 then Spec($\mathcal{R}$) is strongly sequential.

PROOF (OUTLINE). From the Type 1 property we can show that without loss of generality, $\mathcal{R}$ may be assumed to be *dense*, by which we mean that if there exist a substitution σ and two rules R_1 and R_2 of $\mathcal{R}$ such that $lR_1 <_s \sigma lR_1 <_s lR_2$, then for some such substitution σ, σlR_1 is a left-hand side of $\mathcal{R}$. This is so because, given such R_1, R_2, and σ, adding σR_1 to $\mathcal{R}$ does not change either Spec($\mathcal{R}$) or $\Uparrow_{ls}\mathcal{R}$.

When $\mathcal{R}$ is Type 1 and dense, Spec($\mathcal{R}$) can be shown to consist of all the rules in $\Uparrow_{ls}\mathcal{R}$, together with some rules, each of whose left hand sides has the form σlR, where R is in $\Uparrow_{ls}\mathcal{R}$, and σ is an address substitution defined at exactly one address, its value there being a term of the form $F(\bullet)$ where F is a constructor. We already know that Spec($\mathcal{R}$) is orthogonal; the above characterisation of Spec($\mathcal{R}$), and that of strong sequentiality for op-con systems in section 3.5 implies that Spec($\mathcal{R}$) is strongly sequential. $\square$

Examples 1 and 2 are Type 2. Example 3 is Type 1 but not Type 2. Examples 4 and 5 are Type 0 but not Type 1. In example 4, u_s-closure fails; in example 5, there is a thick interval between $f \bullet \bullet$ and $f\,0\,1$.

The particular ways in which the Type 1 and Type 2 properties may fail to hold can be used to modify the original system in order to ensure orthogonality and strong sequentiality of the transformed system. In example 3, we must specify which argument of F should be evaluated first. For example, we may add an instance of the first rule of the form

$$F(2, 0, 1) = \ldots$$

which has the effect of specifying that F is to be strict in its third argument. In example 4, it is necessary to specify which rule is to be applied to a term of the form Or(True, $\bullet$) u_s Or($\bullet$, True). In example 5, it is necessary to close the thick interval by adding a rule whose left-hand side is $f\,0\,\bullet$, or one whose left-hand side is $f \bullet 1$, or both.

We thus see that when a Type 0 system fails to be Type 2, it is possible to isolate the reasons for this failure. The programmer can use this information to add rules which explicitly inform the system of the preferred order of evaluation, in just those cases where the original system left this underspecified.

7. Specificity with sub-root conflicts

Our discussion so far covers operator-constructor systems, and hence the languages ML, Hope, and Haskell. But only a part of Miranda is covered, as a Miranda lawful type is defined by more general rewrite rules[2]. For example, consider the following Miranda definition of a type of lists of even integers:

Example 6.
       elist ::= Enil | Econs num olist
       Econs a x => x, odd(a)

---

[2] In the latest version of Miranda (version 2), lawful types have been removed from the language.

odd is a boolean predicate testing whether its argument is an odd integer. We shall not attempt to give here a semantics for guarded rules, but take the above rule as being a schematic representation for the set of instances where a is an odd integer.

A typical rule for operating on an elist might be:

$$\text{ehead :: elist} \rightarrow \text{num}$$
$$\text{ehead (Econs a x)} = a$$

The semantics of such a lawful type is that, viewed from 'outside', Enil and Econs are constructors, but whenever an attempt is made to pattern-match on an elist term, as with the ehead rule, the elist is first reduced to "head normal form" according to the laws for the type.

Another way of looking at this is to say that laws are no different from rewrite rules: because the rule for Econs obstructs the rule for ehead, the ehead rule may not be applied to an Econs node unless it is known that the Econs node could never in future match the Econs rule. This suggests that the definition of specificity may usefully be extended to such systems.

We modify the previous definition of Spec'(R,$\mathcal{R}$) by imposing different conditions on the substitutions to be applied to R. Firstly, they are weakened: since we are no longer working in an operator-constructor system, σ is not restricted to being a constructor substitution. (It must still be linear.) Secondly, they are strengthened: the condition that σR be non-ambiguous with any rule more specific than R remains, but we add a further condition that σR be chosen to as not to be obstructed by any rule of $\mathcal{R}$.

7.1. DEFINITION. Let $\mathcal{R}$ be a left-linear TRS. Spec($\mathcal{R}$) is the following rule-set:

$$\text{Spec'(R,}\mathcal{R}) = \{ \sigma(l(\text{R})) \mid \sigma \text{ is a linear substitution}$$
$$\wedge \ \forall \text{R'} \in \mathcal{R}. \text{ R' does not obstruct } \sigma\text{R}$$
$$\wedge \ \forall \text{R'} \in \mathcal{R}. \text{ R'} >_{ls} \text{R} \Rightarrow \text{R' and } \sigma\text{R are not ambiguous} \}$$

$$\text{Spec'}(\mathcal{R}) = \bigcup \{ \text{ Spec'(R,}\mathcal{R}) \mid \text{R} \in \mathcal{R} \}$$
$$\text{Spec}(\mathcal{R}) = \Downarrow_s \text{Spec'}(\mathcal{R}) \qquad\qquad\qquad \square$$

We are justified in calling this transformation by the same name as the one previously defined, because for Type 0 systems it is easy to show that it generates the same reduction relation as the Spec($\mathcal{R}$) of the earlier definition. (It is possible that it contains more rules than the previous definition would give, but the extra rules are incapable of applying to any term of the system.)

8. Examples

Applying Spec to the rules for Econs and ehead defined above yields the set consisting of all rules of the forms:

$$\text{Econs } o_1 (\text{Econs } o_2 (...(\text{Econs e x})...)) = \text{ Econs e x}$$
$$\text{ehead (Econs e x)} =. \text{ e}$$

where $o_1, o_2,...$ are odd integers (and there is at least one) and e is an even integer. These are infinite sets, useful as a definition of the semantics, rather than as an implementation.

On this example, Spec yields an orthogonal, strongly sequential system. But as for Type 0 systems, this is not always so.

Example 7.
$$F(G(x, y)) = ...$$
$$G(0, 1) = ...$$

Given a term of the form F(G(..., ...)), to apply the rule for F one must first ensure that the rule for G can never apply to the argument of F. This will require evaluating at least one of the arguments to G, but not necessarily both. In general it is not possible to tell which argument must be evaluated.

9. Conditions for orthogonality and strong sequentiality

To ensure that $\text{Spec}(\mathcal{R})$ is orthogonal, it is sufficient to define an appropriate generalisation of the thin gaps property.

9.1. DEFINITION. $\mathcal{R}$ is *irredundant* if there do not exist rules R_0 and R_1 in $\mathcal{R}$ and a nonempty address u of lR_0 such that $lR_0/u \geq_s lR_1$.

A substitution σ is *thin* if $\sigma(x)$ is thin whenever it is defined.

An *obstruction* is a tuple (t,u,t') where t and t' are terms, u is a proper address of t, and $t/u \uparrow_s t'$. With any obstruction is associated a substitution: that σ having the smallest domain such that $\sigma(t/u) = t/u$ $u_s t'$. The obstruction is thin if σ is thin.

Given two obstructions of the form (t,u,t'), (t',v,t''), if $u \cdot v$ is a proper address of t, then there is an obstruction $(t,u \cdot v,t'')$, This is the *composition* of the two given obstructions.

Given a set of terms T, an obstruction of T is an obstruction (t,u,t') such that t and t' are in T. It is *minimal* if it is not the composition of two obstructions of T.

T is said to have *thin gaps* if every minimal obstruction of T is thin.

A rule system $\mathcal{R}$ is *Type 3* if it is left-linear and irredundant, and the set of its left hand sides is closed under u_s and has thin gaps. $\square$

Note that all Type 0 systems are irredundant, and that for Type 0 systems, the above definition of thin gaps coincides with the earlier one.

The example in the last section did not have thin gaps, for the obstruction $(F(G(x,y)),\langle 1\rangle,G(0,1))$ has the associated substitution $[x:=0, y:=1]$, which is not thin.

The set $\{ F(G(H(\bullet))), H(J(K(\bullet))) \}$ has thin gaps.

The set $\{ F(G(0,1)), G(\bullet,\bullet) \}$ is not irredundant. Note that specificity demands that a term of the form $F(G(0,1))$ may not be reduced unless the subterms matched by this left hand side are all in head normal form. But because of the left hand side $G(\bullet,\bullet)$, this can never be the case. Thus the rule whose left hand side is $F(G(0,1))$ is superfluous.

The u_s-closure (whose definition does not need to be changed) and thin gaps properties will play the same role for left-linear systems as they did for Type 0 systems. Failure of u_s-closure implies that the system contains ambiguities which specificity will not eliminate. Non-thin gaps cause ambiguities in the transformed system (in the first of the above examples, specificity will add rules for both $F(G(1,\bullet))$ and $F(G(\bullet,0))$).

9.2. THEOREM. If $\mathcal{R}$ is Type 3 then $\text{Spec}(\mathcal{R})$ is orthogonal.

PROOF (OUTLINE). It is immediate from the definition of Spec that $\text{Spec}(\mathcal{R})$ can contain no obstructions. If R_1 and R_2 are rules of $\text{Spec}(\mathcal{R})$ which are ambiguous with each other, then (in the same way as for the proof of the same proposition for Type 1 systems) the u_s-closure property implies that they must be instances $\sigma_1(R)$ and $\sigma_2(R)$ of the same rule R of $\mathcal{R}$. However, the thin gaps property rules this out. $\square$

When is $\text{Spec}(\mathcal{R})$ strongly sequential?. A natural generalisation of the Type 2 property suffices.

9.3. DEFINITION. Let $\mathcal{R}$ be Type 3. Let $E(\mathcal{R})$ be the following set of terms:

1. $E(\mathcal{R})$ contains all the left-hand sides of $\mathcal{R}$.
2. For any T and T' in $E(\mathcal{R})$ and nonempty proper address u of T, if $\text{Funct}(T/u) = \text{Funct}(T')$ then $T[u:=T'] \in E(\mathcal{R})$.

3. E($\mathcal{R}$) is as small as possible subject to (1) and (2).

    We call E($\mathcal{R}$) the set of *extended left hand sides* of $\mathcal{R}$.

    R is *Type 4* if every orthogonal subset of E($\mathcal{R}$) is strongly sequential. □

For Type 1 systems, E($\mathcal{R}$) is just the set of left hand sides of $\mathcal{R}$, and Type 4 is equivalent to Type 2. Note that we cannot simply follow the definition of Type 2 and define Type 4 in terms of the set of maximally specific members of E($\mathcal{R}$), since E($\mathcal{R}$) may contain unbounded $\leq_{ls}$-ascending sequences. The situation is illustrated by the pair of left hand sides F(G($\bullet$)) and G(F($\bullet$)), which give rise to extended left-hand sides F(G($\bullet$)), G(F($\bullet$)), F(G(F($\bullet$))), G(F(G($\bullet$))), F(G(F(G($\bullet$)))), G(F(G(F($\bullet$)))), etc. For the example of even lists, E($\mathcal{R}$) happens to be the same as $l(\mathcal{R})$. An example from [19] in which E($\mathcal{R}$) is much larger than $l(\mathcal{R})$ is a type of ordered lists:

$$\text{olist} \quad ::= \quad \text{Onil} \mid \text{Ocons num olist}$$
$$\text{Ocons a (Ocons b x)} \quad \Rightarrow \quad \text{Ocons b (Ocons a x), a<b}$$

$$\text{ohead} :: \text{olist} \rightarrow \text{num}$$
$$\text{ohead (Ocons a x)} \quad = \quad a$$

Computation of E($\mathcal{R}$) for this example is left as an exercise.

9.4. THEOREM. If $\mathcal{R}$ is Type 4 then Spec($\mathcal{R}$) is strongly sequential.

PROOF. Similar to theorem 6.6. □

10.   Summary

The following diagram shows the relations between the various types of TRS. This is a partial order: a line from one class to another indicates containment of the higher class in the lower. Least upper bounds in the diagram are set intersections. Specificity conflicts only occur below the shaded line. The arrows indicate the action of the specificity transformation.

11.   Directions for further work

It is important to establish the complexity and the practicality of the reduction strategy we have described. In the operator-constructor case, calculating the transformed system Spec(R) and applying the

Huet-Lévy strategy will work, but a more direct implementation will very likely be more efficient. In the more general case of Type 4 systems, this is not always possible, as Spec(R) can be infinite (even if the set of function symbols is finite). Here, a more direct implementation is necessary.

The definition of specificity should be extended to guarded rules. For the particular example of section 7, we were able to sidestep this by considering the guard as shorthand for a set of rules, but this is not possible in general.

12. Background

Rule systems with various notions of explicit priorities among or conditions on rules have been studied in [2,3]. However, for many of these notions, the reduction relation is uncomputable or not uniquely defined. This is because of a problem of circularity: to say "this rule shall not be applied to a term unless that rule could never be applied" makes reference to the terms which the given term could be reduced to, by the reduction relation that one is attempting to define. It is necessary to prove that the circular definition is well-defined. In many cases it is not, or if it is, it may be uncomputable. In earlier attempts to formalise the concept of specificity, we encountered the same problem. We avoid it here by restricting attention to the left hand sides of the rewrite rules. We leave open the question of whether information about the right hand sides of the rules can usefully be employed in a more refined definition of specificity.

Laville [15,16] has given a formal semantics for the top-to-bottom, left-to-right strategy by means of a transformation similar to that described here.

Turner [22] defined the semantics of Miranda's laws by translation into an operator-constructor system. Each constructor of a lawful type is replaced by a pair of symbols: an operator and a constructor. Each use of the lawful constructor as the principal function symbol of the left hand side of a law is replaced by the new operator, and every other use is replaced by the new constructor. In addition, a "default" rule of the form $F' x_1 ... x_n = F'' x_1 ... x_n$ is added (where F' is the operator and F'' the constructor replacing some lawful constructor F). Thompson [19] has studied the problem of verification of Miranda programs which use laws, using Turner's transformation to define the semantics, and giving conditions under which equational reasoning is valid. The pattern-matching is still top-to-bottom, left-to-right. However, this does not affect the examples he studies, which, after transformation, happen to be left-sequential [17], for which top-to-bottom, left-to-right pattern-matching is normalising; it is not clear whether his results need to be modified to deal with strongly sequential but non-left-sequential systems such as our Example 2.

It should be possible to show that for left-sequential Miranda programs the semantics we have given coincides with Turner's.

Hope+ [7,18] uses a weaker form of specificity than that described here, called "best-fit" pattern-matching. This is used only to avoid dependency on the order of rules; within a rule, pattern-matching is performed left-to-right, and as a result is not fully lazy.

In a somewhat different vein, Dactl0 [8] is a language of graph rewriting in which specificity conflicts are allowed, and resolved by always choosing the most specific rule. However, the situation is much simpler than for the functional languages considered here, because in Dactl0, pattern-matching and evaluation are independent — in choosing which rule to apply, all that is relevant is the set of rules which could be applied immediately, not the rules which might apply at some time in the future.

References

1. A. Augustsson. A compiler for Lazy ML, ACM Conf. on Lisp and Functional Programming, 1984.

2. J.C.M. Baeten, J.A. Bergstra, and J.W. Klop. Priority rewrite rules, Report CS-R8407, Centrum voor Wiskunde en Informatica, Amsterdam, 1982.

3. J.A. Bergstra and J.W. Klop. Conditional rewrite rules: confluence and termination. J. Comp. Sys. Sci., 32, no.3, 323–362, 1986.

4. G. Berry. Stable models of typed lambda-calculi, in: G. Ausiello and C. Böhm., eds., Proc. 5th Int. Conf. on Automata, Languages, and Programming, Lecture Notes in Computer Science, vol.62 (Springer, 1978)

5. T.H. Brus, M.C.J.D. van Eekelen, M.O. van Leer, and M.J. Plasmeijer. Clean: a language for functional graph rewriting, Report, Computing Science Department, University of Nijmegen, 1987.

6. R.M. Burstall, D.B. MacQueen, and D.T. Sannella. HOPE: an experimental applicative language, in: Proc. 1st ACM Lisp Conference, 136–143, Stanford, 1980.

7. A.J. Field, L.S. Hunt, and R.L. While. Best-fit pattern matching for functional languages. Internal report, Department of Computing, Imperial College, London, 1989.

8. J.R.W. Glauert, J.R. Kennaway, and M.R. Sleep. DACTL: a computational model and compiler target language based on graph reduction. ICL Technical Journal, 5, 509-537, 1987.

9. K. Hammond. Implementing Functional Languages for Parallel Machines, Ph.D. thesis, School of Information Systems, University of East Anglia, 1988.

10. R. Harper, R. Milner, and M. Tofte. The definition of Standard ML, Report ECS-LFCS-88-62, Laboratory for Foundations of Computer Science, University of Edinburgh, 1988.

11. P. Hudak et al. Report on the Functional Programming Language Haskell. Draft Proposed Standard, 1988.

12. G. Huet and J.-J. Lévy. Call by need computations in non-ambiguous linear term rewriting systems, INRIA report 359, 1979.

13. J.W. Klop. Term rewriting systems: a tutorial, Bull. EATCS, no.32, 143–182, June 1987.

14. J.W. Klop. Term rewriting systems, in S. Abramsky, D. Gabbay, and T. Maibaum (eds.) Handbook of Logic in Computer Science, (Oxford University Press, in preparation).

15. A. Laville. Lazy pattern matching in the ML language, INRIA report 664, 1987.

16. A. Laville. Comparison of priority rules in pattern matching and term rewriting, INRIA report 878, 1988.

17. M.J. O'Donnell. Equational Logic as a Programming Language, MIT Press, 1985.

18. N. Perry. Hope+. Internal report, Department of Computing, Imperial College, London, 1988.

19. S. Thompson. Lawful functions and program verification in Miranda, Science of Computer Programming, to appear, 1989.

20. D.A. Turner. SASL language manual. University of St. Andrews, 1979.

21. D.A. Turner. Recursion equations as a programming language, in J. Darlington, P. Henderson, and D.A. Turner (eds.) Functional Programming and its Applications: an Advanced Course, Cambridge University Press, 1982.

22. D.A. Turner. Miranda: a non-strict functional language with polymorphic types. In J.-P. Jouannaud (ed.), Proc. ACM Conf. on Functional Programming Languages and Computer Architecture, Lecture Notes in Computer Science, vol.201, Springer-Verlag, 1985.

23. D.A. Turner. Miranda language manual. Research Software Ltd., Canterbury, U.K., 1987

Graph-based Implementation
of a Functional Logic Language*

Herbert Kuchen, Rita Loogen   Juan José Moreno-Navarro
RWTH Aachen[†]   Universidad Politécnica de Madrid[‡]

Mario Rodríguez-Artalejo.
Universidad Complutense de Madrid[§]

Abstract

We present in this paper a *graph-narrowing abstract machine* which has been designed to support a sequential eager implementation of a functional logic language. Our approach has been to extend a purely functional, (programmed) graph reduction machine by mechanisms capable of performing *unification* and *backtracking*. We describe the structure of the machine and explain the compilation scheme which generates machine code from a given source program. Both the machine and the compilation scheme have been formally specified. A prototype emulator of the machine has been implemented in Occam on a transputer system. Future work is planned for incorporating lazy evaluation and parallelism to the machine.

1 Introduction

During the last years, several approaches have been proposed to achieve an integration of functional and logic programming languages in order to combine the advantages of the two main declarative programming paradigms in a single framework [DeGroot, Lindstrom 86], [Bellia, Levi 86]. Usually one argues that logic languages have more expressive power than functional languages, while the latter have a simpler execution model, particularly suited to parallel implementations.

Roughly, many of the existing approaches to the integration of functional and logic programming can be partitioned into two classes: On the one hand, Horn clause logic languages enhanced with equality and functions; on the other hand, functional languages augmented with logical capabilities. This second class includes the so called functional logic languages [Reddy 85,87], which retain functional syntax but use narrowing — a unification based parameter passing mechanism which subsumes reduction and SLD-resolution — as operational semantics.

We investigate in this paper a sequential, eager implementation of the functional logic language BABEL [Moreno, Rodríguez 89] on a graph narrowing abstract machine. Up to now, BABEL had been developped as a first order, type free language. Here, we extend it to a higher order functional logic language with polymorphic typing.

Our approach has been to extend the sequential kernel of a parallel (programmed) graph reduction machine which has been designed for the execution of functional programming languages [Loogen et al. 89] by the additional features that are necessary to execute functional logic programs, namely,

---

*This work has been partially supported by a german-spanish cooperation action, funded by the german D.A.A.D. and the spanish M.E.C

[†]Lehrstuhl für Informatik II, Ahornstraße 55, 5100 Aachen, West Germany

[‡]Departamento de Lenguajes y Sistemas Informáticos e Ingeniería de Software, Facultad de Informática, Campus de Montegancedo, Boadilla del Monte, 28660 Madrid, Spain

[§]Departamento de Informática y Automática, Facultad de C.C. Matemáticas, 28040 Madrid, Spain

unification and backtracking facilities. For simplicity, we discuss in this paper the realization of an innermost narrowing strategy, i.e. the arguments of a function call are evaluated before the function is applied. However, we have chosen a graph reduction model because our final aim is a distributed parallel machine supporting lazy evaluation. A prototype emulator of the new abstract machine has been programmed in Occam and runs on transputer systems.

A distinctive feature of our approach is that SLD-resolution is subsumed by narrowing, which becomes the single inference mechanism of the language and works both for the Prolog-like part and for the purely functional part. As shown by several researchers [van Emden, Yukawa 87], [Bosco et al. 88], narrowing can be also subsumed by SLD-resolution. Several integrated logic plus functional programming languages — which follow a Horn clause logic based approach for the integration — have chosen some modified form of SLD-resolution as an implementation basis, in order to capitalize on the extensive experience already available for Prolog implementations. The language K-LEAF [Levi et al. 87], [Bosco et al. 89] is a prominent example of this. We have chosen our approach by similar reasons, namely, in order to profit from the available experience in implementation techniques for functional languages. We hope that purely applicative programs will run on the BABEL machine almost as efficiently as in the original graph reduction machine, although some overhead due to the different parameter passing mechanisms cannot be avoided. The narrowing based approach has also the advantage of being conceptually very clear and simple.

This paper is organized as follows. In section 2 we give a short presentation of the language BABEL. The structure of the BABEL abstract machine is described in section 3, where we also explain the compilation of BABEL programs into code for the abstract machine. The compilation rules are very similar to the functional case, because backtracking is not controlled by code, but is instead performed by an implicit mechanism which is started by a special machine instruction. Formal specifications of both the machine and the compilation scheme can be found in [Kuchen et al. 89]. In section 4 we explain in more detail the organization of backtracking, which is the most important novel feature of the machine, since machine instructions for unification are borrowed from Warren's abstract machine for Prolog [Warren 83]. In section 5 we report on the current state of the implementation, which includes some optimizations. Section 6 includes some comments on related works. In section 7 we recapitulate our results and report on some planned future works.

2 The functional logic language BABEL

The language BABEL has been designed by Mario Rodríguez-Artalejo and Juan José Moreno-Navarro to achieve integration of functional and logic programming in a flexible and mathematically well-founded way [Moreno, Rodríguez 88,89], [Moreno 89]. It is based on a constructor discipline and uses narrowing as an evaluation mechanism; cfr. [Reddy 85,87]. In this paper we work with an extension of BABEL that supports polymorphic types and higher-order functions. However, higher-order *logic* variables are *not* allowed, i.e. higher-order variables are never affected by narrowing.

Before we give a formal presentation of BABEL-programs, we consider a small example program:

> typevar A, B.
> type   list(A) = nil | cons (A, list(A)).
>
> fun map: $(A \rightarrow B) \rightarrow list(A) \rightarrow list(B)$.
>   map F []   := [].
>   map F [X|Xs] := [F X | map F Xs].
>
> eval (map (+ 2) [X,3]) = [6,Y].

that will yield the boolean value true with variable bindings {X/4, Y/5}.

Note that we assume numbers and arithmetic operations as well as the equality operator to be predefined. We also allow a PROLOG-like syntax for lists.

The higher-order function map can be used in a very flexible way due to the first-order logic variables. The higher-order variable F can only be used as in applicative programming.

2.1 Syntax

Let $\Sigma = \langle TC_\Sigma, DC_\Sigma, FS_\Sigma \rangle$ be a polymorphic signature, i.e.

- TC_Σ is a set of *ranked type constructors* : tc/n, e.g. nat/0, list/1, ...

- DC_Σ is a set of *typed data constructors*: $c : \tau$, $c' : \tau_1 \times \ldots \times \tau_n \to \tau$ with $\tau = \text{tc}/m\ (\alpha_1, \ldots, \alpha_m)$ and $\tau_i \in \mathbf{CType}_\Sigma$, where $\mathbf{CType}_\Sigma$ is the set of *constructed types* over type variables $\alpha_1, \alpha_2 \ldots \in$ $\mathbf{TVar}_\Sigma$ defined recursively by

$$\tau ::= \alpha \mid \text{tc}/0 \mid \text{tc}/n(\tau_1, \ldots, \tau_n) \quad \% \ n \geq 2$$

and the type variables in $\tau_1, \ldots, \tau_n$ are taken from $\{\alpha_1, \ldots, \alpha_m\}$.

- FS_Σ is the set of *typed function symbols* $f : \tau$ with $\tau \in \mathbf{Type}_\Sigma$, where $\mathbf{Type}_\Sigma$ is the set of *polymorphic types* defined by

$$\tau ::= \alpha \mid \text{tc}/0 \mid \text{tc}/n(\tau_1, \ldots, \tau_n) \mid (\tau \to \tau').$$

In the sequel we assume that "$\to$" associates to the right and omit brackets accordingly.

We assume that Σ contains the predefined types:

- *bool* with data constructors true, false and function symbols $\neg : bool \to bool$ (logic negation), $\wedge : bool \to bool \to bool$ (sequential and), $\vee : bool \to bool \to bool$ (sequential or) and

- *nat* with data constructors 0 and s (successor function) and the usual arithmetic functions.

A special primitive function symbol is the weak equality symbol $=$ with type $\alpha \to \alpha \to bool$ whose definition will be given later.

In example programs we declare constructed types and data constructors in a MIRANDA-like style, cfr. [Turner 85].

We distinguish the following syntactic domains:

- *variables* ranged over by X, Y, Z ... $\in \mathbf{Var}$,

- *terms* ranged over by s, t ... $\in \mathbf{Term}_\Sigma$:

$$
\begin{array}{lll}
t & ::= & X \qquad\qquad\quad \% \text{ variable} \\
  & \mid & c \qquad\qquad\qquad \% \text{ constant (nullary constructor, } c/0 \in DC_\Sigma) \\
  & \mid & c(t_1, \ldots, t_n) \quad \% \ c/n \in DC_\Sigma, \text{ construction, respecting types}
\end{array}
$$

- *expressions* ranged over by B,C,M,N ... $\in \mathbf{Exp}_\Sigma$

$$
\begin{array}{lll}
M & ::= & t \qquad\qquad\qquad\ \% \text{ term} \\
  & \mid & c(M_1, \ldots, M_n) \quad \% \ c/n \in DC_\Sigma, \text{ construction, respecting types} \\
  & \mid & f \qquad\qquad\qquad\ \% \ f \in FS_\Sigma, \text{ function symbol} \\
  & \mid & (MN) \qquad\qquad\ \% \text{ application, respecting types} \\
  & \mid & (D \to M) \qquad\ \% \text{ guarded expression, } B\colon bool \\
  & \mid & (B \to M_1 \square M_2) \quad \% \text{ conditional expression, } B\colon bool, M_1, M_2 : \tau \text{ for some } \tau
\end{array}
$$

Expressions should be well-typed. We omit the formal definition of a type inference system for expressions; cfr. [Milner 78, Damas, Milner 82]. In the sequel we will reserve B, C for boolean expressions.

We remark that $B \to M$ and $B \to M_1 \square M_2$ are intended to mean "if B then M else undefined" and "if B then M_1 else M_2," respectively.

We shall assume that application associates to the left and omit brackets accordingly.

A BABEL-*program* of signature Σ consists of a set of defining rules for the non predefined symbols in FS_Σ. The rules for the predefined symbols are implicitly added to every program, and will be presented later.

Notice that any $f \in FS_\Sigma$ must have type $\tau_1 \to \ldots \to \tau_n \to \tau$, for some $n \geq 0$ and some τ that is not of the form $\tau' \to \tau''$. Here, n is the *type-arity* of f.

Each defining rule for f must have the form

$$\underbrace{f\ t_1 \ldots t_m}_{\text{lhs}} := \underbrace{\underbrace{\{B \to\}}_{\substack{\text{guard} \\ \text{(optional)}}} \underbrace{M}_{\text{body}}}_{\text{rhs}}$$

for some $m \leq n$ (called the *arity* of the rule) and satisfy the following restrictions:

1. *Flatness*: $t_i \in \text{Term}_\Sigma$.

2. *Left Linearity*: $f\ t_1 \ldots t_n$ does not contain multiple variable occurrences.

3. *Well-Typedness*: Under appropriate type assumptions for the variables we may infer the types τ_i for the terms t_i $(1 \leq i \leq m)$, the type *bool* for the guard B and the type $\tau_{m+1} \to \ldots \to \tau_n \to \tau$ for the body M.

4. *Restrictions on free variables*: Any variable that occurs in the rhs but not in the lhs is called *free*. Occurrences of free variables are allowed in the guard, but not in the body. Moreover, free variables must be first-order. By this we mean that their types must be constructed types (under the type assumption used to well-type the rule).

In any program, all rules for a fixed f must have the same arity. This is called the *program-arity* of f, and is less or equal than f's type-arity. Programs are also required to satisfy a nonambiguity condition:

5. *Nonambiguity*: Given any two rules for the same function symbol f:

$$f\ t_1 \ldots t_m := \{B \to\}M$$
$$f\ s_1 \ldots s_m := \{C \to\}N$$

one of the three following cases must hold:

(a) *No superposition*: $f\ t_1 \ldots t_m$ and $f\ s_1 \ldots s_m$ are not unifiable.

(b) *Fusion of bodies*: $f\ t_1 \ldots t_m$ and $f\ s_1 \ldots s_m$ have a most general unifier (m.g.u.) σ such that $M\sigma, N\sigma$ are identical[1].

(c) *Incompatibility of guards*: $f\ t_1 \ldots t_m$ and $f\ s_1 \ldots s_m$ have a m.g.u. σ such that $(B \wedge C)\sigma$ is unsolvable.

This depends on a notion of unsolvability that must be chosen decidable and such that unsolvable boolean expressions cannot yield the value true under any valuation of their variables; cfr. [Moreno, Rodríguez 89].

At this point, a short digression on the *nonambiguity condition* seems appropriate. Some designers of integrated logic plus functional languages, e.g. K-LEAF [Levi et al. 87], have adopted similar nonambiguity conditions in order to guarantee confluence, which in turn is generally believed to be a necessary condition for the completeness of narrowing as an equation solving procedure, cfr. [Hullot 80]. Actually, it is possible to dispose of confluence, provided that the language's semantics is suitably changed to accommodate a notion of nondeterministic function. Nevertheless, some subtle

---

[1] As usual, $M\ \sigma$ denotes the expression M where all variables are replaced according to σ.

semantic problems must be solved in this approach; see [Hussmann 89]. For simplicity, we have chosen to avoid ambiguity in our presentation, though the BABEL machine is able to execute ambiguous programs by backtracking.

We assume some predefined rules for the primitive function symbols and the guarded and conditional expressions. Among them, we have

- Rules for the boolean operations

| $\neg$ false | := | true |
| $\neg$ true | := | false |

| false $\wedge$ Y | := | false |
| true $\wedge$ Y | := | Y |

| false $\vee$ Y | := | Y |
| true $\vee$ Y | := | true |

- Rules for weak equality

$$
\begin{aligned}
(c = c) &:= \text{true} && \% \ c/0 \in DC_\Sigma, \text{ constant} \\
(c(X_1,\ldots,X_n) = c(Y_1,\ldots,Y_n)) &:= (X_1 = Y_1) \wedge \ldots \wedge (X_n = Y_n) && \% \ c/n \in DC_\Sigma \\
(c(X_1,\ldots,X_n) = d(Y_1,\ldots,Y_m)) &:= \text{false} && \% \ c/n \in DC_\Sigma, d/m \in DC_\Sigma \text{ different}
\end{aligned}
$$

- Rules for guarded and conditional expressions

| $(\text{true} \rightarrow X)$ | := | X |

| $(\text{true} \rightarrow X \square Y)$ | := | X |
| $(\text{false} \rightarrow X \square Y)$ | := | Y |

The rules for $\wedge$, $\vee$ reflect the sequential character of these connectives. The rules for weak equality must be used respecting the types of constructors. They specify that an expression $(M_1 = M_2)$ will evaluate to true if M_1, M_2 evaluate both to the same term, and will evaluate to false if M_1, M_2 evaluate to different terms. $(M_1 = M_2)$ will be undefined if the evaluation of M_1 or M_2 does not terminate.

BABEL, as described in [Moreno, Rodríguez 89], supports infinite terms through lazy evaluation. This gives rise to a more sophisticated behaviour of weak equality, since an expression $(M_1 = M_2)$ may be lazily evaluated to false even if the complete evaluation of M_1 or M_2 would not terminate.

As a last remark on BABEL programs, let us mention that pure PROLOG can be straightforwardly translated to BABEL. For instance, the PROLOG program

```
append([], Ys, Ys).
append([X|Xs], Ys, [X|Zs]) :- append(Xs,Ys,Zs).
```

can be translated as follows:

```
typevar A.
type list(A) = nil | cons (A, list(A)).
fun  append : list(A) → list(A) → list(A) → bool.
     append [] Ys Zs := (Zs = Ys) → true.
     append [X|Xs] Ys [Z|Zs] := (Z=X ∧ (append Xs Ys Zs)) → true.
```

The idea is that PROLOG clauses translate into guarded BABEL rules whose body is identical to true. Weak equality must be used to force left linearity, by adding some new equalities between variables to the guard, if needed. Boolean valued functions play the role of predicates. In fact, a concrete BABEL implementation could allow a PROLOG-like syntax as syntactic sugar; in this way, pure PROLOG programs would be legal BABEL programs almost without any syntactic changes, cfr. [Moreno, Rodríguez 89].

Of course, append can also be programmed as a function in BABEL. The point is that the just given version behaves like the PROLOG append predicate under BABEL's evaluation mechanism.

2.2 Narrowing Semantics

A *goal* for a given BABEL Σ-program is any Σ-expression M which includes no higher-order variables. To solve a goal, the BABEL machine tries to reduce it to a normalized form by means of *narrowing*. This means that the lhs of rules for the defined and predefined function symbols are unified with appropriate subexpressions, which are then replaced by the corresponding instance of the rule's rhs. This process is repeated until a normal form N is reached. Then, N is taken as the *result* of the evaluation, and all bindings of variables occurring in M that have been accumulated during the reduction are regarded as the *answer*, similarly as in PROLOG. The combination of result and answer will be called *outcome* in the sequel.

The restrictions imposed on higher-order variables are worthy of being noted carefully. Higher-order variables may occur in the lhs of rules, but are forbidden to occur free in either rhs of rules or goals. This means that they are used only for rewriting, as in functional programming.

The *narrowing semantics* of BABEL is based on the following *narrowing rule*:

Let $f t_1 \ldots t_m := R$ be a variant of a BABEL rule in the program which shares no variables with $(f\ M_1 \ldots M_m)$. If there exists some most general unifier $\sigma \cup \theta$ (where σ binds variables in $(f\ M_1 \ldots M_m)$ and θ binds variables in $(f\ t_1 \ldots t_m)$) with

$$t_i\theta = M_i\sigma \text{ for } 1 \le i \le m,$$

then we may reduce

$$(f\ M_1 \ldots M_m) \longrightarrow_\sigma R\theta.$$

The *one-step narrowing relation*

$$M \Longrightarrow_\sigma N$$

where M, N are BABEL expressions and σ is a finite substitution of some first order variables occurring in M by terms, will be defined as follows

- $M_i \longrightarrow_\sigma N_i$ with $i \in \{1, \ldots, n\}$ implies

$$c(M_1, \ldots, M_i, \ldots, M_n) \Longrightarrow_\sigma c(M_1\sigma, \ldots, N_i, \ldots, M_n\sigma) \text{ and}$$
$$(M_1 \ldots M_i \ldots M_n) \Longrightarrow_\sigma (M_1\sigma \ldots N_i \ldots M_n\sigma)$$

- $B \longrightarrow_\sigma B'$ implies

$$(B \to M) \Longrightarrow_\sigma (B' \to M\sigma) \text{ and } (B \to M_1 \square M_2) \Longrightarrow_\sigma (B' \to M_1\sigma \square M_2\sigma)$$

We write

$$M \stackrel{*}{\Longrightarrow}_\sigma N$$

to indicate the result of *several* narrowing steps, where σ is the composition of the substitutions involved in the single steps, restricted to the variables occurring in M.

Narrowing of a BABEL-expression with constructed type may have the following outcomes:

- *success*: $M \stackrel{*}{\Longrightarrow}_\sigma t$ with $t \in Term_\Sigma$

- *failure*: $M \stackrel{*}{\Longrightarrow}_\sigma N$, N is not further narrowable and $N \notin Term_\Sigma$

- *nontermination*.

For simplicity, we restrict ourselves in this paper to an innermost narrowing strategy. Of course, this implies that infinite objects cannot be used.

We show the innermost evaluation of a goal for the map program. The redex at each step is underlined, and some intermediate steps (corresponding to predefined functions) are skipped.

$$\text{map } (+\ 2)[X, 3] = [6, Y]$$
$$\rightarrow \quad [\underline{(+\ 2\ X)} \mid \text{map } (+\ 2)[3]] = [6, Y]$$
$$\overset{*}{\rightarrow} \quad [s^2(X) \mid \underline{\text{map } (+\ 2)[3]}] = [6, Y]$$
$$\rightarrow \quad [s^2(X), \underline{(+\ 2\ 3)} \mid \text{map } (+\ 2)[\,]] = [6, Y]$$
$$\overset{*}{\rightarrow} \quad [s^2(X), 5 \mid \underline{\text{map } (+\ 2)[\,]}] = [6, Y]$$
$$\rightarrow \quad \underline{[s^2(X), 5] = [6, Y]}$$
$$\rightarrow \quad \underline{(s^2(X) = 6)} \wedge ([5] = [Y])$$
$$\overset{*}{\rightarrow}_{\{X/4\}} \quad \underline{([5] = [Y])}$$
$$\rightarrow \quad (\underline{(5 = Y)} \wedge ([\,] = [\,]))$$
$$\overset{*}{\rightarrow}_{\{Y/5\}} \quad \text{true}$$

The outcome of this derivation consists of result true and answer $\{X/4, Y/5\}$. Some predefined rules for +, = and $\wedge$ have been used.

The BABEL machine tries the program's rules in their textual ordering, tries to evaluate functional expressions before applying them, and evaluates arguments from left to right; it backtracks when a failure or a user's request for alternative solutions occurs.

Primitive symbols are handled as if the user had introduced them through their predefined rules. However, this is not exactly so in all cases: Guarded and conditional expressions are handled in the usual non-strict way, i.e. evaluation of the guard/condition before evaluation of the alternatives. The evaluation of the second member in conjunctions and disjunctions is avoided whenever possible, and weak equality is implemented through unification for the sake of efficiency. This implementation works fine with any equality $t_1 = t_2$ between two terms whose unification either succeeds or finitely fails; but it does not work properly in cases such as $X = c(Y)$, which allow for infinitely many outcomes with result false and different answers, according to the predefined rules of weak equality. The actual implementation will ignore these outcomes. The user can overcome this limitation by explicitly programming his own equality. The price to pay will be a risk of nontermination.

For the first-order fragment of BABEL there is also a declarative semantics, based on algebraic, consistently complete CPOs, and related to a lazy version of narrowing through soundness and completeness theorems; cfr. [Moreno, Rodríguez 89], [Moreno 89]. These results are in the same spirit as those obtained for the language K-LEAF [Levi et al. 87]. Soundness and completeness results are also presented in [Reddy 85] for the eager case, and claimed to hold in [Reddy 87]. However, Reddy's denotational semantics is rather different from our declarative semantics.

3 Structure of the BABEL Machine

The BABEL machine is a sequential abstract graph narrowing machine by which the functional logic language BABEL will be implemented using an innermost evaluation strategy. This strategy has been chosen for simplicity in order to develop a first version of an abstract machine for BABEL.

The main component of the machine is a graph, which contains, among others, so called task nodes which correspond to ordinary activation records but contain much more information. A task node contains e.g. a local data stack for data manipulations and a local program counter. For the organization of backtracking a local trail is necessary. It is used in the same way as in the Warren Abstract Machine (WAM) [Warren 83] to keep track of variable bindings which must be removed in the case of backtracking.

Due to the use of local data stacks and local trails the machine has a very decentralized organization. This will simplify a later parallelization of the machine, i.e. the incorporation of the machine in a parallel environment.

- Task Nodes:

TASK	code address	argument list	local variables	status
status-information (only if status = active or evaluated)				
backtracking information (only if status = active or evaluated)				

- Terminal Nodes:

  - Constructor Nodes:

CONSTR	constructor name	pointers to components

  - Function Nodes:

FUNCTION	code address	partial argument list
number of local variables	number of missing arguments	

- Variable Nodes:

  - Unbound Variable Nodes: | UBV |

  - Bound Variable Nodes: | VAR | Graph-address |

Figure 1: Structure of Graph Nodes

The store of the BABEL machine consists of three components:

- the *program store* which contains the translations of the BABEL rules into machine code,

- the *graph*, which may contain task-, variable- and terminal nodes, and

- the *active task pointer* which points at the task node which corresponds to the currently executed procedure call. A BABEL procedure consists of all program rules corresponding to one function symbol.

Thus, we define

$$BAM := \langle \underset{\text{Store}}{St} , \underset{\substack{\text{Transition} \\ \text{relation}}}{\vdash} \rangle$$

where $St := \text{Program\_store} \times \text{Active\_task\_pointer} \times \text{Graph}$.

A state of the machine is usually denoted by (p,atp,G), where p ∈ Program_store, atp ∈ Active_task_pointer and G ∈ Graph.

3.1 The Graph Component

The graph component is modelled as a mapping from graph addresses into the graph nodes:

$$\text{Graph} := \text{Graph\_addresses} \rightarrow \text{Graph\_nodes, where}$$
$$\text{Graph\_nodes} := \text{Task\_nodes} \cup \text{Terminal\_nodes} \cup \text{Variable\_nodes}.$$

Figure 1 indicates the structure of the different graph nodes. The computation is controlled by the *task nodes* which represent applications.

Each task node contains the address of the first line of code for the corresponding function symbol, pointers to the graph representation of the arguments and a list of pointers to unbound variable nodes which represent local variables. Depending on the status of a task — we distinguish *dormant, active* and *evaluated* tasks — additional information is provided within the task node. The *status-information* of active and evaluated tasks consists of a local stack which is needed for the organization of data manipulations, a program counter which indicates the next instruction and a pointer to the father node, i.e. the node by which the current node has been created. This father pointer is used when a task finishes successfully and the control has to be returned to the father task.

Since BABEL is also a logic language, tasks must be able to perform backtracking. For this reason, active and evaluated task nodes contain certain *backtracking* information. This consists of a local trail which keeps track of variable bindings to be removed in case of backtracking; pointers to the 'previous brother' and the 'last son', which help to find the task to be reactivated when backtracking occurs; a backtrack address, which points to the code that must be executed if backtracking reactivates the task, and finally safe copies of the father's program counter, local stack and local trail, that are needed to restore the machine state in case of backtracking. All this will be explained in detail in section 4, where the organization of backtracking will be discussed.

In addition to the task nodes the graph contains *terminal* and *variable nodes*. Terminal nodes are constructor or function nodes.

Constructor nodes represent structured data. They contain the constructor name and a list of pointers to the graphs of the components of the structure.

Function nodes represent functional data which always correspond to partial function applications. Consequently a function node contains essentially the same base information as a task node (address of first line of code of the function, (partial) list of arguments, number of local variables, i.e. the maximum number of variables occurring in a rule for the function symbol) and additionally the number of arguments that are necessary to make the function application complete.

Variable nodes are needed for the organization of unification. We distinguish nodes for unbound and bound variables. Unbound variable nodes consist only of a tag (UBV). When a variable is bound to some terminal node the graph address of this node is written into the bound variable node which is indicated by the tag VAR. No more information needs to be stored for variables.

3.2 Machine Instructions

This subsection gives a short discussion of the machine instructions of $\mathcal{BAM}$. Five classes of machine instructions are distinguished.

3.2.1 Stack Instructions

Stack instructions are needed for an efficient implementation of some of the primitive functions of BABEL, especially for the logic negation (NOT) and the equality operator (CHECKEQ).

3.2.2 Graph Instructions

Graph instructions are used for the graph manipulation. By LOAD-instructions the addresses of arguments of the active task (LOAD i) or pointers to local variables (LOADX i) can be pushed onto the local stack, i.e. the stack within the task node of the active task.

Constructor nodes are generated by execution of the instruction 'CONSTRNODE (c, m)', where c is the constructor name and m is the number of components whose addresses are taken from the local stack and replaced by the address of the new node.

Task and function nodes are created by the instruction 'NODE (ca, numarg, arity, locals)', which has four parameters: the code address of the function, the number of arguments of the function application that are given on the stack, the program arity of the function, and finally the number of local variables. If enough arguments are given, i.e. numarg = arity, a dormant task node will be constructed. Otherwise, a function node will be created.

To add further arguments to a function node, we use the instruction APPLY i that expects i graph addresses and a pointer to a function node on top of the stack. The i graph addresses are added to the argument list of the function node. If this yields a complete application, a dormant task node is generated. Otherwise, a new function node is built. The existing function node must not be overwritten because of the possibility of sharing.

3.2.3 Unification Instructions

For the organization of unification we need the following instructions.

'UNIFYCONST (c, arity, label)' tries to unify the top element of the local stack with the constructor c. The top element of the data stack points at a constructor node or at a variable node.

In the case of a constructor node with constructor c the argument list of this node is copied onto the stack. Further unification steps will be controlled by the code that follows the UNIFYCONST-instruction. If the constructor name in the node is different from c backtracking occurs.

If the top of the stack points at an unbound variable node, this variable must be bound to a term whose top level constructor will be c. In this case a graph representation for the term must be constructed. The address of the code that generates such a graph representation is given as the third parameter (label) of the UNIFYCONST-instruction. Thus in the case of an unbound variable the program counter of the active task is set to 'label'. After the construction of the graph the binding of the unbound variable to the new graph is performed by executing the instruction BIND, that expects a pointer to an unbound variable node and a pointer to a constructor node on top of the stack and that binds the variable to the term graph whose root is the constructor node.

The 'UNIFYVAR i'-instruction binds the i-th local variable, that will be unbound when executing this instruction due to the linearity restriction of the BABEL-rules, to the graph whose address is on top of the stack. The implementation of an occur-check and a general unification algorithm is not necessary at this place due to the left linearity.

The UNDO-instruction is used to delete variable bindings in case of backtracking.

3.2.4 Control Instructions

Control instructions are jump instructions. The unconditional 'JMP label' sets the program counter of the active task to label. The conditional jump instructions 'JMT label' and 'JMF label' cause a jump only if the boolean value true and false, respectively, is represented by the top element of the stack.

3.2.5 Process Instructions

The activation and termination of tasks is controlled by the process instructions EVALUATE and RET, respectively. The EVALUATE-instruction performs a subroutine call to the dormant task whose address is given on top of the stack. The RET-instruction is executed when a task terminates successfully and the control can be given back to the father task.

For the organization of backtracking the instructions 'BACKTRACK label' and 'FAILRET' are necessary. The BACKTRACK-instruction initializes the backtracking information of a task. FAIL-RET will be executed when a task fails, i.e. no solution can be produced. The 'predecessor' of the task must then be reactivated and forced to evaluate in a different way. For more details, see the explanation of backtracking in section 4.

To control the behaviour of the machine on the top level, some more instructions are necessary.

- The instruction 'MORE' asks the user if more solutions are to be searched.

- The instruction 'FORCE' forces the last successfully terminated task to backtrack and thus to compute more solutions.

- The instruction 'PRINTFAILURE' finishes the whole execution with the output 'no (more) solutions have been found'. The instruction 'PRINTRESULT' is used to output a solution which consists of the result value and bindings of the local variables within the objective.

3.3 Compilation of BABEL-Programs

A BABEL program consists (mainly) of a set of rules and an expression (called the objective or goal), which is to be evaluated using the rules. The rules are grouped according to the function symbol they define. Hence, a BABEL program looks like this:

$$\text{PROC}(f_1, m_1, k_1)$$
$$\cdots$$
$$\text{PROC}(f_n, m_n, k_n)$$
$$\text{OBJECTIVE}(k_0)$$

where $\text{PROC}(f_i, m_i, k_i)$ denotes the set of rules defining function symbol f_i with program-arity m_i and k_i local variables $(1 \le i \le n)$. k_0 is the number of variables within the objective. The machine code for a BABEL program is the following:

```
        0:  NODE (obj, 0, 0, k₀)
        1:  EVALUATE
        2:  PRINTRESULT
        3:  MORE
        4:  JMF end
        5:  FORCE
            proctrans (PROC(f₁, m₁, k₁))
            ...
            proctrans (PROC(fₙ, mₙ, kₙ))
      obj:  BACKTRACK last_fail
            exptrans (OBJECTIVE(k₀))
last_fail:  PRINTFAILURE
      end:  STOP.
```

The first code generates a task node for the objective, starts its evaluation by EVALUATE, and prints the result of the program after a successful evaluation. If the programmer asks for more solutions, the FORCE-instruction is executed and the task of the objective is forced to backtrack.

After this preliminary code, the translation of the procedures follows. This translation is done using the *proctrans* scheme. Finally, code for the objective is produced. The BACKTRACK command stores the label to which to backtrack in case of a failure. The scheme *exptrans* produces code for the evaluation of the objective. If this evaluation fails finally this is reported by the PRINTFAILURE command.

For a function symbol f with program-arity m and defining rules

$$f\, t_{i1} \ldots t_{im} := \text{body}_i \quad (1 \le i \le r)$$

the following code will be generated by the scheme *proctrans*:

```
              BACKTRACK label₁
              ruletrans (f t₁₁...t₁ₘ := body₁ )
    label₁:   UNDO
              BACKTRACK label₂
              ruletrans (f t₂₁...t₂ₘ := body₂ )
    label₂:   UNDO
                ⋮
  label_{r-1}: UNDO
              BACKTRACK labelᵣ
              ruletrans (f t_{r1}...t_{rm} := bodyᵣ )
    labelᵣ:   UNDO
              FAILRET
```

The defining rules of a function symbol are tested in their textual ordering. If all rules fail, the FAILRET command is used to force the predecessor of a task to backtrack.

The translation of each rule consists of code for the unification of the arguments of the function application with the terms on the left hand side of the rule and code for the evaluation of the body. For a rule

$$f\ t_1 \dots t_m := \text{body}$$

the following code will be produced by the scheme *ruletrans*:

> LOAD 1
> *unifytrans* (t_1)
>
> $\vdots$
>
> LOAD m
> *unifytrans* (t_m)
> *exptrans* (body)
> RET

The following translation schemes are used:

- *unifytrans* : $\text{Term}_\Sigma \to \mathcal{BAM}\text{-Code}$ generates code, which unifies an argument of the actual task with the corresponding term on the left hand side of a rule.

  unifytrans uses the scheme

- *graphtrans* : $\text{Term}_\Sigma \to \mathcal{BAM}\text{-Code}$ to produce code for the construction of a graph for a term, that has to be bound to an unbound variable in an argument of the actual task.

- *exptrans* : $\text{Exp}_\Sigma \to \mathcal{BAM}\text{-Code}$ produces code, which evaluates an expression to normal form (in particular the right hand side of a rule).

We will not go further into the general details of the code generation. In figure 2 the translation of the map example (see section 2) is given. The map example contains only one procedure with two rules. The code for the first rule — map F [] := [] — causes the following actions. First the label "nextrule" is stored which is used when the rule fails or backtracking is forced by the user. Then, the arguments of the actual task are loaded onto the stack and unified with the corresponding terms of the rule. To unify the first argument with the variable F, a simple UNIFYVAR instruction is sufficient. The unification of the second argument is more complicated. First it is checked (by UNIFYCONST), whether the argument is the constructor nil. If this is the case, the next instruction is executed, which causes a jump to the code for the right hand side. All arguments have now been unified with the corresponding terms on the left hand side of the rule, and hence, the rule is applicable.

If the argument starts with a constructor different from nil, the rule cannot be applied and a jump to the command referenced by the backtrack label (nextrule) is executed to try the next rule.

Otherwise, the argument must be an unbound variable. To apply the rule, this variable must be bound to the constructor nil. Hence, the UNIFYCONST instruction causes a jump to the code (starting at bindlab) which installs this binding. This code consists of a CONSTRNODE instruction, which leaves a pointer to the desired constructor node on the stack, and a BIND instruction, which overwrites the unbound variable by a variable node which points to this constructor node. The first and third possible actions of the UNIFYCONST command correspond to the read and write mode of the WAM [Warren 83] respectively.

The right hand side of the first rule is very simple. A constructor node with tag nil representing the empty list is produced (by CONSTRNODE) as the result, and control is given back to the calling task.

The code for the second rule — map F [X | Xs] := [F X | map F Xs] — starts with an UNDO-instruction that deletes the bindings that have been produced by the first rule. Then, the backtracking label "fail_lab" is stored in the actual task node. After this, the arguments of the actual task are

0:	NODE (obj, 0, 0, k_0)		LOADX 3
1:	EVALUATE		CONSTRNODE (cons, 2)
2:	PRINTRESULT		BIND
3:	MORE	continue2:	LOADX 1
4:	JMF end		LOADX 2
5:	FORCE		APPLY 1
map:	BACKTRACK nextrule		EVALUATE
	LOAD 1		LOADX 1
	UNIFYVAR 1		LOADX 3
	LOAD 2		NODE (map, 2, 2, 3)
	UNIFYCONST (nil, 0, bindlab)		EVALUATE
	JMP continue		CONSTRNODE (cons, 2)
bindlab:	CONSTRNODE (nil, 0)		RET
	BIND	fail_lab:	UNDO
continue:	CONSTRNODE (nil, 0)		FAILRET
	RET	obj:	BACKTRACK last_fail
nextrule:	UNDO		CONSTRNODE (1, 0)
	BACKTRACK fail_lab		NODE (+, 1, 2, 2)
	LOAD 1		LOADX 1
	UNIFYVAR 1		CONSTRNODE (2, 0)
	LOAD 2		CONSTRNODE (cons, 2)
	UNIFYCONST (cons, 2, bindlab2)		NODE (map, 2, 2, 3)
	UNIFYVAR 2		EVALUATE
	UNIFYVAR 3		RET
	JMP continue2	last_fail:	PRINTFAILURE
bindlab2:	LOADX 2		STOP

Figure 2: $\mathcal{BAM}$-Code for the map Example Program

unified with the corresponding terms on the left hand side of the rule. For the first argument, this is exactly the same as before. For the second argument, it is more complicated, since now the term consists of an application of the binary constructor cons to two variables. If the second argument points at a constructor node for the binary constructor cons, the UNIFYCONST command now leaves pointers to both substructures of this argument on the stack. They are unified with the corresponding parts of the terms on the left hand side of the rule (here using UNIFYVAR commands). If the second argument is an unbound variable, this variable is bound to the appropriate constructor term (by the four commands following bindlab2).

The translation of the body of the rule starts at label continue2. First, the local variable F is applied to the local variable X, and the resulting task is evaluated. Furthermore, a task for map with the local variables F and Xs as arguments is created and evaluated. Both results are combined by a node for the binary constructor cons which points at them. Finally control is given back to the calling task by RET.

If the second and last rule also fails, a jump to the command referenced by the current backtrack label "fail_lab" is performed. All bindings produced by the rule are deleted and backtracking is initiated.

The code for the procedure map is followed by the translation of the objective. This translation is done analogously to the translation of the right hand side of a rule. In fact, the objective can be seen as a definition of a nullary function.

The execution of a $\mathcal{BAM}$-program prog starts with the following initial configuration:

$$(\text{prog}, \text{atp}, G_0)$$

where G_0 is a graph which contains only one node representing the initial task (referenced by atp). This initial task is an active task node with the program counter initialized to 0 and its local stack and local trail are empty.

4 Backtracking

This section describes and justifies the backtracking information in task nodes. The content of the backtracking information that has been described in section 3.1 can be seen in figure 3. All this information is generated each time an EVALUATE command is executed. The local *trail* is a list of graph addresses indicating bound variable nodes, which have to be replaced by unbound variable nodes when an UNDO-instruction is executed. Next, there are two pointers to task nodes in the graph: a so called *backtracking pointer* to the 'previous brother' (the node generated previously by the father) and a so called *last son pointer* to the 'last son' (the last son generated by the task).

local trail	backtracking pointer	last son pointer	backtrack address	safe copies of		
				program counter	local stack	local trail
				of the father		

Figure 3: Backtracking information

The backtracking pointer is used when a task fails — there is no possibility of returning a value — to select the task that must then be re-evaluated. If a task is the first son of its father the backtracking pointer is the address of the father. Otherwise the backtracking pointer points at the task node that was activated by the father node just before this task.

The last son pointer is used to initialize the backtracking pointer of newly generated subtasks. It is also used to find the task to re-evaluate in case of backtracking. Of course, at any moment, the address of the active task is the last son pointer of its father.

Using these pointers one can determine an implicit stack of nodes that reflects the order in which nodes have been activated. The control of the BABEL machine is based on the following ideas:

- A task returning with success (RET command) gives the control to the father which continues its execution.

- A task returning with failure (FAILRET command) gives the control to the previous task in the implicit stack.

The recursive description of this stack in terms of the pointers in the graph is:

- The top of the stack is the right-most bottom-most element of the tree (following the last son pointer of all the nodes, beginning with the very first task generated).

- The predecessor of each task is:

  1. its father if its backtracking pointer points to the father. The task is the first son.
  2. Otherwise the predecessor node is the first node of the stack below the node indicated by its backtracking pointer. The predecessor can be determined by doing one step along the backtracking pointer and then following all the last son pointers.

The following example should clarify this description. Consider the following rules of a BABEL program

$$f\,X := h\,a\,((p\,X) \to (g\,X)\Box(l\,X)).$$
$$p\,X := (q\,X) \land (r\,X).$$
$$q\,a := \text{true}.$$
$$q\,b := \text{false}.$$
$$r\,a := \text{true}.$$
$$g\,X := k\,X.$$
$$l\,X := b.$$
$$k\,a := a.$$
$$h\,a\,b := a.$$

and the objective $(f\,X)$.
The following picture indicates the graph structure with the different pointers:

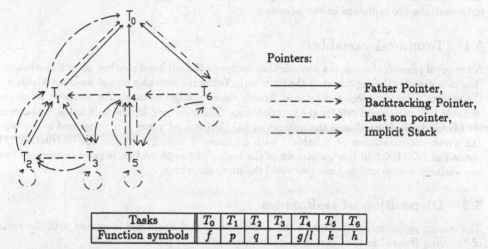

Pointers:

———————→	Father Pointer,
- - - - - - →	Backtracking Pointer,
—·—·—·→	Last son pointer,
—··—··→	Implicit Stack

Tasks	T_0	T_1	T_2	T_3	T_4	T_5	T_6
Function symbols	f	p	q	r	g/l	k	h

Following the policy that a task is not removed from the stack until all its alternatives have been tried it is clear that no answer is lost.

But some other informations for handling backtracking are needed in task nodes. The *backtrack address* is the address of the program where the task must continue in case of backtracking (i.e. the address of the next rule). The rest of the backtracking information is a safe copy of the state of the father: a copy of the program counter, the stack and the local trail (in fact we only need a pointer to the top of the local trail). It is used to restore the state of the father in case of backtracking, undoing all the bad decisions. The copy is made during the execution of the EVALUATE command and the restoring is made along the searching path of the next node to re-evaluate in case of backtracking.

The computation of the previous example shows why these copies are needed. The call to function f creates a task (T_0) that is executed. In order to generate the code for the body of f the first argument of the call to h (constant a) is stored on the local stack. After this, a call to predicate p is done which generates calls to predicates q and r. The first value for p is true binding X to a.

The next step is to continue the execution of the $\mathcal{BAM}$ code for the body of f. The second argument of h is a conditional expression. The "then" expression is selected evaluating g (where evaluation of k is demanded) returning a to the local stack of T_0. Remember that another a was stored on this stack. These two values are eliminated from the stack to construct the task $(h\,a\,a)$. But this task fails (there is no rule for it).

The first task to be re-evaluated is T_5 (for k). In the case that the value of this function changes, we would need to restore the local stack of T_0 to preserve the arguments of h (the first a on the stack).

In our example the backtracking to task T_5 fails as well as the backtracking to T_4 (g). The condition (p X) is re-evaluated. As the boolean value might change, the program counter of T_0 has to be modified to execute again the code for selecting between the "then" or the "else" branch of the conditional. The backtracking to T_3 (r) also fails, and backtracking to T_2 is needed. For this purpose it is necessary to unbind the variable X because T_2 has bound it, i.e. to undo the binding of X noted in the trail of T_2.

5 Implementation

In the implementation of the BABEL Machine we have integrated some extensions and optimizations.

The extensions suppose the inclusion of new nodes: nodes for constants (created at the beginning of the execution and shared for all the nodes that use them) and nodes for numbers. The number nodes lead to new instructions (ADD, SUB, MUL, DIV, MOD) to execute operations, $+$, $-$, $*$, div, mod which can be used in BABEL programs as well as integer literals. The two most important optimizations are explained in the following.

5.1 Temporal variables

A *temporal variable* of a rule is a variable that occurs on the left hand side but not inside a construction (i.e. it is directly the argument of the function). Temporal variables do not need a variable node for themselves. The argument can be used directly instead of the variable. For instance, let us consider variable F in the second rule for the function map. The code used for the unification of this argument is "LOAD 1; Unifyvar 1" and the instruction LOADX is used when F is referenced in the body. We can avoid the unification of variable 1 with argument 1 and directly use the instruction LOAD 1 instead of LOADX 1 in the translation of the body. The optimization is good in memory (we need less variable nodes) and in time (we avoid the unification step).

5.2 Disposition of task nodes

The second optimization deals with the *disposition of task nodes* and is related with the reusability of "binding frames" in the Warren abstract machine.

A task node is no longer needed as soon as the existence of no more alternatives to try is noticed (execution of a FAILRET). But this situation can be found out still earlier, when the task finishes the execution of the last alternative (RET command of the last rule), because the only action that the node can execute is a return with failure. If the information stored in a task node is no longer useful, the node can be deleted from the graph and disposed. From this point of view, the essential information of a task node (w.r.t. the general behaviour of the machine) is the information about its sons (the last son pointer) and bindings that have been made during its execution (the trail). By making a compromise between time and memory efficiency, one could dispose the node of a task that finishes the execution of the last alternative if

- the task has no sons, and

- its trail is empty or

  the task to be re-evaluated in case of failure is the father (its trail is appended to the trail of the father).

This optimization could be handled by a new instruction LASTRET that is used in the translation of the last rule of a function. It is very important because it allows to dispose task nodes (that need a lot of memory), makes the graph smaller and the chains inside it shorter. The performance in memory and execution time is improved because it is faster to find the node to be re-executed in case of backtracking.

5.3 Results

A prototype has been implemented in OCCAM to prepare the development of parallel distributed versions. We are now developping a more serious version in C, with the compiler written in PROLOG. With this version we will have a good measure of the real performance of the machine and compare it with functional languages and PROLOG.

However, the early results show a good behaviour in time (similar to Prolog programs) and a little bit worse in memory. Hence, the optimizations described before are very important. More optimizations need to be included in future versions, for instance a detection of purely functional computations (generating smaller task nodes by avoiding the backtracking information), special treatment of tail recursion and specific instructions for lists.

6 Related Work

Many contributions to the integration of the two main paradigms of declarative programming, logic and functional programming, have been investigated during the last years. [DeGroot, Lindstrom 86] collects significant papers on this field, while [Bellia, Levi 86] analyzes and classifies the main existing approaches to the integration, giving many references. Here, we restrict ourselves to comment some approaches which we find specially related to ours.

Most of the integrated logic plus functional languages proposed up to now are first order. BA-BEL's first order fragment [Moreno, Rodríguez 88,89], [Moreno 89] is quite related to other proposals which use systems of rewrite rules as programs and narrowing as part of the execution mechanism. As representative approaches of this kind let us mention [Reddy 85], where narrowing is proposed as the only execution mechanism, and the work by Dershowitz, Josephson and Plaisted [Dershowitz, Josephson 84], [Dershowitz, Plaisted 85], [Dershowitz 85], [Josephson, Dershowitz 86], where irrevocable (that is, not backtrackable) rewriting is used for simplification, while conditional narrowing is used for solving.

[Reddy 85] distinguishes between constructors and function symbols in the spirit of functional programming. He outlines a denotational semantics and a lazy narrowing strategy; based on [Hullot 80], he presents a soundness and completeness result for innermost narrowing. In first order BABEL, the declarative semantics, soundness and completeness results mentioned in section 2 above are in the spirit of least Herbrand models for Horn clause logic programs, though adapted to lazy evaluation, and much more similar to those for the language K-LEAF [Levi et al. 87] than to Reddy's results. A good discussion of completeness results for conditional narrowing from the point of view of logic plus functional programming can be found in [Giovannetti, Moiso 86].

On the other side, the work by Dershowitz, Josephson and Plaisted is more in the spirit of term rewriting theory. They view narrowing as a particular kind of the superposition operation used in the Knuth-Bendix completion procedure [Knuth, Bendix 70] and adopt an algebraic view, making no attempt to develop a constructor based denotational semantics. In [Josephson, Dershowitz 86], which discusses implementation techniques, it is suggested to use so called conditional terms to simulate conditional narrowing by unconditional rules. An equivalent technique is present in BABEL, where all rules are formally unconditional, but may have as right hand side a guarded expression , whose guard plays the role of a condition which must be narrowed to true before the body can be narrowed.

Some integrated logic plus functional languages with higher order functional programming features have also been proposed. Let us now refer to some representative cases.

[Lindstrom 87] addresses the problem of adding logical variables to a functional language, preserving lazy evaluation, concurrency opportunities, and overall determinacy. The aim is to investigate an efficient implementation on distributed architectures which provides much of the power of AND-parallel logic programming, but without support for OR-parallel search or backtracking.

[Darlington, Guo 88] have extended the functional language HOPE with absolute set abstractions [Darlington et al. 86], whose evaluation uses a kind of lazy narrowing. In this approach, logic variables and unification are restricted to the evaluation of absolute set abstractions. The language has been efficiently implemented.

[Reddy 87] presents a higher order functional logic language, with a denotational semantics and a narrowing based operational semantics. Explicit constructs for nondeterministic choice, existential quantification of logical variables and absolute set abstractions are introduced, and it is claimed that strict constructors are necessary to make good use of the capabilities offered by narrowing. We know of no implementation of this language.

Finally, let us mention the language IDEAL, [Bosco, Giovannetti 86], [Bellia et al. 88], which is a combination of higher order functional programming and PROLOG quite similar in expressiveness to BABEL. IDEAL is not implemented by a machine of its own, but it is instead translated to K-LEAF [Levi et al. 87] by partial evaluation with respect to an equational axiomatization of the λ-calculus; this yields clauses for a first order apply function. K-LEAF, as already discussed in the introduction, is based on Horn clause logic, and has been efficiently implemented by a conservative extension of Warren's abstract machine WAM [Warren 83] with a suspension/reactivation mechanism which emulates demand driven, lazy evaluation of function calls; cfr. [Bosco et al. 89b], [Balboni et al. 89]. This work is based on a theoretical model for emulating narrowing by SLD-resolution [Bosco et al. 88]. BABEL follows a dual approach: Its theoretical model views SLD-resolution as a particular kind of narrowing, and its implementation is achieved by extending a graph reduction machine.

7 Conclusions and Future Work

We have presented an implementation of a higher-order functional logic language by extension of a graph reduction machine. Logic features like unification and backtracking are embedded into this machine. The result is an abstract graph narrowing machine that may allow efficient implementations of the language, especially for functional computations.

To cope with infinite objects and non-strict functions it is necessary to change the evaluation strategy of BAM. The development of a lazy BAM which does not evaluate arguments unless they are needed, is in progress. This machine, on which we will report in a forthcoming paper, evaluates needed arguments of functions only up to head normal form. Sharing of graph nodes is more important for the lazy machine than for the innermost machine.

The main difficulty of the lazy BABEL machine is that the way in which a functional implementation treats lazy evaluation is not quite adequate for a functional logic language. To make a brief discussion we could say that a rule is applied to a subexpression $(fM_1 \ldots M_n)$ following these steps:

1. Demanded arguments by the rule are evaluated until they have head normal form (i.e. there is a constructor at the root).

2. The matching between the head of the rule and the subexpression is tried. If it fails, another rule is applied.

3. The body of the rule is evaluated.

In order to use this approach in BABEL we need to take into account that if an argument does not unify with the corresponding term in the lhs of the rule this does not imply that the rule is not applicable. Another evaluation of the argument could give a new result that unifies with the term. Hence, the utilization of the same mechanism is not possible and it needs to be modified.

Another important research subject is the development of a parallel BABEL machine. In order to simplify the parallelization of BAM, we have chosen a very decentralized structure for BAM. Since we are interested in using large networks of processors, we prefer a loosely coupled architecture, which consists of several processors with local memory communicating by exchanging messages. Tightly coupled architectures are not considered since their number of processors is limited.

The parallel BAM will have a structure similar to the parallel abstract machine PAM [Loogen et al. 89], which has been developped for the parallel implementation of functional languages on a loosely coupled network of processors. Each processing unit of the PAM contains a communication unit and a reduction unit. The communication units are responsible for the exchange of messages, while each reduction unit represents a sequential graph reducer that has been extended for the integration in a parallel machine. In the parallel BAM each reduction unit is replaced by a narrowing unit, which is an analogous extension of the sequential BAM.

The parallelization of the BAM is more complicated than the parallel implementation of a functional language. The reason is the occurrence of side effects caused by logical variables. Thus, more synchronization between parallel processes is needed. In the literature, AND- and OR-parallel implementations of logic programs are investigated. AND-parallelism can be seen as a parallel execution of the arguments of a function. In PROLOG this function is the AND-operation, in BABEL arbitrary functions can be used (as in functional languages). OR-parallelism uses a parallel execution of the different rules for each function symbol.

We are currently working on an AND- and on an OR-parallel version of the BAM, that will be implemented on a transputer system (like the PAM).

References

[Balboni et al. 89] G.P.Balboni, P.G.Bosco, C.Cecchi, R.Melen, C.Moiso, G.Sofi: *Implementation of a Parallel Logic Plus Functional Language*, in: P.Treleaven (ed.), Parallel Computers: Object Oriented, Functional and Logic, Wiley 1989.

[Bellia, Levi 86] M. Bellia, G. Levi: *The Relation between Logic and Functional Languages*, Journal of Logic Programming, Vol.3, 1986, 217–236.

[Bellia et al. 88] M.Bellia, P.G.Bosco, E.Giovannetti, C.Moiso, C.Palamidessi: *A two level approach to logic and functional programming*, CSELT Technical Reports — Vol. XVI, No. 5, August 1988.

[Bosco, Giovannetti 86] P.G.Bosco, E.Giovannetti: *IDEAL: An Ideal DEductive Applicative Language*, IEEE Symp. on Logic Programming 1986, IEEE Comp. Soc. Press, 89-94.

[Bosco et al. 88] P.G. Bosco, E. Giovannetti, C. Moiso: *Narrowing versus SLD–resolution*, Theoretical Computer Science 59, 1988, 3–23.

[Bosco et al. 89] P.G.Bosco, C.Cecchi, E.Giovannetti, C.Moiso and C.Palamidessi: *Using resolution for a sound and efficient integration of logic and functional programming*, in: J. de Bakker (ed.), *Languages for parallel architectures: Design, semantics, implementation models*, Wiley 1989.

[Bosco et al. 89b] P.G.Bosco, C.Cecchi, C.Moiso: *An extension of WAM for K-LEAF: A WAM-based compilation of conditional narrowing*, Int. Conf. on Logic Programming, Lisboa, 1989.

[Damas, Milner 82] L. Damas and R. Milner: *Principal type schemes for functional programs*, ACM Symp. on Principles of Programming Languages, 1982, 207–212.

[Darlington et al. 86] J.Darlington, A.J.Field and H.Pull: *The unification of functional and logic languages*, in: [DeGroot, Lindstrom 86], 37-70.

[Darlington, Guo 88] J.Darlington, Y.Guo: *Narrowing and Unification in Functional Programming — An Evaluation Mechanism for Absolute Set Abstraction*, Working Draft, November 1988.

[DeGroot, Lindstrom 86] D.DeGroot, G.Lindstrom (eds.): *Logic Programming: Functions, Relations, Equations*, Prentice Hall 1986.

[Dershowitz 85] N.Dershowitz: *Computing with Rewrite Systems*, Information and Control 65 ,1985, 122-157.

[Dershowitz, Josephson 84] N.Dershowitz, N.A.Josephson: *Logic Programming by Completion*, 2nd. Int. Conf. on Logic Programming, Uppsala, Sweden, July 1984, 313-320.

[Dershowitz, Plaisted 85] N.Dershowitz, D.A.Plaisted: *Logic Programming cum Applicative Programming*, IEEE Int. Symp. on Logic Programming 1985, IEEE Comp. Soc. Press, 54-66.

[van Emden, Yukawa 87] M.H.van Emden, K.Yukawa: *Logic Programming with Equations*, Journal of Logic Programming, Vol.4, 1987.

[Giovannetti, Moiso 86] E.Giovannetti, C.Moiso: *A completeness result for E-unification algorithms based on conditional narrowing*, Workshop on Foundations of Logic and Functional Programming, Trento, Italy, Dec. 1986, LNCS 306, Springer 1986, 157-167.

[Hullot 80] J.M.Hullot: *Canonical Forms and Unification*, 5th Int. Conference in Automated Deduction, LNCS 87, Springer 1980, 318-334.

[Hussmann 89] H.Hussmann: *Nondeterministic Algebraic Specifications and Nonconfluent Term Rewriting*, Conf. on Algebraic and Logic Programming, LNCS 343, Springer 1989, 31-40.

[Josephson, Dershowitz 86] A.Josephson, N.Dershowitz: *An Implementation of Narrowing: The RITE Way*, Conf. on Logic Programming 1986, IEEE Comp. Soc. Press 1986, 187-197.

[Knuth, Bendix 70] D.E.Knuth, P.B.Bendix: *Simple word problems in universal algebras*, in "Computational Problems in Abstract Algebra", Pergamon, Oxford, U.K., 1970, 263-297.

[Kuchen et al. 89] H.Kuchen, R.Loogen, J.J. Moreno-Navarro, M.Rodríguez-Artalejo: *Graph-based Implementation of a Functional Logic Language*, Aachener Informatik-Berichte Nr. 89-20, RWTH Aachen, 1989.

[Levi et al. 87] G.Levi, C.Palamidessi, P.G.Bosco, E.Giovannetti and C.Moiso: *A complete semantic characterization of K-LEAF, a logic language with partial functions*, IEEE Int. Symp. on Logic Programming 1987, IEEE Soc. Press, 318-327.

[Lindstrom 87] G.Lindstrom: *Implementing logical variables on a graph reduction architecture*, Workshop on Graph Reduction, LNCS 279, Springer 1987, 382-400.

[Loogen et al. 89] R.Loogen, H.Kuchen, K.Indermark, W.Damm: *Distributed Implementation of Programmed Graph Reduction*, Conf. on Parallel Architectures and Languages Europe 1989, LNCS 365, Springer 1989.

[Milner 78] R. Milner: *A theory of type polymorphism in programming*, Journal of Computer and System Sciences, 17(3), 1978.

[Moreno, Rodríguez 88] J.J.Moreno-Navarro, M.Rodríguez-Artalejo: *BABEL: A functional and logic programming language based on constructor discipline and narrowing*, Conf. on Algebraic and Logic Programming, LNCS 343, Springer 1989.

[Moreno, Rodríguez 89] J.J.Moreno-Navarro, M.Rodríguez-Artalejo: *Logic Programming with Functions and Predicates: The Language BABEL*, Technical Report DIA/89/3, Universidad Complutense, Madrid 1989, to appear in the Journal of Logic Programming.

[Moreno 89] J.J.Moreno-Navarro: *Diseño, semántica e implementación de BABEL, un lenguaje que integra la programación funcional y lógica*, Ph.D. Thesis, Facultad de Informática UPM, Madrid, July 1989, (in spanish).

[Reddy 85] U.S.Reddy: *Narrowing as the Operational Semantics of Functional Languages*, IEEE Int. Symp. on Logic Programming, IEEE Computer Society Press, July 1985, 138-151.

[Reddy 87] U.S.Reddy: *Functional Logic Languages, Part I*, Workshop on Graph Reduction, LNCS 279, Springer 1987, 401-425.

[Turner 85] D.A.Turner: *Miranda: A non-strict functional language with polymorphic types*, ACM Conf. on Functional Languages and Computer Architecture 1985, LNCS 201, Springer 1985, 1-16.

[Warren 83] D.H.D.Warren: *An Abstract PROLOG Instruction Set*, Technical Note 309, SRI International, Menlo Park, California, October 1983.

Eureka Definitions for Free!

or

Disagreement Points for Fold/Unfold Transformations

Hanne Riis Nielson & Flemming Nielson
Computer Science Department
Aarhus University, Denmark

Abstract

The fold/unfold framework of Burstall and Darlington is a very powerful framework for transforming function definitions in the form of recursion equation schemes. This may be used to transform a function so as to improve the efficiency of its implementation. However, for this to work the user must supply so-called Eureka definitions and it may require some ingenuity to construct these. This paper shows that a class of these Eureka definitions can be derived in a rather systematic way.

1 Introduction

We shall begin by an example of the fold/unfold framework of Burstall and Darlington [1]. So consider the function

$$\text{lookup (cons (pair x y) xys) z} = \text{IF eq x z THEN y ELSE lookup xys z}$$

that takes a list of pairs as its first argument. It then takes a second argument and recursively looks for it as a first component in one of the pairs in the list and if successful returns the corresponding second component.

This function might be used in a compiler to lookup an identifier in the environment. Typically the identifiers will be known at compile-time whereas the actual values will not be known until run-time. This suggests that more efficient code could be generated if the lookup function was changed so that the compile-time part of the environment could be handled separately from the run-time part because then it would be a compile-time task to determine where some identifier occurs.

We therefore want to *transform* the program so as to *separate* the two components in the list of pairs. A curried version of the transformed lookup function may be written

$$\text{lookup' (cons x xs) z (cons y ys)} = \text{IF eq x z THEN y ELSE lookup' xs z ys}$$

As we shall now see this function can be derived in a systematic way using the *fold/unfold framework*.

The starting point will be a so-called *Eureka definition* and in general this is the step where human ingenuity seems most needed [1]:

$$\text{lookup' xs z ys} = \text{lookup (zip (pair xs ys)) z}$$

Here

$$\text{zip (pair nil nil)} = \text{nil}$$

$$\text{zip (pair (cons x xs) (cons y ys))} = \text{cons (pair x y) (zip (pair xs ys))}$$

will construct a list of pairs from a pair of lists of equal length. We then get

lookup' (cons x xs) z (cons y ys)
  ≡ lookup (zip (pair (cons x xs) (cons y ys))) z   (Eureka definition)
  ≡ lookup (cons (pair x y) (zip (pair xs ys))) z   (unfold zip)
  ≡ IF eq x z THEN y ELSE lookup (zip (pair xs ys)) z (unfold lookup)
  ≡ IF eq x z THEN y ELSE lookup' xs z ys   (fold lookup')

The purpose of this paper is to present a heuristics for how to construct (a class of) Eureka definitions. This centers around systematic type transformations and ways of identifying which type transformations may be useful.

So the starting point will be the type of the lookup function:

lookup: $(\text{LIST } (\text{PAIR } \alpha \ \beta)) \rightarrow \alpha \rightarrow \beta$

Here α and β are type variables that can be instantiated with arbitrary types. As in SML [6], MIRANDA [13] and HASKELL [3] we have type constructors for user defined datatypes. The type constructors needed here may have been introduced by the following equations:

data LIST α = nil + cons α (LIST α)

data PAIR α β = pair α β

The type of the transformed function then is

lookup': $(\text{LIST } \alpha) \rightarrow \alpha \rightarrow (\text{LIST } \beta) \rightarrow \beta$

We shall see later that the corresponding Eureka definition can be produced systematically from the transformations on the types, i.e. from the transformation of the type of lookup into the type of lookup'.

2 Disagreement points

To prepare for this development we first need to identify *where* it might be profitable to apply a type transformation like the one that changed lookup into lookup'. This is facilitated by the the tree representation of types. Here there will be three sorts of nodes in the trees that correspond to types:

- binary nodes labeled →,

- k-ary nodes labeled by type constructors, and

- 0-ary nodes labeled by type variables.

Example: For the type LIST (PAIR STRING INT) → STRING → INT we get the tree:

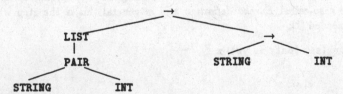

Actually, we always consider a type in a certain context that contains the datatype definitions used in it. To model this we assume that there is a disagreement environment *daenv* that contains the necessary information (to be detailed below). Formally, this means that we always consider pairs consisting of a disagreement environment and a type (represented as a tree).

2.1 Consistently marked trees

To identify disagreement points we shall mark (some of) the nodes in type trees with information about which types should be *separated*. In this paper we shall use marks c and r for this purpose. In general one may have any number of marks but at least for the lookup function it seems sufficient with two marks as we only want to separate two types (using the intuition that one should live at compile-time and the other at run-time). The marks thus correspond to the different *stages* in [4].

We shall say that a tree is *consistently marked*, relative to a disagreement environment *daenv*, if

- all nodes are marked by either c or r,

- if a node for the type constructer *tycon* of arity k is marked d and its k sons are marked d_1, $\cdots$, d_k then $d_1 \cdots d_k d \in daenv(tycon)$,

- if a node for the type variable *tyvar* is marked d then $d \in daenv(tyvar)$,

- if a node for the function space constructor $\rightarrow$ is marked d and its two sons are marked d_1 and d_2 then $d_1 d_2 d \in daenv(\rightarrow)$.

Example: For the tree above we shall assume that $daenv(\texttt{STRING}) = \{c\}$ and $daenv(\texttt{INT}) = \{r\}$ in order to indicate that we want the STRING and INT components separated from one another. For the remaining type constructors we have $daenv(\texttt{PAIR}) = \{ccc, rrr\}$ and $daenv(\texttt{LIST}) = \{cc, rr\}$ to indicate that 'the separations' should be kept separate. We shall further assume that $daenv(\rightarrow) = \{ccc, rrr, rrc\}$ but no harm would result from using $daenv(\rightarrow) = \{ccc, rrr\}$. ∎

The intention thus is that the mark of the root of a subtree indicates in which separation the corresponding subtype should be placed. The general use of $daenv(tycon) = \{c \cdots c, \ r \cdots r\}$ for a k-ary type constructor (k≥1) thus attempts to keep close subtypes together in the same separation if at all possible. Thus $daenv(\rightarrow)$ should contain at least ccc and rrr. By adding rrc one incorporates the intention that at compile-time one may manipulate code, i.e. functions that manipulate run-time entities, but it is beyond the scope of the present paper to go into the philosophical discussions of which choice is likely to be most useful in general.

However, given a type there is no guarantee that the corresponding tree can be made into a consistently marked tree. We shall therefore say that a node N in a partially marked tree is a *disagreement point* if

- each of the subtrees of N can be extended to consistently marked trees, but

- the subtree with root N cannot be extended to a consistently marked tree.

If the tree representation of an annotated type contains a disagreement point then that point indicates where a type transformation may be desired.

Example: For the example above we have two disagreement points. The node labeled PAIR is a disagreement point because its two subtrees can be marked consistently but the subtree itself cannot be. Also the lowest node in the tree labeled $\rightarrow$ is a disagreement point. The node labeled LIST is not a disagreement point since its subtree cannot be marked consistently. This demonstrates that disagreement points are situated as low in the tree as possible. ∎

2.2 Disagreement point analysis

As observed in the above example it follows from the definition of disagreement points that they are as low in the tree as possible. This suggests that an algorithm for identifying disagreement points should perform a bottom-up traversal of the tree while checking the existence of consistently marked extensions of subtrees.

Consider the algorithm of Table 1. Here B is the set of disagreement markings that might apply for

```
INPUT:    a partially marked tree, T, and its disagreement environment, daenv
OUTPUT:   a disagreement point, N₀, if one exists
METHOD:   paint all nodes of T white
          WHILE white nodes remain in T DO
                LET N₀ be a (leftmost) leaf in the subtree of white nodes in T
                LET N₁, ··· Nₖ be the roots of the subtrees of N₀
                CASE label of N₀ OF tycon: LET B = daenv(tycon)
                                    tyvar: LET B = daenv(tyvar)
                                    →:     LET B = daenv(→)
                LET C = B ∩ {d₁··· dₖ d₀ | ∀i: if Nᵢ is marked dᵢ' then dᵢ = dᵢ'}
                IF C = ∅ THEN HALT (with N₀ as disagreement point)
                FOR i = 0, 1, ···, k DO
                      IF πᵢ(C) is a singleton, e.g. {dᵢ"} THEN mark Nᵢ in T with dᵢ"
                paint N₀ black
```

Table 1: Disagreement point analysis algorithm

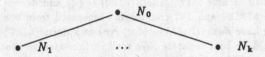

as far as the disagreement environment, *daenv*, is concerned and C is the subset of B that agrees with the markings that have already been placed in the tree. The set $\pi_i(C)$ is obtained by selecting all i'th components, i.e.

$$\pi_i(C) = \{d_i \mid d_1 \cdots d_k \, d_0 \in C\}$$

and note that if N_i is marked with d_i' then $\pi_i(C)$ will be $\{d_i'\}$ so that the node N_i is simply remarked with d_i" $= d_i$'.

The key insight needed to understand the algorithm is to observe that the following invariant holds at each entry to the WHILE-loop:

- all black subtrees may be extended to consistently marked trees, and

- if the root of a black subtree is presently unmarked then this can be done in at least two ways, in one of which the root is marked c and in the other the root is marked r.

Hence the node N_0 should be painted black and the subtrees rooted at each of N_i (for $i = 1, \cdots,$ k) remain black as no problems arise even if N_i was unmarked and is being marked (with the single element in $\pi_i(C)$).

The algorithm is inherently nondeterministic in the selection of candidates, N_0, for disagreement points. As indicated in the algorithm this can be made deterministic by selecting the leftmost candidate. However, the algorithm only finds one disagreement point, e.g. the node labeled PAIR in the example of the previous subsection. To find all disagreement points the algorithm should do OUTPUT N_0, rather than HALT, and the entire path from the root of T to N_0 must be painted black. The next candidate for N_0 now should be the (leftmost) leaf in the *forest* of white nodes in T.

3   Transformations on types

The presence of one or more disagreement points shows that the type is not fully separated. Furthermore, the disagreement points show where we may want to transform the type. After each transformation the intention is that the disagreement point has been removed, has been moved closer to the root of the tree or has been moved from a left subtree to a right subtree. We will, however, not consider this formally in this paper.

3.1 Example: lookup

Based upon the type of the lookup function

LIST (PAIR STRING INT) → STRING → INT

we now show how the detection of disagreement points can be used to transform a type. As we saw above the type is represented as the tree

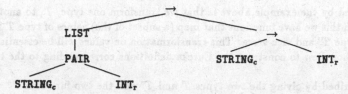

where we have indicated the markings on those subtrees that can be consistenly marked. The disagreement point analysis identifies the roots of the subtypes PAIR STRING INT and STRING → INT as disagreement points. We shall proceed in three stages.

In the *first stage* we can do nothing to solve the problem indicated by the second disagreement point. However, matters can be improved slightly for the first disagreement point by replacing the subtype LIST (PAIR STRING INT) by the *larger*[1] type PAIR (LIST STRING) (LIST INT). The resulting type will be

PAIR (LIST STRING) (LIST INT) → STRING → INT

which has the tree representation

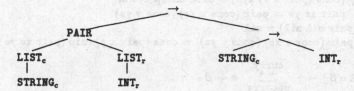

This tree has two disagreement points, the node labeled PAIR and the rightmost node labeled →. Thus the effect of the transformation on the type has been to move a disagreement point (the one that motivated the transformation) closer to the root of the tree while the other disagreement point(s) is unchanged.

In the *second stage* the overall function type is curried so it becomes

(LIST STRING) → (LIST INT) → STRING → INT

with the tree representation

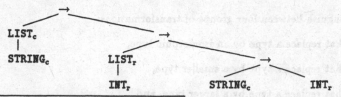

---

[1]'Larger' in the sense of containing more elements.

Now only the rightmost node labeled → is a disagreement point and we see that a disagreement point (the one that motivated the transformation) has been removed.

In the *third stage* we will rearrange the order in which the functions take their arguments. So the type becomes

(LIST STRING) → STRING → (LIST INT) → INT

The corresponding tree has no disagreement points and we are finished. (If we had used $daenv(→)$ = {*ccc*, *rrr*} then the middle node labelled → would still be a disagreement point.)

3.2 A classification of transformations

The general pattern exhibited by the example above is that we transform one type, T, to another type, T', and associated with this we have functions that map (a subset of the) values of type T into (a subset of the) values of type T' and vice versa. This transformation on values will be essential in the next section where we show how to construct the Eureka definitions corresponding to the type transformations.

A transformation is described by giving the two types T and T' and the two functions τ^+ and τ^- that transform the values:

$$T \underset{\tau^-}{\overset{\tau^+}{\rightleftarrows}} T'$$

The transformations corresponding to the example of the previous subsection are given in Table 2.

Transformation 1: LIST (PAIR $\alpha\beta$) $\underset{\text{zip}}{\overset{\text{unzip}}{\rightleftarrows}}$ PAIR (LIST α) (LIST β)

         unzip nil = pair nil nil
         unzip (cons (pair x y) xys) = CASE unzip xys OF
             pair xs ys ⇒ pair (cons x xs) (cons y ys)
         zip (pair nil nil) = nil
         zip (pair (cons x xs) (cons y ys)) = cons (pair x y) (zip (pair xs ys))

Transformation 2: (PAIR $\alpha\beta$) → γ $\underset{\text{uncurry}}{\overset{\text{curry}}{\rightleftarrows}}$ $\alpha → \beta → \gamma$

         curry f x y = f (pair x y)
         uncurry g (pair x y) = g x y

Transformation 3: $\alpha → \beta → \gamma$ $\underset{\text{reorder}}{\overset{\text{reorder}}{\rightleftarrows}}$ $\beta → \alpha → \gamma$

         reorder f x y = f y x

Table 2: Transformations: the lookup example

Intuitively we shall distinguish between four groups of transformations:

- the transformations that replace a type by an isomorphic type,

- the transformations that replace a type by a smaller type,

- the transformations that replace a type by a larger type, and

• the transformations that replace a subtype of one type by a subtype of another type.

The *first group* of transformations is fairly straightforward since it only allows isomorphisms. The two transformation functions on values are then the isomorphisms between the two types. As they are isomorphisms it will always be safe to use such a transformation and an example is Transformation 3 of Table 2.

The *second group* of transformations includes the zip direction of Transformation 1 of Table 2 whereas the *third group* includes the unzip direction of Transformation 1. However, by composing such transformations one easily ends up in the *fourth group*. As a more concrete example of a transformation in the fourth group consider matrix transpose where a matrix is represented as an element of LIST (LIST α): here matrices only correspond to lists of equal-length lists.

This demonstrates that in general we will have to accept that the transformation functions are partial functions unless we want to restrict ourselves to the rather limited class of transformations that fall within the first group.

3.3 Building transformation functions

So far we have considered transformations between entire trees:

$$T \underset{\tau^-}{\overset{\tau^+}{\rightleftarrows}} T'$$

However, usually it will be the case that a subtree in T is replaced, leaving the remainder of the tree unchanged, i.e. $T = T_a[T_b]$ and $T' = T_a[T'_b]$ with

$$T_b \underset{\tau_b^-}{\overset{\tau_b^+}{\rightleftarrows}} T'_b$$

As an example, the actual transformation in the first stage of Subsection 3.1 is on the subtype indicated by Transformation 1 of Table 2.

This then motivates defining τ^+ in terms of τ_b^+ (and τ_b^-). In the following we shall write

$$\tau: T \leftrightarrow T'$$

as an abbreviation for the pair of transformation functions

$$\tau = (\tau^+: T \to T', \ \tau^-: T' \to T)$$

The general idea will be to build τ by a bottom-up traversal over the tree using Reynolds' notion of a domain functor [12].

To do so it is helpful to borrow a few simple notions from category theory. In general, a functor consists of two mappings: one that works on 'types' (called objects) and one that works on 'functions' (called morphisms) and such that the functor laws hold (see later). We have seen that LIST, PAIR and $\to$ construct new types from given types. In a similar way they can be used to construct new functions from given functions. This is easiest for LIST and PAIR where a natural choice might be LIST $f = \text{map}(f)$ and PAIR $f \ g = f \times g$. Here map(f) is the familiar construct for mapping the function f upon each component of a list and $f \times g = \lambda(x,y).(f(x),f(y))$ applies f and g componentwise. To allow for the functions f and g to be partial we shall say that map(f)(z) is defined if and only if all invocations of f on the elements of z are defined and similarly $(f \times g)(x,y)$ is defined if and only if $f(x)$ and $g(y)$ are both defined.

As we consider transformation pairs it is actually more helpful to let LIST and PAIR operate on pairs of partial functions:

LIST $\tau = (\text{map}(\tau^+), \text{map}(\tau^-))$

PAIR $\tau_1 \ \tau_2 = (\tau_1^+ \times \tau_2^+, \ \tau_1^- \times \tau_2^-)$

This also allows to define the effect of function space:

$$\tau_1 \to \tau_2 = (\lambda f. \ \tau_2^+ \circ f \circ \tau_1^-, \lambda g. \ \tau_2^- \circ g \circ \tau_1^+)$$

Note that here the forward direction, i.e. the '+'-direction, of the transformation incorporates the '−'-direction of the τ_1 argument. (In categorical terms: function space is contravariant in its left argument.) This may be clarified by the following diagrams:

$$
\begin{array}{ccc}
T_1 \xleftarrow{\ \tau_1^-\ } T_1' & \qquad & T_1 \xrightarrow{\ \tau_1^+\ } T_1' \\
\Big\downarrow f \qquad \Big\downarrow (\tau_1 \to \tau_2)^+(f) & & \Big\downarrow (\tau_1 \to \tau_2)^-(g) \qquad \Big\downarrow g \\
T_2 \xrightarrow{\ \tau_2^+\ } T_2' & & T_2 \xleftarrow{\ \tau_2^-\ } T_2'
\end{array}
$$

We now have sufficient apparatus in order to define the transformation functions. So consider again the task of replacing a subtree T_b of a tree T by the subtree T_b' and let the transformation pair τ_b be supplied. To handle the remaining type variables and type constructors we shall assume that a *transformation environment*, *trenv*, gives information about how to transform. If a type constructor or type variable has arity k (k ≥ 0) the transformation environment must indicate a function of functionality

$$(T_1 \leftrightarrow T_1') \times \cdots \times (T_k \leftrightarrow T_k') \to (T \leftrightarrow T')$$

where $T = tycon \ T_1 \cdots T_k$ and $T' = tycon \ T_1' \cdots T_k'$ and similarly for the type variables. We then proceed by induction over the tree as follows:

- If the node is the root of the subtree (T_b) to be replaced (by the subtree T_b') we set $\tau = \tau_b$.

- If the node is labeled by a type variable, *tyvar*, we set $\tau = trenv(tyvar)$.

- If the node is labeled by a type constructor, *tycon*, and $\tau_1, \cdots, \tau_k$ are the transformation pairs constructed for its subtrees we put $\tau = trenv(tycon)(\tau_1, \cdots, \tau_k)$.

- If the node is labeled by $\to$, and τ_1 and τ_2 are the transformation pairs constructed for the subtrees we put $\tau = \tau_1 \to \tau_2$.

Example: Consider the first transformation in Subsection 3.1. As indicated in Table 2, the subtree T_b corresponding to the subtype LIST (PAIR STRING INT) is replaced by the subtree T_b' corresponding to PAIR (LIST STRING) (LIST INT). The transformation pair $\tau_b : T_b \leftrightarrow T_b'$ accomplishing this is (unzip, zip). We next define $\tau : T \leftrightarrow T'$, where T is the tree corresponding to the original overall type LIST (PAIR STRING INT) $\to$ STRING $\to$ INT and T' is the tree corresponding to the new overall type PAIR (LIST STRING) (LIST INT) $\to$ STRING $\to$ INT. For this we will assume that the transformation environment, *trenv*, specifies $trenv(\text{STRING}) = id$ and $trenv(\text{INT}) = id$ where $id^+(f) = f$ and $id^-(g) = g$. We then obtain

$$\tau = (\text{unzip, zip}) \to (id \to id)$$

and this amounts to

$$\tau^+(f) = (id \to id)^+ \circ f \circ (\text{unzip, zip})^- = f \circ \text{zip}$$

$$(\text{and } \tau^-(g) = (id \to id)^- \circ g \circ (\text{unzip, zip})^+ = g \circ \text{unzip}).$$

■

4 Construction of Eureka definitions

So far we have seen how the disagreement points can guide the transformation of the *type* of a function. But we have yet to see how the *function definition* itself can be changed. In fact each of the stages in the transformation on the type gives rise to parts of an Eureka definition that will be used to transform the function definition using the fold/unfold framework of Burstall and Darlington.

4.1 Example: lookup

For the example of Subsection 3.1 the *first stage* of the transformation on the type was to replace the list of pairs with a pair of lists. As a result the type was changed from LIST (PAIR STRING INT) $\rightarrow$ STRING $\rightarrow$ INT to PAIR (LIST STRING) (LIST INT) $\rightarrow$ STRING $\rightarrow$ INT and in the previous subsection we saw that the corresponding transformation on values is

$$\tau^+(f) = (\text{id} \rightarrow \text{id})^+ \circ f \circ (\text{unzip}, \text{zip})^- = f \circ \text{zip}$$

The corresponding Eureka definition therefore becomes

$$\text{lookup}_1 = \tau^+(\text{lookup})$$

which is equivalent to lookup_1 (pair xs ys) z = lookup (zip (pair xs ys)) z.

The *second stage* of the transformation on the type is currying. We shall replace the overall type PAIR (LIST STRING) (LIST INT) $\rightarrow$ STRING $\rightarrow$ INT by (LIST STRING) $\rightarrow$ (LIST INT) $\rightarrow$ STRING $\rightarrow$ INT. This is a direct application of one of the transformations of Table 2 and the transformation on values is therefore

$$\tau^+(f) = \text{curry}(f)$$

The corresponding Eureka definition becomes

$$\text{lookup}_2 = \text{curry}(\text{lookup}_1)$$

which is equivalent to lookup_2 xs ys z = lookup_1 (pair xs ys) z.

Finally, the *third stage* of the transformation on the type rearranges the order of the parameters. The type (LIST STRING) $\rightarrow$ (LIST INT) $\rightarrow$ STRING $\rightarrow$ INT is changed to (LIST STRING) $\rightarrow$ STRING $\rightarrow$ (LIST INT) $\rightarrow$ INT. The construction of Subsection 3.3 then gives that the transformation on values is $\tau = \text{id} \rightarrow (\text{reorder}, \text{reorder})$ which means that

$$\tau^+(f)(x) = \text{reorder}(f\ x)$$

The corresponding Eureka definition becomes

$$\text{lookup}_3 \text{ xs} = \text{reorder}(\text{lookup}_2 \text{ xs})$$

which is equivalent to lookup_3 xs z ys = lookup_2 xs ys z.

Putting these definitions together we get

$$\text{lookup}_3 \text{ xs z ys} = \text{lookup}(\text{zip}(\text{pair xs ys}))\text{ z}$$

which is the Eureka definition used in the Introduction. Clearly this Eureka definition could also be obtained as $\text{lookup}_3 = \tau^+(\text{lookup})$ where

$$\tau^+(f)(x) = \text{reorder}(\text{curry}(f \circ \text{zip})\ x)$$

is the composition of the three transformations functions from the transformation stages.

4.2 The general pattern

So far we have derived Eureka definitions without paying much attention to the nature of the transformation functions (τ^+): whether they are isomorphisms, whether they have left or right inverses or whether they are actually defined on their arguments.

To allow for transformation pairs that are pairs of partial functions we shall regard the simplification steps, e.g. $e_1 \equiv e_2$ of the fold/unfold framework as meaning that one side is defined if and only if the other is.

Consider now a transformation pair

$$T \underset{\tau^-}{\overset{\tau^+}{\rightleftarrows}} T'$$

and an application

$$\tau^+(e)$$

As a *first attempt* at defining the existence of this application one might try to simplify $\tau^+(e)$ to an expression e', i.e. $\tau^+(e) \equiv \cdots \equiv e'$, such that e' only contains applications of transformation functions $(\tau_i^+$ or $\tau_i^-)$ in contexts where it can be verified that they will be defined upon their particular arguments. This is too weak, however, as this would not be able to validate the first transformation on the lookup function of Subsection 4.1, because $\tau^+(\text{lookup}) = \text{lookup} \circ \text{zip}$ and when applied to a pair of lists of unequal length the transformations function $\tau_1^+ = \text{zip}$ will not be defined.

To *remedy* this we may note that the existence of lookup $\circ$ zip above is only really of interest when the argument is of a form that could have been produced by unzip. This observation then motivates the following attempt at defining when an application $\tau^+(e)$ *is deemed to exist*: Whenever $\tau^-(\tau^+(e))$ can be simplified to an expression e', i.e. $\tau^-(\tau^+(e)) \equiv \cdots \equiv e'$, such that e' only contains applications of transformation functions $(\tau_i^+$ or $\tau_i^-)$ in contexts where it can be verified that they will be defined upon their particular arguments. Furthermore, the application $\tau^+(e)$ is *deemed to be safe* whenever e' above can be taken to be e.

Example: Consider the transformation upon the lookup function of the previous subsection. There

$$\tau = (\text{id} \to (\text{reorder}, \text{reorder})) \circ (\text{curry}, \text{uncurry}) \circ ((\text{unzip}, \text{zip}) \to (\text{id} \to \text{id}))$$

where composition of pairs of transformation pairs is given by $\tau_1 \circ \tau_2 = (\tau_1^+ \circ \tau_2^+, \tau_2^- \circ \tau_1^-)$. It follows that $\tau^+(f) = \text{reorder} \circ \text{curry}\, (f \circ \text{zip})$ and $\tau^-(g) = \text{uncurry}\, (\text{reorder} \circ g) \circ \text{unzip}$. To validate the application $\tau^+(\text{lookup})$ we calculate

$$
\begin{aligned}
\tau^-(\tau^+(\text{lookup})) &\equiv \text{uncurry}\, (\text{reorder} \circ \text{reorder} \circ \text{curry}\, (\text{lookup} \circ \text{zip})) \circ \text{unzip} \\
&\equiv \text{uncurry}\, (\text{curry}\, (\text{lookup} \circ \text{zip})) \circ \text{unzip} \\
&\equiv \text{lookup} \circ \text{zip} \circ \text{unzip} \\
&\equiv \text{lookup}
\end{aligned}
$$

so that the application is deemed to be safe (as well as to exist). ∎

There would seem to be little interest in an application $\tau^+(e)$ that is deemed to exist but not deemed to be safe. This motivates defining a transformation pair $\tau = (\tau^+, \tau^-)$ to be a *partial isomorphism* if $\tau^-(\tau^+(x)) = x$ whenever the lefthand side is defined and, to allow for change of direction, $\tau^+(\tau^-(y)) = y$ whenever the lefthand side is defined. Thus τ will be a partial isomorphism if and only if (τ^-, τ^+) is.

All of the transformations in Table 2 are partial isomorphisms. Furthermore the property of being a partial isomorphism is being preserved when transformation functions are built in the way indicated in the previous section. For this result to hold we need that LIST, PAIR and $\to$ are so-called *definedness preserving functors*. We shall only explain the conditions for LIST as the other cases are similar. First we need the functor laws:

LIST id $=$ id

LIST $(\tau_1 \circ \tau_2) = (\text{LIST } \tau_1) \circ (\text{LIST } \tau_2)$

Next we need the definedness preserving condition:

τ is a partial isomorphism $\Rightarrow$ LIST τ is a partial isomorphism

By way of digression one may note the close relationship between these definedness preserving functors and what is often called locally monotonic functors: under suitable assumptions the condition that τ is a partial isomorphism may be reformulated as $\tau^- \circ \tau^+ \sqsubseteq \text{id}$ and $\tau^+ \circ \tau^- \sqsubseteq \text{id}$ and the local monotonicity condition

$\tau_1 \sqsubseteq \tau_2 \Rightarrow \text{LIST } \tau_1 \sqsubseteq \text{LIST } \tau_2$

(where $\tau_1 \sqsubseteq \tau_2$ means $\tau_1^+ \sqsubseteq \tau_2^+ \land \tau_1^- \sqsubseteq \tau_2^-$) and the functor laws then imply the definedness preserving condition.

Finally, we may observe that it has been the intention throughout that the transformation pairs only change the overall structure of the types but not the actual data buried there. As an example zip applied to a pair of lists of integers rearranges the order of the integers but does not actually change the integers, e.g. by adding 27 which is then subtracted by unzip. So far this intention has not been made explicit. To do so we may use a well-known remedy from category theory: that the transformations between the functors, e.g. from LIST PAIR α β to PAIR (LIST α) (LIST β), must be natural transformations. We shall therefore say that a transformation pair is a *natural partial isomorphism* if it is a partial isomorphism as detailed above and if furthermore the naturality squares commute. In case of the transformation from LIST PAIR α β to PAIR (LIST α) (LIST β) this demands that

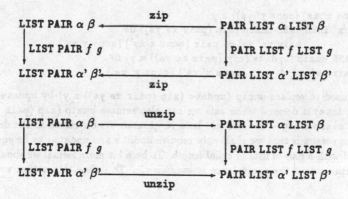

both commute, i.e. we have the equalities (LIST (PAIR f g)) $\circ$ zip $=$ zip $\circ$ PAIR (LIST f) (LIST g) and unzip $\circ$ LIST (PAIR f g) $=$ (PAIR (LIST f) (LIST g)) $\circ$ unzip.

4.3 Example: update

To illustrate the applicability of the technique for constructing Eureka definitions we shall consider yet another example:

update nil x y = cons (pair x y) nil
update (cons (pair x' y') xys) x y = IF eq x x' THEN cons (pair x y) xys
                                                ELSE cons (pair x' y') (update xys x y)

It has the type

$$\text{LIST (PAIR } \alpha\beta) \rightarrow \alpha \rightarrow \beta \rightarrow \text{LIST (PAIR } \alpha\beta)$$

We shall assume that the binding time environment $btenv$ has $btenv(\alpha) = \{c\}$ and $btenv(\beta) = \{r\}$; this means that (as in the lookup example) the first components of the pairs are known early and the second components are known late. We proceed in six stages.

In the *first stage*, disagreement point analysis identifies two disagreement points: the two nodes labeled PAIR. In both cases we shall apply Transformation 1 of Table 2 and the transformation pair becomes

$$\tau_1 = (\text{unzip},\text{zip}) \rightarrow \text{id} \rightarrow \text{id} \rightarrow (\text{unzip, zip})$$

The resulting type will be

$$\text{PAIR (LIST } \alpha) \text{ (LIST } \beta) \rightarrow \alpha \rightarrow \beta \rightarrow \text{PAIR (LIST } \alpha) \text{ (LIST } \beta)$$

From τ_1 we get the transformation functions

$$\tau_1^+ \ f \ (\text{pair xs ys) x y} = \text{unzip} \ (f \ (\text{zip (pair xs ys)) x y})$$

$$\tau_1^- \ g \ \text{xys x y} = \text{zip} \ (g \ (\text{unzip xys) x y})$$

Using that zip o unzip = id it is easy to verify that $\tau_1^-(\tau_1^+(f)) = f$ for all f and thereby that $\tau_1^+(f)$ is deemed to be safe. We now use the Eureka definition

$$\text{update}_1 \ (\text{pair xs ys) x y} = \tau_1^+(\text{update}) \ (\text{pair xs ys) x y}$$
$$= \text{unzip (update (zip (pair xs ys)) x y})$$

Using the fold/unfold framework it is straightforward to get

$$\text{update}_1 \ (\text{pair nil nil) x y} \equiv \text{pair (cons x nil) (cons y nil)}$$

$$\text{update}_1 \ (\text{pair (cons x' xs) (cons y' ys)) x y}$$
$$\equiv \text{IF eq x x' THEN CASE unzip (zip (pair xs ys)) OF}$$
$$\text{pair xs' ys'} \Rightarrow \text{pair (cons x xs') (cons y ys')}$$
$$\text{ELSE CASE unzip (update (zip (pair xs ys)) x y) OF}$$
$$\text{pair xs' ys'} \Rightarrow \text{pair (cons x' xs') (cons y' ys')}$$

Now a fold step can be used to replace unzip (update (zip (pair xs ys)) x y) by update_1 (pair xs ys) x y. Since τ_1^+(update) is deemed to be safe we can also replace unzip (zip (pair xs ys)) by pair xs ys although unzip o zip = id does *not* hold in general. As expressed in the definition of 'deemed to be safe' the reason is that we shall only require update and update_1 to be equivalent when update_1 is supplied with a pair of lists of *equal length*. To be a bit more formal we should write $e_1 \equiv e_2 \ (mod \ \tau_1^-)$ to express that the equivalence is *modulo* τ_1^-. To define this notion we should prefer to write e.g.

$$\text{update}_1 = \lambda(\text{pair nil nil}).\lambda \text{x}.\lambda \text{y}.\text{pair (cons x nil) (cons y nil)}$$

rather than

$$\text{update}_1 \ (\text{pair nil nil) x y} = \text{pair (cons x nil) (cons y nil)}$$

because then $e_1 \equiv e_2 \ (mod \ \tau_1^-)$ would amount to $\tau_1^-(e_1) \equiv \tau_1^-(e_2)$. We arive at the following definition

$$\text{update}_1 \ (\text{pair (cons x' xs) (cons y' ys)) x y}$$
$$\equiv \text{IF eq x x' THEN pair (cons x xs) (cons y ys)}$$
$$\text{ELSE CASE update}_1 \ (\text{pair xs ys) x y OF}$$
$$\text{pair xs' ys'} \Rightarrow \text{pair (cons x' xs') (cons y' ys')}$$

In the *second stage* we observe that the type

Transformation 4: $\alpha \to (\text{PAIR } \beta\gamma) \overset{\text{topair}}{\underset{\text{tofunc}}{\rightleftarrows}} \text{PAIR } (\alpha \to \beta)\,(\alpha \to \gamma)$

topair f = pair g h WHERE g x = CASE f x OF pair u v $\Rightarrow$ u
                            WHERE h x = CASE f x OF pair u v $\Rightarrow$ v
tofunc (pair g h) = f WHERE f x = pair (g x) (h x)

Transformation 5: $\alpha \to \beta \overset{\text{forget}}{\underset{\text{recall}}{\rightleftarrows}} \beta$

forget f = f ?
                    where ? is some element of type α
recall x = f WHERE f y = x

Table 3: Transformations: the update example

$$\text{PAIR } (\text{LIST } \alpha)\,(\text{LIST } \beta) \to \alpha \to \beta \to \text{PAIR } (\text{LIST } \alpha)\,(\text{LIST } \beta)$$

still has two disagreement points: the two nodes labeled PAIR in the tree representation. For the leftmost disagreement point we shall use Transformation 2 of Table 2 and for the rightmost disagreement point we use that $\alpha \to \text{PAIR } \beta\,\gamma$ can be replaced by $\text{PAIR } (\alpha \to \beta)\,(\alpha \to \gamma)$. This transformation (see Table 3) belongs to the first group of transformations described in Subsection 4.2 provided that PAIR and $\to$ are interpreted either as cartesian product and continuous function space or as smash product and strict continuous function space. The transformation pair is

$$\tau_2 = (\text{id} \to \text{id} \to \text{id} \to (\text{topair}, \text{tofunc})) \circ (\text{curry}, \text{uncurry})$$

and the resulting type is $\text{LIST } \alpha \to \text{LIST } \beta \to \alpha \to \text{PAIR } (\beta \to \text{LIST } \alpha)\,(\beta \to \text{LIST } \beta)$. It is fairly straightforward to verify that $\tau_2^-\,(\tau_2^+\,f) = f$ so that the transformation $\tau_2^+(f)$ is deemed to be safe for all f. We now use the Eureka definition

$$\text{update}_2 \text{ xs ys x} = \tau_2^+(\text{update}_1) \text{ xs ys x}$$
$$= \text{topair } (\text{curry update}_1) \text{ xs ys x}$$

and it is fairly straightforward to get

update$_2$ nil nil x $\equiv$ pair g h WHERE g y = cons x nil
                            WHERE h y = cons y nil
update$_2$ (cons x' xs) (cons y' ys) x
        $\equiv$ pair g h WHERE g y = IF eq x x' THEN cons x xs
                            ELSE CASE update$_2$ xs ys x OF pair g' h' $\Rightarrow$ cons x' (g' y)
                    WHERE h y = IF eq x x' THEN cons y ys
                            ELSE CASE update$_2$ xs ys x OF pair g' h' $\Rightarrow$ cons y' (h' y)

In the *third stage* there is only one disagreement point in the type

$$\text{LIST } \alpha \to \text{LIST } \beta \to \alpha \to \text{PAIR } (\beta \to \text{LIST } \alpha)\,(\beta \to \text{LIST } \beta)$$

namely the root of the subtree $\beta \to \text{LIST } \alpha$. We shall here use Transformation 5 in Table 3 to replace the function type $\beta \to \text{LIST } \alpha$ with the list type LIST α. Certainly, such a transformation will not be valid in all cases but if we are in a context in which we only consider constant functions from $\beta \to \text{LIST } \alpha$ then it will indeed be a valid transformation. The transformation we shall apply is

$$\tau_3 = \text{id} \to \text{id} \to \text{id} \to \text{PAIR } (\text{forget}, \text{recall}) \text{ id}$$

and the resulting type is $\text{LIST } \alpha \to \text{LIST } \beta \to \alpha \to \text{PAIR } (\text{LIST } \alpha)\,(\beta \to \text{LIST } \beta)$. Using the Eureka definition

$$\text{update}_3 \text{ xs ys x} = \tau_3^+(\text{update}_2) \text{ xs ys x}$$
$$= \text{CASE update}_2 \text{ xs ys x OF pair g h} \Rightarrow \text{pair (forget g) h}$$

we can use the fold/unfold framework and get

update$_3$ nil nil x $\equiv$ pair (cons x nil) h WHERE h y = cons y nil
update$_3$(cons x' xs) (cons y' ys) x
   $\equiv$ pair (IF eq x x' THEN cons x xs
      ELSE CASE update$_3$ xs ys x OF pair xs' h' $\Rightarrow$ cons x' xs') h
   WHERE h y = IF eq x x' THEN cons y ys
      ELSE CASE update$_3$ xs ys x OF pair xs' h' $\Rightarrow$ cons y' (h' y)

As indicated above it cannot be proved that $\tau_3^+(f)$ is deemed to be safe for all f but one may verify that $\tau_3^+(\text{update}_2)$ is indeed deemed to be safe.

In the *fourth stage* it is observed that the type

$$\text{LIST } \alpha \rightarrow \text{LIST } \beta \rightarrow \alpha \rightarrow \text{PAIR (LIST } \alpha) (\beta \rightarrow \text{LIST } \beta)$$

still has a disagreement point, namely the root of the subtype LIST $\beta \rightarrow \alpha \rightarrow \cdots$. Transformation 3 of Table 2 can be used to swop the order of the second and third arguments so that the overall type becomes

$$\text{LIST } \alpha \rightarrow \alpha \rightarrow \text{LIST } \beta \rightarrow \text{PAIR (LIST } \alpha) (\beta \rightarrow \text{LIST } \beta)$$

The *fifth stage* takes care of the disagreement point corresponding to the subtype LIST $\beta \rightarrow$ PAIR $\cdots$ by applying Transformation 4 of Table 3. The overall type then becomes

$$\text{LIST } \alpha \rightarrow \alpha \rightarrow \text{PAIR (LIST } \beta \rightarrow \text{LIST } \alpha) (\text{LIST } \beta \rightarrow \beta \rightarrow \text{LIST } \beta)$$

The *sixth stage* is similar to stage three and will give a result of type

$$\text{LIST } \alpha \rightarrow \alpha \rightarrow \text{PAIR (LIST } \alpha) (\text{LIST } \beta \rightarrow \beta \rightarrow \text{LIST } \beta)$$

This type has no disagreement points and the transformation process stops. We shall not give the details of the fold/unfold steps of these transformations but only mention that the final function update$_6$ will turn out to be defined by

update$_6$ nil x = pair (cons x nil) h WHERE h nil y = cons y nil
update$_6$ (cons x' xs) x = pair (IF eq x x' THEN cons x xs
      ELSE CASE update$_6$ xs x OF pair xs' h' $\Rightarrow$ cons x' xs') h
  WHERE h (cons y' ys) y = IF eq x x' THEN cons y ys
      ELSE CASE update$_6$ xs x OF pair xs' h' $\Rightarrow$ cons y' (h' ys y)

5 Conclusion

The main point of the present paper was to construct Eureka definitions needed to apply the fold/unfold framework of Burstall and Darlington [1]. This involved systematic definitions of transformation functions so as to perform transformations in context and it involved a way of identifying the points, called disagreement points, where it would be sensible to perform a transformation. However, further work is needed concerning how to choose which disagreement point to work from (in case there are many) and to choose which transformation to apply (in case there are many candidates).

Our approach has been to let the *type of the function* guide the transformation process. This is contrary to the tupling, composition and generalization tactics of [2] where the *structure of the function definition* is used. Rather our work is related to the enhancement developed in [2] for semi-automatically generating directives to the transformation system. In particular the power of the AUTO feature [2] could be increased by using types to indicate what recursive calls to generate.

(This is already implicit in the AUTO feature but in a limited way.) The idea of using the types to guide the transformations can also be found in e.g. [1,11].

In this paper we used an (informal) notion of binding time to determine the disagreement points. A more thorough discussion of binding time analysis may be found in e.g. [9,5,7] and the transformation of programs based on binding time information can also be found in [10,7]. However, our approach is *not* ultimately connected with the use of binding time information. In [8] we show that an annotation based on *processor numbers* can be used to transform programs so as to obtain more parallelism. This is achieved by distributing shared data on individual processors.

Acknowledgement: The title of this paper was inspired by [14]. The work has been supported by the Danish Natural Science Research Council.

References

[1] R. Burstall and J.Darlington. A transformation system for developing recursive programs. *Journal of the ACM*, 1977.

[2] M. S. Feather. A system for assisting program transformation. *ACM Transactions on Programming Languages and Systems*, 1982.

[3] P. Hudak and P.Wadler. *Report on the Functional Programming Language Haskell*. Technical Report, Glasgow University, 1988.

[4] U. Jørring and W.L.Scherlis. Compilers and staging transformations. In *Proc. 13th ACM Symposium on Principles of Programming Languages*, 1986.

[5] J. Launchbury. Projections for specialization. In *Proc. of the IFIP TC2 Workshop on Partial Evaluation and Mixed Computation*, North-Holland, 1988.

[6] R. Milner. The standard ML core language. In *Proc. 1984 ACM Conference on Lisp and Functional Programming*, 1984.

[7] T. Mogensen. Separating binding times in language specifications. In *Proc. of Functional Programming and Computer Architecture*, 1989.

[8] F. Nielson and H. Riis Nielson. *Forced transformations of OCCAM programs*. Technical Report, Aarhus University, 1989.

[9] H. Riis Nielson and F.Nielson. Automatic binding time analysis for a typed λ-calculus. *Science of Computer Programming*, 1988.

[10] H. Riis Nielson and F. Nielson. Transformations on higher-order functions. In *Proc. of Functional Programming and Computer Architecture*, 1989.

[11] W. Polak. *Compiler Specification and Verification*. LNCS 124, Springer, 1981.

[12] J. C. Reynolds. On the relation between direct and continuation semantics. In *Proceedings 2nd ICALP*, Springer LNCS 14, 1974.

[13] D. Turner. Miranda: a non-strict functional language with polymorphic types. In *Functional Programming Language and Computer Architecture*, Springer LNCS 201, 1985.

[14] P. Wadler. Theorems for free! In *Proc. 4th international conference on functional programming language and computer architecture*, ACM Press, 1989.

SYNTHESIS OF EUREKA PREDICATES FOR DEVELOPING LOGIC PROGRAMS

Maurizio Proietti
IASI-CNR
Viale Manzoni 30
I-00185 Roma (Italy)

Alberto Pettorossi
Department of Electronics
University of Roma Tor Vergata
I-00173 Roma (Italy)

ABSTRACT

We consider the problem of inventing new predicates when developing logic programs by transformation. Those predicates, often called eureka predicates, improve program efficiency by eliminating redundant computations and avoiding multiple visits of data structures. It can be shown that no general method exists for inventing the required eureka predicates for a given initial program. We introduce here two strategies, the *Loop Absorption Strategy* and the *Generalization Strategy*, which in many cases determine the new predicates to be defined during program transformation. We study the properties of those strategies and we present some classes of programs in which they are successful.

1. INTRODUCTION AND A PRELIMINARY EXAMPLE

The program transformation methodology is a valuable technique for deriving correct and efficient programs. It has been introduced for functional languages [Burstall-Darlington 77, Darlington 81, Feather 86], but it can also be applied in the case of logic programs (see, for instance, [Azibi 87, Bossi et al. 88, Bruynooghe et al. 89, Debray 88, Hogger 81, Kawamura-Kanamori 88, Nakagawa 85, Tamaki-Sato 84]).

The basic idea of that methodology is the *separation of concerns*, in the sense that the efficiency requirement is separated from the correctness requirement. The latter one is taken into account by allowing only transformation rules which are correctness preserving. (The programmer is left with the problem of termination, which is not captured by the notion of partial correctness.)

The efficiency requirement is taken into account by considering heuristic techniques. This is indeed the best approach which can be adopted, because of the undecidability results we will present in the paper. The programmer is asked to derive from the initial program a more efficient version by inventing suitable auxiliary predicates, the so-called *eureka predicates*. These inventions are hard steps to be made during the program derivation process, but several strategies can be adopted. Two of them are the *Loop Absorption Strategy* and the *Generalization Strategy*, introduced below. They are powerful techniques which are successful in a large number of cases.

The transformation rules which we will use for program derivation are the following ones (they are named after the corresponding rules which are used for the transformation of functional programs):

- *Definition Rule*. It consists in adding a new clause to the current program version. That clause is considered to be a *definition*, with a new head predicate defined in terms of already existing predicates (and not in terms of itself). Each new predicate should occur as head of one definition clause only.

- *Unfolding Rule*. It consists in performing a computation step by applying the SLD-resolution to a chosen clause with respect to a selected atom of its body. The chosen clause is replaced in the current program by *all* those which can be obtained by resolving it with any clause (of the current program) whose head is

This work has been partially supported by the "Progetto Finalizzato Sistemi Informatici e Calcolo Parallelo" of the CNR and by the MPI 40%, Italy.

unifiable with the selected atom.

- *Folding Rule*. It consists in replacing an 'old clause': $H \leftarrow A_1, ...,A_n,A_{n+1},..., A_r$ by a 'new clause':
  $H \leftarrow K\sigma,A_{n+1},...,A_r$, using a 'bridge clause': $K \leftarrow B_1,...,B_n$, where σ is a substitution such that:
  $A_i = B_i \sigma$ for all $i=1,...,n$. This rule can be applied only if: i) unfolding the new clause with respect to the
  atom $K\sigma$ we obtain again the old clause, and ii) the bridge clause is a definition (that is, a clause
  introduced in a previous application of the Definition Rule) and it is different from the old clause.   ■

Our rules are a bit simpler than the ones presented in [Tamaki-Sato 84]. However, they allow the same
transformations, and it is easy to see that they preserve the least Herbrand model semantics of the
predicates occurring in the initial program version (that is, the set of ground facts which are derivable from
the initial program is equal to the set of ground facts derivable in the transformed program).

The above rules will be used for deriving more efficient programs from the given initial versions,
according to the steps of the transformation methodology we now indicate.

The Transformation Methodology.

i)   Given an initial program version the program-transformer (a person or an automatic system) considers
     a clause and selects in its body some atoms which share one or more variables. Indeed, that sharing
     may be the cause of inefficiencies which we would like to avoid, like for instance, repeated visits of
     data, or constructions of unnecessary structures, or redundant computations, etc.

ii) The program-transformer defines a clause C whose body is made out of the selected atoms.

     Notice that if clause C differs from a clause already existing in the program because of the head
     predicate only, the introduction of that clause C can be avoided, and the existing clause can be
     considered as a definition.

iii) The program-transformer looks for a recursive definition of the head predicate of the clause defined at
     Step ii) by applying the unfolding and folding rules. This step of the methodology is motivated by the
     need of removing the cause of inefficiency 'at each level of recursion'. (The examples given in the
     paper will clarify this idea.)

     It is often the case that such recursive definition can only be derived via the introduction of eureka
     predicates (which in turn should be recursively defined). If the process of unfolding clause C generates
     clauses with patterns of atoms which are 'recurrent', the suitable eureka predicates can be determined
     by applying the Loop Absorption Strategy. (The notions occurring here will be formally defined later,
     and a precise description of this step will be given in Section 4 when defining the Loop Absorption
     Procedure.)

iv) Sometimes the required clauses with recurrent patterns of atoms may not be found by unfoldings only.
     In those cases the program-transformer may apply the Generalization Strategy, which will be presented
     in Section 3.   ■

More details about the transformation methodology will also be given when presenting the various
examples. Here is the first one.

Example 1. Maximal-Up-Segments.

Let us consider the problem of computing the maximal length of the up-segments of a given list L. Let L
be a list of integers $[a_1,...,a_n]$. We say that S is an up-segment of L if it is a sublist of L made out of
consecutive elements $a_h,...,a_k$ such that:

i) $a_h \leq a_{h+1} \leq ... \leq a_k$, and

ii) $a_{h-1} > a_h$ and $a_k > a_{k+1}$. We assume that $a_0=+\infty$ and $a_{n+1}=-\infty$.

Here is a logic program which solves that problem by computing: i) the list LL of all up-segments of L,
and ii) the maximal length of the elements of LL.

1. max-ups(L,Max) ← ups(L,LL), maxlength(LL,Max).

2. ups([],[]).

3. ups([H],[[H]]).
4. ups([H,H1|T1],[[H]|Y]) ← H>H1, ups([H1|T1],Y).
5. ups([H,H1|T1],[[H|Y1]|Y]) ← H≤H1, ups([H1|T1],[Y1|Y]).
6. maxlength([],0).
7. maxlength([H|T],M) ← maxlength(T,M1), length(H,N), max(N,M1,M).

We assume the obvious meaning for the base predicates >, ≤, max, and length.

We would like to improve the above program by avoiding the construction of the intermediate list LL of clause 1. We may achieve that objective by applying our proposed program transformation methodology. We consider clause 1 where the atoms ups and maxlength share the variable LL and we look for a recursive definition of max-ups(L,Max). We do not define a new head predicate, because of the remark made at Step ii) of our methodology.

We unfold clause 1 and the clauses derived from it until we obtain a set of clauses such that in the body of each of them either i) there are no calls of ups and maxlength, or ii) there is a pattern of calls of ups and maxlength which is an instance of the pattern of calls occurring in the body of an *ancestor-clause*. (In Section 2 we will formalize the unfolding process as a *tree* of clauses and the notion of ancestor-clause will be the one based on the tree structure). The clauses of type ii) will be called *foldable clauses*, because as we will see later, they will be used as 'old clauses' for performing folding steps. By unfolding clause 1 we get the following semantically equivalent set of clauses:

8. max-ups([],0).
9. max-ups([H],Max) ← length([H],N), max(N,0,Max).
10. max-ups([H,H1|T1],Max) ← H>H1, ups([H1|T1],Y), maxlength(Y,M1), length([H],N),
                                max(N,M1,Max).
11. max-ups([H,H1|T1],Max) ← H≤H1, ups([H1|T1],[Y1|Y]), maxlength(Y,M1), length([H|Y1],N),
                                max(N,M1,Max).

Now, clauses 8 and 9 have bodies without calls of ups and maxlength, and in clause 10 the pattern of atoms 'ups([H1|T1],Y), maxlength(Y,M1)' is an instance of the pattern 'ups(L,LL), maxlength(LL,Max)' in the body of clause 1. However, the pattern 'ups([H1|T1],[Y1|Y]), maxlength(Y,M1)' in clause 11 is *not* an instance of any pattern of atoms occurring in its ancestor-clauses. We continue the unfolding process for clause 11 and we get:

12. max-ups([H,H1],Max) ← H≤H1, length([H,H1],N), max(N,M1,Max).
13. max-ups([H,H1,H2|T2],Max) ← H≤H1, H1>H2, ups([H2|T2],Y), maxlength(Y,M1),
                                  length([H,H1],N), max(N,M1,Max).
14. max-ups([H,H1,H2|T2],Max) ← H≤H1, H1≤H2, ups([H2|T2],[Y1|Y]), maxlength(Y,M1),
                                  length([H,H1|Y1],N), max(N,M1,Max).

At this point we have that:
i)   clauses 8, 9, and 12 do not have calls of ups and maxlength,
ii) the bodies of clauses 10 and 13 have calls of ups and maxlength which are instances of the corresponding calls in the body of their ancestor-clause 1 (thus, clause 10 and 13 are foldable), and
iii) the body of clause 14 has calls of ups and maxlength which are an instance of the corresponding calls in the body of the ancestor-clause 11 (thus, clause 14 is foldable).

We say that we obtained two patterns of the atoms ups and maxlength, which are *recurrent*: the first one in the pairs of clauses 1-10 and 1-13, and the second one in the pair 11-14.

We also say that the foldable clauses 10, 13, and 14 generate the three *clause-loops* 1-10, 1-13, and 11-14 in the tree of unfoldings (see the bold up-arrows in Figure 1 in Section 2).

Now, as we have anticipated, we terminate the unfolding process and we introduce two new predicates, which are the eureka predicates, defined by clauses whose bodies are exactly the recurrent patterns of the atoms ups and maxlength, as they occur in the bodies of the ancestor-clauses 1 and 11.

These steps will be later formalized as applications of the *Loop Absorption Strategy*. The name of this strategy derives from the fact that the ancestor-clauses of the clause-loops 1-10, 1-13, and 11-14 have been *absorbed* into the definitions of the predicates new1 and new2 introduced below.

Since in our case the ancestor-clauses are 1 and 11, the eureka predicates are:

15. new1(L,Max) ← ups(L,LL), maxlength(LL,Max).
16. new2(H1,T1,Y1,M1) ← ups([H1|T1],[Y1|Y]), maxlength(Y,M1).

The variables of the predicate new1 and new2 are determined by the following requirements:

- new1 and new2 should be used in the program for max-ups. Thus, the variables for new1 are those which allow a folding step which uses clause 1 as old clause and clause 15 as bridge clause, and the variables for new2 are those which allow a folding step which uses clause 11 as old clause and clause 16 as bridge clause.
- new1 and new2 should have a recursive definition. Thus, the variables for new1 are also those which allow the folding steps which use clauses 10 and 13 as old clauses and clause 15 as bridge clause, and the variables for new2 are also those which allow a folding step which uses clause 14 as old clause and clause 16 as bridge clause.

During the program derivation process we may avoid the introduction of new predicates when their definition is equal to clauses which already exist in the program. Thus, in our case, we do not introduce the predicate new1: indeed clause 15 is equal to clause 1, apart from the name of the head-predicate.

Now, we can fold clauses 10 and 11 by using the clauses 1 and 16 as bridge clauses, and we obtain:

10.1 max-ups([H,H1|T1],Max) ← H>H1, max-ups([H1|T1],M1), length([H],N), max(N,M1,Max).
11.1 max-ups([H,H1|T1],Max) ← H≤H1, new2(H1,T1,Y1,M1), length([H|Y1],N), max(N,M1,Max).

We are now left with the problem of finding the explicit (recursive) definition of the newly introduced predicate new2. This problem can easily be solved by performing again the unfolding steps which have been performed when deriving clauses 12, 13, and 14 starting from clause 11. Two final folding steps will then be required for the clauses which correspond to clauses 13 and 14. (Recall that in the body of clause 12 no atoms for ups and maxlength occur, and thus for the clause corresponding to clause 12 no folding step is required).

This method of finding the recursive definitions of eureka predicates is a general method. It is always successful simply because the Loop Absorption Strategy is applied only when recurrent patterns of atoms have been found.

The derived program for the predicate new2 is:

17. new2(H,[],[H],0).
18. new2(H,[H1|T1],[H],M) ← H>H1, max-ups([H1|T1],M).
19. new2(H,[H1|T1],[H|Y1],M) ← H≤H1, new2(H1,T1,Y1,M).

The final program for max-ups is given by clauses 8, 9, 10.1, 11.1, 17, 18, and 19.

Minor improvements can be performed by simplifying clauses 9 and 10.1, and we get:

9.1 max-ups([H],1).
10.2 max-ups([H,H1|T1],Max) ← H>H1, max-ups([H1|T1],M1), max(1,M1,Max).

In the derived program the construction of the intermediate list LL between the predicates ups and maxlength has been avoided, as we desired.

As in the initial clause 1, we observe that in clause 11.1 the atoms new2(H1,T1,Y1,M1) and length([H|Y1],N) share the common variable Y1, and in order to avoid the construction of the bindings for that shared variable, we may begin another transformation process starting from the clause:

new3(H,H1,T1,M1,N) ← new2(H1,T1,Y1,M1), length([H|Y1],N).

We leave that derivation to the interested reader. The final program which can be derived is as follows:

```
max-ups([],0).
max-ups([H],1).
max-ups([H,H1|T1],Max) ← H>H1, max-ups([H1|T1],M1), max(1,M1,Max).
max-ups([H,H1|T1],Max) ← H≤H1, new3(H,H1,T1,M1,N), max(N,M1,Max).
new3(H,H1,[],0,2).
new3(H,H1,[H2|T2],M1,2) ← H1>H2, max-ups([H2|T2],M1).
new3(H,H1,[H2|T2],M1,N) ← H1≤H2, new3(H1,H2,T2,M1,N1), N is N1+1.
```

The improvement of the performances of the derived program is due to the fact that during the unfolding process we have found some clauses whose bodies have recurrent patterns of atoms.

The choice of the unfolding steps to be performed for obtaining such clauses is indeed one of the main problems of the program transformation methodology. We address that problem in this paper, and we solve it by defining a rule, called SDR (short for Synchronized Descent Rule), which selects the atoms to be unfolded. Our SDR rule allows us to find recurrent patterns of atoms, if they exist, for some classes of programs which we will specify later. For those classes of programs, during the derivation process nothing is left to the reader's intuition, because once the recurrent patterns of atoms have been found, then the suitable eureka predicates are derived. For that reason we think that our work is a contribution towards making the transformation methodology more automatic and more useful in practice.   □

In Section 2 we formalize the process of unfolding a given clause so that clauses with recurrent patterns of atoms are derived, by introducing the notion of a foldable U-tree. We also formalize the problem of finding foldable U-trees as the *Foldability Problem*, and we show the unsolvability of that problem for various classes of programs, thus providing a theoretical limitation for the transformational approach to program derivation.

In Section 3 we introduce the SDR rule for performing unfolding steps and we also introduce a class of programs for which that rule, together with some applications of the Generalization Strategy, allows us to solve the Foldability Problem. We also consider some interesting subclasses of those programs, in which the Generalization Strategy is not necessary. For those subclasses we extend previously known results.

In Section 4 we describe the Loop Absorption Strategy, which given a foldable U-tree finds the eureka predicates and their recursive definitions, so that program performances can be improved.

Finally, in Section 5 we discuss some problems one may encounter when the order of atoms and clauses affects the semantics of the programs (as in the Prolog case).

2. THE FOLDABILITY PROBLEM

We now present the notion of U-tree for a given program and a given clause. It is a tree of clauses derived by performing unfolding steps. We also present the notion of foldable U-tree, which is a U-tree where some of the derived clauses have bodies with recurrent patterns of atoms. Those recurrent patterns will suggest the definitions of the auxiliary eureka predicates which allow the improvement of program performances.

Let us introduce some preliminary definitions. A program is a definite logic program [Lloyd 87] in which some *base predicates* (like, for instance, equality, concatenation of lists, arithmetic predicates, etc.) have no explicit definition, that is, they do not occur in the heads of the program clauses. The non-base predicates are called *defined predicates*. In the Maximal-Up-Segments Example above, the base predicates are length, max, ≤, and >, while the defined predicates are max-ups, ups, and maxlength. The meaning of a defined predicate can be given in the usual way in terms of the meanings of the base predicates. An atom with a defined predicate is called a *defined atom*.

Let us start off by formalizing the process of unfolding a clause as a tree of clauses. That tree will be called *Unfolding-tree* (or U-tree for short). Since an unfolding step depends on the choice of the atom in the clause to be unfolded, the formalization of the unfolding process also depends on the choice of a selection function, called *Unfolding-selection rule*, or U-selection rule for short. (Thus, the concepts of U-tree and U-selection rule are analogous to those of SLD-tree and computation rule [Lloyd 87].)

DEFINITION 1. (*U-tree.*) Let Prog be a program, C a clause in Prog, and S a U-selection rule. A *U-tree* for <Prog,C> via S is a tree labelled by clauses and constructed as follows:

i) the root is labelled by the clause C, and

ii) let M be a node labelled by a clause of the form: $H \leftarrow A_1,..., A_h,..., A_k$, where A_h is the defined atom selected by the U-Selection rule S. For each clause $A \leftarrow B_1,..., B_s$ in Prog such that there exists a most general unifier σ of A and A_h, M has a son-node N labelled by the clause:

$\quad (H \leftarrow A_1,..., A_{h-1}, B_1,..., B_s, A_{h+1},..., A_k) \sigma.$

We will assume that the rule S is a *partial* function and the clauses for which it is not defined are leaves of the U-tree. Moreover, if the atom selected by S cannot be unfolded because no head can be unified with it, then the corresponding clause is a leaf of the U-tree. ∎

DEFINITION 2. (*Upper portion of a tree.*) Given a tree T we say that a subtree T1 of T is an *upper portion* of T iff i) if a node N is in T1 then every ancestor of N in T is also in T1, and ii) if a node N is in T1 then every brother of N in T is in T1 as well. ∎

One can easily show that the least Herbrand model of a program Prog is equal to the least Herbrand model of (Prog-{C})∪L, where C is a clause of Prog and L is the set of leaves of any upper portion of a U-tree for <Prog, C> via any U-selection rule.

Example 2. The unfolding process for the Maximal-Up-Segments program given in Example 1 can be represented by a U-tree whose finite upper portion is depicted in Figure 1 below (The underlined atoms are the ones selected for unfolding). ▢

DEFINITION 3. (*Foldable clause in a U-tree.*) Let Prog be a program, C a clause in Prog, and S a U-selection rule. A clause D in a U-tree for <Prog,C> via S is said to be *foldable* iff there is an ancestor-clause A of D in the U-tree such that the set of defined atoms in the body of D is an instance of the set of defined atoms in the body of A.

The clause in the path from the root to D which is the nearest to D satisfying the properties of A, will be called 'the' ancestor-clause of D. ∎

DEFINITION 4. (*Foldable U-tree.*) Let Prog be a program, C a clause in Prog, and S a U-selection rule. The U-tree for <Prog,C> via S is said to be foldable iff it has a finite upper portion which satisfies the following condition: for each leaf-clause L such that: i) its body has at least one defined atom, and ii) each defined atom of its body unifies at least one head in Prog, we have that L is a foldable clause.

That portion will be called *foldable upper portion* of the U-tree. ∎

We will often consider the *minimal* foldable upper portion of a U-tree, that is, a foldable upper portion which has no foldable upper portions different from itself. The (minimal) foldable upper portion of a U-tree for <Maximal-Up-Segments program, clause 1> is depicted in Figure 1.

Now we can formalize the *Foldability Problem* as follows: Given a program Prog and a clause C in Prog, is there a U-selection rule S and a foldable U-tree for <Prog,C> via S?

THEOREM 5. The Foldability Problem is partially solvable and it is not solvable.

Proof. (Sketch) Any Turing Machine M and any word w can be encoded into a logic program ProgM and clause C_w, respectively, such that there is a foldable U-tree for <ProgM∪{C_w},C_w> if and only if either M halts or M enters into an infinite cycle when starting on the input word w. Thus the Halting Problem for

Turing Machines can be reduced to the Foldability Problem. (See [Proietti-Pettorossi 89] for a complete proof.) ∎

We will now show that the Foldability Problem is unsolvable also for some restricted classes of programs.
DEFINITION 6. (*Linear recursive programs*.) A program is said to be linear recursive iff there is at most one defined predicate in the body of each clause. ∎
Example 3. The program {p ← p,q.} is linear, while the program {p ← p,q.   q ← q.} is not. The max-ups program of Example 1 is not linear because two defined predicates occur in the body of clause 1. ▫

THEOREM 7. The Foldability Problem for linear recursive programs is not solvable.
Proof. The program ProgM∪{C_w} mentioned in the proof of Theorem 5 is a linear recursive program without base predicates. ∎

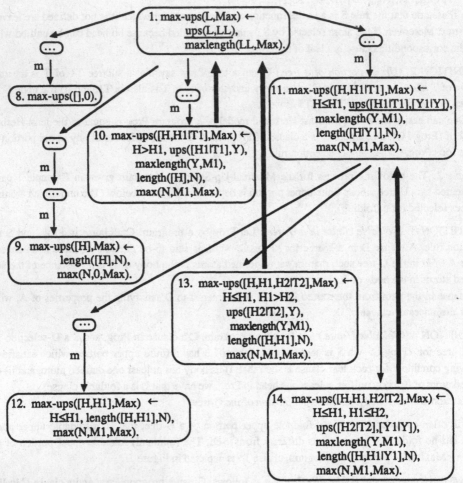

8, 9, and 12 have no defined atoms.
10, 13 and 14 are foldable.
m means 'unfolding maxlength'.
Bold up-arrows denote <ancestor-clause, foldable clause> pairs.

Figure 1. The minimal foldable upper portion of a U-tree for the Maximal-Up-Segments program.

DEFINITION 8. (*Linear terms and linear atoms.*) A term or an atom is linear iff each variable occurs in it at most once. ∎

DEFINITION 9. (*Linear-Term clauses and programs.*) A clause C of a program Prog is said to be a linear-term clause (or LT-clause) iff each defined atom of C is linear. A program Prog is a linear-term program (or LT-program) iff it is made of LT-clauses only. ∎

Example 4. The following clause of the Maximal-Up-Segments program (see Example 1) is a LT-clause:

maxlength([H|T],M) ← maxlength(T,M1), length(H,N), max(N,M1,M).

The following clause of the Maximal-Up-Segments program is *not* a LT-clause:

ups([H,H1|T1],[[H]|Y]) ← H>H1, ups([H1|T1],Y).

because the variable H occurs twice in the head. However, it can be transformed into a LT-clause introducing some equalities (to be considered as base predicates) as follows:

ups([H,H1|T1],[[K]|Y]) ← H=K, H>H1, ups([H1|T1],Y). ❑

Notice that the linearity notions introduced in Definitions 6 and 9 are completely unrelated. The program {p(a). p(t(X,X)) ← p(X).} is linear recursive but not LT, while the program {p(a). p(t(X,Y)) ← p(X), p(Y).} is LT but it is not linear recursive.

THEOREM 10. The Foldability Problem for linear recursive LT-programs is not solvable.
Proof. The program ProgM∪{C_w} mentioned in the proof of Theorem 5 is a linear recursive LT-program without base predicates. ∎

3. SOLVING THE FOLDABILITY PROBLEM FOR NON-ASCENDING PROGRAMS

In this Section we introduce the class of non-ascending programs, and for the programs in that class we will show that we can produce foldable U-trees, if we allow ourselves to apply some generalization steps (they will be formally defined later). Those foldable U-trees will be used for synthesizing suitable eureka predicates and their recursive definitions. We will also present particular subclasses of programs in which the generalization steps are *not* necessary, thus simplifying the program derivation process.

DEFINITION 11. Let X be a variable or a constant and t be a term where X occurs. The depth of X in t, denoted by depth(X,t), is defined by structural induction as follows:
- depth(X,X) = 0, and for any function symbol f:
- if t=f(t_1,...,t_n) then depth(X,t) = max{depth(X,t_i) | X occurs in t_i and i=1,...,n}+1.
Given a term t we denote by maxdepth(t) the depth of its deepest variable or constant.
Given a term t, we denote by var(t) the set of variables occurring in t.
If t and u are linear terms we say that t≤u iff for each variable X in var(t)∩var(u) we have:
depth(X,t) ≤ depth(X,u).

The above definitions of depth, maxdepth, and var, and of the ≤ relation for terms are extended from terms to atoms in the obvious way, by considering the predicate symbols as term constructors. ∎
Notice that the ≤ relation of terms is *not* a partial order. Indeed, it does not satisfy the antisymmetric and transitive properties.

DEFINITION 12. (*Non-Ascending programs.*) Let Prog be a LT-program, and C a clause in Prog of the form: H ← A_1,...,A_m,B_1,...,B_n, where A_1,...,A_m are the defined atoms.
The clause C is said to be non-ascending iff A_i≤H for i=1,...,m.
The program Prog is said to be non-ascending iff all its clauses are non-ascending. ∎

DEFINITION 13. A *Synchronized Descent Rule* (called simply SDR) for a LT-program Prog is a partial function defined as follows. Let D: H ← Body be a LT-clause and {A_1, ..., A_n} be the set of defined atoms (w.r.t. Prog) in Body. If there exists an index i such that $A_j \leq A_i$ for j=1,...,n then SDR(D,Prog) = A_i. If such an index does not exist then SDR is undefined. ∎

Often when referring to a SDR, we will not specify the corresponding clause D and the program Prog, if they can easily be understood from the context.

Notice that for any given clause D and program Prog we can have more than one SDR, because the choice of the index i in the above definition is not always uniquely determined. For simplicity reasons, unless otherwise specified, we may refer to 'the' SDR instead of 'a' SDR, when the statement at hand is valid for any choice of SDR.

However, different choices may determine the derivation of different programs with different behaviours. The problem of anticipating which of the several choices is more advantageous is outside the scope of this paper and we leave it for future research.

We give now the following two lemmas whose easy proofs can be found in [Proietti-Pettorossi 89].

LEMMA 14. By resolving two clauses of a non-ascending program we get a non-ascending clause. ∎

LEMMA 15. Let us consider a non-ascending program and two of its clauses of the form:
$H \leftarrow A_1,...,A_m,...,A_p$ and $K \leftarrow B_1,...,B_n,...,B_q$, where $A_1,...,A_m$ and $B_1,...,B_n$ only are the defined atoms. Let us also consider a defined atom A_s in $\{A_1,...,A_m\}$. Suppose that $A_r \leq A_s$ for r=1,...,m and assume that there exists the most general unifier σ of A_s and K. We have:
- $maxdepth(A_r\sigma) \leq max\{maxdepth(A_s), maxdepth(K), maxdepth(A_r)\}$ for r=1,...,m,
- $maxdepth(B_r\sigma) \leq max\{maxdepth(A_s), maxdepth(K), maxdepth(B_r)\}$ for r=1,...,n. ∎

THEOREM 16. Let Prog be a non-ascending program, C a clause in Prog, and S a SDR for Prog. For each defined atom G in the body of each clause of the U-tree for <Prog, C> via S, we have:
$$maxdepth(G) \leq max\{maxdepth(A) \mid A \text{ is a defined atom in Prog}\}. \qquad (*)$$
Proof. By induction on the construction of the U-tree using Lemmas 14 and 15. ∎

DEFINITION 17. Given a program Prog and a clause C, we denote by G(Prog,C) the context-free grammar with start symbol S and productions Prods defined as the least set such that (we use upper case letters for the non-terminal symbols and lower case letters for the terminal ones):
- if C has the form: $p(...) \leftarrow p_1(...),...,p_m(...),A_1,...,A_n$, where $p_1,...,p_m$ are the defined predicates (w.r.t. Prog), the production: $S \rightarrow P_1...P_m$ is in Prods,
- for each clause of Prog of the form: $q(...) \leftarrow q_1(...),...,q_r(...),B_1,...,B_s$, where $q_1,...,q_r$ (r≥1) are the defined predicates, the production: $Q \rightarrow Q_1...Q_r$ is in Prods,
- for each defined predicate d occurring in the body of some clause, the production: $D \rightarrow d$ is in Prods. ∎

THEOREM 18. Let Prog be a non-ascending program and C a clause in Prog such that the language generated by G(Prog,C) is finite. Let S be a SDR for Prog.
The U-tree T for <Prog, C> via S is foldable if S is defined for all clauses in T with at least a defined atom in their bodies.
Proof. Since S is (always) defined, the set of maximal paths from the root of T to its leaves can be partitioned into: i) paths with leaf-clause whose body does not contain a defined atom, ii) paths with leaf-clause where the atom selected by S cannot be unified with any head in Prog, and iii) infinite paths. For case iii), by Theorem 16 and the hypothesis on G(Prog,C) in any infinite path there is at least one clause which is foldable. Thus, a foldable upper portion of a U-tree, as required by Definition 4, can be constructed by taking paths of type i) and type ii), and minimal initial segments of infinite paths, ending in a foldable clause. ∎

We would like now to revisit the Maximal-Up-Segments Example and show that the technique suggested by the above Theorem 18 can automatically derive for us a foldable U-tree.

Example 5. Maximal-Up-Segments revisited.

The grammar G(Max-ups, clause 1) constructed as indicated by Definition 17 consists of the following set of productions: {S → Ups Maxlength, Ups → Ups, Ups → ups, Maxlength → Maxlength, Maxlength → maxlength}. Therefore the language accepted by G(Max-ups, clause 1) consists of the word 'ups maxlength' only (and thus, it is finite).

In order to use the above Theorem 18, which ensure the existence of a foldable U-tree, we first transform the program for max-ups into a non-ascending one, by using the equality predicates as indicated in Example 4. We then construct the U-tree using a SDR for that program and clause 1. The reader may verify that SDR turns out to be always defined and thus it we get a foldable upper portion of that U-tree. That portion is exactly the one depicted in Figure 1, except for the base atoms in the clauses. In particular, the following clauses should replace the ones in Figure 1 with the same first numbers. (We also have listed here clauses 1 and 8 for the reader's convenience.)

1.   max-ups(L,Max) ← ups(L,LL), maxlength(LL,Max).
8.   max-ups([],0).
9.2   max-ups([H],Max) ← H=K, length([K],N), max(N,0,Max).
10.3 max-ups([H,H1|T1],Max) ← H=K, H>H1, ups([H1|T1],Y), maxlength(Y,M1), length([K],N),
                                       max(N,M1,Max).
11.2 max-ups([H,H1|T1],Max) ← H=K, H≤H1, ups([H1|T1],[Y1|Y]), maxlength(Y,M1),
                                       length([K|Y1],N), max(N,M1,Max).
12.1 max-ups([H,H1],Max) ← H=K, H≤H1, H1=K1, length([K,K1],N), max(N,M1,Max).
13.1 max-ups([H,H1,H2|T2],Max) ← H=K, H≤H1, H1=K1, H1>H2, ups([H2|T2],Y),
                                       maxlength(Y,M1), length([K,K1],N), max(N,M1,Max).
14.1 max-ups([H,H1,H2|T2],Max) ← H=K, H≤H1, H1=K1, H1≤H2, ups([H2|T2],[Y1|Y]),
                                       maxlength(Y,M1), length([K,K1|Y1],N), max(N,M1,Max).   □

As already mentioned, we now state a few more facts which ensure the existence of foldable U-trees for various classes of programs, whereby allowing in those cases the automatic derivation of the auxiliary eureka predicates which are necessary for synthesizing efficient programs, and guaranteeing also the success of our transformation methodology.

From the above Theorem 18 we can easily get the following Theorem.

THEOREM 19. For each linear recursive non-ascending program Prog and for each clause C in Prog there exists a U-selection rule S and a foldable U-tree for <Prog,C> via S.

Proof. In the body of each clause of the U-tree the set of defined atoms is either empty or a singleton. If it is not empty we consider the selection rule which chooses the only defined atom occurring in the body. That rule is a SDR (because ≤ is reflexive), and it is defined for all clauses with at least a defined atom in their bodies. The thesis follows from the fact that G(Prog,C) generates a finite language.   ∎

Now we will prove that foldable U-trees exist for two more classes of programs. The subterm relation is assumed to be reflexive.

THEOREM 20. Let Prog be a linear recursive non-ascending program and C be a non-ascending clause (*not* in Prog) of the form: h(...) ← p₁(...), p₂(...),A₁,...,Aₙ, where the predicates p₁ and p₂ are the only defined predicates (w.r.t. Prog), and h does not occur in Prog. Assume that:

i) for each clause D in Prog of the form: p(...) ← ...,q(...),..., where q is the only defined predicate in the body of D, we have that:
  - for each argument r and s of q and p, respectively, if r has a variable in common with s then r is a subterm of s,
  - distinct arguments of q are not subterms of the same argument of p,
ii) there exist two arguments t₁ and t₂ of p₁(...) and p₂(...), respectively, such that:

ii.1) either t_1 is a subterm of t_2, or t_2 is a subterm of t_1, or $var(t_1) \cap var(t_2) = \emptyset$, and

ii.2) $var(p_1(...)) \cap var(p_2(...)) = var(t_1) \cap var(t_2)$.

Then there is a foldable U-tree for $<Prog \cup \{C\}, C>$.

Proof. First notice that the language accepted by $G(Prog \cup \{C\}, C)$ is finite. Indeed, it is made out of a production of the form: $S \rightarrow P_1 P_2$ (corresponding to C), together with productions of the form $P \rightarrow Q$ (corresponding to the clauses in Prog with exactly one defined atom in their bodies), and productions of the form $P \rightarrow p$ (corresponding to the defined predicates of Prog).

Moreover, condition ii) implies that a SDR is defined for C. Indeed, by the hypothesis that C is a non-ascending clause we have that t_1 and t_2 are linear terms. Therefore, if t_1 is a subterm of t_2 then $t_1 \leq t_2$, and, by hypothesis ii.2, we have that $p_1 \leq p_2$. The case when t_2 is a subterm of t_1 is analogous, and the case when $var(t_1) \cap var(t_2) = \emptyset$ is trivial. We will now show that condition ii) is preserved by unfoldings. Thus SDR is defined for all clauses with at least a defined atom in their bodies, and the thesis follows from Theorem 18.

Let us consider a clause E: $h(...) \leftarrow f(...,i,...), g(...,j,...), ...$, which satisfies hypothesis ii) replacing f, i, g, and j by p_1, t_1, p_2, and t_2, respectively. Let $f(...,i,...)$ be the atom selected for unfolding. (The case for $g(...,j,...)$ is analogous.) Let $f(...,s,...) \leftarrow ..., q(...,u,...), ...$ be a clause, call it D, in Prog where s is the argument which occurs in the same position of i, and u is the argument of q with at least one variable in common with s, if any, otherwise u is *any* argument of q. Notice that by hypothesis i) at most one argument of q may have common variables with s.

By unfolding E using D we get the following clause E1: $(h(...) \leftarrow q(...,u,...), g(...,j,...), ...)\sigma$, where σ is the computed most general unifier. Since $f(...,i,...)$ and $f(...,s,...)$ are linear atoms, and as usual, we assume that D does not have common variables with E, the most general unifier σ can be partitioned into four sets of bindings S_1, S_2, S_3, and S_4 such that:
- S_1 consists of bindings of the form V/a, where $V \in var(i)$ and a is a subterm of s,
- S_2 consists of bindings of the form W/b, where $W \in var(f(...,i,...))-var(i)$ and b is a subterm of an argument of $f(...,s,...)$ different from s (therefore var(b) is a subset of $var(f(...,s,...))-var(s)$), and symmetrically:
- S_3 consists of bindings of the form X/c, where $X \in var(s)$ and c is a subterm of i,
- S_4 consists of bindings of the form Y/d, where $Y \in var(f(...,s,...))-var(s)$ and d is a subterm of an argument of $f(...,i,...)$ different from i (therefore var(d) is a subset of $var(f(...,i,...))-var(i)$).

By hypothesis ii) and by the non-ascending property, we have that in clause E for each argument x and y of f and g different from i and j, respectively, $var(x) \cap var(y) = \emptyset$.

If $var(i) \cap var(j) = \emptyset$, by hypothesis ii.2) we have that $var(f(...,i,...)) \cap var(g(...,j,...)) = \emptyset$, and therefore $var(q(...,u,...)\sigma) \cap var(g(...,j,...)\sigma) = \emptyset$. Hence condition ii) is preserved.

Let us now consider the case when $var(i) \cap var(j) \neq \emptyset$, and j is a subterm of i. (The case when i is a subterm of j is analogous.)

If $var(u) \cap var(s) \neq \emptyset$, u is a subterm of s, by hypothesis i). Therefore $u\sigma$ and $j\sigma$ are subterms of the linear term $i\sigma$ and, thus, condition ii.1) holds for $u\sigma$ and $j\sigma$. Otherwise, if $var(u) \cap var(s) = \emptyset$, the bindings that may apply to u are the ones in S_4 only, and therefore the set of the variables of $u\sigma$ is a subset of those occurring either in an argument of $f(...,i,...)$ different from i or in u. On the other hand, the bindings that may apply to j are the ones in S_1 only, and therefore $var(j\sigma)$ is a subset of $var(j) \cup var(s)$. Hence we have: $var(u\sigma) \cap var(j\sigma) = \emptyset$. Thus, condition ii.1) is preserved by unfoldings.

Notice now that, by hypothesis ii) each variable X occurring in the arguments of $g(...)$ in E different from j occurs neither in $f(...,i,...)$ nor in D. Therefore, X does not occur in $q(...)\sigma$ and $X\sigma = X$. Thus, $var(q(...)\sigma) \cap var(g(...)\sigma)$ is a subset of $var(j\sigma)$.

On the other hand, by hypothesis i), each variable X occurring in the arguments of $q(...)$ in D different from u does not occur in s. Therefore the only bindings that may apply to X are the ones in S_4 and the variables occurring in the arguments of $q(...)\sigma$ different from $u\sigma$ occur either in D or in an argument of $f(...,i,...)$ different from i. Thus, they do not occur in $g(...)\sigma$ and therefore $var(q(...)\sigma)\cap var(g(...)\sigma)$ is a subset of $var(u\sigma)$.

Therefore $var(q(...)\sigma)\cap var(g(...)\sigma)$ is a subset of $var(u\sigma)\cap var(j\sigma)$. The inverse inclusion is obvious. Thus, also condition ii.2) is preserved by unfoldings. This completes the proof. ∎

REMARK. The class of programs which satisfy the hypotheses of the above theorem extends the one of unilinear programs presented in [Pettorossi-Proietti 89]. □

THEOREM 21. Let Prog be a linear recursive non-ascending program and C be a non-ascending clause (*not* in Prog) of the form: $h(...) \leftarrow p_1(...), p_2(...), A_1,...,A_n$, where the predicates p_1 and p_2 are the only defined predicates (w.r.t. Prog), and h does not occur in Prog. Assume that:

i) for each clause D in Prog of the form: $p(...) \leftarrow ...,q(...),...$ where q is the (only) defined predicate in the body of D, we have that:

- for each argument s of $p(...)$ and for each argument r of $q(...)$ $|var(s)\cap var(r)| \le 1$,

- distinct arguments of q do not have common variables with the same argument of p, and

ii) there exist two arguments t_1 and t_2 of $p_1(...)$ and $p_2(...)$, respectively, such that:

  ii.1) $|var(t_1)\cap var(t_2)| \le 1$ (where $|...|$ denotes cardinality), and

  ii.2) $var(p_1(...))\cap var(p_2(...)) = var(t_1)\cap var(t_2)$.

Then there is a foldable U-tree for $<Prog\cup\{C\},C>$.

Proof. It is easy to see that the language accepted by $G(Prog\cup\{C\},C)$ is finite and that condition ii) is preserved by unfoldings. Therefore a SDR is defined for all clauses in any U-tree for $<Prog\cup\{C\},C>$ with at least one defined atom in their bodies, and the thesis follows from Theorem 18. ∎

Notice that the above theorem is a consequence of Theorem 20 if we enforce condition i) by requiring that the arguments of $q(...)$ are variables only.

In the following Example 6 we will apply the results of Theorem 20 and 21, which ensure the existence of a foldable upper portion of a U-tree via SDR, and we will construct that tree.

Example 6. Common-Sublists.

The following program Comsub tests whether or not a list X is a sublist of both Y and Z.

```
1.   comsub(X,Y,Z) ← sub(X,Y), sub(X,Z).
2.   sub([],X).
3.   sub([A|X],[A|Y]) ← sub(X,Y).
4.   sub(X,[A|Y]) ← sub(X,Y).
```

where sub(X,Y) holds iff X is a sublist of Y. The order of the elements should be preserved, but the elements selected by X need not to be consecutive in Y. For instance, [b,d] is a sublist of [a,b,c,d], but [d,b] is not.

Unfortunately, the above program does *not* satisfy the non-ascending hypothesis of Theorems 20 and 21, because the variable A occurs twice in the head of clause 3. We can transform it into a non-ascending program by introducing equalities. Clauses 1, 2, and 4 remain unchanged, while clause 3 becomes:

3.1 sub([A|X],[A1|Y]) ← A=A1, sub(X,Y).

Now we can apply Theorem 20 (or 21) because: i) in clauses 3 and 4 each argument of sub in the bodies is a subterm of the corresponding one in the heads (indeed, it is a single variable), ii.1) in clause 1 sub(X,Y) and sub(X,Z) share the variable X only, and ii.2) $var(sub(X,Y))\cap var(sub(X,Z)) = X = var(X) \cap var(X)$. Thus, we are ensured of the existence of a foldable U-tree for <Comsub, clause 1> via a SDR. The minimal foldable upper portion of that U-tree is depicted in the Figure 2 below. (The underlined atoms are the ones selected for unfolding.) In the following Section we will consider again this example and we will see that by applying the Loop Absorption Procedure, we can derive the suitable eureka predicates and the improved program version. ◻

Unfortunately, Theorem 18 stated above does not ensure us that we can construct a foldable U-tree in the case when, at some point during the unfolding process, we get a clause for which no SDR is defined. For overcoming that difficulty we will now introduce the so called *Generalization Strategy* (see [Boyer-Moore 75] for a similar strategy used in functional programs). However, in order to preserve correctness, we need to use it together with its 'inverse', which is the *Equality Introduction*. This technique will allow us to get foldable U-trees in all cases (but unfortunately, we cannot be sure that the derived programs always have better performances).

DEFINITION 22. (*Generalization + Equality Introduction Rule.*) The application of the 'Generalization + Equality Introduction Rule' (or *Generalization Rule*, for short) to a clause C of the form: $H \leftarrow A_1,..., A_n$, consists in deriving the new clause of the form: $H \leftarrow GenA_1,..., GenA_n, X_1=t_1,..., X_r=t_r$, where: $(GenA_1,..., GenA_n) \theta = (A_1,..., A_n)$ and $\theta = \{X_1/t_1,..., X_r/t_r\}$. ∎

Obviously, when applying the Generalization + Equality Introduction Rule the least Herbrand model is preserved.

We now allow in the program derivation process unfolding steps and generalization steps. That process can be represented as a tree of clauses, which is still called U-tree. As for unfolding steps, when we perform generalization steps we produce a new son-clause. The equality predicates in the son-clauses should be considered as base predicates and, therefore, they will not be unfolded when constructing the U-tree (otherwise the generalization step will be without effect). The notion of foldability is not changed.

By performing suitable generalization steps, it is possible to transform any clause into an equivalent one for which a SDR is defined. Indeed, we can use generalizations so that no pair of defined atoms in the body of a clause has common variables and in that case an SDR is trivially defined. Notice that for doing this, we can restrict ourselves to consider a particular kind of generalization step, whose inverse instantiation is a substitution $\theta = \{X_1/t_1,..., X_r/t_r\}$, where all terms $t_1,..., t_r$ are variables. Thus, by Theorem 18 we have the following fact.

THEOREM 23. Given any non-ascending program Prog and clause C in Prog such that the language generated by G(Prog,C) is finite, there exists a foldable U-tree for <Prog, C>, and it can be constructed using unfolding steps and 'Generalization + Equality Introduction' steps. ∎

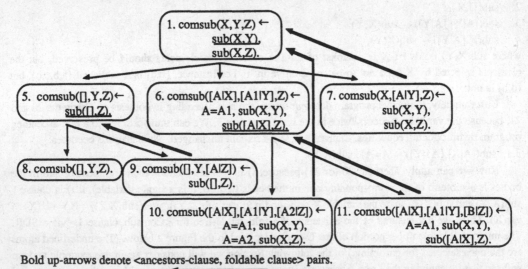

Bold up-arrows denote <ancestors-clause, foldable clause> pairs.

Figure 2. The minimal foldable upper portion of a U-tree for the Comsub program.

Of course, it is not very useful to construct a foldable U-tree at the expense of removing all shared variables among atoms, because if no shared variables occur in the bodies of the foldable clauses of the U-tree, the program we derive does not avoid redundant computations of bindings. Therefore we should use generalization steps with parsimony, so that we may maintain some shared variables among the atoms of the generalized clause. This is always possible because the ≤ relation (see Definition 11) is defined between to atoms with exactly one common variable.

Let us assume, for instance, that a SDR is not defined because a 'cycling' situation among variables occurs, as indicated by the following clause:

$h(X,Y) \leftarrow p(t(X,r(Y))), q(t(Y,r(X)))$.

The depth of X in p is smaller than the depth of X in q and viceversa for Y. In order to break that cycle we introduce by generalization a new variable, and we get:

$h(X,Y) \leftarrow X=X1, p(t(X1,r(Y))), q(t(Y,r(X)))$.

Now for that resulting clause SDR is defined and selects p.

Another simple strategy to avoid unnecessary generalization steps in the U-tree for <Prog,C> is the following one: before generalizing, one may try to unfold one of the defined atoms of the clause where SDR is not defined. If that unfolding step does not produce any atom in the body of a clause with maxdepth greater than the maximal maxdepth of a defined atom in Prog, then we can avoid a generalization step. (In that case, in fact, each atom G obtained after that unfolding step satisfies the property (*) in the statement of Theorem 16, which is used for proving Theorem 18.)

Let us now present an example of the construction of a foldable U-tree and the corresponding improved program version by using the Generalization Strategy.

Example 7. Prefix-Suffix of a list.

A list P is a prefix of a list L if P is either empty or it is an initial segment of L. A list S is a suffix of L if S is either empty or it is a final segment of L. Suppose we want to check whether or not a list PS is both a prefix and a suffix of the list L. We define a relation presuf by means of the following program Presuf:

1. $presuf(PS,L) \leftarrow prefix(PS,L), suffix(PS,L)$.
2. $prefix([],L)$.
3. $prefix([X|P],[X|L]) \leftarrow prefix(P,L)$.
4. $suffix(L,L)$.
5. $suffix(S,[X|L]) \leftarrow suffix(S,L)$.

We would like to avoid the double visit of both the list PS and the list L, while the test of presuf is performed. That objective may be achieved by finding a foldable U-tree for <program Presuf, clause 1>. The existence of that U-tree is not guaranteed by our results because Presuf does *not* satisfy the non-ascending property. Indeed, the variable X occurs twice in the head of clause 3 and the variable L occurs twice in the head of clause 4. However, we can easily obtain a semantically equivalent program, called Presuf1, which is non-ascending, by using equalities for transforming clauses 3 and 4 into the following clauses 3.1 and 4.1:

3.1 $prefix([X|P],[X1|L]) \leftarrow X=X1, prefix(P,L)$.
4.1 $suffix(L,L1) \leftarrow L=L1$.

We can now apply the SDR rule for constructing a foldable U-tree. The unfolding process via SDR generates a U-tree which has a path (starting from the root-clause 1) made out of the following clauses:

1. $presuf(PS,L) \leftarrow prefix(PS,L), suffix(PS,L)$.
6. $presuf([X|Xs],[X1|Ys]) \leftarrow X=X1, prefix(Xs,Ys), suffix([X|Xs],[X1|Ys])$.
7. $presuf([X|Xs],[X1|Ys]) \leftarrow X=X1, prefix(Xs,Ys), suffix([X|Xs],Ys)$.
8. $presuf([X|Xs],[X1,X2|Ys]) \leftarrow X=X1, prefix(Xs,[X2|Ys]), suffix([X|Xs],Ys)$.

(We get 6 from 1 by unfolding prefix, 7 from 6 and 8 from 7 by unfolding suffix).

At this point no SDR is defined because of the cycling situation between the arguments of prefix(Xs,[X2|Ys]) and suffix([X|Xs],Ys); in fact, we have:

depth(Xs, prefix(Xs,[X2|Ys])) ≤ depth(Xs, suffix([X|Xs],Ys)), and

depth(Ys, prefix(Xs,[X2|Ys])) ≥ depth(Ys, suffix([X|Xs],Ys)).

Moreover, if we unfold either prefix or suffix in clause 8 we cause the maxdepth of the other atom to grow bigger than max{maxdepth(A) | A is a defined atom in Presuf1} = 2.

In fact, we get either:

presuf([X,X3|Xs],[X1,X2|Ys]) ← X=X1, X3=X2, prefix(Xs,Ys), suffix([X,X3|Xs],Ys)

where maxdepth(suffix([X,X3|Xs],Ys))=3, or:

presuf([X|Xs],[X1,X2,Y|Ys]) ← X=X1, prefix(Xs,[X2,Y|Ys]), suffix([X|Xs],Ys)

where maxdepth(prefix(Xs,[X2,Y|Ys]))=3.

Thus, in order to construct a foldable U-tree we need to apply a generalization step. We generalize the variable Xs in the atom suffix([X|Xs],Ys) in clause 8 and we obtain:

8.1 presuf([X|Xs],[X1,X2|Ys]) ← X=X1, prefix(Xs,[X2|Ys]), Xs=Z, suffix([X|Z],Ys).

For clause 8.1 SDR is defined and it selects prefix. By continuing the construction of the U-tree from clause 8.1 we get a path made out of the following clauses:

9. presuf([X,X3|Xs],[X1,X2|Ys]) ← X=X1,X3=X2, prefix(Xs,Ys), [X3|Xs]=Z, suffix([X|Z],Ys).

10. presuf([X,X3,X4|Xs],[X1,X2,X5|Ys]) ← X=X1, X3=X2, X4=X5, prefix(Xs,Ys), [X3,X4|Xs]=Z,
                    suffix([X|Z],[X5|Ys]).

11. presuf([X,X3,X4|Xs],[X1,X2,X5|Ys]) ← X=X1, X3=X2, X4=X5, prefix(Xs,Ys), [X3,X4|Xs]=Z,
                    suffix([X|Z],Ys).

(We get 9 from 8.1 and 10 from 9 by unfolding prefix, and 11 from 10 by unfolding suffix).

Now clause 11 is foldable because the defined atoms 'prefix(Xs,Ys), suffix([X|Z],Ys)' are an instance (actually, a renaming) of the corresponding ones in the ancestor-clause 9. For lack of space we do not show here the construction of the complete minimal foldable upper portion of a U-tree for <Presuf1, clause 1>. (It is enough to use the SDR and no more generalization steps will be required.)

Notice that, a different generalization step was possible for clause 8. Indeed, we could derive the following clause:

presuf([X|Xs],[X1,X2|Ys]) ← X=X1, prefix(Xs,[X2|Z]), Z=Ys, suffix([X|Xs],Ys)

where we have generalized the occurrence of the variable Ys instead of Xs. By continuing the derivation process we get a different foldable U-tree and (by applying the Loop Absorption Procedure as indicated in the next Section) a different final program. We do not present any method for anticipating which of the two choices is more advantageous.   ❑

4. SYNTHESIS OF EUREKA PREDICATES AND DERIVATION OF IMPROVED PROGRAMS

The theoretical results presented in the previous Section can be used as a formal justification of the procedure for the synthesis of the eureka predicates indicated in Steps 1-3 below. The success of that technique is guaranteed within the class of non-ascending programs specified by Theorems 19, 20, and 21. If we perform some generalization steps for making the SDR always defined, the success is guaranteed also for the larger class specified by Theorem 23.

Loop Absorption Procedure.

Step 1. *Synthesis of eureka predicates: application of the Loop Absorption Strategy.*

Let us consider a program Prog and a clause C in Prog. For each foldable leaf-clause L of the minimal foldable upper portion T of the foldable U-tree for <Prog, C>: i) we consider the corresponding ancestor-clause A, and ii) we introduce a new eureka predicate newp by a clause N whose body consists of the set of defined atoms in A. The set of variables of newp will be the minimal set which allows to fold both A and L, using N as a bridge clause.

Step 2. *Derivation of the new program version.*

(a) For each clause N introduced at Step 1, relative to the leaf-clause L and the ancestor-clause A, we perform all unfolding and generalization steps corresponding to the subtree of T rooted in A, with the following exception: if during the unfolding and generalization process we have derived a clause, whose corresponding clause in T is *either* a foldable clause *or* the ancestor-clause of a foldable one, then we stop the unfolding and generalization process and we fold that clause by using as bridge clause one which defines a eureka predicate introduced at Step 1. This unfolding-generalization-folding process gives the explicit definition of the predicate defined by the clause N.

(b) We perform the actions described in the above Step 2(a) also for the clause C. (The subtree of T to be considered is T itself, which is rooted in C.)

Step 3. *Simplification.*

We simplify the base predicates, whenever possible. We also eliminate clauses which are subsumed by other clauses and clauses whose bodies contain defined atoms which do not match any head.   ∎

REMARK. We know that if during Step 1 a eureka predicate, say p, turns out to be defined exactly as one of the predicates already present in our program, we may avoid the introduction of p. In that case:

- the folding step relative to a foldable clause which could have been performed at Step 2(a) and Step 2(b) using p, will be performed using instead the corresponding predicate of our program,

- the folding step relative to the ancestor-clause of a foldable clause which could have been performed at Step 2(a) and 2(b) using p, will *not* be performed.

On the contrary, if we choose to introduce the predicate p, nothing goes wrong: we get a final program with redundant clauses (which could be discarded by performing folding and unfolding steps).   □

Example 8. Maximal-Up-Segments revisited.

The reader may easily verify that for the max-ups program, the technique described by the above steps 1-3 gives the same final program derived in Example 1. In particular, with reference to the clauses of Example 5 the pairs <ancestor-clause, foldable clause> are: <1, 10.3>, <1, 13.1>, and <11.2, 14.1>.

The defined atoms in the bodies of the ancestor-clauses 1 and 11.2 give us exactly the definitions of the eureka predicates which we introduced in Example 1 (see clauses 15 and 16).   □

Example 9. Common-Sublists revisited.

Step 1. As the reader may verify from Figure 2, the <ancestor-clause, foldable clause> pairs are the following ones: <5,9>, <1,10>, <6,11>, and <1,7>, where:

1.   comsub(X,Y,Z) ← sub(X,Y), sub(X,Z).
5.   comsub([],Y,Z) ← sub([],Z).
6.   comsub([A|X],[A1|Y],Z) ← A=A1, sub(X,Y), sub([A|X],Z).
7.   comsub(X,[B|Y],Z) ← sub(X,Y), sub(X,Z).
9.   comsub([],Y,[B|Z]) ← sub([],Z).
10. comsub([A|X],[A1|Y],[A2|Z]) ← A=A1, sub(X,Y), A=A2, sub(X,Z).
11. comsub([A|X],[A1|Y],[B|Z]) ← A=A1, sub(X,Y), sub([A|X],Z).

The eureka predicates we introduce by Loop Absorption Strategy are:

newcomsub(A,X,Y,Z) ← sub(X,Y), sub([A|X],Z) due to the pair <6,11>, and

newsub(Z) ← sub([A|X],Z) due to the pair <5,9>.

We do not introduce the eureka predicates relative to the other pairs, because they should have been defined exactly as the predicate comsub, which is already in the initial program version.

Step 2. By performing the unfolding and folding steps (no generalization step is necessary) which correspond to the subtrees rooted in clause 1, 6 and 5 in the U-tree of Figure 2, we get the following recursive definitions of comsub, newcomsub, and newsub, respectively:

12. comsub([],Y,Z).
13. comsub([],Y,[A|Z]) ← newsub(Z).
14. comsub([A|X],[A1|Y],Z) ← A=A1, newcomsub(A,X,Y,Z).
15. comsub(X,[A|Y],Z) ← comsub(X,Y,Z).
16. newcomsub(A,X,Y,[A2|Z]) ← A=A2, comsub(X,Y,Z).
17. newcomsub(A,X,Y,[B|Z]) ← newcomsub(A,X,Y,Z).
18. newsub(Z).
19. newsub([B|Z]) ← newsub(Z).

Step 3. We simplify the equalities in clauses 14 and 16. Moreover, we can eliminate clause 13 which is subsumed by clause 12, and we also eliminate clauses 18 and 19 which become unnecessary. The final program is:

12.   comsub([],Y,Z).
14.1 comsub([A|X],[A|Y],Z) ← newcomsub(A,X,Y,Z).
15.   comsub(X,[A|Y],Z) ← comsub(X,Y,Z).
16.1 newcomsub(A,X,Y,[A|Z]) ← comsub(X,Y,Z).
17.   newcomsub(A,X,Y,[B|Z]) ← newcomsub(A,X,Y,Z).

This program is equal to the one derived in [Tamaki-Sato 84], but through our methodology we have now made all derivation steps easily mechanizable and not based upon the programmer's intuition. □

Example 10. Prefix-Suffix of a list revisited.
Where we show only the derivation which is relative to the path of the foldable U-tree constructed in the above Example 7, leading from clause 1 to clause 11, via clauses 8, 8.1, and 9.
Step 1. From the path under consideration we derive the <ancestor-clause, foldable clause> pair <clause 9, clause 11>, which gives us the following eureka predicate definition:
12. newpresuf(Xs,Ys,X,Z) ← prefix(Xs,Ys), suffix([X|Z],Ys).

Step 2. By performing the unfolding, generalizaton, and folding steps which correspond to the subpath from clause 1 to clause 9, and to the subpath from clause 9 to clause 11, we get the following two clauses:
13. presuf([X,X3|Xs],[X1,X2|Ys]) ← X=X1, X3=X2, [X3|Xs]=Z, newpresuf(Xs,Ys,X,Z).
14. newpresuf([X1|Xs],[Y1|Ys],X,Z) ← X1=Y1, newpresuf(Xs,Ys,X,Z).

Step 3. After the simplification of the equalities, we get the following two clauses:
13.1 presuf([X,X2|Xs],[X,X2|Ys]) ← newpresuf(Xs,Ys,X,[X2|Xs]).
14.1 newpresuf([X1|Xs],[X1|Ys],X,Z) ← newpresuf(Xs,Ys,X,Z).

The reader may complete the derivation of the program for presuf(PS,L) by considering the other paths of the foldable upper portion of the U-tree for <Presuf1, clause 1>. The program which can be derived avoids the double visit of the list L, but because of the generalization step we have performed, it does not avoid the double visit of PS. □

5. FINAL DISCUSSION

We have presented a program transformation methodology and we have applied it to the derivation of some logic programs. We have also characterized our methodology by establishing some theorems which ensure the existence of foldable upper portions of U-trees.
If we have to apply the proposed techniques in the case of Prolog programs (or other programs written in any other logic language in which the order of the atoms and clauses is significant), it may be the case that

we have to perform some extra transformation steps for maintaining the efficiency improvements. Let us consider, in fact, the following situations.

i) If for obtaining the pattern of atoms required for performing a folding step we have to rearrange the order of the atoms, the non-determinism of the derived program may be increased, because some predicates could be evaluated before they are sufficiently instantiated. In those cases we can safely perform the necessary transformations, which interchange the relevant atoms, if the instantiation of the variables satisfies some suitable conditions. Fortunately those conditions, which may require information on calling modes, can often be derived at compile time via standard techniques based on abstract interpretations or data flow analysis [Bruynooghe et al. 87].

ii) The unfolding process may increase the number of generated clauses (see for instance, our Example 10) and therefore at run time each resolution step may need more time when searching for the unifying clause-head. That phenomenon may limit the improvement of efficiency determined by the use of the eureka predicates, but in that case we can profitably apply various techniques based on clause fusion [Debray-Warren 88] or clause abstraction [Sterling-Lakhotia 88] or clause indexing (like in the MacProlog optimizing compiler [Clark et al. 87]).

Now we present the results of some experiments we have performed in our C-Prolog implementation on a VAX 780 under VMS. In the tables below, we compare the time and space performances of the initial program versions with respect to the final ones obtained by introducing eureka predicates.

The Maximal-Up-Segments program.
Computing a solution of max-ups(L,M) where L is a ground list and M is a free variable.
Case (1): $|L|$=200, Case (2): $|L|$=400, where $|L|$ denotes from now on the length of the list L.

Program:	Initial (1)	Final (1)	Initial (2)	Final (2)
Time (sec):	0.110	0.070	0.220	0.140
Space (bytes): global stack	17828	9808	35672	19628
local stack	28108	16224	55560	31916

The Common-Sublists program.
Test 1. The goal is: comsub(X,Y,Z) where X, Y and Z are ground lists, and X is a sublist of Y and Z.
Case (1): $|X|$=40, $|Y|$=310, $|Z|$=231. Case (2): $|X|$=1000, $|Y|$=1270, $|Z|$=1191.

Program:	Initial (1)	Final (1)	Initial (2)	Final (2)
Time (sec):	0.041	0.043	0.165	0.130
Space (bytes): global stack	8744	8092	63380	47500
local stack	17200	19812	81052	51828

Test 2. The goal is: comsub(X,Y,Z) where X, Y, Z are ground lists, and the list X is *not* a sublist of the list Y. $|X|$=11, $|Y|$=28, $|Z|$=28.

Program:	Initial	Final
Time (sec):	0.041	0.064
Space (bytes): global stack	588	980
local stack	1356	2644

Test 3. Computing all solutions of the goal: comsub(X,Y,Z) where X is free variable while Y and Z are ground lists. Case (1): $|Y|$=5, $|Z|$=5. Case (2): $|Y|$=10, $|Z|$=10.

Program:	Initial (1)	Final (1)	Initial (2)	Final (2)
Time (sec):	0.207	0.063	6.516	0.817
Space (bytes): global stack	2388	804	25684	10844
local stack	9340	3260	89260	36860

The Prefix-Suffix program.

Test 1. The goal is: presuf(X,Y) where both X and Y are ground lists. Case (1): |X|=330, |Y|=942.
Case (2): |X|=990, |Y|=2262.

Program:	Initial (1)	Final (1)	Initial (2)	Final (2)
Time (sec):	0.075	0.065	0.228	0.203
Space (bytes): global stack	19052	13772	48092	32252
local stack	33040	24852	77920	51252

Test 2. Computing all solutions of the goal: presuf(X,Y) where X is a free variable and Y is a ground list.
Case (1): |Y|=40, Case (2): |Y|=96.

Program:	Initial (1)	Final (1)	Initial (2)	Final (2)
Time (sec):	0.23	0.16	0.83	0.53
Space (bytes): global stack	1780	1388	4244	3180
local stack	5316	5316	11812	11812

As the reader may notice from the above tables, the efficiency improvements one may expect by the application of our transformation methodology are confirmed by the experimental results. When the evaluations of the predicates tupled together by the introduction of the eureka predicates share common subcomputations then the improvements are particularly substantial.

Moreover, it is often the case that the derived programs realize suitable *synchronizations* among the computations relative to various predicates, thus realizing the so-called *filter promotion* [Bird 84] and improving efficiency.

For instance, in the case of the Common-Sublists example, if using the initial program version we want to generate all common sublists of two lists, say Y and Z, we have first to construct a sublist of Y and then we have to test whether or not it is a sublist of Z.

Instead, if we use the derived program, when an element of a sublist of Y is generated we can check whether or not it occurs also in Z (in the suitable order). That synchronization of the computations allows us to prevent the generation of the entire sublist of Y before discovering, for instance, that it is not a sublist of Z, thus drastically reducing the search space.

Unfortunately, there are some cases in which the performances of the final program versions are *not* better than the initial ones. That phenomenon can be best illustrated by Test 2 of the Common-Sublists program. In that case we have that the goal comsub(X,Y,Z) cannot be satisfied because X is not a sublist of Y. Therefore no computation is necessary for verifying whether or not X is a sublist of Z. The initial program gives the negative result faster because sub(X,Y) immediately fails (indeed X is not a sublist of Y), while in the final program comsub(X,Y,Z) takes some extra time for verifying whether X is a sublist of Z (indeed, it calls the recursively defined predicate newcomsub(A,X,Y,Z)).

Finally, we want to address a point related to the fact that the derived programs may have a large number of clauses, especially for non-toy examples. This is actually the price one pays for applying automatic methods for the development of programs by transformation. For instance, in the Prefix-Suffix example a 'clever transformer' could have invented the new predicate genpresuf, defined by the clause:

genpresuf(PS1,PS2,L) ← prefix(PS1,L), suffix(PS2,L).

starting from the initial clause:

1. presuf(PS,L) ← prefix(PS,L), suffix(PS,L).

Then the derivation process would have been much simpler than the one we have presented using our techniques, but the derived program would have *not* been more efficient. However, we do not see how the invention of the above genpresuf predicate can be derived by easily mechanizable techniques like the ones we have presented here.

6. ACKNOWLEDGEMENTS

We would like to thank the IASI Institute of the National Research Council of Italy and the University of Roma Tor Vergata for providing the necessary facilities and giving the financial support.

Thanks to the anonymous referees, and also to Dr. M. Bruynooghe, Dr. N. Jones, Dr. A. Lakhotia, Dr. J. Maluszynski, and Dr. L. Sterling, who showed much interest in our work.

7. REFERENCES

[Azibi 87] Azibi, N.: "TREQUASI: Un système pour la transformation automatique de programmes PROLOG récursifs en quasi-itératifs, These, Université de Paris-Sud, Centre d'Orsay, 1987.

[Bird 84] Bird, R.S.:"The Promotion and Accumulation Strategies in Transformational Programming", Toplas ACM 6 (4) 1984, pp. 487-504.

[Boyer-Moore 75] Boyer, R.S. and Moore, J.S.: "Proving Theorems about LISP Functions", JACM 22 (1) 1975, pp. 129-144.

[Bossi et al. 88] Bossi, A., Cocco, N. and Dulli S.:"A Method for Specializing Logic Programs", Proc. 3rd Italian Conf. on Logic Programming, GULP 88, Roma, 1988, pp. 97-114.

[Bruynooghe et al. 87] Bruynooghe, M., Janssens G., Callebaut, A., and Demoen, B.: "Abstract Interpretation: Toward the Global Optimization of Prolog Programs", Proc. Symposium on Logic Programming , IEEE Press, 1987, pp. 192-204.

[Bruynooghe et al. 89] Bruynooghe, M., De Raedt, L., and De Schreye D.: "Explanation Based Program Transformation", R. CW-89, Katholieke Universiteit Leuven, Belgium, 1989 (also in Proc IJCAI 89).

[Burstall-Darlington 77] Burstall, R.M. and Darlington, J.: "A Transformation System for Developing Recursive Programs", JACM, Vol. 24, No. 1, January 1977, pp. 44-67.

[Clark et al. 87] Clark, K., McCabe, F., Johns, N., and Spenser, C.: "LPA MacPROLOG Reference Manual" Logic Programming Associates, London [1987].

[Darlington 81] Darlington, J.: "An Experimental Program Transformation and Synthesis System", Artificial Intelligence 16, 1981, pp. 1-46.

[Debray 88] Debray, S.K.: "Unfold/Fold Transformations and Loop Optimization of Logic Programs", Proc. SIGPLAN 88 Conf. on Programming Language Design and Implementation, Atlanta, 1988.

[Debray-Warren 88] Debray, S.K. and Warren, D.S.: "Automatic Mode Inference for Logic Programs", J. Logic Programming 1988, Vol. 5, pp. 207-229.

[Deransart-Maluszynski 85] Deransart, P. and Maluszynski, J.: "Relating Logic Programs and Attribute Grammars" INRIA Report n.393, 1985.

[van Emden-Kowalski 76] van Emden, M.H. and Kowalski, R.: "The Semantics of Predicate Logic as a Programming Language", JACM, Vol. 23, No. 4, October 1976, pp. 733-742.

[Feather 86] Feather, M.S.: "A Survey and Classification of Some Program Transformation Techniques", Proc. TC2 IFIP Working Conf. on Program Specification and Transformation, Bad Tölz, Germany, 1986.

[Hogger 81] Hogger, C.J.: "Derivation of Logic Programs", JACM, No. 28, 2, 1981, pp. 372-392.

[Kawamura-Kanamori 88] Kawamura, T. and Kanamori, T.: "Preservation of Stronger Equivalence in Unfold/Fold Logic Program Transformation", Proc. Int. Conf. on FGCS, Tokyo, 1988, pp. 413-422.

[Lloyd 87] Lloyd, J.W.: "Foundations of Logic Programming", Springer-Verlag, Berlin, Heidelberg, New York, Tokyo, 2nd edition, 1987.

[Nakagawa 85] Nakagawa, H.: "Prolog Program Transformations and Tree Manipulation Algorithms", J. Logic Programming 1985, 2, pp. 77-91.

[Pettorossi-Proietti 89] Pettorossi, A. and Proietti, M.: "Decidability Results and Characterization of Strategies for the Development of Logic Programs", Proc. 6th Int. Conf. on Logic Programming, Lisboa (Portugal) 1989, pp. 539-553.

[Proietti-Pettorossi 89] Proietti, M. and Pettorossi, A.: "The Loop Absorption and the Generalization Strategies for the Development of Logic Programs", Report IASI-CNR, Roma, Italy, (Dec. 1989).

[Sterling-Lakhotia 88] Sterling, L. and Lakhotia, A.: "Composing Prolog Meta-Interpreters", Proc. 5th Int. Conf. on Logic Programming, Seattle, WA (USA), 1988.

[Tamaki-Sato 84] Tamaki, H. and Sato, T.: "Unfold/Fold Transformation of Logic Programs", Proc. 2nd Int. Conf. on Logic Programming, Uppsala, 1984.

[Wadler 84] Wadler, P. L.: "Listless is Better than Laziness" Ph.D. Dissertation, Carnegie-Mellon University, August 1984.

Algebraic Properties of Program Integration

Thomas Reps
Computer Sciences Department
University of Wisconsin—Madison
1210 W. Dayton Street
Madison, WI 53706 USA

The need to integrate several versions of a program into a common one arises frequently, but it is a tedious and time consuming task to merge programs by hand. The program-integration algorithm recently proposed by Horwitz, Prins, and Reps provides a way to create a *semantics-based* tool for integrating a base program with two or more variants. The integration algorithm is based on the assumption that any change in the *behavior*, rather than the *text*, of a program variant is significant and must be preserved in the merged program. An integration system based on this algorithm will determine whether the variants incorporate interfering changes, and, if they do not, create an *integrated* program that includes all changes as well as all features of the base program that are preserved in all variants. To determine this information, the algorithm employs a program representation that is similar to the *program dependence graphs* that have been used previously in vectorizing and parallelizing compilers.

This paper studies the algebraic properties of the program-integration operation. To do so, we first modify the integration algorithm by recasting it as an operation on a *Brouwerian algebra* constructed from sets of dependence graphs. (A Brouwerian algebra is a distributive lattice with an operation $a \div b$ characterized by $a \div b \subseteq c$ iff $a \subseteq b \cup c$.) In this algebra, the program-integration operation can be defined solely in terms of $\cup$, $\cap$, and $\div$. By making use of the rich set of algebraic laws that hold in Brouwerian algebras, the paper establishes a number of the integration operation's algebraic properties.

1. INTRODUCTION

The algorithm recently proposed by Horwitz, Prins, and Reps [5], which we will refer to as the *HPR algorithm*, provides the basis for a tool to integrate (combine) program variants automatically. Given a program *Base* and two variants *A* and *B*, the HPR algorithm makes use of knowledge of the programming language to determine whether the changes made to *Base* to produce *A* and *B* interfere; if there is no interference, the algorithm produces a merged program *M*. One of the virtues of the HPR algorithm is that it is possible to characterize the execution behavior of program *M* in terms of the behaviors of *Base*, *A*, and *B*. (By the execution behavior of a program for some initial state, we mean the sequence of values produced at each program component when the program is run on that state.) Changes in the behavior of *A* and *B* with respect to *Base*—rather than changes in their text—are detected and preserved in the integrated program, along with the unchanged behavior of all three [11]. Although it is undecidable to determine whether a program modification actually leads to a change in execution behavior, it is possible to determine a safe approximation by comparing *A* and *B* with *Base*, using a program representation that is similar to the program dependence graphs used in vectorizing and parallelizing compilers [1, 6].

One aspect of the HPR algorithm that has not been previously addressed is its algebraic properties. These are of interest when dealing with compositions of integrations. For example, if three variants of a given base program are to be integrated by a pair of (two-variant) integrations, it is important to know

This work was supported in part by a David and Lucile Packard Fellowship for Science and Engineering, by the National Science Foundation under grant DCR-8552602, by the Defense Advanced Research Projects Agency, monitored by the Office of Naval Research under contract N00014-88-K-0590, as well as by grants from IBM, DEC, and Xerox.

whether there is a law of associativity to guarantee that it does not matter which two variants are integrated first. (Such a law does hold, and is discussed in Section 4.)

Although the program-integration problem addressed by the HPR algorithm is a greatly simplified one and the algorithm's capabilities are severely limited—the algorithm is developed for a simple language in which expressions contain scalar variables and constants, and the only statements are assignment statements, conditional statements, and while-loops—recent research has made progress towards extending the set of language constructs to which the algorithm is applicable [3, 4], as well as incorporating some alternative techniques [15, 16]. Our hope is that such extensions and modifications will share with the basic HPR algorithm a common set of algebraic properties. However, we would like to avoid having to re-prove that each property holds every time we enhance our techniques. Instead, we would like to have a framework that would not only let us establish the algebraic properties of program integration, but would also allow us to show that a new algorithm possesses these properties merely by demonstrating that the algorithm meets the conditions of the framework. This paper uses lattice theory to provide such a framework.

A novel feature of our study is the use of *Brouwerian algebra*, rather than, for example, Boolean algebra or relational algebra. A Brouwerian algebra [7] is a distributive lattice with a *pseudo-difference* operation, $a \doteq b$, characterized by $a \doteq b \subseteq c$ iff $a \subseteq b \cup c$ (see Section 3). The connection between program integration and Brouwerian algebra is made as follows: we introduce a Brouwerian algebra constructed from sets of dependence graphs; in this algebra, the program-integration operation can be expressed solely in terms of the operations $\cup$, $\cap$, and $\doteq$.

The contributions of the paper can be summarized as follows:

(1) The paper establishes a number of *algebraic properties* that hold for the integration operation. These investigations make use of the rich set of algebraic laws that hold in Brouwerian algebras.

(2) The paper provides a *lattice-theoretic framework* for studying the common properties of different integration algorithms. The operation we define to integrate elements of a Brouwerian algebra is expressed purely in terms of $\cup$, $\cap$, and $\doteq$, and thus has an analogue in all Brouwerian algebras. In Sections 4, 5, and 6, the properties of the integration operation are established using only algebraic identities and inequalities, and thus the results obtained hold for all Brouwerian algebras. Consequently, to show that a proposed program-integration algorithm shares these properties, one merely has to show that the algorithm can be cast as an integration operation in some Brouwerian algebra.

(3) The paper describes how to *eliminate a restriction* that is part of the HPR algorithm. The HPR algorithm assumes that a special program editor is used to create the program variants from the base program: the editor provides a tagging capability so that common statements and predicates can be identified in different versions. As discussed in Section 7, it is possible to do away with this restriction and use Brouwerian algebras whose elements are dependence graphs that do not have tags on their components. Thus, in principle it is no longer necessary for program integration to be supported by a closed system; programs can be integrated even if they are created using ordinary text editors.

(4) The paper identifies a *new criterion* for program integration, based on the operation in our framework that is the *dual* of the integration operation.

The paper is organized into eight sections. Section 2 provides a brief introduction to the HPR algorithm. Section 3 defines Brouwerian algebras, and introduces a particular Brouwerian algebra constructed from sets of dependence graphs. Section 4 defines the operation to integrate elements of a Brouwerian algebra. For the dependence-graph algebra discussed in Section 3, this operation corresponds very closely to the HPR algorithm. Section 5 concerns the operation that is the dual of the integration operation, and shows how the two operations are related. Section 6 discusses an application of program integration. Section 7 describes the relationship of the work described in the paper to previous work; in particular, it compares the integration operation in the dependence-graph algebra with the HPR algorithm. Section 8 briefly describes an implementation of a program-integration tool that incorporates the ideas presented in the paper.

Except in Section 5, all proofs are omitted. Section 5 illustrates the power of the algebraic approach for establishing integration properties; proofs of all other properties cited can be found in [13].

2. OVERVIEW OF THE HPR ALGORITHM FOR PROGRAM INTEGRATION

The HPR algorithm applies to a simplified programming language with the following characteristics: expressions contain only scalar variables and constants; statements are either assignment statements, conditional statements, while loops, or a restricted kind of "output statement" called an *end statement*, which can only appear at the end of a program. An end statement names zero or more of the variables used in the program. The variables named in the end statement are those whose final values are of interest to the programmer; when execution terminates, the final state is defined on only those variables in the end statement. Thus a program is of the form

program
  list-of-statements
end(*id**).

Variables that are used before being defined get their value from the initial execution state.

A full description of the HPR algorithm can be found in [5]; because of space limitations, the description given here will be confined to the case of straight-line code (with end statements). We wish to stress that this does *not* reflect a limitation of the approach described in the paper; our approach applies *in toto* to the more general language handled by the full HPR algorithm.

The integration of A and B with respect to *Base*, which will be denoted by $A[Base]B$, requires combining three structures, $\Delta(A, Base)$, $\Delta(B, Base)$, and $Pre(A, Base, B)$, where $\Delta(A, Base)$ and $\Delta(B, Base)$ represent potentially changed computations of A and B with respect to *Base*, respectively, and $Pre(A, Base, B)$ represents computations that are preserved in all three. To determine this information, the algorithm employs graphs that represent the dependences between program elements. For straight-line code, the vertices represent the program's assignment statements and final uses of variables in the program's end statement; the edges represent write/read dependences (also known as *flow dependences* or *def-use chains*): an edge runs from vertex v to vertex w if (1) v assigns to a variable x, (2) w uses variable x, (3) v precedes w, and (4) there is no intervening assignment to x.

To find potentially changed and preserved computations, the algorithm makes use of an operation called *slicing* [8, 14]. A *slice* of a dependence graph with respect to vertex v consists of all elements on paths to v, which is exactly the set of elements that can affect the value produced at v (*i.e.*, that can affect the behavior of v). For example, when the graph for the program shown below on the left is sliced with respect to the final use of y in the program's end statement, the result is a graph that corresponds to the program shown on the right.

program
  $x := 0; y := x; z := y$
end(*y, z*)

program
  $x := 0; y := x$
end(*y*)

The slice with respect to a set of vertices is the union of the slices taken with respect to the set's members. The slice with respect to a graph H is defined to be the slice taken with respect to the vertex set of H.

The significance of a slice is that it captures a portion of a program's behavior in the sense that, for any initial state on which the program halts, the program and the slice compute the same sequence of values for each element of the slice [11].

THEOREM. (SLICING THEOREM [11]). *Let Q be a slice of program P with respect to a set of vertices. If σ is a state on which P halts, then (1) Q halts on σ, (2) P and Q compute the same sequence of values at each program point of Q, and (3) The final states agree on all variables defined in the final state of Q.*

The HPR algorithm assumes that a special program editor—providing a tagging capability so that corresponding statements can be identified in different versions—is used to create the program variants from the base program. Such correspondences are necessary to determine $\Delta(A, Base)$, $\Delta(B, Base)$, and $Pre(A, Base, B)$: $\Delta(A, Base)$ consists of the slices of A with respect to all vertices v such that either vertex v is not in *Base*, or the slice of *Base* with respect to v differs from the slice of A with respect to v; $\Delta(B, Base)$ is defined similarly for B; $Pre(A, Base, B)$ consists of the slices that are identical in all three graphs. The merged program created by the HPR algorithm corresponds to the graph obtained by taking the union of all these slices.

Example. The following example illustrates the HPR algorithm. The tags on statements are noted between square brackets.

A	Base	B	$\Delta(A, Base)$	$Pre(A, Base, B)$	$\Delta(B, Base)$	A [Base] B
program	program	program	∅	program	program	program
[1] x := 0	[1] x := 0;	[1] x := 0;		[1] x := 0	[1] x := 0;	[1] x := 0;
end(x)	[2] y := x	[2] y := x;		end(x)	[2] y := x;	[2] y := x;
	end(x, y)	[3] z := y			[3] z := y	[3] z := y
		end(x, y, z)			end(z)	end(x, z)

This example illustrates one subtlety of the HPR algorithm: an insertion made in one integrand can "override" a deletion in the other integrand. In the example given above, the insertion of $z := y$ in integrand B overrides the deletion of $y := x$ from integrand A because $z := y$ uses the value assigned to y by $y := x$. Note that the deletion from A of the final use of y does *not* get overridden.

3. USING LATTICE THEORY TO DESCRIBE PROGRAM INTEGRATION

To understand the considerations that led us to recast the HPR algorithm as an operation in a Brouwerian algebra, consider how $Pre(A, Base, B)$ was characterized above: "$Pre(A, Base, B)$ consists of the slices that are identical in all three graphs." This suggests that $Pre(A, Base, B)$ is the meet of A, *Base*, and B in a lattice[1] of dependence graphs ordered by "is-a-slice-of," the meet operation being "greatest common slice." (Here the term "dependence graph" refers to the more general kind used in the full HPR algorithm, not just the kind for straight-line code described in Section 2.) The fact that $\Delta(A, Base)$ and $\Delta(B, Base)$ are then combined with $Pre(A, Base, B)$ suggests that this combination is a join operation. The terms $\Delta(A, Base)$ and $\Delta(B, Base)$ themselves suggest that some sort of difference operation exists for elements of the lattice.

Complicating matters is the fact that the set of dependence graphs ordered by is-a-slice-of is a *lower semi-lattice*, but not a lattice (*i.e.*, it has a meet operation but no join operation). In particular, the

---

[1] A *lattice* is an algebra $(L, \cup, \cap)$, where L is a set of elements that is closed under $\cup$ (join) and $\cap$ (meet), and for all a, b, and c in L the following axioms are satisfied:

$$a \cup a = a \qquad a \cup b = b \cup a \qquad (a \cup b) \cup c = a \cup (b \cup c) \qquad a \cup (a \cap b) = a$$
$$a \cap a = a \qquad a \cap b = b \cap a \qquad (a \cap b) \cap c = a \cap (b \cap c) \qquad a \cap (a \cup b) = a$$

The symbol $\subseteq$ is used to denote the partial order on the elements of L given by $a \subseteq b$ iff $a \cap b = a$. All lattices considered in this paper have a least and a greatest element, which are denoted by $\bot$ and $\top$, respectively.

operation of unioning two dependence graphs, which is used in the HPR algorithm to combine the dependence graphs that represent $\Delta(A, Base)$, $\Delta(B, Base)$, and $Pre(A, Base, B)$, is not a join operation. To see this, consider the union of the dependence graphs for the programs a and b shown below.

a	b
program	**program**
$[1]\ x := 0;\ [2]\ y := x$	$[2]\ y := x;\ [3]\ z := y$
end(y)	**end**(z)

The result of $a \cup b$ is a dependence graph that corresponds to the program

program
$[1]\ x := 0;\ [2]\ y := x;\ [3]\ z := y$
end(y, z).

For $\cup$ (graph union) to be a join operation, both a and b have to be slices of $a \cup b$. However, although both a and b are *subgraphs* of $a \cup b$, only a is a *slice* of $a \cup b$. The graph for b is not a slice of $a \cup b$ because in $a \cup b$ vertex $y := x$ is the target of a flow edge whose source is $x := 0$, which "corrupts" the slices of $a \cup b$ with respect to $y := x$, $z := y$, and the final use of z.

The solution involves defining a lattice whose elements consist of sets of slices, and performing operations on these sets; in particular, the join operation is set union. However, in order for set intersection to capture common slices, it is necessary to work with sets having a particular structure (rather than arbitrary sets of slices). Similarly, ordinary set difference turns out not to capture the notion of $\Delta(A, Base)$ and $\Delta(B, Base)$ from the HPR algorithm, but a variation on set difference that takes into account the ordering relation on slices can be used instead.

Definition. Let G be the set of well-formed program dependence graphs, and let the relation symbol $\leq$ denote the relation "is-a-slice-of," (*i.e.*, $x \leq y$ means that graph x is a slice of graph y).

(i) Define set G_1, the set of all program dependence graphs that are *single-point slices*, to be
$G_1 \triangleq \{ g \in G \mid \exists x \in V(g) \text{ such that } (g/x) = g \}$, where g/x denotes the slice of g with respect to vertex x.

(ii) Define set DCS, the set of all *downwards-closed sets of single-point slices*, to be
$DCS \triangleq \{ S \in P(G_1) \mid \forall x \in G_1 \text{ if } \exists s \in S \text{ such that } x \leq s \text{ then } x \in S \}$, where $P(G_1)$ denotes the power set of G_1.

(iii) For all $x, y \in DCS$, define the operation *pseudo-difference*, denoted by $x \dot{-} y$, to be
$x \dot{-} y \triangleq \{ z \in G_1 \mid \exists p \in (x-y) \text{ such that } z \leq p \}$, where $x-y$ denotes the set difference between x and y. That is, $x \dot{-} y$ is the downwards closure of $x-y$.

Example. The following table illustrates how $\dot{-}$ differs from $-$:

a	b	$a-b$	$a \dot{-} b$	$b-a$	$b \dot{-} a$
$\begin{bmatrix} \textbf{program} \\ x := 0 \\ \textbf{end}() \end{bmatrix}$	$\begin{Bmatrix} \textbf{program} , & \textbf{program} \\ x := 0 & x := 0; \\ \textbf{end}() & y := x \\ & \textbf{end}() \end{Bmatrix}$	$\emptyset\ (= \perp)$	$\emptyset\ (= \perp)$	$\begin{Bmatrix} \textbf{program} \\ x := 0; \\ y := x \\ \textbf{end}() \end{Bmatrix}$	$\begin{Bmatrix} \textbf{program} , & \textbf{program} \\ x := 0 & x := 0; \\ \textbf{end}() & y := x \\ & \textbf{end}() \end{Bmatrix}$

This structure—the set DCS together with the operations of set union, set intersection, and pseudo-difference—is an instance of what is known as a Brouwerian algebra (defined below). The benefit of this fact is that Brouwerian algebras have a rich set of algebraic laws, consisting of identities and inequalities (see the Appendix). These laws provide a convenient way to establish the integration operation's algebraic properties through simple formula manipulations. (For examples, see Section 5.)

Definition. A *Brouwerian algebra* [7] is an algebra $(L, \cup, \cap, \dot{-}, \top)$ where

(i) $(L, \cup, \cap)$ is a lattice with greatest element $\top$.

(ii) L is closed under $\dot{-}$.

(iii) For all a, b, and c in L, $a \dot{-} b \subseteq c$ iff $a \subseteq b \cup c$.

It can be shown that L has a least element, given by $\bot = \top \dot{-} \top$, and that $(L, \cup, \cap)$ is distributive.[2]

THEOREM. $(DCS, \cup, \cap, \dot{-}, G_1)$ *is a Brouwerian algebra, where* $\cup$ *is set union and* $\cap$ *is set intersection.*

4. INTEGRATION OF ELEMENTS OF A BROUWERIAN ALGEBRA

We now introduce a ternary operation on elements of a Brouwerian algebra that, for the dependence-graph algebra discussed in Section 3, corresponds very closely to the HPR algorithm. (The relationship between integration in the dependence-graph algebra and the HPR algorithm is addressed further in Section 7.)

Definition. The *integration* of elements a and c with respect to element b is the element $a[b]c$ defined by $a[b]c \triangleq (a \dot{-} b) \cup (a \cap b \cap c) \cup (c \dot{-} b)$. If $a[b]c = m$, we refer to element b as the *base*, elements a and c as the *integrands*, and element m as the *result* of the integration.

Example. The table shown in Figure 1, which indicates what slices are members of the sets A, *Base*, B, $A \dot{-} Base$, $A \cap Base \cap B$, $B \dot{-} Base$, and $A[Base]B$, illustrates the integration operation (in the dependence-graph algebra) for the example from Section 2. This produces the same result that was obtained in Section 2 with the HPR algorithm; as shown in Figure 1, the set of slices computed for $A[Base]B$ corresponds to the program

program
$\quad x := 0; y := x; z := y$
end(x, z).

Because the integration operation is defined solely in terms of $\cup$, $\cap$, and $\dot{-}$, it has an analogue in all Brouwerian algebras, not just the dependence-graph algebra from Section 3. Because we will study its properties strictly from an algebraic standpoint, our results apply to this operation in *all* Brouwerian algebras. It is not difficult to show that the following basic properties hold for the integration operation:

$a[a]b = b$ $\qquad\qquad\qquad\qquad\qquad a[b]a = a$

$a[\bot]b = a \cup b$ $\qquad\qquad\qquad\qquad a[\top]b = a \cap b$

---

[2] A Brouwerian algebra is quite similar, but not identical, to a Boolean algebra. The relationship between Boolean and Brouwerian algebras can be characterized as follows [7]: for all elements a, define the *Brouwerian complement* by $\neg a \triangleq \top \dot{-} a$; a Brouwerian algebra is Boolean iff $\neg\neg a = a$. Because Boolean algebras are Brouwerian algebras, but not vice versa, some of the properties that hold in Boolean algebras do not hold in Brouwerian algebras. For example, the laws for distributing $\dot{-}$ over $\cup$ and $\cap$ in Brouwerian algebra are somewhat different from the laws for distributing $-$ over $\cup$ and $\cap$ in Boolean algebra. Two of the laws are the same:

(16) $(b \dot{-} a) \cup (c \dot{-} a) = (b \cup c) \dot{-} a$ $\qquad$ (17) $(c \dot{-} a) \cup (c \dot{-} b) = c \dot{-} (a \cap b)$

However, the laws for distributing $\dot{-}$ through $\cap$ on the left and $\cup$ on the right are weaker:

(29) $(a \cap b) \dot{-} c \subseteq (a \dot{-} c) \cap (b \dot{-} c)$ $\qquad$ (32) $c \dot{-} (a \cup b) \subseteq (c \dot{-} a) \cap (c \dot{-} b)$

One can show by means of examples that the inequalities in laws (29) and (32) are, at times, strict.

Term	Slice					
	program $x := 0$ end()	program $x := 0$ end(x)	program $x := 0$; $y := x$ end()	program $x := 0$; $y := x$ end(y)	program $x := 0$; $y := x$; $z := y$ end()	program $x := 0$; $y := x$; $z := y$ end(z)
A	x	x				
$Base$	x	x	x	x		
B	x	x	x	x	x	x
$A \div Base$						
$A \cap Base \cap B$	x	x				
$B \div Base$	x	x			x	x
$A [Base]B$	x	x	x		x	x

Figure 1. Member slices of the sets A, $Base$, B, $A \div Base$, $A \cap Base \cap B$, $B \div Base$, and $A [Base]B$.

$a[b](x_1 \cup x_2) = a[b]x_1 \cup a[b]x_2$ $a[b](x_1 \cap x_2) \subseteq a[b]x_1 \cap a[b]x_2$

$a[b]c$ is monotonic in a $a[b]c$ is antimonotonic in b

$a[b]c \div b = (a \div b) \cup (c \div b)$ $a[b]c \div c = (a \div b) \div c$

The integration operation can be generalized to integrate multiple variants with a given base element simultaneously.

Definition. The *simultaneous integration* of elements $x_1, x_2, \cdots, x_n$ with respect to element b is the element $(x_1[b]x_2, \cdots, x_n)$ defined by

$$(x_1[b]x_2, \cdots, x_n) \triangleq (x_1 \div b) \cup (x_2 \div b) \cup \cdots \cup (x_n \div b) \cup (x_1 \cap x_2 \cap \cdots \cap x_n \cap b).$$

The following associativity theorem shows that a three-variant simultaneous integration can be done as a succession of two-variant integrations (in several different ways).

THEOREM (ASSOCIATIVITY THEOREM).

$(x[b]y)[b]z = x[b](y[b]z) = (x[b]z)[b]y = (x[b]y)[b](x[b]z) = (x[b]y)[x](x[b]z) = (x[b]y, z)$.

5. AN ALTERNATIVE WAY TO PERFORM INTEGRATION

This section concerns a new criterion for program integration, based on the operation that is the dual of the integration operation. After introducing a few new concepts that are needed to define the dual operation, we show how the two operations are related.

Definition. For all x, $y \in DCS$, define the operation *quotient*, denoted by $x \div y$, to be $x \div y \triangleq \{ z \in G_1 \mid \forall p \in (y - x) \, p \nleq z \}$. That is, $x \div y$ is the complement of the upwards closure of $y - x$.

In the definition of $x \div y$, elements of the set $y - x$ represent forbidden (sub-)slices of members of $x \div y$.

Example. The following table illustrates $-$, $\dot{-}$, and $\div$:

a	b	$a-b$	$a \dot{-} b$	$b \div a$
$\begin{bmatrix} \text{program} \\ \quad x := 0 \\ \text{end()} \end{bmatrix}$	$\begin{Bmatrix} \text{program} , \text{program} \\ \quad x := 0 \quad\quad x := 0; \\ \text{end()} \quad\quad y := x \\ \quad\quad\quad \text{end()} \end{Bmatrix}$	$\emptyset \,(= \bot)$	$\emptyset \,(= \bot)$	$G_1 \,(= \top)$

		$b - a$	$b \dot{-} a$	$a \div b$
		$\begin{bmatrix} \text{program} \\ \quad x := 0; \\ \quad y := x \\ \text{end()} \end{bmatrix}$	$\begin{Bmatrix} \text{program} , \text{program} \\ \quad x := 0 \quad\quad x := 0; \\ \text{end()} \quad\quad y := x \\ \quad\quad\quad \text{end()} \end{Bmatrix}$	$G_1 - \begin{bmatrix} s \in G_1 & \text{program} \leq s \\ & \quad x := 0; \\ & \quad y := x \\ & \text{end()} \end{bmatrix}$

Note that because $b - a$ is the singleton set

$\begin{bmatrix} \text{program} \\ \quad x := 0; y := x \\ \text{end()} \end{bmatrix}$

$a \div b$ is the (infinite) set of all single-point slices that do not contain the (sub-)slice

program
   $x := 0; y := x$
end().

Definition. A *double Brouwerian algebra* [7] is an algebra $(L, \cup, \cap, \dot{-}, \div, \top)$ where both $(L, \cup, \cap, \dot{-}, \top)$ and $(L, \cap, \cup, \div, \top \dot{-} \top)$ are Brouwerian algebras. In particular,
(i) L is closed under $\div$.
(ii) For all a, b, and c in L, $a \div b \supseteq c$ iff $a \supseteq b \cap c$.

THEOREM. $(DCS, \cup, \cap, \dot{-}, \div, G_1)$ *is a double Brouwerian algebra, where* $\cup$ *is set union and* $\cap$ *is set intersection.*

Because the dependence-graph algebra is a *double* Brouwerian algebra, it is possible to perform integration using the dual of the operation $a \, [b] c$.

Definition. The *dual integration* of elements a and c with respect to element b is the element $a\{ b \}c$ defined by $a\{ b \}c \triangleq (a \div b) \cap (a \cup b \cup c) \cap (c \div b)$.

Note that, in the dependence-graph algebra, if a, b, and c are all finite sets, then $a \cup b \cup c$ is finite. Hence even though $a \div b$ and $c \div b$ may be infinite, $a\{ b \}c$ is guaranteed to be finite.

We now investigate how $a \, [b] c$ and $a\{ b \}c$ are related; the theorem proven below shows that $a\{ b \}c$ is always less than or equal to $a \, [b] c$. We then give an example for which strict inequality holds.

LEMMA. $(a \dot{-} b) \cup (a \cap b \cap c) = (a \dot{-} b) \cup (a \cap c)$.

PROOF.

$$(a \dot{-} b) \cup (a \cap b \cap c) = ((a \dot{-} b) \cup (a \cap b)) \cap ((a \dot{-} b) \cup c)$$
$$= a \cap ((a \dot{-} b) \cup c) \qquad\qquad \text{by } (26)^3$$
$$= (a \cap (a \dot{-} b)) \cup (a \cap c)$$
$$= (a \dot{-} b) \cup (a \cap c) \qquad\qquad \text{by } (13)$$

$\square$

COROLLARY. $a[b]c = (a \dot{-} b) \cup (a \cap c) \cup (c \dot{-} b)$.

PROOF. Immediate from the definition of $a[b]c$ and the preceding proposition. $\square$

THEOREM. $a\{b\}c \subseteq a[b]c$.

PROOF.

$$a[b]c = (a \dot{-} b) \cup (a \cap c) \cup (c \dot{-} b) \qquad \text{by the preceding corollary}$$
$$= ((a \cup c) \dot{-} b) \cup (a \cap c) \qquad \text{by (16)}$$
$$= (a \cup ((a \cup c) \dot{-} b)) \cap (c \cup ((a \cup c) \dot{-} b))$$
$$= (a \cup (a \dot{-} b) \cup (c \dot{-} b)) \cap (c \cup (a \dot{-} b) \cup (c \dot{-} b)) \qquad \text{by (16)}$$
$$= (a \cup (c \dot{-} b)) \cap (c \cup (a \dot{-} b)) \qquad \text{by (13)}$$

By the dual derivation, we have $a\{b\}c = (a \cap (c \div b)) \cup (c \cap (a \div b))$.

$$a\{b\}c \dot{-} a[b]c = [(a \cap (c \div b)) \cup (c \cap (a \div b))] \dot{-} [(a \cup (c \dot{-} b)) \cap (c \cup (a \dot{-} b))]$$
$$= ((a \cap (c \div b)) \dot{-} [(a \cup (c \dot{-} b)) \cap (c \cup (a \dot{-} b))])$$
$$\cup ((c \cap (a \div b)) \dot{-} [(a \cup (c \dot{-} b)) \cap (c \cup (a \dot{-} b))]) \qquad \text{by (16)}$$
$$= ((a \cap (c \div b)) \dot{-} (a \cup (c \dot{-} b))) \cup ((a \cap (c \div b)) \dot{-} (c \cup (a \dot{-} b))) \qquad \text{by (17)}$$
$$\cup ((c \cap (a \div b)) \dot{-} (a \cup (c \dot{-} b))) \cup ((c \cap (a \div b)) \dot{-} (c \cup (a \dot{-} b)))$$
$$= ((a \cap (c \div b)) \dot{-} (c \cup (a \dot{-} b))) \cup ((c \cap (a \div b)) \dot{-} (a \cup (c \dot{-} b))) \qquad \text{by (4)}$$

$$(a \cap (c \div b)) \dot{-} (c \cup (a \dot{-} b)) = ((a \cap (c \div b)) \dot{-} (a \dot{-} b)) \dot{-} c \qquad \text{by (18)}$$
$$\subseteq ((c \div b) \cap (a \dot{-} (a \dot{-} b))) \dot{-} c \qquad \text{by (28)}$$
$$\subseteq ((c \div b) \cap (a \cap b)) \dot{-} c \qquad \text{by (30)}$$
$$= (((c \div b) \cap b) \cap a) \dot{-} c$$
$$= (c \cap b \cap a) \dot{-} c \qquad \text{by the dual of (14)}$$
$$= \bot \qquad \text{by (4)}$$

Similarly, $(c \cap (a \div b)) \dot{-} (a \cup (c \dot{-} b)) = \bot$. Hence, $a\{b\}c \dot{-} a[b]c = \bot$, and thus, by (4), $a\{b\}c \subseteq a[b]c$. $\square$

Example. Returning once again to the integration example from Sections 2 and 4, Figure 2 shows that the inequality in the above theorem is, at times, strict; the programs shown in Figure 2 have the property that $A\{Base\}B \subset A[Base]B$. In this example, only the maximal single-point slices in each set are listed, rather than the entire downwards-closed set. For instance, the program listed as B,

```
program
    x := 0; y := x; z := y
end(x, y, z),
```

stands for the set

$$\left\{ \begin{array}{llllll} \text{program} & , & \text{program} & , & \text{program} & , & \text{program} & , & \text{program} & , & \text{program} \\ x := 0 & & x := 0 & & x := 0; & & x := 0; & & x := 0; & & x := 0; \\ \text{end}() & & \text{end}(x) & & y := x & & y := x & & y := x; & & y := x; \\ & & & & \text{end}() & & \text{end}(y) & & z := y & & z := y \\ & & & & & & & & \text{end}() & & \text{end}(z) \end{array} \right\}.$$

---

[3] The laws used to justify proof steps are listed in the Appendix.

A	Base	B
program $x := 0$ end(x)	program $x := 0;$ $y := x$ end(x, y)	program $x := 0;$ $y := x;$ $z := y$ end(x, y, z)

A ÷ Base	A ∩ Base ∩ B	B ÷ Base	A [Base]B
$\emptyset \, (= \perp)$	program $x := 0$ end(x)	program $x := 0;$ $y := x;$ $z := y$ end(z)	program $x := 0;$ $y := x;$ $z := y$ end(x, z)

A ÷ Base	A ∪ Base ∪ B	B ÷ Base	A { Base }B
$G_1 - \left\{ \begin{array}{l} s \in G_1 \\ \end{array} \middle| \begin{array}{l} \text{program} \leq s \\ x := 0; \\ y := x \\ \text{end}() \end{array} \right\}$	program $x := 0;$ $y := x;$ $z := y$ end(x, y, z)	$G_1 \, (= \top)$	program $x := 0$ end(x)

Figure 2. An example for which $A \{ Base \}B \subset A [Base]B$.

Because $A \{ Base \}B$ is the *intersection* of $A \div Base$ with $(A \cup Base \cup B) \cap (B \div Base)$, none of the following three single-point slices, which are all members of $A [Base]B$, occur in $A \{ Base \}B$:

program $x := 0; y := x$ end()	program $x := 0; y := x; z := y$ end()	program $x := 0; y := x; z := y$ end(z).

This example illustrates a fundamental difference between integrating by the operation $A [Base]B$ and integrating by $A \{ Base \}B$. With $A [Base]B$ an insertion made in one integrand can "override" a deletion in the other integrand; in the example shown above, the insertion of $z := y$ in integrand B overrides the deletion of $y := x$ from integrand A. By contrast, with $A \{ Base \}B$ a deletion in one integrand can override an insertion in the other integrand; in the example, the deletion of $y := x$ from integrand A overrides the insertion of $z := y$ in integrand B. Consequently, we say that $A \{ Base \}B$ is the *deletion-preserving integration* of A and B with respect to $Base$.

6. COMPATIBLE INTEGRANDS

Program integration deals with the problem of reconciling "competing" modifications to a base program. A different, but related, problem is that of separating *consecutive* edits to a base program into individual edits on the base program. Consider the case of two consecutive edits to base program O; let $O + \Delta A$ be the result of modifying O, and let $O + \Delta A + \Delta B$ be the result of modifying $O + \Delta A$. By "separating consecutive edits," we mean creating a program $O + \Delta B$ that includes the second modification but not the first. The algebraic framework introduced in the previous sections can be used in two different approaches to solving this problem.

6.1. Separating Consecutive Edits by Solving an Equation

One way of formalizing our goal is to say that we are looking for an integrand $O + \Delta B$ that is compatible with base O, integrand $O + \Delta A$, and result $O + \Delta A + \Delta B$; that is, $O + \Delta B$ should satisfy the equation $(O + \Delta A)[O](O + \Delta B) = O + \Delta A + \Delta B$. Thus, our first approach poses the question "Given elements a, b, and m, when does there exist a solution for x in the equation $a[b]x = m$?"

It is possible to show that if solutions to $a[b]x = m$ exist, they form a distributive lattice with a least element and a greatest element. Closed formulas can be given for the least and greatest elements.

THEOREM. *Solutions of $a[b]x = m$ form a distributive lattice with least element $(m \div a) \cup ((a \cap b \cap m) \div (a \div b))$ and greatest element $m \cup (b \cap (m \div a))$.*

Note that the formula for the greatest solution of $a[b]x = m$ makes use of the quotient operation, and thus holds only for double Brouwerian algebras.

6.2. Separating Consecutive Edits by Re-Rooting

It is also possible to take a different approach to the problem of separating consecutive edits. Consider again the case of two consecutive edits to a base program O, where $O + \Delta A$ is the result of modifying O, $O + \Delta A + \Delta B$ is the result of modifying $O + \Delta A$, and we want to create a program $O + \Delta B$ that includes the second modification but not the first. We can re-root the development history $O \rightarrow O + \Delta A \rightarrow O + \Delta A + \Delta B$ so that $O + \Delta A$, rather than O, is the base program. Programs O and $O + \Delta A + \Delta B$ are treated as two variants of $O + \Delta A$. In this case, instead of treating the differences between O and $O + \Delta A$ as changes that were made to O to create $O + \Delta A$, they are now treated as changes made to $O + \Delta A$ to create O: when O is the base program, a statement s that occurs in $O + \Delta A$ but not in O is a "new" statement arising from an insertion; when $O + \Delta A$ is the base program, we treat the missing s in O as if a programmer had deleted s from $O + \Delta A$ to create O. (The status of variant $O + \Delta A + \Delta B$ is unchanged; it is still treated as a variant derived from $O + \Delta A$.) $O + \Delta B$ is created by integrating O and $O + \Delta A + \Delta B$ with respect to base program $O + \Delta A$, that is, by performing the integration $O[O + \Delta A](O + \Delta A + \Delta B)$.

The algebraic framework can be used to demonstrate that re-rooting and then integrating is reasonable in the sense that the program created in this way captures everything that is different between $O + \Delta A + \Delta B$ and $O + \Delta A$. Although in general the approach does not produce an integrand compatible with base O, integrand $O + \Delta A$, and result $O + \Delta A + \Delta B$ (even when a compatible integrand does exist), the element E produced, where $E = O[O + \Delta A](O + \Delta A + \Delta B)$, has the property $(O + \Delta A)[O]E \supseteq O + \Delta A + \Delta B$. This property shows that E captures everything that is different between $O + \Delta A + \Delta B$ and $O + \Delta A$ (as desired), plus more.

THEOREM. *If $a[b]x = m$ has a solution for x, then $a[b](m[a]b) \supseteq m$.*

7. RELATION TO PREVIOUS WORK

In unpublished work, Susan Horwitz and I found proofs of several algebraic properties of the HPR algorithm. The results given in this paper consist of the analogues for Brouwerian algebras of these earlier results, together with a number of new results. However, the method of proof used in this paper is much different than the proof techniques used to establish these earlier results, which involved complicated arguments—with many sub-cases and argument by *reductio ad absurdum*—about operations on dependence graphs. In contrast, the proofs given in this paper are *strictly algebraic* in nature, making use of the rich set of algebraic laws that hold in Brouwerian algebras.

The work described here was motivated by the desire to find a simpler way to prove properties about program integration. In this, I feel it succeeds—proofs in Brouwerian algebra are much less compli-

:ated than direct proofs about dependence graphs. It also provides a framework for studying common properties of variations on or extensions to the program-integration algorithm. The integration operation in a Brouwerian algebra is defined purely in terms of $\cup$, $\cap$, and $\dot{-}$, and thus has an analogue in all Brouwerian algebras. Thus, to show that a proposed program-integration algorithm shares these properties, one merely has to show that the algorithm can be cast as an integration operation in a Brouwerian algebra.

The notation $a[b]c$ that has been used here for the integration operation in Brouwerian algebras is taken from a paper by Hoare in which he investigated some of the properties of $a[b]c$ in Boolean algebras [2]. However, nearly all of the questions examined in this paper (for Brouwerian algebras) were not addressed by Hoare (for Boolean algebras).

The integration operation $a[b]c$ in the Brouwerian dependence-graph algebra provides an alternative method for integrating programs to the HPR algorithm. The two methods do not have exactly the same properties. For example, in the dependence-graph algebra (as well as all other Brouwerian algebras), the operation $a[b]c$ satisfies the properties demonstrated in the paper; however, because the set of dependence graphs does not form a Brouwerian algebra, not all of the results established about integration in Brouwerian algebras hold for the HPR algorithm.

The remainder of this section compares the two program-integration methods. The bottom line is that, in addition to its elegant collection of algebraic properties, the operation $a[b]c$ in the dependence-graph algebra generalizes the HPR algorithm while preserving its most important property—the ability to characterize the execution behavior of the integrated program in terms of the behaviors of the base program and the two integrands.

7.1. Interference Between Integrands

In previous sections, we have not discussed the notion of interfering integrands. In the HPR algorithm, there are two possible ways in which the merged dependence graph M can fail to represent a satisfactory integrated program; we refer to them as "Type I interference" and "Type II interference." The criterion for Type I interference is based on a comparison of slices of the merged graph M with the dependence graphs for programs A and B. The slices $\Delta(A, Base)$ and $\Delta(B, Base)$ represent potentially changed computations of integrands A and B with respect to $Base$, respectively. Thus, there is interference if graph M does not preserve these slices; that is, there is Type I interference if either $\Delta(A, Base)$ or $\Delta(B, Base)$ is not a slice of M.

The final step of the HPR algorithm involves reconstituting a program from dependence graph M. However, if there is no program whose dependence graph is M, we say there is Type II interference (and that graph M is *infeasible*). (See [5] for a discussion of reconstructing a program from the merged dependence graph and the inherent difficulties of this problem.)

The class of integrations that are handled successfully by the integration operation in the Brouwerian dependence-graph algebra coincides with that handled by the HPR algorithm; however, the notion of interference is slightly different. Because the $\cup$, $\cap$, and $\dot{-}$ operations in the dependence-graph algebra can never "corrupt" slices, there is only one notion of interference in the dependence-graph algebra, namely, infeasibility; for an integration $a[b]c$, integrands a and c interfere if there is no program that corresponds to the element $a[b]c$. (This is not to say that it is any easier to test whether an element of the dependence-graph algebra is feasible than it is to test whether an individual dependence graph is feasible, as is done in the HPR algorithm; we are simply pointing out that for integration in the dependence-graph algebra, there is only one notion of interference instead of two.)

Another difference between the two integration algorithms that relates to interference is that in the dependence-graph algebra infeasible elements are subject to the same algebraic laws as feasible elements, which can have certain advantages. For example, when performing a succession of integrations to propagate a change through the development history of a program, some of the intermediate elements produced may be infeasible (indicating interference). Yet subsequent integrations that involve these infeasible elements may, in fact, result in feasible elements. Because Type I interference indicates that a slice has been corrupted, it is not meaningful to perform the analogous integrations with the HPR algorithm.

7.2. Semantic Properties of the Integrated Program

One of the virtues of the HPR algorithm is that there is a theorem that characterizes the execution behavior of the integrated program produced by the HPR algorithm in terms of the behaviors of the base program and the two integrands.

THEOREM. (INTEGRATION THEOREM [11]). *If programs A and B are two non-interfering variants of Base, and program M is the result of integrating A and B with respect to Base (via the HPR algorithm), then for any initial state σ on which A, B, and Base all halt,*

(1) *M halts on σ.*
(2) *If x is a variable defined in the final state of A for which the final states of A and Base disagree, then the final state of M agrees with the final state of A on x.*
(3) *If y is a variable defined in the final state of B for which the final states of B and Base disagree, then the final state of M agrees with the final state of B on y.*
(4) *If z is a variable on which the final states of A, B, and Base agree, then the final state of M agrees with the final state of Base on z.*

For the HPR algorithm, the Integration Theorem follows from two theorems about slices. One, the Slicing Theorem, which was stated in Section 2, demonstrates that a slice captures a portion of a program's behavior in the sense that, for any initial state on which the program halts, the program and the slice compute the same sequence of values for each element of the slice. The other, the Termination Theorem, demonstrates that if a program is decomposed into (two or more) slices, the program halts on any state for which all the slices halt.

THEOREM. (TERMINATION THEOREM [11]). *Let P be a program. Suppose X and Y are sets of vertices such that $G_P = G_P / X \cup G_P / Y$. If P / X and P / Y halt on a state σ, then P halts on σ as well.*

Note that the Termination Theorem and clause (1) of the Slicing Theorem are complementary: clause (1) of the Slicing Theorem asserts that if a program terminates then each slice also terminates; the Termination Theorem asserts that when a program can be decomposed into two slices, if each slice terminates then the program terminates. We can then apply clause (2) of the Slicing Theorem to conclude that the two slices (collectively) compute the same sequence of values as the entire program.

It follows from the Slicing Theorem, the Termination Theorem, the definition of the dependence-graph algebra, and the definition of the operation $A[Base]B$ that the Integration Theorem also holds for $A[Base]B$ in the dependence-graph algebra.

7.3. Integration Without Tags

In the HPR algorithm, it is assumed that a specialized program editor—providing a tagging capability so that common components can be identified in different versions—is used to create the program variants from the base program. This assumption can be relaxed; that is, two different examples of Brouwerian algebras that can be used for integrating programs are (1) the set of downwards-closed sets of *tagged* single-point slices, and (2) the set of downwards-closed sets of *untagged* single-point slices.

It must be noted that the two different definitions of dependence-graph algebras correspond to two different variations on the HPR algorithm. However, although the integration algorithm based on sets of untagged slices produces a somewhat different answer than the algorithm based on sets of tagged slices (both in terms of the final program that is the result of an integration, as well as in the notion of when an integration fails due to interference), the Integration Theorem still holds. That is, for both dependence-graph algebras and the HPR algorithm, we have the same characterization of the execution behavior of the integrated program in terms of the execution behaviors of the base program and the two integrands.

The benefits of doing without tags are two-fold. First, it is no longer necessary for program integration to be supported by a closed system; in principle, programs can be integrated even if they are created using ordinary text editors. Second, the class of integration problems that can be handled successfully in the dependence-graph algebra based on sets of untagged slices is strictly larger than the class that can be handled by the algebra based on tagged slices (which coincides with the class handled by the HPR algorithm).

8. IMPLEMENTATION

A program-integration tool that uses the HPR algorithm has been demonstrable since the summer of 1987 [12]. The integration tool is embedded in a program editor created using the Synthesizer Generator, a meta-system for creating interactive, language-based program development systems [10]. The editor automatically supplies tags on program elements so that common statements and predicates can be identified in different versions. Data-flow analysis of programs is carried out according to the editor's defining attribute grammar and used to construct dependence graphs. An integration command added to the editor invokes the integration algorithm on the dependence graphs, reports whether the variant programs interfere, and, if there is no interference, builds the integrated program.

This implementation has recently been extended to incorporate the ideas described in this paper; we added an editor and interpreter for a higher-order functional language that operates on sets of tagged slices (SLICE_SETs). The primitive operations on SLICE_SETs are join, meet, pseudo-difference, and integration. Functional expressions are built up using lambda-abstraction, application, conditional expressions, and let-clauses. A free variable in an expression (say x) denotes the SLICE_SET created from the program in editing buffer x. If no such buffer exists, the value is $\perp$. An evaluation command added to the editor invokes the interpreter on the expression, and—if the final result is a SLICE_SET—builds the corresponding program (if one exists).

APPENDIX: ALGEBRAIC LAWS FOR BROUWERIAN ALGEBRAS

This appendix covers algebraic laws that hold for Brouwerian algebras. The material presented here is meant to make the paper self-contained; further information about Brouwerian algebras can be found in [7]. (The algebraic properties of $\div$ are dual to those listed below; given a property for $\dot-$, the corresponding property for $\div$ is obtained using the substitution: $\cup$ for $\cap$, $\cap$ for $\cup$, $\div$ for $\dot-$, $\subseteq$ for $\supseteq$, $\supseteq$ for $\subseteq$, and "max" for "min.")

Fundamental Properties of $\dot-$

(a) $a \dot- b \subseteq c$ iff $a \subseteq b \cup c$

Algebraic Properties of $\dot-$

The following properties of Brouwerian algebras are taken from [9] (pp. 59-60); the numbering for laws (4) – (24) follows that given in [9]. (In [9], the laws are expressed in dual form, using a "pseudo-complement" operator, rather than in the form given below, where pseudo-difference is used.)

(4) $b \dot- a = \perp$ iff $a \supseteq b$

(5) $a = b$ iff $b \dot- a = \perp = a \dot- b$

(6) $a \dot- a = \perp$

(7) $\perp \dot- a = \perp$

(8) $b \dot- \perp = b$

(9) $(a \dot- a) \cup b = b$

(10) $a \cup (b \dot- a) \supseteq b$

(11) If $a_1 \supseteq a_2$ then $b \dot- a_2 \supseteq b \dot- a_1$

(12) If $b_1 \supseteq b_2$ then $b_1 \dot- a \supseteq b_2 \dot- a$

(13) $b \supseteq b \dot- a$

(14) $a \cup (b \dot- a) = a \cup b$

(15) $(b \dot- a) \cup b = b$

(16) $(b \dot- a) \cup (c \dot- a) = (b \cup c) \dot- a$

(17) $(c \dot- a) \cup (c \dot- b) = c \dot- (a \cap b)$

(18) $(c \dot- b) \dot- a = c \dot- (a \cup b) = (c \dot- a) \dot- b$

(19) $a \dot- c \supseteq (b \dot- c) \dot- ((b \dot- a) \dot- c)$.

(20) $(b \div a) \cup (c \div b) \supseteq c \div a$

(21) $(b \div a) \supseteq (c \div a) \div (c \div b)$

(22) $a \supseteq (a \cup b) \div b$

(23) $(c \div b) \div a \supseteq (c \div a) \div (b \div a)$

(24) $c \cup ((c \cup b) \div (c \cup a)) = c \cup (b \div a)$

Additional Algebraic Properties of $\div$

The following properties of Brouwerian algebras are taken from [13].

(25) $(u \div b) \div (a \cap b) = a \div b$

(26) $(b \div a) \cup (b \cap a) = b$

(27) $(c \div b) \div a = (c \div a) \div (b \div a)$

(28) $(a \cap b) \div c \subseteq a \cap (b \div c)$

(29) $(a \cap b) \div c \subseteq (a \div c) \cap (b \div c)$

(30) $b \div (b \div a) \subseteq a \cap b$

(31) If $a \div b \subseteq b$, then $a \subseteq b$

(32) $c \div (a \cup b) \subseteq (c \div a) \cap (c \div b)$

(33) $(a \div b) \div (b \div a) = a \div b$

(34) $(a \cup b) \div (a \cap b) = (a \div b) \cup (b \div a)$

ACKNOWLEDGEMENTS

Tony Hoare suggested using the notation $a[b]c$ for the integration operation and pointed out the existence of [2], which discusses properties of $a[b]c$ in Boolean algebras. Susan Horwitz provided many comments and helpful suggestions.

REFERENCES

1. Ferrante, J., Ottenstein, K., and Warren, J., "The program dependence graph and its use in optimization," *ACM Transactions on Programming Languages and Systems* 9(3) pp. 319-349 (July 1987).

2. Hoare, C.A.R., "A couple of novelties in the propositional calculus," *Zeitschr. f. math. Logik und Grundlagen d. Math.* 31 pp. 173-178 (1985).

3. Horwitz, S., Reps, T., and Binkley, D., "Interprocedural slicing using dependence graphs," *Proceedings of the ACM SIGPLAN 88 Conference on Programming Language Design and Implementation*, (Atlanta, GA, June 22-24, 1988), *ACM SIGPLAN Notices* 23(7) pp. 35-46 (July 1988).

4. Horwitz, S., Pfeiffer, P., and Reps, T., "Dependence analysis for pointer variables," *Proceedings of the ACM SIGPLAN 89 Conference on Programming Language Design and Implementation*, (Portland, OR, June 21-23, 1989), *ACM SIGPLAN Notices* 24(7) pp. 28-40 (July 1989).

5. Horwitz, S., Prins, J., and Reps, T., "Integrating non-interfering versions of programs," *ACM Trans. Program. Lang. Syst.* 11(3) pp. 345-387 (July 1989).

6. Kuck, D.J., Kuhn, R.H., Leasure, B., Padua, D.A., and Wolfe, M., "Dependence graphs and compiler optimizations," pp. 207-218 in *Conference Record of the Eighth ACM Symposium on Principles of Programming Languages*, (Williamsburg, VA, January 26-28, 1981), ACM, New York, NY (1981).

7. McKinsey, J.C.C. and Tarski, A., "On closed elements in closure algebras," *Annals of Mathematics* 47(1) pp. 122-162 (January 1946).

8. Ottenstein, K.J. and Ottenstein, L.M., "The program dependence graph in a software development environment," *Proceedings of the ACM SIGSOFT/SIGPLAN Software Engineering Symposium on Practical Software Development Environments*, (Pittsburgh, PA, Apr. 23-25, 1984), *ACM SIGPLAN Notices* 19(5) pp. 177-184 (May 1984).

9. Rasiowa, H. and Sikorski, R., *The Mathematics of Metamathematics*, Polish Scientific Publishers, Warsaw (1963).

10. Reps, T. and Teitelbaum, T., *The Synthesizer Generator: A System for Constructing Language-Based Editors*, Springer-Verlag, New York, NY (1988).

11. Reps, T. and Yang, W., "The semantics of program slicing," TR-777, Computer Sciences Department, University of Wisconsin, Madison, WI (June 1988).

12. Reps, T., "Demonstration of a prototype tool for program integration," TR-819, Computer Sciences Department, University of Wisconsin, Madison, WI (January 1989).

13. Reps, T., "On the algebraic properties of program integration," TR-856, Computer Sciences Department, University of Wisconsin, Madison, WI (June 1989).

14. Weiser, M., "Program slicing," *IEEE Transactions on Software Engineering* SE-10(4) pp. 352-357 (July 1984).

15. Yang, W., Horwitz, S., and Reps, T., "Detecting program components with equivalent behaviors," TR-840, Computer Sciences Department, University of Wisconsin, Madison, WI (April 1989).

16. Yang, W., Horwitz, S., and Reps, T., "A new program integration algorithm," TR-899, Computer Sciences Department, University of Wisconsin, Madison, WI (December 1989).

ARITY RAISER AND ITS USE IN PROGRAM SPECIALIZATION

Sergei A. Romanenko

Keldysh Institute of Applied Mathematics
Academy of Sciences of the USSR
Miusskaya Sq. 4, SU-125047, Moscow, USSR

Experiments on generating compilers by specializing specializers with respect to interpreters have shown that the compilers thus obtained have a natural structure only if the specializer does *variable splitting*. Variable splitting can result in a residual program using several variables to represent the values of a single variable of the original program. In the case of functional programming variable splitting is done by raising the arities of functions. The paper describes the structure and principles of operation of an arity raiser dealing with programs in a subset of pure Lisp.

Keywords: arity raiser, compiler generator, partial evaluation, retyping, specializer, variable splitting.

INTRODUCTION

Program specialization [Dixon 71] seems to be a promising and powerful technique that can lead to new program development methodology.

By *program specialization* we understand constructing, when given a "general-purpose" program and some restriction on its usage, a more efficient "specialized" residual program. Being optimized and simplified version of the original program, the residual program, however, must be equivalent to the original one when used according to the restriction. By *specializer* we understand a system that, given a program and a restriction, will produce a specialized version of the original program.

Program specialization can be achieved by making use of different techniques, such as *driving* [Turchin 72], *fold-unfold method* [Burstall 77], *partial evaluation* [Futamura 71], [Beckman 76], *mixed computation* [Ershov 78], [Bulyonkov 84], the *analysis of computational configurations* [Turchin 79], [Turchin 86], *variable splitting* [Sestoft 86], and *arity raising* [Romanenko 88].

The above techniques deal, for the most part, with two problems: *control restructuring* and *data retyping* (i.e. changing representation of data).

As far as the control restructuring is concerned, various specialization techniques differ in the extent to which the program is reorganized.

In the case of *monovariant* specialization any control point in the original program gives rise to zero or one control point in the residual program.

In the case of *polyvariant* specialization a control point can give rise to more than one control point in the residual program.

In the case of *monogenetic* specialization any control point in the residual program is produced from a single control point of the original program.

In the case of *polygenetic* specialization a control point in the residual program may be produced from several control points of the original program.

As far as the data representation is concerned, various specialization techniques differ in the use they make of *retyping*.

Driving [Turchin 72] and the analysis of configurations [Turchin 79], [Turchin 86], which deal with functional programs, can be classified as polyvariant polygenetic methods with retyping.

Monovariant monogenetic techniques for imperative programs are studied in [Ershov 78]. Papers [Bulyonkov 84], [Barzdin 88] concern polyvariant monogenetic specialization techniques for imperative programs.

The *transformational approach* [Ershov 81], [Ostrovski 88] is believed to include, at least potentially, all conceivable techniques of program specialization, not excluding the polygenetic ones.

Of course, the more powerful techniques tend to be rather expensive, and it is difficult to make them completely automatic. Thus the choice of appropriate specialization techniques depends on the class of problems to be solved.

An interesting application of specializers is compiler generation. It was found by Y.Futamura [Futamura 71] that interpreters can be converted to compilers by specializing a specializer with respect to the interpreters. Several years later it was realized [Beckman 76] that a transformer of interpreters into compilers can be produced by specializing a specializer with respect to a specializer.

To put this approach into practice, we have to overcome the following difficulty. On the one hand, the specializer has to be sophisticated enough to achieve non-trivial specialization. On the other hand, to be specializable, the specializer can't afford to be too complicated.

The group under N.D.Jones at Copenhagen university was the first to overcome the above difficulty [Jones 85], [Sestoft 86], [Sestoft 88]. Since experiments had shown the monovariant specialization to be unsatisfactory for this application, the specializer had to do the polyvariant specialization. Again, the monogenetic specialization proved to be adequate for the purpose (despite there being a lot of problems that have to be dealt with by polygenetic specialization [Turchin 82], [Wadler 88]).

The usefulness of retyping proved to be more problematic. It was found that retyping can be dispensed with at the cost of the residual programs having rather unnatural structure. Suppose, for example, that an interpreter is to be specialized with respect to a program. Since the interpreter is supposed to accept an arbitrary input program, the number of variables in this program cannot be known in advance. Thus the variable's values are likely to be represented in the interpreter as a single value assigned to one of the interpreter's variables. If the specializer is unable to split this variable, the residual program will use a single variable to represent all the values. A reasonable residual program, however, would keep each value in a separate variable [Sestoft 86].

To rectify the drawback, the author suggested that the Copenhagen specializer should be supplemented with an additional phase, whose purpose would be to do variable splitting [Romanenko 88]. In the case of a functional language, variable splitting reduces to increasing the number of functions' parameters, for which reason this additional phase was given the name *arity raiser*. As pointed out by T.Mogensen arity raising is just a special case of retyping, thus any arity raiser is a retyper.

The arity raiser was found to improve the structure of residual programs without making the specializer excessively slow and intricate.

The alternative to the arity raiser is to split variables *on-line*, i.e. at the time the residual program is being generated [Turchin 86], [Mogensen 88]. This approach, however, can result in a mammoth, sluggish specializer.

A short description of the ideas behind the arity raiser can be found in [Romanenko 88]. The present paper gives a detailed account of the structure and principles of operation of an arity raiser dealing with programs in a subset of pure Lisp.

1. THE LANGUAGE MIXWELL

In the following we consider programs written in the language Mixwell, which is a small subset of pure Lisp and was used as the subject language in the Copenhagen specializer MIX [Sestoft 86]. Here is Mixwell's abstract syntax.

pgm	$\in$	Program	programs
fd	$\in$	FnDef	function definitions
exp, e	$\in$	Exp	expressions
f	$\in$	FName	function names
x	$\in$	VName	variable names
$\mathcal{A}$	$\in$	Atom	Lisp atoms
$\mathcal{E}$	$\in$	SExp	Lisp S-expressions

$\text{pgm} ::= \text{fd}_1; \ \ldots \ \text{fd}_n;$

$\text{fd} ::= f(x_1, \ldots, x_m) = \text{exp}$

$\text{exp} ::= x \mid \textbf{quote } \mathcal{E} \mid \textbf{if } \text{exp}_0 \textbf{ then } \text{exp}_1 \textbf{ else } \text{exp}_2 \mid \textbf{call } f(\text{exp}_1, \ldots, \text{exp}_m)$
$\phantom{\text{exp} ::=} \mid \text{car}(\text{exp}) \mid \text{cdr}(\text{exp}) \mid \text{cons}(\text{exp}_1, \text{exp}_2) \mid \text{atom}(\text{exp}) \mid \text{equal}(\text{exp}_1, \text{exp}_2)$

$\mathcal{E} ::= \mathcal{A} \mid (\mathcal{E}_1 \ . \ \mathcal{E}_2)$

A Mixwell program is a list of function definitions, the first function being the goal function. The goal function is to be called first, and inputs to the program are through the parameters of this function.

The body of a function is an expression, which is constructed from variables appearing in the function's formal parameter list, from constants **quote** and operators *car*, *cdr*, *cons*, *atom* and *equal* (as in Lisp), conditionals **if** and defined function calls **call**.

The only data type is well-founded (i.e. non-circular) S-expressions as known from Lisp.

All primitive and defined functions, except the conditional **if**, are strict in all positions. All parameters are called by value.

We use some "sintactic sugar". The keyword **call** is omitted in cases where the name of the function being called is different from the names of the primitive functions. **quote** $\mathcal{E}$ can be written as $'\mathcal{E}$, $\text{cons}(\text{exp}_1, \text{exp}_2)$ as $\text{exp}_1 :: \text{exp}_2$, $\text{equal}(\text{exp}_1, \text{exp}_2)$ as $\text{exp}_1 = \text{exp}_2$. Constants $(\mathcal{E}_1 \ . \ (\mathcal{E}_2 \ . \ \ldots \ (\mathcal{E}_n \ . \ \text{nil}) \ \ldots \ ))$ can be written as $(\mathcal{E}_1 \ \mathcal{E}_2 \ \ldots \ \mathcal{E}_n)$.

2. SPLITTING A FORMAL PARAMETER

Suppose the definition of function f in a program has the form

$f(\ldots, x_k, \ldots) =$ exp. Then the following transformation will be referred to as *the splitting of the function's k-th parameter*.

Let x' and x" be two variables different from all formal parameters of the function f. Then the splitting of x into x' and x" can be done in two steps.

At the first step, the original definition of f is replaced with

$$f(\ldots, x', x'', \ldots) = \exp[x_k \rightarrow \text{cons}(x', x'')]$$

where $\exp[x_k \rightarrow \text{cons}(x', x'')]$ denotes the expression obtained from exp by replacing all occurrences of x_k with cons(x', x").

At the second step, all calls of the function f in all function definitions are transformed, each call of the form call $f(\ldots, e_k, \ldots)$ being replaced with call $f(\ldots, \text{car}(e_k), \text{cdr}(e_k), \ldots)$.

Thus, the original variable x_k is replaced by two new variables x' and x" containing enough information for the value of x_k, if needed, to be reconstructed. To put it more exactly, the value of x_k can be obtained by evaluating the expression cons(x', x").

The fact that the formal parameter x of the function f is to be split into two variables x' and x" will, for the brevity's sake, be written as $f(x \rightarrow x' :: x'')$.

Example. Consider the program f(x) = g(x :: x); g(u) = cdr(u);. By g(u → u1 :: u2) we get the program f(x) = g(x :: x); g(u1, u2) = cdr(u1 :: u2);. Then, by splitting the argument in the calls of g we get f(x) = g(car(x :: x), cdr(x :: x)); g(u1, u2) = cdr(u1 :: u2);.

This program can be locally optimized, which results in f(x) = g(x, x); g(u1, u2) = u2;. Now we see that variable splitting is capable of producing parameters whose values are certain not to be needed. Such parameters can be recognized by a kind of backward analysis [Hughes 88] and eliminated. In the above program we can remove the parameter u1 of the function g, which gives the program f(x) = g(x); g(u2) = u2;.

Thus, the principal use of variable splitting consists in paving the way for other transformations such as local optimization and elimination of unneeded parameters, the latter being, in a sence, a kind of "garbage collection at compile time".

3. CONDITIONS OF THE VARIABLE SPLITTING CORRECTNESS

The program transformation described above can be incorrect. For example, after g(u →, u1 :: u2) for the program f(x) = g('a); g(u) = u; we get f(x) = g(car('a),cdr('a)); g(u1,u2) = u1 :: u2;.

It is evident that the transformed program is not equivalent to the original one, because the original program terminates, with the result being the atom 'a, whereas the transformed program fails to apply *car* or *cdr* to the atom 'a and terminates abnormally. Thus we come to the conclusion:

> Before splitting a parameter, we must make sure that, when the program is run, it is impossible for the parameter's value to be an atom!

Hence, to split a variable, we need to have a description of the structure of its values. Such descriptions will be referred to as *types* of variables.

4. ANALYSIS OF RUN TIME TYPES

To describe the structure of values to be taken by a variable, we use the following set of types.

$t \in$ Type   types
$\mathcal{A} \in$ Atom   Lisp atoms

$t ::= any \mid atom(\mathcal{A}) \mid cons(t_1, t_2) \mid \perp$

We assume the set of types to be equipped with reflexive partial ordering ≤ recursively defined by the following rules:

(i) $\perp \leq t \leq any$ for all types t.

(ii) $cons(t'_1, t'_2) \leq cons(t''_1, t''_2)$ if $t'_1 \leq t''_1$ and $t'_2 \leq t''_2$.

If $t' \leq t''$ and $t' \neq t''$, the type t" is said to be *more general* than the type t'.

The set of types is a lattice, as for all types t',t"∈Type there exist their least upper bound $t' \sqcup t''$ and their greatest lower bound $t' \sqcap t''$. Each set of types T∈P(Type) has its least upper bound $\sqcup T$. Thus the set of types is a pointed continuous partial ordering (CPO) with the bottom ⊥ [Schmidt 86]. It can be easily seen that the set of types has no chains of infinite height. In addition, each *finite* T∈P(Type) has its greatest lower bound $\sqcap T$.

A type represents a set of S-expressions. More specifically, let us define an "abstraction" function Abs mapping sets of S-expressions into types. Abs is defined in terms of an auxiliary function Abs′ mapping S-expressions into types.

Abs ∈ ℙ(SExp) ⟶ Type
Abs′ ∈ SExp ⟶ Type

Abs[E] = ⊔{Abs′[𝛿] | 𝛿∈E}
Abs′[𝒜] = atom(𝒜)
Abs′[(𝛿′ . 𝛿″)] = cons(Abs′[𝛿′], Abs′[𝛿″])

Let us define a "concretization" function Co reconstructing the set of S-expressions from a type:

Co ∈ Type ⟶ ℙ(SExp)

Co[any] = SExp
Co[atom(𝒜)] = {𝒜}
Co[cons(t′,t″)] = {(𝛿′ . 𝛿″) | 𝛿′∈Co[t′] and 𝛿″∈Co[t″]}
Co[⊥] = {}

The following relations hold: Abs[Co[t]] = t and E ⊆ Co[Abs[E]].

Now let x be a variable in a program. The problem is to find a type t such that 𝛿∈Co[t] for all 𝛿 that can be taken as value by x when the program is run. It can be done by *abstract interpretation* [Jones 86] of the program, which amounts to performing the program's computations using abstract values in place of the actual ones.

[Omitted: the type analysis algorithm.]

The type analysis above can, in a sense, be regarded as a monovariant, monogenetic version of the "configuration analysis" as used in the Supercompiler [Turchin 89], [Turchin 86].

5. USING TYPE INFORMATION FOR VARIABLE SPLITTING

The variable splitting transformation as described above splits only one of a function's parameters. However, the information provided by an argument type description is sufficient for all function's parameters to be split at once.

Suppose the type t assigned to a variable x contains some occurrences of the type *any*, which will be referred to as "gaps".

It is obvious that all values of the variable x can be different only at places corresponding to the gaps, and must be congruent at all other places. Therefore, if the type t contains *m* gaps, any S-expression $\mathcal{E} \in Co[t]$ is completely determined by its parts corresponding to the gaps in the type t. This enables the variable x to be *retyped* by replacing it with *m* new variables, which are to be assigned the parts of the variable's values corresponding to the gaps.

For example, if a function's parameter x has the type *cons(cons(any, atom(a)), any)*, then x can be represented by two new parameters u1 and u2, in which case all occurrences of x in the function's body must be replaced with the expression (u1 :: 'a) :: u2.

[Omitted: the algorithm for splitting parameters according their types.]

6. CODE DUPLICATION RISK

<u>Example.</u> Consider the program f(z) = swap(unzip(z,'nil,'nil)); swap(v) = cdr(v) :: car(v); unzip(u,x,y) = if u='nil then x :: y else unzip(cdr(u), car(car(u)) :: x, cdr(car(u)) :: y);.

Any result produced by the function unzip is of the type *cons(any, any)*, hence this type can be assigned to the parameter v of the function swap. Thus we can perform swap(v → v1 :: v2). But this gives rise to two copies of the expression unzip(z,'nil,'nil), which is bad for two reasons. First, duplicating expressions can result in huge programs being produced. Second, code duplication can lead to repeated evaluation of expressions. Both of the problems arise in the above example.

The risk of code duplication and repeated evaluation can be avoided by following the principle of *selector non-introduction*:

> All selectors produced by variable splitting must be eliminable by means of local optimization.

What is the drawback of the type analysis described above? The point is that this analysis tells us whether a selector in the program is certain to be applicable at run time, whereas we need to know whether the selector can be applied *symbolically* at the time the program is being optimized.

The feasibility of the simbolic application of a selector to the expression exp, obviously, depends upon the structure of the expression itself, rather than on the structure of the result to be produced by exp at run time.

If exp has the form **quote** ($\mathcal{E}'$. $\mathcal{E}''$), the symbolic application is feasible, car(exp) being reducible to **quote** $\mathcal{E}'$, and cdr(exp) being reducible to **quote** $\mathcal{E}''$.

If exp has the form exp' :: exp", the symbolic application is feasible, car(exp) being reducible to exp', and cdr(exp) being reducible to exp".

On the other hand, if exp has the form **if** exp_0 **then** exp' **else** exp" or **call** $f(exp_1, \ldots, exp_m)$, it is impossible to make the symbolic application without code duplication.

If exp is a variable x, the symbolic application may seem to be unfeasible. Nevertheless, splitting the parameters throughout the program may result in the variable x being split into a new expression, which may enable the symbolic applicaton.

Example. Consider the program f(x) = g(x :: x); g(u) = h(u); h(v) = cdr(v);. After g(u $\rightarrow$ u1 :: u2), we get f(x) = g(x,x); g(u1,u2) = h(u1 :: u2); h(v) = cdr(v);. Now, after h(v $\rightarrow$ v1 :: v2), we get f(x) = g(x,x); g(u1,u2) = h(u1,u2); h(v1,v2) = v2;.

7. ANALYSIS OF OPTIMIZATION TIME TYPES

As can be seen from the above, we need to know the structure of *symbolic* values assigned to variables at the time the program is being optimized, rather than the structure of ordinary values assigned to variables at the time the program is run. Thus, what we are really interested in are the optimization time types, rather than the run time types.

To find them, we can use the same set of types as has been used for analyzing the run time types.

Suppose we have a program defining functions $f_1, \ldots, f_h$. Let $F = \{f_1, \ldots, f_h\}$, and, for each $f \in F$, $x_{f,j}$ be its j-th parameter, a(f) be its arity, and $body_f$ be its body, so that the definition of f has the form:

$$f(x_{f,1}, \ldots, x_{f,a(f)}) - body_f$$

Let $\theta \in Env = VName \rightarrow Type$ be an *environment* assigning a type to each parameter of a function. Let $\alpha \in ArgDescr = F \rightarrow Env$ be an *argument type description* assigning types to each function's parameters. Let $\rho \in ResDescr = F \rightarrow Type$ be a *result type description* assigning a type to each function's result.

All the sets above are equipped with reflexive partial orderings as follows:

Env: $\theta' \leq \theta'' \Leftrightarrow \forall x \in VName\ \theta'(x) \leq \theta''(x)$
ArgDescr: $\alpha' \leq \alpha'' \Leftrightarrow \forall f \in F\ \alpha'(f) \leq \alpha''(f)$
ResDescr: $\rho' \leq \rho'' \Leftrightarrow \forall f \in F\ \rho'(f) \leq \rho''(f)$

We define two functions R and A to do the abstract interpretation using these ordered sets.

The function R, given an expression exp and an environment θ, computes the type of an expression's result.

$R \quad \in Exp \rightarrow Env \rightarrow Type$

$R[x]\ \theta = \theta(x)$
$R[\textbf{quote}\ \mathcal{E}]\ \theta = Abs'[\mathcal{E}]$
$R[\textbf{if } exp \textbf{ then } exp' \textbf{ else } exp'']\ \theta = any$
$R[\textbf{call } f(exp_1, \ldots, exp_m)]\ \theta = any$

$$R[car(exp)]\ \theta = \begin{cases} any & \text{if } R[exp]\ \theta = any, \\ t' & \text{if } R[exp]\ \theta = cons(t',t''), \\ \bot & \text{otherwise.} \end{cases}$$

$$R[cdr(exp)]\ \theta = \begin{cases} any & \text{if } R[exp]\ \theta = any, \\ t'' & \text{if } R[exp]\ \theta = cons(t',t''), \\ \bot & \text{otherwise.} \end{cases}$$

$R[cons(exp',exp'')]\ \theta = cons(\ R[exp']\ \theta,\ R[exp'']\ \theta\ )$
$R[atom(exp)]\ \theta = any$
$R[equal(exp',exp'')]\ \theta = any$

The function A, given an expression exp, an environment θ, and an argument type description α, computes a new approximation to the final description of each function's parameter types.

$A \quad \in Exp \rightarrow Env \rightarrow ArgDescr \rightarrow ArgDescr$

$A[x]\ \theta\ \alpha = \alpha$
$A[\textbf{quote}\ \mathcal{E}]\ \theta\ \alpha = \alpha$
$A[\textbf{if } exp \textbf{ then } exp' \textbf{ else } exp'']\ \theta\ \alpha$
$\quad = A[exp]\ \theta\ \alpha\ \sqcup\ A[exp']\ \theta\ \alpha\ \sqcup\ A[exp'']\ \theta\ \alpha$

$A[\textbf{call } f(exp_1, \ldots, exp_m)]\ \theta\ \alpha = \alpha_{new}[f \mapsto \alpha_{new}(f)\ \sqcup\ \theta_{new}],$
$\quad \text{where} \quad \alpha_{new} = \sqcup\ \{A[exp_j]\ \theta\ \alpha\}_{j=1,\ldots,m} \quad \text{and}$

$$\theta_{new} = [x_{f,j} \mapsto R[exp_j]\ \theta]_{j=1,\ldots,m}$$

$A[car(exp)]\ \theta\ \alpha = A[exp]\ \theta\ \alpha$
$A[cdr(exp)]\ \theta\ \alpha = A[exp]\ \theta\ \alpha$
$A[cons(exp',exp'')]\ \theta\ \alpha = A[exp']\ \theta\ \alpha\ \sqcup\ A[exp'']\ \theta\ \alpha$
$A[atom(exp)]\ \theta\ \alpha = A[exp]\ \theta\ \alpha$
$A[equal(exp',exp'')]\ \theta\ \alpha = A[exp']\ \theta\ \alpha\ \sqcup\ A[exp'']\ \theta\ \alpha$

We want a final argument type descripton α that is consistent and as low as possible. This must be the least fixed point for the following system of simultaneous equations and relations:

$$\alpha = \sqcup \ \{A[body_f] \ \alpha(f) \ \alpha\}_{f\in F}, \qquad \alpha \geq \alpha_0$$

where α_0 is defined as follows

$$\alpha_0 = [f_1 \mapsto [x_{f_1, j} \mapsto any]_{j=1, \dots, a(f_1)}] \ \sqcup$$
$$[f \mapsto [x_{f, j} \mapsto \perp]_{j=1, \dots, a(f)}]_{f\in F}$$

The description α_0 assigns the type any to the parameters of the goal function f_1, to prevent these parameters from being split. All other parameters, on the contrary, are assigned the type $\perp$, there being no a priori information about their structure.

The least fixed point for the system above does exist because for any given program the ordered sets involved have no chains of infinite height, and the functions A and R are monotonic.

8. USEFULNESS OF VARIABLE SPLITTING

The fact that the parameters of a function f have been assigned the types $t_1, \dots, t_m$, for brevity's sake, will be written as $f(t_1, \dots, t_m)$.

Example. Consider the program

```
f(x) = rev(x, 'a :: 'nil);
rev(u,v) = if u = 'nil then v else rev(cdr(u), car(u) :: v);
```

The analysis of types tells us that $f(any)$, $rev(any, cons(any, any))$. After $rev(v \rightarrow v1 :: v2)$, we get the program

```
f(x) = rev(x, 'a, 'nil);
rev(u,v1,v2) = if u = 'nil then v1 :: v2 else
                    rev(cdr(u), car(u), v1 :: v2);
```

We see that the program obtained is by no means superior to the original one, because no selector has been eliminated owing to variable splitting.

Thus we see that the parameter splitting based exclusively on the information obtained by examining the structure of argument expressions, may well result in the "arity overraising", i.e. increasing the number of parameters without reducing the number of selectors in the program. The types as produced by the above analysis, describing as they do the feasibility of splitting parameters, however, provide no information on the usefulness of this splitting. The arity overraising, nevertheless, can be avoided by "adjusting" the above types in the following way.

Suppose, for example, the type t has been assigned to a parameter x. Then the splitting of the parameter can be restricted by replacing some parts of t having the form $cons(t_1, t_2)$ with *any*. This results in the type t being *generalized*, i.e. changed to some other type t' such that t ≤ t', the depth of splitting being the less the greater the type t'. Thus, for instance, the splitting x → x1 :: (x2 :: x3) corresponds to the type *cons(any, cons(any, any))*, the splitting x → x1 :: x2 to the type *cons(any, any)*, and no splitting to the type *any*.

Thus we are facing the *type generalization problem*: given a *cons* in a type, we have to decide whether this *cons* should be retained or generalized. This decision will be made on the basis of the following *selector elimination principle*:

> A *cons* should be retained only if this causes
> a selector in the program to disappear.

Being formalized as it is, the selector elimination principle gives only an approximate description of the intuitive ideas the humans have about what does it means for a program to have a beautiful and natural structure. Nevertheless, experience has shown this principle to be likely to produce reasonable results, without any danger of the program being spoilt.

9. BACKWARD ANALYSIS

Let us consider the function definition $f(\ldots, x_k, \ldots) = exp$.

The k-th parameter of the function may appear at different places in the function's body exp. Is it any use splitting x_k? To answer this question, we have to consider all occurrences of x_k in exp and to take into account their *contexts* in exp. To take an example, if exp contains the subexpression $cdr(x_k)$, it makes sense to perform the splitting $x_k \to x' :: x''$, since this will cause $cdr(x_k)$ to be replaced with $cdr(x' :: x'')$, the latter being reducible to x''.

Example. f(x) = g(x :: x); g(u) = u; .

In this case the selector elimination principle tells us that it is no use performing the splitting g(u → u1 :: u2).

Example. f(x) = g(x :: x); g(u) = cdr(u);.

In this case the selector elimination principle tells us that the splitting g(u ⟶ u1 :: u2) is worth performing, since it will cause the selector cdr to disappear. And, in fact, after the splitting we get the program f(x) = g(x,x); g(u1,u2) = u2;.

Thus we see that the natural way of getting information about the usefulness of splitting is to make use of some kind of backward analysis [Hughes 88].

10. ACCESS PATHS AND CONTEXTS

Let exp be an expression appearing in a larger expression. We want to consider all attempts by the surrounding expression at accessing the components of exp. For example, if exp is a part of the expression car(cdr(cdr(exp))), then there is an attempt at accessing exp by applying selectors in the following order: cdr, cdr, car. The component to be accessed can be unambiguously identified by a sequence of selectors. This justifies the following definition.

Definition. An *access path* is a finite list (which may be empty) of selector names car and cdr.

We use the following notation. A finite list of elements $a_1, \ldots, a_m$ is written as $[a_1, \ldots, a_m]$, an empty list as $[]$. The concatenation of two lists $A = [a_1, \ldots, a_m]$ and $B = [b_1, \ldots, b_n]$ equal to $[a_1, \ldots, a_m, b_1, \ldots, b_n]$ is denoted by $A^{\char`\^}B$.

The set of all access paths will be denoted by Path. Thus Path = {car, cdr}*.

In some cases the surrounding expression tries to access several components of the expression under consideration. For this reason we have to describe the context by a set of paths, rather than by a single path.

Definition. A set of access paths $\Pi \subset P(Path)$ is an *access context*, if it satisfies the following requirements.

    (i) $[] \in \Pi$
    (ii) If $\pi^{\char`\^}[car] \in \Pi$ or $\pi^{\char`\^}[cdr] \in \Pi$, then $\pi \in \Pi$.

(i) means that an attempt at accessing the expression as a whole must be included into the context. This requirement is useful for technical reasons. (ii) formalizes the obvious fact that a subcomponent can be accessed only by accessing the components in which the subcomponent is included.

The set of all contexts is denoted by Context.

Now consider the function definition $f(\ldots,x_k,\ldots) = $ exp. Suppose that exp contains m occurrences of the parameter x_k in the contexts Π_1, $\Pi_2,\ldots,$ Π_m. What should be the total context for all occurrences of x_k? It is clear that finding all attempts at accessing the parameter x_k amounts to finding all attempts at accessing its occurrences, thus $\Pi_1 \cup \Pi_2 \cup \ldots \cup \Pi_m$ should be considered to be the total context of the parameter x_k.

11. USING CONTEXTS FOR TYPE GENERALIZATION

Let a parameter have the type t and the context Π. Then the function GenType can be easily defined which generalizes t in accordance with Π by replacing all $cons(t_1, t_2)$ unaccessed by Π with any.

GenType : Type $\rightarrow$ Context $\rightarrow$ Type

GenType[t] $\Pi = \sqcap${GenType'[t]π | $\pi \in \Pi$}
GenType' : Type $\rightarrow$ Path $\rightarrow$ Type
GenType'[any]π = any
GenType'[atom($\mathcal{A}$)]π = atom($\mathcal{A}$)
GenType'[cons(t',t'')]([ ]) = any
GenType'[cons(t',t'')]([car]^π) = cons(GenType'[t']π, any)
GenType'[cons(t',t'')]([cdr]^π) = cons(any, GenType'[t'']π)
GenType'[$\perp$]π = $\perp$

It should be noted that for all t$\in$Type and $\pi \in \Pi$ the relation t $\leq$ GenType'[t]π holds, therefore the set {GenType'[t]π | $\pi \in \Pi$} is finite, in spite of the fact that Π may well be infinite. Consequently, the greatest lower bound of this set does exist.

12. LATENT SELECTORS

The above considerations might have produced the expression that the context of a parameter can be determined by examining only the definition of the function concerned, without the program being globally analyzed. This is not really the case, however.

Example. $f(x) = g(x :: 'a)$; $g(u) = h(u)$; $h(v) = cdr(v)$; .

The type analysis tells us that $f(any)$, $g(cons(any, atom(a)))$, $h(cons(any, atom(a)))$. The variable v has the context {[ ], [cdr]}. But what is the context of the variable u? At the first glance, it may appear to be

{[]}, because there seems to be no selectors in the program attempting at accessing the variable u. Thus we, erroneously, come to the conclusion that the types should be generalized as follows: f(*any*), g(*any*), h(*cons*(*any*, *atom*(a))). The only acceptable splitting is therefore h(v → v1 :: v2). By performing it we get f(x) = g(x :: 'a); g(u) = h(car(u),cdr(u)); h(v1,v2) = v2; .

This result is far from being satisfactory, because there have appeared two new selectors car and cdr, not present in the original program. This makes us draw the conclusion that the parameter access analysis has to take into account not only the selectors explicitly appearing in the program, but also the *latent selectors* to be introduced by the splitting of parameters.

Thus, if e_k is an argument expression in the function call call f(...,e_k,...), it would be incorrect to take its context to be {[]}, because there should be taken into account all attempts at accessing e_k due to the splitting of e_k. This can be done in the following way.

Let the k-th formal parameter of the function f be assigned the type t, and the total context of all its occurrences be Π. Let t' = GenType[t]Π. Then the generalized type t' gives all information about the way in which e_k is to be split. The function TypeToContext can be easily defined which converts t' into the context providing the information about all the attempts at accessing e_k due to the splitting of e_k in accordance with t'.

TypeToContext : Type → Context

TypeToContext[*any*] = {[]}
TypeToContext[*atom*(𝒶)] = {[]}
TypeToContext[*cons*(t',t'')] = {[]} ∪
    car*(TypeToContext[t']) ∪ cdr*(TypeToContext[t''])
TypeToContext[⊥] = {[]}

where we use the notation car*Π = {[car]^π | π∈Π}, cdr*Π = {[cdr]^π | π∈Π}.

Now we can determine the context of the expression e_k, assuming the k-th parameter to be assigned the type t, and the total context of all its occurrences to be Π. This context is equal to TypeToContext[GenType[t]Π].

13. SYSTEM OF EQUATIONS FOR FINDING CONTEXTS

For each function f with the definition f($x_{f,1}$,...,$x_{f,m}$) = body$_f$ let $t_{f,1}$, ..., $t_{f,m}$ stand for the types of its parameters, and $c_{f,1}$, ..., $c_{f,m}$ stand for the contexts of its parameters.

Let C x [exp] Π be the total context of all occurrences of the variable x in the expression exp, the expression exp itself being in the context Π.

We have the following set of equations

$$c_{f,j} = \text{TypeToContext}[\ \text{GenType}[t_{f,j}]\ (\ C\ x_j\ [\text{body}_f]\ \{[\,]\}\ )\ ]$$

where C x [exp] Π is defined as follows:

C   ∈ VName → Exp → Context → Context

C x [x] Π = Π
C x [y] Π = {[ ]},   where x≠y.
C x [**quote** &] Π = {[ ]}
C x [**if** exp **then** exp′ **else** exp″] Π =
    C x [exp] {[ ]} ∪ C x [exp′] {[ ]} ∪ C x [exp″] {[ ]}

C x [**call** f(exp$_1$,...,exp$_m$)] Π = ∪{ C x [exp$_j$] $c_{f,j}$ }$_{j=1,...,m}$

C x [car(exp)] Π = C x [exp] ({[ ]} ∪ car*Π)
C x [cdr(exp)] Π = C x [exp] ({[ ]} ∪ cdr*Π)
C x [cons(exp′,exp″)] Π =
    C x [exp′] ({[ ]} ∪ Π/car) ∪ C x [exp″] ({[ ]} ∪ Π/cdr)
C x [atom(exp)] Π = C x [exp] {[ ]}
C x [equal(exp′,exp″)] = C x [exp′] {[ ]} ∪ C x [exp″] {[ ]}

where we use the notation Π/car = {π | [car]^π ∈ Π}, Π/cdr = {π | [cdr]^π ∈ Π}.

We assume the set of contexts to be equipped with natural partial ordering, Π′≤Π″ being equivalent to Π′⊆Π″. The functions TypeToContext, GenType, and C are monotonic with respect to contexts, therefore the minimal fixed point for the above system of equations does exist.

Moreover, since $c_{f,j}$ ⊆ TypeToContext[$t_{f,j}$], there exist only a finite number of contexts that can be taken as value by $c_{f,j}$, hence the minimal fixed point can be found by a finite number of iterations.

The context analysis above resembles, in some respects, the "neighborhood analysis" as used in the Supercompiler [Turchin 86], [Turchin 88].

14. PRACTICAL IMPLEMENTATION OF THE CONTEXT ANALYSIS

Some programming tricks have prove to be useful for implementing the above backward analysis.

First, what we really use in splitting parameters are types generalized with respect to contexts, rather than contexts themselves. Thus, instead of computing $c_{f,j}$, we can compute the type

$$t'_{f,j} = \text{GenType}[t_{f,j}] \, c_{f,j}.$$

Second, since $t_{f,j} \le t'_{f,j}$, we can replace $t_{f,j}$ and $t'_{f,j}$ with a single *marked type* $mt_{f,j}$ having the syntax

```
mt   ∈ MType         marked types
mt   ::= any | atom(𝒜) | cons(t',t") | cons!(mt',mt") | ⊥
```

where each marked *cons!* "belongs" both to $t'_{f,j}$ and $t_{f,j}$, whereas each unmarked *cons* "belongs" only to $t_{f,j}$, the corresponding place in $t'_{f,j}$ being *any*.

The context $c_{f,j}$ can be extracted from $mt_{f,j}$ directly, without finding $t'_{f,j}$, by means of the function Retrieve!.

```
Retrieve!  ∈ MType → Context

Retrieve![any] = {[]}
Retrieve![atom(𝒜)] = {[]}
Retrieve![cons(t',t")] = {[]}
Retrieve![cons!(mt',mt")] = {[]} ∪ car*Retrieve![mt'] ∪ cdr*Retrieve![mt"]
```

Next improvement concerns the representation of contexts. Being sets of paths, contexts are difficult to deal with directly, but we can replace contexts with their representations having the syntax

```
crep      ∈ ContextRep
crep ::=  car(crep) | cdr(crep) | mtype(mt)
```

Given a context's representation, we can reconstruct the context by the function Retrieve.

```
Retrieve   ∈ ContextRep
Retrieve[car(crep)] = {[]} ∪ car*Retrieve[crep]
Retrieve[cdr(crep)] = {[]} ∪ cdr*Retrieve[crep]
Retrieve[mtype(mt)] = Retrieve![mt]
```

All functions the access path analysis involves can be modified so that they will deal with the representation of contexts, rather than with the contexts themselves.

15. GENERALIZATIONS

The first obvious generalization concerns splitting the results of functions. In the language Mixwell each function produces one and only one result, for which reason a defined function call **call** $f(exp_1,\ldots,exp_m)$ cannot be split and, therefore, has to be assigned the type *any*. The language, however, can be extended, so that a function can produce several results, and this device allows the results of a function to be split without splitting the function's definition. A version of the arity raiser with this extension has been implemented by Ruten F. Gurin.

Another possible extension is to make an arity raiser deal with data structures that are more complicated than Lisp S-expressions are. For example, in the case of the languages Refal [Turchin 79], [Turchin 86] and RL [Romanenko 88], the data are arbitrary trees, rather than binary trees, which was taken into account in the arity raiser described in [Romanenko 88].

CONCLUSIONS

In order for the results produced by variable splitting to be reasonable, we need information obtained by two preliminary global analyses of the program. The first, forward, analysis tells us whether the splitting is feasible, whereas the second, backward, analysis tells us whether the splitting is useful.

The information obtained is used to avoid introducing new selectors into the program as well as code duplication, and makes it possible to avoid useless variable splitting that does not cause some selectors in the program to be eliminated.

The experiments made by the author have shown that introducing an arity raiser as a separate phase into a specializer enhances the structure of residual programs generated without affecting the other phases of the specializer. The structure of the specializer, thus, can be kept natural and understandable.

REFERENCES

[Barzdin 88] G. Barzdin. Mixed Computation and Compiler Basis. In D. Bjorner, A. P. Ershov and N. D. Jones, editors, *Partial Evaluation and Mixed Computation*, pages 15-26, North-Holland, 1988.

[Beckman 76] L. Beckman, A. Haraldson, O. Oskarsson, E. Sandewall. A Partial Evaluator, and Its Use as a Programming Tool. *Artificial Intelligence*, 7(4):319-357, 1976.

[Bulyonkov 84] M. A. Bulyonkov. Polyvariant Mixed Computation for Analyzer Programs. *Acta Informatica*, 21:473-484, 1984.

[Burstall 77] R. M. Burstall and J. Darlington. A Transformation System for

Developing Recursive Programs. *Journal of the ACM*, 24(1):44-67, 1977.

[Dixon 71] J.Dixon. The Specializer, a Method of Automatically Writing Computer Programs. Division of Computer Research and Technology, National Institute of Health, Bethenda, Maryland, 1971.

[Ershov 78] On the Essence of Compilation. In E.J.Neuhold, editor, *Formal Description of Programming Concepts*, pages 391-420, North-Holland, 1978.

[Ershov 81] A.P.Ershov. The Transformational Machine: Theme and Variations. In J.Grushka and M.Chytil, editors, *Mathematical Foundations of Computer Science*, Štrbské Pleso, Czechoslovakia, pages 16-32, Lecture Notes in Computer Science, Vol.118, Springer-Verlag, 1981.

[Futamura 71] Partial Evaluation of Computation Process - An Approach to a Compiler-Compiler. *Systems, Computers, Controls*, 2(5):45-50, 1971.

[Hughes 88] J.Hughes. Backward Analysis of Functional Programs. In D.Bjorner, A.P.Ershov and N.D.Jones, editors, *Partial Evaluation and Mixed Computation*, pages 187-208, North-Holland, 1988.

[Jones 85] N.D.Jones, P.Sestoft and H.Sondergaard. An Experiment in Partial Evaluation: The Generation of a Compiler Generator. In J.-P.Jouannaud, editor, *Rewriting Techniques and Applications, Dijon, France*, pages 124-140, Lecture Notes in Computer Science, Vol.202, Springer-Verlag, 1985.

[Jones 86] N.D.Jones and A.Mycroft. Data Flow Analysis of Applicative Programs Using Minimal Function Graphs. In *Thirteens ACM Symposium on Principles of Programming Languages, St.Petersburg, Florida*, pages 296-306, ACM, 1986.

[Jones 88] Automatic Program Specialization: A Re-Examination from Basic Principles. In D.Bjorner, A.P.Ershov and N.D.Jones, editors, *Partial Evaluation and Mixed Computation*, pages 225-282, North-Holland, 1988.

[Mogensen 88] T.Mogensen. Partially Static Structures in a Self-Applicable Partial Evaluator. In D.Bjorner, A.P.Ershov and N.D.Jones, editors, *Partial Evaluation and Mixed Computation*, pages 325-347, North-Holland, 1988.

[Ostrovski 88] B.N.Ostrowski. Implementation of Controlled Mixed Computation in System for Automatic Development of Language-Oriented Parsers. In D.Bjorner, A.P.Ershov and N.D.Jones, editors, *Partial*

Evaluation and Mixed Computation, pages 385-403, North-Holland, 1988.

[Romanenko 88] S. A. Romanenko. A Compiler Generator Produced by a Self-Applicable Specializer Can Have a Surprisingly Natural and Understandable Structure. In D. Bjorner, A. P. Ershov and N. D. Jones, editors, *Partial Evaluation and Mixed Computation*, pages 445-463, North-Holland, 1988.

[Sestoft 86] The Structure of a Self-Applicable Partial Evaluator. In H. Ganzinger and N. D. Jones, editors, *Programs as Data Objects, Copenhagen, Denmark, 1985*, pages 236-256, Lecture Notes in Computer Science, Vol. 217, Springer-Verlag, 1986.

[Schmidt 86] D. A. Schmidt. *Denotational Semantics*. Allyn and Bacon, Boston, 1986.

[Sestoft 88] P. Sestoft. Automatic Call Unfolding in a Partial Evaluator. In D. Bjorner, A. P. Ershov and N. D. Jones, editors, *Partial Evaluation and Mixed Computation*, pages 485-506, North-Holland, 1988.

[Turchin 72] V. F. Turchin. Equivalent Transformation of Recursive Functions Defined in Refal. In *Teoriya Yazykov i Metody Programmirovaniya. Trudy Simposiuma*, pages 31-42, Alushta-Kiev, 1972 (in Russian).

[Turchin 79] V. F. Turchin. A Supercompiler System Based on the Language Refal. *SIGPLAN Notices*, 14(2):46-54, February 1979.

[Turchin 82] V. F. Turchin, R. M. Nirenberg and D. V. Turchin. Experiments with a Supercompiler. In *1982 ACM Symposium on Lisp and Functional Programming, Pittsburgh, Pennsylvania*, pages 47-55, ACM, 1982.

[Turchin 86] V. F. Turchin. The Concept of a Supercompiler. *ACM Transactions on Programming Languages and Systems*, 8(3):292-325, July 1986.

[Turchin 88] V. F. Turchin. The Algorithm of Generalization in the Supercompiler. In D. Bjorner, A. P. Ershov and N. D. Jones, editors, *Partial Evaluation and Mixed Computation*, pages 531-549, North-Holland, 1988.

[Wadler 88] P. Wadler. Deforestation: Transforming Programs to Eliminate Trees. In *European Symposium on Programming*, Lecture Notes in Computer Science, Springer-Verlag, 1988.

Complexity Analysis for a Lazy Higher-Order Language

David Sands [*]

Department of Computing, Imperial College

180 Queens Gate, London SW7 2BZ

email: ds@uk.ac.ic.doc

Abstract

This paper is concerned with the time-analysis of functional programs. Techniques which enable us to reason formally about a program's execution costs have had relatively little attention in the study of functional programming. We concentrate here on the construction of equations which compute the time-complexity of expressions in a lazy higher-order language.

The problem with higher-order functions is that complexity is dependent on the cost of applying functional parameters. Structures called *cost-closures* are introduced to allow us to model both functional parameters *and* the cost of their application.

The problem with laziness is that complexity is dependent on *context*. Projections are used to characterise the context in which an expression is evaluated, and cost-equations are parameterised by this context-description to give a compositional time-analysis. Using this form of context information we introduce two types of time-equation: *sufficient-time* equations and *necessary-time* equations, which together provide bounds on the exact time-complexity.

1 Introduction

This paper is concerned with the time-analysis of functional programs. Techniques which enable us to reason formally about a program's execution costs have had relatively little attention in the study of functional programming. There has been some interest in the mechanisation of program cost analysis, perhaps the main examples being [Weg75, LeM85, Ros89]. These works describe systems which analyse cost by first constructing (recursive) equations which describe the time-complexity of a functional program in a strict first-order language. A closed form expression for cost is obtained in some cases by mechanised manipulation (transformation) of these equations. The average-case solution of such equations is considered in [HC88, Fla85]. We concentrate here on the *first* part of this process—the construction of equations which compute the time-complexity of a given program. For programs written a first-order strict (*i.e.* call-by-value) language this is very straightforward. In the first part of this paper we show how to deal with a strict higher-order language (a fuller development can be found in [San88]). In the remainder of the paper we adapt these ideas to a lazy language. This extension is based on Wadler's use of *context-analysis* in the construction of time equations for a lazy first-order language [Wad88].

The aim is to develop a calculus that enables us to reason about time-complexity. Given a program (which we will consider to be any expression, plus a set of mutually recursive function definitions), the problem is to find a means of constructing equations which describe the cost (in terms of the number of certain elementary operations) of evaluating any expression. In this paper we choose to express cost in terms of the number of non-primitive function applications. One advantage of deriving cost-equations which are themselves expressed in a functional language is that they are amenable to a rich class of program transformation and analysis techniques *c.f.* [LeM85, Ros89]—this paper retains the functional flavour of these approaches.

---

*This work was partially supported by ESPRIT Basic Research Action P3124

The paper is organised as follows. In section 2 we consider the analysis of first and higher-order strict languages. Section 3 introduces a description of *context* that will be used in the analysis of lazy languages. Section 4 presents *sufficient-time* analysis, an upper-bound analysis for a lazy first-order language, which uses contexts that describe information that is *sufficient* to compute a value. Section 5 presents *necessary-time* analysis, a corresponding lower-bound analysis. Section 6 extends these ideas to a higher-order language.

2 Strict Time Analysis

In this section we consider the analysis of strict languages. A full presentation is given in [San88].

2.1 A First Order Language

Firstly we define a simple first-order functional language. We consider a set of mutually recursive function definitions of the form $f_i(x_1, \ldots, x_{n_i}) = e_i$ and an expression to be evaluated in the context of these definitions. Expressions have the following syntax:

$$e ::= f(e_1, \ldots, e_j) \mid ident \mid const \mid \text{if } e_1 \text{ then } e_2 \text{ else } e_3$$

Where f is one of the user-defined functions f_i, or a strict primitive function or constructor p.

For each equation of the form $f_i(x_1, \ldots, x_{n_i}) = e_i$ it is straightforward to construct an equation taking the same arguments as the original function, which computes the cost (in terms of the number of non-primitive function calls) of applying f_i to a tuple of values. The *cost equation* (or *cost-function*) is defined as: $cf_i(x_1, \ldots, x_{n_i}) = 1 + \mathcal{T}[e_i]$ where $\mathcal{T}$ is a syntax-directed abstraction given in figure 1. These rules clearly reflect the call-by-value evaluation order. For example, in the rule for application,

$$
\begin{aligned}
\mathcal{T}[const] &= \mathcal{T}[ident] = 0 \\
\mathcal{T}[\text{if } e_1 \text{ then } e_2 \text{ else } e_3] &= \mathcal{T}[e_1] + \text{if } e_1 \text{ then } \mathcal{T}[e_2] \text{ else } \mathcal{T}[e_3] \\
\mathcal{T}[p(e_1 \ldots e_n)] &= \mathcal{T}[e_1] + \cdots + \mathcal{T}[e_n] \\
\mathcal{T}[f_i(e_1 \ldots e_n)] &= cf_i(e_1 \ldots e_n) + \mathcal{T}[e_1] + \cdots + \mathcal{T}[e_n]
\end{aligned}
$$

Figure 1: First-Order Strict Cost Definition

we sum the cost of evaluating the arguments, in addition to the function application. (*N.B.* We will use infix notation to ease presentation throughout this paper)

Syntax directed derivations of this form, for similar first order languages can be found in [Weg75, LeM85, Ros89]. These works focus on some automatic techniques by which the recursive cost-equations can be manipulated to achieve non-recursive equations.

Example

As a simple example of the above scheme, consider the list-append function defined as:

```
append(x,y) = if null(x) then y else cons(hd(x), append(tl(x),y))
```

From this definition, applying $\mathcal{T}$ we obtain the cost-function which computes the number of non-primitive function applications:

```
cappend(x,y) = 1 + if null(x) then 0 else cappend(tl(x),y)
             = 1 + length(x)
```

The aim of the systems described in the papers cited above is to derive just such a closed-form expression, by means of program transformation. This paper focuses on the process of obtaining the initial cost-functions, for languages using higher-order functions and laziness—a necessary precursor to the derivation of closed-form equations describing, for example, average-case complexity.

2.2 A Higher-Order Curried Language

In this section we outline a means of deriving cost programs for a higher-order language. The time-equations are derived via two mappings. The first modifies the original equations so that functional values are augmented with information needed to describe the cost of their application. The second constructs the time-equations using these modified equations.

Firstly we define our language. We have function definitions of the form $f_i e_1 \ldots e_{n_i} = exp_i$ along with curried primitive functions p_i (of arity m_i). Expressions have the following syntax:

$$exp ::= exp\, e \mid e \qquad e ::= \text{ if } e_1 \text{ then } e_2 \text{ else } e_3 \mid (exp) \mid f_i \mid p_i \mid ident \mid const$$

For each definition $f_i x_1 \ldots x_{n_i} = exp_i$ we wish to construct a cost function $cf_i x_1 \ldots x_{n_i} = exp'_i$ which computes the cost of applying f_i to n_i values.

Suppose we wish to construct a cost-function for an apply function defined as: `apply f x = f x`. The cost function associated with `apply` should have the form:

$$\text{Capply}(f, x) = 1 + \textit{the cost of applying } f \textit{ to } x.$$

But how do we *syntactically* refer to the cost function associated with `f`?

Cost–Closures

In order to reason about the cost of application of functions, as well as the functions themselves, we introduce structures called *cost-closures*. A cost-closure is a triple (f, cf, a) of a function f, its associated cost-function cf and some arity information a. Together with cost-closures we define two (left associative) infix functions ⊙ and c⊙ which define the application of cost-closures and the cost of application. Functions ⊙ and c⊙ satisfy:

$$(f, cf, a) \odot e = \begin{cases} f\, e & \text{if } a = 1 \\ (f\, e, cf\, e, a-1) & \text{otherwise} \end{cases} \qquad (f, cf, n)\, c\odot\, e = \begin{cases} cf\, e & \text{if } n = 1 \\ 0 & \text{otherwise} \end{cases}$$

The arity component of the cost-closure, and its use in the definition of c⊙ is explained by the fact that for reasons of efficiency and simplicity, there is no evaluation of the body of a function until the function is supplied with at least the number of arguments in it's definition (this avoids the potentially expensive resolution of name clashes, and is thus a feature of most functional language implementations).

Cost-closures are used in the following way. We define two syntax-directed translation functions $\mathcal{V}$ and $\mathcal{T}$. The purpose of $\mathcal{V}$ (figure 3) is to modify the original program so that all functional objects are translated into cost-closures, and to perform application via ⊙. $\mathcal{T}$ (figure 4) defines the cost-functions, using c⊙. The cost of evaluating any expression exp with respect to definitions $f_i x_1 \ldots x_{n_i} = exp_i$, $i = 1, \ldots, k$ is then defined by the program given in figure 2.

$$
\begin{aligned}
\text{let} \quad & f'_1 x_1 \ldots x_{n_1} && = && \mathcal{V}[e_1] \\
& && \vdots && \\
& cf_1 x_1 \ldots x_{n_1} && = && 1 + \mathcal{T} \circ \mathcal{V}[e_1] \\
& && \vdots && \\
\text{in} \quad & \mathcal{T} \circ \mathcal{V}[e]
\end{aligned}
$$

Figure 2: Higher-Order Cost-Program Scheme

$$\mathcal{V}[exp\ e] = \mathcal{V}[exp] \ @ \ \mathcal{V}[e]$$
$$\mathcal{V}[\text{if } e_1 \text{ then } e_2 \text{ else } e_3] = \text{if } \mathcal{V}[e_1] \text{ then } \mathcal{V}[e_2] \text{ else } \mathcal{V}[e_3]$$
$$\mathcal{V}[(exp)] = (\mathcal{V}[exp])$$
$$\mathcal{V}[f_i] = (f_i'\ ,\ cf_i\ ,\ n_i\ ) \quad \mathcal{V}[p_i] = (p_i\ ,\ cp_i\ ,\ m_i\ )$$
$$\mathcal{V}[const] = const \quad \mathcal{V}[ident] = ident$$

Figure 3: Function Modification Map, $\mathcal{V}$

$$\mathcal{T}[exp'\ @\ e'] = \mathcal{T}[exp'] + \mathcal{T}[e'] + (exp'\ c@\ e')$$
$$\mathcal{T}[\text{if } e_1' \text{ then } e_2' \text{ else } e_3'] = \mathcal{T}[e_1'] + \text{if } e_1' \text{ then } \mathcal{T}[e_2'] \text{ else } \mathcal{T}[e_3']$$
$$\mathcal{T}[(exp')] = (\mathcal{T}[exp'])$$
$$\mathcal{T}[(p_i\ ,\ cp_i\ ,\ m_i\ )] = \mathcal{T}[(f_i\ ,\ cf_i\ ,\ n_i\ )] = \mathcal{T}[const] = 0$$

Figure 4: Cost-Expression Construction Map, $\mathcal{T}$

$\mathcal{V}$ is defined on the structure of expressions exp and e. $\mathcal{T}$ is consequently defined over the syntax of expressions generated by $\mathcal{V}$.

Some Optimisations

The code derived by the above translation schemes is rather more cumbersome than is necessary. This is because we introduce more @'s and c@'s than are necessary. Some straightforward optimisations simplify the cost program considerably, and can be defined according to the syntactic structure of expressions [San88].

Example

The following simple example illustrates the derivation (and the optimisation):

```
map f x = if (null x) then nil else (cons (f (hd x)) (map f (tl x)))
```

The cost-function derived from this is:

```
cmap f x = 1 + ((null,cnull,1) c@ x) +
            if ((null,cnull,1) @ x) then nil
            else (((cons,ccons,2) c@ (f @ ((hd,chd,1) @ x))) +
((cons,ccons,2)@(f @ ((hd,chd,1)@ x)) c@ ((map',cmap,2)@ f @ ((tl,ctl,1)@ x)))
+ f c@ ((hd,chd,1)@ x) + ((hd,chd,1)c@ x) + ((map',cmap,2)@ f c@ ((tl,ctl,1)@ x))
+ ((map',cmap,2)c@ f) + ((tl,ctl,1)c@ x) )
```

Using simple optimisation schemes, we get the equivalent cost-function definition:

```
cmap f x = 1 + if (null x) then 0 else (f c@ (hd x)) + (cmap f (tl x))
```

2.3 Correctness

The derived program computes the number of times a certain "step" is performed in the evaluation of the program. In [San88] we formalise our intuitive model of "evaluation steps" via an *operational semantics* and prove that the number of steps our derived program computes is correct with respect to the actual operational behaviour of the original program.

3 Lazy Time Analysis: Describing Context

A major obstacle in the time-analysis of lazy languages is the problem of *context sensitivity:* the cost of evaluating an expression depends on the context in which it is used. In order to give a *compositional* treatment of the analysis of lazy-evaluation we must take into account some description of context.

3.1 Modelling Contexts with Projections

The formulation of a context which will be used in our time analysis is that provided by Wadler and Hughes [WH87] in the analysis of *strictness.* Wadler shows how this formulation of context can be useful for time analysis in [Wad88]. Here we provide an introduction to the use of *projections* to model contexts. For a fuller development the reader is referred to [WH87]; a more formal development is given in [DW89].

The basic problem is, given a function, how much information do we require from the argument in order to determine a certain amount of information about the result. Projections, in the domain theoretic sense, can provide a concise description of both the amount of information which is *sufficient* and the amount which is *necessary.*

DEFINITION 3.1 *A projection, α, is a continuous function from a domain $\mathcal{D}$ onto itself, such that $\alpha \sqsubseteq \mathrm{ID}_{\mathcal{D}}$ and $\alpha \circ \alpha = \alpha$, where $\mathrm{ID}_{\mathcal{D}}$ is the identity function on $\mathcal{D}$*

In other words, given an object u, a projection removes information from that object ($\alpha u \sqsubseteq u$), but once this information has been removed further application has no effect ($\alpha(\alpha u) = \alpha u$). A projection is used to represent a context, where the information removed represents information not needed by that context.

In the following the terms *projection* and *context* will be synonymous, and will be ranged over by α and β.

DEFINITION 3.2 Safe Projections: *Given a (first order) function, f, of n arguments, if*

$$\alpha(f(u_1, \ldots, u_n)) = \alpha(f(u_1, \ldots, (\beta u_i), \ldots u_n))$$

for all objects $u_1, \ldots, u_n$, then we say that in context α, β is a safe context for the i'th argument of f. *This is abbreviated by $f^i : \alpha \Rightarrow \beta$.*

Lifted Projections

We will require that projections describe two types of information: what information is *sufficient*, and what information is *necessary.* In order to describe the latter, Wadler and Hughes introduce a new domain element, $\lightning$, called "abort". The interpretation of $\alpha u = \lightning$ is that context α requires a value more defined than u. To make this work, we must have $\lightning \sqsubset \bot$ and all functions are naturally-extended to be strict in $\lightning$, *i.e.,* $f(u_1, \ldots, \lightning, \ldots, u_n) = \lightning$. These technical devices are explained more formally in [Bur90] in terms of *lifting.*

The Projection Lattice

A projection $\alpha : \mathcal{D}_{\lightning} \to \mathcal{D}_{\lightning}$, is called *a projection over $\mathcal{D}$*. Projections over any domain form a lattice, with ordering $\sqsubseteq$, containing at least the following points:

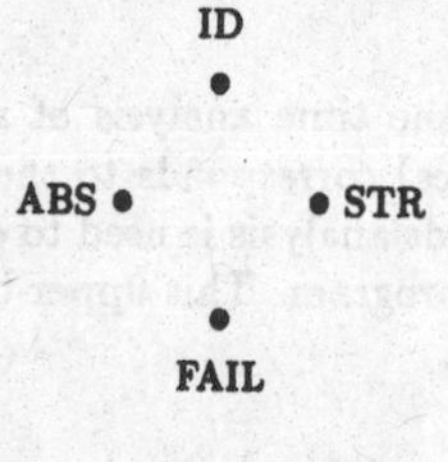

$$\mathrm{ID}\, u = u$$

$$\mathrm{STR}\, u = \begin{cases} \lightning & \text{if } u = \bot \text{ or } u = \lightning \\ u & \text{otherwise} \end{cases}$$

$$\mathrm{ABS}\, u = \begin{cases} \lightning & \text{if } u = \lightning \\ \bot & \text{otherwise} \end{cases}$$

$$\mathrm{FAIL}\, u = \lightning$$

DEFINITION **3.3** *A strict projection is any projection* α *such that* $\alpha(\bot) = \, \text{\reflectbox{?}}$

The largest of such projections is STR, giving us an alternative definition of strict projections: a projection α is strict if and only if $\alpha \sqsubseteq$ STR. Of the non-strict projections, the smallest is the projection ABS. This context is important since if it is safe to evaluate an expression in the context ABS, then the value of the expression will not be needed. FAIL is the unsatisfiable context.

There may be infinitely many projections, which are all either strict (FAIL $\sqsubseteq \alpha \sqsubseteq$ STR) or non-strict (ABS $\sqsubseteq \alpha \sqsubseteq$ ID). The four projections above will be used "polymorphically" to represent the corresponding projection over the appropriate domain.

Given two projections $\alpha \sqsubseteq \beta$, α represents a more precise description of a context than β. The context ID is therefore the least informative. Furthermore, if it is safe to evaluate some expression in a context α, then it is always safe to evaluate in a context $\beta, \alpha \sqsubseteq \beta$.

Contexts for Lists

The following projections are useful for building contexts over the non-flat domain of lists $\mathcal{D}^*$ of elements from some domain $\mathcal{D}$:

$$\text{NIL}\, u = \begin{cases} nil & \text{if } u = nil \\ \text{\reflectbox{?}} & \text{otherwise} \end{cases} \qquad \text{CONS}\,\alpha\,\beta\,u = \begin{cases} cons(\alpha\,x)(\beta\,xs) & \text{if } u = cons\,x\,xs \\ \text{\reflectbox{?}} & \text{otherwise} \end{cases}$$

NIL is the context which requires an empty-list, and CONS $\alpha\,\beta$ is the context which requires a non-empty list whose head is needed in context α and whose tail is needed in context β. For example, the context (CONS STR ABS) requires a non-empty list whose first element is needed, and the rest is not.

Context Analysis

Analysing context is a *backwards analysis* [AH87]. Given a context α for a function f, what can we say about the contexts of the arguments? We need to propagate the information about the result of a function *backwards* to it's arguments. *i.e.*, given a function f of arity n, and a context α we need to find each β_i such that $f^i : \alpha \Rightarrow \beta$.

Ideally we need to find the smallest β_i, since these describe the contexts most precisely. In order to give a computable approximation we may settle for *some* β_i satisfying the above property.

Projection Transformers

A function of α yielding such a β_i is called a *projection transformer*. We will adopt the following notation: The projection-transformer written $f^{\#i}$ is a function satisfying $f^i : \alpha \Rightarrow f^{\#i}\alpha$. *N.B.* Strictly speaking we should distinguish between the syntactic objects—the program defining f, and the semantic objects—the projections, and the denotations given by some semantic function. Following the style of [WH87] we will mix these entities for notational convenience.

Rules for defining recursive equations for the projection transformers are given in [WH87]—an important result here is that a solution to these equations can be determined *automatically* if we work with finite lattices of projections, although it is not difficult to modify the equations to give more accurate projection equations (which are harder to solve).

4 Sufficient-Time Analysis

In this section we show how context information can be used to aid the time analysis of a lazy first-order language; Sufficient-time analysis (with some minor differences) corresponds to the time analysis presented in [Wad88]. The information obtained by the backwards analysis is used to derive equations which compute an upper bound to the precise cost of a given program. This upper-bound

$$T_s[const]\alpha \;=\; T_s[ident]\alpha \;=\; 0$$
$$T_s[\text{if } e_1 \text{ then } e_2 \text{ else } e_3]\alpha \;=\; \alpha \hookrightarrow_s T_s[e_1]\text{ID} + \text{if } e_1 \text{ then } T_s[e_2]\alpha \text{ else } T_s[e_3]\alpha$$
$$T_s[p(e_1 \ldots e_n)]\alpha \;=\; T_s[e_1](p^{\#1}\alpha) + \cdots + T_s[e_n](p^{\#n}\alpha)$$
$$T_s[f_i(e_1 \ldots e_n)]\alpha \;=\; cf_i(e_1 \ldots e_n, \alpha) + T_s[e_1](f_i^{\#1}\alpha) + \cdots + T_s[e_n](f_i^{\#n}\alpha)$$

Figure 5: Definition of T_s

is obtained by using information which tells us what values are *sufficient* to compute an expression. We call the resulting analysis a *sufficient-time* analysis.

4.1 Context-Parameterised Cost Functions

As in the first-order time analysis of section 2, we will define a *cost-function*, cf_i, for each function f_i defined in the original program. As before the cost functions will take as parameters the original arguments to the functions, but in addition they will be parameterised by a *context*, representing the context in which the functions are evaluated.

How can cost-functions make use of context ?

We know that any expression in the context ABS will be ignored, so the cost in this context is zero. In any other context the cost of a function application will be (approximated above by) $1 + $ the cost of evaluating the body of the function, in that context.

We define the cost functions associated with each function $f_i(x_1 \ldots x_{n_i}) = e_i$ to be

$$cf_i(x_1, \ldots, x_{n_i}, \alpha) = \alpha \hookrightarrow_s 1 + T_s[e_i]\alpha$$

where we introduce the notation $\alpha \hookrightarrow_s e$ to abbreviate cost e "guarded" by context α:

$$\alpha \hookrightarrow_s e = \begin{cases} 0 & \text{if } \alpha = \text{ABS} \\ e & \text{otherwise} \end{cases}$$

The syntactic map T_s defined in figure 5 is very similar to that defined in figure 1, but is defined with respect to a particular context. $T_s[e]\ \alpha$ defines the cost of evaluating expression e in context α. It makes use of the context transformers $f_i^{\#1} \ldots f_i^{\#n_i}$ defined for each function f_i, which satisfy the required safety criterion. In particular it will be appropriate to set $f^{\#i}(\text{ABS}) = \text{ABS}$, since if the result of a function is not needed, then neither are its arguments.

The rule for function application tells us that the cost of evaluating a function application is the associated cost-function applied to the arguments (and the context) plus the sum of evaluating the arguments in the contexts prescribed by the context-transformers.

The conditional expression, like any other, has zero cost in the context ABS (guaranteed by the use of $\hookrightarrow_s$). Otherwise we sum the cost of evaluating the condition (which may or may not be evaluated, hence the safe-context for boolean values ID, c.f. [Wad88]) plus either the cost of the alternate or the consequent, depending on the *value* of the condition.

The cost of evaluating any expression in the context ABS is zero, so we have:

PROPOSITION 4.1 *For every expression e, $T_s[e]\text{ABS} = 0$*

PROOF   Straightforward structural induction in e □

A Small Example

Consider the program: hd(cons(not(true),exp)), where not(x) = if x then false else true and exp represents some arbitrary expression. The cost-function for not is

$$\text{cnot}(x,\alpha) = \alpha \hookrightarrow_s 1 + (\alpha \hookrightarrow_s 0 + \text{if } x \text{ then } 0 \text{ else } 0)$$
$$= \alpha \hookrightarrow_s 1$$

We assume a boolean-valued program is evaluated in the context STR, and so the cost program is defined by: $\mathcal{T}_s[\![\text{hd}(\text{cons}(\text{not}(\text{true}),exp))]\!]$ STR, which is, by definition

$$\text{cnot}(\text{true}, \text{cons}^{\#1}(\text{hd}^{\#1}(\text{STR}))) + 0 + \mathcal{T}_s[\![exp]\!] \text{ cons}^{\#2}(\text{hd}^{\#1}(\text{STR}))$$

The context transformers for the primitive functions satisfy

$$\text{hd}^{\#1}(\alpha) = \text{CONS } \alpha \text{ ABS} \quad \text{cons}^{\#1}(\text{CONS } \alpha \, \beta) = \alpha \quad \text{cons}^{\#2}(\text{CONS } \alpha \, \beta) = \beta$$

and so the cost is cnot(true , STR) + $\mathcal{T}_s[\![exp]\!]$ ABS = 1, for any expression exp.

4.2   Approximation and Safety

What are the precise properties of the cost programs? Here we consider the approximation and correctness properties of the "lazy" cost-program.

Approximation

The expression $\mathcal{T}_s[\![e]\!]\alpha$ gives an upper-bound estimate to the cost of lazy evaluation of e in context α. The cost expressions formed by $\mathcal{T}_s$ are a refinement of the call-by-value cost-expression (section 2) in which subexpressions whose values are not needed do not contribute to the cost equation. Since the safety condition for projections does not specify that we require the smallest possible projection, the context ABS may be approximated by any larger projection. This approximation is reflected in the cost-program as an over-estimation of cost. (In the extreme case the context transformers are such that the context ABS is *never* derived in the cost-program, and so the value of the cost program is the same as that given by the strict derivation of figure 1.) Note also that in computing the cost of a function application $f(e)$ in context α the cost due to e will only be counted *once*. The context of e, $f^{\#1}(\alpha)$ will be the net context of the possible contexts in which e is shared, and so the process properly models call-by-*need*.

Safety

Whenever the cost-program terminates yielding a value, that value is indeed an upper bound to the time cost of evaluating the program lazily. A problem with this analysis method is that there are cases when the cost-program does not yield a value when it should do so. Firstly the cost-program may not terminate even when the program does—non-terminating cost expressions can be thought of as "computing" the worst possible upper-bound to the cost. However the approximation in the cost-program can lead to arbitrary run-time errors (*i.e.* not just nontermination). In the next section we introduce *necessary-time* equations which allow us to place a lower-bound on the precise complexity and which have better termination properties.

5   Necessary-Time Analysis

So far we have outlined the use of contexts to derive equations which can give an upper-bound to the time-complexity of an expression in a particular context. As mentioned previously, this idea is based on [Wad88]. The cost-functions which compute this sufficient-complexity are only partially correct in the sense that if they compute a value, then that value is indeed an upper-bound to the time-cost of a program. There is potentially much more information about context using the projections described:

$$
\begin{aligned}
\mathcal{T}_n[const]\alpha &= \mathcal{T}_n[ident]\alpha = 0 \\
\mathcal{T}_n[\text{if } e_1 \text{ then } e_2 \text{ else } e_3]\alpha &= \alpha \hookrightarrow_n \mathcal{T}_n[e_1]\text{STR} + \text{if } e_1 \text{ then } \mathcal{T}_n[e_2]\alpha \text{ else } \mathcal{T}_n[e_3]\alpha \\
\mathcal{T}_n[p(e_1 \ldots e_n)]\alpha &= \mathcal{T}_n[e_1](p^{\#1}\alpha) + \cdots + \mathcal{T}_n[e_n](p^{\#n}\alpha) \\
\mathcal{T}_n[f_i(e_1 \ldots e_n)]\alpha &= cf_i(e_1 \ldots e_n, \alpha) + \mathcal{T}_n[e_1](f_i^{\#1}\alpha) + \cdots + \mathcal{T}_n[e_n](f_i^{\#n}\alpha)
\end{aligned}
$$

Figure 6: Definition of $\mathcal{T}_n$

strict contexts allow us to describe the amount of information which is *necessary* to compute a value. In this section we show how the use of this information can give us equations which describe a lower bound to the precise time-cost (the *necessary-time*) and which overcome the termination deficiencies of sufficient-time analysis. The key to sufficient-time analysis is the use of the context ABS to deduce that an expression will not be evaluated. The key to *necessary-time* is the operational interpretation of the *strict* projections.

5.1 Necessary-Cost Functions

In order to construct functions which compute the necessary-cost of evaluating a function in a particular context, we make the following operational connection between expressions which can be safely evaluated in a strict context, and their operational behaviour.

- If it is safe to evaluate an expression of the form $f(e_1, \ldots, e_n)$ in a strict context, then operationally, we know that this outermost application must be reduced.

Conversely, if an expression is evaluated in a non-strict context then that expression *may or may not* be reduced (only the context ABS allows us to conclude that it *definitely* will not).

Motivated by this observation, we now define the necessary-cost. The cost of evaluating an expression e in a context α is given by $\mathcal{T}_n[e]\alpha$ where $\mathcal{T}_n$ is once again a mapping defined over the syntax of expressions, and assuming some safe context transformers for the user-defined functions.

For each function definition of the form $f_i(x_1 \ldots x_{n_i}) = e_i$ we will define an associated necessary-cost-function $cf_i(x_1, \ldots, x_{n_i}, \alpha) = \alpha \hookrightarrow_n 1 + \mathcal{T}_n[e_i]\alpha$, where we use the notation $\alpha \hookrightarrow_n e$ to abbreviate necessary-cost e modulo context α:

$$
\alpha \hookrightarrow_n e = \begin{cases} e & \text{if } \alpha \sqsubseteq \text{STR} \\ 0 & \text{otherwise} \end{cases}
$$

The definition of $\mathcal{T}_n$ is given in figure 6. The rules are very similar to the definitions for $\mathcal{T}_s$ but we use $\hookrightarrow_n$ in place of $\hookrightarrow_s$. The only other difference is in the translation for the conditional expression.

PROPOSITION 5.1 *For all contexts α, if $\alpha \sqsubseteq \text{STR}$ then*

$$
\alpha(\text{if } u_1 \text{ then } u_2 \text{ else } u_3) = \alpha(\text{if } \text{STR}(u_1) \text{ then } u_2 \text{ else } u_3)
$$

PROOF Straightforward by cases according, $u_1 \sqsupseteq \bot$ and $u_1 \sqsubseteq \bot$. □

This tells us that in any strict context it is safe to evaluate the condition in the context STR, and thus gives us the appropriate context for determining the cost due to the condition in the conditional expression.

5.2 Example

As a example of necessary-time analysis we use insertion-sort (as in [Wad88]). The definitions are given in figure 7. The necessary-time equations constructed according to $\mathcal{T}_n$ are given in figure 8: In this example we wish to consider the cost of evaluating **min** in a strict context. We are not particularly concerned here with the techniques for deriving the safe projection transformers. We

```
insert(x,xs)  =  if null(xs) then cons(x,nil)
                 else if x < hd(xs) then cons(x,xs)
                     else cons(hd(xs),insert(x,tl(xs)))
sort(xs)      =  if null(xs) then nil
                 else insert(hd(xs),sort(tl(xs)))
min(xs)       =  hd(sort(xs))
```

Figure 7: Insertion Sort

```
cinsert(x,xs,α)  =  α ↪ₙ 1 + if null(xs) then 0
                               else if x < hd(xs) then 0
                                   else cinsert(x,tl(xs),cons#2(α))
csort(xs,α)      =  α ↪ₙ 1 + if null(xs) then 0
                               else cinsert(hd(xs),sort(tl(xs)),α) +
                                   csort(tl(xs),insert#2(α))
cmin(xs,α)       =  α ↪ₙ 1 + csort(xs,hd#1(α))
```

Figure 8: Necessary-Cost Functions

note however that the projection transformers needed in this example are members of the finite domains for lists (and integers) described in [WH87] for the purpose of strictness analysis, and as such can be determined mechanically by fixpoint iteration. The equations we require are:

$$hd^{\#1}(\text{STR}) = \text{CONS STR ABS}$$
$$cons^{\#2}(\text{CONS STR ABS}) = \text{ABS}$$
$$insert^{\#2}(\text{CONS STR ABS}) = \text{CONS STR ABS}$$

Now we examine the cost of min:

```
cmin(xs,STR)                =  STR ↪ₙ1 + csort(xs,hd#1(STR))
                            =  1 + csort(xs,CONS STR ABS)
csort(xs,CONS STR ABS)      =  1 + if null(xs) then 0
                                  else cinsert(hd(xs),sort(tl(xs)),CONS STR ABS) +
                                      csort(tl(xs),insert#2(CONS STR ABS))
                            =  1 + if null(xs) then 0
                                  else cinsert(hd(xs),sort(tl(xs)),CONS STR ABS) +
                                      csort(tl(xs),CONS STR ABS)
cinsert(y,ys,CONS STR ABS)  =  1 + if null(ys) then 0
                                  else if y < hd(ys) then 0
                                      else cinsert(y,tl(ys),cons#2(CONS STR ABS))
                            =  1 + if null(ys) then 0
                                  else if y < hd(ys) then 0
                                      else cinsert(y,tl(ys),ABS)
                            =  1
```

and so
```
csort(xs,CONS STR ABS)  =  1 + if null(xs) then 0
                              else 1 + csort(tl(xs),CONS STR ABS)
```

This simple recurrence has the exact solution 1 + 2*length(xs) and so

```
cmin(xs,STR) = 2 + 2*length(xs)
```

In this example the sufficient-time equations derive the same result, since the contexts (CONS STR ABS) and STR are very precise (*i.e.* they are the smallest safe projections). Therefore we can conclude that this is the *exact* time complexity.

5.3 Approximation and Safety

The expression $T_n[e]\alpha$ gives a lower-bound estimate to the cost of the lazy evaluation of e in context α. For a non-strict context α the lower bound must be zero since an expression in such a context *may or may not* need to be evaluated. Proposition 5.2 below establishes this property.

PROPOSITION 5.2 *For every expression* e, ABS $\sqsubseteq \alpha \sqsubseteq$ ID $\Rightarrow T_n[e]\alpha = 0$

PROOF   Structural induction in e.   □

Safety

The necessary-cost programs enjoy better termination properties than the sufficient-cost programs, being at least as well defined as the original program. We state this property in the following way:

THEOREM 5.3 *Given mutually recursive functions* $f_1,\ldots f_m$, *defined by equations:*

$$f_i(x_1,\ldots,x_{n_i}) = e_i,\ i = 1\ldots m$$

then for all objects $u_1,\ldots u_{n_i}$, *and contexts* α

$$\alpha(f_i(u_1,\ldots,u_{n_i})) \sqsupset \bot \Rightarrow cf_i(u_1,\ldots,u_{n_i},\alpha) \sqsupset \bot$$

where cf_i *is defined by the equation* $cf_i(x_1,\ldots,x_{n_i},\alpha) = \alpha \hookrightarrow_n T_n[e_i]\alpha$

PROOF   Omitted—a fixed point induction over the functions and cost-functions simultaneously. □

6   Higher-Order Lazy Time-Analysis

In this section we develop an extension to the techniques for lazy time analysis to incorporate higher-order functions. This is achieved by adaptation of the higher-order analysis given in section 2, illustrated with a conservative extension to the context information available for first-order functions.

6.1   Context Information

The extension of lazy-time analysis to higher-order functions also needs context information. Here we immediately run into some problems. The techniques which we have assumed so far, concerning the form and derivation of context transformers, cannot be directly extended to higher-order functions. Consider, for example, an instance of the apply function, apply f x, in some context α. The problem here is that there is no useful context information that can be propagated to x (by any context function apply#²) which is *independent* of the function f.

Wray's thesis [Wra86] shows how to handle a "second order" language (for strictness analysis) by additional parameterization of the context transformers to include the context transformers for functional arguments. An approach to fully higher-order backwards analysis is outlined in [Hug87]. This is based on a mixture of abstract interpretation (forwards analysis) and first-order backwards analysis. For the purposes of this section it will not be necessary to introduce these devices. Instead we will demonstrate our methods with a sufficient-time analysis using a very simple extension of the context information to higher-order functions. It is expected that the information provided by a full development of context analysis for higher-order functions could be accommodated in the time analysis we present here.

The language we use here is defined by the same grammar as that of the higher-order language in section 2.

6.2 The Projection Transformers

The method we shall describe for constructing the time equations will require the use of the same style of projection transformers that are used for the first-order analysis—for each function definition f_i we will require projection transformers $f_i^{\#k}$ such that $f_i^k \alpha \Rightarrow (f_i^{\#k} \alpha)$.

Since we are working with a higher-order language, we may expect expressions of the form

$$f_i \, e_1 \ldots e_{n_i} e_{n_i+1} \ldots e_m$$

Here the contexts propagated to expressions $e_1 \ldots e_{n_i}$ are determined by the projection transformers of f_i. For a conservative estimate we know it is safe to propagate the context ID to the expressions $e_{n_i+1} \ldots e_m$. In fact, the analysis we present will be able to use more precise information in this instance.

Objects of function type will also require projections to describe the context in which they are needed. A projection of a function gives a function which has less defined results on some of its arguments. For the purpose of time analysis it is sufficient to use the four-point context domain to describe the amount of evaluation of a functional argument (i.e. all or nothing). In an expression of the form $exp \, e$ in a context α, we can safely set the context for exp to be a mapping of α into the four-point domain for functions. For convenience we define a functional $\Diamond$ to perform this task:

$$\Diamond \alpha = \begin{cases} \text{FAIL} & \text{if } \alpha = \text{FAIL} \\ \text{ABS} & \text{if } \alpha = \text{ABS} \\ \text{STR} & \text{if FAIL} \sqsubset \alpha \sqsubseteq \text{STR} \\ \text{ID} & \text{if ABS} \sqsubset \alpha \sqsubseteq \text{ID} \end{cases}$$

6.3 Accumulating Cost-Functions

As in the strict higher-order language we will define for each function in the language a cost function, constructed via two syntactic maps. The first, $\mathcal{V}_L$, plays the same rôle as that of $\mathcal{V}$ in the higher-order strict language — it constructs cost-closures and makes their application explicit via an apply function $\mathbf{@}_L$. The second, $\mathcal{T}_L$, is used to define the cost-expressions. In the following we use the term cost-expression to refer to objects of type context $\to$ cost. The definitions of $\mathcal{V}_L$ and $\mathcal{T}_L$ are given in figures 9 and 10. These definitions will be explained in the following sections.

User-defined functions

For each function defined $f_i \, x_1 \ldots x_{n_i} = e_i$ we define a sufficient-cost function to be

$$cf_i \, (x_1, c_1) \ldots (x_{n_i}, c_{n_i}) \, \alpha = \alpha \hookrightarrow_s 1 + \mathcal{T}_L \circ \mathcal{V}_L [\![e_i]\!] \, \alpha + c_1(f_i^{\#1} \alpha) + \ldots + c_{n_i}(f_i^{\#n_i} \alpha)$$

In addition to the context-transformers, the cost functions require modified versions of functions themselves: $f_i' \, x_1 \ldots x_{n_i} = \mathcal{V}_L [\![e_i]\!]$

Application and it's Cost

The cost-functions defined above now have additional parameterisation in the form of cost-expressions paired with each argument. We will explain this choice by considering the cost associated with function application $exp \, e$.

In the higher-order strict language, application is first translated to $exp' \, \mathbf{@} \, e'$ (were exp' is defined according to $\mathcal{V}$) and the cost of evaluation is $\mathcal{T}[\![exp']\!] + \mathcal{T}[\![e']\!] + exp' \, c\mathbf{@} \, e'$. Suppose we begin by re-using $\mathcal{V}$, and we attempt to define (with respect to some context β) a lazy version of $\mathcal{T}, \mathcal{T}_L$.

In the rule for $\mathcal{T}_L[\![exp' \; @ \; e']\!] \; \beta$ we must propagate the context β to the appropriate cost-expressions. We can map β into a four-point domain (overloading $\Diamond$) to get a safe context for the function exp'. We do not know the appropriate context for e', but we can always safely use the context ID and set

$$\mathcal{T}_L[\![exp' \; @ \; e']\!]\beta = \mathcal{T}_L[\![exp']\!]\Diamond\beta + \mathcal{T}_L[\![e']\!]\text{ID} + (exp' \; c@ \; e') \; \beta$$

Two major problems make this rule unsatisfactory.

1. No useful context information is propagated to e'. The information we have available is the projection transformers, but this is not used since we do not in general know which projection transformer is appropriate.

2. If we have a partial application, for example if exp is cons (exp' is (cons,ccons,2)) then e may not be evaluated at all.

We solve both of these problems by passing both the argument, *and* the cost-expression to the cost function. It is then the cost function's task to apply the appropriate context (which is determined by the projection transformers of the function) to these cost expressions—see the cost-function scheme above. We introduce new versions of @ and c@ to accommodate these requirements.

Cost-closures and the apply function

For these reasons we need to define a new version of $\mathcal{V}$ and a different version of the function @. The "lazy" version of $\mathcal{V}$, $\mathcal{V}_L$ is defined in figure 9. Because, in the rule for application, the cost-closure $\mathcal{V}_L[\![exp]\!]$ is applied to the cost-expression $\mathcal{T}_L[\![e]\!]$, we need a new version of the @ function which satisfies:

$$(f, cf, a) \; @_L \; \langle e, ce \rangle = \begin{cases} f \; e & \text{if } a = 1 \\ (f \; e, cf \; \langle e, ce \rangle, a - 1) & \text{otherwise} \end{cases}$$

Note that cost-closures retain the same *function–costfunction–arity* structure.

Defining the cost-expressions

Figure 10 also defines cost-expressions via a mapping $\mathcal{T}_L$. A significant difference here is that we do not make the definition with respect to a particular context. This is because we wish to pass cost-expressions (functions *context* $\rightarrow$ *cost*) to the cost-functions without applying them to a particular context.

To define $\mathcal{T}_L$ we define a couple of useful functions:

- Addition of cost expressions: we use a specialised addition operator, $\diamond+$, which (for the left operand) maps the context into the four-point projection domain of the left operand: $(ce_1 \; \diamond+ \; ce_2) \; \alpha = (ce_1(\Diamond\alpha)) + (ce_2 \; \alpha)$. By allowing $\Diamond$ to be polymorphic, $\diamond+$ is associative.

- The null cost-expression: the function $\overline{0}$ gives zero-cost in any context, so $\overline{0} \; \alpha = 0$ for any α.

Consider the rule for application: $\mathcal{T}_L[\![exp' \; @_L \; (e', ce')]\!] = \mathcal{T}_L[\![exp']\!] \; \diamond+ \; (exp' \; c@_L \; (e', ce'))$

If we apply this expression to a context β, we get $\mathcal{T}_L[\![exp']\!] \; \Diamond\beta + (exp' \; c@_L \; (e', ce')) \; \beta$. To ensure $c@_L$ gives us a cost expression, only a small change is needed in the definition of c@

$$(f, cf, n) \; c@_L \; \langle e, ce \rangle = \begin{cases} cf \; \langle e, ce \rangle & \text{if } n = 1 \\ \overline{0} & \text{otherwise} \end{cases}$$

Primitive functions

The cost-function associated with a primitive function p_i of arity m_i is

$$cp_i \; (x_1, c_1) \ldots (x_{m_i}, c_{m_i}) \; \alpha = c_1(p_i \; {}^{\#1}\alpha) + \ldots + c_{m_i}(p_i \; {}^{\#m_i}\alpha)$$

$$\mathcal{V}_L[exp\ e] = \mathcal{V}_L[exp]\ \texttt{@}_L\ \langle \mathcal{V}_L[e],\mathcal{T}_L\circ\mathcal{V}_L[e]\rangle$$
$$\mathcal{V}_L[\text{if } e_1 \text{ then } e_2 \text{ else } e_3] = \text{if } \mathcal{V}_L[e_1] \text{ then } \mathcal{V}_L[e_2] \text{ else } \mathcal{V}_L[e_3]$$
$$\mathcal{V}_L[(exp)] = (\mathcal{V}_L[exp])$$
$$\mathcal{V}_L[f_i] = (f_i'\ ,\ cf_i\ ,\ n_i\ )\quad \mathcal{V}_L[p_i] = (p_i\ ,\ cp_i\ ,\ m_i\ )$$
$$\mathcal{V}_L[const] = const \quad \mathcal{V}_L[ident] = ident$$

Figure 9: The function modification map

$$\mathcal{T}_L[exp'\ \texttt{@}_L\ \langle e',ce'\rangle] = \mathcal{T}_L[exp'] \mathbin{\texttt{\o+}} (exp'\ c\texttt{@}_L\ \langle e',ce'\rangle)$$
$$\mathcal{T}_L[\text{if } e_1' \text{ then } e_2' \text{ else } e_3'] = \mathcal{T}_L[e_1'] \mathbin{\texttt{\o+}} \text{if } e_1' \text{ then } \mathcal{T}_L[e_2'] \text{else } \mathcal{T}_L[e_3']$$
$$\mathcal{T}_L[(exp')] = (\mathcal{T}_L[exp'])$$
$$\mathcal{T}_L[(p_i\ ,\ cp_i\ ,\ m_i\ )] = \mathcal{T}_L[(f_i\ ,\ cf_i\ ,\ n_i\ )] = \mathcal{T}_L[const] = \mathcal{T}_L[ident] = \overline{0}$$

Figure 10: The cost-function construction map

Applying the above schemes in the construction of time-equations requires that we remove (partially evaluate) unnecessary instances of $\texttt{@}_L$, and $c\texttt{@}_L$, as we outlined in section 2.2. In addition we need to specialise functions to remove unnecessary parameters—this is because of the additional parameterisation involved in both modified functions, and cost-functions. The (somewhat lengthy) examples have been omitted, but it is worth noting that the process could benefit from some simple mechanical support.

7 Conclusions

We have presented a method of analysing the time complexity of a lazy higher-order functional language. The techniques for a strict higher-order language are more fully developed in [San88]. We have extended of these ideas to give a treatment of lazy higher-order languages, based upon [Wad88]: projections are used to characterise the context in which an expression is evaluated, and cost-equations are parameterised on this context-description. We have introduced two types of time-equation: *sufficient-time* equations (corresponding to the equations in [Wad88]), and *necessary-time* equations, which together provide bounds on the exact time-complexity.

7.1 Related Work

A (non-compositional) means of analysing a call-by-name language is considered in [LeM88]. Le Métayer's solution involves transforming a call-by-name program into a strongly equivalent one with call-by-value semantics. The call-by-value program can be analysed using "strict" techniques (such as those presented in section 2). The translation, however, makes the program significantly more complex, and it not clear that the translation preserves the number of steps that are being counted in the analysis.

Bjerner's time analysis for programs in the language of Martin-Löf type-theory [Bje89] has relevance to the analysis of first-order lazy functional languages, and provided inspiration for Wadler's work. His operational model of contexts, *evaluation degrees* could form an alternative basis for the work presented here. More recently, Bjerner and Holmström [BH89] have adapted the ideas in [Bje89] to give a calculus for the time analysis of a first-order functional language. The equations used to describe context are *precise*, thus specifying an *exact* time-analysis. The problem here is that the equations cannot be solved mechanically. The main correctness theorem developed (independently) in [BH89] (apart from the correctness of the context equations) corresponds very closely to theorem 5.3—if we view their model of context (called "demands") as projections, we get a class of projections for which necessary and sufficient times will always be equal. Equations for this class of "exact" projections can be derived with a straightforward modification of the projection equations in [WH87].

7.2 Further Work

Higher-Order Context Information

The use of first-order context analysis in the analysis of a higher-order language means that, even though cost-expressions are passed as arguments so they are applied to the appropriate context, there are many cases where the contexts derived for higher-order functions are not sufficiently precise. Consider the following function definition: For satisfiable contexts α, the apply function (apply f x = f x) has the following projection transformers: $\text{apply}^{\#1}\alpha = \Diamond\alpha$, and $\text{apply}^{\#2}\alpha = \text{ID}$.

Without knowing about the context of the function apply, the context for x is approximated by the least informative context ID.

The sufficient-time equation constructed with these projection transformers is

$$\text{capply } \langle f,fc \rangle \ \langle x,xc \rangle \ \alpha \ = \ \alpha \hookrightarrow, \ 1 + fc(\Diamond\alpha) + xc \ \text{ID} + (f \ c@ \ \langle x,\bar{0} \rangle) \ \alpha$$

The lack of accurate projection transformers means that the cost-expression xc is applied to the imprecise context ID—it is not difficult to construct examples where this gives an unsatisfactory time analysis. Context-analyses for higher-order languages are not well-developed. As mentioned before, Wray's strictness analysis handles "second order" functions—projection equations can be extended to handle such functions, and the resulting context descriptions can be used by cost-functions presented here. Fully higher-order analyses still present problems for the construction of both approximate and precise context equations.

An alternative solution to this problem further utilises the technique of "passing" cost-expressions. The expression bound to x in the function apply above is evaluated in the context of the function bound to f, so we can pass the cost expression on to the cost function associated with f as follows:

$$\text{capply } \langle f,fc \rangle \ \langle x,xc \rangle \ \alpha \ = \ \alpha \hookrightarrow, \ 1 + fc(\Diamond\alpha) + (f \ c@ \ \langle x,xc \rangle) \ \alpha$$

To generalise this technique we must check that any parameter whose cost-expression we wish to propagate is not shared (i.e. it is not required in more than one context). For a sufficient-time analysis we could propagate to all contexts, while in a necessary-time analysis we could choose to propagate the cost expression to a single context. In addition we need to determine when the propagation is necessary, since unnecessary propagation (i.e. when the context information is sufficiently precise) decreases the compositionality of cost-functions with no additional benefit.

Acknowledgements

Thanks to Jesper Andersen, Chris Hankin, Sebastian Hunt and Daniel Le Métayer for their useful suggestions relating to earlier drafts of this paper.

References

[AH87]   S. Abramsky and C.L. Hankin, editors. *Abstract Interpretation of Declarative Languages*. Ellis Horwood, 1987.

[BH89]   B. Bjerner and S. Holmström. A compositional approach to time analysis of first order lazy functional programs. In *Functional Programming Languages and computer architecture, conference proceedings*. ACM press, 1989.

[Bje89] B. Bjerner. *Time Complexity of Programs in Type Theory*. PhD thesis, Chalmers University of Technology, 1989.

[Bur90] G.L. Burn. A relationship between abstract interpretation and projection analysis (extended abstract). In *17th ACM Symposium on Principals of Programming Languages*, January 1990.

[DW89] K. Davis and P. Wadler. Backwards strictness analysis: Proved and improved. In *Proceedings of Glasgow Workshop on Functional Programming*, August 1989.

[Fla85] P. Flajolet. Mathematical methods in the analysis of algorithms and data structures. Report 400, INRIA, Le Chesnay, France, May 1985.

[HC88] T. Hickey and J. Cohen. Automating program analysis. *J. ACM*, 35:185–220, January 1988.

[Hug87] R. J. M. Hughes. Backwards analysis of functional programs. DoC Research Report CSC/87/R3, University of Glasgow, March 1987.

[LeM85] D. LeMétayer. Mechanical analysis of program complexity. In *ACM SIGPLAN 85 Symposium*, July 1985.

[LeM88] D. LeMétayer. Analysis of functional programs by program transformation. In *Second France–Japan Artificial Intelligence and Computer Science Symposium*. North–Holland, 1988.

[Ros89] M. Rosendahl. Automatic complexity analysis. In *Functional Programming Languages and computer architecture, conference proceedings*. ACM press, 1989.

[San88] D. Sands. Complexity analysis for a higher order language. Technical Report DOC 88/14, Imperial College, October 1988.

[Wad88] P. Wadler. Strictness analysis aids time analysis. In *15th ACM Symposium on Principals of Programming Languages*, January 1988.

[Weg75] B. Wegbreit. Mechanical program analysis. *C.ACM*, 18:528–539, September 1975.

[WH87] P. Wadler and R. J. M. Hughes. Projections for strictness analysis. In *1987 Conference on Functional Programming and Computer Architecture*, Portland, Oregon, September 1987.

[Wra86] S. C. Wray. Programming techniques for functional languages. Technical Report 92, University of Cambridge Computer Laboratory, June 1986.

On the Weak Adequacy
of Branching-Time Temporal Logic

Ph. Schnoebelen and S. Pinchinat*

Laboratoire d'Informatique Fondamentale
et d'Intelligence Artificielle,
Institut Imag - CNRS,
Grenoble - FRANCE

Abstract

We study the adequacy of branching-time temporal logic w.r.t. bisimulation semantics in the framework of non-deterministic programs *without the finitely-branching restriction*. The process equivalence generated by branching-time logic is compared with bisimulation and with two observational equivalences. It is found at best weakly adequate. This further illustrates the strength of the finitely-branching restriction. However, we argue that in connection with branching time temporal logic, one has no better choice than bisimulation as a semantic equivalence: in particular, the equivalence generated by temporal logic is not a congruence w.r.t. usual process operators.

Introduction

When using temporal logic to reason about parallel or non-deterministic programs, a general prerequisite is to investigate the *adequacy* of the logic with the semantics one considers for its (parallel) programs. Basically, the logic should not be able to distinguish two programs that we want to consider as semantically equivalent, or more formally:

$$P \simeq P' \Rightarrow \text{ for all } f \ (P \models f \text{ iff } P' \models f)$$

using $\simeq$ to denote semantic equivalence and writing $P \models f$ when program P satisfies formula f. Let us write $Th(P)$ for $\{f \mid P \models f\}$, so that the previous requirement is written:

$$P \simeq P' \Rightarrow Th(P) = Th(P') \qquad (1)$$

If this requirement is not met, one cannot meaningfully consider the logic as "speaking about" semantic objects. A stronger requirement is

$$P \simeq P' \Leftrightarrow Th(P) = Th(P') \qquad (2)$$

which holds if the logic is sufficiently powerful to distinguish any two semantically different programs (and only these). We say that the logic is adequate when (2) holds, and weakly

*LIFIA-IMAG, 46 Av. Félix Viallet, 38031 GRENOBLE Cedex, FRANCE. E-mail:{phs,sp}@lifia.imag.fr

adequate when we only have (1).

Lamport and Pnueli initiated with [Pnu77,Lam80] the use of temporal logic for reasoning about parallel or non-deterministic programs. [Lam80] also initiated the controversy about branching-time vs. linear-time temporal logic. This debate mainly focused on the different expressiveness of the proposed logics and culminated with the introduction of CTL^* [EH83], a logic including both branching-time and linear-time constructs, and subsuming several other proposals.

The adequacy of a temporal logic was first investigated by Hennessy and Milner [HM85] who studied bisimulation (from [Par81]) as a semantic equivalence for processes (parallel programs). They proved that bisimulation was exactly characterized by a very simple modal language, the so-called Hennessy-Milner Logic: two processes are bisimilar iff they cannot be distinguished by HML temporal formulas. This was a strong point in favor of bisimulation as a semantic equivalence (see also [Abr87,BK89]).

The adequacy result of [HM85] is true of many branching-time temporal logics. However, it only applies to *finitely-branching* systems (i.e. systems where in any given state, there is only a finite number of possible choices), hereafter abbreviated as f.b. systems. In the general case of not necessarily f.b. systems, the proof of [HM85] only yields weak adequacy. However, several parallel languages do not want to restrict themselves to f.b. systems e.g. because these are not closed under some natural operations (communication of values, ...) [BK89,GR83]. We have that same problem with our own FP2 language [SJ89], which led us to investigate the adequacy of the CTL temporal logic (from [CE81]) w.r.t. bisimulation semantics in non-f.b. systems. The technical literature rarely considers non-f.b. systems: we only found [BR83] as directly addressing our problem. Other works (e.g. [HS85]) only mention adequacy results for logics that admit infinite (not necessarily countable !) conjunctions.

In this paper, we show that branching-time temporal logic is only weakly adequate w.r.t. bisimulation (written $\leftrightarrow$):

$$P \leftrightarrow P' \overset{\nLeftarrow}{\Rightarrow} Th(P) = Th(P') \tag{3}$$

Trying to find a different semantics w.r.t. which temporal logic could be adequate, we investigate Milner's original strong observational equivalence (written $\equiv$). We show that it is too broad:

$$P \equiv P' \overset{\Leftarrow}{\nRightarrow} Th(P) = Th(P') \tag{4}$$

There remains one natural intermediate semantic equivalence, adapted from $\equiv$ and written $\approx$, that fits between $\leftrightarrow$ and $\equiv$. We show:

$$P \approx P' \overset{\nLeftarrow}{\nRightarrow} Th(P) = Th(P') \tag{5}$$

Seeing that CTL equivalence fails to match any of three natural semantic equivalences, a question one may ask is "why not consider it as our semantic equivalence ?". We investigated this question in [Sch89] where we show that CTL equivalence does not yield a congruence w.r.t. parallel composition (but it is a congruence w.r.t. several other process operations) so that we end up arguing that if one wants to use branching-time temporal logic without the f.b. restriction, one should stick with bisimulation semantics and be content with weak adequacy. Note also that with the f.b. restriction, everything collapses into:

$$P \leftrightarrow P' \Leftrightarrow P \equiv P' \Leftrightarrow P \approx P' \Leftrightarrow Th(P) = Th(P')$$

In this paper we used CTL for its conceptual simplicity and widespread use but the aforementioned results are general and, modulo some minor details, they apply equally well to other (branching-time) logics (we deal with CTL^* in Appendix A). By contrast, [BR83] only considered logics unable to express eventual termination. As a consequence, (5) was specialized into

$$P \approx P' \overset{\not\Leftarrow}{\Rightarrow} Th(P) = Th(P')$$

As another point of comparison with [BR83], we provide simpler counter-examples based on the ordinal processes of Klop.

In section 1, we recall the basic notions and results we shall use: graphs, bisimulation, the CTL temporal logic and its semantics. Then, the following sections compare CTL with all three equivalences, in turn. The main innovations of the paper are Propositions 3 and 4, relying on the counter-examples developed for Lemmas 2 and 3. The picture is completed with Propositions 1 and 2. Finally, an appendix contains results that are mentioned in the text, but that are out of the precise scope of the paper.

1 Preliminaries

Definition 1 (Graph) *A (directed) graph is a pair $P = (Q, \rightarrow)$ where Q is any set of states, with typical element q, and $\rightarrow \subseteq Q \times Q$ is any transition relation.*

For any $k \in \mathbf{N}$, we write $\overset{k}{\rightarrow}$ for the k-fold composition of $\rightarrow$: $\overset{k}{\rightarrow} = \rightarrow \circ \cdots \circ \rightarrow$ (k-times) and $\overset{0}{\rightarrow} = Id_Q$. We write $q \rightarrow q'$ when $(q, q') \in \rightarrow$ and say that q' is a *successor* of q. A *terminal state* is a state with no successors.

A *path* is a maximal sequence $q_0 \rightarrow q_1 \rightarrow q_2 \rightarrow \cdots$ of states of Q, it may be finite (and ending with a terminal state) or infinite. Given a path $\sigma = q_0 \rightarrow q_1 \rightarrow q_2 \rightarrow \cdots$, we write $|\sigma|$ for the length (number of steps) of σ: it may be infinite, it may also be 0 if q_0 is terminal. When $|\sigma| \geq i$, we write $\sigma(i)$ for the state q_i and σ^i for the suffix path $q_i \rightarrow q_{i+1} \rightarrow \cdots$ We write $\Sigma(q) = \{\sigma, \pi, \ldots\}$ for the set of all paths starting from q and let Σ denote $\bigcup_{q \in Q} \Sigma(q)$.

In the following, only states from a same graph will be compared. This is no loss of generality as any state can be seen as the rooted directed connected sub-graph it canonically induces. Dually, comparing two (rooted) graphs must be understood as comparing their roots in some union graph. In this paper graph nodes, rooted graphs and processes are the same concepts.

We say that $\rightarrow$ is *finitely branching* (or image-finite, or f.b.) if for any $q \in Q$, the set $\{q' \in Q \mid q \rightarrow q'\}$ is finite. *We explicitly do not restrict ourselves to f.b. graphs.*

1.1 Three process equivalences

Given $P = (Q, \rightarrow)$, we define three equivalence relations over Q:

Definition 2 (Bisimulation) $\underline{\leftrightarrow} \subseteq Q \times Q$ *is the largest relation over Q s.t. $q_1 \underline{\leftrightarrow} q_2$ iff:*

- $\forall q_1' \in Q$, *if* $q_1 \rightarrow q_1'$ *then* $\exists q_2' \in Q$ *s.t.* $q_2 \rightarrow q_2'$ *and* $q_1' \underline{\leftrightarrow} q_2'$,

- *and reciprocally,* $\forall q_2' \in Q$, *if* $q_2 \rightarrow q_2'$ *then* $\exists q_1' \in Q$ *s.t.* $q_1 \rightarrow q_1'$ *and* $q_1' \underline{\leftrightarrow} q_2'$.

Definition 3 (Projective equivalences) *We define $q_1 \equiv q_2$ iff $q_1 \equiv_n q_2$ for all $n \in \mathbf{N}$, where $\equiv_n$ is given inductively by:*

- $q_1 \equiv_0 q_2$ *always,*

- $q_1 \equiv_{n+1} q_2$ *iff*

  − $\forall q_1' \in Q$, *if* $q_1 \rightarrow q_1'$ *then* $\exists q_2' \in Q$ *s.t.* $q_2 \rightarrow q_2'$ *and* $q_1' \equiv_n q_2'$,
  − *and reciprocally.*

Similarly, we define $q_1 \approx q_2$ iff $q_1 \approx_n q_2$ for all $n \in \mathbf{N}$, where $\approx_n$ is given inductively by:

- $q_1 \approx_0 q_2$ *always,*

- $q_1 \approx_{n+1} q_2$ *iff*

  − $\forall k \in \mathbf{N}$, $\forall q_1' \in Q$, *if* $q_1 \overset{k}{\rightarrow} q_1'$ *then* $\exists q_2' \in Q$ *s.t.* $q_2 \overset{k}{\rightarrow} q_2'$ *and* $q_1' \approx_n q_2'$,
  − *and reciprocally.*

All three relations are clearly equivalence relations. The name "projective equivalence" comes from [BK87] where, writing $(x)_n$ for the truncation of x at depth n, $x \equiv_n y$ is defined as $(x)_n \underline{\leftrightarrow} (y)_n$.

Another reading of the previous definitions involves a mapping $\mathcal{F}$ over the complete lattice $2^{Q \times Q}$ of relations over Q [Mil88]. For $R \subseteq Q \times Q$, $\mathcal{F}(R)$ is defined by $q_1 \mathcal{F}(R) q_2$ iff $q_1 \rightarrow q_1'$ implies that there exists $q_2 \rightarrow q_2'$ s.t. $q_1' R q_2'$, and reciprocally. $\mathcal{F}$ is monotonic and satisfies $Id_Q \subseteq \mathcal{F}(Id_Q)$. Clearly $\equiv$ is defined as $\bigcap_{m \in \mathbf{N}} \mathcal{F}^n(Q \times Q)$. Similarly, $\approx$ is defined as $\bigcap_{m \in \mathbf{N}} \mathcal{G}^n(Q \times Q)$ for some monotonic $\mathcal{G}$. As $\mathcal{G}(R) \subseteq \mathcal{F}(R)$ for any $R \subseteq Q \times Q$, we get $\approx \subseteq \equiv$. Furthermore, $\underline{\leftrightarrow}$ is defined as the largest fixpoint of $\mathcal{F}$ (or, equivalently, of $\mathcal{G}$). Monotonicity of $\mathcal{F}$ (and of $\mathcal{G}$) entails that $\underline{\leftrightarrow}$ is correctly defined (it is $\bigcup \{R \mid R \subseteq \mathcal{F}(R)\}$) and that $\underline{\leftrightarrow} \subseteq \equiv$ (and $\underline{\leftrightarrow} \subseteq \approx$). It is well-known that if $\rightarrow$ is f.b., $\mathcal{F}$ is anticontinuous, which implies that $\bigcap_{m \in \mathbf{N}} \mathcal{F}^n(Q \times Q)$ is the largest fixpoint of $\mathcal{F}$, i.e. $\equiv = \approx = \underline{\leftrightarrow}$ for f.b. graphs. However, in general, the inclusions are strict (this is already known, but our comparison with CTL will yield another proof).

We extend the notion of bisimulation to paths: $\sigma \underline{\leftrightarrow} \pi$ iff $\sigma(i) \underline{\leftrightarrow} \pi(i)$ for every i. Then, maximality of paths implies that σ and π have same length. Also, this implies that $\sigma^i \underline{\leftrightarrow} \pi^i$ for any i. Note that if $q \underline{\leftrightarrow} q'$ and if $\sigma \in \Sigma(q)$, we can build $\sigma' \in \Sigma(q')$ s.t. $\sigma \underline{\leftrightarrow} \sigma'$.

1.2 Ordinal processes

In several cases, we shall use the ordinal processes of [Klo88], or a variant of them. We recall here their definition and main properties:

Definition 4 (Ordinal processes) *Given any ordinal* λ, *the ordinal process* P_λ *is the graph* $(\lambda, >)$.

Thus, in P_λ we have $\alpha \to \beta$ iff $\beta < \alpha < \lambda$. A basic property is that P_λ has no infinite paths and that $\to$ is transitive. P_λ is non-f.b. as soon as $\lambda > \omega$. Clearly, over P_λ, $\leftrightarrow$ is reduced to equality. Indeed, suppose $\alpha_0 \leftrightarrow \alpha_1$ with $\alpha_1 < \alpha_0 < \lambda$. Then $\alpha_0 \to \alpha_1$, and $\alpha_0 \leftrightarrow \alpha_1$ implies that there exists $\alpha_1 \to \alpha_2$ s.t. $\alpha_1 \leftrightarrow \alpha_2$. Carrying on, we shall build an infinite path $\alpha_0 \to \alpha_1 \to \alpha_2 \to \cdots$ contradicting the well-foundedness of $>$ over ordinals.

Conceptually, all states of an ordinal process are different (w.r.t. bisimilarity). Now, given an equivalence $\sim$ over λ, we say that $\sim$ *distinguishes up to* $\beta \leq \lambda$ iff, for any $\alpha_1, \alpha_2 < \beta$, $\alpha_1 \sim \alpha_2$ implies $\alpha_1 = \alpha_2$. Clearly, $\equiv_n$ distinguishes up to n, so that $\equiv$ distinguishes up to ω. Similarly, it is easy to prove (see Lemma 3 for a similar proof) that $\approx_n$ distinguishes up to $\omega.n$, so that $\approx$ distinguishes up to ω^2. (In this terminology, $\leftrightarrow$ distinguishes up to any λ).

1.3 The CTL temporal logic

Definition 5 (Syntax of CTL)

$$(CTL \ni) \; f, g ::= \top \mid f \wedge g \mid \neg f \mid \mathbf{EX} f \mid \mathbf{E} f \mathbf{U} g \mid \mathbf{A} f \mathbf{U} g$$

Other logical connectives are definable in terms of $\top, \wedge, \neg$ and $\mathbf{EX}$: $\bot$ is $\neg \top$, $f \vee g$ is $\neg(\neg f \wedge \neg g)$, and $\mathbf{AX} f$ is $\neg \mathbf{EX} \neg f$.

CTL formulas denote properties of states in a graph: given a graph $P = (Q, \to)$, a state $q \in Q$ and some formula $f \in CTL$, we write $q \models_P f$ to denote that, in graph P, f holds in q or that q satisfies f. Similarly $q \not\models_P f$ means that f does not hold in q. We always drop the P subscript when it is clear from the context.

We define $\models \subseteq Q \times CTL$ in the standard way, by induction over the structure of formulas:

Definition 6 (Semantics of CTL) *For all* $q, q_0 \in Q$ *and* $f, g \in CTL$:

- $q \models \top$, $q \models f \wedge g$ *and* $q \models \neg f$ *have their obvious definitions.*

- $q \models \mathbf{EX} f$ *iff there exists* $q \to q'$ *s.t.* $q' \models f$.

- $q_0 \models \mathbf{E} f \mathbf{U} g$ *iff there exists a path* $q_0 \to q_1 \to q_2 \to \cdots$ *and some* $n \in \mathbf{N}$ *s.t.* $q_n \models g$ *and* $q_i \models f$ *for all* $i < n$.

- $q_0 \models \mathbf{A} f \mathbf{U} g$ *iff for all paths* $q_0 \to q_1 \to q_2 \to \cdots \in \Sigma(q_0)$ *there is some* $n \in \mathbf{N}$ *s.t.* $q_n \models g$ *and* $q_i \models f$ *for all* $i < n$.

CTL is paradigmatic in the field of branching-time temporal logic because it admits efficient model checking algorithms while remaining very expressive (see [ES89] for a survey). $\mathbf{EX} f$ can be read as "there exists a next state satisfying f", $\mathbf{E}\, f \,\mathbf{U}\, g$ as "there exists a path (starting from here) satisfying f all along until g is eventually satisfied", and $\mathbf{A}\, f \,\mathbf{U}\, g$ as "all paths (starting from here) satisfy f all along until g is eventually satisfied".

Given $(Q, \to)$ and $q \in Q$, we write $Th(q)$ for $\{f \in CTL \mid q \models f\}$ and define $\overset{CTL}{\sim} \subseteq Q \times Q$ by:

$$q \overset{CTL}{\sim} q' \text{ iff } Th(q) = Th(q')$$

(that is, iff q and q' are elementarily equivalent in model-theoretic terminology). This is clearly an equivalence relation. A similar construction applies to any set of formulas, and we shall freely write $q \overset{F}{\sim} q'$ for any set $F \subseteq CTL$. Clearly, $F \subseteq CTL$ implies $\overset{CTL}{\sim} \subseteq \overset{F}{\sim}$.

2 Comparing CTL and $\leftrightarrow$

Proposition 1 *For any graph $(Q, \to)$, and states $q, q' \in Q$:*

$$q \leftrightarrow q' \Rightarrow q \overset{CTL}{\sim} q'$$

This is well-known. One proves that $q \leftrightarrow q'$ implies ($q \models f$ iff $q' \models f$) by induction over the structure of f. As an example let us consider the case where f is $\mathbf{A}\, g_1 \,\mathbf{U}\, g_2$. Assume that $q \not\models f$. Then there is a path $\sigma \in \Sigma(q)$ s.t. no $\sigma(i)$ satisfy g_2, or such that $\sigma(n) \not\models g_1$ for some n with $\sigma(i) \not\models g_2$ for all $i \leq n$. By bisimilarity, we can build a path $\sigma' \in \Sigma(q')$ s.t. $\sigma \leftrightarrow \sigma'$. Then for any i, $\sigma(i) \leftrightarrow \sigma'(i)$, which implies (by ind. hyp.) that $\sigma'(i) \models g_1$ iff $\sigma(i) \models g_1$ (and similarly for g_2). Finally, σ' is such that $q' \not\models f$. All other possible constructions for f are dealt with in the same way.

Of course, the reverse implication does not hold, as a corollary of Proposition 3.

3 Comparing CTL and $\equiv$

A concept we shall need now and later is the *modal height* (w.r.t. $\mathbf{EX}$) of a formula. Formally, we define $d : CTL \to \mathbf{N}$ by:

$$
\begin{aligned}
d(\top) &= 0 & d(\mathbf{EX}\, f) &= d(f) + 1 \\
d(f \wedge g) &= max(d(f), d(g)) & d(\mathbf{A}\, f \,\mathbf{U}\, g) &= max(d(f), d(g)) \\
d(\neg f) &= d(f) & d(\mathbf{E}\, f \,\mathbf{U}\, g) &= max(d(f), d(g))
\end{aligned}
$$

We now consider the fragment HML of CTL, built using only $\top, \neg, \wedge, \mathbf{EX}$:

$$(HML \ni) \; f, g ::= \top \mid f \wedge g \mid \neg f \mid \mathbf{EX}\, f$$

and we stratify it according to the modal heights. More precisely, for any $n \in \mathbf{N}$, we define $HML_n = \{f \in HML \mid d(f) \leq n\}$. We have $HML_0 \subseteq HML_1 \subseteq \cdots \subseteq HML_n \subseteq \cdots \subseteq HML \subseteq CTL$. Modulo our use of unlabeled steps, HML is the so-called Hennessy-Milner logic used in [HM85].

Note that, modulo the usual boolean laws, there exists only a finite number of distinct formulas in any HML_n set, so that any $\overset{HML_n}{\sim}$ equivalence generates only a finite number of equivalence classes.

Lemma 1 *For any graph $(Q, \to)$, and states $q_1, q_2 \in Q$:*

$$q_1 \overset{HML_n}{\sim} q_2 \Leftrightarrow q_1 \equiv_n q_2$$

Proof We proceed by induction on n. The proof of [HM85] relies on the f.b. hypothesis, so that we have to invoke another argument for the "$\Rightarrow$" direction.

($\Rightarrow$): Clearly $\overset{HML_0}{\sim} \subseteq \equiv_0$. Now assume that $\overset{HML_n}{\sim} \subseteq \equiv_n$ and consider two states q_1, q_2 with $q_1 \overset{HML_{n+1}}{\sim} q_2$. If $q_1 \to q_1'$, we partition HML_n, which is finite, into formulas satisfied at q_1' and formulas not satisfied at q_1', that is we write $HML_n = \{f_1, \ldots, f_m\} \cup \{f_{m+1}, \ldots, f_p\}$ with $q_1' \models f_1 \wedge \cdots \wedge f_m \wedge \neg f_{m+1} \wedge \cdots \wedge \neg f_p$. Now, writing f^* for $f_1 \wedge \cdots \wedge f_m \wedge \neg f_{m+1} \wedge \cdots \wedge \neg f_p$, we have $d(f^*) \leq n$ so that (a boolean equivalent of) f^* belongs to HML_n and $\mathbf{EX}\, f^* \in HML_{n+1}$. $q_1' \models f^*$ implies $q_1 \models \mathbf{EX}\, f^*$, and $q_1 \overset{HML_{n+1}}{\sim} q_2$ implies $q_2 \models \mathbf{EX}\, f^*$, which means that there exists some $q_2 \to q_2'$ with $q_2' \models f^*$. Now, if both q_1' and q_2' satisfy f^*, we clearly have $q_1' \overset{HML_n}{\sim} q_2'$ by construction of f^*, which implies $q_1' \equiv_n q_2'$ (by ind. hyp.). This establishes that $q_1 \equiv_{n+1} q_2$. Essentially the same proof appears in [Mil81,GR83].

($\Leftarrow$): Clearly $\equiv_0 \subseteq \overset{HML_0}{\sim}$, so assume $\equiv_n \subseteq \overset{HML_n}{\sim}$. Consider $q_1 \equiv_{n+1} q_2$ and $q_1 \models f$. We show that $q_2 \models f$ by induction on the structure of $f \in HML_{n+1}$. This is obvious if f has the form $\top$, $g \wedge g'$ or $\neg g$. If f is $\mathbf{EX}\, g$ with $g \in HML_n$ then $q_1 \models f$ implies that there exists $q_1 \to q_1'$ with $q_1' \models g$. Now, $q_1 \equiv_{n+1} q_2$ implies that there exists $q_2 \to q_2'$ with $q_1' \equiv_n q_2'$, that is $q_1' \overset{HML_n}{\sim} q_2'$. Then $q_2' \models g$ and $q_2 \models \mathbf{EX}\, g$, that is $q_2 \models f$. Finally, $q_1 \overset{HML_{n+1}}{\sim} q_2$. $\qquad\square$

This lemma entails that $\overset{HML}{\sim} = \equiv$ and has the immediate corollary:

Proposition 2 *For any graph $(Q, \to)$, and states $q_1, q_2 \in Q$:*

$$q_1 \overset{CTL}{\sim} q_2 \Rightarrow q_1 \equiv q_2$$

Of course, the reverse implication does not hold, as a corollary of Proposition 4.

Remark 1 [HM85] proves $\overset{HML}{\sim} = \equiv$ for labeled f.b. graphs, while we proved it for unlabeled non-f.b. graphs. Oddly enough, the "$\Rightarrow$" direction *does not hold* for labeled non-f.b. graphs when the labeling alphabet is infinite (see Appendix B).

4 Comparing CTL and $\approx$

We first exhibit a graph where two states are $\overset{CTL}{\sim}$ without being $\approx$. We consider the ordinal process P_λ with λ infinite and first establish the following lemma:

Lemma 2 *For any $f \in CTL$ and any $\alpha \geq d(f)$ in P_λ, $\alpha \models f$ iff $d(f) \models f$*

In other words, in P_λ any $f \in CTL$ is always true (or always false) from the integer state $d(f)$ onwards.

Proof We prove the lemma by induction over the structure of f.

- Assume $f = \mathbf{EX}\,g$ and $n = d(g)$, and consider $\alpha \geq n + 1$. If $n + 1 \models f$, then $\alpha \models f$. If $n + 1 \not\models f$ then $k \not\models g$ for any $k \leq n$, which implies $n \not\models g$ and then, by ind. hyp., $\beta \not\models g$ for any $\beta \geq n$ because $n = d(g)$. Finally, $\alpha \not\models f$.

- Assume $f = \mathbf{E}\,g_1\,\mathbf{U}\,g_2$ and $n = d(f)$, and consider $\alpha \geq n$. First suppose that $n \models f$. Then $n \models g_1$ or $n \models g_2$. If $n \models g_2$ then $\alpha \models g_2$ (by ind. hyp.) and then $\alpha \models f$. Otherwise $n \models g_1$, and there exists $n \to k$ with $k \models g_2$. Now $\alpha \models g_1$ (by ind. hyp.) and as $\alpha \to k$, we have $\alpha \models f$. The other possibility is $n \not\models f$, and then $n \not\models y_2$, implying $\alpha \not\models g_2$ (by ind. hyp.). If now $\alpha \models f$ then $\alpha \models g_1$ (and then $n \models g_1$) and there exists $\alpha \to \beta$ with $\beta \models g_2$. As β must be less than n or else we would have $n \models g_2$, we have $n \to \beta$, contradicting $n \not\models f$.

A similar proof applies to the $\mathbf{A}\,g_1\,\mathbf{U}\,g_2$ case, and the remaining cases are obvious. $\qquad\square$

This lemma has the immediate corollary:

Proposition 3 $q_1 \overset{CTL}{\sim} q_2$ *does not imply* $q_1 \approx q_2$

Indeed, the previous lemma shows that in $P_{\omega+2}$, $\omega \overset{CTL}{\sim} \omega + 1$, while $\omega \not\approx \omega + 1$.

We now consider the graph P obtained from the ordinal process P_{ω^2+2} by adding a transition $\omega^2 + 1 \to \omega^2 + 1$. We begin with the following lemma:

Lemma 3 *For all* $n \in \mathbf{N}$ *and* $\alpha_1, \alpha_2 \geq \omega.n$, *we have* $\alpha_1 \approx_n \alpha_2$ *in* P.

Proof We proceed by induction over n. The result is clear for $n = 0$, so assume it holds for n and consider $\alpha_1, \alpha_2 \geq \omega.(n + 1)$. If $\alpha_1 \overset{k}{\to} \beta_1$, β_1 may be less than $\omega.n$ or not. If $\beta_1 < \omega.n$, then also $\alpha_2 \overset{k}{\to} \beta_1$. If $\beta_1 \geq \omega.n$ then we can consider $\alpha_2 \overset{k}{\to} \omega.n$ and have $\beta_1 \approx_n \omega.n$ by ind. hyp. Finally we obtain $\alpha_1 \approx_{n+1} \alpha_2$, which completes the proof. $\qquad\square$

The same proof generalizes the result we mentioned after Definition 4 by allowing any transitions $\alpha_1 \to \alpha_2$ to be added in P_λ, provided that α_1 and α_2 are above ω^2. This lemma has the immediate corollary:

Proposition 4 $q_1 \approx q_2$ *does not imply* $q_1 \overset{CTL}{\sim} q_2$

Indeed, we just saw that in P, $\omega^2 \approx \omega^2 + 1$, though there exists an infinite path starting from $\omega^2 + 1$ and none from ω^2. This is easily expressed in CTL and for $f = \mathbf{A}\,\top\,\mathbf{U}\,\neg\mathbf{EX}\,\top$ we have $\omega^2 \models f$ and $\omega^2 + 1 \not\models f$.

Conclusion

As stated in the introduction, this paper was written to answer some questions that arose naturally in the semantics of FP2 [SJ89]. The implications of our findings are clear: we cannot use CTL to reason about FP2 programs without adopting a semantics at least as discriminating as $\overset{CTL}{\sim}$ (e.g. bisimulation). The use of $\approx$ or $\equiv$ (as in [GR83,BBK87]) is simply not compatible with CTL. Furthermore we cannot use $\overset{CTL}{\sim}$ itself as a semantic equivalence for it is not a congruence [Sch89].

Further, we think these results are more widely interesting. They illustrate the strength of the f.b. restriction. Indeed, several examples suggest that the equivalences generated by temporal logics are very sensitive to this restriction [BR83,Sch89].

The ordinal processes were used by Klop to show that $\approx$ and $\underset{\leftrightarrow}{}$ do not coincide: the earlier proof of [San82] used much more complicated counter-examples. In this paper they provided us with "simple" generic counter-examples. Indeed, the study of process theory and process logics in the non-f.b. framework requires such a collection of paradigmatic examples and counter-examples. We believe that the temporal theory of ordinal graphs deserves to be studied in its own right, generalizing results like Lemmas 2 and 4.

Acknowledgements

We would like to thank Hubert Comon for his patient and thorough criticism of the draft.

Appendix

A   The CTL^* logic

In this section, we show that the results we developed for CTL are still valid for CTL^*, a richer logic introduced in [EH83]. In the paper, we preferred to concentrate on CTL because it has a very simple presentation, and does not mix state and path formulas the way CTL^* does. Indeed, the use of path formulas in CTL^* leads one to define in a less direct way the equivalence generated over states.

We follow Stirling and define CTL^* in the following way:

Definition 7 (Syntax of CTL^*)

$$(CTL^* \ni) \; f,g ::= \top \mid f \wedge g \mid \neg f \mid \mathbf{X} f \mid f \mathbf{U} g \mid \forall f$$

where now truth is defined w.r.t. to a path σ of $(Q, \rightarrow)$.

Definition 8 (Semantics of CTL^*)

- $\sigma \models \top$, $\sigma \models f \wedge g$ and $\sigma \models \neg f$ have their obvious definitions.
- $\sigma \models \mathbf{X} f$ iff $|\sigma| \geq 1$ and $\sigma^1 \models f$.
- $\sigma \models f \mathbf{U} g$ iff there exists $n \in \mathbf{N}$ s.t. $|\sigma| \geq n$, $\sigma^n \models g$ and $\sigma^i \models f$ for all $0 \leq i < n$.
- $\sigma \models \forall f$ iff $\sigma' \models f$ for all $\sigma' \in \Sigma(\sigma(0))$.

Given $q \in Q$, we write $q \models f$ iff $\sigma \models f$ for all $\sigma \in \Sigma(q)$. Note that $q \not\models f$ does not imply $q \models \neg f$. Again, we write $\sigma \overset{CTL^*}{\sim} \sigma'$ and $q \overset{CTL^*}{\sim} q'$ with obvious definitions.

CTL^* subsumes CTL in the sense that every formula $f \in CTL$ can be directly translated into a formula $f^* \in CTL^*$ s.t. $q \models_{CTL} f$ iff $q \models_{CTL^*} f^*$. This is easy and well-known.

The modal height $d(f)$ of CTL^* formulas is defined as with CTL: $d(\forall f) = d(f)$ and $d(f \mathbf{U} g) = max(d(f), d(g))$.

Proposition 5 *For any graph $(Q, \rightarrow)$, and paths $\sigma_1, \sigma_2 \in \Sigma$:*

$$\sigma_1 \underline{\leftrightarrow} \sigma_2 \;\Rightarrow\; \sigma_1 \overset{CTL^*}{\sim} \sigma_2$$

Again, the proof is by induction over the structure of a formula $f \in CTL^*$. This proposition has the immediate corollary:

Proposition 6 *For any graph $(Q, \rightarrow)$, and states $q, q' \in Q$:*

$$q \underline{\leftrightarrow} q' \;\Rightarrow\; q \overset{CTL^*}{\sim} q'$$

The reverse implication does not hold in general: a simple cardinality argument shows that CTL^* cannot distinguish between more than $\aleph_1$ states while there exist ordinal graphs of larger size. However, we believe the stronger:

Conjecture 1 *In P_λ, $\omega \overset{CTL^*}{\sim} \omega + 1$.*

which would entail

$$q_1 \overset{CTL^*}{\sim} q_2 \text{ does not imply } q_1 \approx q_2$$

We uncovered an error in our earlier proof of Conjecture 1. In particular, an extension to CTL^* of Lemma 2 proved incorrect:

Lemma 4 *There exist formulas $f \in CTL^*$ and states $\alpha \geq d(f)$ in P_λ such that $\alpha \not\models f$ while $d(f) \models f$*

We need some notation for our example. Write $(\geq n)$ for $\neg\forall\neg\mathbf{X}^n\top$, $(= n)$ for $(\geq n) \wedge \neg(\geq n+1)$ and $(\ni n)$ for $\top \mathbf{U} (= n)$. Then $\sigma \models (\geq n)$ iff $\sigma(0) \geq n$, $\sigma \models (= n)$ iff $\sigma(0) = n$ and $\sigma \models (\ni n)$ iff $\sigma(i) = n$ for some $i \leq |\sigma|$. Now consider

$$f_n = (\ni n - 1) \vee \mathbf{X} \neg (\geq n - 1)$$

f_n has depth n. For $n \geq 2$ in P_λ, we have

$$n \models f \text{ while } n + 1 \not\models f \tag{6}$$

There exist other examples where the strict $n = d(f)$ is not required. Consider

$$f_n = \neg\mathbf{X}\mathbf{X}\top \vee (\ni n - 2) \vee (\ni n - 3) \vee \mathbf{X}\mathbf{X}\neg(\geq n - 3)$$

where $d(f_n) = n - 1$ and where (6) holds for $n \geq 3$.

B Labeled graphs

We assume an infinite set $A = \{a, \ldots\}$ of action names. A graph is now a pair $(Q, \rightarrow)$ where $\rightarrow \subseteq Q \times A \times Q$. We write $q \overset{a}{\rightarrow} q'$ when $(q, a, q') \in \rightarrow$. The definitions of bisimulation and of the two other equivalences are adapted in the usual way. The first problem is to incorporate these actions in the temporal logic. The Hennessy-Milner Logic has one modal combinator per action: **EX** is replaced by all $\langle a \rangle$ (for $a \in A$), with the semantics:

$$q \models \langle a \rangle f \text{ iff } \exists q \overset{a}{\rightarrow} q' \text{ s.t. } q' \models f$$

However, this only allows references to actions in the **EX** combinator, not in the two other ones. A more general solution is to include atomic propositions "**after** a" (for any $a \in A$) with the semantics:

$$q \models \text{after } a \text{ iff } \exists q' \overset{a}{\rightarrow} q$$

Note that $\langle a \rangle f$ can be written **EX** $(f \wedge \text{after } a)$. We adopt this extension and end up with a new logic: CTL_A. As we expect the semantics of **after** a to match our intuition, we restrict ourselves to labeled graphs *that are trees*. A rooted-graph can be unfolded into an equivalent (bisimilar) tree, so that there is no loss of generality.

Of course all our negative results still hold in this framework. Furthermore, we still have:

$$q_1 \underset{}{\leftrightarrow} q_2 \Rightarrow q_1 \overset{CTL_A}{\sim} q_2$$

with an almost identical proof.

More interesting is the following:

$$q_1 \overset{HML_A}{\sim} q_2 \overset{\Leftarrow}{\underset{\not\Rightarrow}{}} q_1 \equiv q_2$$

where the "$\Leftarrow$" direction is proved exactly as in Lemma 1. The "$\Rightarrow$" direction only holds when A is finite. Our counter-example needs some more definitions. We write $\mathcal{P}(A)$ for the sets of subsets of A and $\mathcal{P}_{cf}(A)$ for the sets of finite or cofinite[1] subsets of A. Given $B \subseteq A$, we define $P_B = \Sigma_{b \in B} b.Nil$ (with standard CCS-like definitions for $+$, action-prefixing and Nil). Note that $P_B \equiv_1 P_{B'}$ iff $B = B'$. Now, if we pick any $a \in A$ and define $P = \Sigma_{B \in \mathcal{P}(A)} a.P_B$ and $P' = \Sigma_{B \in \mathcal{P}_{cf}(A)} a.P_B$, we have $P \overset{HML_A}{\sim} P'$ while $P \not\equiv_2 P'$. (We do not include the proof).

As we also have $P \overset{CTL_A}{\sim} P'$, we end up with:

$$q_1 \overset{CTL_A}{\sim} q_2 \overset{\not\Leftarrow}{\underset{\not\Rightarrow}{}} q_1 \equiv q_2$$

References

[Abr87] S. Abramsky. Observation equivalence as a testing equivalence. *Theoretical Computer Science*, 53:225–241, 1087.

[BBK87] J. C. M. Baeten, J. A. Bergstra, and J. W. Klop. On the consistency of Koomen's fair abstraction rule. *Theoretical Computer Science*, 51(1):129–176, 1987.

---

[1] i.e. having a finite complement.

[BK87]   J. A. Bergstra and J. W. Klop. *A Convergence Theorem in Process Algebra*. Research Report CS-R8733, CWI, 1987.

[BK89]   J. A. Bergstra and J. W. Klop. Process theory based on bisimulation semantics. In *Linear Time, Branching Time and Partial Order in Logics and Models for Concurrency, Noordwijkerhout, LNCS 354*, pages 50–122, Springer-Verlag, 1989.

[BR83]   S. D. Brookes and W. C. Rounds. Behavioural equivalence relations induced by programming logics. In *Proc. 10th ICALP, Barcelona, LNCS 154*, pages 97–108, Springer-Verlag, July 1983.

[CE81]   E. M. Clarke and E. A. Emerson. Design and synthesis of synchronization skeletons using branching time temporal logic. In *Proc. Logics of Programs Workshop, Yorktown Heights, LNCS 131*, pages 52–71, Springer-Verlag, May 1981.

[EH83]   E. A. Emerson and J. Y. Halpern. "Sometimes" and "Not Never" revisited: on branching versus linear time. In *Proc. 10th ACM Symp. Principles of Programming Languages, Austin, Texas*, pages 127–140, January 1983.

[ES89]   E. A. Emerson and J. Srinivasan. Branching time temporal logic. In *Linear Time, Branching Time and Partial Order in Logics and Models for Concurrency, Noordwijkerhout, LNCS 354*, pages 123–172, Springer-Verlag, 1989.

[GR83]   W. G. Golson and W. C. Rounds. Connections between two theories of concurrency: metric spaces and synchronization trees. *Information and Control*, 57, 1983.

[HM85]   M. Hennessy and R. Milner. Algebraic laws for nondeterminism and concurrency. *Journal of the ACM*, 32(1):137–161, January 1985.

[HS85]   M. Hennessy and C. Stirling. The power of the future perfect in program logics. *Information and Control*, 67:23–52, 1985.

[Klo88] J. W. Klop. *Bisimulation Semantics*. Lectures given at the REX School/Workshop, Noordwijkerhout, NL, May 1988.

[Lam80] L. Lamport. "Sometimes" is sometimes "Not Never". In *Proc. 7th ACM Symp. Principles of Programming Languages, Las Vegas*, pages 174–185, January 1980.

[Mil81] R. Milner. A modal characterisation of observable machine-behaviour. In *Proc. CAAP 81, Genoa, LNCS 185*, pages 25–34, Springer-Verlag, March 1981.

[Mil88] R. Milner. *Operational and Algebraic Semantics of Concurrent Processes*. Research Report ECS-LFCS-88-46, Lab. for Foundations of Computer Science, Edinburgh, February 1988. To appear in the *Handbook of Theoretical Computer Science*.

[Par81] D. Park. Concurrency and automata on infinite sequences. In *Proc. 5th GI Conf.*, pages 167–183, Springer-Verlag, March 1981.

[Pnu77] A. Pnueli. The temporal logic of programs. In *Proc. 18th IEEE Symp. Foundations of Computer Science, Providence*, pages 46–57, 1977.

[San82] M. T. Sanderson. *Proof Techniques for CCS*. PhD thesis, Univ. Edinburgh, November 1982. Available as Report CST-19-82.

[Sch89] Ph. Schnoebelen. *Congruence Properties of the Process Equivalence Induced by Temporal Logic*. 1989. Submitted for publication.

[SJ89]   Ph. Schnoebelen and Ph. Jorrand. Principles of FP2. Term algebras for specification of parallel machines. In J. W. de Bakker, editor, *Languages for Parallel Architectures: Design, Semantics, Implementation Models*, chapter 5, pages 223–273, Wiley, 1989.

The Value Flow Graph: A Program Representation for Optimal Program Transformations

Bernhard Steffen *   Jens Knoop †   Oliver Rüthing†

Abstract

Data flow analysis algorithms for imperative programming languages can be split into two groups: first, into the *semantic* algorithms that determine *semantic equivalence* between terms, and second, into the *syntactic* algorithms that compute complex program properties based on syntactic term identity, which support powerful optimization techniques like for example *partial redundancy elimination*. *Value Flow Graphs* represent semantic equivalence of terms syntactically. This allows us to feed the knowledge of semantic equivalence into syntactic algorithms. The power of this technique, which leads to modularly extendable algorithms, is demonstrated by developing a two stage algorithm for the optimal placement of computations within a program wrt the *Herbrand interpretation*.

1   Introduction

There are two kinds of data flow analysis algorithms for imperative programming languages. First, the *semantic* algorithms that determine *semantic equivalence* between terms, e.g. the classical algorithm of Kildall [Ki1,Ki2]. Second, *syntactic* algorithms that compute complex program properties on the basis of syntactic term identity, which support powerful optimization techniques, e.g. Morel/Renvoise's algorithm for determining partial redundancies [MR]. *Value Flow Graphs* represent semantic equivalence syntactically. This allows us to feed the knowledge of semantic equivalence into syntactic algorithms. We will demonstrate the power of this technique by developing a two stage algorithm for the optimal placement of computations within a program wrt the *Herbrand interpretation*, which is structured as follows:

1. Construction of a Value Flow Graph for the Herbrand interpretation:

   (i) Determining term equivalence wrt the Herbrand interpretation (in short *Herbrand equivalence*) for every program point (Section 4.1).

   (ii) Computing a sufficiently large syntactic representation of the semantic equivalences for each program point (Section 4.2).

   (iii) Connecting the representations of equivalence classes of 1.(ii) according to the actual data flow. This results in a Value Flow Graph (Section 4.3).

2. Optimal placement of the computations:

   (i) Determining the computation points wrt the Value Flow Graph of step 1.(ii) by means of a Boolean equation system (Section 5.1).

   (ii) Placing the computations (Section 5.2).

---

*Department of Computer Science, University of Aarhus, DK-8000 Aarhus C — The work was done in part at the Laboratory for Foundations of Computer Science, University of Edinburgh

†Institut für Informatik und Praktische Mathematik, Christian-Albrechts-Universität, D-2300 Kiel 1 – The authors are supported by the Deutsche Forschungsgemeinschaft grant La 426/9-1

This is the only known algorithm of its kind that is (proved to be) optimal wrt the *Herbrand interpretation* for arbitrary control flow structures. It therefore generalizes and improves the known algorithms for common subexpression elimination, partial redundancy elimination and loop invariant code motion.

Rosen, Wegman and Zadeck developed an algorithm with a similar intent. However, they used a weaker representation for global semantic equivalence, the *static single assignment form* (SSA form), to represent global equivalence properties [RWZ]. Thus they could not apply the elegant and structurally independent technique of Morel and Renvoise [MR]. Rather they developed their own more complicated algorithm, which only works for particular program structures (reducible flow graphs). Moreover, their algorithm is only optimal for *acyclic* flow graphs (note, Herbrand equivalence is called *transparent equivalence* in [RWZ]).

It is worth mentioning that Steffen [St1,St2] and later Rosen, Wegman and Zadeck [RWZ] were the first who dealt with the *second order effects* of code motion. In our algorithm these effects are an automatic consequence of its optimality (see Corollary 5.7).

Practical experience with an implementation of our algorithm, which is implemented in a joint project with the NORSK DATA company, shows its practicality. In particular, all examples in this paper are computed by means of this implementation.

2   An Example

The following example illustrates the main features of our two stage algorithm. First, it works for arbitrary nondeterministic flow graphs (note that the loop construct of Figure 2.1 is not even reducible). Second, it considers semantic equivalence between terms.

The diagrams below represent the *nondeterministic branching structure* as arrows and *parallel assignments* as nodes:

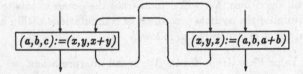

Figure 2.1

This program fragment has the following property:

while looping "$a+b$" and "$x+y$" evaluate to the same value

which suggests an optimization with the following result:

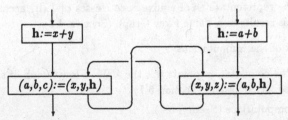

Figure 2.2

Already the basic variant (see 4.2) of our algorithm achieves this optimization. The following discussion demonstrates the effects of the five steps of our two stage algorithm.

The semantic analysis of step 1.(i) designates the flow graph with partitions characterizing all term equivalences wrt the Herbrand interpretation, i.e. all equivalences being valid independent of specific properties of the term operators (Figure 2.3). In particular, it detects the equivalence of "$a+b$" and "$x+y$" after the execution of either assignment.

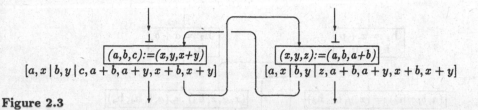

Figure 2.3

Afterwards, step 1.(ii) extends this designation for every program point to a syntactic representation of semantic equivalences which is large enough to perform our optimization:

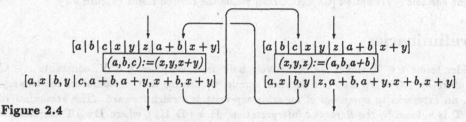

Figure 2.4

Subsequently, step 1.(iii) produces the corresponding Value Flow Graph, whose relevant part is shown in Figure 2.5:

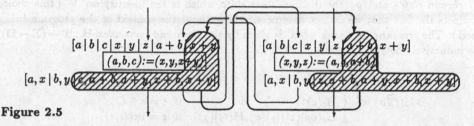

Figure 2.5

The placement procedure only refers to term equivalences that are explicit in the Value Flow Graph under consideration, i.e. two terms are equivalent at a program point if they are displayed as members of the same equivalence class in the Value Flow Graph at this point. Applying a modification of Morel/Renvoise's algorithm (step 2.(i)) to the Value Flow Graph above yields:

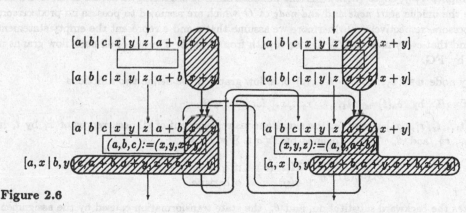

Figure 2.6

The inserted nodes are the optimal computation points (the insertion of synthetic nodes is common for code motion, see Section 5). – Now, application of step 2.(ii) results in:

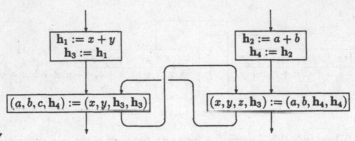

Figure 2.7

Subsequent *variable subsumption* [Ch,CACCHM] yields the desired result (Figure 2.2).

3 Preliminaries

We consider terms $t \in \mathbf{T}$ which are inductively built from variables $v \in \mathbf{V}$, constants $c \in \mathbf{C}$ and operators $op \in \mathbf{Op}$. To keep our notation simple, we assume that all operators are two-ary. However, an extension to operators of an arbitrary arity is straightforward. The *semantics* of terms of $\mathbf{T}$ is induced by the *Herbrand interpretation* $\mathbf{H} = (\mathbf{D}, \mathbf{H_0})$, where $\mathbf{D} =_{df} \mathbf{T}$ denotes the non empty data domain and $\mathbf{H_0}$ the function which maps every constant $c \in \mathbf{C}$ to the datum $\mathbf{H_0}(c) = c \in \mathbf{D}$ and every operator $op \in \mathbf{Op}$ to the total function $\mathbf{H_0}(op) : \mathbf{D} \times \mathbf{D} \to \mathbf{D}$, which is defined by $\mathbf{H_0}(op)(t_1, t_2) =_{df} (op, t_1, t_2)$ for all $t_1, t_2 \in \mathbf{D}$. $\Sigma = \{\sigma \mid \sigma : \mathbf{V} \to \mathbf{D}\}$ denotes the set of all *Herbrand states* and σ_0 the distinct *start state* which is the identity on $\mathbf{V}$ (this choice of σ_0 reflects the fact that we do not assume anything about the context of the program being optimized). The *semantics* of terms $t \in \mathbf{T}$ is given by the *Herbrand semantics* $\mathbf{H} : \mathbf{T} \to (\Sigma \to \mathbf{D})$, which is inductively defined by: $\forall \sigma \in \Sigma \ \forall t \in \mathbf{T}$.

$$\mathbf{H}(t)(\sigma) =_{df} \begin{cases} \sigma(v) & \text{if } t = v \in \mathbf{V} \\ \mathbf{H_0}(c) & \text{if } t = c \in \mathbf{C} \\ \mathbf{H_0}(op)(\mathbf{H}(t_1)(\sigma), \mathbf{H}(t_2)(\sigma)) & \text{if } t = op(t_1, t_2) \end{cases}$$

As usual, we represent imperative programs as *directed flow graphs* $G = (N, E, \mathbf{s}, \mathbf{e})$ with node set N and edge set E. (These flow graphs are obtainable for example by the algorithm of [All]). Nodes $n \in N$ represent *parallel assignments* of the form $(x_1, ., x_r) := (t_1, ., t_r)$, where $r \geq 0$ and $x_i = x_j$ implies $i = j$, edges $(n, m) \in E$ the nondeterministic branching structure of G, and $\mathbf{s}$ and $\mathbf{e}$ denote the unique *start node* and *end node* of G which are assumed to possess no predecessors and successors, respectively. Furthermore we assume that $\mathbf{s}$ and $\mathbf{e}$ represent the empty statement "skip" and that every node $n \in N$ lies on a path from $\mathbf{s}$ to $\mathbf{e}$. The set of all such flow graphs is denoted by $\mathbf{FG}$.

For every node $n \equiv (x_1, ., x_r) := (t_1, ., t_r)$ of a flow graph G we define two functions

$$\delta_n : \mathbf{T} \to \mathbf{T} \quad \text{by} \quad \delta_n(t) =_{df} t[t_1, ., t_r / x_1, ., x_r] \text{ for all } t \in \mathbf{T},$$

where $t[t_1, ., t_r / x_1, ., x_r]$ stands for the simultaneous replacement of all occurrences of x_i by t_i in t, $i \in \{1, ., r\}$, and $\theta_n : \Sigma \to \Sigma$, defined by: $\forall \sigma \in \Sigma \ \forall y \in \mathbf{V}$.

$$\theta_n(\sigma)(y) =_{df} \begin{cases} \mathbf{H}(t_i)(\sigma) & \text{if } y = x_i, \ i \in \{1, ., r\} \\ \sigma(y) & \text{otherwise} \end{cases}$$

δ_n realizes the backward substitution, and θ_n the state transformation caused by the assignment of node n. Additionally, let $\mathcal{T}(n)$ denote the set of all terms which occur in the assignment represented by n.

A *finite path* of G is a sequence $(n_1, .., n_q)$ of nodes such that $(n_j, n_{j+1}) \in E$ for $j \in \{1, .., q-1\}$. $\mathbf{P}(n_1, n_q)$ denotes the set of all finite paths from n_1 to n_q and ";" the concatenation of two paths. Now the backward substitution functions $\delta_n : \mathbf{T} \to \mathbf{T}$ and the state transformations $\theta_n : \Sigma \to \Sigma$ can be extended to cover finite paths as well. For each path $p = (m \equiv n_1, .., n_q \equiv n) \in \mathbf{P}(m, n)$ we define $\Delta_p : \mathbf{T} \to \mathbf{T}$ by $\Delta_p =_{df} \delta_{n_q}$ if $q = 1$ and $\Delta_{(n_1, .., n_{q-1})} \circ \delta_{n_q}$ otherwise, and $\Theta_p : \Sigma \to \Sigma$ by $\Theta_p =_{df} \theta_{n_1}$ if $q = 1$ and $\Theta_{(n_2, .., n_q)} \circ \theta_{n_1}$ otherwise. The set of all *possible states* at a node $n \in N$ is given by

$$\Sigma_n =_{df} \{\sigma \in \Sigma \mid \exists p = p'; (n) \in \mathbf{P}(\mathbf{s}, n) : \Theta_{p'}(\sigma_0) = \sigma\}$$

Now, we can define:

Definition 3.1 *Let* $t_1, t_2 \in \mathbf{T}$ *and* $n \in N$. *Then* t_1 *and* t_2 *are* Herbrand equivalent *at node* n *iff* $\forall \sigma \in \Sigma_n. \ \mathbf{H}(t_1)(\sigma) = \mathbf{H}(t_2)(\sigma)$.

4 Construction of a Value Flow Graph

The following subsections correspond to the three construction steps of a Value Flow Graph for a flow graph G, which we consider as to be given from now on.

4.1 Determining Local Semantic Equivalence

The semantic analysis determines all equivalences between program terms wrt the Herbrand interpretation (see 1.Optimality Theorem 4.6). These are expressed by means of structured partition DAGs (cp. [FKU]), which are directed, acyclic multigraphs, whose nodes are labeled with at most one operator or constant and a set of variables. Given a structured partition DAG, two terms are equivalent iff they are represented by the same node of the DAG. – To define the notion of a structured partition DAG precisely, let $\mathcal{P}_{fin} =_{df} \{T \mid T \subseteq (\mathbf{V} \cup \mathbf{C} \cup \mathbf{Op}) \land |T| \in \omega \setminus \{0\}\}$.

Definition 4.1 *A* structured partition DAG *is a triple* $D = (N_D, E_D, L_D)$, *where*

- (N_D, E_D) *is a directed acyclic multigraph with node set* N_D *and edge set* $E_D \subseteq N_D \times N_D$.
- $L_D : N_D \to \mathcal{P}_{fin}$ *is a labelling function, which satisfies*
  1. $\forall \gamma \in N_D. \ |L_D(\gamma) \setminus \mathbf{V}| \leq 1$ *and*
  2. $\forall \gamma, \gamma' \in N_D. \ \gamma \neq \gamma' \Rightarrow L_D(\gamma) \cap L_D(\gamma') \subseteq \mathbf{Op}$
- *Leaves of* D *are the nodes* $\gamma \in N_D$ *with* $L_D(\gamma) \cap \mathbf{Op} = \emptyset$.
- *An inner node* γ *of* D *possesses exactly two successors, which we denote by* $l(\gamma)$ *and* $r(\gamma)$.
- $\forall \gamma, \gamma' \in N_D. \ L_D(\gamma) \cap L_D(\gamma') \cap \mathbf{Op} \neq \emptyset \ \land \ l(\gamma) = l(\gamma') \ \land \ r(\gamma) = r(\gamma') \Rightarrow \gamma = \gamma'$.

If N_D *is finite,* D *is called a* finite structured partition DAG. *The set of all structured partition DAGs and the set of all finite structured partition DAGs are denoted by* $\mathcal{PD}$ *and* $\mathcal{PD}_{fin}$, *respectively.*

A node $\gamma \in N_D$ of a structured partition DAG is meant to represent an equivalence class of program terms:

$$\mathbf{T}_D(\gamma) = ((\mathbf{V} \cup \mathbf{C}) \cap L_D(\gamma)) \cup \{(op, t, t') \mid op \in (\mathbf{Op} \cap L_D(\gamma)) \land (t, t') \in \mathbf{T}_D(l(\gamma)) \times \mathbf{T}_D(r(\gamma))\}$$

Thus a full DAG represents a partition (or equivalence relation) on:

$$\mathbf{T}(D) =_{df} \bigcup \{\mathbf{T}_D(\gamma) \mid \gamma \in N_D\} \subseteq \mathbf{T}$$

This can be illustrated as follows:

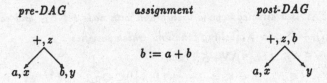

$$partition \longleftrightarrow DAG$$

$$[a, x \mid b, y \mid a + b, a + y, x + b, x + y, z]$$

Figure 4.2

Viewing DAGs as equivalence relations makes $\mathcal{PD}$ a complete lattice, with inclusion defined set theoretically as usual. This guarantees existence and well definedness of $\mathcal{H}(P)$ in:

Definition 4.3 *Let $D \in \mathcal{PD}$. Then*

1. $\mathcal{H}(D)$ *is the smallest structured partition DAG with $D \subseteq \mathcal{H}(D)$ and $\mathbf{T}(\mathcal{H}(D)) = \mathbf{T}$.*
2. *$t_1, t_2 \in \mathbf{T}$ are syntactically D-equivalent, iff D possesses a node γ with $t_1, t_2 \in \mathbf{T}_D(\gamma)$.*
3. *$t_1, t_2 \in \mathbf{T}$ are semantically D-equivalent, iff they are syntactically $\mathcal{H}(D)$-equivalent.*

We have (cf. [St2]):

Theorem 4.4 *Let $t_1, t_2 \in \mathbf{T}$, $n \in N$, and $pre[n] \in \mathcal{PD}_{fin}$ be the structured partition DAG of the entry information at node n computed by Algorithm A.1. Then t_1 and t_2 are Herbrand equivalent at node n iff they are semantically $pre[n]$-equivalent.*

Structured partition DAGs characterize the domain which is necessary to compute all term equivalences which do not depend on specific properties of the term operators. Moreover, they allow us to compute the effects of assignments essentially by updating the position of the left hand side variable:

$$pre\text{-}DAG \qquad assignment \qquad post\text{-}DAG$$

$$b := a + b$$

Figure 4.5

As a consequence of Theorem 4.4 we obtain:

Theorem 4.6 (1.Optimality Theorem)
Given an arbitrary flow graph, Algorithm A.1 terminates with a DAG-designation which exactly characterizes all equivalences of program terms wrt the Herbrand interpretation.

4.2 Computing the Syntactic Representation

In the last section we constructed finite structured partition DAGs that characterize Herbrand equivalence semantically (Definition 4.3(3)). However, the placement procedure (Section 5.1) considers the pre-DAGs and post-DAGs of a designation of a flow graph as purely syntactical objects, i.e. terms are considered equivalent iff they are syntactically equivalent (Definition 4.3(2)). Of course, it is not possible to finitely represent all Herbrand equivalences syntactically. However, it is possible to represent finite subsets that are sufficient for obtaining our optimality results (see Section 5.3). This is done by computing for every node n of G a finite set of terms T_{suf} that is sufficient to represent all necessary equivalences at n syntactically, i.e. as the restriction of $\mathcal{H}(D)$ to T_{suf}.

Here, we sketch two strategies for the construction of such term closures. The first strategy associates every node n with the set of terms representing values that *must* be computed on every continuation of paths from s to n that end in e, and the second strategy with the set of terms representing values that *may* be computed on a continuation of a path from s to n ending in e. Both term closures are computed by backward analysis. The first strategy algorithm iteratively computes approximations of the closure for a node as the *meet* over the current approximations of the closures of its successors. The second strategy algorithm is essentially dual. However, it is necessary to constrain the iteration here because the straightforward dual algorithm would not terminate. These two strategies define the *basic* and *full* variant of our two stage algorithm.

There is another important variant of our algorithm, which we call RWZ-variant. It is based on a strategy for computing closures, which starts by invoking the first strategy algorithm. Subsequently, it applies this algorithm to all flow graphs that result from considering nodes as end nodes which possess at least one "brother".

4.3 The Value Flow Graph

A Value Flow Graph connects the term equivalence classes of a DAG designation according to the data flow. Essentially, its nodes are the equivalence classes and its edges representations of the data flow. For technical reasons we define the nodes of a Value Flow Graph as pairs of equivalence classes. However, identifying these pairs with their second component leads back to the original intuition, which will be referred to in the next section.

In the following let us assume that every node n of G is designated by a pre-DAG $\mathbf{pre}(n)$ and a post-DAG $\mathbf{post}(n)$ according to the results of Section 4.2. For the sake of readability we abbreviate $\dot{\bigcup}_{n \in N} (N_{\mathbf{pre}(n)} \times N_{\mathbf{post}(n)})$ by Γ and define a subset $\xleftarrow{\delta} \subseteq \Gamma$ (in the following $\gamma \xleftarrow{\delta} \gamma'$ stands for $(\gamma, \gamma') \in \xleftarrow{\delta}$) by:

$$\forall (\gamma, \gamma') \in \Gamma. \ \gamma \xleftarrow{\delta} \gamma' \Longleftrightarrow_{df} \exists n \in N. \ \mathbf{T}_{\mathbf{pre}(n)}(\gamma) \supseteq \delta_n(\mathbf{T}_{\mathbf{post}(n)}(\gamma')).$$

Let now $\odot$ denote a new symbol, and $pred_G$ and $succ_G$ functions that map a node of G to its set of predecessors and successors, respectively. Then the technical definition of the Value Flow Graph for the DAG designation under consideration is as follows:

Definition 4.7 *A* Value Flow Graph **VFG** *is a pair (VFN,VFE) consisting of*

- *a set of nodes* $VFN \subseteq \dot{\bigcup}_{n \in N} ((N_{\mathbf{pre}(n)} \cup \{\odot\}) \times (N_{\mathbf{post}(n)} \cup \{\odot\}))$, *where*

$$\nu = (\gamma_1, \gamma_2) \in VFN \Longleftrightarrow_{df} \begin{cases} \gamma_1 \xleftarrow{\delta} \gamma_2 & \text{if } \gamma_1 \neq \odot \wedge \gamma_2 \neq \odot \\ \not\exists \gamma_3. \gamma_1 \xleftarrow{\delta} \gamma_3 & \text{if } \gamma_1 \neq \odot \wedge \gamma_2 = \odot \\ \not\exists \gamma_3. \gamma_3 \xleftarrow{\delta} \gamma_2 & \text{if } \gamma_1 = \odot \wedge \gamma_2 \neq \odot \end{cases}$$

- *a set of edges* $VFE \subseteq VFN \times VFN$, *where*

$$(\nu, \nu') \in VFE \Longleftrightarrow_{df} \begin{cases} \nu'{\downarrow}_1 \neq \odot \wedge \nu{\downarrow}_2 \neq \odot \wedge \\ \mathcal{N}(\nu') \in succ_G(\mathcal{N}(\nu)) \wedge \\ \mathbf{T}_{\mathbf{pre}(\mathcal{N}(\nu'))}(\nu'{\downarrow}_1) \subseteq \mathbf{T}_{\mathbf{post}(\mathcal{N}(\nu))}(\nu{\downarrow}_2) \end{cases}$$

where "${\downarrow}_1$" and "${\downarrow}_2$" denote the projection of a node ν to its first and second component respectively, and $\mathcal{N}(\nu)$ the node of the flow graph that is related to ν.

Thus, nodes ν of the Value Flow Graph are pairs (γ_1, γ_2), where γ_1 is a node of the pre-DAG and γ_2 a node of the post-DAG of a node n of G, such that γ_1 and γ_2 represent the same values, i.e. satisfy the inclusion $\mathbf{T}_{\mathbf{pre}(n)}(\gamma_1) \supseteq \{t \mid \exists t' \in \mathbf{T}_{\mathbf{post}(n)}(\gamma_2).\ t = \delta_n(t')\}$. Edges of the Value Flow Graph are pairs (ν, ν'), such that $\mathcal{N}(\nu)$ is a predecessor of $\mathcal{N}(\nu')$ and values are maintained along the connecting edge, i.e. $\mathbf{T}_{\mathbf{pre}(\mathcal{N}(\nu'))}(\nu' \downarrow_1) \subseteq \mathbf{T}_{\mathbf{post}(\mathcal{N}(\nu))}(\nu \downarrow_2)$. Finally, given a Value Flow Graph VFG, we define:

$$VFN_\mathbf{s} =_{df} \{\nu \mid \mathcal{N}(pred_{\mathbf{VFG}}(\nu)) \neq pred_G(\mathcal{N}(\nu)) \vee \mathcal{N}(\nu) = \mathbf{s}\}$$

and

$$VFN_\mathbf{e} =_{df} \{\nu \mid \mathcal{N}(succ_{\mathbf{VFG}}(\nu)) \neq succ_G(\mathcal{N}(\nu)) \vee \mathcal{N}(\nu) = \mathbf{e}\}$$

where $pred_{\mathbf{VFG}}$ and $succ_{\mathbf{VFG}}$ denote functions that map a node of $\mathbf{VFG}$ to its set of predecessors and successors, respectively.

5 Optimal Placement of Computations

The placement procedure is optimal in its own right. It works for any Value Flow Graph, which need not be produced by the first stage algorithm or restricted to Herbrand equivalence.

Before going into details, let us mention a technicality, which is typical for code motion (cf. [RWZ]). Edges, leading from a node with more than one successor to a node with more than one predecessor, are split by insertion of a synthetic node. This is necessary in order to avoid "deadlock" during the code motion process, which may arise as illustrated in Figure 5.1(a). There the computation of "$a+b$" at node 3 is partially redundant wrt to the computation of "$a+b$" at node 1. However, this partial redundancy cannot safely be eliminated by moving the computation of "$a+b$" to node 2, because this may introduce a new computation on a path which leaves node 2 on the right branch. On the other hand, it can safely be eliminated by moving the computation of "$a+b$" to the synthetic node 4 as it is displayed in Figure 5.1(b).

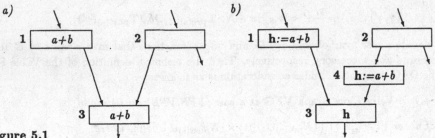

Figure 5.1

The following consideration assumes this simple transformation. In fact, the corresponding transformation of the Value Flow Graph is trivial as well, because all the inserted nodes represent skip-statements.

5.1 Determination of the Computation Points

The point of the placement procedure for computations is the solution of the following Boolean equation system (see Equation System 5.2), which we modified to work on Value Flow Graphs rather than flow graphs directly, in order to capture semantic equivalence. Following [MR], the names of the predicates are acronyms for the properties "*local anticipability*", "*availability*" and "*placement possible*":

Equation System 5.2 (Boolean Equation System)

- The Frame Conditions (Local Properties):

$$\mathbf{ANTLOC}(\nu) \Longleftrightarrow \nu{\downarrow_1} \cap \mathcal{T}(\mathcal{N}(\nu)) \neq \emptyset$$

$$\mathbf{AVIN}(\nu) = \mathbf{PPIN}(\nu) = \mathit{false} \text{ if } \nu \in \mathit{VFN_s}$$

$$\mathbf{PPOUT}(\nu) = \mathit{false} \text{ if } \nu \in \mathit{VFN_e}$$

- The Fixed Point Equations (Global Properties):

$$\mathbf{AVIN}(\nu) \iff \prod_{\nu' \in pred(\nu)} \mathbf{AVOUT}(\nu')$$

$$\mathbf{AVOUT}(\nu) \iff \mathbf{AVIN}(\nu) \vee \mathbf{PPOUT}(\nu)$$

$$\mathbf{PPIN}(\nu) \iff \mathbf{AVIN}(\nu) \wedge (\mathbf{ANTLOC}(\nu) \vee \mathbf{PPOUT}(\nu))$$

$$\mathbf{PPOUT}(\nu) \iff \prod_{m \in succ(\mathcal{N}(\nu))} \sum_{\substack{\nu' \in succ(\nu) \\ \mathcal{N}(\nu') = m}} \mathbf{PPIN}(\nu')$$

Algorithm A.2 computes the greatest solution of this system, which determines the computation points by means of

$$\mathbf{INSERT}(\nu) =_{df} \mathbf{PPOUT}(\nu) \wedge \neg \mathbf{PPIN}(\nu)$$

5.2 Placing the Computations

The placement Algorithm A.3 proceeds in three steps:

1. It marks all nodes of the Value Flow Graph that occur on paths that lead from nodes satisfying **INSERT** to nodes satisfying **ANTLOC**.

2. It associates with every marked node of the Value Flow Graph an auxiliary variable. This is a new auxiliary variable, if the marked node either satisfies **INSERT** or has more than one predecessor in the Value Flow Graph. Otherwise the auxiliary variable of its unique predecessor in the Value Flow Graph is taken.

3. It initializes at every node of the Value Flow Graph satisfying **INSERT** its associated auxiliary variable by its initialization term. (Initialization terms of a node ν of the Value Flow Graph are minimal representatives of its corresponding equivalence class $\nu{\downarrow_2}$.)

   If two marked nodes which are associated with different auxiliary variables, say $\mathbf{h}_k$ and $\mathbf{h}_l$, are connected by an edge in the Value Flow Graph, a trivial assignment $\mathbf{h}_l := \mathbf{h}_k$ is added at the end of the first node.

   Finally, original computations of the flow graph are replaced by the corresponding auxiliary variables.

Note, in order to eliminate all redundancies at once, the initializations of auxiliary variables are split into sequences of assignments that only have a single operator in their right hand side expression.

5.3 Optimality Results

An analysis of the Boolean Equation System 5.2 delivers not only the correctness of the derived program transformation, but also its optimality. Intuitively, a flow graph is defined to be optimal wrt a Value Flow Graph if it is "best" in the class of branching structure preserving flow graphs that are "safe" and "complete" for it. Here "best" means that it possesses a minimal number of computations on every path, and "safe" ("complete") that it computes on every path at most (at least) as many values. A formal definition of this notion of optimality is complicated, because all these properties need to be defined in terms of the Value Flow Graph. We will therefore only sketch the formal treatment. For this purpose we will assume (without loss of generality) that the synthetic nodes are already inserted, that linear sequences of nodes are abbreviated by a single node (basic block), and that the Value Flow Graph *covers* all computations of the underlying flow graph, i.e.:

$$\forall n \in N \ \forall t \in T(n) \ \exists \nu \in VFN. \ \mathcal{N}(\nu) = n \wedge t \in \mathbf{T}_{\mathbf{pre}(n)}(\nu \downarrow_1)$$

Now, let **VFG** be a Value Flow Graph for a flow graph $G = (N, E, \mathbf{s}, \mathbf{e})$, and $G' = (N', E', \mathbf{s}', \mathbf{e}')$ a branching structure preserving flow graph for G, i.e. there exists a graph isomorphism Ψ from G' onto G with $\Psi(\mathbf{s}') = \mathbf{s}$ and $\Psi(\mathbf{e}') = \mathbf{e}$. Furthermore assume that $p \in \mathbf{P}(\mathbf{s}, \mathbf{e})$ and $p' = (n_1, .., n_q) \in \mathbf{P}(\mathbf{s}', \mathbf{e}')$ with $\Psi(p') = p$, and let **VFG**(p) denote the graph that results from unrolling **VFG** along the path p. Then **VFG**(p) is a collection of trees, which we will refer to as the **VFG**-values of p. This notion is motivated by the fact that **VFG**(p) defines an equivalence relation on (potential) term occurrences wrt p whose equivalence classes contain computations that evaluate to the same value during the execution of p, and that these classes are maximal such wrt **VFG**. Given a **VFG**-value C of p, $rg_p(C) =_{df} \{n_i \mid \exists \nu \in VFN_C. \ \mathcal{N}(\nu) = n_i\}$ denotes the *range* of C. A computation t' of p' at node n_i is Ψ-*covered* by a **VFG**-value C of p if $\Psi(n_i) \in rg_p(C)$ and if t' is covered by C at $\Psi(n_i)$, or if $\delta_{n_{i-1}}(t')$ is Ψ-covered by C at n_{i-1}. This complicated definition is necessary because a computation in p' need not match a term in **VFG**, for example because of additional (auxiliary) variables in G'. $C_{\mathbf{VFG}}(p)$ denotes the set of all **VFG**-values of p that cover at least one computation of p, and $C_{\mathbf{VFG}}(\Psi, p')$ the maximal set $\top$, or the smallest set of **VFG**-values of p which Ψ-cover all computations of p', if such a set exists.

After this preparation we are able to define the central notions of our optimality concept. G' is **VFG**-*safe* for G if $C_{\mathbf{VFG}}(\Psi, p') \subseteq C_{\mathbf{VFG}}(\Psi(p'))$, and it is **VFG**-*complete* for G if $C_{\mathbf{VFG}}(\Psi, p') \supseteq C_{\mathbf{VFG}}(\Psi(p'))$ for all $p' \in \mathbf{P}(\mathbf{s}', \mathbf{e}')$. Moreover, p' is *better* than p if it contains at most as many (non trivial) computations as p, and G' is *better* than G if p' is better than $\Psi(p')$ for all $p' \in \mathbf{P}(\mathbf{s}', \mathbf{e}')$. Finally, G is **VFG**-*optimal* if it is better than any branching structure preserving G' that is **VFG**-safe and **VFG**-complete for G.

Theorem 5.3 (2.Optimality Theorem)
Every flow graph transformed by the second stage of our algorithm is **VFG**-*optimal.*

Let us now consider the combined effect of the two stages of our algorithm. As mentioned already, it is not possible to finitely represent all Herbrand equivalences syntactically. However, using the 1.Optimality Theorem 4.6 we can show that there exists an infinite Value Flow Graph **VFG**$_\infty$ that even represents all global Herbrand equivalences. This Value Flow Graph is the natural extension of a given Value Flow Graph where all partition DAGs D are replaced by $\mathcal{H}(D)$, see Definition 4.3.

Definition 5.4 A **VFG**$_\infty$-*optimal program is called* Herbrand optimal.

We have:

Theorem 5.5 (Herbrand Optimality)
Every flow graph transformed by our two stage algorithm in the full variant is Herbrand optimal.

Herbrand optimal transformations may cause unboundedly many reinitializations of auxiliary variables in order to eliminate a single redundant computation. Thus, the costs of these reinitializations can easily exceed the costs of the eliminated computation. Motivated by this problem Rosen, Wegman and Zadeck introduced a notion of optimality, which is based on an additional technical constraint (see [RWZ] for details). Referring to this notion as RWZ-optimality we can prove:

Theorem 5.6 (*RWZ*-Optimality)
Every flow graph transformed by our two stage algorithm in the RWZ-variant is RWZ-optimal.

As usual for code motion, our algorithm is devoted to the costs of computations. However, costs for register loading and storing are subsequently taken care of by variable subsumption. An algorithm based on the graph coloring techniques of [Ch,CACCHM] is implemented for this purpose.

Finally, let Trans : **FG** → **FG** be the operator specified by the full variant of our algorithm. Then we obtain by means of the 2.Optimality Theorem 5.3:

Corollary 5.7 Trans *is idempotent, i.e.* $\forall G \in \mathbf{FG}.$ Trans$(G) =$ Trans(Trans$(G))$.

In particular, the full variant of our algorithm covers all second order effects (cf. [RWZ]).

6 Complexity

The second stage of our algorithm can be applied to arbitrary Value Flow Graphs, yielding optimal results relative to the equivalence information represented (see 2.Optimality Theorem 5.3). We therefore estimate the worst case time complexity, which as usual is based on the assumption of *constant branching* and *constant term depth*, independently for both stages. This requires the following three parameters: the number of nodes of a flow graph n, the complexity of computing the meet of two equivalence informations m, and the maximal number of Value Flow Graph nodes which are associated with a single node of the underlying flow graph, μ. This yields for the complexity of the five steps of our algorithm:

1. Construction of a Value Flow Graph for the Herbrand interpretation:

   (i) Determination of semantic equivalences: $O(n^2*m)$. Here "n^2" reflects the maximal length of a descending chain of annotations of a flow graph. In fact, the number of analysis steps of Algorithm A.1 is linear in this chain length. This can be achieved by adding those nodes to a workset whose annotations have been changed. Then processing a worklist entry consists of updating the annotations of all its successors. This can be done in $O(m)$ because of our assumption of constant branching.

   To our knowledge, the exact nature of m is not studied in previous papers. This is probably due to the fact that, in practice, this effort hardly increases linearly in the size of the analysed program, and therefore is regarded as harmless. However, DAGs that arise during the analysis may represent sets of terms which increase exponentially in n. Inspite of this fact, we conjecture that the compact representation of these sets by means of structured partition DAGs, together with the constraint that the DAGs arise during the analysis of a particular program, allows us to show that the number of nodes in such a DAG only increases quadratically in n. This conjecture would suffice to prove an overall complexity of $O(n^4)$ for the first step, because we know that the meet of two DAGs can be computed essentially linearly in the size of the resulting DAG.

(ii) Computation of the syntactic representation of the semantic equivalences: This complexity depends on the variant chosen. Whereas the basic variant and the RWZ-variant are both $O(n^3)$, the full variant seems to be exponential in n.

(iii) Construction of the Value Flow Graph: $O(n*\mu)$. This is based on two facts. First, if there exists an edge in the Value Flow Graph between two nodes ν_1 and ν_2 then the corresponding nodes $\mathcal{N}(\nu_1)$ and $\mathcal{N}(\nu_2)$ of the flow graph are connected as well. Thus every edge of the Value Flow Graph is associated with an edge of the original flow graph. Second, the effort to construct all edges of the Value Flow Graph that correspond to a single edge (n, m) in the original flow graph is linear in the number of Value Flow Graph nodes that annotate n, which can be estimated by μ.

2. Optimal placement of the computations:

(i) Determination of the computation points: $O(n*\mu)$. The argument needed here is based on that of the first step, however, we do not have constant branching, and the algorithm here is bidirectional. This leads to the product $n*\mu$ because all nodes of the Value Flow Graph can be updated once by executing only two elementary operations per edge of the Value Flow Graph, and the number of edges in a Value Flow Graph can be estimated by $O(n*\mu)$.

(ii) Placing the computations: $O(n*\mu)$. This is straightforward.

Let us finally give an estimation of the worst case time complexity of the practically motivated RWZ-variant. Here, $O(\mu)$ can be approximated by $O(n^2)$. In fact, exploiting the specific nature of the RWZ-closure already during the first step, we arrive at an algorithm with an overall complexity of $O(n^4)$. Assuming our conjecture, this result is also true for the RWZ-variant of our two stage algorithm presented above.

7   Conclusion

We have shown, how to combine semantic algorithms with syntactic ones, in order to obtain maximal optimization results. This technique, which is based on the introduction of Value Flow Graphs, has been illustrated by developing a two stage algorithm for the optimal placement of computations within a program.

In addition to their optimality, algorithms developed by means of this technique are easily to extend, because the separation of their semantic part from their (independently optimal) syntactic transformation part makes them modular. This modularity allows to independently enhance the semantic properties by modifying the first stage, and the transformation capacity by strenghtening the second stage. In our current implementation, the first stage is extended to deal with *constant propagation* and *constant folding* (see [SK1,SK2]). An extension of the second stage to *strength reduction* ([ACK,CK,JD1,JD2]) is under development.

Acknowledgements

The presentation in this paper profited from discussions with Torben Hagerup, Mark Jerrum, Barry Rosen and Ken Zadeck.

References

[All]   F. E. Allen. *"Control Flow Analysis"*. ACM Sigplan Notices, July 1970

[ACK]   F. E. Allen, J. Cocke and K. Kennedy. *"Reduction of Operator Strength"*. In: St. S. Muchnick and N. D. Jones, editors. "Program Flow Analysis: Theory and Applications", Prentice Hall, Inc., Englewood Cliffs, New Jersey 07632, 1981

[Ch]   G. J. Chaitin. *"Register Allocation and Spilling via Graph Coloring"*. IBM T. J. Watson Research Center, Computer Science Department, P.O. Box 218, Yorktown Height, N. Y. 10598, 1981

[CACCHM] G. J. Chaitin, M. A. Auslander, A. K. Chandra, J. Cocke, M. E. Hopkins and P. W. Markstein. *"Register Allocation via Coloring"*. IBM T. J. Watson Research Center, Computer Science Department, P.O. Box 218, Yorktown Height, N. Y. 10598, 1980

[CK]   J. Cocke and K. Kennedy. *"An Algorithm for Reduction of Operator Strength"*. Communications of the ACM, 20(11):850-856, 1977

[FKU]   A. Fong, J. B. Kam and J. D. Ullman. *"Application of Lattice Algebra to Loop Optimization"*. 2nd POPL, Palo Alto, California, 1 - 9, 1975

[JD1]   S. M. Joshi and D. M. Dhamdhere. *"A Composite Hoisting-Strength Reduction Transformation for Global Program Optimization – Part I"*. Internat. J. Computer Math. 11, 21 - 41, 1982

[JD2]   S. M. Joshi and D. M. Dhamdhere. *"A Composite Hoisting-Strength Reduction Transformation for Global Program Optimization – Part II"*. Internat. J. Computer Math. 11, 111 - 126, 1982

[Ki1]   G. A. Kildall. *"Global Expression Optimization during Compilation"*. Technical Report No. 72-06-02, University of Washington, Computer Science Group, Seattle, Washington, 1972

[Ki2]   G. A. Kildall. *"A Unified Approach to Global Program Optimization"*. 1st POPL, Boston, Massachusetts, 194 - 206, 1973

[MR]   E. Morel and C. Renvoise. *"Global Optimization by Suppression of Partial Redundancies"*. Communications of the ACM, 22(2):96-103, 1979

[RWZ]   B. K. Rosen, M. N. Wegman and F. K. Zadeck. *"Global Value Numbers and Redundant Computations"*. 15th POPL, San Diego, California, 12 - 27, 1988

[St1]   B. Steffen. *"Optimal Run Time Optimization. Proved by a New Look at Abstract Interpretations"*. TAPSOFT'87, Pisa, Italy, LNCS 249, 52 - 68, 1987

[St2]   B. Steffen. *"Abstrakte Interpretationen beim Optimieren von Programmlaufzeiten. Ein Optimalitätskonzept und seine Anwendung"*. PhD thesis, Christian Albrechts-Universität Kiel, 1987

[SK1]   B. Steffen and J. Knoop. *"Finite Constants: Characterizations of a New Decidable Set of Constants"*. 14th MFCS, Porąbka-Kozubnik, Poland, LNCS 379, 481 - 491, 1989

[SK2]   B. Steffen and J. Knoop. *"Finite Constants: Characterizations of a New Decidable Set of Constants"*. Extended version of [SK1], LFCS Report Series, ECS-LFCS-89-79, Laboratory for Foundations of Computer Science, University of Edinburgh, 1989

A Appendix: The Algorithms

Algorithm A.1 (The Semantic Analysis of Step 1.(i))

Input: *An arbitrary flow graph* $G = (N, E, \mathsf{s}, \mathsf{e})$ *with unique start node* s *and unique stop node* e, *which are assumed to possess no predecessors and no successors, respectively.*

Output: *A designation of* G *with pre-DAGs (stored in pre) and post-DAGs (stored in post), characterizing valid and complete equivalence information at the entrance and at the exit of every node* $n \in N$, *respectively.*

Remark: $\perp$ *denotes the "empty" data flow information and* $\top$ *its complement, the "universal" data flow information, which is assumed to "contain" every data flow information.* $[\![\ ]\!]$ *denotes the* local *analysis component and* $\sqcap$ *the* meet *operation.* ($[\![\ ]\!]$ *and* $\sqcap$ *operate on DAG-structures).* $pred(n) =_{df} \{m \mid (m, n) \in E\}$ *and* $succ(n) =_{df} \{m \mid (n, m) \in E\}$ *denote the set of all predecessors and successors of a node* n, *respectively. The variable* workset *controls the iterative process, and the auxiliary variable* meet *stores the result of the most recent meet operation.*

(Initialization of the designation arrays pre and post and the variable workset)
FOR *all nodes* $n \in N$ **DO**
  IF $n = \mathsf{s}$
    THEN $(pre[n], post[n]) := (\perp, [\![n]\!](\perp))$
    ELSE $(pre[n], post[n]) := (\top, \top)$ **FI**
OD;
$workset := \{\mathsf{s}\}$;

(Iterative fixed point computation)
WHILE $workset \neq \emptyset$ **DO**
  LET $n \in workset$
    BEGIN
      $workset := workset \backslash \{n\}$;
      (Update the "environment" of node n *)*
      FOR *all nodes* $m \in succ(n)$ **DO**
        $meet := pre[m] \sqcap post[n]$;
        IF $pre[m] \sqsupset meet$
          THEN
            $pre[m] := meet$;
            $post[m] := [\![m]\!](pre[m])$;
            $workset := workset \cup \{m\}$
        FI
      OD
    END
OD.

Algorithm A.2 (Solution of the Boolean Equation System (Step 2(i)))

Input: *A Boolean equation system which is completely initialized wrt the local property* **ANTLOC**.

Output: *The greatest solution of the Boolean equation system.*

Remark: *With every node of the Value Flow Graph the predicates* **ANTLOC, AVIN, AVOUT, PPIN** *and* **PPOUT** *are associated. However, only the later four are involved in the fixed point iteration, which therefore operates on the fourfold cartesian product of the complete semi-lattice* $\{false, true\}$ *with* $false \sqsubset true$. $pred(\nu) =_{df} \{\mu \mid (\mu, \nu) \in VFE\}$ *and* $succ(\nu) =_{df} \{\mu \mid (\nu, \mu) \in VFE\}$ *denote the set of all predecessors and successors of a node* ν, *respectively. The variable* workset controls the iterative process. For notational convenience we abbreviate $(AVIN(\nu)$, $AVOUT(\nu)$, $PPIN(\nu)$, $PPOUT(\nu))$ by $\vec{p}_\nu$. The auxiliary variable $\vec{p}$ stores the result of the most recent application of the local analysis component, and avin and ppout are further auxiliary variables.

(Initialization)
FOR all nodes $\nu \in VFN$ DO $\vec{p}_\nu := (true, true, true, true)$ OD;
FOR all nodes $\nu \in VFN_s$ DO $(AVIN(\nu), PPIN(\nu)) := (false, false)$ OD;
FOR all nodes $\nu \in VFN_e$ DO $PPOUT(\nu) := false$ OD;
$workset := VFN_s \cup VFN_e$;

(Iterative fixed point computation)
WHILE $workset \neq \emptyset$ DO
  LET $\nu \in workset$
    BEGIN
      $workset := workset \setminus \{\nu\}$;
      (Update the "environment" of node ν)
      FOR all nodes $\mu \in pred(\nu) \cup succ(\nu)$ DO
        IF $\mu \in pred(\nu)$
          THEN
            $ppout := PPOUT(\mu) \wedge \Sigma \{PPIN(\lambda) \,|\, \lambda \in succ(\mu) \wedge \mathcal{N}(\lambda) = \mathcal{N}(\nu)\}$;
            $\vec{p} := (AVIN(\mu), AVIN(\mu) \vee ppout, AVIN(\mu) \wedge (ANTLOC(\mu) \vee ppout), ppout)$
          ELSE
            $avin := AVIN(\mu) \wedge AVOUT(\nu)$;
            $\vec{p} := (avin, avin \vee PPOUT(\mu), avin \wedge (ANTLOC(\mu) \vee PPOUT(\mu)), PPOUT(\mu))$

        FI;
        IF $\vec{p}_\mu \sqsupset \vec{p}$
          THEN
            $\vec{p}_\mu := \vec{p}$;
            $workset := workset \cup \{\mu\}$ FI
      OD
    END
OD.

Algorithm A.3 (The Optimizing Program Transformation (Step 2(ii)))

INPUT: *A flow graph G and an accociated Value Flow Graph VFG with attached predicate designation characterizing the greatest solution of the Boolean Equation System 5.2.*

OUTPUT: *The transformed flow graph G_T. In G_T auxiliary variables are initialized at the optimal computation points by their minimal computation forms wrt to the equivalence information expressed by VFG. Original computations are replaced by auxiliary variables.*

REMARK: *The algorithm consists of three phases, namely*

- *Marking of the definition-use chains in VFG.*
- *Allocating of the auxiliary variable numbers.*
- *Transforming of the flow graph, namely*
  - *Initializing auxiliary variables at their computation points by their computation forms.*
  - *Introducing spill code for the generated auxiliary variables.*
  - *Substituting original computations by a reference to their covering auxiliary variable.*

The marking of a node $\nu \in VFN$ is indicated by the predicate $mark(\nu)$, the number of an associated auxiliary variable is denoted by $nr(\nu)$ and the variable *count* indicates the number of the last generated auxiliary variable.

(Phase 1: Marking of the definition-use chains in **VFG** *)*
FOR all nodes $\nu \in VFN$ **DO** $mark(\nu) := false$ **OD**;
$workset := \{ \nu \in VFN \,|\, \text{ANTLOC}(\nu)\}$;
WHILE $workset \neq \emptyset$ **DO**
  LET $\nu \in workset$
    BEGIN
      $workset := workset \setminus \{\nu\}$;
      $mark(\nu) := true$;
      IF $\neg\text{INSERT}(\nu)$ **THEN** $workset := workset \cup \{\nu' \in pred(\nu) \,|\, \neg\, mark(\nu') \}$ **FI**
    END
OD;

(Phase 2: Allocating auxiliary variable numbers)
$count := 0$;
FOR all nodes $\nu \in VFN$ **DO** $nr(\nu):=0$ **OD**;
$workset := \{\nu \in VFN \,|\, \text{INSERT}(\nu)\}$;
WHILE $workset \neq \emptyset$ **DO**
  LET $\nu \in workset$
    BEGIN
      $workset := workset \setminus \{\nu\}$;
      $mark(\nu) := false$;
      IF $\text{INSERT}(\nu) \vee |pred(\nu)| \geq 2$
        THEN
          $count := count + 1$;
          $nr(\nu) := count$
        ELSE *(assume $pred(\nu) = \{\nu'\}$)*
          $nr(\nu):= nr(\nu')$
      FI;
      $workset := workset \cup \{\nu' \in succ(\nu) \,|\, mark(\nu) \}$
    END
OD;

(Phase 3: Transformation of the flow graph)
(Initializing auxiliary variables at their computation points by their computation forms)
FOR all nodes $n \in N$ **DO**
  $workset := \{\nu \in VFN \,|\, \text{INSERT}(\nu) \wedge \mathcal{N}(\nu)=n \}$;
  WHILE $workset \neq \emptyset$ **DO**
    LET $\nu \in \{\nu' \in workset \,|\, \forall \bar\nu \in workset \,.\, \bar\nu\!\downarrow_2 \notin succ^*(\nu'\!\downarrow_2)\}$
      BEGIN
        $workset := workset \setminus \{\nu\}$;
        IF $L_{\text{post}(n)}(\nu\!\downarrow_2) \cap (V \cup C) \neq \emptyset$
          THEN
            LET $x \in L_{\text{post}(n)}(\nu\!\downarrow_2) \cap (V \cup C)$
              BEGIN
                Attach the assignment $\boxed{h_{nr(\nu)} := x}$ at the end of node n
              END

ELSE
    LET $op \in L_{\mathbf{post}(n)}(\nu\downarrow_2),$
           $\nu' \in VFN. \ \nu'\downarrow_2 = l(\nu\downarrow_2),$
           $\bar{\nu} \in VFN. \ \bar{\nu}\downarrow_2 = r(\nu\downarrow_2)$
    BEGIN
      Attach the assignment $\boxed{h_{nr(\nu)} := h_{nr(\nu')} \, op \, h_{nr(\bar{\nu})}}$ *at the end of node* n
    END
    FI
  END
OD
OD;

(Introducing spill code for the generated auxiliary variables)
FOR *all nodes* $\nu, \nu' \in \{\bar{\nu} \in VFN \mid nr(\bar{\nu}) \neq 0\}$ **DO**
  IF $\nu \in pred(\nu') \wedge nr(\nu) \neq nr(\nu')$
    THEN
      Attach a component of spill code $\boxed{(.., h_{nr(\nu')}, ..) := (.., h_{nr(\nu)}, ..)}$ *at the end of node* $\mathcal{N}(\nu)$
  FI
OD;

(Substituting original computations by a reference to their covering auxiliary variable)
FOR *all nodes* $n \in N$ **DO**
  $workset := \{\nu \in VFN \mid ANTLOC(\nu) \wedge \mathcal{N}(\nu) = n\};$
  WHILE $workset \neq \emptyset$ **DO**
    LET $\nu \in \{\nu' \in workset \mid \forall \bar{\nu} \in workset. \ \bar{\nu}\downarrow_1 \notin pred^*(\nu'\downarrow_1)\}$
    BEGIN
      $workset := workset \setminus \{\nu\};$
      Replace all original computations $t \in \mathcal{T}(n) \cap \mathbf{T}_{\mathbf{pre}(n)}(\nu\downarrow_1)$ *by* $h_{nr(\nu)}$
    END
  OD
OD.

Type Inference and Implicit Scaling

Satish Thatte

Department of Mathematics and Computer Science
Clarkson University, Potsdam, NY 13676, USA

Abstract

We describe a novel application of subtyping in which a small orthogonal set of structural subtyping rules are used to capture the notion of scaling—an unusual variety of polymorphism found in APL-like languages which is attracting renewed interest due to its applications in data parallel programming. The subtyping approach allows us to provide a simple coercion-based semantics for a generalized interpretation of scaling that goes well beyond what is available in APL dialects.

1 Introduction

Data parallelism [HS86,Bre88,Vis89] has gained increasing favor recently due to its conceptual simplicity and the high speedup available whenever the technique can be used effectively. Conceptually, data parallelism covers a broad range from traditional vector processing to techniques for programming Transputer networks [Vis89] and the Connection Machine [HS86]. In this paper, we are concerned with one of the main techniques used for data parallel programming: the technique of *scaling*, which goes back all the way to APL [Ive62] where it was introduced for its expressive power in array manipulation rather than as a way of expressing parallelism. Our concern will be with the implications of scaling for static typing—specifically, we explore a novel subtyping approach to the static type analysis of a very general interpretation of scaling.

Recall that in APL, many scalar operations also accept array arguments and "scale" their meaning accordingly. In later dialects like APL2, the arguments may also be arbitrarily nested arrays. For instance, the scaling and shifting of a vector is usually written as $a+b\mathbb{v}$ where $\mathbb{v}$ is a vector and a and b are real constants. Representing $\mathbb{v}$ by a 1-D array V, one can simply write this expression as a+b*V in APL. In Standard ML [Mil84], using a list V, the same expression might be written as map (op +) (distl (a, map (op *) (distl (b, V)))) where the distl primitive is borrowed from FP [Bac78]. Besides the obvious implicit parallelism, the gain in expressive power as a result of scaling is striking.

The price paid for implicit scaling is added complexity in the semantics of the language. Existing explanations of scaling in APL [Ben85,JM78] treat only the operations involved (such as "+" and "*" above) as being polymorphic. The range of possible behaviors of such operations, especially when nested structures are allowed as arguments, is hard to capture in a single principle type expression, or even in a finite number of expressions. This is the main difficulty in doing static type analysis of scaled expressions. Our innovation in this paper is to show that an alternative approach based on coercive structural subtyping accounts very effectively for scaling. In effect, our type system coerces the APL-like version of the expression given above to the Standard ML version. We expect that a realistic compiler using our system can derive enough information from the typing process to generate more efficient (sequential or data parallel) code than the naive synthesized version implies.

The generality achieved by our solution goes well beyond what is available in APL dialects. Scaling is no longer limited to syntactic operators—all functions including user-defined ones can be scaled up in the same way. The extension of the subtype structure relative to type constructors captures all the natural implications of scaling for components of structures, higher-order functions, and so forth (see examples in Section 3). The notion of scaling itself is more general. As an example, suppose "++" denotes vector concatenation, and the vector consisting of $x_1, x_2, ..., x_n$ is denoted by $[x_1, x_2, ..., x_n]$. The expressions $[[1,2],[3,4]]$ ++ $[[5,6],[7,8]]$ and $[[1,2],[3,4]]$ + $[[5,6],[7,8]]$ both work correctly: the former yields $[[1,2,5,6], [3,4,7,8]]$ and the latter $[[6,8], [10,12]]$. Note that the grain of scaling is different in the two cases. We do not know of any APL dialect which *automatically* adjusts the grain of scaling to the needs of the application in this way. Our technique is also quite robust under many kinds of enrichments of the underlying language—for instance with mutable variables. Compatibility with parametric polymorphism poses some interesting problems, which are discussed in Section 8.

The basis of our solution is a small set of orthogonal subtyping rules (with corresponding coercions) which capture most cases of scaling. As in the case of subtyping with labeled record types [Car88] subtyping is based on the structure of type expressions. Although easy to understand and motivate, the structural relationships turn out to be unusually complex. Even the antisymmetry of the subtype relation needs a nontrivial proof. The proof of the coherence of subsumptions (subtyping judgements), *i.e.*, the property that each subsumption implies a semantically unique abstract coercion, requires a normalization result for derivations of subsumptions. The subtype structure is consistently complete, but this is not obvious, and the algorithms for finding LUBs and GLBs (required in the typechecking algorithm) are quite complex. In spite of this complexity, we believe that the subtype structure is intuitively natural and will be "user-friendly" in practice.

The subtyping rules define the rest of the problem, which is to verify that they can be applied within a standard general framework of the kind given in [Rey85] to give unambiguous meanings to scaled expressions. Standard typing rules allow derivation of types and coerced (unscaled) versions for all meaningful scaled expressions and each coerced version can be given a meaning using the standard semantics of the λ-calculus. To show that each scaled expression has a *unique* meaning, we need two further properties: the existence of a minimal typing judgement for each well-typed expression, and semantic coherence—the property that the meaning of an expression depends only on the typing judgement applied to it, not on the derivation used to reach that judgement. Since each use of a subsumption in a typing derivation implies the insertion of a coercion, the meaning of an expression seems to depend on the particular derivation. Coherence asserts that this apparent ambiguity is semantically inconsequential: all the different coerced versions for the same judgement have the same meaning. The notion of coherence was first discussed explicitly in [BC+89]. Reynolds' discussion of coercions and overloaded operators [Rey85] is based on the same intuition. As Reynolds (implicitly) points out, coherence of typing is closely related to coherence of subsumptions. The additional complication in our case comes from the fact that each function-valued expression is "overloaded" with an infinite number of potential meanings. However, it can be shown that at most one of these overloaded meanings is usable in any particular application. This fact, together with coherence of subsumptions, turns out to be sufficient for coherence of typing.

In the rest of the paper, following a brief discussion of related work and some preliminaries in Sections 2 and 3, we begin by deriving the subtype structure in Section 4. Section 5 gives an outline of the coercion-based semantics. The proofs of the major properties of the subtype

$$
\begin{array}{llllll}
e ::= & x & \text{(identifiers)} & \mid \lambda x_\tau.\, e & \text{(typed abstractions)} & \mid e_1\, e_2 & \text{(applications)} \\
& \mid e_1, e_2 & \text{(pairs)} & \mid e \downarrow i & \text{(projections, } i=1,2) & \mid \underline{\text{nil}}_\tau & \text{(empty list)} \\
& \mid e_1;\, e_2 & \text{(cons)} & \mid \underline{\text{hd}}\ e & \text{(list head)} & \mid \underline{\text{tl}}\ e & \text{(list tail)} \\[4pt]
\tau ::= & \iota & \text{(scalar types)} & \mid \tau_1 \times \tau_2 & \text{(product types)} & & \\
& \mid [\tau] & \text{(list types)} & \mid \tau_1 \to \tau_2 & \text{(function types)} & &
\end{array}
$$

Figure 1: Syntax of Object and Type Expressions

structure are outlined in Section 6. Section 7 gives the typing algorithms, and Section 8 concludes with a discussion of the problems involved in adding parametric polymorphism. Many technical details and all actual proofs are omitted in this version for lack of space.

2 Related Work

Type inference using subtypes structures has proved to be a fruitful idea in a variety of applications. It was originally introduced by Reynolds [Rey80] to systematize the semantics of automatic coercions between types. Such subtyping might be called *coercive*, to contrast it with the *inclusive* variant used in theories of inheritance [Car88], quantified types [Mit88] and partial types [Tha88], where subtypes are taken to be subsets. Most applications of the coercive variant have been concerned with relationships between *atomic* types, such as "integer ≤ real". An underlying theme in this paper is that coercive *structural* subtyping—subtyping based on the structure of type expressions—can be very useful as a tool to provide coercion based semantics for many interesting language features that pose problems for other semantic approaches. A similar approach is used in [BC+89] to give an alternative semantics for inheritance. We have elsewhere [Tha90] explored an application to dynamic typing in static languages.

3 Type and Object Languages

The object language is a simply typed dialect of the λ-calculus. For definiteness, the language includes a linear list or sequence structure for the application of scaling. However, this fact is nowhere used in an essential way, and substituting sequences with any other data structure suitable for set representation (such as trees or arrays) would require no change in the treatment except for the substitution of appropriate new conversion functions. The grammars for type and object expressions are given in Figure 1, where the metavariable e ranges over expressions, x over identifiers, ι over scalar types and τ over all type expressions. Scalar types in this context need not include only atomic types. Any type which is not a product or function type and is not a structure type involved with scaling can be thought of as a scalar type. The set of all type expressions will be denoted by *Typexprs*.

Besides the constructors × and → for product and function types, we have an outfix type constructor [ ]; [τ] is list-of-τ. We need to provide the list primitives as syntactic operators in order to allow them to be generic. Note that the type intended for each use of <u>nil</u> must be given (this can be avoided by introducing the "universal" type described by Reynolds [Rey85]). In a simply typed dialect of the λ-calculus such as ours, recursion must normally be provided by an explicit construct which computes least fixed points of functions. The reason for omitting the construct in the grammar above is that fixpoint constructs are incompatible with minimal typing in our context—the counterexample is omitted here for lack of space. This does *not* mean that the language cannot include fixpoint constructs. It does mean that the typing constraints for such constructs cannot be described using nondeterministic typing rules as in the case of the other constructs. It is easy to infer the *natural* type of instances of the fix construct, and the fix case in the minimal typing algorithm Type in Section 7 does exactly that.

4 The Subtype Structure

The essence of our approach is to capture the semantics of scaling in a small orthogonal set of structural subtyping rules. The subtype structure must find a balance between two conflicting principles—orthogonality and coherence. Orthogonality—the treatment of all (data and function) types as first-class citizens in the subtyping scheme—is what gives the solution its simplicity, generality and expressive power. Unrestricted orthogonality leads to loss of coherence, but the coherent solution derived below retains sufficient orthogonality for most practical purposes.

It is helpful to start with some examples to outline the desired range of applicability of the subtype structure. The primitive coercions we shall need are provided in FP [Bac78] as primitives—"•" (function composition), α (a *curried* version of map), distl, distr and trans. The function trans transforms any pair of lists of equal size into a list of pairs of corresponding elements in the obvious way; distl "distributes" its first argument by pairing it with elements of its second (list/sequence) argument, and distr is exactly the same except it takes its arguments in the reverse order. We treat these coercions as though they possess polymorphic types because they are used only in places where their type is both correct and manifest. The use of FP primitives as basic coercions is especially interesting because FP has been influenced by many APL ideas and idioms but lacks a notion of scaling. The reason (presumably) is that the semantics of implicit scaling in APL is rather complex and *ad hoc*. We restore scaling (for homogeneous structures) in a semantically simple way by *implicitly* using the same coercions FP programmers must use *explicitly*.

We use $[e_1, e_2, \dots, e_n]$ as an abbreviation for $e_1; (e_2; (\dots; (e_n; \text{nil}_\tau) \dots))$ (where τ is the component type) and the form $e \twoheadrightarrow e'$ to mean that the expression e is (expected to be) coerced to e' by a minimal typing derivation. Thus,

$$\text{square } [1, 2, 3] \quad \twoheadrightarrow \quad (\alpha \text{ square}) [1, 2, 3] \quad = \quad [1, 4, 9]$$
$$1 + [1, 2, 3] \quad \twoheadrightarrow \quad (\alpha +) (\text{distl } (1, [1, 2, 3])) \quad = \quad [2, 3, 4]$$
$$[1, 2, 3] + 1 \quad \twoheadrightarrow \quad (\alpha +) (\text{distr } ([1, 2, 3], 1)) \quad = \quad [2, 3, 4]$$
$$[1, 2, 3] + [2, 3, 4] \quad \twoheadrightarrow \quad (\alpha +) (\text{trans } ([1, 2, 3], [2, 3, 4])) \quad = \quad [3, 5, 7]$$

Scaling is not limited to one "level" in a structure. Thus,

$$1 + [[1, 2], [2, 3]] \quad \twoheadrightarrow \quad (\alpha (\alpha +)) ((\alpha \text{ distl}) (\text{distl } (1, [[1, 2], [2, 3]]))) \quad = \quad [[2, 3], [3, 4]]$$

For an example with nonscalar operands, let $f = \lambda x_{\text{int} \times [\text{int}]}. x{\downarrow}1; x{\downarrow}2$,

$$f (0, [[1, 2], [2, 3]]) \quad \twoheadrightarrow \quad (\alpha f) (\text{distl } (0, [[1, 2], [2, 3]])) \quad = \quad [[0, 1, 2], [0, 2, 3]]$$

We wish to capture the implicit coercions implied by these examples in a few orthogonal structural subtyping rules. Subtyping judgements will be presented in the "natural deduction" style. Each subtyping judgement has the form $\vdash \tau1 \le \tau2 \Rightarrow f$ where f is the corresponding coercion. The simple scaling of functions as in square [1, 2, 3] can be captured in its full generality by the rule

SCL: $\quad \vdash \quad \tau1 \rightarrow \tau2 \quad \le \quad [\tau1] \rightarrow [\tau2] \quad \Rightarrow \quad \alpha$

which uses the (polymorphic) operator α to convert any function of type $\tau1 \rightarrow \tau2$ to a function of type $[\tau1] \rightarrow [\tau2]$, where $\tau1$ and $\tau2$ are arbitrary types. For instance, consider the expression square $[[1, 2], [2, 3]]$. Here the type of square is coerced to $[[int]] \rightarrow [[int]]$ by two iterations of SCL, and square itself is coerced to α (α square). An interesting consequence of SCL is that one *never* needs to use the α (map) operator explicitly, even in order to scale up an argument of a higher-order function (see inner product example at the end of the section).

Evaluation of expressions like $[1, 2, 3] + [2, 3, 4]$ can be seen as a two step process in which a *zipping* step collates the two operands to yield $[(1,2), (2,3), (3,4)]$ and a *scaling* step coerces "+" to "α +". The first step can be captured by the rule

ZIP: $\vdash$ $[\tau1] \times [\tau2]$ $\leq$ $[\tau1 \times \tau2]$ $\Rightarrow$ trans

with the semantic proviso (enforced by trans) that the two lists must have the same length. This generalizes pleasantly to examples like

$$[[1, 2], [3, 4]] + [[2, 3], [4, 5]]$$
$$\rightarrow \;\; (\alpha\,(\alpha +))\,((\alpha\,trans) \bullet trans\,([[1, 2], [3, 4]], [[2, 3], [4, 5]])) \;\; = \;\; [[3, 5], [7, 9]]$$

The argument type $[[int]] \times [[int]]$ is transformed to $[[int \times int]]$ by two iterations of ZIP, and "+" is then applicable by two iterations of SCL. The second iteration of ZIP uses a naturally induced subtyping relationship between list types (incorporated into rule LIST in Figure 2). ZIP implies that all explicit uses of our version of trans can also be eliminated.

This leaves examples like $1 + [1, 2, 3]$. The argument type here is $int \times [int]$ and it needs to be subsumed to $[int \times int]$. The coercion involves *replication* of the first argument to match the second. Replication cannot be separated from zipping since the degree of replication is determined by the context—1 is replicated three times in this example because the *other* argument of "+" is a list of length three. We might therefore propose the symmetric rules

$\vdash \; \tau1 \times [\tau2] \; \leq \; [\tau1 \times \tau2] \; \Rightarrow \;$ distl   and $\vdash \; [\tau1] \times \tau2 \; \leq \; [\tau1 \times \tau2] \; \Rightarrow \;$ distr

Unfortunately, these rules are incompatible with coherence. The problem can be seen with a simple example — two semantically distinct derivations for $[int] \times [int] \leq [[int \times int]]$:

$[int] \times [int] \leq [int \times [int]] \leq [[int \times int]]$ $[int] \times [int] \leq [[int] \times int] \leq [[int \times int]]$

The coercion for $[int] \times [int] \leq [[int \times int]]$ is distl $\bullet$ distr in the first derivation, and distr $\bullet$ distl in the second: $([1,2],[3,4])$ would be converted to $[[(1,3),(1,4)], [(2,3),(2,4)]]$ by the first derivation and to $[[(1,3),(2,3)], [(1,4),(2,4)]]$ by the second. We therefore impose the restriction that replicated values must be *scalars*.

The basic cases of the subtype relation are defined by rules SCL, ZIP, REPL and REPR in Figure 2. The other rules in Figure 2 are standard for all subtype relations (see, *e.g.*, [Rey85]). Of these, LIST, PROD, and FUN allow the basic rules to be applied to *subexpressions* of a type expression in a natural way. In the coercion for PROD, we have used FP's selection functions **1** and **2** as projections from pairs, and FP's *construction* form in its dyadic version—the construction "$\{f_1, f_2\}$" denotes a function such that $\{f_1, f_2\}\, x = (f_1\, x, f_2\, x)$.

Clearly, the coercions in Figure 2 are naive. In a serious sequential implementation, one would expect to optimize the implementation of standard combinations to avoid actual zipping and replication whenever possible, to produce code that is comparable in efficiency to (say) equivalent hand-coded C programs. In programming for the Connection Machine on the other hand, actual replication appears to be the standard practice [HS86]. The detection and

$$\text{SCL: } \vdash \tau_1 \rightarrow \tau_2 \leq [\tau_1] \rightarrow [\tau_2] \Rightarrow \alpha \qquad \text{ZIP: } \vdash [\tau_1] \times [\tau_2] \leq [\tau_1 \times \tau_2] \Rightarrow \text{trans}$$

$$\text{REPL: } \vdash \iota \times [\tau] \leq [\iota \times \tau] \Rightarrow \text{distl} \qquad \text{REPR: } \vdash [\tau] \times \iota \leq [\tau \times \iota] \Rightarrow \text{distr}$$

$$\text{RFLX: } \vdash \tau \leq \tau \Rightarrow \text{id}$$

$$\text{TRNS: } \frac{\vdash \tau_1 \leq \tau_2 \Rightarrow f \qquad \vdash \tau_2 \leq \tau_3 \Rightarrow g}{\vdash \tau_1 \leq \tau_3 \Rightarrow g \cdot f}$$

$$\text{LIST: } \frac{\vdash \tau_1 \leq \tau_2 \Rightarrow f}{\vdash [\tau_1] \leq [\tau_2] \Rightarrow \alpha f}$$

$$\text{PROD: } \frac{\vdash \tau_1 \leq \tau_2 \Rightarrow f \qquad \vdash \tau_3 \leq \tau_4 \Rightarrow g}{\vdash \tau_1 \times \tau_3 \leq \tau_2 \times \tau_4 \Rightarrow \{f \cdot \mathbf{1}, g \cdot \mathbf{2}\}}$$

$$\text{FUN: } \frac{\vdash \tau_1 \leq \tau_2 \Rightarrow f \qquad \vdash \tau_3 \leq \tau_4 \Rightarrow g}{\vdash \tau_2 \rightarrow \tau_3 \leq \tau_1 \rightarrow \tau_4 \Rightarrow \lambda h. \, g \cdot h \cdot f}$$

Figure 2: Subtyping Rules and Coercions

transformation of optimizable combinations of coercions can be made a part of the typechecking algorithm. The details are clearly nontrivial, and will have to await another paper.

To illustrate the use of a number of rules working together, consider a slightly more complex example involving higher-order functions. In FP, the inner product function is defined by the expression $(/+) \cdot (\alpha *) \cdot \text{trans}$, where "/" is APL's *reduce* operator, which has type (real $\times$ real $\rightarrow$ real)$\rightarrow$[real]$\rightarrow$real in this context. Given that explicit uses of α and trans are unnecessary, we should be able to express inner product as $(/+) \cdot *$. The expression should have the type $\tau = [\text{real}] \times [\text{real}] \rightarrow \text{real}$. "/+" clearly has type [real]$\rightarrow$real. The type of "*" is coerced from real $\times$ real $\rightarrow$ real to [real $\times$ real] $\rightarrow$ [real] using SCL to fit the composition, giving the (minimal) type $\sigma = [\text{real} \times \text{real}] \rightarrow \text{real}$ for the overall expression. It is easy to see that the required type τ is a supertype of σ—[real] $\times$ [real] $\leq$ [real $\times$ real] by ZIP and hence $\tau \geq \sigma$ by FUN. The standard behavior is therefore *inherited* by our version, which is more general than the usual inner product. In addition to a pair of real sequences, it could also be applied to a real constant and real sequence, or to a sequence of real pairs.

The subtype structure defined here appears to have few unexpected consequences of the kind that made coercions in PL/I notorious. A possible exception is that some nonhomogeneous list expressions, instead of producing type errors, are automatically homogeneized:

$$[(3, [1,2]), ([4,5], 6)] \rightarrow [\text{distl} (3, [1,2]), \text{distr} ([4,5], 6)] = [[(3,1),(3,2)], [(4,6),(5,6)]]$$

It should be noted that in all of the examples in this section, whenever automatic coercion is required, the resulting converted expression is not unique. Given an apparently mismatched

$$A \vdash x \Rightarrow x : A(x) \qquad\qquad A \vdash \underline{nil}_\tau \Rightarrow \underline{nil}_\tau : [\tau]$$

$$\begin{array}{c} A \vdash e_1 \Rightarrow e_1' : \tau \\ A \vdash e_2 \Rightarrow e_2' : [\tau] \\ \hline A \vdash e_1; e_2 \Rightarrow e_1'; e_2' : [\tau] \end{array} \qquad \begin{array}{c} A \vdash e \Rightarrow e' : \tau_1 \times \tau_2 \\ \hline A \vdash e{\downarrow}i \Rightarrow e'{\downarrow}i : \tau_i \end{array} \quad i = 1, 2$$

$$\begin{array}{c} A \vdash e \Rightarrow e' : [\tau] \\ \hline A \vdash \underline{hd}\ e \Rightarrow \underline{hd}\ e' : \tau \end{array} \qquad \begin{array}{c} A \vdash e \Rightarrow e' : [\tau] \\ \hline A \vdash \underline{tl}\ e \Rightarrow \underline{tl}\ e' : [\tau] \end{array}$$

$$\begin{array}{c} A + x : \tau \vdash e \Rightarrow e' : \tau' \\ \hline A \vdash \lambda x_\tau.e \Rightarrow \lambda x_\tau.e' : \tau \to \tau' \end{array} \qquad \begin{array}{c} A \vdash e_1 \Rightarrow e_1' : \tau_1 \to \tau_2 \\ A \vdash e_2 \Rightarrow e_2' : \tau_1 \\ \hline A \vdash e_1 e_2 \Rightarrow e_1' e_2' : \tau_2 \end{array}$$

$$\begin{array}{c} A \vdash e_1 \Rightarrow e_1' : \tau_1 \\ A \vdash e_2 \Rightarrow e_2' : \tau_2 \\ \hline A \vdash e_1, e_2 \Rightarrow e_1', e_2' : \tau_1 \times \tau_2 \end{array} \qquad \begin{array}{c} A \vdash e \Rightarrow e' : \tau 1 \qquad \vdash \tau 1 \le \tau 2 \Rightarrow f \\ \hline A \vdash e \Rightarrow f\ e' : \tau 2 \end{array}$$

Figure 3: Typing Rules

application, one can either coerce the function part to adapt to the argument or *vice versa*. The individual coercions themselves can be carried out in many ways. The important point is that, as a result of the coherence property, this flexibility does not cause any semantic ambiguity.

5 The Semantics in Outline

The semantics of the object language is based on transforming scaled expressions—all expressions are assumed to be scaled—to unscaled ones based on the subtype structure of the last section. The "engine" for the transformation is type inference, specified by a set of typing rules. We use typing rules in which the insertion of coercions is made explicit, departing from previous usage [CW85, Rey85] for systems based on subtypes. One reason is that the statements and proofs of several theorems are made clearer and simpler by the change. We also use the new form to emphasize that our subtype scheme is coercive rather than inclusive. Many recent papers on type inference with subtypes [Car84, Mit88, Tha88] use inclusive subtyping. Coercive subtyping allows relationships that are semantically more *ad hoc*, and need more justification through properties such as coherence. The general form of a typing rule is $A \vdash e \Rightarrow e' : \tau$, which can be read as: "Given a set A of typing assumptions for free variables, the expression e is coerced to e' which has the type τ." The expression e' is the unscaled version of e. The typing rules are given in Figure 3. The most notable rule is the last rule in the right column, which uses a coercion function to account for the use of a subsumption.

The semantics of the coerced expressions derived by type inference is meant to be transparent. This is equivalent to saying that given $A \vdash e \Rightarrow e' : \tau$, the assertion "$e'$ has the type τ" is *prima facie* sound. Suppose there are functions **E** and **T** which map syntactic expressions in the object and type languages to their respective denotations (the details of the definitions of **E** and **T** are standard: see, *e.g.*, [Car88]). The function **E** uses an additional environment argument η as is usual in denotational semantics. We use $\eta \vDash A$ to mean that the environment η satisfies the type assumptions in A. Note that **E** only assigns *transparent* meanings (without any attempt to resolve scaling) and is only meant to be applied to unscaled expressions.

Semantic Soundness Theorem. $\quad A \vdash e \Rightarrow e' : \tau \quad$ implies $\quad \forall \eta \vDash A. \mathbf{E}[\![e']\!]\eta \in \mathbf{T}[\![\tau]\!]$.

Given that $\mathbf{E}[\![f]\!]\eta \in \mathbf{T}[\![\tau1{\to}\tau2]\!]$ for the coercion f in the subtyping rule, the proof of this theorem is easy by induction on the stucture of e, and is left as an exercise. Although typing is sound, it is highly nondeterministic. Suppose we define:

$$\mathsf{Type}(A,e) = \{\tau \mid A \vdash e \Rightarrow e' : \tau \text{ for some } e'\} \qquad \mathsf{Expr}(A,e,\tau) = \{e' \mid A \vdash e \Rightarrow e' : \tau\}$$

$\mathsf{Type}(A,e)$ is not a singleton for most well-typed e, and $\mathsf{Expr}(A,e,\tau)$ is not a singleton for most types τ in $\mathsf{Type}(A,e)$. However, as we describe in Sections 6 and 7, $(Typexprs, \leq)$ is a poset and each nonempty $\mathsf{Type}(A,e)$ contains a minimal element, which we denote by $\mathsf{MinType}(A,e)$. Moreover, although $\mathsf{Expr}(A,e,\tau)$ may contain many expressions, the semantic coherence theorem in Section 7 asserts that this is semantically inconsequential since all members of $\mathsf{Expr}(A,e,\tau)$ always have the same (transparent) meaning. To be more precise, the semantic coherence theorem asserts that for all distinct e_1 and e_2 in any $\mathsf{Expr}(A,e,\tau)$, $\forall \eta \vDash A$, $\mathbf{E}[\![e_1]\!]\eta = \mathbf{E}[\![e_2]\!]\eta$, and therefore **E** can be applied to $\mathsf{Expr}(A,e,\tau)$. We can now define the new semantic function **SE** which gives meaning to *scaled* expressions directly. Assuming $\eta \vDash A$:

$$\mathbf{SE}[\![e]\!]\eta = \text{if } \mathsf{Type}(A,e) = \varnothing \text{ then } \mathbf{wrong} \text{ else } \mathbf{E}[\![\mathsf{Expr}(A,e,\mathsf{MinType}(A,e))]\!]\eta$$

where **wrong** is a special semantic value that denotes type error.

6 Properties of the Subtype Structure

In this section we discuss the two major properties of our subtype structure which are needed to validate the semantics outlined in the last section, namely, partial ordering and semantic coherence. The former is needed for the existence of minimal types and the latter for the coherence of typing judgements. A subtype relation is naturally reflexive and transitive (a preorder), as reflected in rules RFLX and TRNS in Figure 2. We begin by showing that $(Typexprs, \leq)$ is antisymmetric as well. We then outline a proof of the coherence of subtyping judgements, *i.e.*, the property that $\vdash \tau1 \leq \tau2 \Rightarrow f$ and $\vdash \tau1 \leq \tau2 \Rightarrow g$ implies $f = g$ (extensionally). The property is needed because each subsumption $\tau_1 \leq \tau_2$ can usually be derived in a number of different ways, leading to superficially different coercion functions. For instance:

$$\vdash [\text{int} \times \text{int}] \to \text{int} \leq [[\text{int}] \times [\text{int}]] \to [\text{int}] \Rightarrow (\lambda g. \, g \bullet (\alpha \text{ trans})) \bullet \alpha$$

$$\vdash [\text{int} \times \text{int}] \to \text{int} \leq [[\text{int}] \times [\text{int}]] \to [\text{int}] \Rightarrow \alpha \bullet (\lambda g. \, g \bullet \text{trans})$$

via two derivations for the same subsumption. The details are left as an exercise.

The key to the entire analysis in this section is an analogy between derivations of subtyping judgements and term rewriting sequences. There is room here only to sketch the development. The new technical notion underlying the analogy is that of a *unit* subsumption, corresponding to a single rewriting step. The derivation of a unit subsumption involves exactly one use of one of the *basic* rules (SCL, ZIP, REPL, REPR), along with possible uses of other (nonbasic) rules.

We use the notation $\vdash \tau \lhd \sigma \Rightarrow f$ for unit subsumptions, or just $\tau \lhd \sigma$ for short, whenever we can ignore the coercion f. It is not hard to see that the coercion for a unit subsumption is unique. Moreover, any derivation of a subtyping judgement $(\tau_1 \leq \tau_2)$ can be presented in the form of a sequence $\tau_1 = \tau_{11} \lhd ... \lhd \tau_{1n} = \tau_2, n \geq 0$, where the overall coercion is the composition of the unit coercions. The proof of this observation requires a rearrangement of the derivation along the lines of the (quite different) rewriting system described in [CG89]. This constitutes a *partial* normalization of the derivation of the subtyping judgement: there are in general many such sequences for a given judgement. The main result we wish to prove is that all sequences of unit subsumptions for a given subtyping judgement are semantically equivalent, *i.e.*, there is a *unique* representative sequence which represents the subsumption semantically (in terms of the implied coercion). This amounts to a full normalization result for derivations of subtyping judgements.

Note that each step $\tau_i \lhd \tau_{i+1}$ involves replacement of a single subexpression within τ_i by the corresponding expression according to the *basic* rule involved. This is very similar to a term rewriting step and would be just ordinary rewriting based on a set of first-order rewrite rules if not for the antimonotonicity of "$\rightarrow$" in its first argument. To make the analogy more precise, we need to partition occurrences of subexpressions in type expressions into positive and negative ones in order to indicate whether they are monotonically or antimonotonically related to the overall expression. An *occurrence* is a *binary* string specifying a *path* to the subexpression concerned. The subexpression reached by (occurring at) p in τ is denoted by τ/p. The idea is the same as in rewriting, with type constructors and constants playing the role of function symbols. The concatenation of occurrences p and q is denoted by $p \cdot q$. The set of all occurrences in an expression τ will be denoted by $O(\tau)$. The root occurrence Λ is positive. There are four inductive cases for extensions of each $p \in O(\tau)$.

1. $\tau/p = \iota$: there are no occurrences extending p.
2. $\tau/p = [\tau']$: $p \cdot 0$ has the same sign as p.
3. $\tau/p = \tau_1 \times \tau_2$: $p \cdot 0$ and $p \cdot 1$ have the same sign as p.
4. $\tau/p = \tau_1 \rightarrow \tau_2$: $p \cdot 0$ has the opposite and $p \cdot 1$ has the same sign as p.

We wish to think of the basic rules SCL, ZIP, REPL, and REPR as rewrite rules, except that they may be used in either direction depending on the sign of the occurrence being replaced. A "redex" will be either a positive occurrence of an instance of a LHS or a negative occurrence of an instance of a RHS of a basic rule. The corresponding reducts will be the corresponding instances of the RHS and LHS respectively. It is easy to show that τ_1 can be "rewritten" to τ_2 in one step according to this description *iff* $\tau_1 \lhd \tau_2$. Whenever we wish to emphasize the occurrence p involved in a step $\tau_1 \lhd \tau_2$, we shall write it as $\tau_1 \lhd_p \tau_2$.

6.1 Antisymmetry

To prove that $\leq$ is antisymmetric, we define a linearly ordered "measure" for types which strictly grows with $\lhd$. The measure uses the auxiliary functions D, F and S. Of these, D will play a central role throughout this and the next section. $D(\tau)$ can be thought of as the depth of (list) structure in τ. We define the measure here and leave the proof to the reader for lack of space.

$$D(\tau) = \text{Case } \tau \text{ of}$$

ι:	0		$\tau_1 \rightarrow \tau_2$:	0
$[\tau']$:	$1 + D(\tau')$		$\tau_1 \times \tau_2$:	$\max(D(\tau_1), D(\tau_2))$

One of the useful properties of $\mathbf{D}$ is that $\tau_1 \leq \tau_2$ implies $\mathbf{D}(\tau_1) = \mathbf{D}(\tau_2)$. Suppose $<k_1,...,k_n>$ denotes the (lexicographically ordered) sequence of integers k_i, $1 \leq i \leq n$, $P_i(\tau)$ is the number of *positive* occurrences and $N_i(\tau)$ is the number of *negative* occurrences of length i and form $[\tau']$ in τ, and $Depth(\tau)$ is the length of the longest occurrence in $O(\tau)$. Let $\chi_\tau(p)$ denote -1 if p is a negative occurrence in $O(\tau)$ and 1 otherwise.

$$F(\tau) = <k_0, \ldots, k_{Depth(\tau)}> \qquad \text{where } k_i = P_i(\tau) - N_i(\tau), \ 0 \leq i \leq Depth(\tau)$$

$$S(\tau) = \sum_{p \in O(\tau)} \chi_\tau(p)^* s_\tau(p) \qquad\qquad s_\tau(p) = \begin{cases} \mathbf{D}(\tau 1) + \mathbf{D}(\tau 2), & \tau/p = \tau 1 \rightarrow \tau 2 \\ 0, & \text{otherwise} \end{cases}$$

The required measure is the lexicographically ordered pair $(F(\tau), S(\tau))$.

6.2   Coherence of Subsumptions

The key idea in proving coherence of subsumptions is that of *permutations* of sequences of unit subsumptions. The idea is again taken from work on term rewriting [HL79]. A permutation of a sequence is a reordering of the steps in it, preserving the end points. All permutations of a given sequence constitute a *permutation class*. The first step in the proof of coherence of subsumptions is to show that all sequences in the same permutation class are semantically equivalent, given that the basic coercions obey a set of algebraic laws. The second step shows that all sequences for a given subtyping judgement belong to a single permutation class; in other words, there is a unique sequence for each subsumption *modulo* permutations.

Suppose we identify sequences of unit subsumptions by names. Let $B, C, \ldots$ range over sequences. We shall write $B : \tau_1 \leq \tau_2$ to indicate that B is a sequence for $\tau_1 \leq \tau_2$. Clearly, there is a *unique* coercion from τ_1 to τ_2 associated with a given *sequence* $B : \tau_1 \leq \tau_2$. This coercion will be denoted by $\mathbf{C}_B$. Coherence of subsumptions can now be paraphrased as the

Unique Coercion Theorem. $B : \tau_1 \leq \tau_2$ and $C : \tau_1 \leq \tau_2$ implies $\mathbf{C}_B = \mathbf{C}_C$.

Permutations can be defined by using an idea analogous to the classical notion of *residuals* in rewriting [HL79]. It is not hard to show that each redex occurrence except p in τ_1 leaves exactly one residual occurrence in τ_2 when $\tau_1 \lhd_p \tau_2$. Moreover, the residual of a redex is a redex. If $q \neq p$ is such a redex occurrence in τ_1, then let $q \backslash p$ denote its residual in τ_2. Similarly, let $p \backslash q$ denote the residual of p after the alternative step $\tau_1 \lhd_q \tau_3$ which is obviously possible as well. The basic fact we are interested in is that in this situation there is always a τ_4 such that both $B: \tau_1 \lhd_p \tau_2 \lhd_{q \backslash p} \tau_4$ and $C: \tau_1 \lhd_q \tau_3 \lhd_{p \backslash q} \tau_4$ are possible. Note that this does *not* imply that the rewrite relation ($\lhd$) is strongly locally confluent since it assumes that p and q are *distinct*. We shall say that B and C are *direct* permutations of each other, denoted by $B \approx C$. Also, if $B' : \tau_0 \leq \tau_1$ and $C' : \tau_4 \leq \tau_5$ are any other sequences, then $B' \cdot B \cdot C' \approx B' \cdot C \cdot C'$ where $B \cdot C$ denotes the concatenation of sequences B and C.

The general permutation relation, which is the reflexive, transitive and symmetric closure of $\approx$, will be denoted by "$\equiv$". A permutation class is just an equivalence class of "$\equiv$". The justification for using the equivalence notation is that permutations are *semantically* equivalent, i.e., $B \equiv C$ implies $\mathbf{C}_B = \mathbf{C}_C$. To show this we need only prove that the sequences B and C used in defining "$\approx$" correspond to the same coercion. When neither of the two occurrences p and q is a prefix of the other, the two coercions are obviously independent. Suppose one *is a* prefix of the other. There are four cases depending on which of the four *basic* rules (SCL, ZIP, REPL, REPR) is applicable to the *larger* of the two subexpressions (reached by the prefix occurrence). Suppose SCL is applicable, and the smaller subexpression occurs in the argument part of the type. For instance, suppose $f : \tau 1 \rightarrow \tau 2$, and there is a type $\tau 3 \lhd \tau 1$, with the corresponding direct coercion g. We have the two sequences

1. $\tau 1 \rightarrow \tau 2 \lhd [\tau 1] \rightarrow [\tau 2] \lhd [\tau 3] \rightarrow [\tau 2]$ 2. $\tau 1 \rightarrow \tau 2 \lhd \tau 3 \rightarrow \tau 2 \lhd [\tau 3] \rightarrow [\tau 2]$

We must show that the equation

$$(\text{SCL}) \quad (\alpha f) \cdot (\alpha \; g) \;=\; \alpha \; (f \cdot g)$$

for the corresponding coercion functions holds irrespective of the values of f and g. This is easy to verify—the equation is given in [Bac78] as equation III.4. It is also easy to see that this equation implies the equality of the two coercions derived in the example at the beginning of Section 6. The same equation suffices (with f and g reversing roles) if the smaller subexpression occurs in the result part $(\tau 2)$. The other cases require verification of similar simple equations. We list the equations corresponding to ZIP, REPL and REPR below, and leave their derivation and verification to the reader.

$$(\text{ZIP}) \quad (\alpha \; \{ f \cdot 1, g \cdot 2 \}) \cdot \text{trans} \;=\; \text{trans} \cdot \{ (\alpha \; f) \cdot 1, (\alpha \; g) \cdot 2 \}$$
$$(\text{REPL}) \quad \text{distl} \cdot \{ 1, \alpha f \cdot 2 \} \;=\; (\alpha \; \{ 1, f \cdot 2 \}) \cdot \text{distl}$$
$$(\text{REPR}) \quad \text{distr} \cdot \{ \alpha f \cdot 1, 2 \} \;=\; (\alpha \; \{ f \cdot 1, 2 \}) \cdot \text{distr}$$

These equations imply the semantic equivalence of permutations:

Lemma 1: $B \equiv C$ implies $C_B = C_C$.

To prove that all sequences for a given subsumption $\tau 1 \leq \tau 2$ belong to the same permutation class is not hard but is technically rather complicated. The main idea is that any sequence can be permuted to a standard form. This is possible because any sequence consists conceptually of a number of subsequences, each corresponding to a single step of scaling. For instance, the algorithm Φ defined in the next section gathers subsequences for zipping and replication together whenever possible. That is, if the set $S = \{ [\tau'] \mid \tau 1 \times \tau 2 \leq [\tau'] \}$ is nonempty, then $\Phi(\tau 1 \times \tau 2)$ is its *least* member, otherwise $\Phi(\tau 1 \times \tau 2)$ fails. Similar properties apply to subsequences for scaling. This leads to:

Lemma 2: $B : \tau_1 \leq \tau_2$ and $C : \tau_1 \leq \tau_2$ implies $B \equiv C$.

The Unique Coercion Theorem is a direct consequence of Lemmas 1 and 2.

7 Typing Algorithms

The main result in this section is a minimal typing algorithm for the typing system of Sections 4 and 5. More precisely, we give an algorithm **Type** which, given a set of type assumptions and an expression, will return a coerced expression and its type, and will satisfy the following three properties.

Correctness. If **Type**(A,e) succeeds and returns e', τ then $A \vdash e \Rightarrow e' : \tau$.

Minimality of typing. If $\text{Type}(A,e) \neq \varnothing$ then $\text{Type}(A,e)$ succeeds and returns $(e', \text{MinType}(A,e))$ (for some e').

Suppose we define the relation $(\equiv_A)$ of "semantic equivalence *modulo* a set A of typing assumptions" by: $e_1 \equiv_A e_2 \Leftrightarrow \forall \eta \vDash A. \; E[\![e_1]\!]\eta = E[\![e_2]\!]\eta$.

Minimality of coercion. If $\tau \in \mathsf{Type}(A,e)$, $e' \in \mathsf{Expr}(A,e,\tau)$, $\mathbf{Type}(A,e) = e_0, \tau_0$, and $\vdash \tau_0 \le \tau. \Rightarrow f$, then $e' \equiv_A (f\ e_0)$.

Minimality of coercion asserts that **Type** not only finds a minimal type but also a minimal coerced version in a precise sense. It is easy to see that this implies coherence of typing, *i.e.*, the property that $A \vdash e \Rightarrow e_1 : \tau$ and $A \vdash e \Rightarrow e_2 : \tau$ implies $e_1 \equiv_A e_2$.

Not surprisingly, the interesting part of type inference in our system is the inference of subsumptions. The subtyping rules of Section 4 are complex enough to make this nontrivial. Reynolds [Rey85] points out that minimal typing for sufficiently rich languages—those with "cons" operators or conditional expressions for instance—actually requires inference of least upper bounds (LUBs) and greatest lower bounds (GLBs) for pairs of types which have upper and lower bounds respectively. Subsumption is a special case where the LUB of two types is equal to one of them. We therefore begin with the (mutually recursive) algorithms **LUB** and **GLB**, and then give the minimal typing/coercion algorithm **Type**.

The basic idea in finding the LUB of types $\tau1$ and $\tau2$ is to coerce them both to the same outward form with as little change as possible, and then apply the idea recursively to their parts. When one is a product and the other a list type, the product type must be coerced to a list type to achieve compatibility. This is done by the algorithm Φ given below.

$$\Delta(\tau) = \text{if } \tau = \tau' \times \tau'' \text{ then return } \Phi(\tau)$$
$$\text{else if } \tau = [\tau'] \text{ then return } \tau \text{ else fail}$$

$$\Phi(\tau_1 \times \tau_2) = \text{if } \tau_1 = \tau_2 = \iota \text{ then fail}$$
$$\text{else if } \tau_1 \ne \iota \text{ then let } [\tau_1'] = \Delta(\tau_1) \text{ else let } \tau_1' = \tau_1$$
$$\text{if } \tau_2 \ne \iota \text{ then let } [\tau_2'] = \Delta(\tau_2) \text{ else let } \tau_2' = \tau_2$$
$$\text{return } [\tau_1' \times \tau_2']$$

Example: $\Phi([\text{int} \to \text{int}] \times ([\text{int}] \times \text{int})) = [(\text{int} \to \text{int}) \times (\text{int} \times \text{int})]$

It is easy to see that $\tau \le \Phi(\tau)$ whenever $\Phi(\tau)$ succeeds. If the set $S = \{\ [\tau']\ |\ \tau1 \times \tau2 \le [\tau']\ \}$ is nonempty, then $\Phi(\tau1 \times \tau2)$ is its *least* member, otherwise $\Phi(\tau1 \times \tau2)$ fails. Likewise, if $S = \{\ [\tau']\ |\ \tau \le [\tau']\ \}$ is nonempty, then $\Delta(\tau)$ is its *least* member, otherwise $\Delta(\tau)$ fails.

The GLB algorithm needs a similar function Γ with properties which are the reverse of Φ — it requires a list type to be "uncoerced" to a product type by a *reverse* subsequence. This is a little tricky since given a list type $\tau2$, the "closest" product type $\tau1$ for the required minimal subsumption $\tau1 \le \tau2$ is not unique. It is therefore necessary to provide Γ with *both* the (product and list) types for which a GLB is required, so that it can find a starting point for the sequence which is compatible with the given product type. Let $[\tau]^k$ denote the k-fold application of the list constructor to τ. The product and list types are the first and second arguments of Γ:

$$\Gamma(\tau_{11} \times \tau_{12}, \tau_2) = \text{if } \tau_2 \ne [\tau_{21} \times \tau_{22}]^k \text{ then fail}$$
$$\text{else let } k_1 = D(\tau_{11}) - D(\tau_{21}) \text{ and } k_2 = D(\tau_{12}) - D(\tau_{22})$$
$$\text{if } (k_1 < k \text{ and } \tau_{21} \ne \iota) \text{ or } (k_2 < k \text{ and } \tau_{22} \ne \iota) \text{ then fail}$$
$$\text{else if } (k_1 \ne k \text{ and } k_2 \ne k) \text{ or } k_1 > k \text{ or } k_2 > k \text{ then fail}$$
$$\text{else return } [\tau_{21}]^{k_1} \times [\tau_{22}]^{k_2}$$

Example: Suppose $\tau = [\text{int} \times ([\text{int}] \to [\text{int}])]$.
$\Gamma(\text{int} \times ([[\text{int}]] \to [[\text{int}]]), \tau) = \text{int} \times [[\text{int}]] \to [\text{int}]$ $\quad$ $\Gamma([\text{int}] \times [[\text{int}]] \to [\text{int}]], \tau) = [\text{int}] \times [[\text{int}]] \to [\text{int}]$

LUB (τ_1, τ_2) = Case τ_1 of

ι: if $\tau_2 = \iota$ then return ι else fail

$\tau_{11} \to \tau_{12}$: if $\tau_2 \neq \tau_{21} \to \tau_{22}$ then fail

else if not $(k = D(\tau_{11}) - D(\tau_{21}) = D(\tau_{12} - D(\tau_{22}))$ for some k then fail

else if $k = 0$: return **GLB**$(\tau_{11}, \tau_{21}) \to$ **LUB**(τ_{12}, τ_{22})

$k > 0$: return **LUB**$(\tau_1, [\tau_{21}]^k \to [\tau_{22}]^k)$

$k < 0$: return **LUB**$([\tau_{11}]^k \to [\tau_{12}]^k, \tau_2)$

$\tau_{11} \times \tau_{12}$: if $\tau_2 = [\tau_2']$ then return **LUB**$(\Phi(\tau_1), \tau_2)$

else if $\tau_2 \neq \tau_{21} \times \tau_{22}$ then fail

else if $D(\tau_{11}) \neq D(\tau_{21})$ or $D(\tau_{12}) \neq D(\tau_{22})$ then return **LUB**$(\Phi(\tau_1), \Phi(\tau_2))$

else return **LUB**$(\tau_{11}, \tau_{21}) \times$ **LUB**(τ_{12}, τ_{22})

$[\tau_1']$: if $\tau_2 = [\tau_2']$ then return $[$**LUB**$(\tau_1', \tau_2')]$

else if $\tau_2 \neq \tau_{21} \times \tau_{22}$ then fail

else return **LUB**$(\tau_1, \Phi(\tau_2))$

GLB (τ_1, τ_2) = Case τ_1 of

ι: if $\tau_2 = \iota$ then return ι else fail

$\tau_{11} \to \tau_{12}$: if $\tau_2 \neq \tau_{21} \to \tau_{22}$ then fail

else if not $(k = D(\tau_{11}) - D(\tau_{21}) = D(\tau_{12} - D(\tau_{22}))$ for some k then fail

else if $k = 0$: return **LUB**$(\tau_{11}, \tau_{21}) \to$ **GLB**(τ_{12}, τ_{22})

$k > 0$: return **GLB**$([\tau_{11}]^{-k} \to [\tau_{12}]^{-k}, \tau_2)$

$k < 0$: return **GLB**$(\tau_1, [\tau_{21}]^k \to [\tau_{22}]^k)$

$[\tau_1']$: if $\tau_2 = [\tau_2']$ then return $[$**GLB**$(\tau_1', \tau_2')]$

else if $\tau_2 \neq \tau_{21} \times \tau_{22}$ then fail

else return **GLB**$(\Gamma(\tau_2, \tau_1), \tau_2)$

$\tau_{11} \times \tau_{12}$: if $\tau_2 = \tau_{21} \times \tau_{22}$ then return **GLB**$(\tau_{11}, \tau_{21}) \times$ **GLB**(τ_{12}, τ_{22})

else if $\tau_2 = [\tau_2']$ then return **GLB**$(\tau_1, \Gamma(\tau_1, \tau_2))$

else fail

Figure 5: LUB and GLB Algorithms

Note the extensive use of the "depth of list structure" function **D** in both Γ and in the **LUB/GLB** algorithm. There is no room here for a complete explanation of its role, but the function is used to measure the mismatch in degree of scaling and/or zipping/replication between type expressions. The **LUB**, **GLB** algorithms are given in Figure 5. Given Δ, **LUB** and **GLB**, the algorithm **Type** for inference of minimal types and coercions—given in Figure 6—is straightforward except for the application case, which needs to resolve the overloading of the

$Type(A, e)$ = Case e of

x: return x, Ax ; $\underline{nil}_\tau$: return $\underline{nil}_\tau$, $[\tau]$

e_1, e_2: let $e_3, \tau_3 = Type(A,e_1)$ and $e_4, \tau_4 = Type(A,e_2)$ in return (e_3, e_4), $\tau_3 \times \tau_4$

$e \downarrow i$: if $Type(A, e) \neq e'$, $\tau_1 \times \tau_2$ then fail else return $e' \downarrow i$, τ_i $(i = 1$ or $2)$

$e_1; e_2$: let $e_3, \tau_3 = Type(A,e_1)$ and $e_4, \tau_4 = Type(A,e_2)$ in

let $\tau_5 = LUB(\tau_3, \tau_4)$ in return $(C_{\tau_3 \leq \tau_5}\, e_3, C_{\tau_4 \leq \tau_5}\, e_4)$, $[\tau_5]$

$\underline{hd}\ e$: let $e', \tau = Type(A, e)$ in if $\Delta(\tau)$ returns $[\tau']$ then return $\underline{hd}\ (C_{\tau \leq [\tau']}\, e')$, τ' else fail

$\underline{tl}\ e$: let $e', \tau = Type(A, e)$ in if $\Delta(\tau)$ returns $[\tau']$ then return $\underline{tl}\ (C_{\tau \leq [\tau']}\, e')$, $[\tau']$ else fail

$\lambda x_\tau.e$: let $e', \tau' = Type(A+x{:}\tau, e)$ in return $\lambda x_\tau.e'$, $\tau \to \tau'$

$\underline{fix}\ e$: if $Type(A, e) \neq e'$, $\tau_1 \to \tau_2$ for some e', τ_1, τ_2 then fail

else if $LUB(\tau_1, \tau_2) \neq \tau_1$ then fail else return $e' \cdot C_{\tau_2 \leq \tau_1}$, τ_2

$e_1\ e_2$: if $Type(A, e_1) \neq e_1'$, $\tau_1 \to \tau_2$ for some e_1', τ_1, τ_2 then fail

else let $e_2', \tau_3 = Type(A, e_2)$ and $k = D(\tau_3) - D(\tau_1)$ in

if $k < 0$ or $LUB([\tau_1]^k, \tau_3) \neq [\tau_1]^k$

then fail else return $(\alpha^k\ e_1')\ (C_{\tau_3 \leq [\tau_1]^k}\ e_2')$, $[\tau_2]^k$

Figure 6:   Algorithm   Type

function part—the constant k derived in the analysis of this case (using D again) captures the only meaning of the function part that could possibly be appropriate in that application.

8   Concluding   Remarks

We have described a coercion based semantics for implicit scaling which rests on just four structural subtyping rules. The rest of the system simply works out the consequences of applying these rules within a standard general framework of the kind described in [Rey85]. We regard this as a nice illustration of the way coercive structural subtyping can be used—at little cost in semantic complexity—to raise the expressive power of a language by eliminating a class of programming chores. For other applications of the idea, see [BC+89, Tha90].

The compatibility of the subtype structure described here with parametric polymorphism is an interesting topic for further investigation. Combining our system with the *implicit* parametric polymorphism of the Hindley-Milner system [DM82] may result in the loss of semantic coherence. Consider for instance our operator $\underline{hd}$. Under parametric polymorphism, $\underline{hd}$ is usually a polymorphic *function* which possesses all types of the form $[\tau] \to \tau$. Assuming loosely that the set A of type assumptions can supply any of the types possessed by such a function $\underline{hd}$, we would have

$A \vdash \underline{hd} \Rightarrow \underline{hd}$: $[[int]] \to [int]$, since $A(\underline{hd}) = [[int]] \to [int]$

$A \vdash \underline{hd} \Rightarrow \alpha\, \underline{hd}$: $[[int]] \to [int]$, since $A(\underline{hd}) = [int] \to int \leq [[int]] \to [int]$

where the two converted expressions obviously have different meanings in most applications.

One way to overcome this difficulty is to avoid treating the operations on the "structure of interest" as functions. This may be more natural in some cases (*e.g.*, arrays) than in others (*e.g.*, lists). It might be possible to avoid this dilemma in a combination with *explicit* bounded abstraction over types [CW85]. Besides generalizing our system, a successful combination with the latter would provide some insight into general techniques for combining coercive subtyping with parametric polymorphism. A similar combination has been studied in [BC+89] for a coercive interpretation of structural subtyping for labeled records.

References

[Bac78] Backus, J. Can Programming be Liberated from the von Neumann Style? A Functional Style and Its Algebra of Programs. CACM **21**, 613-641 (1978)

[Ben85] Benkard, J. P. Control of Structure and Evaluation. In: Proc. APL'85 Conference.

[BC+89] Breazu-Tannen, V., Coquand, T., Gunter, C. and Scedrov, A. Inheritance and explicit coercion. In: Proceedings of Fourth LICS Symposium. IEEE 1989

[Bre88] Breuel, T.M. Data Level Parallel Programming in C++. In: Proc. of 1988 USENIX C++ Conf., pp. 153-167.

[Car88] Cardelli, L. A Semantics of Multiple Inheritance. Info. and Comp. **76**,138-164 (1988)

[CG89] Curien, P-L. and Ghelli, G. Coherence of Subsumption. Manuscript. 1989

[CW85] Cardelli, L. and Wegner, P. On Understanding Types, Data Abstraction and Polymorphism. Computing Surveys **17** (4) (1985)

[DM82] Damas, L. and Milner, R. Principle Type-schemes for Functional Programs. In: Proc. 9th POPL Symposium, Albuquerque, NM. ACM 1982

[HL79] Huet, G. and Levy, J-J. Computations in Nonambiguous Linear Term Rewriting Systems. Tech. Rep. 359, INRIA-Le Chesney, France, 1979

[HS86] Hillis, W.D. and Steele, G.L., Jr. Data Parallel Algorithms. CACM **29** (12) (1986)

[Ive62] Iverson, K.E. A Programming Language. Wiley, New York, 1962

[JM78] Jenkins, M.A. and Michel, J. Operators in an APL Containing Nested Arrays. CIS Dept., Queen's University, Kingston, Ontario. Tech. Rep. 78-60. 1978

[Mil84] Milner, R. A Proposal for Standard ML. In: Proc. 1984 ACM Symp. on LISP and Functional Programming, Austin, TX., pp. 184-197. ACM 1984

[Mit88] Mitchell, J.C. Polymorphic Type Inference and Containment. Information and Computation **76**, 211-249 (1988)

[Rey80] Reynolds, J.C. Using Category Theory to Design Implicit Conversions and Generic Operators. In: Semantics Directed Compiler Generation (N.D.Jones, Ed.), pp. 211-258, Lecture Notes in Computer Science, Vol. 94. Springer-Verlag 1980

[Rey85] Reynolds, J.C. Three Approaches to Type Structure. In: Proc. TAPSOFT 1985, Lecture Notes in Computer Science, Vol. 186. Springer-Verlag 1985

[Tha88] Thatte, S.R. Type Inference with Partial Types. In: Proc. 15th ICALP. Lecture Notes in Computer Science, Vol. 317, pp. 615-629. Springer-Verlag 1988

[Tha90] Thatte, S.R. Quasi-static Typing. In: Proc. of the 17th POPL Symposium, San Francisco, CA. ACM 1990

[Vis89] Vishnubhotla, P. Data Parallel Programming on Transputer Networks. In: Proc. of 2nd Conf. of North American Transputer Users Group, G.S. Stiles (Ed.). April 1989

TOWARDS THE THEORY OF PROGRAMMING IN CONSTRUCTIVE LOGIC

A.A.Voronkov

Institute of Mathematics

Universitetski Prospect 4

630090 Novosibirsk 90

USSR

Abstract. We develop an approach to the theory of extracting programs from proofs based on constructive semantics of the first order formulas called *constructive truth*. The underlying ideas are discussed. Using this notion of truth we define an appropriate notion of *constructive calculus*. Some results on relations between our theory and well known notions of constructive logic and the theory of enumerated models are proved.

1. Introduction. Extracting programs from proofs: the main ideas and problems

The extraction of programs from proofs or programming in constructive logic is based on the idea that under some restrictions proofs can be considered as programs. The general scheme of extracting programs from proofs is the following: at the beginning one writes a specification of the problem in some formal logical language (usually a variant of type theory). Then a formal proof of this specification is constructed and the program is extracted from this proof according to one of the known methods. Sometimes the last step can be absent because already the proof can serve as the program.

There are many distinctions between classical and constructive proofs. The main difference which allows one to consider constructive proofs as programs is the explicit definability property or ∃-property: if a proof Π of a closed formula $\exists xA$ is given then one can effectively construct a term t

such that $A(t)$ holds (in some appropriate sense). If there are free variables $x_1,\ldots,x_n$ in A then such a proof can be considered as an algorithm
meeting "specification" A (i.e. algorithm α such that $A(x_1,\ldots,x_n,$
 $\alpha(x_1,\ldots,x_n))$ holds for every $x_1,\ldots,x_n$.

From the classical point of view the information sufficient for an
adjustment of formula of the form $\forall \bar{x} \exists y \varphi(\bar{x},y)$ is the following: given any
 $\bar{x}$ one can find (generally speaking unclear in what way) an y such that
 $\varphi(\bar{x},y)$ hold. From the constructive viewpoint the adjustment of this formula
means much more: there should be some general method (or *construction*) that
allows to find such an y for given $\bar{x}$. The constructive proofs have the
property that they implicitly contain an information sufficient for extracting such general method, which is in fact a program computing y by $\bar{x}$.

There are essentially two groups of methods of extracting programs from
proofs. The first group uses syntactical methods like normalization of natural deduction proofs or cut elimination in sequential proofs. The second
group is based on constructive semantics of formulas developed from Kleene's
realizability. We briefly explain the basic ideas of these methods.

The normalization of proofs consist of syntactical transformations of
the natural deduction proofs [Prawitz 1965] called *reductions.* The reductions are repeatedly applied to a proof while it is possible. The proof in the
form where no application of reductions is possible is called normal proof
or proof in normal form. Any normal proof of closed formula $\exists x \varphi(x)$ in e.g.
intuitionistic predicate calculus or intuitionistic arithmetic takes the
form

$$\frac{\begin{array}{c} \Pi \\ \varphi(t) \end{array}}{\exists x \varphi(x)}$$

Let a proof of a formula $\forall \bar{x} \exists y \varphi(x,y)$ is given:

$$\frac{\Pi}{\forall \bar{x} \exists y \varphi(x,y)}$$

Then one can use it as a program in the following way. Let $\bar{t}$ is a tuple of
"input values" for the variables $\bar{x}$. To obtain an "output value" for y it
is sufficient to normalize the proof obtained from the above proof by adding
the $\forall$ -elimination rule:

$$\frac{\begin{array}{c}\Pi\\\forall x \exists y \varphi(x,y)\end{array}}{\exists y \varphi(\bar{t},y)}$$

Its normal form takes the form

$$\frac{\begin{array}{c}\Pi_1\\\varphi(\bar{t},s)\end{array}}{\exists y \varphi(\bar{t},y)}$$

Thus s is the intended value for y.

There are many lacks of normalization listed below.

(i) The proof is too large object to deal with and it is extremely inefficient to implement normalizations on proofs. So systems essentially based on normalization usually use not proofs but some structures coding only computationally useful information from proofs.

(ii) In the proofs of some particular theories there can be many introduction and elimination rules. In this case for each pair introduction rule - elimination rule for the same connective or quantifier it is needed to introduce new reduction rule and to prove normalization theorem for this extended calculus.

(iii) Reductions are not very expressible tool - as a matter of fact they are too simple. For example normalization lacks for the Markov's principle

$$\frac{\forall x(\varphi(x) \vee \daleth\varphi(x)) \qquad \daleth\daleth\exists x \varphi(x)}{\exists x \phi(x)}$$

where x is variable ranging over natural numbers. The algorithm implicit in this rule is the following: using $\forall x(\varphi(x) \vee \daleth\varphi(x))$ verify $\varphi(0)$, $\varphi(1)$, $\varphi(2)$...until a number n with $\varphi(n)$ is found. There is no reduction rule for the Markov's principle because to find such n one should normalize proofs of $\varphi(0) \vee \daleth \varphi(0)$, $\varphi(1) \vee \daleth\varphi(1)$...

In our opinion all this lacks of normalization lie in its syntactical nature. There is another techniques allowing to extract programs from proofs - realizability-like semantics of formulas. There are many such semantics developed from original Kleene's realizability [Kleene 1945]. These semantics reflect the constructive meaning of logical connectives first discovered by Kolmogorov [1932]. We consider the general scheme of realizability and discuss some lacks of existing realizability-like semantics.

Roughly speaking in this scheme we associate with any formula φ a relation $r \oplus \varphi$. If there is some element a with $a \oplus \varphi$ then we say that a "realizes" φ. The set of possible elements a depends on the used realizability. The idea is that such an a contains information which is sufficient to adjust φ. The general scheme of realizability is the following:

1. For atomic φ the relation $r \oplus \varphi$ is given and depends on the kind of realizability. Usually the "realizations" of atomic formulas are very simple elements (with no inner structure) and an atomic formula is realizable iff it is true or provable.

2. "Realizations" of $\varphi \wedge \psi$ are ordered pairs $<a,b>$ such that $a \oplus \varphi$ and $b \oplus \psi$.

3. "Realizations" of $\varphi \vee \psi$ are ordered pairs $<0,a>$ such that $a \oplus \varphi$ or ordered pairs $<1,b>$ with $b \oplus \psi$. (This is not particularly important that we choose 0 and 1 to distinguish between the two cases. Instead of 0 and 1 can be taken any two different elements of the set R of possible realizations.)

4. "Realizations" of $\varphi \supset \psi$ are "algorithms" α which given any a with $a \oplus \varphi$ give an output $\alpha(a)$ such that $\alpha(a) \oplus \psi$.

5. "Realizations" of $\exists x \varphi(x)$ are pairs $<t,a>$ such that $a \oplus \varphi(t)$.

6. "Realizations" of $\forall x \varphi(x)$ are "algorithms" α such that for every t $\alpha(t) \oplus \varphi(t)$.

This general scheme can be refined in many ways. For example in original Kleene's realizability for arithmetic instead of pairs and algorithms the Gödel numbers of these pairs and Kleene's number of the partial recursive function are taken. Realizability can be used for extracting programs from proofs as follows. Using the constructive proof of the formula $\forall \bar{x} \exists y \varphi(\bar{x}, y)$ one can construct an element realizing this formula. By the above definition this element is an algorithm α such that for any tuple $\bar{a}$ of input values for $\bar{x}$ $\alpha(\bar{a})$ is a pair $<b,c>$ with $b \oplus \varphi(c)$. So c is the intended value for y.

Realizability seems more flexible than normalization in many aspects, but there are some lacks in existing definitions of realizability. First of all realizability-like semantics have one undesirable property: realizability (even in the case of arithmetic) contradicts to classical logic. There are classically false but realizable formulas. It means that the definition of calculus in which the proofs are constructed can not rely only upon realizability - if we do not want to obtain from the proof of $\exists x \varphi(x)$ an a

such that $\phi(a)$ is false (but realizable).

The second undesirable property of realizability is that the usual definitions of realizability were designed for some special theories but there was not a definition suitable for large classes of theories. But if we are going to extract from proofs *programs* then the proofs must handle various data types: lists, numbers, functions etc. To treat such data types properly the notion of realizability is needed which can cover many various data types and many constructive theories describing properties of these data types.

Realizability and normalization have many common features. For example Mints [1974] proved that the two methods give equivalent programs in the case of intuitionistic predicate calculus. Similarly all we said about data types can as well be related to normalization.

One of the most important problems common for all existing approaches is the following: how to define constructive systems in which the proofs are constructed and how to construct algorithms for extracting programs from proofs? To solve this problem one needs a general theory for programming in constructive logic - a theory which explains what is a constructive calculus and how such constructive calculi are related to programs to be extracted. The existing approaches are either too particular or too general. Too particular means that it covers one particular calculus, such as arithmetic. To obtain generality all other theories are usually interpreted in this core theory. But to interpret e.g. lists in arithmetic is about the same as implementing list processing programs in machine codes. Too general means that one choose some very expressive type theory which allows to interpret everything and is (as any too general concepts) quite inefficient and unnatural.

In other words the following questions arise:

(1) what is the program? and

(2) what is the extraction of program? and

(3) what is the semantic relations between the proof and the extracted program?

The most general answer to the question (1) is that the program is an "algorithm". There is no problem with this answer because there are many well known approaches to the formal notion of algorithm and they are essentially (or more exactly extensionally) the same. The extraction of program is some algorithmic process transforming the proof to a description of algorithm. Proofs are conducted in formal systems. But the roots of formal systems are some domains of objects and proofs usually describe properties of these objects. For example proofs in formal arithmetic describe properties of natural numbers. If we agree with such treatment of proofs then we come to the following conclusion: the program extracted from a constructive proof of existence of an element with the desired property have to show a way to construct the element of the underlying model (or if we deal with a class of models then a way to construct the appropriate element for any model of this class). Since programs are algorithms then this way should be algorithmic. There is a generally adopted way to reason about the elements of these models - to encode or enumerate them.Thus we naturally come to the theory of enumerated models [Ershov 1980].

The notion of provability is secondary for models, the primary is the notion of truth. Thus the algorithm for extracting programs from proofs should be based on this notion. To implement such an approach the following things are to be done:

(1) It is necessary to express the truth of formulas algorithmically (the constructive encoding of formulas, or the constructive adjustment of truth).

(2) Proofs in formal systems should not give formulas that have no this constructive decoding;

(3) It is necessary to have an algorithm which constructs by the proof of a formula this constructive adjustment of truth of this formula.

In the rest of this paper we develop a formal theory intended to give the theoretical foundations for extracting programs from proofs based on above ideas. The more formal papers on this subject are [Voronkov 1988b, 1989b]. But a long list theorems as in [Voronkov 1989b] can try the most patient reader so here we will explain only the most essential results in this direction. The origins of such semantics can be traced to modified realizability [Kreisel 1959]. Very close to our classical realizability is the semantics studied by Läuchly [1970]. The first semantics suitable for several models was introduced in [Prank 1981]. Then Nepeivoda and Sviridenko [1982] proposed a semantics based on enumerable sets [Ershov 1977] but this paper contained some errors making definition of realizability incorrect. The correct presentation was given in [Voronkov 1985]. The similar semantics was independently discovered by Plisko [1987] but his semantics is closer to n-realizability from [Voronkov 1985] than to the semantics presented here.

2. The main auxiliary definitions

This section contains auxiliary definitions concerning the theory of enumerated models and higher type functionals. All definitions are given for one-sorted case but they can easily be generalized for many-sorted models.

Definition 1. Let S be a set. An *enumeration* of S is any mapping of the set of all natural numbers N <u>onto</u> S. An *enumerated set* is any pair (S,ν) where S is a set and ν is an enumeration of S.

Let $\mathfrak{R} = \langle M, P_0, P_1, \ldots, f_0, f_1, \ldots \rangle$ is a model of signature σ.

Definition 2. An *enumeration* of the model $\mathfrak{R}$ is any enumeration $\nu: N \rightarrow M$ of the domain M of $\mathfrak{R}$ such that there exists a binary total recursive function F such that for any $n, y_1, \ldots, y_{m_n} \in N$

$$f_n(\nu y_1, \ldots, \nu y_{m_n}) = \nu F(n, \langle y_1, \ldots, y_{m_n} \rangle),$$

where $\langle y_1, \ldots, y_{m_n} \rangle$ is the Gödel number of the tuple $y_1, \ldots, y_{m_n}$. The pair $(\mathfrak{R},\nu)$ where $\mathfrak{R}$ is a model of signature σ, and ν is its enumeration is called an *enumerated model* of the signature σ.

Let $(\mathfrak{R},\nu)$ be an enumerated model of the signature σ and the (extended) signature Σ is the enrichment of σ with elements $\nu 0, \nu 1, \ldots$ Using ν we can effectively construct some Gödel numbering μ of formulas of the signature Σ.

Definition 3. An enumerated model $(\mathfrak{R},\nu)$ is called *recursive* iff the set of all μ-numbers of quantifier-free formulas of the signature Σ is recursively enumerable. $(\mathfrak{R},\nu)$ is called *decidable* model iff the set of all μ-numbers of quantifier-free formulas of the signature Σ is decidable.

For correct definition of our semantics we need some formalization of functionals of higher types. As a suitable formalization we use elements of Scott's information systems [Scott 1982]. (Some another formalizations can be used as well, e.g. A-spaces [Ershov 1973] or f-spaces [Ershov 1977].) There is no place to write all formal definitions concerning information systems, so below we give only some informal explanations. Information systems allow one to define domains of functionals of higher types. For any information systems A,B there exist the information systems $A + B$, $A \times B$ and $A \rightarrow B$. We refer reader to [Scott 1982] for complete definitions. The set of all elements of an information system A, or simply the *domain* of A is denoted by A. In any information system A there always exists the least element $\perp_A$. The domain $A + B$ is essentially the disjoint union of the domains A and B plus the element $\perp_{A+B}$. The domain $A \times B$ consists of pairs $<a,b>$ with $a \in A$, $b \in B$. The elements of $A \to B$ are *continuous mappings* from A to B.

The elements of information systems are by definition sets of data objects. Suppose that we have a set of *elementary* information systems with natural numbers as data objects. Then set of data objects of the complex domains constructed from elementary ones according to definitions of $+$, $\times$, $\to$ is the subset of the set of *hereditarily finite sets over* N. If we take some Gödel numbering of this set then we can speak about *computable elements*. An element (represented by some set A) is computable iff the set of Godel numbers of members of A is recursively enumerable.

The information system I_ω [Voronkov 1988b] is such that elements of I_ω are either $\perp$ or natural numbers $0, 1, \ldots$ The information system 1 is defined in such a way that it has the only bottom element $\perp_1 = \{0\}$.

3. Constructive truth

In this section we define a constructive semantics of first order formulas in such a way that the set of constructively true formulas is the subset of classically true ones.

Let $(\mathfrak{R}, \nu)$ be an enumerated model of the signature σ. We assign to each formula φ of an extended signature Σ an information system A_φ and the relation $a \, c\!l \, \varphi$ (a classically realizes φ) where $a \in A_\varphi|$. If φ is a formula with free variables $x_0, \ldots, x_n$ then $\forall \varphi$ will denote the formula $\forall x_0 \ldots \forall x_n \varphi$. If there are no free variables in φ then $\forall \varphi \leftrightarrow \varphi$.

Definition 4. (The relation $c\!l$). In (i)-(vi) all formulas are closed.

(i) $A_\varphi \leftrightarrow 1$ for atomic φ and $\perp_1 c\!l \, \varphi$ iff φ is true in $\mathfrak{R}$.

(Generally speaking the definition of $c\!l$ depend of the model $(\mathfrak{R}, \nu)$, so we ought to write $c\!l_{(\mathfrak{R}, \nu)}$ instead of $c\!l$, but we will omit indices where it will not cause ambiguities).

(ii) $A_{\varphi \wedge \psi} \leftrightarrow A_\varphi \times A_\psi$ and $<a,b> c\!l \, \varphi \wedge \psi$ iff $a \, c\!l \, \varphi$ and $b \, c\!l \, \psi$.

(iii) $A_{\varphi \vee \psi} \leftrightarrow A_\varphi + A_\psi$ and, for $r \in A_{\varphi \vee \psi}$, $r \, c\!l \, \varphi \vee \psi$ iff either for some $a \in A_\varphi$ $r = inl(a)$ and $a \, c\!l \, \varphi$, or for some $b \in A_\psi$ $r = inr(b)$ and

$b \ cl \ \psi$, where *inl* and *inr* are natural embeddings of A_φ and A_ψ into $A_{\varphi \lor \psi}$.

(iv) $A_{\varphi \to \psi} \leftrightarrow A_\varphi \to A_\psi$ and, for $f \in A_\varphi \to A_\psi$, $f \ cl \ \varphi \to \psi$ iff for every $a \ cl \ \varphi \quad f(a) \ cl \ \psi$.

(v) $A_{\exists x \varphi(x)} \leftrightarrow I_{(\mathfrak{R},\nu)} \times A_{\varphi(t)}$, where t is an arbitrary closed term and $\langle n, a \rangle \ cl \ \exists x \varphi(x)$ iff $a \ cl \ \varphi(\nu n)$.

(vi) $A_{\forall x \varphi(x)} = I_{(\mathfrak{R},\nu)} \to A_{\varphi(t)}$, and, for $f \in A_{\forall x \varphi(x)}$, $f \ cl \ \forall x \varphi(x)$ iff for every $n \in \mathbb{N} \quad f(n) \ cl \ \varphi(\nu n)$.

(vii) If there are free variables in φ then $A_\varphi \leftrightarrow A_{\forall \varphi}$, and $a \ cl \ \varphi$ iff $a \ cl \ \forall \varphi$.

The following theorem explains why this semantics is called "classical realizability":

Theorem 5. There exist an a such that $a \ cl_{(\mathfrak{R},\nu)} \varphi$ iff $\mathfrak{R} \vDash \varphi$. ∎[1]

You may ask: so what is the need to introduce the new notion equivalent to the classical notion of truth? We made it because now we can easily define a constructive notion of truth such that the set of constructively true formulas are the subset of classically true ones:

Definition 6. Let $a \in A_\varphi$. Then $a \ con \ \varphi$ iff $a \ cl \ \varphi$ and a is computable. If $a \ con \ \varphi$ then we will say that a *constructively realizes* φ. A formula φ is said to be *constructively true* in the enumerated model $(\mathfrak{R},\nu)$ (denoted by $(\mathfrak{R},\nu) \vDash_{con} \varphi$) iff there is an a with $a \ con_{(\mathfrak{R},\nu)} \varphi$.

Thus we define the constructive notion of truth which does not diverse with the classical one, so the first part of our aim is satisfied. The second important property of our definition is that it is correct *for any denumerable model* and hence for any data type represented by such a model. Indeed, in [Voronkov 1986c] we investigated the properties of constructive truth for such an important data type as the type of lists with atoms from some model. It is also possible to generalize our definitions and technique for *parametric data types,* for example *lists(T),* where T is any data type, but in this case all needed definitions will take some space. (The papers on these developments are in preparation).

In the theory of enumerated models the most simple models are the decidable ones. The following theorem shows that if a model is "good" from the viewpoint of the theory of enumerated models then the constructive truth is identical to the classical truth for this model.

---

[1] We omit all proofs because of lack of space.

Theorem 7. Let $(\mathfrak{R},\nu)$ be decidable enumerated model, and φ be a formula. Then $(\mathfrak{R},\nu) \vDash \varphi$ iff $(\mathfrak{R},\nu) \vDash_{con} \varphi$.

The proof of this theorem is very simple but it shows that we are on the right way: for decidable models there is no difference between classical and constructive notion of truth. Some other results on relations between classical and constructive truth can be found in [Starchenko, Voronkov 1988] and [Voronkov 1988b, 1989b].

The next interesting question is the following: for what class of formulas the two notions of truth are equivalent independently of interpretation? This problem is closely related to the problem of eliminating computationally irrelevant parts from mechanically extracted proofs (see. e.g. [Goad 1980a,b, Henson 1989]). The following theorem partially gives an answer to this question:

Theorem 11. Let φ be a Harrop formula [Harrop 1960]. Then for every enumerated model $(\mathfrak{R},\nu)$ $\mathfrak{R} \vDash \varphi$ iff $(\mathfrak{R},\nu) \vDash_{con} \varphi$.

There are several another classes of formulas having this property but Harrop formulas are the most famous ones (see [Harrop 1960] and [Goad 1980b]).

4. Constructive theories

In this section we introduce the definition of constructive theory (constructive logic, constructive calculus) based on the above definition of constructive truth. We shown that the known first order theories are constructive in the precise sense of our definitions. It is proved that the intuitionistic predicate calculus is not complete for constructive truth. The very interesting result is given in Theorem 21: the intuitionistic arithmetic has only one (constructive) model (*categoricity* of intuitionistic arithmetic).

In what follows we will sometimes use informal notions (e.g. saying that the set of formulas is decidable). But all formal notions can of course be given.

Definition 9. The *inference figure* of signature σ is a finite sequence of formulas $\varphi_1, \ldots, \varphi_n, \varphi$, where $n \geq 0$. The *calculus* $\mathcal{L}$ is any effectively enumerable set of inference figures.

The *provability* of a formula in a calculus $\mathcal{L}$ is defined as usual: φ is provable iff there is an inference figure of the form $\varphi_1,\ldots,\varphi_n,\varphi$ in $\mathcal{L}$ such that for all $i \in \{1,\ldots,n\}$ φ_i are provable in $\mathcal{L}$.

The following definition is given in informal terms:

Definition 10. The calculus $\mathcal{L}$ is *constructive* for an enumerated model $(\mathfrak{R},\nu)$ iff there exists an algorithm α which by any inference figure $\varphi_1,\ldots,\varphi_n,\varphi$ of $\mathcal{L}$ and any $a_1,\ldots,a_n$ such that $a_1 \mathrel{\mathcal{Cl}} \varphi_1,\ldots, a_n \mathrel{\mathcal{Cl}} \varphi_n$ gives an a such that $a \mathrel{\mathcal{Cl}} \varphi$.

The following theorem shows soundness of the notion of constructive calculus w.r.t. constructive truth:

Theorem 11. Let $\mathcal{L}$ be constructive for $(\mathfrak{R},\nu)$ and $\vdash_{\mathcal{L}} \varphi$. Then $(\mathfrak{R},\nu)$ $\vdash_{con} \varphi$. Moreover, an element a with $a \mathrel{con} \varphi$ can be found effectively by a proof of φ in $\mathcal{L}$.

The application of Theorem 11 in program synthesis is immediate:

Theorem 12. Let $\mathcal{L}$ be constructive for $(\mathfrak{R},\nu)$. Then given any proof Π of a closed formula $\forall \bar{x} \exists y \psi(x,y)$ one can effectively construct a general recursive function g such that for any tuple $\bar{n}$ of natural numbers $\mathfrak{R} \vdash \varphi(\nu\bar{n},\nu g(\bar{n}))$.

To show that our definitions are generally applicable we have to show at least that the known constructive calculi are constructive in the sense of our definitions. The following theorems show the constructiveness of the intuitionistic first order predicate calculus, intuitionistic arithmetic (the analog of Nelson's theorem [Nelson 1947]) and constructiveness of the Markov's principle.

Theorem 13. Intuitionistic predicate calculus is constructive for every enumerated model $(\mathfrak{R},\nu)$.

Theorem 14. Intuitionistic arithmetic is constructive for the standard model of arithmetic $(\mathbb{N}, \mathrm{id}_{\mathbb{N}})$.

Theorem 15. The calculus $\mathcal{L}$ consisting of all instances of Markov's principle is constructive for every enumerated model $(\mathfrak{R},\nu)$[2].

Now we make some remarks about Markov's principle. In many papers on constructive logic and especially on program synthesis it is suggested that the constructive proof can have classical parts. (Many considerations but no formal definition on this subject are in [Goad 1980a,b].) There is one obs-

---

[2] Let us note: not only for natural numbers!

tacle to give semantics for such *mixed* proofs using traditional approaches because in the known realizability semantics there are formulas that are realizable but classically false. But in our semantics it is not so! Thus slightly changing our definitions we can prove the constructiveness of the following mixed inference figure[3]:

$$\frac{\vdash_{con} \varphi \vee \neg \varphi \qquad \vdash_{cl} \exists x \varphi}{\vdash_{con} \exists x \varphi}$$

The definition of constructive calculi depends of an enumerated model. It is interesting to describe the class of formulas which are constructively true in any enumerated model. This suggests the following definition.

Definition 16. The formula φ is called *constructively valid* iff for any enumerated model $(\mathbb{R}, \nu)$ $(\mathbb{R}, \nu) \vdash_{con} \varphi$.

Plisko [1988] showed that for a similar semantics the class of valid formulas is Π_1^1-complete and is hence even more complicated than the class of classically true formulas of arithmetic. However his proof can not be adapted to our semantics. All we are able to say now about the class of constructively valid formulas is the following theorem:

Theorem 17. There exist a constructively valid formula φ which is not provable in the intuitionistic predicate calculus.

There is one syntactical criterion of constructiveness which is (explicitly or implicitly) used in many papers:

Definition 18. A calculus $\mathcal{L}$ is called *syntactically constructive* iff the following two conditions hold:

1. If $\vdash_{\mathcal{L}} \varphi \vee \psi$, where φ, ψ are closed, then either $\vdash_{\mathcal{L}} \varphi$ or $\vdash_{\mathcal{L}} \psi$.

2. If $\vdash_{\mathcal{L}} \exists x \varphi(x)$, where $\exists x \varphi(x)$ is closed, then for some term t we have $\vdash_{\mathcal{L}} \varphi(t)$.

This definition is not very natural but one can hardly find the right definition based on syntactical considerations. We introduce a semantic criterion of constructivity:

Definition 19. A calculus $\mathcal{L}$ is called *semantically constructive* iff there is an enumerated model $(\mathbb{R}, \nu)$ such that $\mathcal{L}$ is constructive for $(\mathbb{R}, \nu)$.

There is one curious corollary of the last definition: the *classical*

---

[3] I do not who first proposed using this mixed principle. I learned it from N.N.Nepeivoda.

first order predicate calculus is semantically constructive! But why one can not use classical logical when studying e.g. finite models? This example shows that there are semantically constructive calculi which are not syntactically constructive. The following theorem shows that the converse is also true:

Theorem 20. There exists a calculus $\mathcal{L}$ of a finite signature σ such that

1. there exists a model of $\mathcal{L}$;
2. $\mathcal{L}$ is syntactically constructive;
3. $\mathcal{L}$ is not semantically constructive.

It is well known that the first order language is not very expressive from the model-theoretical point of view. For example any sufficiently rich theory have many non-isomorphic (countable) models. The following theorem shows that the constructive semantics can make the language more expressive:

Theorem 21. Any two constructive models of the Heyting arithmetic are recursively isomorphic.

Another results on expressibility of the language with constructive semantics are published in [Starchenko, Voronkov 1988, Voronkov 1988b].

References

Basin D.A. [1989]. *Building theories in Nuprl.* - In: Logic at Botic'89, LNCS 363, 1989, 12-25.

Bates J.L., Constable R.L. [1985] *Proofs as programs.* - ACM Trans. on Programming languages and systems, 1985, v.7, no.1, p.113-136.

Beeson M. J. [1978a] *Some relations between classical and constructive mathematics.* - J. Symb. Logic, 1978, v.43, no.2, p.228-246.

Beeson M.J. [1986] *Proving programs and programming proofs.* - In: VII Int. Congress on Logic, Methodology and Philosophy of Science, Elsevier Sci. Publishers, 1986, p.51-82.

Bertoni A., Mauri G., Miglioli P., Ornaghi M. [1984] *Abstract data types and their extension within a constructive logic.* - Semantics of Data Types, LNCS 173, 1984, 177-195.

Bishop E. [1970] *Mathematics as a numerical language.* In: Intuitionism and Proof Theory, North Holland, 1970, p.53-71.

Bresciani P., Miglioli P., Moscato U., Ornaghi M. [1986] *PAP - proofs as programs (Abstract).* - JSL 51(3), 1986, 852-853.

Chisholm P. [1987] *Derivation of a parsing algorithm in Martin-Lof's theory of types.* - Science of Computer Programming, 1987, v.8, no.1, p.1-42.

Constable R.L. [1972] *Constructive mathematics and automatic program writers.* - In: IFIP'71, North Holland, 1972, p.229-233.

Constable R.L. [1983] *Programs as proofs: a synopsis.* - Information Processing Letters, 1983, v.16, no.3, p.105-112.

Constable R.L. e.a. [1986] *Implementing mathematics with the Nuprl proof development system.* - Prentice Hall, 1986.

Coquand T., Huet G. [1988] *The calculus of constructions.* - Information and computation, 1988, v.74, no.213, p.95-120.

Dragalin A.G.[1967] *To the basing of Markov's principle.* - Soviet Mathematical Doklady, 1967, v.177.

Dragalin A.G. [1978] *Mathematical intuitionism. Introduction to the proof theory* (Russian). - Moscow, Nauka, 1978.

de Bruin N.G. [1980] *A survey of the project AUTOMATH.* - In: To H.B.Curry; Essays on Combinatory Logic, Lambda Calculus and Formalism, Academic Press, 1980, p.579-606.

Diller J. [1980] *Modified realization and the formulae-as-types notion.* In: Festschrift on the occasion of H.B.Curry's 80th Birthday, Academic Press, N.Y., 1980, p.491-502.

Ershov Yu.L. [1973] *The theory of A-spaces.* - Algebra i Logica, 12(4), 1973.

Ershov Yu.L. [1977] *The theory of enumerations* (in Russian). - Moscow, Nauka, 1977.

Ershov Yu.L. [1980] *Decidability problems and constructive models* (in Russian). - Moscow, Nauka, 1980.

Feferman S. [1979] *Constructive theories of functions and classes.* - In: Logic Colloquium'78, North Holland, 1979, p.159-224.

Feferman S. [1984] *Between constructive and classical mathematics.* - In: Computation and proof theory, Lecture Notes in Math 1104, 1984, p.143-162.

Goad C.A. [1980a] *Proofs as descriptions of computation.* - 5th CADE, LNCS 87, 1980, p.39-52.

Goad C.A. [1980b] *Computational uses of the manipulation of formal proofs.* - Stanford Univ. Department of CS, TR no. STAN-CS-80-819, 1980, 122p.

Gödel K. [1958] *Uber eine noch nicht benutzte Erweiterung des finiten Standpunktes.* - Dialectica, 1958, v.12, no. 3/4, p.280-287.

Goto S. [1979b] *Program synthesis from natural deduction proofs.* - 6th IJCAI, 1979, v.1, p.339-341.

Harrop R. [1960] *Concerning formulas of the types $A \rightarrow B \vee C$, $A \rightarrow (Ex)B(x)$ in intuitionistic formal system.* - J. Symb. Logic, v.17, 1960, pp.27-32.

Hayashi S., Nakano H. [1988] *PX: a computational logic.* - MIT Press, 1988.

Henson M.C. [1989a] *Information loss in the programming logic TK.* - Draft, Univ. of Essex, Department of Computer Sci., October, 1989.

Henson M.C. [1989b] *Realizability models for program construction.* - In: J.L.A. van de Snepsheut (Ed.), Mathematics of Program Construction, LNCS 375, 1989, 256-272.

Huet D. [1986] *Computation and deduction.* - Carnegie Mellon Univ., 1986.

Kleene S.C. [1952] *Introduction to metamathematics.* - Van Nostrand P.C., Amsterdam, 1952.

Kleene S.C. [1973] Realizability: a retrospective survey. - LNM 337, 1973.

Kolmogorov A.N. [1932] *Zur Deutung der Intuitionistischen Logik.* - Mathematische Zeitschrift, v.35, 1932, p.58-65.

Kreisel G. [1958] *Interpretation of analysis by means of constructive functionals of finite types.* - In: Constructivity in Mathematics, North Holland, 1958, p.101-128.

Läuchly H. [1970] *An abstract notion of realizability for which intuitionistic predicate calculus is complete.* - In: Intuitionism and Proof Theory, North Holland, 1970, p.227-234.

Manna Z., Waldinger R. [1979] *Synthesis: dreams -> programs.* - IEEE Trans. Software Engineering, 1979, v.5.,no.4, p. 294-328.

Markov A.A., Nagorny N.M. [1986] *Theory of algorithms.* - Moscow, Nauka, 1986.

Miglioli P., Moscato U., Ornaghi M. [1989] *Semi-constructive formal systems and axiomatization of abstract data types.* - TAPSOFT'89, LNCS 351, 337-351.

Mints G.E. [1974] *E-theorems* (in Russian). - Zapiski Nauchnyh seminarov LOMI, 1974, v.40, p.110-118.

Nelson D. [1947] *Recursive functionals and intuitionistic number theory.* - Trans. Amer. Math. Soc., v.61, 1947, p.307-368.

Nepeivoda N.N. [1979a] *An application of proof theory to the problem of con structing correct programs.* - Kibernetika, 1979, no.2.

Nepeivoda N.N. [1979b] *A method of constructing correct programs from correct subprograms.* - Programmirovanie, 1979, no.1.

Nepeivoda N.N., Sviridenko D.I. [1982] *Towards the theory of program synthesis (in Russian).* - In: Trudy Instituta Matematiki, v.2, Novosibirsk, Nauka, 1982, p.159-175.

Nordstrom B., Peterson K. [1983] *Types and specifications.* - IFIP'83, NH, 1983, 915-920.

Nordstrom B., Smith J.M. [1984] *Propositions, types and specifications of programs in Martin-Lof's type theory.* - BIT, 24(3), 1984, 288-301.

Plisko V.E. [1987] *On languages with constructive logical connectives.* - Soviet Mathematical Doklady, v.296, no.1., 1987.

Prank R.K. [1981] *Expressibility in elementary theory or recursively enumerable sets with realizability logic.* - Algebra i Logica, 20(4), 1981.

Prawitz D. *Natural deduction.* - Stockholm, Almquist and Wicksell, 1965.

Petersson K. [1982] *A programming system for type theory.* - LPM Memo 21, Dpt of CS, Chalmers Univ. of Technology, Goteborg, 1982.

Scott D.S. [1982] *Domains for denotational semantics.* In: Lecture Notes in Computer Science 140, 1982, pp.577-612.

Starchenko S.S., Voronkov A.A. [1988] *On connections between classical and constructive semantics.* - In: COLOG-88 (papers presented at the Int. Conf. on Computer Logic), Part 1, Tallinn, 1988, p.101-112.

Voronkov A.A. [1985] *A generalization of the notion of realizability.* - Unpublished Manuscript, 25pp. (Abstract was published in Siberian Mathematical Journal, 1986).

Voronkov A.A. [1986a] *Logic programs and their synthesis* (Russian). Preprint no. 23, Institute of Mathematics, Novosibirsk, 1986.

Voronkov A.A. [1986b] *Synthesis of logic programs* (Russian). Preprint no. 24, Institute of Mathematics, Novosibirsk, 1986.

Voronkov A.A. [1986c] *Intuitionistic list theory* (Russian). - In: Abstracts of the 8th All-union Conf. on Mathematical Logic, Moscow, 1986.

Voronkov A.A. [1987a] *Constructive logic: a semantic approach.* - In: Abstracts of the 8th Int. Congress on Logic, Methodology and Philosophy of Sci., v.5, part 1, Moscow, Nauka, 1987, p.79-82.

Voronkov A.A. [1987b] *Deductive program synthesis and Markov's principle.* - In: Fundamentals of computation theory, LNCS v.278, 1987, p.479-482.

Voronkov A.A. [1988a] *Constructive calculi and constructive models.* - Soviet Mathematical Doklady, 299(1), 1988.

Voronkov A.A. [1988b] *Model theory based on the constructive notion of truth.* - In: Model Theory and Applications, Trudy Instituta Matematiki, v.8, Novosibirsk, 1988.

Voronkov A.A. [1989a] *Program synthesis using proofs in first order logic.* (Russian). - To be published in Vychislitelnye sistemy, 1989, 50pp.

Voronkov A.A. [1989b] *A theory for programming in constructive logic.* - presented to the 3rd Int. Conf. on Computer Sci. Logic, Kaiserslautern, October, 1989.

Author Index

Vol. 379: A. Kreczmar, G. Mirkowska (Eds.), Mathematical Foundations of Computer Science 1989. Proceedings, 1989. VIII, 605 pages. 1989.

Vol. 380: J. Csirik, J. Demetrovics, F. Gécseg (Eds.), Fundamentals of Computation Theory. Proceedings, 1989. XI, 493 pages. 1989.

Vol. 381: J. Dassow, J. Kelemen (Eds.), Machines, Languages, and Complexity. Proceedings, 1988. VI, 244 pages. 1989.

Vol. 382: F. Dehne, J.-R. Sack, N. Santoro (Eds.), Algorithms and Data Structures. WADS '89. Proceedings, 1989. IX, 592 pages. 1989.

Vol. 383: K. Furukawa, H. Tanaka, T. Fujisaki (Eds.), Logic Programming '88. Proceedings, 1988. VII, 251 pages. 1989 (Subseries LNAI).

Vol. 384: G. A. van Zee, J. G. G. van de Vorst (Eds.), Parallel Computing 1988. Proceedings, 1988. V, 135 pages. 1989.

Vol. 385: E. Börger, H. Kleine Büning, M. M. Richter (Eds.), CSL '88. Proceedings, 1988. VI, 399 pages. 1989.

Vol. 386: J.E. Pin (Ed.), Formal Properties of Finite Automata and Applications. Proceedings, 1988. VIII, 260 pages. 1989.

Vol. 387: C. Ghezzi, J. A. McDermid (Eds.), ESEC '89. 2nd European Software Engineering Conference. Proceedings, 1989. VI, 496 pages. 1989.

Vol. 388: G. Cohen, J. Wolfmann (Eds.), Coding Theory and Applications. Proceedings, 1988. IX, 329 pages. 1989.

Vol. 389: D.H. Pitt, D. E. Rydeheard, P. Dybjer, A.M. Pitts, A. Poigné (Eds.), Category Theory and Computer Science. Proceedings, 1989. VI, 365 pages. 1989.

Vol. 390: J.P. Martins, E.M. Morgado (Eds.), EPIA 89. Proceedings, 1989. XII, 400 pages. 1989 (Subseries LNAI).

Vol. 391: J.-D. Boissonnat, J.-P. Laumond (Eds.), Geometry and Robotics. Proceedings, 1988. VI, 413 pages. 1989.

Vol. 392: J.-C. Bermond, M. Raynal (Eds.), Distributed Algorithms. Proceedings, 1989. VI, 315 pages. 1989.

Vol. 393: H. Ehrig, H. Herrlich, H.-J. Kreowski, G. Preuß (Eds.), Categorical Methods in Computer Science. VI, 350 pages. 1989.

Vol. 394: M. Wirsing, J.A. Bergstra (Eds.), Algebraic Methods: Theory, Tools and Applications. VI, 558 pages. 1989.

Vol. 395: M. Schmidt-Schauß, Computational Aspects of an Order-Sorted Logic with Term Declarations. VIII, 171 pages. 1989. (Subseries LNAI).

Vol. 396: T. A. Berson, T. Beth (Eds.), Local Area Network Security. Proceedings, 1989. IX, 152 pages. 1989.

Vol. 397: K. P. Jantke (Ed.), Analogical and Inductive Inference. Proceedings, 1989. IX, 338 pages. 1989. (Subseries LNAI).

Vol. 398: B. Banieqbal, H. Barringer, A. Pnueli (Eds.), Temporal Logic in Specification. Proceedings, 1987. VI, 448 pages. 1989.

Vol. 399: V. Cantoni, R. Creutzburg, S. Levialdi, G. Wolf (Eds.), Recent Issues in Pattern Analysis and Recognition. VII, 400 pages. 1989.

Vol. 400: R. Klein, Concrete and Abstract Voronoi Diagrams. IV, 167 pages. 1989.

Vol. 401: H. Djidjev (Ed.), Optimal Algorithms. Proceedings, 1989. VI, 308 pages. 1989.

Vol. 402: T. P. Bagchi, V. K. Chaudhri, Interactive Relational Database Design. XI, 186 pages. 1989.

Vol. 403: S. Goldwasser (Ed.), Advances in Cryptology – CRYPTO '88. Proceedings, 1988. XI, 591 pages. 1990.

Vol. 404: J. Beer, Concepts, Design, and Performance Analysis of a Parallel Prolog Machine. VI, 128 pages. 1989.

Vol. 405: C. E. Veni Madhavan (Ed.), Foundations of Software Technology and Theoretical Computer Science. Proceedings, 1989. VIII, 339 pages. 1989.

Vol. 407: J. Sifakis (Ed.), Automatic Verification Methods for Finite State Systems. Proceedings, 1989. VII, 382 pages. 1990.

Vol. 408: M. Leeser, G. Brown (Eds.), Hardware Specification, Verification and Synthesis: Mathematical Aspects. Proceedings, 1989. VI, 402 pages. 1990.

Vol. 409: A. Buchmann, O. Günther, T. R. Smith, Y.-F. Wang (Eds.), Design and Implementation of Large Spatial Databases. Proceedings, 1989. IX, 364 pages. 1990.

Vol. 410: F. Pichler, R. Moreno-Diaz (Eds.), Computer Aided Systems Theory – EUROCAST '89. Proceedings, 1989. VII, 427 pages. 1990.

Vol. 411: M. Nagl (Ed.), Graph-Theoretic Concepts in Computer Science. Proceedings, 1989. VII, 374 pages. 1990.

Vol. 412: L. B. Almeida, C. J. Wellekens (Eds.), Neural Networks. Proceedings, 1990. IX, 276 pages. 1990.

Vol. 413: R. Lenz, Group Theoretical Methods in Image Processing. VIII, 139 pages. 1990.

Vol. 414: A. Kreczmar, A. Salwicki, M. Warpechowski, LOGLAN '88 – Report on the Programming Language. X, 133 pages. 1990.

Vol. 415: C. Choffrut, T. Lengauer (Eds.), STACS 90. Proceedings, 1990. VI, 312 pages. 1990.

Vol. 416: F. Bancilhon, C. Thanos, D. Tsichritzis (Eds.), Advances in Database Technology – EDBT '90. Proceedings, 1990. IX, 452 pages. 1990.

Vol. 417: P. Martin-Löf, G. Mints (Eds.), COLOG-88. International Conference on Computer Logic. Proceedings, 1988. VI, 338 pages. 1990.

Vol. 419: K. Weichselberger, S. Pöhlmann, A Methodology for Uncertainty in Knowledge-Based Systems. VIII, 136 pages. 1990. (Subseries LNAI).

Vol. 420: Z. Michalewicz (Ed.), Statistical and Scientific Database Management, V SSDBM. Proceedings, 1990. V, 256 pages. 1990.

Vol. 421: T. Onodera, S. Kawai, A Formal Model of Visualization in Computer Graphics Systems. X, 100 pages. 1990.

Vol. 423: L. E. Deimel (Ed.), Software Engineering Education. Proceedings, 1990. VI, 164 pages. 1990.

Vol. 424: G. Rozenberg (Ed.), Advances in Petri Nets 1989. VI, 524 pages. 1990.

Vol. 425: C. H. Bergman, R. D. Maddux, D. L. Pigozzi (Eds.), Algebraic Logic and Universal Algebra in Computer Science. Proceedings, 1988. XI, 292 pages. 1990.

Vol. 426: N. Houbak, SIL – a Simulation Language. VII, 192 pages. 1990.

Vol. 427: O. Faugeras (Ed.), Computer Vision – ECCV 90. Proceedings, 1990. XII, 619 pages. 1990.

Vol. 428: D. Bjørner, C. A. R. Hoare, H. Langmaack (Eds.), VDM '90, VDM and Z – Formal Methods in Software Development. Proceedings, 1990. XVII, 580 pages. 1990.

Vol. 429: A. Miola (Ed.), Design and Implementation of Symbolic Computation Systems. Proceedings, 1990. XII, 284 pages. 1990.

Vol. 430: J. W. de Bakker, W.-P. de Roever, G. Rozenberg (Eds.), Stepwise Refinement of Distributed Systems. Models, Formalisms, Correctness. Proceedings, 1989. X, 808 pages. 1990.

Vol. 431: A. Arnold (Ed.), CAAP '90. Proceedings, 1990. VI, 285 pages. 1990.

Vol. 432: N. Jones (Ed.), ESOP '90. Proceedings, 1990. IX, 436 pages. 1990.

This series reports new developments in computer science research and teaching – quickly, informally and at a high level. The type of material considered for publication includes preliminary drafts of original papers and monographs, technical reports of high quality and broad interest, advanced level lectures, reports of meetings, provided they are of exceptional interest and focused on a single topic. The timeliness of a manuscript is more important than its form which may be unfinished or tentative. If possible, a subject index should be included. Publication of Lecture Notes is intended as a service to the international computer science community, in that a commercial publisher, Springer-Verlag, can offer a wide distribution of documents which would otherwise have a restricted readership. Once published and copyrighted, they can be documented in the scientific literature.

Manuscripts

Manuscripts should be no less than 100 and preferably no more than 500 pages in length.
They are reproduced by a photographic process and therefore must be typed with extreme care. Symbols not on the typewriter should be inserted by hand in indelible black ink. Corrections to the typescript should be made by pasting in the new text or painting out errors with white correction fluid. Authors receive 75 free copies and are free to use the material in other publications. The typescript is reduced slightly in size during reproduction; best results will not be obtained unless the text on any one page is kept within the overall limit of 18 x 26.5 cm (7 x 10½ inches). On request, the publisher will supply special paper with the typing area outlined.
Manuscripts should be sent to Prof. G. Goos, GMD Forschungsstelle an der Universität Karlsruhe, Haid- und Neu-Str. 7, 7500 Karlsruhe 1, Germany, Prof. J. Hartmanis, Cornell University, Dept. of Computer Science, Ithaca, NY/USA 14850, or directly to Springer-Verlag Heidelberg.

Springer-Verlag, Heidelberger Platz 3, D-1000 Berlin 33
Springer-Verlag, Tiergartenstraße 17, D-6900 Heidelberg 1
Springer-Verlag, 175 Fifth Avenue, New York, NY 10010/USA
Springer-Verlag, 37-3, Hongo 3-chome, Bunkyo-ku, Tokyo 113, Japan

ISBN 3-540-52592-0
ISBN 0-387-52592-0